# Handbook of Forensic Science

# Handbook of Forensic Science

Edited by

## Jim Fraser and Robin Williams

**WILLAN**
**PUBLISHING**

Published by

Willan Publishing
Culmcott House
Mill Street, Uffculme
Cullompton, Devon
EX15 3AT, UK
Tel: +44(0)1884 840337
Fax: +44(0)1884 840251
e-mail: info@willanpublishing.co.uk
website: www.willanpublishing.co.uk

Published simultaneously in the USA and Canada by

Willan Publishing
c/o ISBS, 920 NE 58th Ave, Suite 300
Portland, Oregon 97213-3644, USA
Tel: +001(0)503 287 3093
Fax: +001(0)503 280 8832
e-mail: info@isbs.com
website: www.isbs.com

First published 2009

Hardback
ISBN-978-1-84392-312-1
Paperback
ISBN-978-1-84392-311-4


British Library Cataloguing-in-Publication Data

A catalogue record for this book is available from the British Library

**FSC**
**Mixed Sources**
Product group from well-managed
forests and other controlled sources
Cert no. SGS-COC-2482
www.fsc.org
© 1996 Forest Stewardship Council

Project management by Deer Park Productions, Tavistock, Devon
Typeset by GCS, Leighton Buzzard, Beds
Printed and bound by T.J. International, Padstow, Cornwall

# Contents

## Part 1 Forensic Science Practice

### Section 1: Identifying individuals

### Section 2: Identifying and comparing materials

## Part 2 Forensic Science as Investigative Support

## Part 3 Forensic Reasoning and the Evaluation of Scientific Evidence

# List of figures and tables

**Figures**

## Tables

# List of abbreviations

| | |
|---|---|
| AAA | American Anthropological Association |
| AAFS | American Academy of Forensic Science |
| AATCC | American Association of Textile Chemists and Colorists |
| ABC | American Board of Criminalistics |
| ABFA | American Board of Forensic Anthropology |
| ACF | Arson Control Forum |
| ACPO | Association of Chief Police Officers |
| ACPOS | Association of Chief Police Officers (Scotland) |
| AFIS | Automatic Fingerprint Identification Systems |
| AP | acid phosphatase |
| APA | Association of Police Authorities |
| APB | Arson Prevention Bureau |
| AQF | Australian Qualifications Framework |
| ASCLAD | Association of Crime Laboratory Directors |
| ATF | Inter-Agency Arson Task Forces |
| BAFO | British Society of Forensic Odontologists |
| BCU | Basic Command Unit |
| BIA | Behavioural investigative Advisers |
| BPA | Bloodstain Pattern Analysis |
| CCRC | Criminal Cases Review Commission |
| CE | capillary gel |
| CHEA | Council for Higher Education Accreditors |
| CIA | Central Intelligence Agency |
| CIT | Canberra Institute of Technology |
| CJ | criminal justice |
| CJA | Criminal Justice Act 2003 |
| CJPA | Criminal Justice and Police Act 2001 |
| CODIS | combined DNA index system |
| CPD | continuing professional development |
| CPS | Crown Prosecution Service |

| | |
|---|---|
| CRFP | Council for the Registration of Forensic Practitioners |
| CSE | Crime Scene Examiner |
| CSI | Crime Scene Investigator |
| DAD | diode array detection |
| DAG | directed acyclic graph |
| DMAC | p-dimethylaminocinnamaldehyde |
| DMORT | Disaster Mortuary Operational Response Teams |
| DNA-ases | non-specific enzymes |
| EDNAP | European DNA Profiling Group |
| EDPS | European Data Protection Supervisor |
| EFG | European Fibres Group |
| ENFSI | European Network of Forensic Science Institutes |
| ENFSI DWG | European Network of Forensic Science Institutes Drugs Working Group |
| ESDA | Electrostatic Detection Apparatus |
| FATF | G8 Financial Action Task Force |
| FBI | Federal Bureau of Investigation |
| FEPAC | Forensic Education Program Accreditation Committee |
| FFLM | Faculty of Forensic and Legal Medicine |
| FFT | Fast Fourier Transform |
| FID | flame ionisation detector |
| FLINTS | Forensic Led Intelligence System |
| FSS | Forensic Science Service |
| FTIR | Fourier transform infrared spectroscopy |
| GBL | gamma butyrolactone |
| GC | gas chromatography |
| GDC | General Dental Council |
| GHB | gamma hydroxybutyric acid |
| GMC | General Medical Council |
| HCA | hierarchical cluster analysis |
| HE | higher education |
| HEI | higher education institution |
| HMIC | Her Majesty's Inspectors of Constabulary |
| HOSDB | Home Office Scientific Development Branch |
| HPLC | high performance liquid chromatography |
| HSE | Health and Safety Executive |
| IAAI | International Association of Arson Investigators |
| IABPA | International Association of Blood Pattern Analysts |
| IAI | International Association for Identification |
| ICP-MS | inductively coupled plasma mass spectrometry |
| IFE | Institute of Fire Engineers |
| INCB | International Narcotics Control Board |
| IOB | Institute of Biology |
| IOP | Institute of Physics |
| IPS | Institute of Forensic Science |
| IRMS | Isotope ratio mass spectroscopy |
| ISFG | International Society of Forensic Genetics |
| ITAI | Institute of Traffic Accident Investigators |

| | |
|---|---|
| JPAC | Joint Prisoner of War/Missing in Action Accounting Command |
| KM | Kastle Meyer |
| LCN | low copy number |
| LDIS | local laboratory systems |
| LGC | Laboratory of the Government Chemist |
| LMG | Leucomalachite Green |
| LR | likelihood ratio |
| LSD | Lysergic acid diethylamide |
| MDA 1971 | Misuse of Drugs Act 1971 |
| MIR | Major Incident Room |
| MLP | multilocus probe |
| MLSC | management of linked series crime |
| MO | *modus operandi* |
| MOJ | miscarriages of justice |
| MPFSL | Metropolitan Police Forensic Science Laboratory |
| MS | mass spectrometer |
| MSSC | management of serious series crime |
| mtDNA | mitochondrial DNA |
| MUP | methyl umbelliferyl phosphate reagent |
| NAFIS | National Automatic Fingerprint Identification System |
| NCF | National Crime Faculty |
| NCIS | National Criminal Intelligence Model |
| NCOF | National Crime and Operations Faculty |
| NCPE | National Centre for Policing Excellence |
| NDNAD | National DNA Database of England and Wales |
| NFFID | National Firearms Forensic Intelligence Database |
| NIDB | National Injuries Database |
| NIFS | National Institute of Forensic Science |
| NIM | National Intelligence Model |
| NMC | Nursing and Midwifery Council |
| NOS | UK National Occupational Standard |
| NPIA | National Policing Improvement Agency |
| NRC | National Research Council |
| NTC | National Training Centre |
| PABS | physiologically altered bloodstains |
| PACE | Police and Criminal Evidence Act 1984 |
| PCA | principal component analysis |
| PCP | phencyclidine |
| PCR | polymerase chain reaction |
| PGC | pyrolysis-gas chromatography |
| PGC-MS | pyrolysis-gas chromatography-mass spectrometry |
| PLR | polarised light microscopy |
| PMK | piperonylmethylketone or 3,4methylenedioxyphenyl-2-propanone |
| PPAF | Police Performance Assessment Framework |
| PPP | Public Private Partnership |
| PRA | Police Reform Act 2002 |

| | |
|---|---|
| PSA | prostate specific antigen |
| PSU | Home Office's Police Standards Unit |
| RFPL | restriction fragment length polymorphism |
| RMNE | random man not excluded |
| RPL | recognition of prior learning |
| RSC | Royal Society of Chemistry |
| RSS | Royal Statistical Society |
| RTO | Registered Training Organisation |
| SA | Specialist Adviser |
| SAG | Scientific Advisory Group |
| SCRO | Scottish Criminal Record Office |
| SDIS | state system |
| SEM/EDS | scanning electron microscope fitted with an energy dispersive X-ray spectrometer |
| SEMTA | Science, Engineering, Manufacturing Technologies Alliance |
| SEW | Society of Expert Witnesses |
| SIDS | Sudden infant death syndrome |
| SLP | single locus probe |
| SMANZFL | Senior Managers Australian and New Zealand Forensic Science Laboratories |
| SNP | single nucleotide polymorphisms |
| SOC | Scene of Crime |
| SOCO | Scene of Crime Officer |
| SOPs | Standard Operating Procedures |
| SSU | Scientific Support Unit |
| STR | Short tandem repeat |
| SWG | Scientific Working Group |
| SWGDE/SWGIT | Scientific Working Group for digital and multimedia evidence |
| SWGDRUG | Scientific Working Group for the Analysis of Drugs |
| SWGFAST | Scientific Working Group for latent fingerprints |
| SWGFEX | Scientific Working Group for fire and explosives |
| SWGGUN | Scientific Working Group for firearms and tool marks |
| SWGMAT | Scientific Working Group for Materials Analysis |
| SWIM | Scientific Work Improvement Model |
| SWOR | sampling without replacement |
| SWR | sampling with replacement |
| TEN-T | Trans-European Transport Network |
| TLC | thin layer chromatography |
| UKAS | United Kingdom Accreditation Service |
| UNODC | United Nations Office on Drugs and Crime |
| UV-vis | ultraviolet-visible spectroscopy |
| VET | Vocational Education and Training |
| VNTR | variable number of tandem repeat |

# Acknowledgements

We have accumulated many debts during the time that we have been preparing this Handbook. Numerous academic and professional colleagues have supported our efforts and endured our conversations about it, and we are grateful to them all. We also acknowledge the work done by the anonymous referees of our original proposal, and the huge efforts made by the many authors who have supplied chapters for this Handbook. We cannot name all of those individuals whose advice we have sought and valued, but amongst them are: David Chaney, Jason Ditton, Keith Fryer, Martin Innes, Gary Pugh, Peter Stelfox, and our publisher Brian Willan. Chris Lawless has supported all of our editorial work and also took responsibility for the preparation of the Glossary. Finally we need to thank our respective partners, Celia Lloyd and Erica Haimes for their patient endurance of the many times that 'one last telephone call' or 'one last email' about 'the Handbook' meant that we were delayed in meeting our commitments to them.

We hope that all of those listed above feel that their – and our – efforts have been worthwhile.

*Jim Fraser, University of Strathclyde*
*Robin Williams, Durham University*

# Notes on contributors

**Colin Aitken** is Professor of Forensic Statistics at The University of Edinburgh. He is a Fellow of the Royal Statistical Society (RSS), a Fellow of the Forensic Science Society, a member of the International Statistical Institute and a Chartered Statistician. He has a long-standing research interest in the interface of statistics, law and forensic science and has published many papers on the subject. He is a co-author of *Statistics and the evaluation of evidence for forensic scientists* and *Bayesian networks and probabilistic inference in forensic science*. He is Chairman of the RSS' working group on Statistics and the Law, an associate member of the European Academy of Forensic Sciences committee on research and development, a member of the US National Institute of Justice/National Institute of Science and Technology expert working group on Human Factors in Latent Print Analysis, and co-chairman of FORSTAT, an annual series of workshops on statistics in forensic science for members of the European Network of Forensic Science Institutes. He is the Chief Editor of the journal *Law, Probability and Risk*. He has also been consulted as an expert in many criminal cases.

**Julie Allard** is a Consultant Forensic Scientist at the London laboratory of the Forensic Science Service. She has over 35 years' experience as a forensic scientist, reporting biological evidence types such as body fluids, DNA, blood patterns and crime scenes. Throughout her career she has been particularly involved in the analysis of sexual assault findings and has authored or co-authored several papers on the subject. She also has a keen interest in the application of the case assessment and interpretation model. She is currently a National Scientific Lead for the organisation, advising on casework, standards, quality and training matters in relation to body fluids.

**David Barclay** is a consultant forensic scientist and senior lecturer at Robert Gordon University, Aberdeen. He obtained an MSc (For Sci) from Strathclyde before undertaking a long career in Forensic Science casework and then management with the Forensic Science Service (FSS). He was attached to

National Crime Faculty on its inception in 1996 and was head of physical evidence there until he retired in 2005. During that period he reviewed around 235 undetected murders in the UK and abroad, and over the last few years has worked extensively on undetected cold cases and alleged miscarriages of justice in several countries, including over 10 murder cases in Australia, and in the USA, Holland and the UK. He has had a long standing interest in improving the utility of physical evidence and intelligence to criminal investigations. In 2007 Dave was made a Fellow of the Forensic Science Society.

**Bob Bramley** had a career with the Forensic Science Service from 1970 to 2004. From 1996 until his retirement he was the Chief Scientist. He was also Custodian of the National DNA Database from 1996 to 2006. Since his retirement he has continued as a consultant supporting the Home Office in development of the Forensic Regulator role and a national quality standard for providers of forensic science services to the criminal justice system. In the wider forensic science community, both nationally and internationally, he has lectured and published widely on quality, standards and the DNA Database. In 2003, he was awarded the Distinguished Contributor Award by the European Network of Forensic Science Institutes and in 2005 he was appointed CBE for his contribution to forensic science.

**Hilary Buchanan** studied mathematics and education at Taylor University in Indiana, and then moved to Scotland where she obtained an MSc (with Distinction) in Forensic Science from the University of Strathclyde. Following a placement with Strathclyde Police in Glasgow, which led to published work on the recovery of fingerprints from untreated wood, she embarked on studies towards a PhD at the University of Strathclyde. The PhD thesis from this period of research, on the applicability of isotope ratio mass spectrometry for the profiling of MDMA, is currently approaching completion, and some of the results have been published already. Hilary has also been a student member of the Forensic Science Society and the Royal Society of Chemistry for the duration of her postgraduate studies.

**Paul Chamberlain** is a senior forensic scientist with the Forensic Science Service Ltd, specialising in the detection, recovery and comparison of fingerprints. He has a BSc from the Open University and is a registered forensic practitioner. Previously he worked for the Metropolitan Police, Bedfordshire Police and Hertfordshire Constabulary and has over 25 years' casework experience. On moving to the Forensic Science Service in 2000, he has continued to undertake casework and taken a leading role in the development of fingerprint services, quality management and research initiatives. He is currently the Chair of the European Network of Forensic Science Institutes (ENFSI) Fingerprint Working Group, working extensively on the Groups Fingerprint Best Practice Manual, and a regional representative of the International Association for Identification.

**Christophe Champod** received his MSc and PhD (*summa cum laude*) both in Forensic Science, from the University of Lausanne, in 1990 and 1995 respectively. He remained in academia, eventually holding the position of assistant professor in forensic science. From 1999 to 2003, he led the Interpretation Research Group of the Forensic Science Service (UK), before taking a professorship at the School of Criminal Sciences (ESC)/Institute of Forensic Science (IPS) of the University of Lausanne. He is in charge of education and research on identification methods (detection and identification). He is a member of the International Association for Identification and in 2004 was elected a member of the FBI-sponsored SWGFAST. His research is devoted to the statistical evaluation of forensic identification techniques. The value of fingerprint evidence is at the core of his interests.

**Tim Clayton** is currently a consultant forensic scientist and has worked for 20 years as an expert witness in the Criminal Justice System. He obtained a BSc (Hons) degree from the University of East Anglia before studying for a PhD in molecular genetics at the John Innes Institute in Norwich. After a brief period of postdoctoral research he joined the Home Office Forensic Science Service. He is also a qualified barrister, having been called to the Bar by Middle Temple in 2007. Through his career, he has specialised in forensic biology and in particular DNA profiling. He has lectured and published widely on the subject of forensic DNA profiling. His current area of interest is in the regulation of experts, the setting of quality standards in forensic science and the rules governing the admissibility of expert evidence in the English courts.

**Amanda Cooper** spent six years as a Medical Laboratory Scientific Officer in the NHS; she worked in the Haematology and Blood Transfusion department in two hospitals in Oxfordshire and gained professional qualifications relating to this work. She then moved to a commercial DNA-testing laboratory based at Abingdon and was engaged in testing for paternity, immigration and forensic cases and genetic diagnostics, progressing through the organisation to become Operations Manager. In 2002 Amanda joined Thames Valley Police as the Scientific Support Manager. This role enabled her to gain significant involvement in the Association of Chief Police Officers (ACPO) Forensic Portfolio and she undertook a number of pieces of work within national programmes. Amanda is currently the Director of Information and Strategy and is a Member of the Institute of Directors.

**Niamh Nic Daéid** received her Bachelor of Science degree in Chemistry and Mathematics from Trinity College, Dublin. She completed her PhD in Chemistry at the Royal College of Surgeons in Ireland. She is currently a Senior Lecturer in Forensic Science at the Centre for Forensic Science at Strathclyde University. Over the past 13 years or so she has been involved in education, training and research in many aspects of forensic practice including drug analysis and drug profiling. She has published and presented over 90 research papers and conference presentations in forensic science and manages one of the largest academic-based research groups in the discipline in the UK. She also undertakes independent casework and is authorised under the Criminal Procedures (Scotland) Act as a forensic chemist. Niamh is involved with a number of ENFSI (the European Network of Forensic Science Institutes) working groups and acts as a lead assessor for the the Council for Registration of Forensic Practitioners. She is a member of the Council for the Forensic Science Society and is the current editor of *Science and Justice*.

**Martin Evison** is Associate Professor of Anthropology at the University of Toronto and Director of the University's Forensic Science Program. He has a PhD in Ancient DNA from the University of Sheffield, and from 1994 until 2005 he was the forensic anthropologist at Sheffield Medico-Legal Centre, where he led a research group focusing on computational and molecular methods of human identification. He has undertaken casework on five continents; in forensic archaeology and anthropology, facial identification and contamination or innocent transfer of DNA. He has published in *Journal of Forensic Sciences* and *Forensic Science Communications* among other journals, and is currently co-editing (with R.W. Vorder Bruegge) a report on *Computer-Assisted Forensic Facial Comparison* (published by Taylor and Francis in 2009).

**Jim Fraser** is Professor of Forensic Science and Director of the University of Strathclyde's Centre for Forensic Science. He is Associate Director of the Scottish Institute for Policing Research, Chair of the European Academy of Forensic Science and a past President of the Forensic Science Society. He has extensive experience as an expert witness in criminal courts in the UK and has been involved in many high-profile cases. Jim has significant experience in strategic and policy matters in relation to forensic science in the UK and internationally. He has advised a range of agencies on forensic, scientific and investigative matters, including the ACPO, ACPOS, HMIC, the Home Office and the Scottish and Westminster Parliaments.

**Mick Gardiner** is the Chief Executive of Gardiner Associates Fire Ltd, a multi-discipline team of consultants who provide a range of fire/arson investigation training programmes. Until his retirement from the London Fire Brigade in 1995, the last 11 years of his service were devoted to fire investigation. In that role he carried out numerous investigations, many involving fatalities, serious injury and criminal activities. He has spoken at training events in Europe and the USA. He has contributed to a number of publications and is author of the FM Global *Pocket Guide to Fire and Arson Investigation* (UK 2000 edition). Mick has provided professional advice and assistance to organisations such as the Institution of Fire Engineers (IFE); Arson Prevention Bureau (APB); Arson Control Forum (ACF); and the Council for the Registration of Forensic Practitioners (CRFP), and is currently a CRFP Lead Assessor. He assisted in the design of the UK National Occupational Standard (NOS) and is a member of the International Association of Arson Investigators (IAAI) Training and Education group. Mick is a recipient of the 'Pete Ganci' award which was presented to him in January 2009 by the IAAI UK chapter for having excelled and being positively proactive within his field.

**Peter Gill** PhD FIBiol is currently Professor of Legal Medicine at the University of Oslo and Senior Lecturer at the University of Strathclyde.

Previously he had worked for 26 years at the Forensic Science Service, UK. He specialises in all areas of DNA profiling technology, but has a special interest in statistics, computation and interpretation of evidence. Peter has more than 100 publications to his credit. He is Chair of the European Network of Forensic Science Institutes (ENFSI) methods, analysis and interpretation subgroup of the DNA working group, and is a member of the European DNA profiling group (EDNAP). He has chaired several DNA commissions of the International Society of Forensic Genetics (ISFG), producing several publications (such as recommendations on the interpretation of mixtures) that have become standard throughout the EC.

**Max M. Houck** is the Director of the West Virginia University Forensic Science Initiative, a programme that develops training and resources for the forensic industry. He is also Director of Forensic Business Development in the WVU College of Business and Economics. He has co-authored and edited numerous books and journal articles. He is a Fellow of the American Academy of Forensic Sciences, among other professional organisations, and Chairman of the Forensic Science Educational Program Accreditation Commission. He also serves on the editorial boards of several journals and is founding co-editor, along with Jay Siegel, of the journal *Forensic Science Policy and Management*.

**Graham Jackson** is Consultant Forensic Scientist with *Advance Forensic Science* and Visiting Professor of Forensic Science at the University of Abertay Dundee. He provides advice, support and training in case assessment and interpretation (CAI) to forensic science providers in the UK and abroad. He worked for over 30 years for the Forensic Science Service in a wide range of roles and has been co-author, along with fellow members of a CAI team, of a number of papers on case assessment and interpretation. Several of these CAI papers gained awards from the European Academy of Forensic Sciences and the Forensic Science Society. His most recent contribution is a chapter on 'Case Assessment and Interpretation (CAI)' written along with co-author Phil Jones for *Encyclopedia of Forensic Science* to be published by Wiley in 2009.

**Alan Kershaw's** career has been in administrative management, specialising since 1983 in professional regulation. For 16 years he worked at the General Medical Council, dealing with all aspects of the regulatory business and focusing on the definition, description and delivery of high-quality professional standards. His culminating position was as Director of Education and Standards. Between 1999 and 2007 he worked as Chief Executive of the Council for the Registration of Forensic Practitioners, whose work he describes in Chapter 20 of this book. Since the late 1990s he has served as a lay member on the boards of several premier regulatory bodies, including the Royal Pharmaceutical Society of Great Britain, the Solicitors Regulation Authority, the Royal Institution of Chartered Surveyors, the Nursing and Midwifery Council. He helped to found the General Osteopathic Council and authored *Pursuing Excellence,* its Code of Conduct for registered osteopaths. At present he holds a number of lay member positions, primarily the Chairmanship of ILEX Professional Standards Ltd, the regulatory arm of the Institute of

Legal Executives. In all he has been involved in standards setting for some 35 professional groups, has published numerous articles on the subject in professional journals and has delivered papers at national and international conferences.

**Adrian Linacre** is a Senior Lecturer at the Centre for Forensic Science, University of Strathclyde, where he has been employed since 1994. He has a DPhil in molecular genetics and his research is on low-level DNA typing from non-human samples. He is on the editorial board of *Forensic Science International: Genetics*, a co-author of *An Introduction to Forensic Genetics* (Wiley 2007) as well as editor of, and contributor to, *Forensic Science in Wildlife Investigations* (Taylor and Francis 2009). He is a Registered Forensic Practitioner in the area of human contact traces and an assessor for the Council for the Registration of Forensic Practitioners.

**Lucy Mason** joined the Ministerial Delivery Unit at the Department of Innovation, Universities and Skills following more than five years working in the Thames Valley Police, most recently as Force Risk Manager and previously as Executive Research Officer to the Chief Constable. She is a Research Associate of the Centre for Criminology, University of Oxford, and has published various papers on police accountability, counter-terrorism, organised crime, and the future of policing, as well as serving as Review Editor for *Policing: A Journal of Policy and Practice* published by Oxford University Press. She has a doctorate in Archaeological Science from the University of Oxford, following her undergraduate degree in Archaeology and Anthropology at the University of Cambridge.

**James Munday** joined the Metropolitan Police Forensic Science Laboratory in 1972, working mainly in criminalistics, and moved into full-time fire and explosion investigation in 1979. He left the Laboratory in 1998 to set up a private consultancy in the UK. In 2003 he relocated to New South Wales, Australia although his services are available worldwide. He has investigated almost 3,000 fire scenes including over 350 fatal incidents, and carried out laboratory tests on materials from more than 1,000 others. During the past ten years Jim has been heavily involved in devising and delivering training programmes and helping to create national standards of competence for investigators. He also has a special interest in the interpretation of thermal damage distribution on people involved in fires. A frequent lecturer, with many publications, most recently the *Disaster and Emergency Management Handbook* (Butterworth Tolley 2003), he is also a Member of the Institution of Fire Engineers, holds the Diploma of the Forensic Science Society in Fire Investigation and is an IAAI Certified Fire Investigator. In 2007 Jim was made a Fellow of the Forensic Science Society.

**Terrence Napier** joined the Metropolitan Police Forensic Science Laboratory in 1988 having completed a degree in Applied Chemistry. He started his forensic career in the department that examined marks and traces and later joined the Serious Crimes Unit which specialised in the examination of major crime scenes, particularly using a wide array of enhancement methods. Terrence then joined West Yorkshire Police as a Forensic Science Manager, being tasked with increasing the use of footwear evidence within West Yorkshire Police. In 2002 Terrence left West Yorkshire Police to run his own business as a forensic supplier to police forces and has worked with numerous forces in England and Wales. To date he has examined in excess of 60,000 crime scenes marks and many thousands of footwear items.

**Paul Roberts** is Professor of Criminal Jurisprudence and Co-Director of the LLM programme in the University of Nottingham School of Law, where he researches and teaches in the fields of criminal evidence and criminal justice with particular emphasis on philosophical, international and comparative perspectives. His principal publications include Roberts and Zuckerman, *Criminal Evidence* (OUP 2004); Roberts and Redmayne (eds), *Innovations in Evidence and Proof* (Hart 2007); and Roberts and Willmore, *The Role of Forensic Science Evidence in Criminal Proceedings* (HMSO 1993). He is a member of the Royal Statistical Society's Working Group on Statistics and the Law and sits on the Board of Foreign Advisers of the Institute of Evidence Law and Forensic Science at the China University of Political Science and Law (CUPL) Beijing, has advised the UK Law Commissions and conducted research for the Crown Prosecution Service, and regularly lectures to the legal profession on topics of criminal evidence and procedure.

**James Robertson** was appointed as the first non-police head of the forensic group with the Australian Federal Police in 1989. Under his leadership the group has grown from modest beginnings to a forensic leader in Australia. Orginally a lecturer in forensic science at the University of Strathclyde, Dr Robertson has maintained a strong interest in academia and research. Included in his publications are the *Forensic Examination of Fibres* and the *Forensic Examination of Hairs*. He is an Adjunct or Honorary Professor at three universities. He has contributed to several major enquiries into miscarriages of justice and has a strong interest in the role of forensic science in the rule of law. Dr Robertson holds the Australian Public Service Medal for services to forensic science and law enforcement.

**Claude Roux** is Professor of Forensic Science and the founding Director of the Centre for Forensic Science at the University of Technology, Sydney, Australia. He obtained a BSc and a PhD in forensic science from the University of Lausanne, Switzerland. He has 19 years' experience in providing forensic expertise, training and research. His areas of activities and interests cover a broad spectrum of forensic science and include chemical criminalistics, finger mark detection, questioned documents, forensic education and training and management. Claude is an Editorial Board member for *Forensic Science International* and *Science and Justice*. He is also involved in a number of scientific and advisory groups in Australia and overseas. His service as Chair of the Australian and New Zealand Association of Forensic Science Educators and Researchers is of particular relevance for the current contribution.

**Nick Tilley** is currently attached to the Jill Dando Institute of Crime Science, University College London. He was previously at Nottingham Trent University, where he is now an emeritus professor. His research interests lie in policing, crime prevention and programme evaluation methodology. He is author or editor of some 10 books and more than 100 chapters, journal articles and published research reports. His most recent book is *Crime Prevention* (Willan 2009). *Evaluating Crime Reduction Initiatives*, which he is editing with Johannes Knutsson, is due also to be published in 2009 (Criminal Justice Press and Willan).

**Michael Townsley** is a lecturer in the School of Criminology and Criminal Justice, Griffith University. Before joining Griffith University he was a Senior Research Fellow at the Jill Dando Institute of Crime Science, University College London. Trained as a statistician, he has focused his research on crime analysis, problem-oriented policing and quantitative methods in a criminal justice setting, all with a view to preventing crime. His current research projects include the spatial and temporal modelling of crime and the analysis of large novel data sets.

**Adrian Wain** is a National Scientific Lead in the field of body fluids with the Forensic Science Service. He has 25 years' experience in body fluid analysis, DNA profiling and blood pattern interpretation. His work has led to his continued involvement in some high-profile homicide cases from crime scene to court room. He is also an assessor for Human Contact traces and the newly formed Natural Sciences specialty with the Council for Registration of Forensic Practitioners. His current interests lie mainly with the setting and maintenance of quality standards within forensic science.

**Robin Williams** is Professor Emeritus in the School of Applied Social Sciences at Durham University and Professor in the school of Applied Sciences at Northumbria University. He previously worked at the Universities of Cardiff, Southampton and Manchester. He has carried out several research studies of the police uses of forensic science in the UK and in Continental Europe. His book (co-authored with Paul Johnson) on the growth of forensic DNA databases was published in 2007, and he has also written a number of academic papers and reports on operational and policy issues relating to the development and use of forensic genetics. He has been a member of the Harvard Workshop on DNA Fingerprinting and Civil Liberties, funded by the American Society of Law, Medicine and Ethics, and of the Nuffield Council on Bioethics Working Party on the Forensic Uses of Bioinformation. His work has been funded by the Home Office, the Wellcome Trust and the Nuffield Foundation. He is a member of the Policy, Ethics and Life Sciences Institute at the University of Newcastle.

**Sheila Willis** is Director of the Forensic Science Laboratory in Ireland where she has been a career forensic scientist since the early years of the laboratory, having joined in 1979. She trained as a chemist and completed a PhD in 1977. As a practising forensic scientist, she was particularly involved in physical trace evidence including fibres, paint and glass as well as fire accelerants and explosives. She is interested in how forensic evidence can best be exploited such that the potential and limitations of the findings are clearly understood and is very conscious that this demands good communication with all stakeholders, particularly those from the legal domain.

**Tim Wilson** is a Professor of Forensic Sciences and Public Policy in the School of Applied Sciences at Northumbria University. His research interests centre on the use of forensic and clinical sciences in the criminal justice system and the resulting interfaces with ethics, public health, economics and politics. He is also Visiting Fellow at PEALS (Policy Ethics and Life Sciences) at Newcastle University, where he is currently co-researching projects on the future of bioinformation and the long-term sustainability of forensic pathology in England and Wales supported by respectively the Nuffield Foundation and the Wellcome Trust. He chairs the National Policing Improvement Agency forensic pathology committees for professional discipline, and registration and training. Previously he was a member of the Senior Civil Service where his career spanned the Home Office, the Ministry of Justice and HM Treasury. His additional expertise in financing public infrastructure and service modernisation resulted in secondments to WS Atkins and later – for an EC funded cooperation project in Russian with government, the legislature and academia – the International Labour Organisation. He did similar work in South Africa during the Mandela Presidency.

# Preface

The significance, influence and visibility of forensic science in criminal justice systems have risen notably in recent years. Factors likely to have contributed to this development can be tentatively identified although their precise role as causative, influential or peripheral agents is more difficult, perhaps impossible, to establish. This situation is not solely a consequence of progress in technical or scientific expertise from within forensic science but arises in combination with features of the external environment including cultural, social, economic, legal and political factors. For example, developments in DNA technology have been accompanied by major investments by governments around the world in the establishment and expansion of DNA databases on the assumption that such investments will contribute to improvements in the effectiveness of criminal justice. And within the UK, changing political priorities have resulted in new structures for the provision of forensic science with the creation of an entirely commercial market in England and Wales, albeit accompanied by a more traditional public sector approach in Scotland.

The primary aim of this book is to present and examine contemporary forensic science practice against this broader background; to set the activities, procedures, usage, value and expectations of forensic science in this context; and to comment critically and authoritatively on the role of forensic science in the criminal justice system. In doing so, technical aspects of forensic science are presented in a manner that is relevant to experts, but also enables non-specialist readers including police officers, lawyers, social scientists, criminologists and researchers to gain an advanced understanding of the nature and scope of forensic science and the potential benefits and risks that accompany its uses.

What now constitutes forensic science, its essence, extent, methods and purpose, is a matter of current debate within the community and beyond. Most forensic practitioners are specialists and many are expert witnesses. As such they are trained to remain within their expertise – whether it is DNA analysis, anthropology, fingerprints, or whatever – and they are often reluctant to stray beyond their specialism. From the perspective of expert testimony such behaviour is to risk attacks on their integrity and competence. For this reason, forensic science could be portrayed as an activity in which expert practitioners inhabit deep troughs of knowledge characterised by historically distinctive practices and procedures, with few cross-cutting paths that allow these to be compared; in effect an intensification of the old adage that the nature of science is to know more and more about less and less. The most extreme example of this is the differing approaches to interpretation and evaluation of DNA and fingerprints. Despite their common purpose, in criminal justice terms, fingerprints and DNA methodologies are, for the most part, conceptually, procedurally, culturally and professionally separate. It has taken academic and other commentators from outside the fields of operational practice (Saks and Koehler 2005; Cole 2001) and controversial cases like that of Shirley McKie (Justice 1 Committee 2007) to highlight such inconsistencies.

Many authors have attempted to define the necessary and essential features of forensic science in order to demarcate it from closely related enterprises. Our strategy in this book is to do without – at least at the beginning – a formal definition of forensic science. Instead, we have sought to describe and characterise the range of activities that are included in contemporary discussions of the term, and only then have we tried to determine their family resemblances. So we have taken an approach that identifies common themes and practices whilst recognising the variety of technical, disciplinary and cognitive resources that forensic scientists draw on in carrying out their work. Our aim is to examine and illustrate these commonalities and differences as we explore forensic science, and also to reflect and comment on the issues that arise from this effort. This approach is very different from most other books on the subject, many of which have a much narrower disciplinary scope and a specific technical focus. In exploring such a broad canvas in a single volume there are practical matters to address. The investigation of a single case such as a road traffic incident resulting in a death could involve a large number of disciplines, including for example engineering, physics, chemistry, biology, statistics, mathematics and computer science. Such a case may also require the interpretation of complex legal issues in addition to trade specifications and international standards. Few individuals are likely to have this range of knowledge, particularly if they come from non-scientific disciplines, and so it would be impossible to take the broad perspective of this book and to cover the entire technical range of forensic science. Instead we select some of the dominant disciplines and kinds of forensic science and present them in sufficient depth to draw out the key features of each area. In addition, several editorial chapters seek to identify common themes and issues present in a number of chapters.

In Chapter 1 we introduce the range of material covered in the handbook and set out a guide to the scientific, legal, social, political and economic issues of relevance. This includes an examination of the intersections between these areas, particularly where contests over knowledge and authority have arisen in ways relevant to contemporary forensic science practice.

In Part 1 of the Handbook we consider a number of key areas of forensic science practice. Section 1 deals with the identification of individuals by DNA (Chapter 2), fingerprints (Chapter 3) and forensic anthropology (Chapter 4).

A comparison of the content of these chapters illustrates the common as well as divergent practices in identifying individuals. Section 2 examines the identification and comparison of materials and artifacts. This includes drugs (Chapter 5), body fluids in sexual offences (Chapter 6), trace evidence (Chapter 7) and marks (Chapter 8). In the final section of Part 1, we explore the reconstruction of events in a legal and investigative context, considering bloodstain pattern analysis (Chapter 9) and fire investigation (Chapter 10). Each of these sections contain chapters which focus on specific areas of forensic science which, in addition to providing detail on the main theme, are illustrative of more general practices and principles such as interpretation and reasoning processes.

Part 2 examines how forensic science is used as investigative support in the UK and describes how police organisations and laboratories configure resources and relationships in the investigation of crime. 'Forensic resources and criminal investigations' (Chapter 11) describes the structures and processes used by police forces and the recent development of new roles and working practices involved in effective use of forensic science. The *modus operandi* of the DNA databases in England and Wales, Scotland and Northern Ireland are considered in Chapter 12. The chapter describes the development and implementation of the databases and their varying legislative frameworks, governance and impact in criminal investigations. Chapter 13, (on forensic science in major crime inquiries), describes how scientific expertise has come to play a central part in the investigation of serious and major crime in the UK. Recent developments such as the role of 'specialist advisers' and the increasing use of forensic science to investigate 'cold cases', amongst other developments, are reviewed. The next chapter, 'Forensic science in UK policing: strategies, tactics and effectiveness' (Chapter 14), considers recent efforts by key stakeholders in UK forensic science to develop a coherent strategy for the use of science and technology in policing as well as several other significant initiatives such as the DNA Expansion Programme, HMIC thematic reports on forensic science and joint ACPO/FSS projects.

Part 3 of the Handbook, 'Forensic Reasoning and the Evaluation of Scientific Evidence', is concerned with the analysis of the logical and discursive methods and models used by investigators and forensic scientists to structure, communicate and evaluate evidence and intelligence in the course of investigations, as well as how forensic science expertise is represented by and incorporated into the legal process. Following this, Chapter 15, provides a summary account of recent debates on the role of statistics in forensic science. It considers the history of the differing ways in which probability has been theorised and expressed and concludes that the role of statistical and probabilistic reasoning in the administration of justice is set to increase. This is in part due to the increased sensitivity of analytical technology available but also a consequence of the so-called 'paradigm shift' described by Saks and Koehler (2005). Chapter 16, 'Understanding forensic science opinions', considers how operational scientists and academic scholars recently have tried to describe and prescribe the logic of forensic investigation. Such efforts have produced a range of assertions: from those that insist on the necessity for deliberate hypothetico-deductive theorising by crime scene examiners, to those that provide more nuanced accounts of the use of abductive reasoning by a range of scientific investigators. Chapter 17, 'The science of proof: forensic science evidence in English criminal trials', describes the range of issues that arise when courts seek to determine the admissibility of differing claims to expertise and their relevance for fact-finders. It considers the legal principles that lie behind the need for and use of expert witnesses, their responsibilities, and recent case law relating to expert evidence. A number of key cases in England and Wales are analysed in order to consider the dynamics of a system in which there are no standardised formulations of scientific and related expertise of the kind that exist in other jurisdictions, for example 'Daubert and Frye' hearings in the USA. It also considers the effect of current judicial understandings of scientific evidence on how reports are written and how their providers may be interrogated in the courtroom setting.

Part 4 of the Handbook, 'Themes and Debates in Contemporary Forensic Science', considers current and emerging issues in contemporary forensic science practice. Each of the chapters is concerned with the ways in which legal, ethical, political, professional and economic factors impinge on the organisation and use of forensic science in support of justice in general and criminal investigation in particular. In Chapter 18, 'Forensic science and the internationalisation of policing', consideration is given to the application of forensic science knowledge to interjurisdictional investigations and prosecutions, and the ways in which this process is shaped by differing political and judicial systems. This chapter also considers the sources and effects of the strategic proliferation of UK forensic expertise and practice through international collaboration and the increasing interest in transnational intelligence gathering and data sharing. Chapter 19, 'Forensic science, ethics and criminal justice', explores accounts of the seeming disparity between the universal values of scientific inquiry and the contingencies of adversarial legal practice. It discusses the necessity for forensic scientists to formulate and defend their expert opinions in ways that are responsive to these two different approaches to knowledge and deliberation and goes on to portray some of the difficulties they can encounter in seeking to achieve this.

Chapter 20, 'Professional standards, public protection and the administration of justice', considers the nature of professionalism, ethics and standard setting for the extensive range of practitioners who are involved in forensic science. In particular it describes the history, development, implementation and role of the recently abandoned Council for Registration of Forensic Practitioners in the UK. Despite efforts to set such standards it challenges the manner in which lawyers select expert witnesses and the implications of this for forensic practice and criminal justice.

The significant and recent growth of forensic science programmes in higher education is considered in Chapter 21, 'The development and enhancement of forensic expertise: higher education and in-service training'. The expansion of the role of higher education has been the source of much commentary within the community of operational forensic scientists in particular, as well as policing agencies and academia in general. This chapter describes this expansion and considers its significance for the future of forensic science and its development. It also discusses the relationship between academic provision and in-service training by the police and forensic science providers.

In the concluding chapter, 'The future(s) of forensic investigation', we consider some of the important issues that will face forensic science in the UK and elsewhere during the first decade of the twenty-first century. These include: the management of growing political and public expectations of the contribution of science to criminal investigation; the increasing commercialisation of forensic science provision; the equality of prosecution and defence access to scientific resources; the implications of developments in forensic surveillance and the databasing of forensic intelligence; the effectiveness of efforts to improve the scientific literacy of police users of forensic science support; and the uneven development of research-based teaching of forensic science in UK universities.

## References

Cole, S.A. (2001) *Suspect Identities: A History of Fingerprinting and Criminal Identification.* Cambridge Mass.: Harvard University Press.

Justice 1 Committee (2007) *Inquiry into the Scottish Criminal Records Office and the Scottish Fingerprint Service.* Edinburgh: The Scottish Parliament.

Saks, M. and Koehler, J. (2005) 'The coming paradigm shift in forensic identification science', *Science*, 309: 892–895.

# Chapter 1

# The contemporary landscape of forensic science

*Jim Fraser and Robin Williams*

## Introduction

> Physical evidence cannot be wrong, it cannot perjure itself, it cannot be wholly absent. Only human failure to find it, study and understand it, can diminish its value.
>
> (Kirk: 1974)

> Some place their faith in forensic science to the degree that they are under the impression that it is absolute, infallible and unassailable. In truth it is a manmade construct, dependent on manmade machinery, man-calibrated accuracy, man-led action under manmade protocols and analyzed by man – an altogether human construct.
>
> (American Academy of Forensic Sciences cited in Pyrek (2007: 2)

> Forensic science plainly has something of value to offer to criminal investigators and the courts. Why, then, does so much of it cling, instead, to an untenable absolutism and committed subjectivity?
>
> (Saks 1998: 1090)

Differing understandings of the nature of forensic science and of the value of its contribution to criminal justice, like those captured in the varying claims quoted above, are found throughout the many celebratory and critical commentaries that articulate its contemporary condition and future promise. There is general agreement amongst the majority of observers that technical progress in a number of forensic science disciplines, along with growing police and judicial confidence in the robustness of their analyses, facilitates an increasing and exceptional contribution to criminal investigations and prosecutions in advanced industrial societies.[1] For some scholars and practitioners, this phenomenon needs no special explanation, being simply one of the ways in which seemingly objective scientific discoveries are increasingly brought to bear on rational decision-making and collective actions in such societies. For others, including many of those involved in the profession of forensic science itself, a more cautious attitude may be discerned. Underlying such caution is the observation of the (under-appreciated) heterogeneity of forensic science practice, along with the persistent absence of agreement on how best to determine and formulate any underpinning commonality of ambition, reasoning or practice amongst its constituent elements.[2] Despite the efforts of writers like Inman and Rudin (2001) to develop statements of common principles and practice, and notwithstanding notable generic advances (for example in the deployment of Bayesian reasoning) as well as developments in individual forensic disciplines (for example in DNA profiling), there remain significant conceptual and empirical dissonances that hamper efforts to arrive at a shared understanding of many of the most basic features of the forensic endeavour.[3] In addition, the multiplicity of ways in which forensic science is applied to individual cases, and the heterogeneity that inevitably follows variation in legal procedures in different jurisdictions, act as further barriers to the widespread standardisation of forensic science knowledge and practice.

This chapter is no more than an initial foray into this complex discursive and practical terrain; terrain that subsequently will be navigated in much more detail by the many distinguished contributors to this Handbook. Accordingly, the next few pages are limited to a sketch of the overall intellectual, legal, organisational and policy contexts in which we locate the several sections and many chapters that make up the book as a whole. In this introduction then, we merely make visible the factors we have sought to consider in our own efforts to analyse and understand the condition and role of forensic science in contemporary criminal justice processes. These considerations include: the theoretical underpinnings of forensic science in general, and of specific advances in particular; the developing operational uses of a range of forensic technologies to support investigations; the authority accorded to forensic expertise by criminal justice actors in particular and by wider publics in general; the underlying, and often tense relationship between the epistemic idioms of science and the law; and the interplay of state, public and commercial interests in the expansion and regulation of forensic science and its criminal justice applications. We attempt a transnational perspective on the many issues under consideration since, although some are specific to UK jurisdictions, we believe such developments are of interest and relevance to other jurisdictions given the increasing internationalisation of crime and policing, the avowedly universal character of scientific knowledge, and the increasing rate of knowledge transfer across national boundaries.

We begin by acknowledging the many terminological complexities that arise in efforts to characterise the predominant features of this field of theory and practice. Such complexities are immediately obvious with regard to the underlying notion of 'science' and the scope of its application to a bewildering variety of disciplines and investigative processes. In fact, even the conventional use of the singular noun in the term 'forensic science' can work to conceal the multiplicity of scientific disciplines that claim a place in this domain as well as differences in the ways in which they are applied in varying forensic contexts.[4] Despite these uncomfortable facts, however, the use of the plural form 'forensic sciences' remains rare and will hardly be found in the pages of this Handbook. Terminologically, it can also be argued that there are many occasions when the expressions 'forensic technology' or 'forensic technologies' should be preferred to that of 'forensic science', since usually what is described is not a body of theoretical knowledge, but rather the practical application of one or several bodies of knowledge, albeit through disciplined human procedures and the use of a variety of instruments and tools. Throughout this text we assume that references to 'technology' will remind readers of the fact that specific forensic innovations cannot be understood without reference to the social desires and strategies that occasioned their development (even where – as is the case with DNA profiling, for example – the original impetus may have come from outside the field of criminal investigation).[5]

Indeed, it is worth noting that the term 'forensic science' is one that is most associated with the Anglophone world, or perhaps the common law jurisdictions typical of that world. The term is much less common in continental Europe and has no direct equivalent in a number of European languages. In Germany the word 'kriminalistik' was coined to represent the activities of applied forensic investigators, and has been widely taken up in the USA (in the terms 'criminalistics' and 'criminalist') and in some European countries to describe a certain subset of forensic activities, although it is still sometimes used synonymously with 'forensic science' (see Houck and Siegal 2006). In Finland, the nearest equivalent is 'technical crime investigation', recognising that whatever this set of activities contains, they are subsets of investigation that engage technological means rather than subsets of science. Indeed it is possible to argue that careful evaluation of the numerous roles and activities sometimes included under the heading of forensic science practice may establish that many of these are only loosely related to formal principles of scientific knowledge and practice (see Fraser 2007b).

Many other difficulties and differences arise in the effort to capture, even on a preliminary basis, the constitutive features of forensic science.[6] For this reason, when commissioning contributions to this Handbook, we have worked with a deliberately inclusive understanding of the distinctiveness of forensic science as a collection of expert practices whose ambition is to draw on a body of universally valid scientific knowledge, apply reliable technologies and robust methodologies to individual cases, and link underlying principles to localised practical reasoning in support of the goals of criminal justice. Thus, whilst forensic science is concerned with the exploration, explication and evaluation of fundamental facts such as the identity, origin and life history of materials, substances and artefacts by scientific methodologies and technologies, its approach to the discovery and interpretation of all such local instances of these facts is necessarily conditioned by the requirement to provide disciplined conclusions that are both relevant to practical investigative decisions and also recognised by legitimate judicial authority. The authors of the chapters that follow this introduction do not necessarily share our perspective on all of these matters (indeed some may disagree with our comments or our emphases), but we hope that this initial overview of an extensive and varied field of applied systematic practice will usefully orientate readers who go on to read what our colleagues have written in the body of the Handbook.

**Mapping forensic science**

Strong positive images of the authority of contemporary forensic science are everywhere. They provide a resource for governmental actors concerned to show their commitment to increasingly effective crime control, they frame the technological commodities and services offered to such actors by both public sector and commercial providers, and they are the stuff of endless factual and fictional media representations.[7]

For example, in an account of what seems an instance of an unusually effective government programme, the Forensic Science and Pathology Unit of the UK Home Office (2005a) state that the presence of forensic evidence, more specifically DNA, increases the likelihood of detection of dwelling-house burglaries by almost threefold (from 16 per cent to 41 per cent). However, the significance of this claim as an account of the effectiveness of DNA collection and analysis is not universally accepted and the causal relationship between the presence of forensic evidence and the successful detection of an offence (let alone the successful prosecution of an offender) remains little explored and largely unexplained. A recent US report (Roman et al. 2008) provides the first substantive large-scale study of the effectiveness and cost effectiveness of DNA in volume crime, and this work did show that property offences in which DNA was discovered at the crime scene and subsequently analysed had twice as many suspects arrested (and more than twice as many cases accepted for prosecution) as those that did not. However, the use of a randomised control trial methodology in this study has yet to be followed in any other study of the use of forensic science in support of criminal investigations.

Despite this general shortcoming, the availability of forensic science evidence in individual cases of serious crime can often be shown to have had especially dramatic effects. An example of such cases was also included in the UK Home Office publication mentioned above. In this instance, two young girls (aged eleven and nine) were raped and indecently assaulted in Canterbury, Kent in 1988. Whilst the perpetrator was not identified at the time, 13 years later and over 175 miles away in Derby, a shoplifter was arrested and his DNA sample taken. The resulting profile was automatically uploaded to the National DNA Database of England and Wales (NDNAD) and was found to match the 1988 crime scene samples. On arrest, the suspect admitted his guilt, was speedily tried and sentenced to a term in jail. Such an example can – and invariably is – used to illustrate, in powerful and emotive terms, the impact of DNA technology and its use as an inceptive tool for the investigation of crime. Without the availability of crime scene and subject genetic samples, there would have been little or no prospect of an arrest let alone a prosecution or conviction in this, and many other similar cases. In addition, the guilty plea by this particular suspect confirms the overwhelming authority of the DNA in the absence of virtually any other substantive evidence. Such instances do much to foster the impression that forensic evidence has no boundaries or limitations to its application, being able to reach back almost indefinitely in time in this and other cases.[8]

In turn, such positive investigative outcomes have prompted the retrospective systematic review of many historic controversial cases (for example those of

James Hanratty, Stephen Downing, and others)[9] as well as the resolution of significant miscarriages of justice, such as the case of those convicted in 1990 of the murder of Lynette White, a young prostitute, who was murdered in 1988. In this case, and two years later, the Court of Appeal overturned the conviction of the 'Cardiff Three' and questioned the reliability of the interview and confession evidence presented at the original trial. Following a series of unsuccessful reviews of the case, a final review found small specks of blood on a cellophane wrapper from a condom and the key ring of the flat, which were insufficient for analysis in 1988 (and which had also been overlooked in previous reviews). A complete reassessment of the crime scene by a behavioural scientist and the forensic scientist working together, and re-enactment of the incident, led to reconsideration of recovered fingermarks and retained materials such as some sections of wallpaper. DNA profiles obtained from these materials eliminated all previous suspects including the 'Cardiff Three', but did not match any profile then held on the NDNAD. In 2002, the relatively novel technique of 'familial searching' the NDNAD, on this occasion based on the presence of a rare allele found in the crime scene profile, resulted in a request for a voluntary intelligence sample from Jeffrey Gafoor, a local security guard whose relative was on the database and with whom he shared a 'familial' pattern. After providing the confirmatory buccal sample, Jeffrey Gafoor unsuccessfully attempted suicide, and in July 2003 he pleaded guilty to the murder – 15 years after the crime.

However, despite the appeal of these, and other such affirmative accounts, there exist many less optimistic understandings of the nature of forensic science in general, its relationship with the law, and the effectiveness of its deployment in efforts to detect crime and prosecute offenders.[10] Jurists, policymakers and a variety of critics have constantly revisited the claims of forensic science to 'speak truth to justice', the former sometimes encountering the difficulty of translating from legal to scientific discourse and vice versa. Questions have arisen either in response to seeming miscarriages of justice resulting in part from the inappropriate deployment of specific technologies, or as part of more general inquiries into the costs and benefits of the uses of forensic science to support the criminal justice processes of contemporary liberal democracies.[11]

An example of the former can be found in the case of Sion Jenkins who was arrested and charged with the murder of his stepdaughter Billie-Jo Jenkins in 1998. Other than circumstantial evidence, the only evidence against him was the presence of fine blood spatters on his clothing. At the heart of this case was a dispute about the interpretation of such spatters. The prosecution argued that these incriminated Sion Jenkins since they could only have arisen from his assault of the victim. The defence contended that such fine spatters could be caused by 'expired blood' of the kind that would have come from the 'dying breath' of the victim. A large number of experts, including forensic and academic scientists drawn from a number of disciplines, as well as pathologists, were involved in three trials over nine years. Following the third trial in 2007 Sion Jenkins was released when the jury were unable to reach a verdict.

In addition to these kinds of technological contestations, other conceptual aspects of forensic science such as the statistical methodologies underpinning many routine interpretative aspects of practice (especially those used in DNA interpretation) continue to present difficulties and cause confusion for courts and juries. In an especially significant case, the solicitor Sally Clark was convicted of the murder of her two sons in 1999, a conviction upheld on appeal in 2000 (*R v. Clark* [2000] WXCA Crim 54). In fact, the conviction relied on flawed statistical evidence presented by Sir Roy Meadow, an experienced paediatrician. Meadow used a published figure for the frequency of sudden infant death syndrome (SIDS) in families and proceeded to square this figure to obtain a value of 1 in 73 million for the frequency of two such deaths in the same family. In a statement issued by the Royal Statistical Society, this approach was characterised as 'statistically invalid' and one that could only be justified if SIDS arose independently in families. There was no empirical evidence to support such an assumption and good *a priori* reasons for supposing it to be false, given the genetic and environmental factors shared within families. In addition to this basic statistical issue a more complex one arose in some of the press reports about the 1 in 73 million figure which was presented as the 'chance that the deaths of the two children were accidental'. Such an assertion is in fact an example of the 'prosecutor's fallacy', an issue which had already played a role in a number of high-profile cases involving DNA interpretation in the 1990s.

There are also occasions on which the apparent absence of forensic evidence can cause controversy, confusion and issues of interpretation. Michael Stone was convicted of the murders of Lin and Megan Russell in 1998 following their deaths in 1996. After a successful appeal he was convicted for a second time in 2001. During the period between the murders and the second conviction there were extensive developments in DNA technology that required constant review of the forensic materials in the case. Despite this, no significant forensic evidence to link Stone to the victims or their murder was found. Stone was convicted largely on the basis of a confession he made to a fellow inmate in Canterbury prison.[12] However, there was an assumption in this case (and there continue to be in many others) that such events cannot take place without forensic evidence being transferred and therefore that it will be subsequently found. Despite Kirk's assertion quoted at the beginning of this chapter, it is clear that in many cases no forensic evidence is found and one must question the realism of his statement that the only explanation for the seeming absence of such evidence is human failure.

Such cases illustrate a number of important themes in the application of forensic science that are a consequence of the lack of declared legal standards for the admissibility of scientific and expert evidence in the United Kingdom and elsewhere. In the absence of these standards the technological and epistemological limits of such evidence remain unexplored in any systematic manner outside the court system and, consequently, judgements are made within the contingencies of individual cases. Some jurisdictions (for example, the United States) attempt to supplement case law with more principled inclusionary rules in order to provide guidance and restrictions on the admissibility of expert and scientific evidence in the courts.[13]

## Theory and practice in forensic science

The observations of the American Academy of Forensic Sciences cited by Pyrek at the beginning of this chapter provide a strong signal that the seemingly simple notion of forensic science as a 'human construct' has a number of complex ramifications. In its least contentious version, it is a reminder of the fact that forensic science – as with all such theoretical and practical endeavours – has a history. But telling this history as a progressive narrative of the gradual accumulation of incontrovertible facts of nature and the reliable application of such facts to improve investigative and judicial decision-making will serve only to reinstate another – albeit historicised – account of forensic science practice as able to represent 'reality' with increasing precision.[14] Yet the observations of the Academy of Forensic Sciences can be seen to have wider implications than this, since they explicitly emphasise the constructed (and reconstructed) nature of this enterprise by the rhetorical repetition of 'manmade machinery, man-calibrated accuracy, man-led action under manmade protocols and analyzed by man'. The emphasis of the authors of the statement on the human shaping of forensic science provides a powerful rationale for reflecting on its various historical journeys and social uses in different communities. It also reminds us of the importance of examining the ways in which the objects and practices of this heterogeneous enterprise may be distinguished from other kinds of scientific endeavours with their roots in, and their growth fed by, different kinds of social imaginaries.[15]

Finally, we need to acknowledge that our efforts to grasp the essential features of forensic science theory and practice, as well as account for its current status, need to recognise the instability and permeability of its shifting boundaries, the difficulty of establishing legitimate membership of its 'community' (Roberts and Willmore 1993), and the lack of an agreed definition of its core ontological and methodological preferences (Inman and Rudin 2001). As Thornton and Peterson (2002: 3) assert, 'Forensic science is, in many ways, an untidy, scruffy sort of discipline. In an anthropomorphic sense, it has dirty fingernails and hair growing out of its ears. Those using forensic science have had trouble in deciding what they want from it, and those practicing it have had trouble in deciding what they will allow themselves to become.'

So an acknowledgement of the historically and socially constructed character of forensic science and its associated technologies demands that we pay attention to the more intricate trajectories of particular forensic science disciplines and practices as well as the influences exerted by developments in one such discipline over others.[16] Not all of these histories are glorious ones. In the seeming absence of a commonly agreed methodological basis for the assessment of the validity and reliability of specific – sometimes long-standing – forensic practices, the deployment of faulty reasoning or faulty procedures can surely lead to wrongful convictions, or at least unsafe convictions, based in part on subsequently discredited scientific evidence. For example, the recent 'permanent abandonment' by the US Federal Bureau of Investigation Laboratory of 'Bullet Lead Analysis' (which determines the amounts of particular trace elements in fired bullets and compares them with unfired bullets potentially associated with the gun) has led to the review of all cases in which such evidence was presented in support of prosecutions between the early 1980s and 2004.[17]

Moreover, our attentiveness to all of these issues needs to be informed by an awareness of the background of wider (and often contested) cultural expectations of the nature and role of techno-scientific theory and practice in contemporary social, especially legal, life. We have already commented on the increasingly demanding political and public expectations that seem to be placed on forensic science, but it is also important to note that these expectations have themselves been fed by narratives of the current (or potential future) success of forensic science at resolving outstanding investigative uncertainties, trial disputes, and even disputed convictions. The life-course of all forensic science innovations is determined not simply by collective agreement on the validity of the science itself, nor by the robustness of its technological realisation. Instead, it is conditioned by social factors extrinsic to these material issues, by the desires, needs and experiences of actual and potential users. These social factors are visible both in the shaping of such technologies in the first place, including the ways that 'scientists and engineers configure users and contexts of use as integrated parts of technological development' (Oudshoorn 2003: 209), and also their subsequent acceptance, rejection, or modification, by relevant communities of users and stakeholders.[18]

## Using forensic science

The second set of questions most often raised about the uses of forensic science in contemporary criminal investigations refer not to problems over the deployment of specific areas of forensic evidence in the prosecution of offenders, but instead challenge the adequacy of current knowledge of the effectiveness and cost effectiveness of its wider and routine applications in support of police investigations. Here particular attention has focused on policy issues that relate to the taking, retention and speculative searching of particular types of bio-information, and there has been an increasingly lively debate on the legislative framework and police utilisation of the National DNA Database and IDENT1.[19]

Scientific investigations are not limited to the provision of theoretical representations of the world; most such inquiries involve active and persistent interventions in the world – through experimentation and technological innovation.[20] However, the kinds of interventions, both actual and potential ones, which constitute forensic science are aimed to facilitate the identification, collection, analysis and interpretation of physical evidence in order to serve the common interest in 'truth' shared by all those involved – as victims, suspects, accused persons, litigants, investigators, judges, advocates, and members of juries – in criminal and civil justice processes. This requirement involves not only a particular pragmatic shaping of the scientific activity in question, but also brings its practice into a sometimes tense relationship with the expectations and requirements of the very different epistemic priorities and routines of legal, especially adversarial, reasoning.

Jasanoff (1995) encapsulates the distinction neatly when she asserts that 'Facts established by law do not generally need to travel beyond the context of the particular case. Scientific representations, by contrast, seek to capture generalities that recur in nature, are independent of places and persons, and can be relied on for future investigations.' Some scholars, for example, Goldberg (1994), emphasise the ways in which science is privileged by the law; others, for example Faigman *et al.* (2002), see signs of an 'emerging integration' of what are often presented as incompatible legal and scientific cultures in the US Supreme Court decision in *Daubert v. Merrell Dow Pharmaceuticals*. Finally, Jasanoff (1995) emphasises the continual conflict between law and science over knowledge – the traditional preserve of science, and responsibility – the traditional preserve of the law. For her, these conflicts are continually shaping and reshaping science and the law but not necessarily to each other's satisfaction.[21]

From our perspective, the varying practices of science and the law derive from differences in their underlying epistemic priorities, fundamental contrasts in the mechanisms by which each seeks to achieve these priorities, and the professional cultural and procedural norms that consequently follow as each searches to establish and maintain their autonomy and authority. The scientific method combines empiricism, the direct observation of phenomena, with an experimental approach that removes the influence of external factors and prejudices inherent in many other forms of truth seeking. The objective testing of hypotheses, ideally by formal statistical means, and their continual retesting in a publicly accessible manner leads to knowledge with widely accepted authority. However, there exist many debates over the principles that safeguard such claims. For example, the role of 'falsification' as a key feature of scientific method (which has been adopted as a required feature of 'Daubert' recognition) is a matter of continued philosophical dispute. Not all (at least provisionally) accepted science is able to conform to the rigours of Popperian falsification, and neither is it clear that deductive theorising always informs the generation of hypotheses which clearly and exactly provide the rationale for, and shape of, empirical testing. Such a monolithic approach is contrary to the variation inherent in scientific practice in which hypotheses may be formed or modified during interim stages of investigation. What matters more to science is a commitment to the rigorous testing of the hypotheses at some point if legitimate claims for knowledge production are to be established and maintained. It is only in this way that the 'universality' of scientific method can be used to support the growth of knowledge and truth on a grand scale. The objectivity of science provides epistemic authority in any debate over 'truth' including a number of widely accepted yet counter-intuitive physical phenomena. The most frequently cited example of such a phenomenon is wave particle duality, i.e. that an electron can behave as both a wave and a particle contrary to our common-sense understandings of the world.

In law on the other hand, the difficult relationship between 'truth' and 'common understandings' is further mediated by a concern with 'justice'. In its pursuit of its aims, the law proceeds by stipulative authority, is characterised by extensive variety and pragmatism in its approach to truth determining with different rules in different legal contexts, different rules of evidence in different jurisdictions and different standards of proof. All of these rules derive from the law itself without reference to any external standard; in other words the law is normative, being the sole arbiter of truth in its particular context. The law therefore determines what is true by a set of organic, highly variable, subjective, internally referenced and sometimes seemingly contradictory rules, contrasting markedly with scientific truth seeking.

There are two main families of legal systems: inquisitorial (or Civil Law)[22] and adversarial (or Common Law), each of which has different approaches based on different philosophical principles. Within these two families, the law is 'local' and closely aligned with nation states or political entities (federations, counties, cantons, etc.) often known as 'jurisdictions'.[23] Almost all the contributors to this Handbook present their material from the perspective of an adversarial legal process and in relation to the processes of criminal investigation in common law systems.[24] In such systems the authority of the law and its means of determining truth are based on statutes, i.e. a set of codified rules, and decisions made in previous cases of a similar nature (stated cases) which are more or less binding depending on circumstances.

The scope, nature and means of presentation of evidence to criminal courts is determined by the rules of evidence, an essentially *ad hoc* collection of mainly exclusionary rules, which vary in detail from jurisdiction to jurisdiction. In order to be considered in any hearing, evidence must be admissible within these rules and relevant to the matter before the tribunal. Within common law systems, irrespective of whether a jury is involved, guilt or innocence (more strictly 'non-guilt') is determined by a common-sense interpretation of the evidence presented to the court based on the extent to which the evidence supports the prosecution case. The standard of proof, the bar that has to be overcome, is 'beyond reasonable doubt', a criterion that is necessarily situationally and locally determined.

Most relevant to the concerns of this Handbook, and arising out of the differing perspectives of science and the law, are the large number of issues that arise in the presentation of expert evidence in which scientific findings must be translated into common-sense or at least 'common' language by the expert witness for others involved in the legal process. Here again we encounter wide variation in practices and philosophies between jurisdictions as each attempts to control the use and scope of potentially available evidence; what Jasanoff refers to as the 'complex archaeology of the courtroom'. In this environment, where the determination of the admissibility and validity of the evidence is central to the relationship between science and law, Roberts and Zuckerman reflect that 'more and more the problem of expert qualification and the risk of biased scientific evidence appear to stem from the institutional demands and limitations of criminal proceedings rather than reflecting the inadequacies of scientific method or failure of individual experts' (Roberts and Zuckerman 2004).

In contrast to the large and expanding body of scholarship – in the US, the UK and elsewhere – which has attempted to describe the differences between scientific and legal knowledge and reasoning as well as the ways in which each shapes the others' practice,[25] there is much less research on the relationship between forensic science and other criminal justice disciplines, especially that of policing. This is especially strange since, for the most part, it is the police who largely control the ways in which forensic science enters the criminal justice process. It is the police who are the largest users of forensic science, and as such are especially influential in defining and articulating the needs and interests which shape the production of forensic science knowledge as well as favour the technologies through which it is delivered and utilised.

Published audits from a number of sources consistently highlight poor knowledge of forensic science in the police service, even in such high-risk areas as homicide investigation. *Using Forensic Science Effectively* (ACPO/FSS/ Audit Commission 1996), a seminal document published over a decade ago, found that 'awareness of scientific support is poor and often insufficient for purpose' and that there was 'almost a complete absence of forensic science content in probationer [constable] or refresher training' (*ibid*: 23). Four years later *Under the Microscope* (HMIC 2000), which included as an appendix a summary of the methodology, findings and recommendations of this earlier report, found that 'despite repeated reminders in successive reports from diverse sources, there is no national policy that operational staff receive "awareness" training'. Furthermore, 'Despite several revisions of the content of training for inspectors or sergeants ... national supervisory training does not at present provide any input on scientific and technical support.' Two years later, a follow-up thematic inspection by HMIC (2002: 22) found only patchy improvements: 'A recurrent theme of the inspection was the lack of awareness [of forensic science] at all levels, particularly the operational level, of what could be achieved.' It was also directly critical of ACPO: 'The lack of full engagement amongst Chief Officers was reflected in many of the responses from the forces assessed in this revisit.' In spite of the fact that many years have passed since the publication of these reports, it is not clear that the problems they describe have been fully solved.

Whilst these two turn-of-the-century reports focused on the use of forensic science in support of volume crime, the situation in relation to serious crime investigations seemed no more encouraging. For example, Nicol *et al.* (2004) identified among six main areas of failure in homicide reviews 'forensics (exhibit management and submission)'. They go on to identify forensic science as an area of particular concern as there was routine failure to comply with standard procedures, as well as a number of cases where potential forensic evidence had been completely overlooked and not submitted for laboratory examination.

There is ample evidence therefore that the use of forensic science to achieve the aims of criminal justice is suboptimal. The development of new technology arises through commercial or academic routes and draws on the universal and international knowledge base of science. At the same time, the law is notoriously resistant to new technology and embedded in a culture of the written word that requires complex real world events to be reduced to linear narratives capable of being reconstructed in courtrooms. Furthermore, the police may often seek to apply technology and science as a symbol of contemporary currency and modernity yet fail properly to embed or understand such technology in any systematic manner. Both institutions use 'common sense' as their primary reasoning mechanism and arbiter of significance, relevance and value, and for this reason alone, remain uneasy bedfellows alongside the more reflective approach typical of natural science.

The culture, norms and tacit behaviour of the law attenuate both the rate and uptake of science and technology. The application of technology happens in an incremental and disconnected manner rather than a systematic or coordinated approach based on perceived benefits and risks. The extensive involvement of the numerous and varied actors in the criminal justice process – 'first responder', crime scene investigator, detective, chemist, biologist, solicitor, barrister, judge, etc. – all ensure that the environment and application of forensic science remains complex and difficult.

## Learning forensic science

Until recently, most learning in forensic science happened in the course of training by specialist police organisations for CSIs (and other police personnel such as fingerprint examiners), and in scientific institutions for graduate scientists. The entry qualifications for CSI and related roles were good secondary school grades, and for scientists a good, relevant first degree. In the past 10 years or so there has been a spectacular and worldwide increase in vocational training and education in forensic science, a detailed account of which is provided by Roux and Robertson in Chapter 21 of this Handbook. The cause of this sudden growth and the implications of it are unclear at present and are likely to remain so until a systematic retrospective analysis of the phenomenon takes place. Notwithstanding this, a number of contributory factors – at least to UK developments – can be identified at this stage.

Following the general expansion of forensic science which took place in the UK as a consequence of government investment in new technologies (particularly DNA but also fingerprints and other areas), forensic science became increasingly visible as a positive contributor to the criminal justice process and lauded by the media for its ability to solve by technological means cases that hitherto were insoluble. The public's perennial interest in fictional crime investigation has probably played a part in this phenomenon, adding to its visibility with many dramatic and romanticised portrayals of forensic science and forensic scientists. At the same time there has been a significant decrease in students interested in studying the more traditional academic science subjects, particularly chemistry, which has caused the newer universities to examine their educational portfolios in the light of the rise in interest in forensic science. A separate general phenomenon has been the increased influence of industry on training and education that, supported by governments, has led to the development of vocational standards and training in a wide range of areas including forensic science.

Given that many staff of the university departments who teach forensic science today in the UK have variable professional or research backgrounds in the subject it is difficult to see how the increased provision of undergraduate training can itself contribute to improved knowledge in the field (Fraser

2008). Whilst forensic science has clearly caught the attention of potential students looking for a role or career that is both interesting, and has demonstrable social relevance, there remain questions about the educational and occupational value of their forensic science qualification in the light of the seemingly shrinking market for employment – even in criminal justice – in England and Wales.

At the same time, and given the recurrent issue of how poor knowledge in the police service limits the potential contribution of forensic science, such developments in training ought to be welcome. However, the weaknesses in knowledge of forensic science within police organisations does not lie in the specialist roles of those working within forensic science support, but with police officers more generally especially first responders and investigators. Previous reviews of how the police acquire this knowledge in England and Wales (for example Fraser 2007a) have identified major weaknesses in the forensic science training infrastructure and planning for the whole of policing. Strategic statements concerning forensic training and learning were almost completely absent from the business plans and strategic documents of CENTREX, the central police training authority in England and Wales. However, since April 2007, the National Policing Improvement Agency (NPIA) has replaced CENTREX, and whilst it is too early to assess the extent to which NPIA perspectives will repair this situation, there are ambitious plans and allocated funding of around £10 million (NPIA 2008a) to address the 'forensic competence' of police officers and specialist practitioners. Currently these plans and funding are invoked and marshalled in order to achieve 'effective use of forensic science in the investigation of crime ... [by addressing] all aspects of forensic science learning and competence, including crime scene investigating, fingerprinting and footwear training' (NPIA 2008b).

## Governing forensic science

The later decades of the last century witnessed the gradual realisation among academics and policymakers that the capacity of governments to exercise direct controls over crucial social processes, including criminal justice processes, was increasingly limited. This was nicely summarised in an important paper by Kickert (1993: 275) in which he argued that 'The control capacity of government is limited for a number of reasons: lack of legitimacy, complexity of policy processes, complexity and multitude of institutions concerned, etc. ... Deregulation, government withdrawal and steering at a distance are all notions of less direct government regulation and control, which lead to more autonomy and self-governance for social institutions.'

Accordingly, new images of governance have arisen and been realised in the twenty-first century, images of networks of semi-autonomous actors involved in a multitude of human and material processes '... in which no single actor has enough power to dominate the others and in which decision-making is a bargaining process and decisions are compromises ...' (Kickert 1993.) The recent history of UK forensic science instantiates this emerging form of network governance in which (despite the control of much of policing by traditional state mechanisms) 'an increasingly dispersed set of subjects and objects' (Hindmarsh and Du Plessis, in press) are ruled not by 'hard law', but by other forms of regulation, including self-regulation, procedural 'standardisation', and a variety of other codes – including ethical codes – of scientific and professional practice.

A small number of institutional actors dominated UK forensic science in the last half of the twentieth century, in particular several units of the Home Office, the Association of Chief Police Officers (ACPO) and the Forensic Science Service (FSS). The work of these actors is visible in the construction of a variety of forensic science policy resources including several formal strategic statements and plans,[26] the introduction of new forensic science provision regimes, an increasing emphasis on auditing the effectiveness and efficiency of police uses of forensic science, and the encouragement of particular technological and operational innovations. The interests of these actors, as well as the accounts of the nature and prospects for forensic science that they formulated and disseminated, also informed a series of legislative and organisational changes that reinforced lay and professional views of the growing importance of forensic science within the UK criminal justice system during this time. In addition, some of these actors envisaged the capacity of forensic science to serve as a lever for the improvement of other areas and practices of policing.[27]

In the early years of this century, the widely recognised success of the DNA Expansion Programme (Forensic Science and Pathology Unit Home Office 2005a) was seized upon and deployed by the Forensic Science Policy Unit of the Home Office and ACPO to inform the formation and adoption of the 'Forensic Integration Strategy' (Forensic Science and Pathology Unit Home Office 2005b). The strategy, to be realised through a number of separate but related 'workstreams', combined an interest in improving traditional measures of forensic effectives (for example, the amount of physical evidence recovered from crime scenes, and the number of offenders identified through the analysis of such evidence) with an interest in the normalisation of 'recognised best practice' in the design and operation of the 'forensic process' across the 43 police forces of England and Wales. In addition, the strategy also focused attention on what it called 'procurement reform' in an effort to improve the position and the discipline of individual forces when faced with decisions about the purchase of forensic science services from an increasingly varied group of commercial suppliers. The more recent iteration of such a strategy for forensic science in policing – Forensics21 – will be discussed in our final editorial chapter on the future of forensic science.

## Conclusion

In the course of this introduction to the *Handbook of Forensic Science* we have covered a number of recent and current debates on the status and uses of forensic science in support of criminal justice. We have tried to indicate the reasons for the increased interest in forensic science in both investigative and prosecutorial contexts, as well as the nature of the difficulties that recur in attempts to define its scope. We have also discussed the relationship between scientific and operational policing practice and the differing outlooks of the two. In the sections and chapters that follow this opening foray into the field, individual contributors provide appropriately detailed accounts of these general matters by reference to fields of inquiry in which they have acknowledged expertise.

We will return to some of the issues raised in this introduction and elsewhere in the Handbook as a whole when we survey the current situation of forensic science – especially in the UK – in order to consider its changing shape and its ability to meet the challenges of the next decades.

## Notes

1  From a police perspective, for example, the authors of the recently published *Senior Investigating Officers' Handbook* (Cook and Tattersall 2008) approvingly cite recent research (Roycroft 2007) which asserts that 'forensic material' was the single most significant factor contributing to the 'solvability' of cases of serious crime.

2  For example, it is more than 40 years since Kirk noted that 'With all of the progress that has been made in this field [for Kirk, 'criminalistics'], and on a wide front, careful examination shows that for the most part, progress has been technical rather than fundamental, practical rather than theoretical, transient rather than permanent.' (Kirk 1963: 235). Thornton and Peterson's (2002: 3) version of this same claim suggests that it still remains true in the first decade of the twenty-first century: 'Forensic science has historically been troubled by a serious deficiency in that a heterogeneous assemblage of technical procedures, a pastiche of sorts, however effective or virtuous they may be in their own right, has frequently been substituted for basic theory and principles.'

3  Consider for example Evett and Weir's (1998: 238–245) explication of the different ways in which philosophical and pragmatic issues of 'identification' and 'individuality' are conceptualised and attested in fingerprint comparison and in DNA profile analysis.

4  The overinclusive use of the term 'forensic' is of course equally problematic, especially where it is seemingly used as a synonym for adjectives like 'careful' or 'detailed'.

5  The omnibus term 'technoscience' as developed in Science and Technology Studies, although hardly used at all by commentators within forensic science, further alerts us to the fact that these technologies themselves are not merely socially conditioned *derivatives* of science, but instead play an important part in the *shaping* and *stabilisation* of claims to the scientific knowledge that underpins their authoritative deployment. Discussions of these issues – largely, but not exclusively beyond the forensic domain – can be found elsewhere (see for example Hackett *et al.* 2007).

6  Definitions of 'forensic science' vary hugely from the cursory (for example '... the application of science in the resolution of legal disputes' in Jackson and Jackson 2004: xiii) through the laudatory  ('... a wondrous intersection where science, medicine and the law meet, with a final disposition being the adjudication of criminal cases.' (Pyrek 2007: 4) to the analogical (Like medicine or engineering, the forensic analysis of physical evidence is an applied science, resting firmly on a foundation of the basic scientific principles of physics, chemistry and biology.' (Inman and Rudin 2001: 8).

7   The recursive relationship between factual and fictional representations of contemporary forensic science is shown by numerous claims for the existence of a 'CSI Effect', although whether such an effect exists (and if it does, what form it takes) remains heavily contested. For a range of claims and views on this topic, see Ramsland (2006), Tyler (2006) and Cole and Dioso-Villa (2007).

8   UK police forces have recently enhanced their reputation for the investigation of 'cold cases' where their conspicuous successes have depended in large measure on the application of developments in forensic – especially DNA – technology.

9   In 2000, the Court of Appeal overturned the conviction of Stephen Downing for the 1973 murder of Wendy Sewell in a Derbyshire graveyard. A subsequent reinvestigation by Derbyshire Police failed to eliminate Downing who has refused to be interviewed and cannot be rearrested under the law as it stands. In another prominent case, James Hanratty was convicted of murder in 1961 and subsequently hanged. In 1999 the case was referred to the Criminal Case Review Commission and in March 2001 DNA from Hanratty's exhumed body was matched to samples from the crime scene. Lord Woolf, the Lord Chief Justice, stated, 'In our judgement ... the DNA evidence establishes beyond doubt that James Hanratty was the murderer.'

10  Some sense of this range may be obtained by comparing the accounts given of the nature and conditions of contemporary forensic science by the following: Broeders (2007); Inman and Rudin (2001); James and Nordby (2003); Kiely (2006); Moriarty and Saks (2005); Saferstein (2004); Saks and Koehler (2005).

11  Both of these kinds of inquiries constantly return to questions of 'trust' – in science in general, in policing actions, and most crucially, trust in the joint application of these two powerful forms of contemporary ruling.

12  Following referral by the Criminal Cases Review Commission to the Court of Appeal Stone's appeal was upheld.

13  More detail on these issues can be found in Paul Roberts's Chapter in this Handbook.

14  When Jasanoff (2008: 771) claims that science 'perennially sheds it own history', we take her to be referring to the fact that the teaching and learning of seemingly universal forms of contemporary scientific and technological practice require no principled attentiveness to previous incarnations. This does not contradict the fact that the practitioners in many forensic science domains do narrate the histories of their particular fields, but it may explain their preference for Whiggish progressivism and technological determinism in the accounts they provide – especially in textbooks and in the framing of other instructional materials.

15  Central to the specific character of forensic science is of course its ineradicable but contested relationship with law, a complex issue, more discussed in legal than scientific texts, but summarised nicely by Jasanoff (2006: 329) in her comment that 'The use of scientific evidence ... in court brings into collaboration two institutions with significantly different aims and normative commitments. In their by no means friction-free encounters, neither science nor law completely retains or completely relinquishes its autonomy.'

16  The recent debate over the scientific status of fingerprint comparison is an interesting example of a revisionist approach to the history of this particular forensic discipline. This is discussed in more detail by Champod and Chamberlain's Chapter 3 in this volume. See also Champod (2008), Mnookin (2008), Haber and Haber (2008a and b), Federal Bureau of Investigation (2007: 2), Cole (2004), Dror and others (Dror and Charlton 2006; Dror, Charlton and Peron 2006; Dror *et al.* 2005; Dror and Rosenthal 2008).

17 Following receipt of a report by the National Research Council of the National Academy of Science, the FBI Laboratory determined that 'scientists and manufacturers' were unable 'to definitively evaluate the significance of an association between bullets made in the course of a bullet lead examination' (2004). For the original report, see National Research Council (2004), and for a critical commentary on some of its conclusions, see Kaye (2005). Other forensic science enterprises that have recently come under critical scrutiny – in some cases devastating scrutiny – include ear print comparison, hair microscopy, and bite mark identification. In the latter two cases in particular, the availability of DNA profiling has permitted an alternative methodology for testing the robustness of conclusions based on other kinds of analytical practices.

18 There are many general accounts of the social shaping of technology, and the relationship between 'users' and specific technological innovations (for example, Bijker, Hughes and Pinch 1989; Hackett *et al.* 2007; Law 1991; Oudshoorn and Pinch 2003; Williams 1974). A very useful example of one such study in the forensic realm is Aronson's account of the development of DNA profiling (Aronson 2007).

19 IDENT1 is the national automated fingerprint system in the UK (previously NAFIS).

20 The value of thinking about much scientific activity as actively participating in the world rather than passively reflecting it is strongly advocated by Hacking (1983).

21 There are many other accounts of the relationship between science and the law that offer valuable insights into the tensions and the mutual affordances that exist between the two enterprises. Two important books which provide valuable assessments of the UK context are Roberts and Zuckerman (2004) and Redmayne (2001).

22 Also referred to as Continental Law.

23 More strictly this refers to the ambit of the court, i.e. the extent of its authority to determine a legal outcome.

24 One contributor (Champod) practises and teaches within an inquisitorial legal system but this has little bearing on the content of the chapter.

25 A good example of this is the development of case law and scientific practice in relation to the 'prosecutor's fallacy'. The central issue in the 'prosecutor's fallacy' is confusion of the DNA match probability (a matter for the scientist) with the probability of guilt or innocence (a matter for the jury). An increasingly complex series of disputes over the interpretation of DNA statistics in the English courts ultimately led to a definitive judgement, but although this clarified the issue in many respects, the legal phraseology that replaced statistical terminology is proving unsatisfactory to scientists and statisticians. Accordingly another series of skirmishes may soon take place across this particular frontier.

26 For some recent examples that have extended this work into the current century, see several iterations of the Home Office Police Science and Technology Strategy, the Home Office Strategic Plan and the National Policing Plan.

27 See for example: '… the sort of intelligence produced by Forensic Science will be a catalyst for modernisation throughout the CJS, enhancing professionalism and moulding workforce practices around the efficient use and collection of valuable evidence.' (Forensic Science and Pathology Unit Home Office 2005b).

## References

ACPO/FSS/Audit Coimmission (1996) *Using Forensic Science Effectively*. London: HMSO.

Aronson, J.D. (2007) *Genetic Witness: Science, Law and Controversy in the Making of DNA Profiling*. New Brunswick, NJ: Rutgers University Press.

Bijker, W., Hughes, T.P., and Pinch, T. (eds), (1989) *The Social Construction of Technological Systems: New Directions in the Sociology and History of Technology*. Cambridge Mass.: MIT Press.

Broeders, A.P.A. (2007) 'Principles of Forensic Identification Science', pp. 303–37, in T. Newburn, T. Williamson and A. Wright (eds), *Handbook of Criminal Investigation*. Cullompton: Willan Publishing.

Champod, C. (2008) 'Fingerprint examination: towards more transparency', *Law, Probability and Risk*, 7: 111–118.

Cole, S.A. (2004) 'Fingerprint Identification and the Criminal Justice System: Historical Lessons for the DNA Debate', pp. 63–90, in D. Lazer (ed), *DNA and the Criminal Justice System*. Cambridge, Mass.: MIT Press.

Cole, S.A. and Dioso-Villa, R. (2007) 'CSI and its effects: media, juries and the burden of proof', *New England Law Review*, 41, 435–470.

Cook, T. and Tattersall, A. (eds) (2008) *Blackstone's Senior Investigating Officers' Handbook*. Oxford: Oxford University Press.

Dror, I.E. and Charlton, D. (2006) 'Why Experts Make Errors', *Journal of Forensic Identification*, 56, 600–616.

Dror, I.E. Charlton, D. and Peron, A. (2006) 'Contextual Information Renders Experts Vulnerable to Making Erroneous Identifications', *Forensic Science International*, 156: 74–78.

Dror, I.E., Peron, A., Hind, S.-L. and Charlton, D. (2005) 'When Emotions Get the Better of Us: The Effect of Contextual Top-down Processing on Matching Fingerprints', *Applied Cognitive Psychology*, 19, 799–809.

Dror, I.E. and Rosenthal, R. (2008) 'Meta-analytically Quantifying the Reliability and Biasability of Forensic Experts', *Journal of Forensic Sciences*, 53: 900–903.

Evett, I.W. and Weir, B.S. (1998) *Interpreting DNA Evidence – Statistical Genetics for Forensic Scientists*. Sunderland: Sinauer Associates Ltd.

Faigman, D.L. Kaye, D.H., Saks, M.J. and Sanders, J. (eds). (2002) *Science in the Law: Forensic Science Issues*. St Paul, Minn.: West Group.

Federal Bureau of Investigation (2007) Press Release: 'FBI Laboratory to Increase Outreach in Bullet Lead Cases', from http://www.fbi.gov/pressrel/pressrel07/bulletlead111707.htm. Accessed February 2009.

Forensic Science and Pathology Unit Home Office (2005a) *DNA Expansion Programme 2000–2005: Reporting Achievement*. London: Home Office.

Forensic Science and Pathology Unit Home Office (2005b) *Forensic Integration Strategy 2005–2008*. London: Home Office.

Fraser, J. (2007a) 'The Application of Science to Criminal Investigations', in T. Newburn, T. Williamson and A. Wright (eds), *Handbook of Criminal Investigation* (381–402). Cullompton: Willan Publishing.

Fraser, J. (2007b) 'Setting Context in Context', *Forensic Science Society Annual General Meeting*. Glasgow.

Fraser, J. (2008) 'Why We Need More Research', *Forensic Science Society Annual General Meeting*. Wyboston.

Goldberg, S. (1994) *Culture Clash: Law and Science in America*. New York: New York University Press.

Haber, L. and Haber, R.N. (2008a) 'Experiental or scientific expertise', *Law, Probability and Risk*, 7: 143–150.

Haber, L. and Haber, R.N. (2008b) 'Scientific validation of fingerprint evidence under Daubert', *Law, Probability and Risk,* 7: 87–109.

Hackett, E.J., Amsterdamska, O., Lynch, M. and Wajcman, J. (eds) (2007) *The Handbook of Science and Technology Studies* (3rd edn). Cambridge, Mass.: MIT Press.

Hacking, Ian (1983) *Representing and Intervening.* Cambridge: Cambridge University Press.

Hindmarsh, R. and Du Plessis, R. (in press) 'The new civic geography of life science governance: perspectives from Australia and New Zealand', *New Genetics and Society.*

HMIC (2000) *Under the Microscope: Thematic Inspection Report on Scientific and Technical Support.* London: Home Office.

HMIC (2002) *Under the Microscope Refocused.* London: Home Office.

Houck, M.M. and Siegal, J.A. (2006) *Fundamentals of Forensic Science.* Burlington: Elsevier.

Inman, K. and Rudin, N. (2001) *Principles and Practice of Criminalistics: The Profession of Forensic Science.* London: CRC Press.

Jackson, A.R.W. and Jackson, J.M. (2004) *Forensic Science.* London: Pearson Prentice Hall.

James, S.H. and Nordby, J.J. (eds) (2003) *Forensic Science: An Introduction to Scientific and Investigative Techniques.* Boca Raton, FL: CRC Press.

Jasanoff, S. (1995) *Science at the Bar: Law, Science and Technology in America.* Cambridge, Mass.: Harvard University Press.

Jasanoff, S. (2005) 'Law's knowledge: Science for justice in legal settings', *American Journal of Public Health,* 95, Supplement 1: S49–S58.

Jasanoff, S. (2006) 'Just evidence: the limits of science in the legal process', *Journal of Law, Medicine and Ethics,* 34: 328–341.

Jasanoff, S. (2008) 'Making Order: Law and Science in Action', in E.J. Hackett, O. Amsterdamska, M. Lynch and J. Wajcman (eds), *The Handbook of Science and Technology Studies* (3rd edn., pp. 761–786). Cambridge, Mass.: MIT Press.

Kaye, D.H. (2005) 'The NRC Bullet-Lead Report: should science committees make legal findings?', *Jurimetrics,* 46, 91–105.

Kickert, W.J.M. (1993) 'Autopoiesis and the science of (public) adminstration: essense, sense and nonsense', *Organization Studies,* 14: 261–278.

Kiely, T.F. (2006) *Forensic Evidence: Science and the Criminal Law.* London: Taylor and Francis.

Kirk, P.L. (1963) 'The Ontogeny of Criminalistics', *Criminology and Police Science,* 54: 235–238.

Kirk, P.L. (1974) *Crime Investigation* (2nd edn., p. 2). New York: Wiley.

Law, J. (ed.) (1991) *A Sociology of Monsters.* London: Routledge.

Mnookin, J. (2008) 'The validity of latent fingerprint identification: confessions of a fingerprinting moderate', *Law, Probability and Risk,* 7: 127–141.

Moriarty, J.C. and Saks, M.J. (2005) 'Forensic Science: grand goals, tragic flaws, and judicial gatekeeping', *Judges' Journal,* 44: 16–33.

National Policing Improvement Agency (2008a) *Business Plan 2008–2011.* London: Home Office.

National Policing Improvement Agency (2008b) http://www.npia.police.uk/en/10432.htm. Accessed 2 April 2009.

National Research Council (2004) *Committee on Scientific Assessment of Bullet Lead Elemental Composition Comparison, Forensic Analysis: Weighing Bullet Lead Evidence.*

Nicol, C., Innes, M., Gee, D. and Feist, A. (2004) *Reviewing Murder Investigations: An Analysis of Progress Reports from Six Forces.* London: Home Office.

Oudshoorn, N. (2003) 'Clinical trials as a cultural niche in which to configure the gender identities of users: the case of male contraceptive development', in Oudshoorn, N. and Pinch, T. (2003) (eds) *How Users Matter: The Co-Construction of Users and Technologies* (pp. 209–228). Cambridge, Mass.: MIT Press.

Pyrek, K.M. (2007) *Forensic Science Under Siege*. Amsterdam: Elsevier Press.

Ramsland, K. (2006) *The CSI Effect*. New York: Berkley Boulevard Books.

Redmayne, M. (2001) *Expert Evidence and Criminal Justice*. Oxford: Oxford University Press.

Roberts, P. and Zuckerman, A. (2004) *Criminal Evidence*. Oxford: Oxford University Press.

Roberts, P. and Willmore, C. (1993) 'The Role of Forensic Science Evidence in Criminal Proceedings', *Royal Commission on Criminal Justice Study 11*. London: HMSO.

Roman, J.K., Reid, S., Reid, J., Chalfin, A., Adams, W. and Knight, C. (2008) *The DNA Field Experiment: Cost-Effectiveness Analysis of the Use of DNA in the investigation of High-Volume Crimes*. Washington, DC: Urban Institutes.

Roycroft, M. (2007) 'What Solves Hard to Solve Murders', *Journal of Homicide and Major Incident Investigation*, 3.

Saferstein, R. (2004) *Criminalistics: An Introduction to Forensic Science*. New York: Prentice Hall.

Saks, M.J. (1998) 'Merlin and Solomon: Lessons from the Law's Formative Encounters with Forensic Identification Science', *Hastings Law Journal*, 49 (April): 1069–1141.

Saks, M. and Koehler, J.J. (2005) 'The coming paradigm shift in forensic science', *Science*, 309, 892–895.

Thornton, J.I. and Peterson, J.L. (2002) 'The General Assumptions and Rationale of Forensic Identification', in D.L. Faigman, D.H. Kaye, M.J. Saks and J. Sanders (eds), *Science in the Law: Forensic Science Issues* (pp. 1–112). St Paul, Minn.: West Group.

Tyler, T.R. (2006) 'Viewing CS and the threshold of guilt: managing truth and justice in reality and fiction', *Yale Law Journal*, 115: 1052–1085.

Williams, R. (1974) *Television, Technology and Cultural Form*. London: Fontana Books.

**Part 1**

# Forensic Science Practice

# Introduction

## Jim Fraser and Robin Williams

The purpose of Part 1 is to describe forensic practice by selecting particular areas in order to illustrate the range of practical, procedural, conceptual and cognitive activities involved, and also to identify, anatomise and clarify its characteristic features. It is evident from the material presented that forensic practice exhibits a wide disciplinary range and an extensive variety of ways of working. Inherent differences between disciplines are exemplified by the range and complexity of technology used for comparison and analysis: genetic analysers (DNA), gas chromatography mass spectrometry (drugs profiling) and sophisticated software algorithms (automated fingerprint comparison) to give a few examples. The relentless pressure of new and developing technologies is likely to maintain this variation, acting as a constant force for change. Bloodstain pattern analysis (Wain and Linacre), which still relies almost exclusively on the observational skills and knowledge of the individual scientist, is perhaps the sole exception to this. Two other sources of variation are notable: the influence of police practices in relation to particular types of investigation (e.g. fires, homicide) and the requirement to meet legal and procedural needs in different jurisdictions. Munday and Gardiner describe the history and development of increasingly cooperative approaches to fire investigation with the aim of achieving common standards and working practices. They stress the interdependent nature of relationships between scientists, investigators, fire services and other agents, the need for effective communication, and acceptance of shared aims to achieve desired outcomes in this complex environment. Allard also highlights the need for such an approach, stressing the importance of understanding the specific aims of an investigation before an effective forensic examination strategy can be implemented in the laboratory, and the findings evaluated. The variation between jurisdictional practices resulting in highly localised application of scientific methods is one of the distinctive features of forensic practice and stands in stark contrast to the 'universality' of science as applied in other domains such as medicine. Notwithstanding, several contributors (Gill and Clayton, Evison, and Nic Daeid and Buchanan) anticipate growing international collaboration in their particular spheres of activity.

Despite this variation between disciplines, a number of common themes and issues are presented in individual chapters. Fundamental themes discussed by almost all contributors (albeit with varying viewpoints and approaches) are identification, classification and categorisation of physical evidence. This includes processes for identifying people (Gill and Clayton – DNA; Champod and Chamberlain – Fingerprints and Evison – body parts and tissues); natural materials and substances (Houck – hairs; Allard – body fluids; Nic Daeid and Buchanan – drugs); synthetic materials and substances (Houck – fibres, paint, glass; Nic Daeid and Buchanan – drugs); and manufactured items and artefacts (Houck – textiles; Napier – shoes).

Although the technological and instrumental means of establishing identity or classification vary enormously, the primary purpose of this is common: an association (inclusion) or elimination (exclusion) of relevance to a criminal investigation, by physical evidence. Two divergent approaches to identification are evident, each of which uses different reasoning processes: probabilistic and categoric. Most contributors advocate a probabilistic approach and outline the factors essential to take into consideration in doing so. Again, despite the differences in detail between disciplines, the relevant factors are reducible to fundamental elements. Understanding and assessing in an objective manner the inherent variation in materials (natural and synthetic) and artefacts (such as shoes, glass) is touched on by several contributors (for example Houck, Napier, Nic Daeid and Buchanan). The specific context of a crime or incident (the activity, location, timings and circumstantial information) are considered important by most contributors for the evaluation of evidence and the formulation and assessment of alternative explanations.

The major exception to this is the evaluation of fingerprints. Champod and Chamberlain are critical of the approach that uses categoric identification and lacks transparency in how such judgements are reached. They contend that this approach is illogical and does not serve the criminal justice system well. They are also critical of a range of other practices in fingerprint examination that are at odds with most other forensic practices. Similar views have been expressed by a number of other commentators (for example Cole 2001 and 2004: Dror and Charlton 2006; Dror, Charlton and Peron 2006; Dror and Rosenthal 2008; Mnookin 2008; Saks and Koehler 1991) who consider DNA to be the 'gold standard' in forensic evidence. However, categoric identification is also used for shoe mark comparison as described by Napier albeit on the basis of a clearer rationale and in a more transparent and accountable manner, and it is therefore not the sole province of fingerprint examination.

Forensic practice is generally confined to comparatively restricted and enclosed environments: the courtroom, laboratory or crime scene. In only a small number of cases are more detailed workings, deliberations or accounts exposed to a wider audience. Two cases are described involving DNA (Gill and Clayton – the Omagh bombings) and bloodstain pattern analysis (Wain and Linacre – the murder of Billie-Jo Jenkins), that provide some indication of the extent to which legal systems are willing to rely on expert evidence, and the potential limitations of such evidence.

Although the nine chapters in Part 1 represent a limited selection from the wide range of forensic practice, the breadth of disciplinary activity is striking. It is also evident that there are common themes and threads, as described by a number of contributors. We believe these common themes are representative of the greater part of forensic practice and that their major features are exposed and explored by the contributors to this part of the Handbook. On this basis we are led to the conclusion that it is not necessary to understand the full extent or variety of forensic disciplines in order to grasp the essential nature or the central issues of forensic science.

## References

Cole, S.A. (2001) *Suspect Identities: A History of Fingerprinting and Criminal Identification*. Cambridge, Mass.: Harvard University Press.

Cole, S.A. (2004) 'Fingerprint Identification and the Criminal Justice System: Historical Lessons for the DNA Debate', pp. 63–90, in D. Lazer (ed.), *DNA and the Criminal Justice System*. Cambridge, Mass.: MIT Press.

Dror, I.E. and Charlton, D. (2006) 'Why Experts Make Errors', *Journal of Forensic Identification*, 56: 600–616.

Dror, I.E., Charlton, D. and Peron, A. (2006) 'Contextual Information Renders Experts Vulnerable to Making Erroneous Identifications', *Forensic Science International*, 156: 74–78.

Dror, I.E. and Rosenthal, R. (2008) 'Meta-analytically Quantifying the Reliability and Biasability of Forensic Experts', *Journal of Forensic Sciences*, 53: 900–903.

Mnookin, J. (2008) 'The validity of latent fingerprint identification: confessions of a fingerprinting moderate', *Law, Probability and Risk*, 7: 127–141.

Saks, M.J. and Koehler, J.J. (1991) 'What DNA "Fingerprinting" Can Teach the Law about the Rest of Forensic Science', *Cardozo Law Review*, 13: 361–372.

**Section 1**

# Identifying individuals

# Chapter 2

# The current status of DNA profiling in the UK

*Peter Gill and Tim Clayton*

## Introduction

Although a number of different DNA analysis techniques are available to the forensic scientist, without doubt, the use of short tandem repeat (STR) DNA sequences is of fundamental importance because they have become the recognised world standard to construct national DNA databases. Consequently, considerable effort has been expended to develop multiplexed (one tube) reactions that analyse several loci simultaneously and now at least four commercial multiplex kits are available to the forensic community.

Most jurisdictions use a standard number of polymerase chain reaction (PCR) amplification cycles designed to limit the sensitivity of the test. By increasing the number of PCR amplification cycles, it is possible to dramatically boost the sensitivity of the system so that just a handful of cells may be successfully analysed. However, interpretation is much more complex since the origin of DNA profiles may be less certain and is complicated by issues such as contamination; there is also the potential for 'innocent' transfer of DNA and a predominance of mixtures to consider.

Additional forensic DNA analysis techniques have also been developed. These include mitochondrial DNA (mtDNA) – a less informative marker that can assist in the detection of very highly degraded material such as bone; Y-chromosome markers which are male specific and can offer potential advantages in certain cases where there are, for example, a male component in a mixture that is predominantly female and single nucleotide polymorphisms (SNPs).

This review provides a brief historical background of the development of DNA profiling in forensic casework that has culminated in the instigation of national DNA databases across the globe. We concentrate on the most topical areas that have not been covered previously: the development of the UK and international DNA databases and the future; the development of new multiplexes; the reporting and interpretation strategies; the role of the international scientific societies in development and standardisation of DNA profiling.

## The role of the European scientific societies

Within Europe, there are two predominant scientific societies that have a special interest in DNA profiling: the oldest is the International Society of Forensic Genetics (ISFG) which dates from 1968. This society is also the home of the DNA Commission. The DNA Commission comprises a peer review body of recognised experts from all over the world (not just Europe) who regularly meet to discuss and to formulate recommendations relating to new techniques or areas that may be controversial. Recent work includes Y chromosome STR analysis (Gusmao *et al.* 2006) and the interpretation of mixtures (Gill *et al.* 2006b). A full list of publications is to be found on the ISFG website. These publications reflect and attempt to define the consensus view of the forensic community – consequently, they are an important source of potential court-going documents.

Also under the ISFG umbrella is the European DNA Profiling Group (EDNAP) http://www.isfg.org/ednap/ednap.htm. This group came into being in 1988. Currently there are representatives from 16 European countries. The group is very active and practically orientated. This group was responsible for originally recognising the potential of short tandem repeat (STR) analysis – see for example reference (Gill *et al.* 2006b) – and was the first to demonstrate uniformity of results across different laboratories. The STRs and methods originally developed by EDNAP have since become acknowledged as worldwide standards.

The DNA working group of the European Network of Forensic Science Institutes (ENFSI) http://www.enfsi.org/ewg/dnawg/ first met in 1995. This is probably the largest group with 27 European countries and close US affiliation. The group is very active and is involved with several different areas: database legislation; QA, QC, sampling kits, training, standards for the ENFSI QA programme; methods, analysis and interpretation of evidence; a European population database is available: www.str-base.org.

## Historical development of multiplexed systems

Early multiplexes consisted of relatively few loci based on simple STRs. The 4 locus 'quadruplex' was the first multiplex to be used in casework, and was developed by the Forensic Science Service (FSS) (Kimpton *et al.* 1993). Because it consisted of just four STRs, there was a high chance of a random match – 1 in 10,000. In 1995, the FSS re-engineered the multiplex, producing a 6 locus STR system combined with the amelogenin sex test (Sullivan *et al.* 1993). This acquired the name 'second generation multiplex' (SGM). The addition of complex STRs D21S11 and HUMFIBRA/FGA (Mills *et al.* 1992), which have greater variability than simple STRs, decreased the chance of a random match to about 1 in 50 million. In the UK, the introduction of SGM in 1995 facilitated the implementation of the UK national DNA database (NDNAD) (Werrett 1997). As databases become much larger the number of pairwise comparisons increases dramatically and so it becomes necessary to ensure that the match probability of the system is sufficient to minimise the chance of two unrelated individuals matching by chance (otherwise known as an adventitious match). Consequently, as the UK NDNAD grew in its first four years of operation, a new system known as the AMPFlSTR®SGM Plus™ (Cotton *et al.* 2000), was introduced in 1999 that comprised 10 STR loci with amelogenin, replacing the previous SGM system. To ensure continuity of the DNA database, to enable the new system to match samples that had been collated in previous years, all six loci of the older SGM system were retained in the new AMPFlSTR®SGM Plus™ system. At the time of writing, more than 3.5 million samples are stored on the database. Probability of a match between two unrelated people is approximately $10^{-13}$ using the SGM Plus™ system. For a full DNA profile in court, the UK practice is to report a 'generic' match probability of less than 1 in 1 billion (1,000 million). Recently, there has been much discussion about how the national DNA database should evolve. For example, the House of Commons Science and Technology Committee 'Forensic Science on trial' http://www.publications.parliament.uk/pa/cm200405/cmselect/cmsctech/96/96i.pdf (pages 40–41) recommended that an additional six markers be deployed in order to increase the discriminating power of the test in order to further safeguard against the possibility of an adventitious match. The merits of this proposal are considered below.

### Development and harmonisation of national DNA databases

Harmonisation of STR loci has been achieved by collaboration at the international level. Notably, the European DNA profiling group (EDNAP) carried out a series of successful studies to identify and to recommend STR loci for the forensic community to use. This work began with an evaluation of the simple STRs HUMTH01 and HUMVWFA (Kimpton *et al.* 1995). Subsequently, the group evaluated D21S11 and HUMFIBRA/FGA (Gill *et al.* 1997). Recommendations on the use of STRs have been published by the International Society of Forensic Genetics (Bar *et al.* 1997, Olaisen *et al.* 1998).

To date, a number of European countries have legislated to implement national DNA databases that are based upon STRs (Schneider and Martin 2001). In Europe, there has been a drive to standardise loci across countries, in order to meet the challenge of increasing cross-border crime. In particular, a European Community (EC)-funded initiative led by the European Network of Forensic Science Institutes (ENFSI) was responsible for coordinating collaborative exercises to validate commercially available multiplexes for general use within the EC (Gill *et al.* 2000a). For example, national DNA databases were introduced in 1997 in Holland and Austria; 1998 in Germany, France, Slovenia and Cyprus; 1999 in Finland, Norway and Belgium; 2000 in Sweden, Denmark, Switzerland, Spain, Italy and the Czech Republic; 2002 in Greece and Lithuania; 2003 in Hungary; 2004 in Estonia and Slovakia (Martin 2004) (http://www.dur.ac.uk/p.j.johnson/European_Database.xls)

A parallel process has occurred in Canada (Fregeau 1998; Walsh 1998) and in the US (Hoyle 1998) where standardisation is based on 13 STR loci which has become known as the combined DNA index system (CODIS) (Table 2.1).

**Table 2.1**  The combined DNA index system (CODIS)

There are 13 CODIS designated loci denoted in green and red, and 8 ENFSI loci that are denoted in red and blue; i.e. there are currently 7 loci that are in common use across both North America and Europe. Other loci (not standardised) are denoted in black type

| Locus | AMP *Fl* STR Profiler plus | AMP *Fl* STR COfiler | Powerplex 1.1 | Powerplex 2.1 | Powerplex 16 | SGM | SGM Plus | AMP *Fl* STR Identifiler |
|---|---|---|---|---|---|---|---|---|
| D16S539 |  | * | * |  | * |  |  | * |
| D7S820 | * | * | * |  | * |  |  | * |
| D13S317 | * |  | * |  | * |  |  | * |
| D5S818 | * |  | * |  | * |  |  | * |
| CSF1PO |  | * | * |  | * |  |  | * |
| TPOX |  | * | * | * | * |  |  | * |
| HUMTH01 |  | * | * | * | * | * | * | * |
| HUMVWFA/31A | * |  | * | * | * | * | * | * |
| HUMFIBRA/FGA | * |  |  | * | * | * | * | * |
| D21S11 | * |  |  | * | * | * | * | * |
| D8S1179 | * |  |  | * | * | * | * | * |
| D18S51 | * |  |  | * | * | * | * | * |
| D3S1358 | * | * |  | * | * | * | * | * |
| Amelogenin | * |  | * |  | * | * | * | * |
| Penta D |  |  |  |  | * |  |  |  |
| Penta E |  |  |  | * | * |  |  |  |
| D16S539 |  |  |  |  |  |  | * | * |
| D2S1388 |  |  |  |  |  |  | * | * |
| D19S433 |  |  |  |  |  |  | * | * |

Based on the initial EDNAP exercises, and on recommendations by ENFSI and the Interpol working party (Leriche 1998), four systems were defined as the European standard set of loci – HUMTH01, HUMVWFA31, D21S11 and HUMFIBRA/FGA. Three further loci were added to this set – D3S1358, D8S1179 and D18S51. These loci are the same as the standard set of loci identified by Interpol for the global exchange of DNA data and are included in the multiplexed commercial systems manufactured by Applied Biosystems (AB) and Promega (Table 2.1).

One of the great advantages of STRs is that designations of alleles are robust and reliable across a variety of analysis platforms. Typically, automated fluorescent detection platforms are utilised. The trend is moving away from traditional slab polyacrylamide gels to capillary electrophoresis. For high throughput laboratories processing thousands of samples per year, the norm is utilisation of multi-channel capillary gel (CE) instruments (e.g. AB 3100CE).

### The UK national DNA database

The UK National DNA database (Werrett 1997) is projected to reach a target of 5 million samples within the next few years. The system operates by analysis of buccal (mouth) scrapes or hair roots taken from any individual arrested for any criminal offence. These are known as criminal justice (CJ) samples. Results are stored on computer in the form of an alphanumeric code that is based on the nomenclature of each STR. During criminal casework, operational laboratories carry out analysis of biological material such as semen or bloodstains. The STR profiles derived from these samples are compared against the CJ samples in the existing database. If a match is found then the investigating authorities are informed of the identity of the individual, to enable further investigations to be carried out. The NDNAD is an intelligence database.

Initially, DNA profiling was confined to use in serious crimes, but now has been extended to volume crimes such as burglary from which the majority of matches now originate. The database also intercompares profiles from crime scenes and is able to identify linked scenes and therefore serial offenders. It is relatively common to find links between minor offences and more serious offences.

Novel applications are possible. In particular the use of the database for familial searching (Jobling and Gill 2004; Bieber et al. 2006) has recently been implemented in the UK. If a perpetrator is not recorded on the NDNAD, then no match will result. However, close relatives such as brothers or father and son will have many alleles in common. This can be used to good effect – rather than search for a complete match, a search that relies on >50% alleles matching will yield a list of potential suspects. If prioritised by locality, this list may provide additional investigative leads. Additional confirmatory tests using Y-chromosome or mitochondrial DNA can be used to narrow the field. Obviously, the familial search method is firmly part of the investigative stage of an inquiry – once potential suspects are identified, then a sample may subsequently confirm a match with the crime stain.

An indication of ethnicity is also possible, either from the genetic STR genotype of the perpetrator, or from the Y-chromosome – see ISFG DNA commission recommendations (Gill *et al.* 2001; Gusmao *et al.* 2006) and review Jobling and Gill (2004) for more details. Whereas these markers can give a useful indication of ethnicity, they are never 100 per cent accurate. Their use is in prioritising a list of potential suspects for investigative purposes.

### Population databases

Population databases are distinct from intelligence databases and are often referred to as 'frequency databases'. The former are used to calculate the relative rarity of a profile in a population in order to give an indication of the weight of the DNA evidence to a court. Because allele frequencies differ between racial groups, it is the normal practice to prepare databases for the major racial groups that comprise the commonest population groups of a country. For example, there are three different databases that are used in forensic casework in the UK: White Caucasian, Afro-Caribbean and Asian (Indian subcontinent). The greatest differences are found between broad racial groupings. Relatively minor differences are found between subgroups within the same racial group but from (for example) distinctly different geographical locations. A key question is whether the frequency database that is utilised is representative, given that most databases used for forensic purposes are based on broad random collections of racial groups that do not usually take account of sub-population structure. The Asian database comprises people whose ancestors originated from a very wide geographical and cultural background. Can we be sure that a single database is representative for all subgroups within the entire subcontinent?

The National Research Council (NRC) report (National Research Council 1996) took the view that the actual 'subgroup' to which the suspect belongs is irrelevant, since in evaluating the evidence one is considering the probability of the evidence if the suspect was not the source of the DNA. Accordingly, Foreman *et al.* (1998) pointed out that it is the ethnicity of the offender that is relevant and not the ethnicity of the defendant. However, if the court wishes to evaluate the scenario where it is claimed that the sub-population of the offender is the same as that of the suspect (for example if all potential suspects are from a particular locality or a particular group of people) then the question does arise as to whether the database is representative.

To answer this question, fairly extensive studies have been carried out to measure genetic differences between different groups of people (Balding *et al.* 1996; Budowle *et al.* 1999; Foreman and Evett 2001; Gill and Evett 1995). These studies support the notion that differences between sub-populations are low and discernible differences are unlikely within cosmopolitan populations. However, theoretical variation between sub-populations can be accommodated by the use of a correction factor ($F_{ST}$) (Balding and Nichols 1994). Measured differences between sub-populations appear minor and $F_{ST}<1\%$ (unless the population is highly inbred). This means that inferences derived about frequencies of alleles in a specific sub-population for which a database is not available can be accommodated by using a general database so long as $F_{ST}$ is included in the calculation. Gill *et al.* (2000a) showed from a comparison of 24 different populations that a single pan-European database could suffice for white Caucasians (http://www.str-base.org/).

*Assessing the strength of the evidence following a match derived from the intelligence database*

The strength of the DNA evidence resulting from an intelligence database match is always presented as a conditioned match probability or as a likelihood ratio, as calculated from a relevant population database. The question of whether searching a large intelligence database for a match subsequently affected the strength of the evidence was addressed by the NRC report (National Research Council 1996: 133–135). They originally recommended that an adjustment was applied by multiplying the match probability (*Pm*) by the number of people on the database. Using an example of an intelligence database of N= 1,000 and a multiplex with Pm of $10^{-6}$ this would result in N x Pm of 0.001. Intuitively, this appears wrong, since the exclusion of 999 other individuals ought to strengthen the evidence.

Balding and Donnelly (1996) have criticised the above approach on the grounds that the weight of the evidence for a DNA database search can be expressed as Pm provided that there is other non-DNA evidence in the case. This is a crucial point. The meaning of the match probability is unaffected by the fact that the match was derived from a database search, provided that the evidence is supported by non-DNA evidence – i.e. DNA evidence is not intended as sole-plank evidence.

Suppose that there are 1 million samples in an intelligence database. If a multiplex system is used that has a match probability (*Pm*) of $2 \times 10^{-8}$ (as for the original SGM system) then the chance of an adventitious match is $N \times Pm = 0.02$. Taking the reciprocal demonstrates that approximately one in 50 samples that are compared to a database this size will match by chance.

Much lower match probabilities are needed to accommodate large intelligence databases, and this illustrates the reason why the original SGM profiling system was superseded by the more powerful SGM Plus system.

It is projected that databases of several million will exist within the next few years. The question arises, therefore, how low should the *Pm* be?

As the database grows, it is implicit that the probability of a match needs to be reduced in order to keep the potential number of adventitious matches to a minimum. To fulfil this requirement, in the UK the SGM system was upgraded in 1999. The six original loci were supplemented by four additional loci to produce the AMP*F*lSTR®SGM Plus™ system (Table 2.1). Consequently, a much lower average random match probability was achieved. For a full profile the probability of a chance match for white Caucasians varies between Pr=$10^{-10}$ and $10^{-16}$ (Gill *et al.* 2000a; Foreman and Evett 2001).

To assess the impact of an adventitious match, the only relevant comparisons are between criminal justice (reference or known) samples and crime (or unknown) samples, rather than pairwise comparisons within the database itself. Approximately 3.5 million DNA profiles are currently retained on the database and to date they have been compared against approximately 280,000 samples taken from crime scenes – this is 3.5m $\times$ 280,000 = $9.8^{11}$ pairwise comparisons in total. Applying a match probability of $10^{-13}$ (the SGM Plus average), this gives a 62 per cent chance of one or more adventitious matches. Further work would be needed to clarify the position further given the spread of match probabilities that exist within SGM Plus. We can conclude that it is certainly possible that adventitious matches could occur between crime samples and the database, but, a) they will be very rare; b) provided that the match is treated purely as an investigative lead and not conclusive proof of guilt, an adventitious match will not be problematical.

If a match is believed to be adventitious then testing further STR loci or using other typing systems should easily demonstrate this.

Additional loci decrease the match probabilities further. This may be important for countries where the population is much larger than that of the UK and the consequent target size of the database may be larger. The Promega 16-plex (Powerplex 16) and the ABD 16-plex (AMPFlSTR®Identifiler™) systems have match probabilities in the region of $10^{-17}$, making adventitious matches less likely to occur. When considering the chance of a random match it must be noted that there are two other important effects that require attention:

- Databases will contain pairs of relatives (especially brothers) with increased probability of chance matching. Between a pair of siblings the probability is approximately 1 in 10,000 for the SGM Plus system.

- Partial DNA profiles will have much higher match probabilities and therefore a much higher chance of adventitious match.

- However, complex DNA multiplexes are difficult to manufacture, and may not be as robust. Paradoxically, this increases the number of partial profiles and consequently the number of adventitious matches rises. Consequently, introducing more loci into a single multiplex may not be the solution.

In cases where there is little non-DNA evidence, or the non-DNA evidence suggests that the defendant is innocent, then the overall combined strength of the evidence against the suspect is decreased. This can be demonstrated mathematically (Evett and Weir 1998). However, juries currently assess all of the evidence in a case using an intuitive approach to decide guilt or innocence.

### A process for the evolution of national DNA databases

How will DNA databases evolve over time? Given that the database markers are decided based on the best available technology at the time, this does not mean to say that this will be true several years later.

At the date of writing, it appears that STRs are certainly the best markers of choice. There has been much discussion about alternative markers – Single Nucleotide Polymorphisms (SNPs) but these suffer from the drawback that at least 50 are required in multiplex; furthermore their characteristics are not conducive to the interpretation of complex mixtures (Gill et al. 2004). It is easier to produce smaller multiplexes of 10 STRs; their characteristics are ideal to interpret complex mixtures.

The platforms, or the technology used to analyse STRs have evolved independently. Automated systems capable of processing thousands of samples are now commonplace. The development of new processing methods does not compromise the database because the markers remain the same.

EDNAP has recently described a rationale for database markers to evolve in order to keep pace with new developments. However, the reasons to change need to be carefully considered. Briefly they can be summarised as follows:

(a) to improve discriminating power;
(b) to improve the sensitivity of testing so that smaller amounts of DNA may be detected;
(c) to improve the robustness or the quality of a result.

Obviously, adding more loci will improve the discriminating power, but this may not improve the quality of the result. There is a general consensus view that new loci are required, but the driver is predominantly related to improving the quality of the result, rather than to increasing the discriminating power (Gill *et al*. 2006c; Gill *et al*. 2006d).

The commonest reason for the partial profile is either because DNA is present in low amounts, or because of degradation. DNA is acted on by non-specific enzymes (DNA-ases). The effect is to cleave or cut the DNA molecule into smaller fragments. The longer the DNA fragment is, the greater the chance that a cleavage will occur in the target sequence, and the greater the chance of degradation. To analyse degraded material then it makes sense to design new STRs that are much shorter in order to reduce this risk. This is known as the 'short amplicon' strategy.

Recent discussions by the ENFSI group have proposed at least three new STR markers, and a redesign of the existing multiplex in order to enable detection of shorter DNA fragments. Not only would there be quality improvements but the chance of an adventitious hit on the national DNA database is reduced accordingly. It is also proposed that these additional markers are added to the current list of Interpol loci, bringing the total to 10. Manufacturers of multiplexes have participated in the discussions. However, this is not a trivial issue. Because of the difficulties of designing and producing robust multiplexes it is anticipated that it may take two years or more to develop multiplex kits that are compatible with current databases and which employ the 'short amplicon strategy'.

## *Uniqueness*

Now, the issue of whether a DNA profile can be considered to be 'unique' is considered. By 'unique' it is meant that there is no other person in the population under consideration that possesses those relevant characteristics – in this case the STR genotype.

The preceding text considered the chance that a DNA profile will match someone in a hypothetical DNA database. An assessment of whether a DNA profile is unique in an unsampled population has been considered by Balding (1999). Clearly, a profile is either unique or it is not but without testing everyone it is only possible to address the issue probabilistically. To estimate this probability Balding uses data from the DNA frequency databases and population genetics theory and asks: 'Given that we know there is one person with this profile, what is the probability that there is at least one other person with the same genotype?' He takes account of familial relationships within the population by factoring in an 'arbitrary' number of relatives of known genetic distance (for example brothers, uncles, nieces). Accordingly, Balding (1999) utilises the following definition: Where $U$ is the event that the DNA profile of $S$, the defendant, matches the crime scene profile, with probability $p$ and there is no matching individual in a population of $N$ unprofiled individuals. $U$ is evaluated against *all* of the evidence ($E$) presented in the case.

$$P(U|E) = \frac{(1-p)^N}{1+Np}$$

Using an arbitrary $\Pr(U|E) > 99.9\%$, Balding (1999) shows that the 99.9 per cent criterion for uniqueness is nearly always achieved when >11 STR loci are used and the population size is $10^7$. The assumption is made that the defendant is as likely to have left the crime stain as any member of some specified population. Interestingly, the more STR loci used, the smaller the contribution to the overall calculation from unrelated individuals – the calculation becomes dominated by brothers and near relatives.

Budowle *et al.* (2000) also consider the conditions where a multiple locus DNA profile may be considered to be unique within the context of a case (source attribution). It is emphasised that an assessment within the context of a world population is not particularly relevant since the pool of potential suspects must always be of limited size – for example children under the age of 10 would not be regarded as potential suspects of a rape.

Whereas Balding (1999) recommends calculation of both related and unrelated individuals in the population, Budowle *et al.* (2000) prefer to consider relatives in a separate calculation only if relevant to the specific case. It may be that the suspect has no relatives that could be considered to be alternative suspects or, if he does, that for a number of other reasons it is considered that relatives could not have had access to the crime scene. If the case scenario requires a consideration of relatives, then clearly the population of suspects must be very much smaller than for a general population. Chakraborty *et al.* (1999) report that the most common conditional probability for a 13 STR locus (CODIS) DNA profile is expected to occur in no more than 1 in 40,000 among full siblings. The most expedient method to deal with the issue of relatives is to test that person. However, in many jurisdictions it is not permissible to obtain samples legally; or the issue may be raised in court by the defence (when it is effectively too late to carry out additional testing).

Balding asserts that source attribution is impossible if there is substantial non-DNA evidence that supports the innocence of the defendant. Conversely, the US DNA advisory board (DNA_Advisory_Board 2000) stated: 'If the DNA evidence appears to have come from the defendant, then the only reasonable explanation is that it did come from the defendant and other explanations of the data should be examined.' In particular the relevance of the evidence may be an issue – it is possible that there are innocent reasons for the presence of a DNA profile (this is an especially important consideration relating to low copy number DNA profiling where transfer of DNA may not be attributable to a particular body fluid). The combination and weighting of different kinds of evidence to decide guilt or innocence (of which the DNA evidence is but one facet) is a question for the jury and is certainly outside the province of the scientist.

The assertion that any given full DNA profile is 'unique', although it could well be true, is not very helpful in the courtroom context because of its emotive impact. This may in turn imply guilt – although not explicitly stated – and it tends to cloud the more important issues: what is the relevance of this evidence; how did the evidence come to be there? Consequently, conventional reporting practice in the UK is not to assert uniqueness since it may be seen as implying guilt.

## Reporting DNA evidence using likelihood ratios

Recently, the International Society of Forensic Genetics DNA Commission reviewed the interpretation of complex DNA profiles (Gill *et al.* 2006a). They recommended a method known as the 'likelihood ratio' approach. A typical analysis of crime sample evidence (E) requires the scientist or other evaluator to consider at least two alternative hypotheses – the prosecution hypothesis $(H_p)$ and the defence hypothesis $(H_d)$. For a profile with more than one contributor, the prosecution may hypothesise that the suspect (S) and one unknown (U) person were the contributors, whereas the defence may hypothesise that there were two unknown contributors $U_1$ and $U_2$. The likelihood ratio (LR) compares the probabilities of the evidence under these alternative hypotheses:

$$LR = \frac{\Pr(E|H_p)}{\Pr(E|H_d)}$$

If the LR is greater than one, then the evidence favours $H_p$ but if it is less than one then the evidence favours $H_d$. The evidence is then expressed in terms of the two alternative hypotheses. One of the attractive features of this approach is that it enables the scientist to simultaneously consider and to compare the alternative defence and prosecution scenarios. It enables a framework that allows for different hypotheses to be considered if necessary – for example the defence may contend that there are three unknown contributors instead of one. Much has been written on the subject of the likelihood ratio. The reader is referred to Buckleton (2005) for a review. However, it is important to point out that there are alternative 'frequentist' methods to evaluate evidence that are sometimes used in the UK and in many other jurisdictions such as North America.

### Alternative methods to report DNA evidence

*The Doheny Adams appeal court ruling*
In the appeal of R v. Doheny and Adams (1 Cr App R 369) the court considered the presentation of evidence derived from population statistics, recommending that the rarity of a DNA profile should be expressed in terms of the size of a population of suspects (for example the relevant population of the town or city where the crime was committed). The recommendation was:

Provided that he has the necessary data, and the statistical expertise, it may be appropriate for him to say how many people with the matching characteristics are likely to be found in the United Kingdom – or perhaps in a more limited relevant sub-group, such as for instance, the white Caucasian sexually active males in the Manchester area.

Both prosecution and defence agreed that the perpetrator was from a population consisting of 800,000 people, living in the area of Manchester. The DNA profiling evidence combined with conventional blood grouping concluded a likelihood ratio of 40,000, called by the judges the 'random occurrence ratio' of 1 in 40,000. The term 'random occurrence ratio' is taken to mean the chance of observing a profile in a random set of (unrelated) people. This is interpreted to mean a match probability. The judges recommended that this should be explained to a jury in terms of the number of individuals in the target population of 800,000 in this case who would possess the 'relevant characteristics'. In this example there could be 20 other people with the same DNA profile. The judges concluded that 'this figure still renders it an extremely unlikely coincidence that both the Appellant and another of this small cohort should have been in the vicinity of the crime at about the same time that it was committed'.

Currently, in the UK, this statement format is not commonly employed. However, an example is given here (*R v. Wilkinson*) where a partial DNA profile with a match probability of 1 in 33,000 was calculated. In accordance with the court recommendations, the scientist attempted to indicate the number of individuals that would possess the relevant characteristics in a local population, a regional population and in the national population, using the government census data. The offence (a rape) occurred in the Durham area of England. By presenting the results in this way, clear guidance can be given to the jury on the impact of the relative size of the 'suspect' population and help place in context the evidential value of the match. The decision of which target population to 'accept' as the relevant population is always the court decision, and not that of the scientist – a suitable format is given in Table 2.2.

The number of potential individuals who could match is always rounded up to an integer or whole number as the obvious solution to counter the suggestion that fractions are of little meaning to a jury (Evett *et al.* 2000a).

**Table 2.2** Presentation of data in *R v. Wilkinson*

| Geographical population | Number of men (rounded to the nearest 1,000) | Expected number of men with matching characteristics |
| --- | --- | --- |
| National (UK) | 30 million | 867 |
| Regional (north-east region) | 1,219,000 | 37 |
| Local (Easington area) | 46,000 | 2* |
| | | (*rounded up from 1.4) |

Whereas it is relatively easy to apply the recommendations of the appeal court ruling to examples from single stains, it is not so easy to do this when mixtures or complex DNA profiles are observed.

Mixtures are often encountered in casework. The likelihood ratio method is the preferred (but not the only way) to interpret them. In general, there are three types of approach to their statistical evaluation. The 'frequentist' approach is to calculate the probability of inclusion (*pI*), or its converse, the probability of exclusion (*pE*) or random man not excluded (RMNE). The Bayesian approach is to calculate a likelihood ratio (LR). However, the complexity of the latter method requires the use of expert systems which are now in routine use (Bill *et al.* 2005; Gill *et al.* 2006e). These systems follow the principles described by Gill *et al.* (1998, 2000b).

### Probability of Inclusion method

The frequentist methods are commonly used throughout the US and Europe (DNA_advisory_board 2000; Ladd *et al.* 2001) and Australia; most experts report mixtures using probability of exclusion (*pE*), which addresses 'the probability that a random person would be excluded as a contributor to the observed DNA mixture'. It is possible to turn this statement round and ask: 'What is the probability that a random person would be included as a contributor to the observed DNA mixture?'

This is referred to as the probability of Inclusion (*pI*) and is considered more suited to UK reporting as it follows the central recommendation of the Doheny/Adams appeal court ruling (*R v. Doheny and Adams* 1997 1 Cr App R 369, 374) where the judgement focused on the question: 'How many people with the matching characteristics are likely to be found in the United Kingdom or a more limited relevant subgroup?'

There has been some criticism of the *pI* method and care is certainly needed in its use. The predominant argument against has been that it wastes information compared to the likelihood ratio method. However, in some evidential stains there is uncertainty about the number of contributors, which may render the likelihood ratio method difficult to apply. Under this circumstance, if the only remaining alternative would be to effectively report the evidence as inconclusive, then the *pI* method can be used. The issues are summarised by Gill *et al.* (2006a) – there are some important caveats: the evidential alleles must be well represented so that the chance of dropout and any potential confusion with stutter is minimised.

### The developing interpretation strategy

Over the years, divergent practices have arisen in laboratories worldwide. Consequently, it is important to recognise that there is always more than one method to report DNA evidence – there is no single method to be advocated, to the exclusion of all others.

The ISFG DNA Commission recently reviewed procedures currently used within the EU and has published a number of recommendations for users (Gill *et al.* 2006a). These recommendations are a result of consensus international agreement on ways to interpret difficult DNA profiles, especially those that are low level, where the minor profile is subject to the phenomenon of allele dropout or where stutters may confuse interpretation. Some methods may be more powerful than others, but the task of the Commission was to consider all methods that are valid for scientific purposes and to identify the limitations where possible. It was not the intention to be prescriptive.

This work continues; the aim is to consult widely between the major scientific societies, ENFSI, EDNAP, in order to produce additional authoritative documents. It is proposed that the next steps will be to publish European ISO 17025 standard guidelines.

### Increasing the sensitivity of biochemical tests (post 1990s)

The development of the PCR technique (Mullis *et al.* 1986; Mullis and Faloona 1987; Saiki *et al.* 1985) was responsible for a dramatic increase in the sensitivity of the DNA profiling technique and enabled the analysis of much smaller amounts of DNA than had hitherto been possible. The actual amount of DNA required for analysis was decreased by approximately one thousandfold. For samples amplified by PCR between 250 pg–1 ng is routinely analysed, compared to (50 ng–1μg) when minisatellites were used.

### Increased range of evidence types

The improved sensitivity also led to an increase in the different evidence types that could be analysed, concurrently improving the success rates of DNA profiling techniques on evidence types that had previously proven to be problematical or largely unsuccessful. For example, the analysis of saliva was demonstrated on cigarette butts (Hochmeister *et al.* 1991), envelope flaps and stamps. It was also demonstrated that DNA profiles could be recovered from saliva associated with bite marks (Sweet *et al.* 1997) and from debris underneath fingernails (Wiegand *et al.* 1993).

The utility of STRs to analyse highly degraded DNA samples in real casework was dramatically demonstrated by the identification of human remains from disasters such as Waco, Texas (Clayton *et al.* 1995a; Clayton *et al.* 1995b; Whitaker *et al.* 1995); the Spitzbergen disaster (Olaisen *et al.* 1998); TWA flight 800 (Ballantyne 1997); Swiss-air flight 111 (Leclair *et al.* 2004); the 1998 Philippines air-crash (Goodwin *et al.* 1999). However, Olaisen was able to use minisatellites in the Spitzbergen disaster with a 100 per cent success rate because prior to collection, the bodies were at an ambient temperature of ~0°C and were well preserved. Conversely, with the Waco disaster bodies were badly burned and subsequently highly decomposed after several days at an ambient temperature of ~30°C, hence minisatellite analysis was not possible with these samples. The success rate (with STRs) was 66–83 per cent. A similar success rate was achieved with the TWA-800 disaster where bodies were decomposed and often skeletonised. The World Trade Center 9/11 disaster was particularly challenging – a total of 2,819 individuals died (reviewed by Marchi (2004)) and the entire gamut of forensic DNA techniques was employed. The greatest challenges are the results of war and genocide – in former Yugoslavia more than 30,000 people went missing and in Bosnia-

Herzegovina alone more than 10,000 bodies required identification (reviewed by Huffine *et al.* (2001)).

One area that has received much attention is the use of fingerprint enhancement chemicals on fingerprints in blood. For example, Fregeau *et al.* (2000) showed that chemicals tested had no adverse effect on PCR provided that stains were less than 54 days old. Andersen and Bramble (1997) also demonstrated that light sources used to enhance bloody fingerprints did not affect the success of PCR provided that short-wave UV was not used.

The retrieval of DNA profiles from latent hand or finger-prints, where no body fluid was apparent (van Oorschot and Jones 1997), began a new area of exploitation of the DNA profiling technique. van Oorschot (1997) recovered DNA profiles from surfaces that had been touched – such as handles of leather briefcases and telephone handsets (primary transfer) – furthermore, the amount of DNA that could be recovered by swabbing was surprisingly high. Between 2–150 ng was estimated; this allowed analysis using conventional STR techniques. In addition, it was claimed that DNA could be transferred from an object to a person's hands (secondary transfer). However, Ladd *et al.* (1999) were only able to recover 1–15 ng from surfaces after following a similar experimental design; secondary transfer from individuals consisted of DNA profiles that were close to background and was considered to be uninterpretable. Van Renterghem *et al.* (2000) were able to analyse partial profiles (or better) from 38 out of 116 fingerprints lifted from glass slides, using conventional analysis with AMP*Fl*STR Profiler plus.

### Increasing the sensitivity by increasing the PCR cycle number (low copy number)

Generally, the lower limits of sensitivity recommended by manufacturers of STR multiplex systems are in the region of 250 pg. Multiplexes usually work at their optimum efficiency when 1 ng of DNA is analysed (Sparkes *et al.* 1996a; Sparkes *et al.* 1996b) and not more than 28–30 cycles of amplification are carried out. Interpretation of DNA profiles is assisted by utilising systems that are not too sensitive and this is important because the scientist often needs to associate the presence of a bloodstain (or other body fluid) with the DNA profile itself. A highly sensitive system that may reveal DNA from sources other than the body fluid analysed would require careful consideration when the evidence was interpreted. For this reason, validation exercises often include studies on the effect of rough handling, coughing or sneezing on to garments to determine if it is possible casually to transfer DNA to evidential material.

Forensic scientists always seek to increase the sensitivity of their methods and the easiest way to do this is simply to raise the number of PCR amplification cycles. Findlay *et al.* (1997) demonstrated that single cells (buccal) could be analysed when 34 cycles were used with SGM multiplex system. Interpretation, however, was not straightforward – additional alleles (known as drop-in products) were occasionally observed. The size of stutter artefacts was enhanced and allele dropout was common. However, such profiles may be interpreted using a framework that takes into account this phenomenon.

Subsequently, increasing the sensitivity of PCR by raising the number of cycles has been used to increase the range of evidence types available to analysis. For example Wiegand and Kleiber (1997) analysed epithelial cells transferred from an assailant after strangulation using 30–31 cycles of PCR. Van Hoofstat et al. (1998) analysed fingerprints from grips of tools with 28–40 cycles. Analysis of STRs from telogen hair roots and hair shafts in the absence of the root has been reported (Barbaro et al. 2000; Hellmann et al. 2001; Szibor et al. 2006).

Increased PCR cycles are routinely used by anthropologists and forensic scientists to identify ancient DNA from bones. Gill et al. (1994) used 38–43 cycles to analyse STRs from 70-year-old bone from the Romanov family. Schmerer et al. (1999, 2000) and Burger et al. (1999) analysed STRs from bone thousands of years old (60 and 50 PCR cycles respectively). Some authors have used modified PCR methods, for example, a nested primer PCR strategy was used by Strom and Rechitsky (1998). This utilised a first round amplification with 40 cycles, with subsequent analysis of a portion with a further 20–30 cycles. This method was used to analyse DNA from charred human remains and minute amounts of blood.

Gill et al. (2000b) compared different methods available to analyse DNA, where the target quantity was <100 pg. By varying cycling conditions between 28–60 cycles, they concluded that the optimum for both SGM and AMP*Fl*STR®SGM Plus™ systems was 34 cycles. There was little to be gained by increasing the cycle number further since it did not result in increased sensitivity, but caused significant deterioration in profile quality. The extreme sensitivity of the method suggested that analysis should only be attempted in a carefully controlled environment in order to reduce the possibility of contamination from personnel and other sources within the laboratory itself.

A fundamental misconception exists that analysis of low copy number (LCN) DNA occurs when elevated cycle numbers are used. This definition of LCN is not based on the technique used to produce the profile, but on the number of template molecules input into the PCR.

All methods used to analyse low quantities of DNA suffer from the same basic disadvantages of stochastic variation. When present in low numbers, a DNA molecule will be delivered in variable quantities as a result of sampling variation. This leads to variability in the PCR and the preferential amplification of alleles. There are therefore several consequences that cannot be avoided:

- Locus dropout.
- Allele dropout may occur because one of a pair of alleles at a heterozygote locus fails to be amplified to a detectable level.
- Stutters may increase in size relative to the progenitor allele.

This means that different DNA profiles observed after replicate PCR analyses may not be fully representative. In addition, random contamination events could add spurious alleles to the profile. Taberlet et al. (1996) suggested a method of replicated analyses that comprised a rule that an allele could only be scored if observed at least twice in replicate samples. This theory was expanded by Gill et al. (2000b) who adopted Taberlet's duplication rule and demonstrated that it was conservative in relation to a new likelihood ratio (LR) method that assessed DNA profiles in relation to sporadic allelic contaminants, stutters and allelic dropout. Provided that the level of sporadic contamination was not high (<30% per locus) then the duplication method was demonstrated to be conservative relative to the likelihood ratio method.

Recently a new mathematical method has been introduced into casework. Based on the original theory published by Gill *et al.* (2000b), the solution has been programmed into an expert system called *LoComatioN* (Gill *et al.* 2006e). The advantages of this system are that it utilises an advanced statistical theory, and can interpret results from multiple contributors. Recently a complex four-person mixture was successfully reported using this method (Gill *et al.* 2008b).

### Association of the DNA profile with the evidential material analysed

There are two broad categories of evidence types – discrete (e.g. bone, hair) and non-discrete (e.g. body fluid stains). When using LCN, it is generally easier to associate a DNA profile with a discrete evidence type. This is because analysis of bone samples is not attempted without removing the outermost layer by physical methods (e.g. sanding) in order to minimise the possible contamination from extraneous DNA. Similarly, hair shafts can be washed in a detergent solution to remove adhering DNA. This cannot be done with evidence types that are not discrete, e.g. bloodstained cloth, hence the chance is increased that a DNA profile may not be directly associated with the evidential body fluid that is 'apparently' analysed. Because there is a serious possibility of transferring LCN DNA from an extraneous source, to both minimise the chance of contamination and to identify an occurrence and when it happens the following guidelines are generally used:

- DNA extractions and setting up PCR reactions are carried out in a dedicated laboratory.
- Personnel wear disposable lab coats, gloves and face masks.
- Benches and equipment are frequently treated with bleach (or equivalent) and the laboratory equipment irradiated with UV light each night.
- PCR amplification is carried out in a separate laboratory or laboratory area.
- Negative controls are used with every test to monitor laboratory environment and reagents used.
- PCR tests are duplicated or triplicated where possible.
- All DNA profiles are compared against elimination databases (these include staff, other lab personnel, as well as a log of unsourced contamination events from negative controls.
- A database to eliminate investigators of crime scenes as potential contributors is also under preparation.

### Defining when DNA transfer can occur

Consider a general model to illustrate the potential transfer of DNA before, during and after a crime (Figure 2.1).

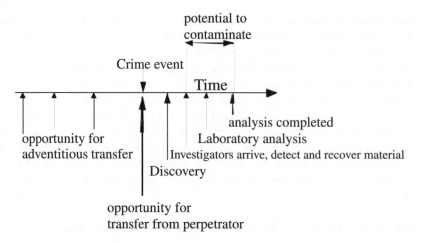

**Figure 2.1** A timeline illustrating the potential for DNA transfer

Before and after a crime event there is the potential for adventitious transfer of cells. Note the term contamination is reserved for transfer of DNA *after* the crime event. Adventitious transfer and laboratory contamination usually involve low levels of DNA.

The association of body fluid and the DNA profile is not implicit (Gill 2001). If the body fluid giving a positive presumptive test is small or degraded then the DNA profile may have originated from an alternative source. For example a small degraded spot that has given a positive presumptive test for blood might be masked by a fresh saliva stain that instead contributes to the observed result. The scientist cannot infer either the type of cell donating the DNA or the time when the cells were deposited.

An estimate of the quantity of DNA is useful to assist in the interpretation of the relevance of a DNA profile. For example, if a visible fresh bloodstain yields several micrograms of DNA, it is not unreasonable to associate the DNA profile with the bloodstain. However, the association is uncertain if the bloodstain is minute, old and yields just a few picograms of DNA. Inevitably, there is a direct relationship between the quantity of DNA present and the relevance of the evidence.

The interpretation of the case can only follow after an assessment of all the available evidence, taking into consideration the scenarios offered by prosecution and defence lawyers.

### An assessment of contamination risks

From Figure 2.1 it can be seen that DNA can be transferred at any time before, during and after the crime. The foregoing discussion has covered the possibility of adventitious transfer at a period before the crime and it is implicit that the DNA profile matches a suspect. If the DNA profile does not match the suspect then post-crime transfer must be considered. Contamination is transfer of DNA after the crime event. Potential sources of contamination are:

(a) investigative officers/pathologists etc. at the crime scene;
(b) laboratory staff;
(c) cross-contamination from samples processed in the laboratory, e.g. by aerosol;
(d) plastic-ware contamination (may be contaminated at the manufacturing source).

Whereas (a) and (b) can be covered by reference to staff databases, and databases of investigating officers, (c) and (d) are more difficult to detect but are minimised by good laboratory design, staff wearing anti-contamination clothing and facemasks, and UV sterilisation of plastic-ware.

Transfer of DNA by individuals unassociated with the crime before the crime event itself is defined as adventitious transfer. When a DNA profile does *not* match the suspect the following possibilities apply:

(a) The suspect is not the source and the perpetrator profile has been visualised.
(b) Cells have been transferred by an innocent individual before the crime (perpetrator has not shed cells) – 'adventitious transfer'.
(c) Cells have been transferred by an investigator after the crime event (perpetrator has not shed cells) – 'contamination'.

Note that mixtures may show DNA profiles arising from a combination of the three different events listed.

The circumstances of the victim leading up to the crime event are unknown to the scientist, hence the possibilities of adventitious transfer cannot be directly ascertained. Once the crime has been discovered, the scene and the associated evidence enter a controlled environment, where the risk of contamination is minimised by the adoption of good laboratory and investigative practice.

The primary risk of contamination is wrongful exclusion – particularly if the contaminant masks the perpetrator's profile. For the converse to apply – wrongful inclusion, either tube mix-up or gross contamination (such as use of pipette tips contaminated in the laboratory – e.g. used twice) would be required. Good laboratory practice renders this a virtual impossibility and it is not considered further here.

### Transfer and persistence

There is currently considerable lack of understanding about issues of transfer and persistence. Further work is being undertaken in this area. Ways by which DNA may be transferred to objects can be subdivided into two categories (Lowe *et al.* 2002):

*primary transfer* – where DNA is transferred as a result of physical contact. There is marked variation between the extents to which different individuals shed DNA from physical contact with objects (unpublished results). The amount of DNA remaining at a crime scene may depend upon the time since contact, with the best chance of recovery immediately after an incident. The persistence of DNA will also depend upon the extent of contact by other individuals.

*secondary transfer* – for example where DNA of a person (x) is transferred to an object by a different person (y). This may occur if the suspect and victim have physical contact, for example shake hands. Secondary transfer may also occur if two objects are in contact. Currently there is some evidence (Lowe *et al.* 2002) to support secondary transfer from person to object, although only mixtures have been encountered so far.

### Statement writing

In conjunction with the increased use of DNA profiling, there has been a parallel development in interpretation methodology. In particular, Cooke *et al.* (1998, 1999) and Evett *et al.* (2000b) introduced the notion of the 'hierarchy of propositions'. This has led to a much deeper understanding of the interpretative process. Because of uncertainties that surround persistence and transfer, the statements are written to reflect this. Examples of the wording used in statements are given below. Interpretation is dependent upon a full analysis of the circumstances of the crime and based on a careful consideration of all of the non-DNA evidence.

*Observation of mixtures*:

With LCN, mixtures are commonly encountered. It cannot be determined whether recovered DNA profiles are associated with a crime event. An example statement follows:

> 'The observation of mixed DNA STR profiles (i.e. from more than one individual) can be anticipated. For example, from past experience it is not unusual to detect DNA profiles on items that match the profile of an individual who has habitually worn that item. However, currently we have no information to assist with questions of transfer and persistence of low levels of DNA on items such as clothing. Thus consideration should be given as to how the DNA detected has been transferred to that item, and consequently to the relevance of finding profiles matching the individuals in the case.'

*In the following, two alternatives are considered. No reference is made about the origin of the body fluid type – it is simply stated that DNA was recovered from the item.*

> **Either**: 'The majority of the DNA originated from Mr X.'

> **Or**: 'The majority of the DNA originated from someone other than and unrelated to Mr X. If this DNA had in fact originated from Mr X then I would expect to obtain matching profiles.'

*In the summary section the following paragraphs are included – this statement was specifically written for a case where DNA from a watch-strap matched a suspect.*

When very small amounts of DNA are analysed special considerations arise as follows:

- Although a DNA profile has been obtained, it is not possible to identify the type of cells from which the DNA originated, neither is it possible to state *when* the cells were deposited.
- It is not possible to make any conclusion about transfer and persistence of DNA in this case. It is not possible to estimate when the suspect last wore the watch if it is his DNA.
- Because the DNA test is very sensitive it is not unexpected to find mixtures. If the potential origins of DNA profiles cannot be identified, it does not necessarily follow that they are relevant to this case; since transfer of cells can occur as a result of casual contact.

Effectively, the strength of the LCN DNA evidence is decreased compared to conventional DNA analysis. This inevitably arises from uncertainties relating to the method of transfer of DNA to a surface and uncertainties relating to when the DNA was transferred. It is emphasised that the relevance of the DNA evidence in a case can only be assessed by a concurrent consideration of all the non-DNA evidence. Research is currently being undertaken to devise a probabilistic Bayesian method that encapsulates both the DNA and non-DNA evidence (Evett *et al*. 2002).

### Comments relating to the Omagh judgement

Recently, the Omagh judgement (2007) has raised concerns about the application of the *low copy number* technique in relation to the relevance of evidence. Some brief comments on this case are given here.

It is unfortunate that the low copy number technique was linked with the application of 34 PCR cycles. Undoubtedly, this amount of amplification is capable of detecting low levels (a few picograms of DNA) but the method was invented some years ago when methods (flat bed gels) were less sensitive. Since then, the introduction of capillary gel electrophoresis has dramatically increased the sensitivity of the method. Recently the UK technical working group (Gill *et al*. 2008a) observed (section 2.9.1):

> We have demonstrated experimentally that some laboratories achieve results from ca. 50 pg of DNA using standard 28 PCR cycles. Since these consequences are common to all methods of DNA analysis and are not restricted to 34 cycles, we do not consider the LCN label for 34 cycle work to be useful, or particularly helpful, and propose to abandon it as a scientific concept because a clear definition cannot be formulated.

Instead, the term *low-level* is now proposed to describe partial profiles, independent of the method used. It is the quality of the result rather than the method by which it was derived that is important.

A *conventional* result is one that is *unambiguous* and no special procedures are required to interpret the match probability. It follows that a conventional result may be obtained from a system that employs any methodology, regardless of the cycle number used – the requirement is that the profile is fully represented.

An *ambiguous* DNA profile is one that does not match the suspect: either because alleles are missing or because there are additional alleles. This is typical of a *low-level* DNA profile and these consequences arise independently of the methodology used.

Another common example of an *ambiguous* DNA profile is a mixture. Often a mixture may comprise alleles from a major versus minor contributor. The ISFG DNA Commission (Gill *et al.* 2006b) considered the interpretation of mixtures where the minor component was of evidential value and included examples where alleles were missing (i.e. dropped out) or where stutter interfered with the interpretation. Gill *et al.* (2007) have reviewed the position and suggested changes to the terminology. For example, it is implicit that a mixture of a major and minor contributor comprises both *conventional* and *low-level* DNA profiles.

It is important not to confuse the strength of evidence of the DNA profile with the matter of how the profile was transferred. They are two separate questions. If there is a perfect match with DNA from a suspect, then the scientist cannot necessarily give an indication of when the DNA profile was transferred (Figure 2.1) – the evidential strength of the profile itself is unaffected but crucially, a match does not translate into guilt. This seems to have been the main issue with the recent Omagh trial. Some crime stains recovered were complete and unambiguous conventional profiles (not low copy number). But the issue for the court was to determine whether the DNA profile was coincident with the activity of the crime itself, or whether the transfer of DNA was by an innocent method. If the court considered that the presence of the profiles could have been attributed either to contamination, or evidence tampering, then these are issues of relevance of the evidence, and not an issue of the match probability itself. Scientifically, these subjective probabilities could be explored using a Bayes net solution (Evett *et al.* 2002).

Whilst advocating a Bayes solution to evaluate subjective probabilities, it is worth highlighting that this approach has been used before in the case of *R v. Doheny and Adams* (1997). However, the complexity of the approach led to it being ruled inadmissible as evidence as it trespassed upon the territory of the jury. The jury combines evidence by *intuitive* processes and the appeal court concluded that there was little hope that they could understand the complexity of the Bayesian probabilistic approach that was put to them.

To summarise, with *low-level* DNA profiling, we are not really concerned with a particular technique or method, rather it is the *philosophy* of the approach that is important. The uncertainty of the method of transfer does not diminish the fact of the matching DNA profile – the former does not invalidate the latter, but the method of transfer is clearly a concern for the court to consider, and is not necessarily one for the scientist. This is why it is important to present *low-level* DNA evidence in the context of supporting *non-DNA* evidence. In recognition, the Crown Prosecution Service (CPS) of England and Wales do not use DNA as sole-plank evidence. But in the Omagh trial, it was clear that there was insufficient *non-DNA* evidence that could be adduced as evidence.

Recent events highlight a general need for continuing discussion, debate and education to explore new ways of presenting complex scientific methods in court that can be readily understood by the layperson.

### Other DNA markers

It is important not to lose sight of other genetic markers used in forensic analysis. A brief summary is included here. The interested reader is referred to the more extensive review of Jobling and Gill (2004) for further details. Mitochondrial DNA is commonly used to analyse very old degraded materials such as bones and hair shafts. Autosomal genetic markers can be used to provide information about the phenotype of the individual such as race (Lowe *et al.* 2001) and hair colour (Grimes *et al.* 2001). Y-chromosome markers also assist with the interpretation of male/female mixtures where the former is in particularly low concentration. There is considerable interest in the use of Y-chromosome analysis in order to provide information on racial origin; also there is the potential to use Y-chromosome markers to give an indication of surname (Immel *et al.* 2006; King *et al.* 2006; Moore *et al.* 2006). However, the major disadvantage of systems other than core STR loci is that the profiles are not stored in national DNA databases.

For high-throughput laboratories there are obvious attractions to utilising multicapillary electrophoresis machines. Concurrent developments also include automation of extraction, quantification, PCR set-up, PCR and post-PCR set-up. In addition to these developments, the interpretation is also currently the subject of developing expert systems that will effectively result in substantial automation of the entire process from start to finish.

Looking further to the future, platform development will result in faster, cheaper methods, particularly in relation to miniaturisation that may enable analysis at a scene of crime.

Finally, since the first introduction of DNA profiling in forensic analysis in 1986, the subsequent introduction of STRs into casework made the national DNA database possible, and this has led to a massive change in the way in which forensic science is used by the police. In particular the expansion of DNA analysis to include both serious crimes and volume crimes such as burglary has resulted in the strategic use of DNA to actively reduce levels of crime (by virtue of increasing detection rates and acting as a deterrent).

### References

(1997) R v. Doheny and Adams [1997] 1 Crim App R 369.

(2007) Queen v. Sean Hoey, Neutral Citation no. [2007] NICC 49.

Anderson, J. and Bramble, S. (1997) 'The effects of fingermark enhancement light sources on subsequent PCR-STR DNA analysis of fresh bloodstains', *Journal of Forensic Sciences*, 42: 303–6.

Balding, D.J. (1999) 'When can a DNA profile be regarded as unique?', *Sci Justice*, 39: 257–60.

Balding, D.J. and Donnelly, P. (1996) 'Evaluating DNA profile evidence when the suspect is identified through a database search', *Journal of Forensic Sciences*, 41: 603–7.

Balding, D.J., Greenhalgh, M. and Nichols, R.A. (1996) 'Population genetics of STR loci in Caucasians', *Int J Legal Med*, 108: 300–5.

Balding, D.J. and Nichols, R.A. (1994) 'DNA profile match probability calculation: how to allow for population stratification, relatedness, database selection and single bands', *Forensic Science International*, 64: 125–40.

Ballantyne, J. (1997) 'Mass disaster genetics', *Nat Genet*, 15: 329–31.

Bar, W., Brinkmann, B., Budowle, B., Carracedo, A., Gill, P., Lincoln, P., Mayr, W. and Olaisen, B. (1997) 'DNA recommendations. Further report of the DNA Commission of the ISFH regarding the use of short tandem repeat systems. International Society for Forensic Haemogenetics', *Int J Legal Med*, 110: 175–6.

Barbaro, A., Falcone, G. and Barbaro, A. (2000) 'DNA typing from hair shaft', *Progress in Forensic Genetics*, 8: 523–525.

Bieber, F.R., Brenner, C.H. and Lazer, D. (2006) 'Human genetics. Finding criminals through DNA of their relatives', *Science*, 312: 1315–6.

Bill, M., Gill, P., Curran, J., Clayton, T., Pinchin, R., Healy, M. and Buckleton, J. (2005) 'PENDULUM – a guideline-based approach to the interpretation of STR mixtures', *Forensic Science International*, 148: 181–9.

Buckleton, J. (2005) 'A framework for interpreting evidence', in J. Buckleton, C.M. Triggs and S.J. Walsh (eds), *Forensic DNA evidence interpretation*. Boca Raton: CRC Press.

Budowle, B., Chakraborty, R., Carmody, G. and Monson, K. (2000) 'Source attribution of a forensic DNA profile', *Forensic Science Communications*.

Budowle, B., Moretti, T.R., Baumstark, A.L., Defenbaugh, D.A. and Keys, K.M. (1999) 'Population data on the thirteen CODIS core short tandem repeat loci in African Americans, U.S. Caucasians, Hispanics, Bahamians, Jamaicans, and Trinidadians', *Journal of Forensic Sciences*, 44: 1277–86.

Burger, J., Hummel, S., Hermann, B. and Henke, W. (1999) 'DNA preservation: a microsatellite-DNA study on ancient skeletal remains', *Electrophoresis*, 20: 1722–8.

Chakraborty, R., Stivers, D.N., Su, B., Zhong, Y. and Budowle, B. (1999) 'The utility of short tandem repeat loci beyond human identification: implications for development of new DNA typing systems', *Electrophoresis*, 20: 1682–96.

Clayton, T.M., Whitaker, J.P., Fisher, D.L., Lee, D.A., Holland, M.M., Weedn, V.W., Maguire, C.N., Dizinno, J.A., Kimpton, C.P. and Gill, P. (1995a) 'Further validation of a quadruplex STR DNA typing system: a collaborative effort to identify victims of a mass disaster', *Forensic Science International*, 76: 17–25.

Clayton, T.M., Whitaker, J.P. and Maguire, C.N. (1995b) 'Identification of bodies from the scene of a mass disaster using DNA amplification of short tandem repeat (STR) loci', *Forensic Science International*, 76: 7–15.

Cooke, R., Evett, I., Jackson, G., Jones, P. and Lambert, J. (1998) 'A hierarchy of propositions: Deciding which level to address in casework', *Sci Justice*, 38: 231–239.

Cooke, R., Evett, I., Jackson, G., Jones, P. and Lambert, J. (1999) 'Case preassessment and review in a two way transfer case', *Sci Justice*, 39: 103–111.

Cotton, E.A., Allsop, R.F., Guest, J.L., Frazier, R.R., Koumi, P., Callow, I.P., Seager, A. and Sparkes, R.L. (2000) 'Validation of the AMPFlSTR SGM plus system for use in forensic casework', *Forensic Science International*, 112: 151–61.

DNA_ADVISORY_BOARD (2000) 'Statistical and population genetics issues affecting the evaluation of the frequency and occurrence of DNA profiles calculated from pertinent population databases', *Forensic Science Communications*, http:/www.fbi.gov/hq/lab/fsc/backissu/july2000/dnastat.htm.

Evett, I.W., Foreman, L.A., Jackson, G. and Lambert, J.A. (2000a) 'DNA profiling: A discussion of issues relating to the reporting of very small match probabilities', *Criminal Law Review*, 341–355.

Evett, I.W., Gill, P.D., Jackson, G., Whitaker, J. and Champod, C. (2002) 'Interpreting small quantities of DNA: the hierarchy of propositions and the use of Bayesian networks', *Journal of Forensic Sciences*, 47: 520–30.

Evett, I.W., Jackson, G. and Lambert, J.A. (2000b) 'More on the hierarchy of propositions: Exploring the distinction between explanations and propositions' *Sci Justice*, 40: 3–10.

Evett, I.W. and Weir, B. (1998) *Interpreting DNA evidence. Statistical Genetics for forensic scientists*. Sinauer Associates, Sunderland, Mass., USA.

Findlay, I., Taylor, A., Quirke, P., Frazier, R. and Urquhart, A. (1997) 'DNA fingerprinting from single cells', *Nature*, 389: 555–6.

Foreman, L.A. and Evett, I.W. (2001) 'Statistical analyses to support forensic interpretation for a new ten-locus STR profiling system', *Int J Legal Med*, 114: 147–55.

Foreman, L.A., Lambert, J.A. and Evett, I.W. (1998) 'Regional genetic variation in Caucasians', *Forensic Science International*, 95: 27–37.

Fregeau, C.J. (1998) 'National casework and the national DNA database: the Royal Canadian Mounted Police perspective', *Progress in Forensic Genetics*, 7: 541–543.

Fregeau, C.J., Germain, O. and Fourney, R.M. (2000) 'Fingerprint enhancement revisited and the effects of blood enhancement chemicals on subsequent profiler Plus fluorescent short tandem repeat DNA analysis of fresh and aged bloody fingerprints', *Journal of Forensic Sciences*, 45: 354–80.

Gill, P. (2001) 'Application of low copy number DNA profiling', *Croat Med J*, 42: 229–32.

Gill, P., Brenner, C., Brinkmann, B., Budowle, B., Carracedo, A., Jobling, M.A., De Knijff, P., Kayser, M., Krawczak, M., Mayr, W.R., Morling, N., Olaisen, B., Pascali, V., Prinz, M., Roewer, L., Schneider, P.M., Sajantila, A. and Tyler-Smith, C. (2001) 'DNA Commission of the International Society of Forensic Genetics: recommendations on forensic analysis using Y-chromosome STRs', *Forensic Science International*, 124: 5–10.

Gill, P., Brenner, C.H., Buckleton, J.S., Carracedo, A., Krawczak, M., Mayr, W.R., Morling, N., Prinz, M., Schneider, P.M. and Weir, B.S. (2006a) 'DNA commission of the International Society of Forensic Genetics: Recommendations on the interpretation of mixtures', *Forensic Science International*, 160: 90–101.

Gill, P., Brown, R., Fairley, M., Lee, L., Smyth, M., Simpson, M., Irwin, B., Dunlop, J., Greenhalgh, M., Way, K., Westacott, E.J., Ferguson, S.J., Ford, L.V., Clayton, T. and Guiness, J. (2008a) 'National recommendations of the technical UK DNA working group on mixture interpretation for the NDNADB and for court going purposes', *Forensic Sci Int: Genetics*, 2: 76–82.

Gill, P., Curran, J. and Neumann, C. (2007) 'Interpretation of complex DNA profiles using Tippett plots', in N. Morling (ed.), *Progress in Forensic Genetics*. Elsevier: Copenhagen, Denmark.

Gill, P., Curran, J., Neumann, C., Kirkham, A., Clayton, T., Whitaker, J.P. and Lambert, J. (2008b) 'Interpretation of complex DNA profiles using empirical models and a method to measure their robustness', *Forensic Sci Int: Genetics*.

Gill, P., D'Aloja, E., Andersen, J., Dupuy, B., Jangblad, M., Johnsson, V., Kloosterman, A.D., Kratzer, A., Lareu, M.V., Meldegaard, M., Phillips, C., Pfitzinger, H., Rand, S., Sabatier, M., Scheithauer, R., Schmitter, H., Schneider, P. and Vide, M.C. (1997) Report of the European DNA profiling group (EDNAP): an investigation of the complex STR loci D21S11 and HUMFIBRA (FGA). *Forensic Science International*, 86: 25–33.

Gill, P. and Evett, I. (1995) 'Population genetics of short tandem repeat (STR) loci', *Genetica*, 96: 69–87.

Gill, P., Fereday, L., Morling, N. and Schneider, P.M. (2006c) 'The evolution of DNA databases – recommendations for new European STR loci', *Forensic Science International*, 156: 242–4.

Gill, P., Fereday, L., Morling, N. and Schneider, P.M. (2006d) 'New multiplexes for Europe-Amendments and clarification of strategic development', *Forensic Science International*.

Gill, P., Ivanov, P.L., Kimpton, C., Piercy, R., Benson, N., Tully, G., Evett, I., Hagelberg, E. and Sullivan, K. (1994) 'Identification of the remains of the Romanov family by DNA analysis', *Nat Genet*, 6: 130–5.

Gill, P., Kirkham, A. and Curran, J. (2006e) 'LoComatioN: A software tool for the analysis of low copy number DNA profiles', *Forensic Science International*, 166(2): 128–138.

Gill, P., Sparkes, R., Fereday, L. and Werrett, D.J. (2000a) 'Report of the European Network of Forensic Science Institutes (ENSFI): formulation and testing of principles to evaluate STR multiplexes', *Forensic Science International*, 108: 1–29.

Gill, P., Sparkes, R., Pinchin, R., Clayton, T., Whitaker, J. and Buckleton, J. (1998) 'Interpreting simple STR mixtures using allele peak areas', *Forensic Science International*, 91: 41–53.

Gill, P., Werrett, D.J., Budowle, B. and Guerrieri, R. (2004) 'An assessment of whether SNPs will replace STRs in national DNA databases – joint considerations of the DNA working group of the European Network of Forensic Science Institutes (ENFSI) and the Scientific Working Group on DNA Analysis Methods (SWGDAM)', *Sci Justice*, 44: 51–3.

Gill, P., Whitaker, J., Flaxman, C., Brown, N. and Buckleton, J. (2000b) 'An investigation of the rigor of interpretation rules for STRs derived from less than 100 pg of DNA', *Forensic Science International*, 112: 17–40.

Goodwin, W., Linacre, A. and Vanezis, P. (1999) 'The use of mitochondrial DNA and short tandem repeat typing in the identification of air crash victims', *Electrophoresis*, 20: 1707–11.

Grimes, E.A., Noake, P.J., Dixon, L. and Urquhart, A. (2001) 'Sequence polymorphism in the human melanocortin 1 receptor gene as an indicator of the red hair phenotype', *Forensic Science International*, 122: 124–9.

Gusmao, L., Butler, J.M., Carracedo, A., Gill, P., Kayser, M., Mayr, W.R., Morling, N., Prinz, M., Roewer, L., Tyler-Smith, C. and Schneider, P.M. (2006) 'DNA Commission of the International Society of Forensic Genetics (ISFG): an update of the recommendations on the use of Y–STRs in forensic analysis', *Forensic Science International*, 157: 187–97.

Hellmann, A., Rohleder, U., Schmitter, H. and Witig, M. (2001) 'STR typing of human telogen hairs – a new approach', *Int J Legal Med*, 114: 269–73.

Hochmeister, M.N., Budowle, B., Jung, J., Borer, U.V., Comey, C.T. and Dirnhoffer, R. (1991) 'PCR-based typing of DNA extracted from cigarette butts', *Int J Legal Med*, 104: 229–33.

Hoyle, R. (1998) 'Forensics. The FBI's national DNA database', *Nat Biotechnol*, 16: 987.

Huffine, E., Crews, J., Kennedy, B., Bomberger, K. and Zinbo, A. (2001) 'Mass identification of persons missing from the break-up of the former Yugoslavia: structure, function, and role of the International Commission on Missing Persons', *Croat Med J*, 42: 271–5.

Immel, U.D., Krawczak, M., Udolph, J., Richter, A., Rodig, H., Kleiber, M. and Klintschar, M. (2006) 'Y-chromosomal STR haplotype analysis reveals surname-associated strata in the East-German population', *Eur J Hum Genet*, 14: 577–82.

Jobling, M.A. and Gill, P. (2004) 'Encoded evidence: DNA in forensic analysis', *Nat Rev Genet*, 5: 739–51.

Kimpton, C., Gill, P., D'Aloja, E., Andersen, J.F., Bar, W., Holgersson, S., Jacobsen, S., Johnsson, V., Kloosterman, A.D., Lareu, M.V. *et al.* (1995) 'Report on the second EDNAP collaborative STR exercise. European DNA Profiling Group', *Forensic Science International*, 71: 137–52.

Kimpton, C.P., Gill, P., Walton, A., Urquhart, A., Millican, E.S. and Adams, M. (1993) 'Automated DNA profiling employing multiplex amplification of short tandem repeat loci', *PCR Methods Appl*, 3: 13–22.

King, T.E., Ballereau, S.J., Schurer, K.E. and Jobling, M.A. (2006) 'Genetic signatures of coancestry within surnames', *Curr Biol*, 16: 384–8.

Ladd, C., Adamowicz, M.S., Bourke, M.T., Scherczinger, C.A. and Lee, H.C. (1999) 'A systematic analysis of secondary DNA transfer', *Journal of Forensic Sciences*, 44: 1270–2.

Ladd, C., Lee, H.C., Yang, N. and Bieber, F.R. (2001) 'Interpretation of complex forensic DNA mixtures', *Croat Med J*, 42: 244–6.

Leclair, B., Fregeau, C.J., Bowen, K.L. and Fourney, R.M. (2004) 'Enhanced kinship analysis and STR-based DNA typing for human identification in mass fatality incidents: the Swissair flight 111 disaster', *Journal of Forensic Sciences*, 49: 939–53.

Leriche, A. (1998) 'Final report of the Interpol Working Party on DNA profiling. Proceedings from the 2nd European Symposium on Human Identification', *Promega Corporation*, 48–54.

Lowe, A., Murray, C., Whitaker, J., Tully, G. and Gill, P. (2002) 'The propensity of individuals to deposit DNA and secondary transfer of low level DNA from individuals to inert surfaces', *Forensic Science International*, 129: 25–34.

Lowe, A.L., Urquhart, A., Foreman, L.A. and Evett, I.W. (2001) 'Inferring ethnic origin by means of an STR profile', *Forensic Science International*, 119: 17–22.

Marchi, E. (2004) 'Methods developed to identify victims of the World Trade Center disaster', *American Labor*, 36: 90–96.

Martin, P.D. (2004) 'National DNA databases – practice and practicability. A forum for discussion', *Progress in Forensic Genetics*, 10: 1–8.

Mills, K.A., Even, D. and Murray, J.C. (1992) 'Tetranucleotide repeat polymorphism at the human alpha fibrinogen locus (FGA)', *Hum Mol Genet*, 1: 779.

Moore, L.T., McEvoy, B., Cape, E., Simms, K. and Bradley, D.G. (2006) 'A Y-chromosome signature of hegemony in Gaelic Ireland', *Am J Hum Genet*, 78: 334–8.

Mullis, K., Faloona, F., Scharf, S., Saiki, R., Horn, G. and Erlich, H. (1986) 'Specific enzymatic amplification of DNA in vitro: the polymerase chain reaction', *Cold Spring Harb Symp Quant Biol*, 51, Pt 1: 263–73.

Mullis, K.B. and Faloona, F.A. (1987) 'Specific synthesis of DNA in vitro via a polymerase-catalyzed chain reaction', *Methods Enzymol*, 155: 335–50.

National_Research_Council (1996) *The evaluation of forensic DNA evidence*. Washington, DC: National Academy Press.

Olaisen, B., Bar, W., Brinkmann, B., Budowle, B., Carracedo, A., Gill, P., Lincoln, P., Mayr, W.R. and Rand, S. (1998) 'DNA recommendations 1997 of the International Society for Forensic Genetics', *Vox Sang*, 74: 61–3.

Saiki, R.K., Scharf, S., Faloona, F., Mullis, K.B., Horn, G.T., Erlich, H.A. and Arnheim, N. (1985) 'Enzymatic amplification of beta-globin genomic sequences and restriction site analysis for diagnosis of sickle cell anemia', *Science*, 230: 1350–4.

Schmerer, W.M., Hummel, S. and Herrmann, B. (1999) 'Optimized DNA extraction to improve reproducibility of short tandem repeat genotyping with highly degraded DNA as target', *Electrophoresis*, 20: 1712–6.

Schmerer, W.M., Hummel, S. and Herrmann, B. (2000) 'STR-genotyping of archaeological human bone: experimental design to improve reproducibility by optimisation of DNA extraction', *Anthropol Anz*, 58: 29–35.

Schneider, P.M. and Martin, P.D. (2001) 'Criminal DNA databases: the European situation', *Forensic Science International*, 119: 232–8.

Sparkes, R., Kimpton, C., Gilbard, S., Carne, P., Andersen, J., Oldroyd, N., Thomas, D., Urquhart, A. and Gill, P. (1996a) 'The validation of a 7-locus multiplex STR test for use in forensic casework. (II), Artefacts, casework studies and success rates', *Int J Legal Med*, 109: 195–204.

Sparkes, R., Kimpton, C., Watson, S., Oldroyd, N., Clayton, T., Barnett, L., Arnold, J., Thompson, C., Hale, R., Chapman, J., Urquhart, A. and Gill, P. (1996b) 'The validation of a 7-locus multiplex STR test for use in forensic casework. (I). Mixtures, ageing, degradation and species studies', *Int J Legal Med*, 109: 186–94.

Strom, C.M. and Rechitsky, S. (1998) 'Use of nested PCR to identify charred human remains and minute amounts of blood', *Journal of Forensic Sciences*, 43: 696–700.

Sullivan, K.M., Mannucci, A., Kimpton, C.P. and Gill, P. (1993) 'A rapid and quantitative DNA sex test: fluorescence-based PCR analysis of X-Y homologous gene amelogenin', *Biotechniques*, 15:, 636–8, 640–1.

Sweet, D., Lorente, J.A., Valenzuela, A., Lorente, M. and Villanueva, E. (1997) 'PCR-based DNA typing of saliva stains recovered from human skin', *Journal of Forensic Sciences*, 42: 447–51.

Szibor, R., Plate, I., Schmitter, H., Wittig, H. and Krause, D. (2006) 'Forensic mass screening using mtDNA', *International Journal of Legal Medicine*, November 120(b): 372–6.

Taberlet, P., Griffin, S., Goossens, B., Questiau, S., Manceau, V., Escaravage, N., Waits, L.P. and Bouvet, J. (1996) 'Reliable genotyping of samples with very low DNA quantities using PCR', *Nucleic Acids Research*, 24(16): 3189–3194.

Van Hoofstat, D., Deforce, D., Brochez, V., de Pauw, I., Janssens, K., Mestdagh, M., Millecamps, R., Van Geldre, E. and Van Den Eeckhout, E. (1998) *DNA typing of fingerprints and skin debris: sensitivity of capillary electrophoresis in forensic applications using multiplex PCR*. Proceedings of the 2nd European Symposium on Human Identification, pp. 131–7. Promega Corporation.

van Oorschot, R.A. and Jones, M.K. (1997) 'DNA fingerprints from fingerprints', *Nature*, 387: 767.

Van Renterghem, P.V., Leonard, D. and De Greef, C. (2000) 'Use of latent fingerprints as a source of DNA for genetic identificatio', *Progress in Forensic Genetics*, 8: 501–503.

Walsh, J.J. (1998) 'Canada's proposed forensic DNA evidence bank', *Can. Soc. Forens. Sci. J.*, 31: 113–125.

Werrett, D. (1997) 'The national DNA database', *Forensic Science International*, 88: 33–42.

Whitaker, J.P., Clayton, T.M., Urquhart, A.J., Millican, E.S., Downes, T.J., Kimpton, C.P. and Gill, P. (1995) 'Short tandem repeat typing of bodies from a mass disaster: high success rate and characteristic amplification patterns in highly degraded samples', *Biotechniques*, 18: 670–7.

Wiegand, P., Bajanowski, T. and Brinkmann, B. (1993) 'DNA typing of debris from fingernails', *Int J Legal Med*, 106: 81–3.

Wiegand, P. and Kleiber, M. (1997) 'DNA typing of epithelial cells after strangulation', *Int J Legal Med*, 110: 181–3.

# Chapter 3

# Fingerprints

*Christophe Champod and Paul Chamberlain*

## Introduction and terminology

The term *friction ridge skin* refers to a specific type of skin, the surface of which has ridges and furrows, formed by folds in the skin surface. It can be observed on the distal phalanges of the fingers and thumbs, and also on the palms, toes and soles of the feet. We call these surfaces the volar surfaces. It is believed that the biological function of these surfaces is to increase the grip and the mechanical sensitivity of the skin to pressure, movement and vibration.

The *general flow* of the ridges forms various patterns. Three main categories: arches, loops and whorls can be defined. These patterns are formed by the conjunction of ridge systems that are articulated around key focal points called *core(s)* and *delta(s)*.

Closer inspection reveals that the ridges may break (bifurcate), end, or may be limited in length, sometimes forming little more than a dot. These latter events are termed *minutiae* in this chapter, although various other terms such as points, characteristics, or Galton points are also used. Minutiae can also form combined arrangements such as lakes (formed by two opposing bifurcations), islands (formed by two connected ridge endings) or spurs (formed from a bifurcation and ridge ending). The terminology regarding these latter formations lacks standardisation. The *ridges* bear *pores* indented in their summit. Their function is to allow the secretion of sweat from eccrine glands embedded in the dermis. The pores themselves vary in shape and relative position along the ridge. The edges of the ridges are also irregular, often with distinctive shapes. The above described features are often categorised into three levels: Level 1 relating to the general ridge flow of the ridges, Level 2 to minutiae (or large deviation of the ridge path) and Level 3 to pores and ridge edge or other details (Figure 3.1). In addition there are other features that may be observed. Creases (some of which are permanent, particularly when associated with flexures) may have distinctive shapes. Trauma to the skin such as warts, blisters and scars may also be seen.

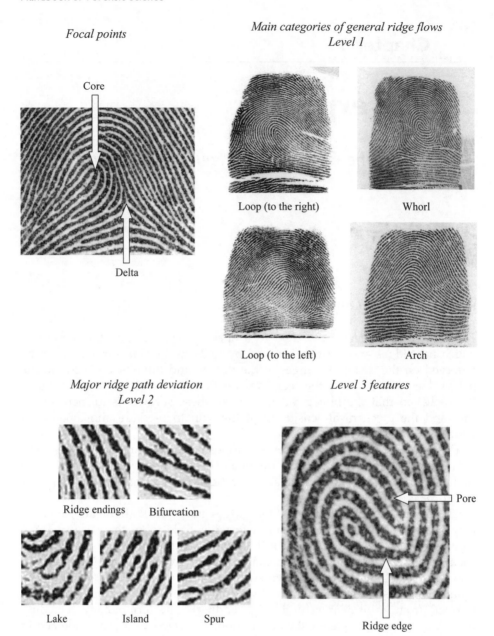

*Focal points*

*Main categories of general ridge flows*
*Level 1*

Core

Delta

Loop (to the right)

Whorl

Loop (to the left)

Arch

*Major ridge path deviation*
*Level 2*

*Level 3 features*

Ridge endings    Bifurcation

Lake    Island    Spur

Pore

Ridge edge

**Figure 3.1**  Illustration of the three levels of details

The term *fingerprint* refers to an impression left by a friction ridge skin area of a finger. Likewise, a *palm print* is an impression from the palm. By convention a *print* is then a reference from a known sample taken with cooperation and under controlled conditions either using an inking process or an optical device (essentially a digital scanner commonly referred to as *livescan*) (Maltoni *et al.* 2003). Because of their pristine acquisition conditions, prints are a near perfect representation of the friction ridge skin.

The friction ridge skin area can also leave a representation of its characteristics when it comes into direct contact with any surface. We refer to these impressions as *marks*. They are made of sweat residues, a complex mixture of compounds originating from eccrine and sebaceous glands. The friction ridge skin area acts here as a 'stamp' contaminated with sweat residues. Marks are then left adventitiously when one touches an object without gloves or footwear. By the uncontrolled nature of the deposition, marks are often of varying quality compared to the prints. If the term mark is qualified as in *finger marks* or *palm marks*, it means that the corresponding position on the friction ridge skin area has been established, otherwise the term mark alone will refer to an impression of any friction ridge skin area. The reader may also have come across the term *latent* mark, print or impression. The term latent has often been used to designate the large proportion of marks that cannot be seen without the application of detection techniques. The term *area of friction ridge detail* is also sometimes encountered.

Marks may not be complete; sections of the ridge flow may not be reproduced. The finger may be placed on a surface for a very short period of time thus reducing the transfer of residue, may be in contact for longer time or placed on the same surface multiple times. This gives rise to visible differences: marks may be fragmentary with broken ridge flow; distorted by pressure which may sometimes cause the residue to be pushed into the furrows, thus changing the appearance of the mark, or overlaid (superimposed).

The term *quality* is an assessment of accuracy of the representation of the impression (either a mark or a print) compared with the actual friction ridge skin surface. Prints tend to be of high quality when taken in appropriate conditions, whereas marks may vary due to the uncontrolled circumstances of their deposition (Figure 3.2).

In the UK fingerprint practitioners engaged in comparison are generally called *fingerprint experts*. Here we will use the term fingerprint examiner to mean a practitioner trained to competency.

The basis of all fingerprints examination is that configurations of fingerprint features have a high level of specificity or 'uniqueness' (the term often used); that configurations of ridges in sequence, minutiae, pores or ridge edge details do not change with time and that such configurations will reform more or less exactly (except where there is heavy damage as the result of trauma). Because of the above attributes, the comparison of friction ridge skin impressions helps to address issues of identity of individuals.

## Short historical perspective focused on the UK

Fingerprints are used in two related but distinct ways within the criminal justice system. First as a biometric, that is a method for the identification of arrested individuals, for example, to establish if they have come to police notice previously. Second to attribute finger or palm marks recovered from a crime scene to an individual to provide information for investigators.

The systematic use of fingerprints for identification purposes in the UK can be traced to the turn of the twentieth century. At that time the anthropometric

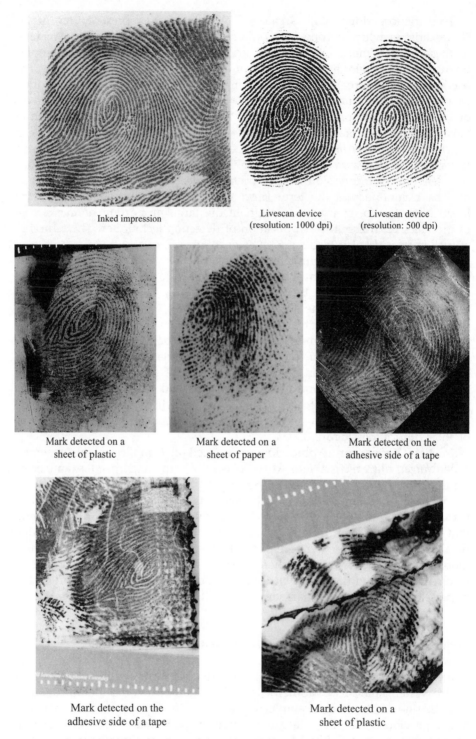

Inked impression

Livescan device
(resolution: 1000 dpi)

Livescan device
(resolution: 500 dpi)

Mark detected on a
sheet of plastic

Mark detected on a
sheet of paper

Mark detected on the
adhesive side of a tape

Mark detected on the
adhesive side of a tape

Mark detected on a
sheet of plastic

**Figure 3.2** Illustration of the range of quality obtained for the same finger on prints (depending on the acquisition techniques) and on marks (depending on the deposition)

system (developed in 1881 by Bertillon in France) using specific measurements of the human body (length of index finger, length of arm, circumference of head etc.), was the prevalent biometric method of personal identification, alongside the developing photographic technologies. The principles were the following: (1) bone lengths remain constant during adult age, but (2) vary from individual to individual and (3) they can be measured with reasonable precision. Bertillon proposed the use of the description of the iris's colour combined 11 precise measurements. A classification method was also developed in order to structure these distinctive characteristics. It addressed the increasing issues of identification with great success although its limitations were becoming evident as the size of databases increased. The limitations of this technique were: (1) uneven distributions of the measures in the population; (2) the correlation between features; (3) inter-operator variations due to lack of training, the quality of the (very expensive) instrumentation or non-cooperative subjects; and (4) the need of the body and the absence of anthropometric 'traces' left on crime scenes.

Francis Galton in England, and specific government committees (Troup and Belper) were tasked to assess the merits of Bertillon's method and prepare recommendations for the UK government. The work of British scientists in the development of fingerprinting, namely H. Faulds, W. Herschel, F. Galton and E. Henry is well covered in recent monographs (Beavan 2001; Cole 2001; Sengoopta 2003). William Herschel, a colonial administrator in India, proposed the use of fingerprints to identify individuals, especially prisoners, as a result of his use to identify employees. His work over some 30 years also supported the concept of permanence. At the same time, Henry Faulds, who studied at Andersons College in Glasgow (now the University of Strathclyde), then a medical missionary in Japan, proposed in 1880 to use fingerprints for investigative purposes, as fingermarks could be detected at crime scenes. As a natural addition to that, Faulds designed a classification system based on ridge flow pattern and core characteristics. The main forensic operational contribution came from the work of Francis Galton. He presented in 1892 the basic axioms of fingerprinting, which are the notion of permanence (based on Herschel's work and data), and uniqueness. He also suggested the possibility of reliably classifying fingerprint patterns into three basic types. The first classification method of Galton was judged unsuitable to handle large collections of individuals. The method was then greatly improved by Edward Henry (helped by his Indian colleagues). This Galton-Henry classification allowed the storage and retrieval of a particular set of fingerprints from extremely large databases. This development was instrumental in persuading the Troup committee to adopt fingerprints as the main method of personal identification in the UK.

The first cases in the UK of the use of marks left on crime scenes to identify its donors are well documented: *Jackson* (1902) and *Stratton* brothers (1905).

Due to these early successes and combined with a strong belief in the new modern virtues of science in the early twentieth century, the use of fingerprints as a means of personal identification became established and essentially remained unchallenged until fairly recently.

Until the 1990s New Scotland Yard maintained the national fingerprint database, whilst a similar collection was maintained for Scotland by SCRO (Scottish Criminal Record Office). Each arrestee would be fingerprinted, generally when charged with an offence although additional powers to fingerprint in respect of particular investigations existed. Outside of the London Metropolitan Police area two sets of fingerprints were taken, one for the national collection and one for the local police fingerprint department. The national collections formed the heart of the criminal record offices. Each set received was coded according to the Henry classification and searched to determine if the individual had previously come to notice. Sets were taken when the individuals were held in prisons and retained to prove previous convictions.

In the 1970s the New Scotland Yard collection was moved to videotape and whilst the Henry classification was still used as the filing method, speed of access increased. In the 1980s AFIS (i.e. Automatic Fingerprint Identification Systems) technologies were developed. The book by Komarinski serves as a good introduction to forensic AFIS systems (Komarinski 2005), the development in the UK is briefly outlined by Blain (2002). New Scotland Yard introduced a system and several provincial forces purchased stand-alone systems. In the early 1990s a consortium of forces purchased a networked system that allowed a degree of national searching. This was followed in 1996 by the roll-out of NAFIS (National Automated Fingerprint Identification System), the first truly national system. With the advent of NAFIS individual police forces undertook shared maintenance of the national database. Recent years have seen the increased use of new technology with the development of electronic scanning of fingerprints (using livescan devices), first in custody suites and latterly using mobile technologies.

The utilisation of these collections for investigation required the ability to search a mark from a crime scene. Originally the Henry coding system was refined to allow such searching with reasonable accuracy although this was highly labour intensive. In the 1930s the Battley single finger system further extended this ability by introducing a coding system for single prints and marks. The advent of videotape systems, albeit restricted to New Scotland Yard, extended the searching ability. It was however the introduction of the AFIS systems and in particular NAFIS that provided the first national search facility. NAFIS has moved now to IDENT1, offering in its extension both finger and palm print search capabilities (Suman and Whitaker 2005).

In parallel with the development of fingerprint comparison techniques, there has been an increase in the range and complexity of techniques to detect and recover crime scene marks. The original powdering technique remains widely used in view of its reasonable sensitivity and ease of use. But other chemical reagents have been introduced extending the ability to recover marks as well as the range of surfaces that can be examined. Both selectivity and sensitivity of the techniques have been increased by combining them in sequence, allowing targeting of specific compounds of the sweat residue. Researchers in the UK have pioneered innovation in this area. The review paper by Goode and Morris (1983) can be considered to be a landmark publication and subsequently the research programmes of the Home Office

Scientific Development Branch, the Metropolitan Police Forensic Science Laboratory and the Forensic Science Service have contributed significantly to the ongoing development of techniques.

## Use of fingerprint in investigations

Three fingerprint processes can be identified:

| | |
|---|---|
| *Print to prints*: | The comparison of the fingerprints from an unknown individual (living or dead) against a database of known prints (or declared as such) from individuals, to prove identity. The comparison can be undertaken from the unknown material to the known or vice versa. |
| *Mark to prints*: *(Prints to marks)* | The comparison of a mark left in circumstances of interest to an investigation with a reference collection of prints from known (or declared as such) individuals. The converse is also possible, meaning the search of the features from a new set of ten-prints (ten-prints is a term used to refer to a control set of finger and palm prints) against the database of (unresolved) marks. |
| *Mark to marks*: | The comparison of marks recovered from different offences to establish a connection. |

The first two uses are by far the most prevalent in operational practices and we will concentrate on them hereinafter.

### Print to prints

Currently, in England and Wales, fingerprints are taken on the arrest of an individual, retained permanently in a national database called IDENT1 and accessed using AFIS technology. Fingerprinting on arrest is a relatively new change included in the Criminal Justice Act 2005. It replaced the system, still in force in Scotland, whereby fingerprints were taken only at charge or caution and subsequently destroyed where there were no proceedings or the individual was acquitted. Current AFIS technology will search an inquiry print against database and then present a selection of fingerprints for comparison. Examiners have the opportunity to review all fingers and palms should they wish. The accuracy of systems when searching fingerprints taken under controlled conditions is such that the single respondent produced is generally found to correspond. AFIS system accuracies are now such that, when comparing prints, the concept of 'lights out' identification is being actively investigated. This means that the computer systems will be allowed to make the 'call' without human intervention. This allows a round-the-clock accurate identification system which when coupled to various mobile devices clearly benefits police and other agencies.

Ten-print forms are input to the system either through the capture of inked prints using scanners or more commonly through direct capture of the fingers and palm by livescan devices. Essentially a specialised scanner, this device captures digital images, which can be rapidly searched by direct transmission to the AFIS system. However, this kind of apparatus still requires a degree of operator training and experience to obtain a high quality set of ten prints: it is often subject to the loss of certain areas of the finger and palm, particularly tips of fingers and the centre area of palms. The latter has little impact on the ten-print search facility but may be important in processing of crime scene marks. Whilst the accuracy of the identification and the maintenance of the database are to the highest standard, the identification process should not be considered to be without error. Most of the errors are not related to the fingerprint comparison, however, but to such activities as: poorly taken fingerprints, fingerprints being associated to the wrong individual, duplication of fingers etc. Errors such as these are rare but do occur.

### Mark to prints (or prints to marks)

Marks are searched either manually against prints (when for example the investigation has reduced the scope to a limited number of individuals), or in conjunction with the AFIS system. Over recent years the use of AFIS systems has become widespread and to a certain extent the traditional practice of police agencies nominating potential suspects for a comparison has diminished. Nonetheless such work does still take place. Within the UK the traditional approach of using life size photographs and a handheld magnifier is common. Enlargements are used occasionally. Some computer-based on screen comparison systems do exist but are not in regular use at this time. The accuracy in AFIS searching marks against prints is lower than that of prints against prints as a result of the lower quality of the marks. Unlike good quality prints, encoding programs are not sufficiently sophisticated to automatically detect the features of lower quality marks. Where a hit has been achieved using AFIS, it is still common practice for the mark and print to be compared by an examiner using a handheld magnifier. AFIS systems do not in fact 'identify' the mark but provide a list of potential candidates. Various algorithms exist but all AFIS systems work on broadly similar lines by comparing a dataset from the enquiry mark with templates obtained from the ten prints in the database, and generating a score value based on the similarity of the datasets. As the systems accuracy improves the likelihood of the actual match appearing in first place on the candidate list increases. It is a common misconception that AFIS systems have replaced the traditional examination and the examiner. However, although it is possible to conceive the development of a fully automatic comparison system, such is not yet feasible.

The use of crime scene marks requires the detection of the marks on items and their recovery by a suitable method or sequence of techniques that will allow the search and then comparison.

## Finger marks detection techniques

Crime scene marks may be *patent*, i.e. visible to the naked eye or *latent*, formed of sweat residue or other substances that are not readily visible. Marks may also be formed in such substances as dust, paint or blood. Latent marks are more often encountered in criminal investigation, in particular planned crimes where the offender has taken some precautions against detection. Considerable investment has been made in a range of techniques to visualise these marks. Agencies such as the HOSDB (Home Office Scientific Development Branch), FSS (Forensic Science Service) and a number of universities have research programmes, to develop new techniques and improve those currently used. HOSDB forms the main advisory body to the UK police and is influential in which techniques are utilised. Their long-standing research programmes have provided significant data on the efficiency of various techniques as well as their safety. Its main publication (*Manual of Fingerprint Development Techniques*) can be considered as the most influential publication in this area (Bowman 2004).

Latent marks are generally formed from sweat left on the surface of ridges. The deposited residue is composed of mainly water, proteins, amino acids, fatty acids, inorganic salts, cholesterol and squalene. The amount of residue left by an individual depends on a large number of variables, such as: the conditions in which the friction ridge surface has been kept, the diet, age, sex and physical condition of the donor. This variation implies that some detection techniques may prove successful for 'good' donors only. Also the residue will degrade with time, since the deposit and the ability to detect marks may vary as a function of time for certain detection techniques.

The strategy adopted for the detection of marks is to choose reagents based on:

- the nature of the substrate (porous – such as paper, semi-porous or non-porous such as glass and plastic surfaces);
- the case circumstances (fire scene, outdoor wetted object);
- the ability to transport the items to the laboratory versus the ability to deploy a technique directly on site;
- the potential detrimental effect of the technique on the item;

Judgements are made on the effectiveness of the technique although practical issues such as availability, examination time and safety have a significant influence. The use of many techniques in sequences to maximise the likelihood of recovery is not routine and often reserved for serious crimes.

Marks left on a porous surface have shown persistence for decades, the residue being absorbed and fixed by the surface. On the contrary, marks on a non-porous surface are prone to abrasion. Their persistence is therefore significantly influenced by the subsequent handling of the item.

Detection techniques may be broadly categorised into optical, physical or chemical and are covered in details elsewhere (Champod *et al.* 2004b). The advances on the detection techniques are reviewed every three years for the

Interpol Forensic Science Symposium (Champod *et al.* 2004a; Becue *et al.* 2007).

Optical techniques take advantage of the interaction between light and the surface to produce a suitable contrast, often without any adverse effect on the marks themselves, thus allowing the use of follow-up detection techniques. The surface can be searched using different wavelengths (from ultraviolet to infrared), different illumination conditions (diffuse/reflective mode, dark field examination, etc.) or in luminescence conditions. These techniques are the cornerstone of a successful detection process of marks, applied either at the outset of the examination or after each physical or chemical technique. Many marks are relatively easy to photograph; however, others require sound photographic knowledge to obtain a usable image. In any case, photographic and written documentation should indicate the position of the detected mark on the object, its relationship to the other marks, as well as a close-up view of the mark itself with sufficient resolution to optimise its quality (as defined previously). Each recorded image should carry a scale (using a ruler on the image itself, for example).

The oldest and most common form of physical detection is the use of powder. A number of commercial powders are available in differing materials, particle size, particle shape and colours. Powders have a tendency to adhere to the fatty components of the residue. Generally effective only on non-porous surfaces and with limited sensitivity, they have the advantage of simplicity. Marks are developed using powders and then transferred on an appropriate medium (such as gelatine or adhesive lifter). Occasionally they are only photographed. Another physical technique is vacuum metal deposition. Metals tend to condense differently on a surface when it bears latent mark residues, resulting in contrast between the mark and the substrate.

A range of chemical reagents is also available. These reagents rely on specific chemical reactions between the reagent and one or more constituents of the residue. Ninhydrin (and its analogues) or DFO react with amino acids to form a visible purple compound or a fluorescent product visible under specific wavelengths of light. These are the methods of choice for porous surfaces. They may be followed by techniques targeted at lipid components (such as the physical developer). Fumes from heated cyanoacrylate (a constituent of superglues) tend to polymerise preferentially on the residue and form a white polymer on the ridges. It is a very efficient method on non-porous surfaces that is often followed by dye staining of the glued impressions to increase their visibility. Marks left in blood or on adhesive surfaces require specific detection techniques to target the heme, proteins or other specific content of the residue (Figure 3.3).

Increasingly digital imaging systems are being used. These provide a range of tools to capture and optimise images. Some sophisticated systems may use such techniques as FFT (Fast Fourier Transform) to remove backgrounds. A key issue with any digital technology is the ability to significantly alter the image. Any system or process must therefore record and maintain the raw image and subsequent optimised images with an appropriate audit trail (Russ 2001, Reis 2007).

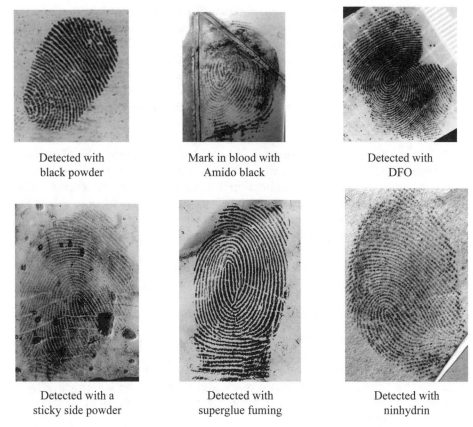

| | | |
|---|---|---|
| Detected with black powder | Mark in blood with Amido black | Detected with DFO |
| Detected with a sticky side powder | Detected with superglue fuming | Detected with ninhydrin |

**Figure 3.3**  Examples of marks detected with various detection techniques

## Method of comparison and associated conclusions

### Basic premises

The premises of friction ridge skin identification are twofold:

(1) Friction ridge skin arrangements are *extremely discriminating,* and reflect the variability between donors (fingerprint examiners would probably use the term 'unique', but we feel that this term is often misused). The discriminating power is expressed in the capacity of an examiner to distinguish between arrangements from different sources. The discriminating capability is rooted in the morphogenesis of the friction ridge skin. General flow alone presents variation that will allow a fair discrimination although the number of possible classes for the general pattern is not infinite. Some patterns may however be less frequent than others. Arches represent roughly 5 per cent of the patterns observed on fingertips, whereas some loops account for 60 per cent. The factors (genetic and epigenetic) influencing the general flow are known (Kücken 2007). The discrimination is drastically increased by the specific arrangements

67

of ridges in sequence. The morphogenesis of ridges is highly epigenetic and leads to arrangements with various lengths (ridges end with either endings or bifurcations) and sequences (Ashbaugh 1999; Wertheim and Maceo 2002). The between sources variability of these arrangements of ridges in sequence is extreme to the point that no two individuals showing the same arrangements have ever been found. Finally, the shape of ridge edges as well as the form and relative position of pores is also very discriminative.

(2) Friction ridge skin arrangements are *persistent*. From about the 25th week of foetal life until decomposition of tissues after death, the arrangement of ridges will remain permanent in all respects (with the exception of size as the result of natural growth). Scars are permanent only when the dermis is damaged by the incident, otherwise the friction ridge skin will regenerate according to the 'template' held on the dermis (Maceo 2005).

It is due to this variability and persistency that friction ridge skin has gained the status of 'gold standard' for inferring identity.

### Protocol for a mark to print comparison: ACE-V[1]

In general most examiners subscribe to the ACE-V methodology or a comparable protocol (Ashbaugh 1999). ACE-V is an acronym that stands for *analysis, comparison, evaluation* and *verification* and implies four distinct stages to the comparison between a mark and print. In the UK practice (and elsewhere), it is common to find little distinction, or clear-cut separation, between its stages.

*Analysis* requires the examiner to examine the mark without the print in order to assess and locate the friction ridge skin features that may be used for further comparison. The analysis also allows an assessment of the quality of the mark and factors such as distortion, pressure, amount of residue and the nature of the substrate and of the detection technique used. Taking these factors into account will help to set the *tolerances* (or boundaries) that the examiner will have to allow for considering a potential correspondence. When the quality of the print is poor, a similar analysis will be carried out on the print (without undertaking any comparison work). Tolerances may then also be assigned to the print, when for example a blurred area is observed. It is advised to document the analysis phase by writing contemporaneous case notes, especially when the mark or print is of very limited quality. Another outcome of the analysis stage is a decision from the examiner regarding the capacity of the mark to be *compared* against known prints (a limited number of forms or using AFIS). In some instances, the analysis stage concludes as to whether or not the mark is expected to be *identified* should the corresponding source be available.

*Comparison* means locating the corresponding features from the mark in the print of interest. It takes the form of a side-by-side comparison. The print either constitutes the output of a potential candidate from an AFIS search or a print from a form that showed some initial similarity. All features (from level 1 to level 3) should be considered for that phase, starting from general features to particulars. The comparison should always entail observation of features in the mark followed by their location in the print. The reverse process, from the print to the mark, should only be made with care (and being documented). It is only when the general pattern is within tolerances that the comparison continues with ridge arrangements. Instead of focusing on minutiae during the comparison process, it is advised to compare every ridge and furrow (assessing comparatively their length and sequence) and then the shape of pores and edges if the quality of the mark allows. The comparison stage is essentially factual and should lead to a documentation of the features that have been found in correspondence and the features that have been described as dissimilar. Documentation of this crucial stage is sometimes sparse due to time constraints and it is not common practice to produce any form of chart to record the information (an example is given Figure 3.4). The absence of documentation may lead to difficulties in disputed cases and we would advise systematic documentation of the comparison stage.

*Evaluation* is the fundamental inferential step of the process. It will lead to the formulation of a conclusion. There are three conclusions that are commonly used in the discipline: *individualisation* (generally referred to as an *identification*), *exclusion* and *inconclusive* (often termed *'not identified'*). An individualisation means that the mark and the print have an identical source to the exclusion of all other potential donors. An exclusion means that the mark and the print(s) do not have the same source. Inconclusive indicates that neither of the previous conclusions (individualisation or exclusion) has been reached. Observed differences in ridge flow (for example the mark being a loop and the print showing a whorl pattern) will enable an examiner to exclude the print from being from the same friction ridge skin area as the mark. In fact, as soon as a difference is observed between the mark and the print that cannot be reconciled in the light of the tolerances defined during the analysis stage, then an exclusion conclusion will be reached. Logically, the absence of any irreconcilable discrepancy is a prerequisite for identification.

In the absence of dissimilarities, the examiner will weigh the corresponding features in reference to the standards for identification (see below). In a nutshell, the individualisation will be reached when the examiner observes a level agreement (across the three levels of legible features) that exceeds the highest level of correspondence he observed through his/her training and experience in comparisons involving *non-matching* entities. An identification is then concluded when the mark shows sufficient quality (clarity) of friction ridges in agreement with the print so that the probability for such a match to happen if a print from another source is submitted is deemed to be impossible.

For all other cases, the comparison will be deemed 'inconclusive' even if there are significant and perhaps highly probative correspondences between the mark and print. Corroborative evidence of this type (i.e. less than 'certain') based on friction ridge skin impressions is rarely brought to the attention of the Criminal Justice System despite its potential to help address the issue of identity. We regret that the profession has adopted such a cautious approach as it precludes the trier of fact from having the advantage of potentially very

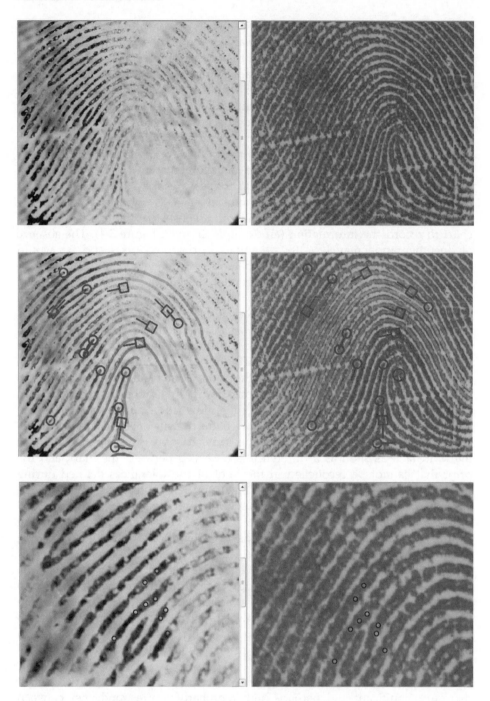

**Figure 3.4** Example of a comparison chart. On the top a close-up of the comparison without annotation (the mark on the left and the print on the right). In the middle, illustration of the agreement in terms of ridges in sequence and level 2 features with an indication of the minutiae found in correspondence. On the bottom, a close-up of some of the level 3 features retained during the comparison process

strong corroborative evidence (Champod and Evett 2001). This traditional and very conservative approach limits the potential of fingerprint evidence. This situation arises from the misconception that fingerprint evidence must be categoric, and from the unwillingness of the majority of examiners to accept the relevance of probabilistic evaluation. Indeed most examiners would feel at ease to express an opinion as to the definitive source or otherwise of a mark, but would refrain from providing an informed judgement in terms of likelihood of common or different sources. Our view is that the development of statistical models (as discussed below) will provide the necessary tools to the development of a spectrum of conclusions, similar to other forensic disciplines. The perception that this will in some way 'water down' fingerprint evidence by removing its simplistic black or white (identification or no identification) approach is, in our opinion, outweighed by the strengthening of the process through the introduction of objectivity and the potential additional evidence.

*Verification* is defined as the examination by another qualified examiner resulting in the same conclusion. This examination process is called the verification stage. Its objective is for another examiner to independently review the conclusion of the first examiner, following the Analysis, Comparison and Evaluation (ACE) protocol. Most departments will use the verification stage as the ultimate quality assurance measure. Such importance means that this stage needs to be fully documented and that the department needs to have processes in place to handle dissenting opinions. The weight to be given to this quality mechanism is directly related to the departmental standard operating procedures, which are adopted in cases of failure to verify the original conclusion. In an ideal world, we would expect the verification stage to be blind, meaning that the second examiner would have no information regarding the examination details and conclusions reached by the first. However, the whole concept of independent review is difficult to ensure in small departments or where there are heavy case workloads. Also few departments have regular checks of non-identified marks. Whilst there may well be practical reasons for this in terms of manpower, it also may reflect the way in which the outcomes are valued. A third check of the identification is still rooted in the UK practices. The third identification check is much hailed as a failsafe, but in fact the simple process of adding further quasi-independent checks may not provide the degree of assurance that is required. This is particularly where the working environment is not receptive to the possibility of error and is dominated by the concept that longer service equates to more skill.

### Standards for identification

The standards for identification are essentially the same whether we consider print to prints or mark to prints comparisons. The section that follows can apply without distinction to both scenarios.

The basis of identification is first empirical and founded on the fact that no two individuals have been found to have the same fingerprints. This is undoubtedly true for complete sets of fingerprints and provides a suitable basis for use as a biometric tool. However, when dealing with marks from crime scenes that by their very nature are poor quality, from single fingers and partial representations, this basis can be questioned.

Fingerprint identification in the UK and around the world is understood to mean that a mark has been attributed to a particular individual to the exclusion of all others, although it is seldom articulated in this way. 'Others' refers often to any human in the world, living or dead. In fact such a claim may be unnecessary as in all but a few scenarios, the suspect [or source] may be from a much smaller or restricted population. It is therefore interesting that examiners have felt the need to make a much greater claim, presumably to increase the perceived evidential value of the identification.

Prior to 2001, UK practice required that 16 minutiae in agreement (without discrepancies) between a mark and a print was required for an 'identification'. The 16-points standard, although termed a standard, was, to all intents and purposes, a numerical threshold above which it was safe to claim identification. It was adopted in 1924 after a poor-quality reproduction of a photograph submitted by Alphonse Bertillon of two prints allegedly from two individuals and charted to show 16 minutiae in agreement was sent to the head of the Scotland Yard fingerprint department. Having examined the material Superintendent Collins decided that he could see only 10 in agreement and consequently increased this standard to 16. This standard was a recommendation that was used with flexibility before the 1950s. The number of 16 became a Home Office working agreement in 1953, following a case where the fingerprint evidence was made of two fingerprint identifications with respectively 12 and 15 points in agreement. The standard was regularly discussed; however, it remained unchanged by fingerprint practitioners, since no substantive erroneous decisions were apparent. The concept of the 16-points standard reenforced the unfounded belief in the accuracy and robustness of fingerprint identification in the UK. It was higher than those applied elsewhere in the world (many countries adopting 12 with reference to the work of Edmond Locard (Locard 1914)). A rather crude probabilistic calculation was used to show that such a 16-point configuration would give a probability smaller than the inverse of the world population although examiners were advised never to make such an argument in court (Balthazard 1911). Note that the 16-points standard was never given legal force.

During the 1970s some variation was seen in the application of the standard. This may have been a reflection of the 1973 IAI (International Association for Identification) resolution that declared there to be no numerical basis for a fingerprint individualisation. For a period of time so called 'non-provable (or partial) identifications' were presented in serious cases. These were comparisons where the threshold could not be met but where there were sufficient minutiae for an examiner to have some degree of confidence that the source of the fingerprint and the mark were the same. Later guidelines allowed two marks with between 10 and 16 minutiae in agreement to be reported as a full identification and single marks of 10 minutiae in agreement to be determined as full identifications where it was a serious crime and the examiner had 'significant experience'.

The Home Office undertook a full review in England and Wales of the 16-points rule in the mid 1980s and discovered that the paper by Bertillon mentioned above, had been largely misunderstood. The purpose of the original image (and text) was to draw attention to the importance of dissimilarities more than of gross similarities (Champod *et al*. 1993). The Home Office review resulted in a landmark report by Evett and Williams which drew attention to certain practices within the fingerprint community associated with the use of the numerical standard (Evett and Williams 1996). The report indicated that there was considerable variation in the number of minutiae seen by examiners in any one mark. The range of variation on the number of minutiae annotated was so large that the concept of a 'standard' became clearly questionable. The review concluded that the 16-points standard was not an efficient way of ensuring quality; other mechanisms should be explored such as: performance testing of experts, file audits and blind trials.

By the 1990s the 16-point standard had fallen into disuse with many decisions in court accepting identifications without 16 points. In the cases of *R v. Thomas McAteer* (1993), *R v. Craig Eyre* and *Ian Andrew Reid v. DPP* (1996) we find the courts accepting fingerprint evidence with less than 16 minutiae in agreement; in fact in the case of McAteer with just eight. In North America the development of ACE-V as a methodology and the growing use of other elements of the mark such as pore positions, ridge edge detail, creases etc. began to influence the UK.

In 1996 ACPO (the Association of Chief Police Officers) for England and Wales initiated a working party that resulted in the abandonment of the 16-points standard and in favour of a non-numerical or holistic approach with a fingerprint profession supported by a strong training and quality assurance programme. The 16-points standard was abandoned in England and Wales in July 2001, whereas Scotland adopted the same non-numerical approach in 2007. This meant that fingerprint experts could give their opinions unfettered by any arbitrary numerical thresholds. The determination of identification therefore rests solely with the trained examiner's experience. If he/she determines that the number of corresponding fingerprint features is sufficient (without discrepancies) then an identification will be declared. The ultimate safeguard is a verification process whereby two other examiners 'independently' assess the conclusion reached.

This holistic approach is fully in line with the practice in North America, Australia and the Nordic countries, which all adhere to the IAI 1973 resolution, modified slightly in Ne'Urim, Israel (1995) which states: 'No scientific basis exists for requiring that a predetermined minimum number of friction ridge features must be present in two impressions in order to establish a positive identification.'

In the rest of Europe, the minimum standard is generally 12 (Italy is the exception with 16 to 17 points), although agencies have found mechanisms to bypass the rigid standard; for example where the pattern is clearly visible or there is a skin trauma present or perhaps through the assignment of greater weight to certain features.

From a logical perspective, there is no argument to recommend any predetermined minimum number of features for the following main reasons:

(1) The relative frequency of general flow varies greatly from class to class. Some types of arches would reduce the population of potential donors 10 times more than whorls. A numerical standard system would not make a distinction between general patterns.

(2) Minutiae frequency varies greatly as a function of their type and their position. Hence any system suggesting a fixed addition of points cannot be supported from a statistical perspective. Recent studies of statistical evaluation of partial fingermarks have shown that the discrimination offered by partial fingermarks is very high, even down to configurations of three minutiae. The random match probabilities involved compete with DNA profiling (Neumann *et al.* 2006; Neumann *et al.* 2007).

(3) When quality allows, small features such as pore positions and shapes and the topography of the edges of the ridges can add to the identification process. No numerical standard would account for these third-level details.

Allowing the whole range of features to be accounted for in the identification process is referred to as *ridgeology* and has been promoted by David Ashbaugh (Ashbaugh 1999). It is this holistic approach that has been adopted as a policy for fingerprint identification in the UK.

Quality management systems have been introduced but the emphasis to date has been on the management systems through ISO9002 rather than the more in depth assessments such as ISO17025. Thus the policy and management procedures are covered but the fundamental standards are as yet not externally verified. At the time of writing no uniform competence or proficiency scheme is employed across all UK fingerprint departments although plans exist for its introduction. Only lately have development courses been established for long-serving examiners. With most examiners in the employ of police the necessary ability to maintain independence that the court would wish to see may be open to challenge.

### Bias and errors in fingerprint identifications

Research aimed at identifying the potential bias to which examiners may be susceptible has made significant recent progress (Dror 2005; Dror *et al.* 2005; Dror and Charlton 2006; Dror *et al.* 2006). This empirical research highlights the existence and the need of a full awareness of the impact of contextual information on the final decision making of fingerprint examiners. The studies by Dror *et al.* are mainly focused on the final decision arising from the comparison. We believe that a strict adherence to the ACE-V protocol with a distinct analysis and comparison stage is critical to mitigate the risk. Clearly there are dangers here that may be more pronounced given the close working relationship between the examiners and the police investigators. A clear and documented analysis, which would minimise this risk, is not universally seen in the UK and it is unlikely that marks are regularly analysed in this fashion.

The fingerprint profession claimed for numerous years that a misidentification was not a possible outcome (with the exception of intentional or fraudulent evidence). Recent academic interest in the area has led to the publication of accounts of 22 cases of misidentifications (Cole 2005; Cole 2006b). Although Cole (2005) is suggesting that these cases represent the tip of the iceberg, the accuracy of this statement remains unknown. Among these 22 cases, two are from the UK and neither is accepted as misidentification.

The first case is against McNamee who was convicted in 1987 in England for conspiracy to cause explosions. He had been identified as the man who left a thumbmark on a battery recovered from an explosive device in London by fingerprint examiners from the Metropolitan Police. During his appeal in 1998, numerous fingerprint experts were called to comment on the identification. Some experts identified that mark to McNamee's print (although their conclusions were based on different sets of features), others maintained that the mark was not sufficient for individualisation. The original verdict was set aside by the Court of Appeal (*R v. Gilbert Thomas Patrick McNamee*, No. 9704481 S2, The Court of Appeal, Criminal Division, 17 December 1998).

The second case is the supposed misattribution (with allegedly 16 points in agreement) of a mark found on a scene in Scotland to the thumbprint of Shirley McKie. The McKie case is covered by a recent book (McKie and Russell 2007) and a full inquiry of the Scottish Criminal Record Office and Scottish Fingerprint Service has been undertaken by the Justice 1 committee of the Scottish parliament.[2] In this case, there is not a complete consensus. A minority of latent print examiners continue to claim that McKie was indeed the source of the disputed mark, whereas the majority have declared an exclusion in this case. This lack of consistency between examiners is a worrying fact.

The other famous case of known misattribution is the FBI misidentification related to the terrorist attacks in Madrid, Spain, in 2004. Various reports of critical importance have followed the discovery of the wrong individualisation of one Brandon Mayfield. The main recommendations of the internal review team were (Smrz *et al.* 2006; Stacey 2004): revisions in the latent print training programme, revisions to evidence-acceptance policies, detailed revisions to SOPs (Standard Operating Procedures) and casework documentation policies and procedures, revisions to SOPs regarding the decision-making process when determining the comparative value of a latent mark, and more stringent verification policies and procedures. An internal scientific review team explored the main issues facing the fingerprint profession (Budowle *et al.* 2006). A report of the office of the Inspector General regarding this case has also been released (United States Department of Justice and Office of the Inspector General – Oversight and Review Division 2006). Four critical areas have been identified:

(1) the fact that the known impression from Brandon Mayfield was showing a degree of similarity (10 minutiae could be described as in correspondence) with the true source;

(2) the fact that circular reasoning could have convinced examiners of the presence of distinctive features on the mark whereas their visibility was established on the known impression first;

(3) the misleading conclusions from the analysis stage with regards to the number of marks revealed (double tap or superimposition) and a questionable reliance on level 3 features;

(4) the potential bias of the verification stage caused by the knowledge of the conclusions of the first examiner when the mark was checked by the next.

These reports should be considered by any laboratory doing friction ridge skin individualisation. The possibility for a misattribution exists and the standard operating procedures should recognise this.

### From identification issues to activity issues

The examination of marks allows the association of an individual with a particular surface or item. A contact between the donor and the surface or item is a prerequisite. At present, there is no scientific method that allows a reliable estimate of timeframe in which the mark was left on the surface. Patent marks, particularly those in blood, provide significant evidence other than that of identity. For example, whether a mark was made in the blood of a victim, or by deposition of the blood of the victim already on the hand is clearly of significance. Such determinations are possible as the ridges and pores may show distinct differences.

An area of particular interest in the detection of criminal activities is the interpretation of mark placement. In certain cases it is possible to provide an opinion, either on the activity or the position of the hand when the mark was made. Of course, in many scenarios there will be more than one activity that could result in the observed marks. It is therefore important to consider all possible propositions. It is interesting to observe that many fingerprint examiners in the UK (and elsewhere) are unwilling to provide such opinions. There is a tendency to limit the evidence to that of association rather than explore the potential for more informative opinions regarding the activity of the person who touched the object. We believe that when the real issues in the case are in relation to both the source of the marks and the activity associated with them (handling or sequence of events), then the duty of the expert witness is to inform the trier of facts on both aspects.

Similarly, where no marks are found we find quite often that this fact is sometimes misinterpreted by investigators and legal professionals. Bearing in mind the number of factors that affect both the persistence and the detection of a mark, the inability to find any mark cannot be used to ascertain that there was no contact between the item or surface and the particular individual. This may not be made clear in statements and reports. Where some history can be associated to the item it may be possible to draw some inference as to why no marks were found. For example the expectation of finding marks on items that have been wetted. The limitation in such an approach is the availability of data and the number of conflicting factors that need to be considered.

## Provision of fingerprint services in the UK

The majority of fingerprint examinations in the UK are provided by departments (traditionally called bureaux) attached to police forces. In England and Wales these departments are essentially autonomous although increasingly they are subject to the policies and direction of the National Fingerprint Board set up by ACPO. In Scotland the fingerprint departments were amalgamated into the Scottish Police Services Authority in 2007 (a merger not unconnected to the debate with regard to the McKie case).

In England and Wales each department deals with submissions relating to crime within the geographical area of the police force. There are some exceptions to this, in particular terrorist investigations that are more often undertaken by the Metropolitan Police and other larger forces.

The police services are supported in terms of research and development by HOSDB (Home Office Scientific Development Branch). Training is supplied by centralised organisations and therefore a degree of consistency has been achieved. In England and Wales training is provided by the National Policing Improvement Agency (NPIA). Central instruction is given to provide basic skills and in-house training provided within the student's own department mentored by a local trainer. A portfolio of work is prepared and a final assessment is undertaken covering basic knowledge, comparison skills and court presentation. In Scotland training is provided from within the Scottish Police Services Authority. The traditional 'apprenticeship' of five years has been removed although the idea that length of service and therefore experience can be utilised as some measure of competence is still embedded. What may be missing in the training is the general concept of forensic science in terms of a philosophical basis. Such studies may be all the more important as the majority of examiners work within police organisations and may therefore be subjected to conflicting influences with regard to balanced and transparent reporting and pursuit of the investigation.

In addition to the police, a number of commercial organisations also provide fingerprint services. LGC/ Alliance provides fingerprint services in association with a police force and the FSS provides a range of services including specialist detection and recovery to police forces and government agencies. The FSS also maintains a programme of research and development. In recent years several smaller companies have been formed to deliver fingerprint expertise for the defence and undertake some contracted casework.

The UK national AFIS system is known as IDENT1 (formerly NAFIS although this term is still in general use). It is managed by the NPIA. The system comprises terminals within each of the force departments that provide access to the national fingerprint database and a link directly to the police national computer. Fingerprints taken in force areas are handled by the local departments who search the fingerprints, create new records and update police criminal records as necessary.

The Home Office has invested in Livescan technology for all charging stations. This has helped ensure that the biometric identification of individuals is fairly rapid. However, the quality of images being filed into the database may not be as consistently high as was envisaged. The algorithm supplied most recently by SAGEM (Défense Sécurité (SAFRAN Group, France)) is highly effective, to the point that automatic identifications (based solely on technology without check by an examiner) using mobile technologies are opening future possibilities for identity checking.

## Fingerprint Evidence in court

The first successes for fingerprints date from the early twentieth century. The first murder case, *R v. Stratton* (1905) is well documented. But two cases served to provide the necessary precedents for future use, *R v. Castleton* (3 Cr App R 74, 1909) and *HM Advocate v. Hamilton* (JC 1 1933). These set the tone of the legal response to fingerprints by accepting the system as 'practically infallible' and admissible as the sole grounds of identification. This is perhaps a reflection of the legal systems in the UK or the social conditions that prevailed. However, no significant challenge was made to the validity of fingerprint identification for some considerable time. This is indeed similar to other jurisdictions; however, notable challenges have arisen in the USA in recent years. In *Hamilton*, the High Court of Judiciary clearly refrained from accepting using the term 'infallible' as a qualifier of the fingerprint evidence, but suggested the term 'reliable'. In *R. v. R.J. Buckley* (Court of Appeal, criminal division, 143 SJ LB 159, *The Times* 12 May 1999), their Lordships reviewed the previous cases in the UK where fingerprint evidence had been admitted without 16 points of correspondence, the historical aspects of the 16-points standard and the associated review process undertaken under ACPO. Lord Justice Rose laid down the following guidelines in his decision (extracts from the decision):

(a) If there are fewer than eight similar ridge characteristics, it is highly unlikely that a judge will exercise his discretion to admit such evidence and, save in wholly exceptional circumstances, the prosecution should not seek to adduce such evidence.

(b) If there are eight or more similar ridge characteristics, a judge may or may not exercise his or her discretion in favour of admitting the evidence. How the discretion is exercised will depend on all the circumstances of the case, including in particular:

    (i) the experience and expertise of the witness;
    (ii) the number of similar ridge characteristics;
    (iii) whether there are dissimilar characteristics;
    (iv) the size of the print relied on, in that the same number of similar ridge characteristics may be more compelling in a fragment of print than in an entire print; and
    (v) the quality and clarity of the print on the item relied on, which may involve, for example, consideration of possible injury to the person who left the print, as well as factors such as smearing or contamination.

(c)   In every case where fingerprint evidence is admitted, it will
      generally be necessary, as in relation to all expert evidence, for
      the judge to warn the jury that it is evidence opinion only, that
      the expert's opinion is not conclusive and that it is for the jury to
      determine whether guilt is proved in the light of all the evidence.

This ruling is very similar to Locard's tripartite rule (Locard 1914), with the
exception that the admissibility of fingerprint evidence has been limited to
cases where at least eight corresponding minutiae are observed, whereas
Locard opened the door to the use of marks of very limited quality as
corroborative evidence (Champod 1995). As Lord Justice Rose said: 'It may
be that in the future, when sufficient new protocols have been established to
maintain the integrity of fingerprint evidence, it will be properly receivable as
a matter of discretion, without reference to any particular number of similar
ridge characteristics.' Indeed we referred earlier to recent statistical studies that
establish the high evidential contribution of very limited marks (in terms of
number of minutiae) (Neumann et al. 2006; Neumann et al. 2007). On average,
a configuration with three minutiae will be observed in the population with a
match probability in the order of one in a thousand. We obtain one in 10,000
for four minutiae and one in a million for six minutiae. Hence fingerprint
evidence below eight points of coincidence may contribute very significantly
in deterring crime. The above argument is heavily focused on minutiae, but
a similar point can be made invoking level 3 details such as pores and edge
structure if the mark and the alleged corresponding print are of adequate
quality. Cases of individualisation when the number of corresponding
minutiae is very limited have been published (Reneau 2003).

The debate regarding fingerprint evidence in UK courts contrasts with
the polarised arguments in the US courts especially in the follow-up of the
*Daubert* (*Daubert v. Merrell Dow Pharmaceuticals* [1993] 509 US 579) decision
setting new guidelines for the admissibility of scientific evidence (Berger
2000).

Until January 2002, all *Daubert* hearings led to the admissibility of fingerprint
evidence in US courtrooms. In January 2002 the first decision that limited
(briefly) expert testimony on fingerprint identification was made. In *US v. Llera
Plaza* (*US v. Llera Plaza, Acosta and Rodriguez* US District Court of the Eastern
District of Pennsylvania [2002] Criminal No. 98-362-10,11,12), Judge Pollack
held that a fingerprint expert could not give an opinion of identification and
required that the expert limit his testimony to outlining the correspondences
observed between the mark and the print, leaving to the court the assessment
of the significance of these findings. Asked to reconsider his opinion, Judge
Pollack later reversed his decision, and admitted the evidence, mainly due
to the consideration of the UK Court of Appeal ruling in *R v. Buckley*. That
decision led to increased scrutiny of and interest in the fingerprint area in the
scientific literature with unprecedented press coverage and reactions from the
legal community (Steele 2004). Later, in *Mitchell* (*United States v. Byron Mitchell*
Court of Appeals for the Third Circuit [2004] No. 02-2859 (29 April 2004)), the
Appeal Court gave, while accepting fingerprint evidence under *Daubert*, a fair
assessment of the field: on balance the probative benefits outweigh the risks,

but the field lacks clear standards and the debate is marred by the ill-defined concept of the criteria for sufficiency.

The scientific status of identification evidence and in particular fingerprint evidence still receives critical attention from scholars and commentators (Saks and Koehler 2005; Zabell 2005; Harmon *et al.* 2006). Simon Cole in particular published a series of papers pointing out some critical weaknesses in latent fingerprint identification (Cole 2004a; Cole 2004b; Cole 2005; Cole 2006a; Cole 2006b).

The present situation is that the UK courts accept the non-numerical standard and for the most part do not challenge the identification. The reasons for this may be twofold. First the general perception amongst the public (including judiciary) is that fingerprint evidence is irrefutable and safe. This view is consistently reinforced by the media. Second there may be a lack of adequate defence expertise. The defence therefore tend to try to devalue the evidence through claims to legitimate access, attacks on the chain of evidence or occasionally discrediting the examiner. In fact there are a number of other lines of questioning that may be appropriate (especially in the aftermath of the Mayfield case): for example the lack of a demonstrable process, issues relating to ongoing competence of the examiner and lack of contemporaneous notes and detailed records of the conclusion and its basis.

Examiners supply statements in accordance with the prevailing rules. However, in general, these statements do little more than offer the opinion of the examiner and provide rather limited detail on how the conclusion has been drawn. The practice of charting the mark and print to demonstrate the features in agreement is no longer common. Thus the transparency of the examination process may be questioned. There is a common practice within the fingerprint community to document factually *what* has been done without documenting *why* a given conclusion has been drawn.


## The future


There continues to be a large investment in technologies to recover fingerprints. This will continue and therefore one may expect some extension in the types of surfaces that may reveal marks. Other associated research such as aging of marks may also bring benefits to the criminal justice system.

AFIS technologies continue to improve and the acceptance of 'lights out' checking for biometric use may not be too far in the future. Wireless transfer of mark images from crime scenes will also become standard, offering rapid turnaround of identifications.

But probably the most important development will be the design of statistical models to evaluate low features matches. Recent studies indicate a potential for extending the number of marks on which evidence can be given. Such research may also represent an adequate and sought-after response to the current debate (mainly in the USA) regarding the admissibility of fingerprint evidence. We foresee the fingerprint profession moving from the current situation where the strength of the opinion is mainly associated with the expert and his/her experience to a time where fingerprint evidence will be supported by statistical models and a full documentation of the process used to draw a conclusion from a comparison.

Finally the terms quality assurance and proficiency testing will tend to dominate the debate regarding fingerprint evidence in the future. It is a move towards transparency and accountability that will bring the fingerprint field to be held to the same standards as all other forensic evidence types.

## Notes

1  We limit our presentation to the case where a mark is compared against a print, but the protocol remains essentially the same when prints are compared against prints. The only difference is the *quality* of the information on one side of the comparison process.
2  http://www.scottish.parliament.uk/business/committees/justice1/reports.htm

## References

Ashbaugh, D.R. (1999) *Qualitative-Quantitative Friction Ridge Analysis – An Introduction to Basic and Advanced Ridgeology*. Boca Raton: CRC Press.

Balthazard, V. (1911) 'De l'identification par les empreintes digitales', *Comptes rendus des séances de l'Académie des Sciences*, 152: 1862–1864.

Beavan, C. (2001) *Fingerprints – The Origins of the Crime Detection and the Murder Case that Launched Forensic Science*. New York: Hyperion.

Becue, A., Champod, C. and Margot, P.A. (2007) 'Fingermarks, Bitemarks and other Impressions (Barefoot, Ears, Lips) – A Review' (September 2004–July 2007). *Proceeding of the 15th Interpol Forensic Science Symposium*, www.interpol.int/Public/ Forensic/ IFSS/meeting15/ReviewPapers.pdf.

Berger, M.A. (2000) 'The Supreme Court's Trilogy on the Admissibility of Expert Testimony', in Federal Judicial Center (ed.), *Reference Manual on Scientific Evidence*. Washington: Federal Judicial Center, 9–38.

Blain, B. (2002) 'Automated Palm Identification', *Fingerprint Whorld*, 28: 102–107.

Bowman, V. (ed.) (2004) *Manual of Fingerprint Development Techniques*. Sandridge: Home Office Scientific Research and Development Branch.

Budowle, B., Buscaglia, J. and Schwartz Perlman, R. (2006) 'Review of the Scientific Basis for Friction Ridge Skin Comparisons as a Means of Identification: Committee Findings and Recommendations', *Forensic Science Communications*, 8, http://www. fbi.gov/hq/lab/fsc/current/research/2006_01_research02.htm.

Champod, C. (1995) 'Locard, Numerical Standards and "Probable" Identification', *Journal of Forensic Identification*, 45: 132–159.

Champod, C., Egli, N. and Margot, P.A. (2004a) 'Fingermarks, Shoesoles and Footprint Impressions, Tire Impressions, Ear Impressions, Toolmarks, Lipmarks, Bitemarks – A Review (2001–2004). *Proceeding of the 14th Interpol Forensic Science Symposium*, www.interpol.int/Public/Forensic/ IFSS/meeting14/ReviewPapers.pdf.

Champod, C. and Evett, I.W. (2001) 'A Probabilistic Approach to Fingerprint Evidence', *Journal of Forensic Identification*, 51: 101–122.

Champod, C., Lennard, C. and Margot, P.A. (1993) 'Alphonse Bertillon and Dactyloscopy', *Journal of Forensic Identification*, 43: 604–625.

Champod, C., Lennard, C.J., Margot, P.A. and Stoilovic, M. (2004b) *Fingerprints and other Ridge Skin Impressions*. Boca Raton: CRC Press.

Cole, S. (2001) *Suspect Identities: A History of Fingerprinting and Criminal Identification*. Harvard University Press.

Cole, S.A. (2004a) 'Fingerprint Identification and the Criminal Justice System: Historical Lessons for the DNA Debate', in D. Lazer (ed.), *DNA and the Criminal Justice System*. Harvard: MIT Press, 63–90.

Cole, S.A. (2004b) 'Grandfathering Evidence: Fingerprint Admissibility Rulings from *Jennings* to *Llera Plaza* and Back Again', *American Criminal Law Review*, 41: 1189–1276.

Cole, S.A. (2005) 'More than Zero: Accounting for Error in Latent Fingerprint Identification', *The Journal of Criminal Law and Criminology*, 95: 985–1078.

Cole, S.A. (2006a) 'Is Fingerprint Identification Valid? Rhetorics of Reliability in Fingerprint Proponents' Discourse', *Law and Policy*, 28: 109–135.

Cole, S.A. (2006b) 'The Prevalence and Potential Causes of Wrongful Conviction by Fingerprint Evidence', *Golden Gate University Law Review*, 37: 39–105.

Dror, I. (2005) 'Experts and technology: Do's & Don'ts', *Biometric Technology Today*, 13: 7–9.

Dror, I.E. and Charlton, D. (2006) 'Why Experts Make Errors', *Journal of Forensic Identification*, 56: 600–616.

Dror, I.E., Charlton, D. and Péron, A.E. (2006) 'Contextual Information Renders Experts Vulnerable to Making Erroneous Identifications', *Forensic Science International*, 156: 74–78.

Dror, I.E., Péron, A., Hind, S.-L. and Charlton, D. (2005) 'When Emotions Get to the Better of us: The Effect of Contextual Top-Down Processing on Matching Fingerprints', *Applied Cognitive Psychology*, 19: 799–809.

Evett, I.W. and Williams, R. (1996) 'A Review of the Sixteen Points Fingerprint Standard in England and Wales', *Journal of Forensic Identification*, 46: 49–73.

Goode, G.C. and Morris, J.R. (1983) 'Latent Fingerprints: A Review of their Origin, Composition and Methods for Detection'. Aldermaston, UK: Atomic Weapons Research Establishment, AWRE Report No. 022/83.

Harmon, R., Budowle, B., Langenburg, G. and Houck, M.M. (2006) 'Letters: Questions About Forensic Science (with response)', *Science*, 311: 607–610.

Komarinski, P. (2005) *Automated Fingerprint Identification Systems (AFIS)*. New York: Elsevier Academic Press.

Kücken, M. (2007) 'Models for Fingerprint Pattern Formation', *Forensic Science International*, 171: 85–96.

Locard, E. (1914) 'La preuve judiciaire par les empreintes digitales', *Archives d'anthropologie criminelle, de médecine légale et de psychologie normale et pathologique*, 29: 321–348.

Maceo, A.V. (2005) 'The Basis for the Uniqueness and Persistence of Scars in the Friction Ridge Skin', *Fingerprint World*, 31: 147–161.

Maltoni, D., Maio, D., Jain, A.K. and Prabhakar, S. (2003) *Handbook of Fingerprint Recognition*. New York: Springer Verlag.

McKie, I. and Russell, M. (2007) *Shirley McKie: The Price of Innocence*. Edinburgh: Birlinn Ltd.

Neumann, C., Champod, C., Puch-Solis, R., Egli, N., Anthonioz, A. and Bromage-Griffiths, A. (2007) 'Computation of Likelihood Ratios in Fingerprint Identification for Configurations of Any Number of Minutiae', *Journal of Forensic Sciences*, 52: 54–64.

Neumann, C., Champod, C., Puch-Solis, R., Meuwly, D., Egli, N., Anthonioz, A. and Bromage-Griffiths, A. (2006) 'Computation of Likelihood Ratios in Fingerprint Identification for Configurations of Three Minutiae', *Journal of Forensic Sciences*, 51: 1255–1266.

Reis, G. (2007) *Photoshop® CS3 for Forensics Professionals*. Indianapolis, USA: Wiley Publishing, Inc.

Reneau, R.D. (2003) 'Unusual Latent Print Examinations', *Journal of Forensic Identification*, 53: 531–537.

Russ, J.C. (2001) *Forensic Uses of Digital Imaging*. Boca Raton: CRC Press.

Saks, M.J. and Koehler, J.J. (2005) 'The Coming Paradigm Shift in Forensic Identification Science', *Science*, 309: 892–895.

Sengoopta, C. (2003) *Imprint of the Raj – How Fingerprinting Was Born in Colonial India*. London: Macmillan.

Smrz, M.A., Burmeister, S.G., Einseln, A., Fisher, C.L., Fram, R., Stacey, R.B., Theisen, C.E. and Budowle, B. (2006) 'Review of FBI Latent Print Unit Processes and Recommendations to Improve Practices and Quality', *Journal of Forensic Identification*, 56: 402–434.

Stacey, R.B. (2004) 'A Report on the Erroneous Fingerprint Individualization in the Madrid Train Bombing Case', *Journal of Forensic Identification*, 54: 706–718.

Steele, L.J. (2004) 'The Defense Challenge to Fingerprints', *Criminal Law Bulletin*, 40: 213–240.

Suman, A. and Whitaker, G. (2005) 'Benchmarking the Operational Search Accuracy of a National Identification System', *Biometric Technology for Human Identification II, Proceedings of the SPIE*, 5779: 232–241.

United States Department of Justice and Office of the Inspector General – Oversight and Review Division (2006) *A Review of the FBI's Handling of the Brandon Mayfield Case (unclassified and redacted)*. Washington, DC.

Wertheim, K. and Maceo, A. (2002) 'The Critical Stage of Friction Ridge and Pattern Formation', *Journal of Forensic Identification*, 52: 35–85.

Zabell, S.L. (2005) 'Fingerprint Evidence', *Journal of Law and Policy*, 13: 143–179.

## Acknowledgements

We would like to thank Cédric Neumann for commenting on the draft and Flore Bochet and Damien Dessimoz for helping us with the illustrations.

# Chapter 4

# Forensic anthropology and human identification from the skeleton

*Martin Evison*

He first took my Altitude by a Quadrant, and then with Rule and Compasses, described the Dimensions and Out-Lines of my whole Body; all which he entered upon Paper, and in six Days brought my Cloths very ill made, and quite out of Shape.

*(Jonathan Swift, Gulliver's Travels)*

## Introduction

This chapter will consider the role of forensic anthropology within forensic science. The nature and methods of routine practice will be reviewed and relationships with other disciplines described. In discussing the future prospects of forensic anthropology, the chapter will consider both the potential for scientific advance, and the value of the development of anthropology as a general field within criminal justice system and public safety policy.

## What is forensic anthropology?

Anthropology is the study of people. It encompasses social practices, language and communication, archaeology and human evolution, and the physical or biological attributes of human groups. By implication, forensic anthropology could refer to any or all of these subfields pursued in the interest of the courts. In practice, however, a much narrower definition applies: forensic anthropology usually refers to the analysis of skeletonised or partially skeletonised human remains in the context of a criminal investigation. There is, of course, an inevitable and growing overlap with other areas of anthropology and human biology.

The forensic anthropologist's primary role is to analyse the skeleton and offer a profile of the individual – by age at death, sex, stature, ancestry and other individuating features – that may assist in the identification of the individual and to interpret any evidence from the skeleton that may relate to the cause of death. The forensic anthropologist's wider role is to assist in the detection and recovery of human remains, to offer an evidence-based opinion about any mechanism of dismemberment or disposal and of time since death, and, if necessary, to undertake a forensic facial reconstruction from which the individual might be recognised.

When a presumptive identification has been provided, this identification is routinely confirmed by DNA analysis or forensic odontology – that is, dental records. Forensic anthropology often has more investigative than probative value in human identification. Careful and explicit distinction between individual and class evidence, and the presumptive and positive modalities of identification is critical. This can also be the case in the assessment of probable mechanisms of disposal, time since death and cause of death, especially in jurisdictions where firearms are rarely used in homicides.

## The nature of casework in forensic anthropology

The frequency and variety of casework encountered in forensic anthropology varies according to three major parameters: homicide rate, population density and environment.

The overall rate of homicide can vary immensely according to jurisdiction. For 1998 to 2000, for example, reported rates of homicide in England and Wales were 1.5 per 100,000, in Canada 1.85, in the European Union 1.70, in Australia 1.87 and in the United States 5.87 (Barclay and Tavares 2002: 10). Elsewhere, rates may be considerably higher than those experienced in Western Europe and North America. For 1998 to 2000, reported rates of homicide in Russia were 20.52 per 100,000 and in South Africa 54.25 (Barclay and Tavares 2002: 10). Homicide rates in Brazil doubled between 1980 and 2002, from 11.4 per 100,000 to 28.4 (Gawryszewski and Mercy 2004).

Population density will affect the frequency at which forensic anthropology cases are encountered, as it influences both opportunity for concealment and opportunity for prompt detection of human remains. Estimates for 2006 from the Central Intelligence Agency's World Factbook (CIA 2007) yield population densities per square kilometre for England and Wales of 250.88, for Canada 3.64, for Australia 2.66 and for the United States 35.57. Within any jurisdiction, homicide rates may also vary according to locality. Individual cities possess distinctive trends (Barclay and Tavares 2002: 11) which, along with the environment of the surrounding catchment, may affect the frequency and nature of body disposal and forensic anthropology casework. The process of decomposition generally advances more rapidly in warm, humid environments and is arrested in cold or freezing conditions. Climate, season and weather may have considerable influence on rates of decomposition. More proximate environmental factors affecting specific cases include the immediate surroundings, clothing, extent of concealment or interment, method of disposal or dismemberment, faunal activity, and so on.

Put simply, homicide in England and Wales – for example – is infrequent, bodies are difficult to conceal, and the climate does not generally lend itself to rapid skeletonisation. The United States, by contrast, has a relatively high homicide rate, numerous sparsely populated regions offering opportunities for easy concealment of human remains, and many climatic zones that will promote rapid skeletonisation.

A further consideration with regard to jurisdiction is the investigation of homicides resulting from civil rights abuses, war and war crimes – including those investigations supported by the United Nations. There have been many highly publicised investigations of alleged and proven government-sponsored atrocities over the last 30 years that have included Latin American countries; the Balkans, in particular Bosnia and Herzegovina, and Kosovo; Rwanda; Cambodia; and East Timor. Recently, changing political circumstances have led to investigations of alleged historic civil rights related homicides in countries as diverse as Brazil (see Adam 2003; Guimarães 2003), Cyprus and Spain. For many years it has been the practice of the United States Government to identify and repatriate the remains of its fallen servicemen and women, and forensic anthropologists form part of US teams investigating fatalities arising from the Vietnam and Korea Wars, and other conflicts. Whilst historical remains of British service personnel are occasionally exhumed and identified, the battlefield cemetery and grave were traditional prior to the Korean war.

As a consequence of local historical political conditions and government policies, forensic anthropology practice has become highly developed in countries such as Argentina and the United States. Argentina, for example, possesses a highly experienced forensic anthropology team in the *Equipo Argentino de Antropologia Forense* (EAAF 2008), formed as a consequence of the need to investigate alleged homicides resulting from Argentina's periods of military dictatorship in the 1970s and 1980s. The United States possesses a specialist command for the identification of missing service men and women – the Joint Prisoner of War/Missing in Action Accounting Command or JPAC (JPAC 2008), emergency disaster response teams – the Disaster Mortuary Operational Response Teams or DMORTs (DMORT 2008, Saul *et al.* 2002), and a well-regarded system of accreditation for forensic anthropologists – the American Board of Forensic Anthropology (ABFA 2008). A summary of the role of the forensic anthropologist in mass fatality incidents is offered by Saul *et al.* (2002).

Not all forensic anthropologists practise on a continuous basis. The level of casework is low in Western jurisdictions, nearly all of which have low homicide rates. Sheffield Medico-Legal Centre in England, for example, serves a catchment population of about six million (about 10 per cent of the United Kingdom population) and receives only one or two skeletonised or partially skeletonised suspicious deaths per annum, although the amount of material examined – which would also include archaeological human remains and faunal remains – is much higher. In such circumstances, forensic anthropologists often find themselves employed in university Departments of Anatomy, Anthropology, Archaeology and Forensic Science, and will supplement their case experience by contributing to the investigation of human rights abuse, war crimes and major fatality incidents overseas. Irrespective of jurisdiction, forensic anthropology can play a role in the investigation of major fatality incidents resulting from natural and human-made disasters, and accidents. The popular media profile of forensic anthropology may contrast considerably with the amount of local casework, however, and lead to unrealistic career expectations amongst young people, who have a range of undergraduate and graduate course offerings available to them at numerous universities.

## Forensic anthropology in practice

### A team-based approach to investigation

Forensic anthropologists work as part of investigative teams made up of police officers, police or civilian forensic scientists, forensic pathologists and odontologists, and a range of other experts. In the investigation of human rights abuses, teams may be further extended to include military personnel, governmental officials, social workers, and lawyers or other representatives of non-governmental organisations. The forensic anthropologist has two roles in an investigation: to offer appropriate expert counsel to the investigative team; and to liaise closely with other forensic specialists, such as the ecologist, entomologist, pathologist, toxicologist or odontologist, when undertaking the recovery and analysis of skeletal remains.

### Detection and recovery

The forensic anthropologist may be expected to contribute to the detection and recovery of human remains (see Boyd 1979; Killam 1990; Bass and Birkby 1978; Hunter *et al.* 1996). There are known patterns to clandestine body disposals. Remains are frequently dumped close to paved roads or other 'hard standing', but out of view of other motorists or passers-by. The forensic anthropologist may be asked to prioritise search areas on the basis of this or similar information, aerial photographs (including infrared images which may detect elevated heat from a recent disposal), and geological and topographic maps. An understanding of the local topography, climate and weather, vegetation, geomorphology, and land use may inform such an assessment and should – wherever possible – be supported by a first-hand visual survey of the area. Daily or seasonal patterns of land or road use may be an important consideration, both generally and in the context of a specific suspect or suspects. Disposal localities are frequently known to the offender. Bodies are difficult to bury in frozen ground or where underlying bedrock or vegetation will impede rapid disposal. There may be visual evidence of disturbance to vegetation or the ground surface. Good field craft and good intelligence are invaluable in searches. Given the almost limitless number of potential hiding places in a large search area and the less than perfect nature of criminal intelligence, it is not unusual for extensive searches to fail to yield human remains. Conversely, whilst small domestic dwellings present a narrow context within which to work, bodies have been missed in such searches!

Having identified potential 'hot spots', non-invasive search methods may be employed. Magnetometry, electrical resistivity and ground-penetrating radar can each be used to establish whether there is evidence of subsoil disturbance. Metal detectors can be helpful in contexts where false positive signals are not a prohibitive factor. Cadaver dogs may be used to detect signs of human decomposition. Fibre-optic cameras may be used to investigate cavities and spaces in buildings. Ultimately, the sure and final course of action often is to dig. In certain contexts, most notably alleged war crimes investigations, it may first be necessary to ensure expert assistance has been used to establish that both the vicinity and immediate scene is clear of mines, booby traps or unexploded ordnance.

Forensic archaeology (see Bass and Birkby 1978; Hunter *et al.* 1996; Burns 2007: 232–56) involves application of archaeological excavation techniques in the recovery of buried evidence or remains. The following techniques, which are routine in archaeology, are some of those that may be employed:

- topographic survey (e.g. with laser or electronic distance measuring equipment);
- excavation (including grid systems, baulking, etc.);
- three-dimensional recording using manual or optical methods;
- visual recording (photographic and diagrammatic);
- sieving (systematic recovery of objects according to size).

Forensic archaeology plays an equally important role in interpretation of the scene. The forensic archaeologist should be able to understand the significance of subsurface strata, and plant material or geological inclusions present, and – in particular – how disturbances to local naturally occurring patterns may be related to postulated scenarios of excavation, spoil, scatter, body disposal, backfill, tools used, and so on. Weather effects – such as flooding, faunal activity and natural changes to the vegetation – can be misinterpreted as having an artificial cause and collaboration with a forensic ecologist may be essential.

The forensic archaeologist should be able to assist the investigator in identifying and recognising exhibits; and in interpreting naturally and artificially occurring changes, marks or features in relation to possible mechanisms of interment, and the local ecology and weather. The forensic anthropologist should have adequate archaeological skill and training to undertake a forensic excavation, and be capable of preliminary evaluation of geomorphological, botanical and faunal material recovered at the scene, not least to ensure that the option of involving other experts – ecologist, entomologist, geomorphologist, botanist or palynologist – is not missed and relevant evidence not disrupted.

Recovery of any remains should be coordinated with the forensic pathologist and other forensic scientists. Recovery of skeletonised human remains frequently occurs under very challenging conditions, where there is some potential to obliterate evidence or introduce contamination. DNA and low copy number DNA awareness are important, as is awareness of good practice and evidential handling at the crime scene. It is routine for the forensic anthropologist to provide a DNA profile for elimination purposes (see ACPO 2005).

Archaeological niceties are not always practicable. Necessity may dictate the use of mechanical excavation equipment. Although not particularly desirable, this is not unusual and the equipment can be very deftly handled by a skilled operative.

On completion of the recovery procedure, the forensic anthropologist should be able to offer a comprehensive description and interpretation of the site of and possible method of disposal, without overstating the strength of any conclusions drawn, and with careful delineation between evidence of investigative and probative value. Any alteration or damage caused to the remains during recovery should be recorded – this is sometimes unavoidable.

## *Preparation*

A radiological – x-ray – survey of the remains is advisable prior to further analysis or modification of the remains in preparation for osteological analysis. In routine investigations, the survey may give positional information relating to apparently insignificant or fragmentary skeletal material that may be lost if the elements of the skeleton become commingled during the preparation process. In war crimes investigations, the survey serves to ensure ammunition or explosive devices present can be removed prior to further analysis, as well as to assist in the location of any spent projectiles that may relate to injury or the cause of death. Portable fluoroscope and digital X-ray systems offer considerable utility for use in the field.

In the case of partially skeletonised human remains or those where more recent bodies are the subject of an anthropological investigation, examination of clothing, the exterior of the body and the internal organs is normally the province of the forensic pathologist. The clothing and autopsy findings, and manner of autopsy, may have bearing on the subsequent analysis of the skeleton, however, and the anthropologist should consider fully the significance of a post mortem examination and its findings.

In most Western jurisdictions it is the forensic dentist, not the anthropologist, who reports on the dentition. Anthropologists lack familiarity with oral pathology, dental restorations and prosthodontic treatment. The anthropologist should have an adequate understanding of dental development and variation, however, especially as applied to age and ancestry estimation, and be able to provide a provisional odontological assessment for identification purposes. Any dermatoglyphic fingerprint or DNA samples should be collected promptly and appropriate guidelines followed to avoid loss or contamination of evidence.

There are two commonly used methods for cleaning the skeleton. Dermestid beetles (see, for example, Hefti *et al.* 1980) effectively remove soft tissue, but require special facilities for their maintenance and containment. A common manual method involves heating the remains in warm water ($\leq 90\ °C$) in the presence of papain, which digests proteins, and a domestic detergent that removes fats. Industrial methylated spirits can be used to degrease cleaned bones prior to handling. Cleaning the skeleton via the manual method – of which there are many variations – can take days or weeks and can result in fragile or friable bones. Any relevant findings, alteration or damage caused to the remains during preparation should be recorded.

In human rights abuse investigations, the circumstances may dictate that more rapid means are used to remove or expose for analysis those parts of the skeleton most pertinent to age and sex estimation, without recourse to a complete osteological analysis. This is a less than ideal practice, but may be appropriate if the overall balance of forensic and humanitarian investigation necessitates it. Forensic anthropologists frequently encounter cases involving incomplete skeletons, where the material is of uncertain provenance – brought in by a member of the public, for example, or found during construction work and brought in by a police officer concerned that he or she may have a murder inquiry on their hands. In such cases a prompt and reliable opinion as to whether the material is human and recent enough to be of forensic interest is required.

Finally, forensic anthropologists are frequently involved in cases involving fleshed or burned human remains, as well as skeletonised cases and those stages in between, where their expertise often complements that of the forensic pathologist.

## Forensic osteological analysis

A forensic osteological analysis can yield information relating to the following:

- whether the remains are of forensic interest – i.e. not faunal or archaeological;
- the minimum number of individuals present;
- time since death – or post-mortem interval;
- age at death;
- sex;
- ancestry;
- other individual or class evidence, pathology and trauma.

Several excellent manuals are available that describe in detail the methods of forensic osteology, and the equipment and facilities needed to undertake them, as well as ethical, judicial and admissibility issues, and reporting practices (e.g. White and Folkens 2005; Bass 2005; Burns 2007; Byers 2005; Schwartz 2007). Bass (2005) provides a very useful field guide to human osteology and Burns (2007) a comprehensive introduction to forensic anthropology. Scheuer and Black (2000) offer a reference for the subadult skeleton. Rathburn and Buikstra (1984) and Fairgrieve (1999) provide collections of case studies. This section is intended to offer a brief overview of the main methods of analysis.

### Faunal and archaeological remains

Faunal material or human bone of archaeological age is rarely of forensic significance. The species and age of the material are therefore of primary importance (see Bass 2005: 308–16 for an introduction). Species of bone and teeth can usually be readily determined by gross morphology. Where the material is too fragmentary for visual identification, molecular (see Stoeckle

2003 for a broadly applicable approach) or, alternatively, histological (Mulhern and Ubelaker 2001) methods may be employed.

Guidance to the age of human skeletal material is offered by the fragility, colour and odour of the skeleton. Recent human remains tend to be waxy and robust, relatively light or white in colour and retain a smell of ammonia. Entomological or other evidence of recent decomposition may be present. Archaeological human bone tends to be odourless – apart from smells conferred from soil – relatively fragile or friable, and tea-stained in appearance. These parameters will vary according to climate and geography, and in any event they involve a gradual process of change. Material of Victorian age, for example, may be difficult to interpret unequivocally.

Context can offer support to an interpretation – if the material arose from the site of a known archaeological or municipal cemetery, for example. Unwanted teaching skeletons may show evidence of labelling or wiring, and archaeological skeletal collections may yield a number of individuals rather implausible in a forensic context. Dental restorations are rare in material of archaeological age. Clothing, jewellery and other possessions may assist in the interpretation of the age of the skeleton and time since death. If a determination is not possible, an assessment may allow the anthropologist to give some guidance to an investigator in forming an opinion as to whether further analysis or investigative effort is warranted. The equivocal nature of such guidance should be made clear. If these parameters do not permit estimation of time since death, it can sometimes be estimated using physico-chemical methods (see Byers 2005: 126), including – under specific circumstances – C bomb-pulse dating (see ORAU 2007).

## Minimum number of individuals

It is traditional practice to lay out the bones in anatomical order prior to analysis. This assists in completing an inventory of skeletal elements and, in the case of commingled remains, establishing the minimum number of individuals present. In the event that more than one individual is present in an assemblage of commingled remains, provisional assignment of bones to an individual skeleton can be undertaken on the basis of bone size, morphology and appearance. Where the individuals were of a similar age and build, and so on, this can be difficult.

## Assessment of age at death

Techniques for the assessment of age from soft tissue remains are limited. As Knight (1996: 101) remarks:

> … Ageing a living person can be difficult and a wide margin of error exists, especially as age advances, so the same exercise in a corpse can be expected to be even less exact. Where the body is relatively intact, the usual criteria known to the man in the street are applied to make a general estimate …

This comment reflects the limited investigative role of forensic pathology in human identification, relative to odontology and anthropology.

A variety of books and scientific papers describing methods for the estimation of age from the skeleton have accumulated in a rather piecemeal way over the course of the century and continue to grow as a result of further research. Initially based on the analysis of gross morphology or measurement of the skeleton, the methods have been supplemented by histological and radiometric techniques. At the same time, the use of statistics has allowed the resolution of age estimation methods to be improved and degrees of inherent error to be established. Occasionally, novel skeletal collections consisting of individuals of known age at death have allowed the accuracy of established age assessment methods to be reassessed in controlled studies, often with disappointing results.

Physical and forensic anthropologists now recognise a suite of age estimation techniques which can be applied to human skeletal material. The value of the techniques will vary according to the developmental stage concerned. Some techniques are applicable only to juveniles, others only to adults. All of them are based on the assignment of remains to identifiable stages in the normal growth, development and ageing of the skeleton.

It is widely recognised that the processes of bodily development vary from individual to individual and from one skeletal trait to another within a single individual. A variety of developmental factors, illness, diet, cultural practices and known or unknown genetic predispositions may each affect skeletal development independently. Not only are the processes of development non-uniform, their assessment and assignment is subject to varying degrees of inter- and intra-observer error. For all of these reasons any age or age range established from the skeleton is regarded as probable rather than determined.

### Which age estimation methods are preferred?

There are differences in the accuracy of the age estimation methods themselves and in their appropriateness for use in the context of any particular investigation. Methods in forensic odontology – dental eruption – are favourable for the analysis of juvenile material, accompanied by the assessment of epiphyseal development and diaphyseal length of the skeletal elements. In adults, the use of multifactorial methods of age estimation – which combine the results derived from the separate techniques – is generally preferable to relying on only a single method, in principal at least (Lovejoy et al. 1985a; Mensforth and Lovejoy 1985; Schwarz 2007: 257–8). However, proponents of one technique – such as the pubic symphysis method – may doubt the utility of adjusting the age estimate derived by that means on account of results obtained from a less precise method (see Lovejoy et al. 1985a: 3; White and Folkens 1991: 319–20). A particular method of estimation may be preferred if it is based on a collection of standard material which is more representative of the subject under investigation on the basis of sex, ethnic origin or other factors. A further consideration may be the extent to which it is ethical, or otherwise acceptable, to interfere with the body in the course of investigation. Radiographic analysis of changes in bone structure (Walker and Lovejoy 1985) is a non-invasive method; morphological analyses require exposure of the bone and microscopic analysis of histological changes to the bone (Frost 1987a, b; Stout 1988, 1989), which is a destructive process.

*Practical guidelines*

Methods of age estimation from the skeleton are based on empirical studies of development and ageing. A number of primary (diaphyseal) and secondary (epiphyseal) centres of ossification are laid down during the growth of the foetus. The process continues following birth with the epiphyses at the ends of the long bones being particularly important in enabling longitudinal development of the skeleton. Fusion of the epiphyses to the centres of primary ossification is characteristic of later development as adulthood is approached. Throughout adult life the skeleton experiences continual and characteristic processes of remodelling and wear, with the latter factor predominating in later years.

The assessment of age from the skeleton requires that the maximum amount of useful material should be recovered and prepared for analysis with the minimum amount of damage or loss. Special care is required in the analysis of infant or foetal material, which is particularly subject to post-mortem degradation *in situ* and easily lost or damaged during excavation and post-excavation processing. It is also necessary to ascertain whether or not one is dealing with a single individual or with commingled skeletal elements.

A brief summary follows. For further discussion of the estimation of age at death the reader is referred to Reichs (1986), Krogman and Isçan (1986), Ubelaker (1989), Isçan and Kennedy (1989) and White and Folkens (1991). Articles relevant to craniofacial identification are presented in Clement and Ranson (1998). Post-mortem degenerative and depositional processes are discussed in Haglund and Sorg (1997). All age estimation methods are subject to varying degrees of error and it is important to recognise that it is an estimate of age which is produced, not a true determination. In many cases, however, even an estimation of age within a range of values may be critical to an investigation.

*Ageing of subadult remains*

Patterns of ossification and dental development are the key factors in the estimation of age in subadults. Reviews of the methods are provided by Ubelaker (1987, 1989: 63–73), Johnston and Zimmer (1989) and Hillson (1986: 177–201). Age estimation in neonates and in the foetus can be derived from the traditionally recognised patterns of growth in the living (Stowens 1966: 5–6), from more recent studies (Mercer *et al.* 1987; Goldstein *et al.* 1988; Amato *et al.* 1991) and from methods directed specifically at skeletal remains (Olivier and Pineau 1958, 1960; Fazekas and Kósa 1978; Weaver 1986). Huxley (1998) reported good correspondence between foetal ages derived from foot length and diaphyseal length in a single case of known age.

*Dental development*

Ubelaker (1989: 63–69) has provided a systematic description of dental development typical of a number of age classes and the chronology of dental development has recently been summarised by Dykes and Clark (1998). Development of the dentition is commonly regarded as being under relatively strict genetic control and therefore far less liable to environmental interference than other skeletal traits. Age estimation from the dentition thus offers a relatively accurate means of classification of the younger age ranges, although it is not without potential error (see White and Folkens 1991: 308–11).

### Epiphyseal closure

The fusion of the epiphyses of the postcranial skeleton follows a regular pattern, but may occur over a range of chronological ages varying from individual to individual. Fusion of the epiphysis is usually scored on a 0–4 scale, with zero unfused and 4 fully fused. The medial clavicle epiphysis is fused in the majority of individuals in their late twenties, but may remain unfused in approximately 10 per cent of thirty-year-olds. Fusion of the epiphyses progresses at earlier ages in males than females, but varies considerably from individual to individual (see Ubelaker 1987 and White and Folkens 1991: 313–4 for further references).

### Long bone length

Estimation of age from the length of the long bones is a less exact method of age estimation and relies on comparison with bone length and age in a comparable skeletal series (Ubelaker 1987, 1989: 70–74). The method can also be applied to diaphyseal length in foetal and neonatal material (Weaver 1986). In foetal and neonatal skeletons there is likely to be a paucity both of material recovered and recognisable classes against which skeletal age can be assessed.

### Arc length of cranial bones

Long bone development is relatively retarded in comparison to the bones of the skull. Arc length of the cranial bones may offer complementary means of estimating foetal age (Weaver 1986: 93, 96). The reconstructed skull may offer a further means of age estimation – or the estimation of a minimum age – on the basis of the relationship with head circumference in living individuals (Stowens 1966: 5).

### Ageing of adult remains

It is evident from the pattern of dental development and epiphyseal closure that developmental stages which can be used in age classification are only applicable into the late twenties, and offer much more resolution in earlier age ranges. Age estimation in older age groups is based on changes attributable to wear and other ageing processes. The methods are summarised in Isçan and Loth (1989) and Ubelaker (1989: 74–95).

### Pubic symphysis surface

Probably the most popular means of estimating adult age from the skeleton is from the pubic symphysis surface. A series of phases of age-related changes to the morphology of the pubic symphysis surface was first proposed by Todd (1920, 1921) and later supplemented by McKern and Stewart (1957). More recent studies have led to a reassessment of the accuracy of earlier methods and a number of revisions have been proposed (Suchey et al. 1986; Meindl et al. 1985a; Suchey and Katz 1986; Brooks and Suchey 1990).

*Auricular surface of the ilium*

The auricular surface of the ilium is also believed to undergo age-related changes in morphology (Lovejoy *et al.* 1985b) which permit age estimation into the later age ranges where the pubic symphysis surface does not, albeit via a more technically demanding system (White and Folkens 1991: 318).

*Sternal rib end*

Following earlier observations of age-related changes to the costochondral junction of the rib, Isçan *et al.* (1985; Isçan and Loth 1986) presented a series of age estimation standards for the sternal rib end, based on the analysis at autopsy of 230 White individuals of known age at death. A modification for Black specimens was later proposed (Isçan *et al.* 1987). A series of nine age phases were identified, offering the unusual potential for age discrimination during the later years, within broad age categories, but based only on the fourth rib. The sternal rib end is easily eroded as a consequence of post-mortem or post-depositional processes, however.

*Cranial suture closure*

The closure of the cranial sutures is believed to follow an age-related pattern, but one which has proved difficult to quantify and apply reliably in age estimation. Meindl and Lovejoy (1985; and see Novotný *et al.* 1993: 74–5) used a four-stage scale to assign the degree of suture closure of the lateral-anterior sutures of the cranium to derive a more reliable method. One feature in particular – the sphenooccipital synchondrosis – fuses at between 20 and 25 years of age in 95 per cent of individuals (see White and Folkens 1991: 313; and Briggs 1998: 57–8). Mann *et al.* (1987) analysed the pattern of maxillary suture closure in males and females, and suggested that maxillary suture closure pattern may be used to corroborate age estimates derived using other methods.

*Dental wear*

In adults where dental development is near complete, age estimation from the dentition is based on a presumed relationship between age and the extent of tooth wear. Age estimation methods directed at the adult dentition have briefly been reviewed by Xiaohu *et al.* (1992) and Clement (1998: 75–80). Lovejoy (1985) established a systematic method for the classification of dental wear from Native American skeletal material, which is probably not applicable to modern attrition rates.

*Histological and radiological methods*

Novel methods for age estimation from the skeleton continue to be proposed. Walker and Lovejoy (1985) found an inverse relationship between bone density assessed radiographically and age at death applicable to the clavicle and proximal femur. Age-related changes in trabecular bone morphology in the proximal femur – and the humerus – can also be assessed macroscopically (Schranz 1959; Acsádi and Nemerskéri 1970; Leutert 1974). Microscopic examination of patterns of bone remodelling in skeletal material of known age has indicated that numbers of osteons and other histological structures can be used as a means of age estimation (Kerley and Ubelaker 1978; Frost 1987a, b; Stout 1988, 1989). As White and Folken (1991: 319) observe, these techniques have not been widely tested and are sometimes based on small sample sizes.

The most reliable method of age estimation from the adult skeleton is probably that of Johanson (1971) and Gustafson (1950), based on attrition and translucency assessed histologically.

## Assessment of sex

Assessment of sex relies on sexual dimorphism in adult humans that chiefly affects the pelvic girdle. Sex estimation in juveniles is not reliable. Methods of sex assessment are presented in White and Folkens (2005), Burns (2007), Byers (2005) and Schwartz (2007).

### Morphology of the pelvis and sacrum

Examination of the pubis and ilium offers the most reliable method for sex assessment, a wider pelvic inlet and outlet having developed in females as it is better able to facilitate childbirth. The pubis of females is relatively elongated horizontally and possesses a ventral arc and wider sub-pubic angle. The ilium of females has a wider sciatic notch and may possess a preauricular sulcus. Schwarz (2007: 294) offers a comprehensive list of features of the pelvis and sacrum that may be used to distinguish males and females. In some cases, parturition marks develop on the dorsal surface of the pubis of women who have undergone childbirth.

### Morphology of the skull and mandible

Sexual dimorphism may be evident in the skull, but may not be as clear as in the pelvis – a distinction that can be affected by ancestry. Of the distinguishing features in males, superciliary barring 'brow ridges', the zygomatic arch projecting beyond the external auditory meatus, marked nuchal lines on the occipital bone and a pronounced mental eminence on the mandible are the most prominent. Schwarz (2007: 293) provides a comprehensive list.

### Other potential skeletal indicators of sex

Schwarz (2007: 287–95) reviews statistical approaches based on discriminant function equations that may be used to estimate sex from the skull and mandible, pelvis, and a number of elements of the postcranial skeleton. Rogers (1999) has proposed a visual method for sex estimation from the distal humerus.

## Assessment of ancestry

The skull, mandible and dentition offer the primary means of assessment of ancestry. The nasal aperture of White people tends to be tall and narrow, with a pinched nasal bridge and a sharp nasal sill at the margin of the nasal base. Black people tend to possess a broad and short nasal aperture, with a flat nasal bridge and a smooth margin at the nasal sill. Persons of Oriental ancestry are, approximately, intermediate. A number of features of dental morphology occur at distinctive frequencies in different populations (for example, see Burns 2007: 168). Schwarz (2007: 305) and Bass (2005: 83–92) review assessment of ancestry. Bass (2005: 88–91) introduces quantitative methods for assessing ancestry and FORDISC (Ousely and Jantz 2005) offers a software application tool based on an accumulated database of craniometric measurements from a variety of populations. The femur may also be used in ancestry estimation (see Burns 2007: 203–4).

### Other individuating features, pathology and trauma

Estimation of stature by projection from long bone length is routine (see Bass 2005). Handedness may be crudely assessed by comparing the size of muscle attachment sites on the bones of the upper limbs and shoulder girdle (see also Burns 2007 and Byers 2005: 417–420). Other potentially individuating features include many that can be assessed radiologically. A classic example is the morphology of the frontal sinuses (Christensen 2005), which are assessed radiologically and compared with ante-mortem radiographs, if available. A large potential range of other features may be visible on a radiograph that can be used to infer or – equally importantly – exclude identification. There are a plethora of non metric traits that an individual may possess, which may occur at distinct frequencies in different populations, some of which may be comparable to ante-mortem data. Schwarz (2007: 266–8) provides a comprehensive list. Finally, numerous forms of pathology may leave observable marks on the skeleton (Aufderheide and Rodriguez-Martin 1998; Roberts and Manchester 2007). Various forms of arthritis, osteoarthritis, Schmorl's nodes, kyphosis, scoliosis and osteophytosis are frequently encountered and may also be observable on ante-mortem radiographs. Dental caries and periodontitis are common forms of dental pathology and their patterns and treatments greatly assist the forensic odontologist in identification from dental records.

Injury to the skeleton can be loosely divided into ante-mortem, peri-mortem and post-mortem trauma. Ante-mortem trauma – healed fractures, for example – are potentially unique and may offer strong evidence of identity when compared with medical records. Peri-mortem trauma – occurring around the time of death – can be problematic as it may be difficult to state conclusively whether an injury was sustained after or before death occurred, but the key significance may be whether the trauma could be the proximate or ultimate cause of death. Ante-mortem trauma may also be a potential cause of death in the event of the victim dying some time after an injury was sustained. Early healing may be visible radiographically. Post-mortem fractures tend to be different in shape from peri-mortem, as a consequence of dehydration and decomposition. The morphology and distribution of injuries is significant. Gunshot entry and exit wounds, blunt force trauma, cut marks due to stabbing, and saw, cut or chop marks – often resulting from dismemberment – are usually distinctive in shape and pattern (see Byers 2005: 295–354 and Symes et al. 2002). Forensic anthropologists may contribute to the investigation of cause of death in skeletonised, partially skeletonised and fresh fleshed cases (see Saul and Saul 2002, 2005).

### The osteobiography concept

The concept of the 'osteobiography' was developed to encourage archaeologists and physical anthropologists working on ancient remains to go further than simply looking at measurements – relating to age, sex, stature, etc. – and to develop a more comprehensive history of the individual as written on bone (Frank Saul, personal communication). It extends the biological profile to encompass health status, build, habitual activities and postures and so on (see Saul and Saul 1989, Capasso *et al.* 1998). The term occupational marker may be misleading as more than one activity may cause an identical bony change. Nevertheless, activities with cultural – squatting, chewing "khat" – and occupational – motorcycle dispatch riding, coal distribution and cutlery polishing (see Bovenzi *et al.* 1986) – dimensions have been reflected, albeit ambiguously, in forensic cases.

### Forensic facial reconstruction

Forensic facial reconstruction is a technique that permits the reconstruction of approximate facial appearance from the skull (Gerasimov 1968; Prag and Neave 1999; Wilkinson 2004). Its value is in cases where there are no candidates – a missing person, for example – for pursuing positive identification by forensic odontology, DNA, and so on. Its role is to create media interest that might generate 'leads' – names put forward by the public, which can be prioritised for further investigation and positive identification by other means. There are two traditional methods of facial reconstruction: the 'Russian' method, which relies on the approximate modelling of the craniofacial musculature in clay (or another modelling material), and the 'American' method, which relies on estimating the facial surface by interpolating in clay between pegs inserted at known tissue depths at about 30 points on the skull. A number of routes to computerised forensic facial reconstruction have been explored (Vanezis *et al.* 1989; Miyasaka *et al.* 1995; Evison 1996, Evison *et al.* 1998; Clement and Marks 2005), which are essentially analogous to the two plastic approaches.

## Areas of controversy

### Estimation or determination?

Methods of osteological analysis possess limited degrees of accuracy, with the estimation of sex being most accurate, with reported rates in the region of 80–90 per cent, when applied to skeletal material of known sex. Estimation of ancestry is less reliable. Stature estimates usually have error ranges of several centimetres. Age estimation also tends to generate broad age ranges, with adults – especially older adults – being particularly difficult to age precisely. The term 'determination' frequently encountered in forensic anthropology textbooks and scientific publications, is a misnomer. These attributes are estimates – an issue of critical importance in a forensic investigation where the value is investigative and not probative, and some circumspection is warranted. The reasons for the limited accuracy of estimates of osteological parameters relate to the representativeness of the skeleton under investigation to the population from which the method of estimation was derived, the effect of inter- and intra-observer error, and accuracy and bias in the method.

### Representativeness of the population from which the method of estimation method was derived

Methods for the estimation of age from the skeleton are derived from the study of standard material of known age at death. Major reference collections in the United States include the Hamann-Todd Collection at Case Western Reserve University and the Terry Collection held at the Smithsonian Institution in Washington. The Hamann-Todd Collection consists of 3,592 skeletons of White and Black individuals derived from low socio-economic groups from urban areas accumulated from local hospitals between 1912 and 1938 (see White and Folkens 1991: 307). Lovejoy *et al.* (1985a: 5) observed that only about 16 per cent of the individuals in the Hamann-Todd Collection had age at death reliably assigned. The Terry Collection consists of around 1,600 skeletons of adult Black and White individuals derived from both rural and urban populations accumulated at around the time of the American Civil War (1861–1865). The material used by Todd (1920, 1921) in the first systematic study of ageing from the pelvic bones was derived from the Western Reserve skeletal collection, which originated from dissections of White and Black individuals accumulated during the early 1900s (see Suchey *et al.* 1986: 33). More recent material used in the development of age estimation standards includes a collection of skeletons of US Korean War dead (McKern and Stewart 1957) and post-mortem skeletal specimens collected by the Los Angeles County Department of the Chief Medical Examiner-Coroner (Suchey *et al.* 1986).

Because of environmental factors such as diet, health, occupation, and genetic factors (which may be related to ethnic group), the extent to which the skeleton under investigation is representative of the standard population may be critical to the accuracy of the age estimate. The age profile of the standard material may also influence the degree of error. Suchey *et al.* (1986: 35–36) observe that individuals in the Western Reserve collection analysed by Todd tend to fall into the older age ranges. The accompanying records were not always found to be accurate and the assignment of 'known' age seems frequently to have been based on a physical assessment of the cadaver prior to dissection, not on reliable accompanying documentation. The collection of Korean War dead (McKern and Stewart 1957) consists of 349 skeletons, but is derived entirely from male individuals with a limited distribution of ages (30 years or younger). Most of the individuals are White. The Los Angeles County material – which has been used to derive 'corrections' of the Todd and McKern-Stewart methods – derives from 739 individuals aged from 14 to 92 years, but consists only of the pubic bones of males (Suchey *et al.* 1986). Suchey and co-workers (see Suchey and Katz 1997) have attempted to improve the methods of age estimation from the pubic symphysis surface, extending their analysis to collections of female material and material of diverse ancestry. Suchey *et al.* (1986: 42–3) assigned 'race' on the basis of a physical assessment supported by accompanying documental records, and the difficulties and ambiguities involved in applying this often nebulous concept are apparent. On the basis of these assignments, however, the sample consisted of 18.6 per cent Black, 2.0 per cent Oriental and 10.6 per cent Mexican individuals, with the remainder being classified as White (65.8 per cent) or being assigned to an ambiguous 'other' category (2.7 per cent). Whilst pragmatism may indicate it is advisable to group these sub-samples together, ignoring potential genetic influences may present its own risks.

Clearly both genetic and environmental factors must be assessed in establishing the most applicable standard to use in the estimation of age. Todd (1920, 1921) carried out separate studies on White and Black populations, Suchey et al. (1986) used a combined 'multi-ethnic' data set in their study. Isçan and Miller-Shaivitz (1986: 109–10) noted, with regard to sex estimation from the skeleton, that the Hamann-Todd Collection was preferable to the Terry Collection as a standard when applied to the analysis of a skeleton originating from an urban population. Sex, as well as ethnic group, may influence the outcome of age estimation (Suchey et al. 1986: 48). It may be noted that the assessment of age in prehistoric populations is likely to introduce further sources of variability due to unknown genetic and environmental factors (see White and Folkens 1991: 308). Similar issues apply to methods of sex, stature and ancestry estimation, as well as to estimation of age. Populations are not static over time: as Jantz (2001: 284–7) reported from a large study, cranial vaults have become higher and narrower, and faces narrower, over the period 1850 to 1975.

### Inter- and intra-observer error

A systematic analysis of inter-observer error was completed by Suchey et al. between 1978 and 1983, in a study involving ageing from the pelvis using the McKern-Stewart method conducted by 25 forensic anthropologists (Suchey et al. 1986: 48–57). Participants were asked to assign the 0–5 score of McKern and Stewart (1957: 75–9) to each pair of pubic bones for the three components: the dorsal plateau, the ventral rampart and the symphyseal rim.

The most notable finding was a surprising discrepancy in precision between assessments of males and females, with females being assessed far more indecisively than males. The early age ranges were also subject to more indecisive assessments. Overall, only 65 per cent of the assessments covered the known age of the individual. Although Suchey et al. were able to use the results of this study to suggest modifications to the McKern-Stewart method (Suchey et al. 1986: 57–65), the results provide an indication of the influence of the observer on the outcome of age estimation from the skeleton – using one of the more reliable methods. Age estimation methods have rarely been extensively tested, a consideration which is particularly applicable to the more recent techniques.

### Accuracy and bias inherent in the age estimation method

The natural continuum in physical changes due to ageing and their variation from individual to individual and body part to body part lead to inherent inaccuracy in age estimation. Because of the number of developmental stages that can be identified it is easier to age individuals before maturity than afterward – when changes to the skeleton are driven only by the ageing process and environmental factors. The completeness of the skeletal assemblage will also affect the accuracy and precision of age estimation. Certain bone elements are particularly useful in the assignment of age from the skeleton; others are less precise – or cannot be used in age estimation at all. Under ideal circumstances a skeletal series – a number of individual skeletons investigated together – would provide the opportunity to reduce the amount of inherent error encountered in analysing isolated skeletons. Although it often may be possible to seriate archaeological remains in this way, such opportunities are rare in forensic contexts. The degree of accuracy will also be reduced when the skeleton under investigation is not representative of the standard material used in the development of the age estimation method (see above). Further consideration of the accuracy and precision of age estimation is provided in Meindl *et al.* (1985b) and White and Folkens (1991: 306–7).

Bias in the methods of age estimation is chiefly expressed in tendencies for over- or under-ageing. In particular, ageing from the pubic bones has tended to lead to systematic under-ageing of the material (Meindl *et al.* 1985a, b). According to Lovejoy *et al.* (1985a: 12), '… The best single indicator for determining age at death in skeletal populations is dental wear. It is consistently without bias and probably presents the highest accuracy as well.' Given the commonly acknowledged influence of diet, especially, on dental wear this claim should be treated with circumspection in forensic contexts.

Reassessments of osteological methods of assessment are continually produced (e.g. Baker 1984; Suchey *et al.* 1986; Meindl *et al.* 1985a; Suchey and Katz 1986; Brooks and Suchey 1990; Key *et al.* 2005; Falys *et al.* 2005; Powers 1962; Hershkovitz *et al.* 1997). These reassessments are not based on new technological developments, but on new comparisons with skeletal samples of known age at death. Whilst these reassessments may offer some refinements, the fundamental implication is that the methods of forensic anthropology are prone to intra- and inter-observer error, systematic bias, and the affects of lack of representativeness of the skeleton under investigation to the sample used in methodological development.

These observations signal that the prudent approach to age estimation is to examine all available indicators of age to arrive at an age range within which the true value will fall. The range should be broad enough such that the pitfall of an accidental exclusion – of, say, an 'outlier' – may be avoided.

### Why not just use DNA?

The favoured methods for reliable human identification are DNA profiling, dermatoglyphic fingerprinting and forensic odontology. DNA profiles have been obtained from decades-old forensic specimens since the early 1990s (e.g. Jeffreys *et al.* 1992; Gill *et al.* 1994; Evison *et al.* 1997). Although technically challenging, the methods are now routine, meaning that a high-resolution DNA profile can be anticipated from skeletal remains. In the absence of a candidate – offering ante-mortem dental records, a comparative DNA profile from relatives or personal possessions, or an ante-mortem fingerprint – DNA, fingerprints and forensic odontology are, however, of limited immediate use.

The predominant value of forensic anthropology and facial reconstruction in human identification is their investigative role, offering a biological profile, osteobiography and approximate facial image that can be used to elicit and prioritise candidates. Following a process of elimination, identity can be confirmed by DNA, fingerprints or dental records. When this evidence cannot be obtained, unusual or unique osteological evidence – such as frontal sinus morphology or ante-mortem trauma or surgery – may be sufficient.

### Race is a redundant concept

The term 'race' continues to be used by some forensic anthropologists and forensic scientists. It is an entirely flawed and redundant concept in human biology. Although expressions such as 'ancestry' or 'geographic ancestry' are not without semantic problems, they are conceptually nearer to scientific understanding of global genetic and phenotypic variation: the term 'race' perpetuates a misguided and unscientific view and – despite the popular use of the term including, unfortunately, in the social sciences – it should be abandoned.

### The ambiguous value and lack of scientific probity of forensic facial reconstruction

Facial reconstruction produces a resemblance of the deceased, not an exact likeness. The term 'facial approximation' is more accurate and is favoured by many practitioners. The artistic quality of facial reconstructions is evidently variable, but there is no evidence that artistic quality has any bearing on the chances of success in obtaining identification. Facial reconstruction is largely an artistic process with a limited and dubious quantitative and scientific basis, the accuracy of which has often been overstated (see, for example, Macho 1986, 1989; Tyrell et al. 1997; Evison 1996; Stephan 2001, 2002, 2003).

Even in the absence of an extensive scientific basis for facial reconstruction or a proper understanding of exactly what role – if any! – the approximated face plays in generating leads from publicity in the media, it is clear that facial reconstructions are instrumental in leading to identifications in roughly 50 to 75 per cent of cases where they are used. These are inevitably cases where other routes were becoming exhausted.

## Future prospects

### New osteological and physical methods

New methods for age estimation continue to be derived based on macroscopic, histological, radiological and molecular methods. Relatively untried techniques include ageing from the pattern of ossification of the thyroid cartilage (Cerny 1983 cited in Krogman and Işcan 1986: 127) or from radiography of the second metacarpals (Kimura 1992). Controlled studies of the reliability of new or existing age estimation methods based on large samples are rare, however, although the value of the medial clavicle epiphysis to age estimation has recently been reviewed (Kreitner *et al.* 1998). In partial contrast to Walker and Lovejoy (1985), Pocock *et al.* (1989) found that muscle strength, physical fitness and weight, but not age predicted femoral neck bone mass (see also Leutert 1974 and Schranz 1959). Tooth cementum annulation (see Wittwer-Backofen *et al.* 2004 for a recent validation study) and dental microstructure analyses (see Huda and Bowman 1995 for a historical application) are emerging as alternatives to the well-regarded Johanson/Gustafson method of ageing from the dentition.

Molecular methods of ageing have been proposed which are based on the gradual conversion of L- to D-aspartic acid following initial deposition into the skeletal material. These have been derived for dentine (Ogino *et al.* 1985; Ogino and Ogino 1988; Ritz *et al.* 1990), cartilage (Pfeifer *et al.* 1995a) and bone (Pfeifer *et al.* 1995b). Dentine is particularly useful as it is relatively inert following initial deposition and there is little aspartic acid turnover. Bone is constantly remodelled, however. Finally, stable isotope analysis has emerged as a valuable tool in understanding diet and provenance (see, for example, Fraser *et al.* 2006).

Refinement of existing techniques using skeletal collections of known history as comparative controls will continue to be important. These include current collections such as the Los Angeles County material, growing collections like that of the University of Tennessee Forensic Anthropology Data Bank (FDB 2008) and new potential sources of reference material, such as the Texas State Forensic Research Facility (FACTS 2008).

### New molecular methods

Advances in genetics offer several potential new opportunities in human identification from the skeleton (see Jobling and Gill 2004). The assumption that a DNA profile from a skeleton is no use without a comparative profile from personal possessions or relatives of the candidate is becoming questionable. The accumulation of forensic DNA databases means that it is now theoretically possible to search a database for similar DNA profiles to that of the unidentified skeleton – 'familial searching' – in order to detect a relative, with the aim of leading to a positive identification. Research on the genetics of common characteristics may allow prediction of aspects of appearance from a trace forensic DNA sample – red hair and fair skin, for example (Branicki *et al.* 2007). DNAPrint Genomics, Inc. (Sarasota, FL), offered a product permitting the inference of ancestry from a DNA profile (Frudakis *et al.* 2004).

### Studies of taphonomy and detection of human remains

General studies of post-mortem processes have gained popular notoriety through the activities of the University of Tennessee Anthropological Research Facility begun in 1972 by Dr William M. Bass. Davenport *et al.* (1992) reported a coordinated programme for the investigation of detection and recovery of human remains. The understanding of post-mortem process or time since death may be amenable to investigation via the study of physico-chemical changes which, for example, Hiller *et al.* (2003) employed in the study of experimental heating of bone and Brandão *et al.* (2007) employed in the study of heating of dental materials.

### Developments in quantitation, imaging and visualisation modelling

In forensic facial reconstruction, Stephan (2001, 2002, 2003, 2006) has done much to introduce theoretical and quantitative rigour. Data collection from living individuals using medical imaging techniques – such as from magnetic resonance imaging data (Evison 1996; Evison and Wilkinson forthcoming – offer further developments. Computerised approaches generally have the advantage of rapidity, portability and flexibility – the ability to address uncertainties such as age, obesity or ancestry (Green and Evison 1999), and the potential for 3-D visualisation on the Internet (Evison and Green 1999). Virtual reality offers wider potential for the visualisation and demonstration of post-mortem findings (March *et al.* 2004). Forensic facial identification for the courts demands anthropometric and image-based investigation (Evison 2005; Evison and Vorder Bruegge 2008).

### The other anthropologies

The value to the criminal justice system and public safety of the sub-fields of anthropology – other than physical or biological and archaeological – is little explored. Forensic linguistics tends to reside in linguistics departments of the universities. Socio-cultural practices in relation to public safety, crime, investigation and identification are little explored from an anthropological perspective – in contrast to the psychological, sociological and criminological – although socio-cultural anthropologists are sometimes called upon to provide expert opinion both for and against the land rights claims of indigenous peoples. Archaeologists may provide similar expert opinion in relation to the criminal international black market trade in precious artefacts.

The involvement of socio-cultural anthropologists embedded with the United States military in Iraq has been the source of heated controversy resulting in a special investigation by the American Anthropological Association (AAA 2007). This report provides interesting insight into important debate surrounding an ethically divisive issue, as well as the sophomoric politics of academic anthropology. 'Working for the military' is unacceptable to some anthropologists, despite the contribution forensic anthropology has undoubtedly made to the identification of victims of the regime of Saddam Hussein (e.g. BBC 2004) or – under the auspices of NATO/KFOR – Slobodan Milošević. Whilst the American Anthropological Association opposes the investigation of Americans based on – for example – their 'race', religion, or even travel patterns (AAA 2008), it does not seem clear how the policing or intelligence agencies are meant to ethically respond in the face of – for the sake of discussion – White Supremacist or Islamic Extremist terrorism.

## Conclusion

The forensic anthropologist forms part of a team of investigators and scientists, where their general role is to advise and offer options, as well as expert assistance – from survey through to recovery and analysis of evidence. Liaison with related disciplines – ecology, entomology, pathology, odontology – is important during both the investigative and analytical phases. Forensic anthropologists may contribute to the investigation of fresh fleshed, partly skeletonised and skeletonised remains.

Forensic anthropology plays an important investigative role, but is best viewed as a complement to more positive methods of human identification such as DNA analysis. Biological parameters generated during an osteological analysis are often more properly termed estimates, rather than determinations. It is important that presumptive and positive modalities of identification are clearly delineated, and that biographical parameters – age range, for example – are left sufficiently broad to avoid unwarranted exclusions.

Forensic anthropology will remain an important tool in the identification of the victims of war and war crimes, and mass fatality incidents. The United States offers the best international model for good practice via ABFA and DMORT. Many European jurisdictions suffer a comparative disadvantage in that their caseloads are limited and professional organisations correspondingly small. It may be the criminal justice system and public safety policies of emerging economies such as Brazil, China and India that enjoy the most rapid incorporation of contemporary best practice in the medium term. A century of previous research suggests that significant methodological developments based on the gross morphology of bone are probably exhausted. New scientific approaches – molecular or computational – are likely to be more productive and may, importantly, be applicable to the living as well as the deceased.

## Acknowledgements

I am grateful to Frank and Julie Saul, and Jerry Melbye for offering extensive and helpful comments on an earlier draft of this chapter. Any errors or oversights are my own.

## References

AAA (2007) AAA commission on the engagement of anthropology with the US security and intelligence communities – final report [Web]. Accessed 29 August 2008. http://www.aaanet.org/_cs_upload/pdf/4092_1.pdf

AAA (2008) House racial profiling letter [Web]. Accessed 29 August 2008. http://www.aaanet.org/issues/policy-advocacy/upload/House-racial-profiling-letter.pdf

ABFA (2008) American Board of Forensic Anthropology, Inc. ABFA [Web]. Accessed 29 August 2008. http://www.csuchico.edu/anth/ABFA/

ACPO (2005) ACPO DNA good practice manual [Web]. Accessed 29 August 2008. http://www.acpo.police.uk/asp/policies/Data/dna_good_practice_manual_2005.doc

Acsádi, G. and Nemerskéri, J. (1970) *History of human life span and mortality*. Budapest: Akademiai Kiado.

Adam, D. (2003) 'Brazilian forensic medicine: back from the dead', *Nature*, 423: 13–4.

Amato, M., Huppi, P. and Claus, R. (1991). 'Rapid biometric assessment of gestational age in very low birth weight infants', *J Perinatal Med*, 19: 367–71.

Aufderheide, A.C. and Rodriguez-Martin, C. (1998) *The Cambridge Encyclopedia of Human Palaeopathology*. Cambridge: Cambridge University Press.

Baker, R.K. (1984) 'The relationship of cranial suture closure and age analyzed in a modern multiracial sample of males and females', California State University, Fullerton (Unpublished MA Thesis).

Barclay, G. and Tavares, C. (2002) 'International comparisons of criminal justice statistics 2000'. Research, Development and Statistics Directorate Communications and Development Unit. London: Home Office.

Bass, W.M. (2005) *Human osteology: a laboratory and field manual* (5th edn). Columbia, MO: Missouri Archaeological Society.

Bass, W.M. and Birkby, W.H. (1978) 'Exhumation: the method could make the difference', *FBI Law Enforcement Bulletin*, July: 6–11.

BBC (2004) 'Babies found in Iraq mass grave' [Web]. Accessed 29 August 2008. http://news.bbc.co.uk/2/hi/middle_east/3738368.stm

Bovenzi, M., Fiorito, A. and Volpe, C. (1986) 'Bone and joint disorders in the upper extremities of chipping and grinding operators', *Int Arch Occup Environ Health*, 59(2): 189–98.

Boyd, R.M. (1979) 'Buried body cases', *FBI Law Enforcement Bulletin*, February: 1–7.

Brandão, R.B., Martin, C.C.S., Catirse, A.B.C.E.B., de Castro e Silva, M., Evison, M.P. and Guimarães, M.A. (2007) 'Heat induced changes to dental resin composites: a reference in forensic investigations?', *J Forensic Sci*, 52(4): 913–9.

Branicki, W., Brudnik, U., Kupiec, T., Wolanska-Nowak, P. and Wojas-Pelc, A. (2007) 'Determination of phenotype associated SNPs in the MC1R gene', *J Forensic Sci*, 52: 349–54.

Briggs, C.A. (1998) 'Anthropological assessment', pp. 49–61, in J.G. Clement and D.L. Ranson (eds), *Craniofacial identification in forensic medicine*. London: Arnold.

Brooks, S. and Suchey, J.M. (1990) 'Skeletal age determination based on the os pubis: a comparison of the Ascadi-Nemeskeri and Suchey-Brooks methods', *Hum Evol*, 5: 227–38.

Burns, K.R. (2007) *Forensic anthropology training manual* (2nd edn). New Jersey: Pearson.

Byers, S.N. (2005) *Introduction to forensic anthropology: a textbook* (2nd edn). New York: Pearson.

Capasso, L., Kennedy, K. and Wilczak, C.A. (1998) 'Atlas of occupational markers on human remains', *J Paleopathol Monographic Publications*, 3: 1–184.

Cerny, M. (1983) 'Our experience with estimation of an individual's age from skeletal remains of the degree of thyroid cartilage ossification', *Acta Universitatis Palackianae Olomucensis*, 3: 121–44.

CIA (2007) *The World Fact Book 2007*. Central Intelligence Agency [Web]. Accessed 6 June 2007. https://www.cia.gov/library/publications/the-world-factbook/index.html

Christensen, A.M. (2005) 'Testing the reliability of frontal sinuses in positive identification', *J Forensic Sci*, 50: 18–22.

Clement, J.G. (1998) 'Dental identification', pp. 63–81, in J.G. Clement and D.L. Ranson (eds), *Craniofacial identification in forensic medicine*. London: Arnold.

Clement, J.G. and Marks, M.K. (2005) *Computer-graphic facial reconstruction*. New York: Academic Press.

Clement, J.G. and Ranson, D.L. (1998) (eds) *Craniofacial identification in forensic medicine*. London: Arnold.

Davenport, G.C., France, D.L., Griffin, T.J., Swanburg, J.G., Lindemann, J.W., Tranunell, V., Armbrust, C.T., Kondrateiff, B., Nelson, A., Castellano, K. and Hopkins, D. (1992) 'A multidisciplinary approach to the detection of clandestine graves', *J Forensic Sci*, 37(6): 1445–58.

DMORT (2008) 'Disaster Mortuary Operational Response Teams', DMORT [Web]. Accessed 29 August 2008. http://www.dmort.org/

Dykes, E. and Clark, D.H. (1998) 'Chronology of dental development', pp. 279–81, in J.G. Clement and D.L. Ranson (eds), *Craniofacial identification in forensic medicine*. London: Arnold.

EAAF (2008) 'Argentine forensic anthropology team. Equipo Argentino de Antropologia Forense' [Web]. Accessed 29 August 2008. http://www.eaaf.org/

Evison, M.P. (1996) '3-D facial reconstruction. Assemblage 1' [Web]. Accessed 8 June 2007. http://www.shef.ac.uk/~assem/1/evison.html

Evison, M.P. (2005) (ed.) 'Computer aided forensic facial comparison: scientific and technical report', Technical Support Working Group (unpublished technical report, 285 pages).

Evison, M.P., Finegan, O.M. and Blythe, T.C. (1998) 'Computerised 3-D facial reconstruction: research update. Assemblage 4' [Web]. Accessed 8 June 2007. http://www.assemblage.group.shef.ac.uk/4/4evison.html

Evison, M.P. and Green, M.A. (1999) 'Presenting three-dimensional forensic facial simulations on the Internet using VRML', *J Forensic Sci*, 44(6): 1219–23.

Evison, M.P., Smillie, D.M. and Chamberlain, A.T. (1997) 'Extraction of single-copy genomic DNA from forensic specimens with a variety of post-mortem histories', *J Forensic Sci*, 42(6): 1030–6.

Evison, M.P. and Vorder Bruegge, R.W. (2008) 'The Magna database: a database of 3-D facial images for research in crime prevention and detection', *Forensic Sci Comm*, 10(2) [Web]. Accessed 29 August 2008. http://www.fbi.gov/hq/lab/fsc/backissu/april2008/research/2008_04_research01.htm

Evison, M.P. and Wilkinson, I.D. A head and neck MR image database [submitted for publication July 2008].

FACTS (2008) Forensic Anthropology Center at Texas State [Web]. Accessed 29 August 2008. http://www.txstate.edu/anthropology/facts/

Fairgrieve, S.I. (1999) (ed.) *Forensic osteological analysis: a book of case studies*. Springfield, IL: Charles C. Thomas.

Falys, C.G., Schutkowski, H. and Weston, D.A. (2005) 'The distal humerus – a blind test of Rogers' sexing technique using a documented skeletal collection', *J Forensic Sci*, 50(6): 1289–93.

Fazekas I.G. and Kósa, K. (1978) *Forensic foetal osteology*. Budapest: Akadémiai Kiadó Publishers.

FDB (2008) Forensic Anthropology Data Bank [Web]. Accessed 29 August 2008. http://web.utk.edu/~anthrop/FACdatabank.html

Fraser, I., Meier-Augenstein, W. and Kalin, R.M. (2006) 'The role of stable isotopes in human identification: a longitudinal study into the variability of isotopic signals in human hair and nails', *Rapid Commun. Mass Spectrom*, 20: 1109–16.

Frost, H.M. (1987a) 'Secondary osteon populations: an algorithm for determining mean bone tissue age', *Yearbook Phys Anthropol*, 30: 221–38.

Frost, H.M. (1987b) 'Secondary osteon population densities: an algorithm for estimating the missing osteons', *Yearbook Phys Anthropol*, 30: 239–54.

Frudakis, T., Venkateswarlu, K., Thomas, M.J., Gaskin, Z., Ginjupalli, S., Gunturi, S., Ponnuswamy V., Natarajan, S. and Nachimuthu, P.K. (2004) 'A classifier for the SNP-based inference of ancestry', *J Forensic Sci*, 48(4): 771–82.

Gawryszewski, V.P. and Mercy, J.A. (2004) 'Homicide trends and characteristics – Brazil, 1980–2002', *Morbidity and Mortality Weekly Report*, 53(08): 169–71 [Web]. Accessed 6 June 2007. http://www.cdc.gov/mmwr/preview/mmwrhtml/mm5308a1.htm

Gerasimov, M.M. (1968) *The face finder*. London: Hutchinson and Co.

Gill, P., Ivanov, P.L., Kimpton, C., Piercy, R., Benson, N., Tully, G., Evett, I., Hagelberg, E. and Sullivan, K. (1994)' Identification of the remains of the Romanov family by DNA analysis', *Nature Genet*, 6: 130–5.

Goldstein, I., Reece, E. and Hobbins, J. (1988) 'Sonographic appearance of the fetal heel ossifications centers and foot length measurements provide independent markers of gestational age estimation', *Amer J Obst Gynecol*, 159: 923–26.

Green, M.A. and Evison, M.P. (1999) 'Interpolating between computerized three-dimensional forensic facial simulations', *J Forensic Sci*, 44(6): 1224–8.

Guimarães, M.A. (2003) 'The challenge of identifying deceased individuals in Brazil: from dictatorship to DNA analysis', *Sci Just*, 43(4): 215–8.

Gustafson, G. (1950) 'Age determination on teeth', *J Am Dent Assoc*, 41: 45–54.

Haglund, W.D. and Sorg, M.H. (1997) *Forensic taphonomy: the postmortem fate of human remains*. Boca Raton, FL: CRC Press.

Hefti, E., Trechsel, U., Rüfenacht, H. and Fleisch, H. (1980) 'Use of dermestid beetles for cleaning bones', *Calcified Tissue Int*, 31(1): 45–7.

Hershkovitz, I., Latimer, B., Dutour, O., Jellema, L.M., Wish-Baratz, S., Rothschild, C. and Rothschild, B.M. (1997) 'Why do we fail in aging the skull from the sagittal suture?' *Amer J Phys Anthropol*, 103(3): 393–9.

Hiller, J.C., Thompson, T.J.U., Evison, M.P., Chamberlain, A.T. and Wess, T.J. (2003) 'Bone mineral change during experimental heating: an X-ray scattering investigation', *Biomaterials*, 24(28): 5091–7.

Hillson, S. (1986) *Teeth*. Cambridge: Cambridge University Press.

Huda, T.F.J. and Bowman, J.E. (1995) 'Age determination from dental microstructure in juveniles', *Amer J Phys Anthropol* 97: 135–50.

Hunter, J., Roberts, C. and Martin, A. (1996) *Studies in crime: an introduction to forensic archaeology*. London: Batsford.

Huxley, A.K. (1998) 'Comparability of gestational age values derived from diaphyseal length and foot length from known forensic foetal remains', *Med Sci Law*, 38(1): 42–51.

Işcan, M.Y. and Kennedy, K.A.R. (1989) (eds) *Reconstruction of life from the skeleton*. New York: Alan R. Liss.

Işcan, M.Y. and Loth, S.R. (1986) 'Estimation of age and determination of sex from the sternal rib', pp. 68–89, in K.J. Reichs (ed.) *Forensic osteology: advances in the identification of human remains*. Springfield, IL: Charles C. Thomas.

Işcan, M.Y. and Loth, S.R. (1989) 'Osteological manifestations of age in the adult', pp. 23–40, in M.Y. Işcan and K.A.R. Kennedy (eds) *Reconstruction of life from the skeleton*. New York: Alan R. Liss.

Işcan, M.Y., and Miller-Shaivitz, P. (1986) 'Sexual dimorphism in the femur and tibia', pp. 101–111, in K.J. Reichs (ed.) *Forensic osteology: advances in the identification of human remains*. Springfield, IL: Charles C. Thomas.

Işcan, M.Y., Loth, S.R. and Wright, R.K. (1985) 'Age estimation from the rib by phase analysis: white females', *J Forensic Sci*, 30(3): 853–63.

Işcan, M.Y., Loth, S.R. and Wright, R.K. (1987) 'Racial variation in the sternal extremity of the rib and its effect on age determination', *J Forensic Sci*, 32(2): 452–66.

Jantz, R.L. (2001) 'Cranial changes in Americans: 1850–1975', *J Forensic Sci*, 46: 784–7.

Jeffreys, A.J., Allen, M.J., Hagelberg, E. and Sonnberg, A. (1992) 'Identification of the skeletal remains of Josef Mengele by DNA analysis', *For Sci Int*, 56: 65–76.

Jobling, M.A. and Gill, P. (2004) 'Encoded evidence: DNA in forensic samples', *Nat Rev Genet*, 5(10): 739–51.

Johanson, G. (1971) 'Age determinations from human teeth', *Odontologisk Revy*, 22 (Suppt): 27–39.

Johnston, F.E. and Zimmer, L.O. (1989) 'Assessment of growth and age in the immature skeleton', pp. 11–21, in M.Y. Işcan and K.A.R. Kennedy (eds), *Reconstruction of life from the skeleton*. New York: Alan R. Liss.

JPAC (2008) Joint POW/MIA Accounting Command. JPAC [Web]. Accessed 29 August 2008. http://www.jpac.pacom.mil/

Kerley, E.R. and Ubelaker, D.H. (1978) 'Revisions in the microscopic method of estimating age at death in human cortical bone', *Amer J Phys Anthropol*, 49: 545–6.

Key, C.A., Aiello, L.C. and Molleson, T. (2005) 'Cranial suture closure and its implications for age estimation', *Int J Osteoarchaeol*, 4(3): 193–207.

Killam, E.W. (1990) *The Detection of Human Remains*. Springfield: Charles C. Thomas.

Kimura, K. (1992) 'Estimation of age at death from second metacarpals', *Zeitshr Morphol Anthropol* 79(2): 169–181.

Knight, B. (1996) *Forensic pathology*. London: Arnold.

Kreitner, K.F., Schweden, F.J., Reipert, T., Nafe, B. and Thelen, M. (1998) 'Bone age determination based on the study of the medial extremity of the clavicle', *Eur Radiol* 8 (7): 1116–22.

Krogman, W.M. and Işcan, M.Y. (1986) *The human skeleton in forensic medicine*. Springfield, IL: Charles C. Thomas.

Leutert, G. (1974) 'Alternsveränderungen im Bereich des Schenkelhalses aus morphologischer Sicht', *Beitr Orthopäd*, 21: 457–62.

Lovejoy, C.O. (1985) 'Dental wear in the Libben population: its functional pattern and role in the determination of adult skeletal age at death', *Amer J Phys Anthropol*, 68: 47–56.

Lovejoy, C.O., Meindl, R.S., Mensforth, R.P. and Barton, T.J. (1985a) 'Multifactorial determination of skeletal age at death: a method and blind tests of its accuracy', *Amer J Phys Anthropol*, 68: 1–14.

Lovejoy, C.O., Meindl, R.S., Pryzbeck, T.R. and Mensforth, R.P. (1985b) 'Chronological metamorphosis of the auricular surface of the ilium: a new method for the determination of adult skeletal age at death', *Amer J Phys Anthropol*, 68: 15–28.

Macho, G. (1986) 'An appraisal of plastic reconstruction of the external nose', *J Forensic Sci*, 31: 1391–403.

Macho, G. (1989) 'Descriptive morphological features of the nose – an assessment of their importance for plastic reconstruction', *J Forensic Sci*, 34: 1021–36.

Mann, R.W., Symes, S.A. and Bass, W.M. (1987) 'Maxillary suture obliteration: aging the human skeleton based on intact or fragmentary maxilla', *J Forensic Sci*, 32(1): 148–57.

March, J., Schofield, D., Evison, M.P. and Woodford, N. (2004) 'Three-dimensional computer visualization of forensic pathology data', *Amer J Forensic Med Pathol*, 25(1): 60–70.

McKern, T.W. and Stewart, T.D. (1957) 'Skeletal age changes in young American males', Technical Report EP-45. Natick, MA: US Army Quartermaster Research and Development Center, Environmental Protection Research Division.

Meindl, R.S. and Lovejoy, C.O. (1985) 'Ectocranial suture closure: a revised method for the determination of skeletal age at death based on the lateral-anterior sutures', *Amer J Phys Anthropol*, 68: 57–66.

Meindl, R.S., Lovejoy, C.O. and Mensforth, R.P. (1985a) 'A revised method of age determination using the Os pubis, with a review and tests of accuracy of the other current methods of pubic symphyseal ageing', *Amer J Phys Anthropol*, 68: 29–45.

Meindl, R.S., Lovejoy, C.O., Mensforth, R.P. and Carlos, L.D. (1985b) 'Accuracy and direction of error in sexing of the skeleton, implications for paleodemography', *Amer J Phys Anthropol*, 68: 79–85.

Mensforth, R.P. and Lovejoy, C.O. (1985) 'Anatomical, physiological, and epidemiological correlates of the ageing process: a confirmation of multifactorial age determination in the Libben skeletal population', *Amer J Phys Anthropol*, 68: 87–106.

Mercer, B., Sklar, S., Shariatmadar, A., Gillieson, M. and D'Alton, M. (1987) 'Fetal foot length as a predictor of gestational age', *Amer J Obst Gynecol*, 156: 350–5.

Miyasaka, S., Yoshino, M., Imaizumi, K. and Seta, S. (1995) 'The computer-aided facial reconstruction system', *Forensic Sci Int*, 74(1–2): 155–65.

Mulhern, D.M. and Ubelaker, D.H. (2001) 'Differences in osteon banding between human and non-human bone', *J Forensic Sci*, 46: 220–2.

Novotný, V., Isçan, M.Y. and Loth, S.R. (1993) 'Morphologic and osteometric assessment of age, sex, and race from the skull', pp. 71–88, in M.Y. Isçan, and R.P. Helmer, (eds), *Forensic analysis of the skull*. New York: Wiley-Liss.

Ogino, T. and Ogino, H. (1988) 'Application to forensic odontology of aspartic acid racemization in unerupted and supernumerary teeth', *J Dental Res*, 67 (10): 1319–22.

Ogino, T., Ogino, N. and Nagy, B. (1985) 'Application of aspartic acid racemization to forensic odontology: postmortem designation of age at death', *For Sci Int*, 29: 259–67.

Olivier, G. and Pineau, H. (1958) 'Détermination de l'age du foetus et de l'embryon', *Arch D'Anatomie (La Semaine des Hôpitaux)* 6: 21–8.

Olivier, G. and Pineau, H. (1960) 'Nouvelle détermination de la taille foetale d'après les longueurs diaphysaires des os longs', *Ann Méd Légale*, 40: 141–4.

ORAU (2007) 'Radiocarbon dating in forensic science', Oxford Radiocarbon Accelerator Unit [Web]. Accessed 6 June 2007. http://c14.arch.ox.ac.uk/embed.php?File=leaf_forensic.html

Ousley S.D. and Jantz, R.L. (2005) 'The next FORDISC: FORDISC 3', *Proc Amer Acad Forensic Sci*, 11: 294–5.

Pfeifer, H., Mornstad, H. and Teivens, A. (1995a) 'Estimation of chronologic age using the aspartic acid racemization method. I: On human rib cartilage', *Int J Legal Med*, 108 (1): 19–23.

Pfeifer, H., Mornstad, H. and Teivens, A. (1995b) 'Estimation of chronologic age using the aspartic acid racemization method II: On human cortical bone', *Int J Legal Med*, 108 (1): 24–6.

Pocock, N., Eisman, J., Gwinn, T., Sambrook, P., Kelly, P., Freund, J. and Yeates, M. (1989) 'Muscle strength, physical fitness, and weight but not age predict femoral neck bone mass', *J Bone Mineral Res*, 4 (3): 441–8.

Powers, R. (1962) 'The disparity between known age and age as estimated by cranial suture closure', *Man* 62: 52–4.

Prag, A.J.N.W. and Neave, R. (1999) *Making faces: using forensic and archaeological evidence* (2nd edn). London: British Museum Press.

Rathbun, T.A. and Buikstra, J.E. (1984) *Human identification – case studies in forensic anthropology*. Springfield, IL: Charles C. Thomas.

Reichs, K.J. (1986) (ed.) *Forensic osteology: advances in the identification of human remains*. Springfield, IL: Charles C. Thomas.

Ritz, S., Schultz, H.W. and Schwarzer, B. (1990) 'The extent of aspartic acid racemization in dentine: a possible method for a more accurate determination of age at death?' *Zeitschr für Rechtsmedizin*, 103 (6): 457–62.

Roberts, C.A. and Manchester, K. (2007) *The archaeology of disease* (3rd edn]. New York: Cornell University Press.

Rogers, T.L. (1999) 'A visual method of determining the sex of skeletal remains using the distal humerus', *J Forensic Sci*, 44(1): 57–60.

Saul, F.P. and Saul, J.M. (1989) 'Osteobiography: A Maya Example', pp. 287–302, in M.Y. Işcan and K.A.R. Kennedy (eds), *Reconstruction of life from the skeleton*. New York: Alan R. Liss.

Saul, F.P. and Saul, J.M. (2002) 'Forensics, archaeology and taphonomy: the symbiotic relationship', pp. 71–98, in: W.D. Haglund and M.H. Sorg (eds), *Advances in forensic taphonomy: method, theory and archaeological perspectives*. Boca Raton, FL: CRC Press.

Saul, F.P. and Saul, J.M. (2005) ' "The game is afoot!" – feet help solve forensic puzzles in the United States and Overseas', pp. 359–74, in J. Rich, D.E. Dean and R.H. Powers (eds), *Forensic Science and Medicine Forensic Medicine of the lower extremity: human identification and trauma analysis of the thigh, leg and foot*. Totowa, NJ: Humana Press 359-74.

Saul, F.P., Sledzik, P.S. and Saul, J.M. (2002) 'The Disaster Mortuary Operational Response Team (DMORT) model for managing mass fatality incidents (MFIs) in the United States of America (with special emphasis on the role of the forensic anthropologist)', *Revista Colombiana de Ciencias Forenses*, 1: 66–73.

Scheuer, L. and Black, S. (2000) *Developmental juvenile osteology*. London: Academic Press.

Schranz, D. (1959) 'Age determination from the internal structure of the humerus', *Amer J Phys Anthropol*, 17: 273–8.

Schwartz, J.H. (2007) *Skeleton keys: an introduction to human skeletal morphology, development and analysis* (2nd edn). Oxford: Oxford University Press.

Stephan, C.N. (2001) 'Building faces from dry skulls: are they recognised above chance rates?', *J Forensic Sci*, 46 (3): 432–40.

Stephan, C.N. (2002) 'Do resemblance ratings measure the accuracy of facial approximation?', *J Forensic Sci*, 47 (2): 239–43.

Stephan, C.N. (2003) 'Facial approximation: an evaluation of mouth-width determination', *Amer J Phys Anthropol*, 121(1): 48–57.

Stephan, C.N. (2006) 'Beyond the Sphere of the English Facial Approximation Literature: Ramifications of German Papers on Western Method Concepts', *J Forensic Sci*, 51(4): 736–9.

Stoeckle, M. (2003) 'Taxonomy, DNA, and the bar code of life', *BioScience*, 53: 2–3.

Stout, S.D. (1988) 'The use of histomorphology to estimate age', *J Forensic Sci*, 33 (1): 121–5.

Stout, S.D. (1989) 'Histomorphometric analysis of human skeletal remains', pp. 41–52, in M.Y. Işcan and K.A.R. Kennedy, (eds), *Reconstruction of life from the skeleton*. New York: Alan R. Liss.

Stowens, D. (1966) *Pediatric Pathology*. Baltimore: Williams, Wilkins.

Suchey, J.M. and Katz, D. (1986) 'Skeletal age standards derived from an extensive multi-racial sample of modern Americans', *Amer J Phys Anthropol*, 69: 269 (abstr.).

Suchey, J.M. and Katz, D. (1997) 'Applications of pubic age determination in a forensic setting', pp. 204–36, in K.J. Reichs (ed.), Forensic osteology: advances in the identification of human remains. Springfield, IL: Charles C. Thomas.

Suchey, J.M., Wiseley, D.V. and Katz, D. (1986) 'Evaluation of the Todd and McKern-Stewart methods for ageing the male Os pubis', pp. 36–67, in K.J. Reichs (ed.) *Forensic osteology: advances in the identification of human remains*. Springfield, IL: Charles C. Thomas.

Swift, J. (1735) *Gulliver's Travels* (reissue edition 1999). London: Signet Classics.

Symes, S.A., Williams, J.A., Murray, E.A., Hoffman, J.M., Holland, T.D., Saul, J.M., Saul, F.P. and Pope, E.J. (2002) 'Taphonomic context of sharp-force trauma in suspected cases of human mutilation and dismemberment', pp. 403–34, in W.D. Haglund and M.H. Sorg (eds), *Advances in forensic taphonomy: method, theory and archaeological perspectives*. Boca Raton, FL: CRC Press.

Todd, T.W. (1920) 'Age changes in the pubic bone: I. The male white pubis', *Amer J Phys Anthropol* 3: 285–334.

Todd, T.W. (1921) 'Age changes in the pubic bone: II. The pubis of the male Negro-white hybrid; III. The pubis of the white female; IV. The pubis of the female Negro-white hybrid', *Amer J Phys Anthropol*, 4: 1–70.

Tyrrell, A.J., Evison, M.P., Chamberlain, A.T. and Green, M.A. (1997) 'Forensic three-dimensional facial reconstruction: historical review and contemporary developments', *J Forensic Sci* 42(4): 653–61.

Ubelaker, D.H. (1987) 'Estimating age at death from immature human skeletons: an overview', *J Forensic Sci*, 32: 1254–63.

Ubelaker, D.H. (1989) *Human skeletal remains: excavation, analysis, interpretation*. Washington, DC: Taraxacum.

Vanezis, P., Blowes, R.W., Linney, A.D., Tan, A.C., Richards, R. and Neave, R. (1989) 'Application of 3-D computer graphics for facial reconstruction and comparison with sculpting techniques', *For Sci Int*, 42: 69–84.

Walker, R.A. and Lovejoy, C.O. (1985) 'Radiographic changes in the clavicle and the proximal femur and their use in the determination of skeletal age at death', *Amer J Phys Anthropol* 68: 67–78.

Weaver, D.S. (1986) 'Forensic aspects of fetal and neonatal specimens', pp. 90–100, in K.J. Reichs (ed.) *Forensic osteology: advances in the identification of human remains*. Springfield, IL: Charles C. Thomas.

White, T.D. and Folkens, P.A. (1991) *Human osteology*. San Diego, CA: Academic Press.

White, T.D. and Folkens, P.A. (2005). *The human bone manual*. Burlington, MA: Elsevier Academic Press.

Wilkinson, C. (2004) *Forensic facial reconstruction*. Cambridge: Cambridge University Press.

Wittwer-Backofen, U., Gampe, J and Vaupel, J.W. (2004) 'Tooth cementum annulation for age estimation: results from a large age-know validation study', *Amer J Phys Anthropol*, 123(2): 119–29.

Xiaohu, X., Philipsen, H.P., Jablonski, N.G., Pang, K.M. and Jiazhen, Z. (1992) 'Age estimation from the structure of adult human teeth: review of the literature', *For Sci Int*, 54: 23–8.

**Section 2**

# Identifying and comparing materials

# Chapter 5

# Drugs of abuse

*Niamh Nic Daéid and Hilary Buchanan*

## Introduction

The aim of this chapter is to give the reader a brief introduction to the types of illicit drugs currently encountered and some background to their production and analysis. This is both in terms of identification (qualitative analysis) and purity (quantification). We also wish to draw to the attention of the reader some of the difficulties associated with drug analysis such as the methods of sampling large drug seizures and the chemical characterisation of drugs (drug profiling) including the robustness of the information it can provide. Finally we wish to present some insight into the new technologies available to drug analysts.

According to the United Nations Office on Drugs and Crime (UNODC), the global illicit drug trade is worth (US) $322 billion and impacts almost every level of human security, from individual health to safety and social welfare (2005). The drugs in question come from a wide range of sources, both through clandestine chemical synthesis and through chemical modifications of natural products. The complexity of controlling the global drug problem was addressed in the 2005 annual report of the International Narcotics Control Board (INCB). The illicit drug manufacturing process is often an elaborate network of clandestine laboratories, each one responsible for a different stage of the process such as obtaining or synthesising precursors, production of the illicit drug, tabletting or packaging, and dumping of waste. Ecstasy tablets in Europe, for instance, may be synthesised (as MDMA powder) in Belgium and the Netherlands, and then transported to Portugal for tabletting (Europol 2006). The separation of sites affords a layer of protection to the criminal groups; if the authorities shut down one clandestine site, another one in the chain can fill the gap so that the production process will continue relatively unhindered.

Fortunately, the spreading out of the manufacturing process may also benefit the authorities. Separation of sites necessitates trafficking between them, and the more often a drug is in transit, the greater the opportunity for its seizure.

The importance of discovering these trafficking routes is, therefore, vital for the control and containment of the world drug problem.

## Natural products

### Cannabis

The botanical name of cannabis is *cannabis sativa*. It is often referred to as marijuana or grass (herbal cannabis) and hashish or hash (cannabis resin). Cannabis grows over a wide variety of geographic terrains, altitudes and latitudes and is native to the mountainous areas of central and south Asia. Although the plant prefers the higher temperatures and longer growing seasons of the equatorial areas, it has been cultivated as far north as 60 degrees latitude. Approximately 40 million Europeans use cannabis each year, with an estimated one in four 15–34-year-olds having smoked cannabis either as herbal material or cannabis resin.

A number of forms of the drug may be encountered, including plant material, resin and 'hash oil'. The active ingredient in all of these formulations is $\Delta^9$-tetrahydrocannabinol ($\Delta^9$-THC, Figure 5.1). Also found is $\Delta^9$-tetrahydrocannabinolic acid, which is converted to $\Delta^9$-THC through smoking, and the compounds $\Delta^8$-tetrahydrocannabinol ($\Delta^8$-THC), cannabidiol (the precursor of $\Delta^9$-THC), and cannabinol (the degradation product of $\Delta^9$-THC).

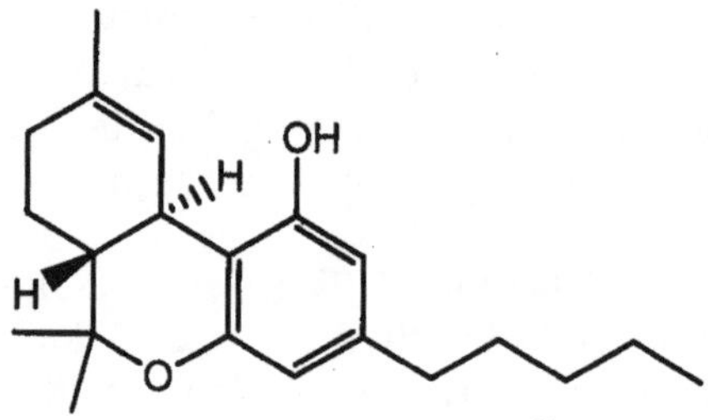

**Figure 5.1**  Structure of $\Delta^9$-THC

It is estimated that 20,000 to 30,000 tons of cannabis are produced worldwide per annum. Southern Africa (South Africa, Lesotho, Malawi and Swaziland) is one of the biggest producing regions, far exceeding that of Morocco which used to be the world leader in production. Most of the cannabis grown in this part of the world is intended for local consumption, although large shipments are also sent to Europe and North America. Mexico, the biggest cannabis producing country in the Americas, is the primary supplier of herbal cannabis to the United States. Jamaica supplies large quantities of cannabis to Canada, either directly or through the United States.

Most resin is brought in through Spain from Morocco, with lesser amounts transported from Pakistan, Afghanistan and Central Asia via Eastern Europe. Herbal cannabis originates mainly from Columbia, Jamaica, and Africa (South Africa, Nigeria and Ghana) and is transported by sea into Spain and Portugal for distribution throughout Europe.

*Fresh plant material*
The plant grows from 30 cm to 6 m in height and reaches maturity in about three months. Leaves are coated with various different types of hairs called trichomes, some of which contain the THC. The greatest concentration of THC-rich trichomes is in the flowering tops of the plants, and those of the female plant have a greater concentration than those of the male. In recent years, the increase in hydroponic growth of cannabis has resulted in the predominance of flowering female plants and a product with a much higher THC content (so called 'skunk' cannabis).

Low-quality dried plant material generally contains stalks, seeds, leaves and flowering tops, which may be compressed into blocks or left loose. High-quality material contains mostly flowering tops.

*Resin (hashish)*
Some of the trichomes produce a resin which is scraped from the surface of the plant and pressed into blocks. Cannabis resin typically contains about 2–10 per cent by weight of $\Delta^9$-THC. When examining resin, several observations are recorded, such as colour and layers within the resin block, whether or not the seized blocks fit together, or the presence of striation marks (cutting marks) which might be linked to a cutting instrument.

*Hash oil*
Hash oil is produced by extracting the whole plant material using a solvent (such as alcohol). On extraction, the resulting oil can contain between 10–30 per cent by weight of $\Delta^9$-THC. The oil is used in various ways, including smoking with tobacco.

## Tryptamines and mushrooms

Tryptamines is the generic name given to a group of alkaloids which occur naturally in approximately 1,500 plants and other life forms from around the world. Dimethyltryptamine, or DMT (Figure 5.2), is of particular interest as it is the active component in various forms of South American snuff, known as YOPO or COHOBA, and has been the subject of synthetic production and consequent abuse.

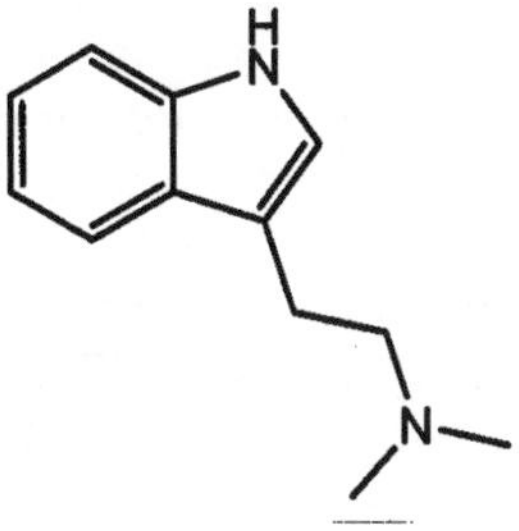

**Figure 5.2**   Structure of DMT

Psilocybin and psilocin (Figure 5.3) are derived primarily from various species of mushrooms which belong to the genus *psilocybe, panaeolus* and *conocybe*. The examination of a seizure containing mushrooms involves the characterisation of the plant including shape, size, colour and any parts which may be present.

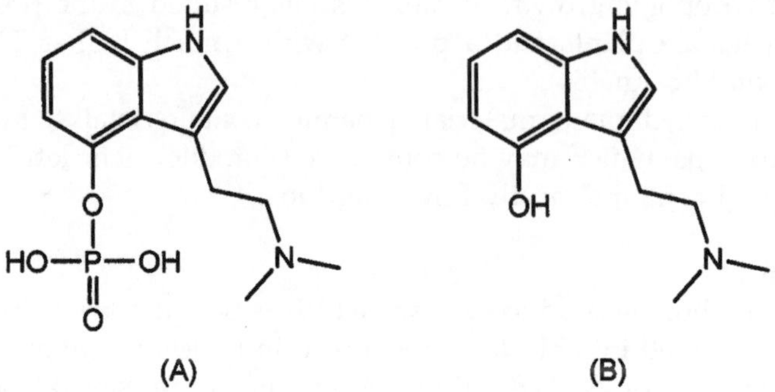

**Figure 5.3** Structures of psilocybin (A) and psilocin (B)

Illicit trafficking of cacti, which contain the psychoactive agent mescaline (Figure 5.4), is also known. This drug occurs in at least three species of cacti.

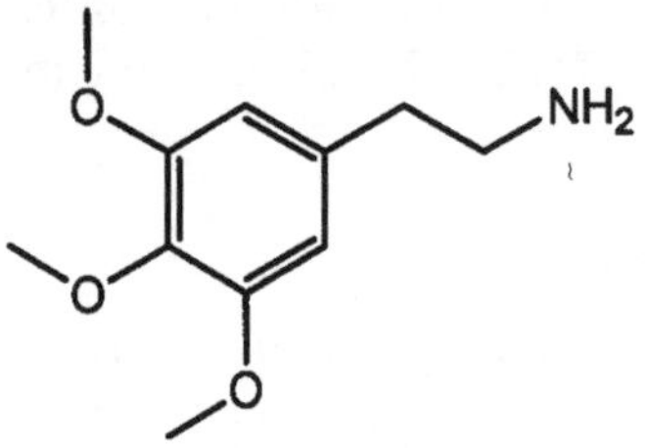

**Figure 5.4** Structure of mescaline

## Semi-synthetic drugs

### Heroin

Diamorphine, the main constituent of heroin, is a semi-synthetic drug derived from opium, which comes from the poppy (*papaver somniferum*). Opium contains a number of alkaloids, such as morphine, thebaine, papaverine, codeine and noscapine. Morphine can be extracted and converted to diamorphine (Figure 5.5). In the UK, 'heroin' is the term used to refer to powder sold on the street containing diamorphine (Strathclyde Police 2006). Many regions of the world, however, use the terms 'heroin' and 'diamorphine' synonymously.

Often associated with human trafficking (Europol 2006), heroin continues to be a major drug of abuse, with Asia having the largest number of heroin abusers and accounting for almost half of the global total (United Nations Office on Drugs and Crime 2006a). Although heroin abuse in western and

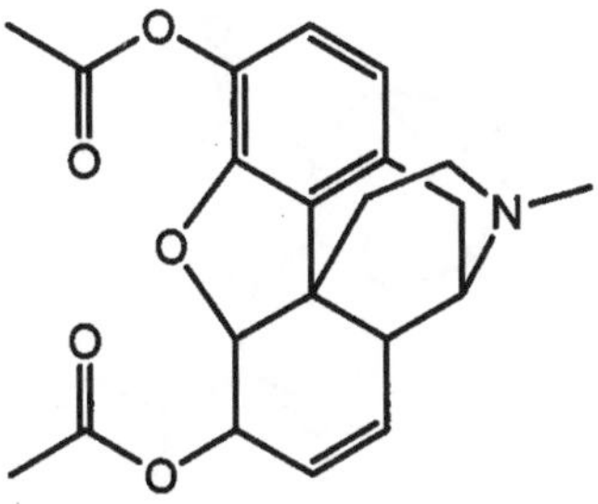

**Figure 5.5** Structure of diamorphine

central Europe has been stable over the past few years, the number of heroin abusers in Europe as a whole is estimated to be larger than in the Americas. The UNODC reports that eastern Europe now has more heroin abusers than both western and central Europe combined (United Nations Office on Drugs and Crime 2006a).

Ninety per cent of opiates[1] in Europe originate in Afghanistan, and they are primarily trafficked via the Balkan Route with two-way traffic occurring as MDMA is exported from Europe along this path (Europol 2006; United Nations Office on Drugs and Crime 2006a). According to Interpol, the Balkan Route has developed into three arms, all originating in Turkey. The southern route progresses via Greece, Albania and Italy; the central route exploits Bulgaria and the Former Yugoslav Republic of Macedonia (FYROM), Serbia and Montenegro, Bosnia and Herzegovina, Croatia, Slovenia, and Italy or Austria; and the northern route utilises Bulgaria and Romania to Hungary, Austria, the Czech Republic, and Poland or Germany (Interpol 2005).

Other routes are emerging for heroin trafficking from this region of the world. The Silk Route, which originates in Afghanistan and progresses through Central Asia and the Russian Federation into Europe, facilitates two-way traffic as heroin precursors are trafficked back to Afghanistan (Europol 2006). A further heroin trafficking route was reported in 2004 which was by air from Pakistan, and approximately 25 per cent of heroin in the United Kingdom is reported to enter the country in this way (United Nations Office on Drugs and Crime 2005).

### Cocaine

Cocaine (Figure 5.6) is a semi-synthetic drug produced from the South American coca plant (*erythroxylon*). 'Crack' cocaine is cocaine base, and the salt form of the drug is sometimes called 'snow' cocaine (King 2003).

Cocaine is produced primarily in three countries in the Andean region: Columbia, Peru and Bolivia. Ninety-nine percent of the global total was reported by these three countries. The processing of coca leaf into coca paste/base and then the final product, cocaine, usually occurs near the cultivation sites. Cocaine seizures have risen steadily over the last few decades. This increase is reportedly due to better sharing of intelligence information and cooperation between law enforcement agencies (United Nations Office on Drugs and Crime 2006a).

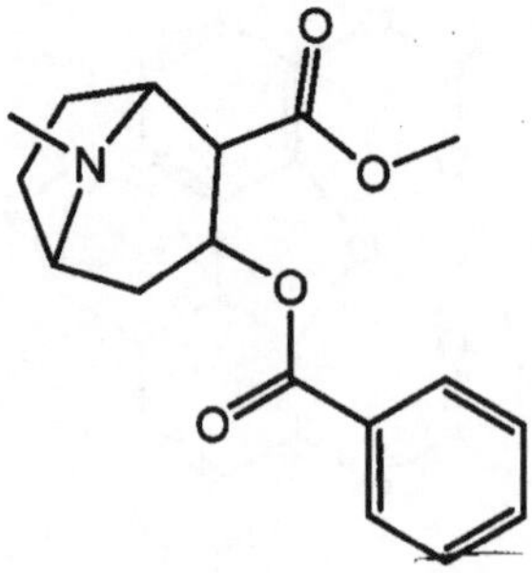

**Figure 5.6** Structure of cocaine

Cocaine is often concealed within the packaging or goods of legitimate consignments, such as coffee beans, or within the body of a vehicle (Europol 2006). For example, the United States estimates that 70 per cent of cocaine exported from Peru leaves the country by sea in legitimate consignments (United Nations Office on Drugs and Crime 2006a). Common means of transportation include speedboats, cargo freighters or container ships, but consignments can also be dropped into international waters by aircraft (Europol 2006).

### Lysergic acid diethylamide (LSD)

Lysergic acid diethylamide (LSD, Figure 5.7) is a semi-synthetic drug first synthesised in 1938. The starting materials are lysergic acid compounds of ergot, a spore capsule of a parasite mushroom. On the illicit drug market, LSD has been sold in the form of impregnated paper (blotters/trips), microdots, thin squares of gelatine (window panes), or impregnated on sugar cubes. Stamps or blotters are the common dose form. These papers are 'trade marked' with various designs.

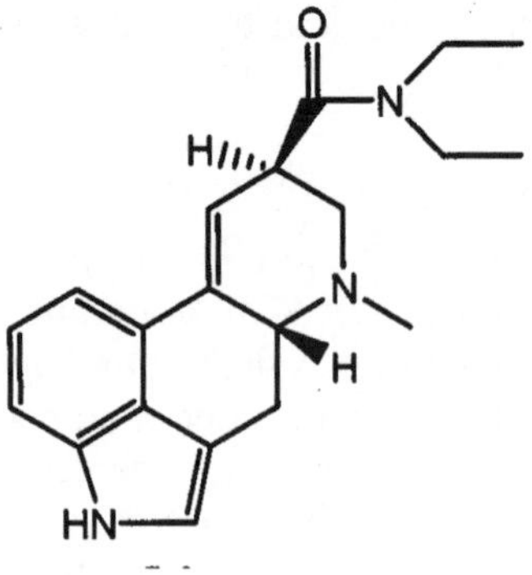

**Figure 5.7** Structure of LSD

## Synthetic drugs

### Phenethylamines – ecstasy and amphetamines

According to Europol's *Drugs 2006* report, the 'production and trafficking of drugs are the main activities of criminal groups in the European Union'. Cannabis, amphetamine and ecstasy[2] (Figure 5.8) are the most widely abused drugs in the European Union. Indeed, Europe is the major supplier of ecstasy worldwide (United Nations Office on Drugs and Crime 2006a). The most significant European ecstasy laboratories are located in Belgium and the Netherlands with Belgian and Dutch criminal groups controlling production and distribution (Europol 2006). Belgium and the Netherlands are the two countries most often cited by other countries as their main source of ecstasy.

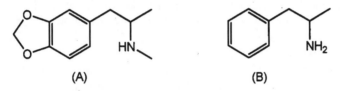

(A)                                    (B)

**Figure 5.8** Structures of MDMA (A) and amphetamine (B)

In 2000, 75 per cent of dismantled ecstasy laboratories were in Europe; in 2004 this had dropped to 23 per cent. Eighty-one per cent of the worldwide ecstasy seizures in 1994 were in Europe compared with 53 per cent in 2004 (United Nations Office on Drugs and Crime 2006a). The frequency of substantial ecstasy seizures in the European Union declined in 2005, perhaps as a result of a waning supply of the drug due to effective control of precursor chemicals.

The UNODC reports an increase in 2004 for the production of ecstasy worldwide: global ecstasy seizures rose by 87 per cent, and global precursor seizures rose by 113 per cent (United Nations Office on Drugs and Crime 2006a). This latter figure is reportedly due to seizures of PMK, the major precursor for the manufacture of ecstasy. PMK (piperonylmethylketone or 3,4-methylenedioxyphenyl-2-propanone) can be synthesised from safrole or isosafrole, and these are often referred to as 'pre-precursors' for ecstasy. Most ecstasy precursors are seized in east and south-east Asia, Europe and North America.

The apparent decrease in European ecstasy production in the face of a global increase in production can be explained by production increases in other parts of the world. According to the UNODC, approximately, 48 per cent of dismantled ecstasy laboratories were located in the United States and Canada (United Nations Office on Drugs and Crime 2005). The growing popularity of ecstasy in North America is also confirmed by an increase in precursor seizures. The spread of ecstasy manufacture to the rest of the world is similarly revealed by the shutdown of clandestine labs in recent years in south-east Asia, Oceania, Africa and parts of South America (United Nations Office on Drugs and Crime 2006a).

The trafficking of ecstasy within Europe has historically been controlled by many small criminal groups who buy the illicit drug(s) in Holland and Belgium and transport the substance(s) to other European distribution centres (United Nations Office on Drugs and Crime 2006a), facilitated by differing legislation and the abolition of internal border control among EU member states (Europol 2006). European ecstasy is also trafficked internationally, with North America and Asia seen as large consumer markets (Europol 2006; United Nations Office on Drugs and Crime 2006a).

### Barbiturates and benzodiazepines

Barbiturates are therapeutically used as sedatives, hypnotics, anaesthetics and anti-convulsants. Virtually all barbiturates on the illicit drug market come from licit sources. There are 12 barbiturates recognised and scheduled by the United Nations. They occur mainly as capsules or tablets and in some cases as injectable solutions. Seized illicit barbiturates are often mixed with other substances, such as caffeine, codeine or even heroin, but they may also be mixed with other barbiturates.

Benzodiazepines were introduced to replace barbiturates and methaqualone as tranquillisers, hypnotics, anti-convulsants and muscle relaxants. Currently there are 33 benzodiazepines on the control list, all of which appear as tablets or capsules, though some also appear as liquids or powders for preparation for injection. As with barbiturates, benzodiazepines appear to be diverted from the licit market rather than synthesised in clandestine laboratories. Various benzodiazepines show more prominence on the illicit market than others; these are primarily temazepam, diazepam (Valium) and flunitrazepam (Rohypnol, Figure 5.9).

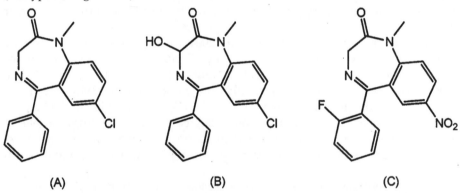

(A)  (B)  (C)

**Figure 5.9** Structures of diazepam (A), temazepam (B) and flunitrazepam (C)

### Methaqualone and mecloqualone

Methaqualone (Figure 5.10) and mecloqualone were prepared as nonbarbiturate sleeping tablets, though they have also legally been used as hypnotics in some European countries. They appear on the illicit drug market either through diversion from the legitimate pharmaceutical trade or through illicit synthesis. The illicit samples are usually brown or grey powders with varying degrees of purity. Methaqualone is used sometimes as a cutting agent for heroin.

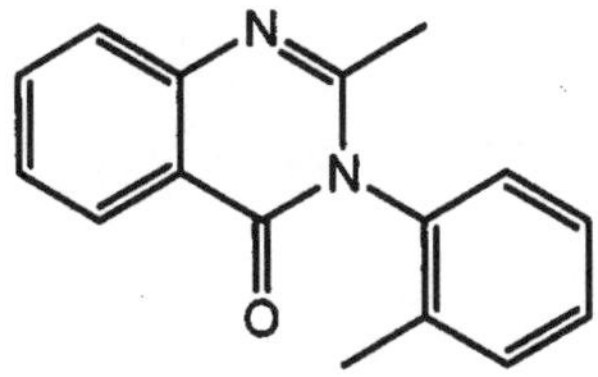

**Figure 5.10** Structure of methaqualone

## Phencyclidine (PCP) and analogues

Phencyclidine (PCP, Figure 5.11), was synthesised in the early 1950s and eventually marketed as a veterinary anaesthetic. PCP entered the illicit drug market in the 1960s. The laboratory synthesis of the drug is relatively straightforward and the substance is most commonly obtained as a powder, crystalline material or tablet.

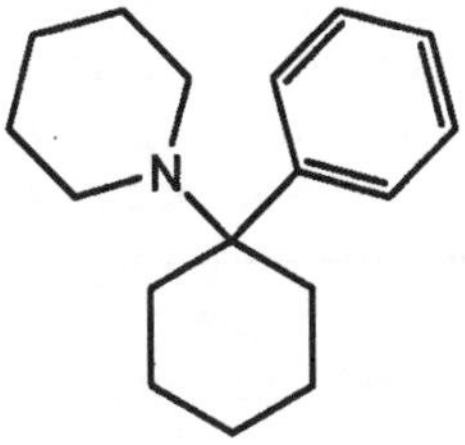

**Figure 5.11** Structure of PCP

A structurally related anaesthetic, ketamine (Special K, Figure 5.12), is sometimes encountered in ecstasy.

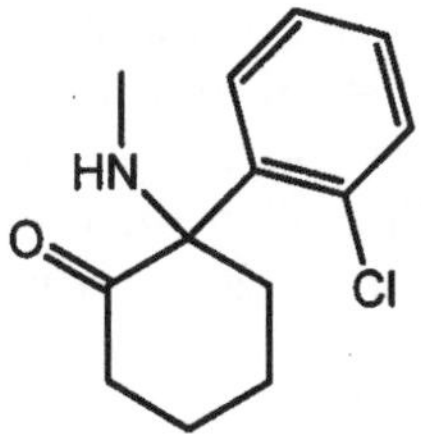

**Figure 5.12** Structure of ketamine

## Gamma hydroxybutyric acid (GHB)

Gamma hydroxybutyric acid (GHB, Figure 5.13) is the sodium salt of 4-gammahydroxybutyric acid and is easily synthesised by alkaline hydrolysis of gamma butyrolactone (GBL), a common industrial solvent.

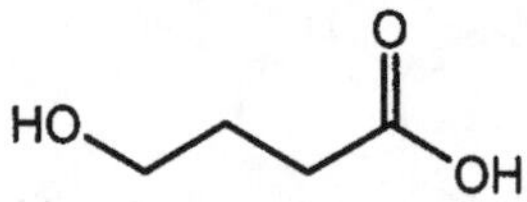

**Figure 5.13** Structure of GHB

## Law and legislation

A century ago, the international effects of the 'national' Chinese heroin problem were addressed with the creation of The Shanghai Opium Commission in 1909 (United Nations Office on Drugs and Crime 2006a). From this was derived the first mechanism for the international legislation of drugs, the Hague Opium Convention of 1912. Countries party to this convention were required to implement domestic legislation restricting drugs to medical use. The Shanghai Opium Commission and the Hague Opium Convention were the catalysts for international drug control as it is today.

Half a century later, the UN created the first of three major international drug control treaties which are currently in effect: the Single Convention on Narcotic Drugs 1961. As with any international convention, signatories are required to implement domestic legislation in accordance with the recommendations set out therein, and they are obligated to evaluate the policies against the international standard (United Nations Office on Drugs and Crime 2006a). More than 160 countries are party to these three treaties (International Narcotics Control Board 2004). The UN regularly names the countries who have not signed the treaties and continually urges them to do so (International Narcotics Control Board 2005).

The 1961 Single Convention on Narcotic Drugs was formed out of a need to combine many different nations' legislation on narcotic drugs into one primary instrument. It seeks to limit the manufacture, possession and use of drugs to science and medicine. Countries party to this convention are required to provide annual statistical returns and estimates for the use of and need for drugs covered by this convention. It also encourages international cooperation as a tool for fighting illicit international drug trafficking (United Nations Office on Drugs and Crime 2006b; United Nations 1961).

The second international treaty on drug control is the Convention on Psychotropic Substances 1971, which was written in response to the widening range of drugs of abuse. This convention establishes control over the use of psychotropic substances, including many synthetic drugs, based on their potential harm and therapeutic value (United Nations Office on Drugs and Crime 2006b; United Nations 1971).

In contrast to the 1961 and 1971 treaties which seek to limit the trade in and use of controlled substances to legitimate scientific and medical purposes, the third major treaty was formed in an effort to deal with the growing problem of drug trafficking. The Convention Against the Illicit Traffic in Narcotic Drugs and Psychotropic Substances 1988 provides for the extradition of drug traffickers, and it offers provision against money laundering and the divergence of precursors (United Nations Office on Drugs and Crime 2006b; United Nations 1988).

The effectiveness of this international drug control system is difficult to evaluate due to patchy data over the years; a concealed, illegal activity does not lend itself to simple quantitative monitoring. However, reports published annually by the UN now highlight the worldwide drug situation in yearly increments based in part on statistics provided by signatories to the major conventions.

## UK legislation

Two main pieces of legislation govern the use of controlled drugs in the UK. The Misuse of Drugs Act 1971 (MDA 1971) corresponds to the UN conventions and sets out what is *restricted* in relation to the listed substances. The details of control are specified in the Misuse of Drugs Regulations 2001 (MDR 2001), which explains what *can* be done with the listed substances (King 2003).

### The Misuse of Drugs Act 1971

The MDA 1971 introduced the concept of 'controlled drugs' and created the Advisory Council on the Misuse of Drugs. The Council's role is to advise the government on substances which are likely to be misused and are capable of posing a social problem (King 2003).

The MDA 1971 prohibits possession, possession with intent to supply, production (and allowing premises to be used for production), and import/ export of controlled drugs listed in Schedule 2 of the Act. Within Schedule 2, the substances are divided into three classes (A–C) based on their perceived capacity to cause social harm (King 2003).

Class A (Part I of Schedule 2) drugs carry the most severe penalty. They are defined to include (for example) cocaine, diamorphine, LSD, methadone, methamphetamine, morphine and psilocin. The penalty for possessing a Class A drug is imprisonment of up to seven years and/or an unlimited fine, and the penalty for supplying is up to life imprisonment and/or an unlimited fine. Amphetamine (unless prepared for injection, in which case it becomes Class A), codeine and methaqualone are Class B drugs. This class carries a penalty for possession of up to five years in prison and/or an unlimited fine. Penalty for supply is up to 14 years' imprisonment and/or an unlimited fine (King 2003). Examples of Class C drugs include cannabis and cannabis resin, diazepam, and ketamine. The penalty for possession of a Class C drug is up to two years in prison and/or an unlimited fine, and the penalty for supply is up to 14 years' imprisonment and/or an unlimited fine (King 2003).

The contents of each class are amended as necessary to reflect the changing opinion on controlled substances over time. For example, cannabis and cannabis resin were downgraded from Class B to Class C on 29 January 2004 (Office of Public Sector Information 2003), following a report in which cannabis was deemed less dangerous than other Class B drugs (Home Office 2006). On 18 January 2007, methamphetamine was reclassified from Class B to Class A (Office of Public Sector Information 2006).

A number of generic controls are also provided for in the MDA 1971. For example, stereoisomers, salts esters and ethers of controlled substances, unless specifically excluded by name, are controlled to the same degree as the parent molecule (King 2003).

*The Misuse of Drugs Regulations 2001*

Whilst the MDA 1971 details what should *not* be done with controlled substances, the MDR 2001 sets out what *can* be done. It divides controlled substances into five schedules (1–5) according to their value as medicines versus their potential for abuse. This piece of legislation controls the manufacture, prescription and record keeping of the listed substances (King 2003).

## Analysis of drugs of abuse

The analysis of suspected drugs of abuse occurs over a number of stages. Moreover, the particular technique or series of examinations required usually depends upon the requirements of the analysis. Generally this includes the identification or confirmation of the presence of a controlled substance. It may also include determining the quantity of a controlled substance present within the sample. Chemical profiling may also be undertaken in which synthetic by-products and/or reaction impurities within the sample are characterised with the aim of linking samples together. The preparation of the analytical space and the physical examination of the item, including its packaging, sampling strategy and the analysis required are all important aspects of the examination.

There are various analytical techniques commonly used in the forensic examination of suspected drugs, and these include presumptive testing (colour/spot tests), thin layer chromatography (TLC), high performance liquid chromatography (HPLC) and gas chromatography (GC) with either flame ionisation detector (FID) or mass spectrometer (MS). Other techniques such as Fourier transform infrared spectroscopy (FTIR), ultraviolet-visible spectroscopy (UV-vis) and Isotope ratio mass spectroscopy (IRMS) may occasionally be used in particular cases and circumstances. Not every technique will be used in each case; rather the most appropriate techniques will be chosen depending on the sample type/amount and the analysis requested.

Forensic drug analysis should also follow strict quality assurance mechanisms. In most forensic laboratories, the drug section's processes and protocols will be accredited to ISO 17025 or a similar standard. This will include a requirement to validate all of the analytical processes, including the determination of measurement uncertainty for the analytical measurements undertaken.

*Preparation of the analytical space*

One of the most important and fundamental parts of the examination of samples suspected of containing controlled substances is the initial preparation of the space where the analysis is to take place. Benches should be washed down with detergent and dried. Depending on laboratory operating procedures the bench may also be swabbed and the swabs retained for analysis if required. Fresh bench covering should be laid on the bench for each examination. Sample packages should be opened individually, and the bench should be cleaned and re-covered in between the opening of subsequent packages. Gloves must be changed frequently and such changes noted.

### Physical examination

Once drug samples are presented for examination, the packaging should be checked to ensure that it is intact. Any breach of the packaging should be reported and a decision taken as to whether the analysis of that item should continue.

Each item should be described fully (with diagrams if appropriate), including a description of colour, smell and any packaging materials which may be present. If there are logos (such as with ecstasy tablets) or marks on the items (for example, blocks of resin or packages of drugs), these should be fully described and possibly photographed. Microscopic examination may also be used to examine the morphological characteristics of the material. This includes descriptions of different types of crystals or other solids which may be present, the structure of tablets, the presence of different types of trichomes in plant material, and so on.

The analytical strategy undertaken will depend upon whether that item is considered a bulk or trace sample. A trace sample is considered to be one which is barely visible to the naked eye. Trace samples may be present on the insides of reaction vessels, scales, knives and other drug paraphernalia. In many cases, trace samples are swabbed from these items and analysed using confirmatory chromatographic techniques. Such samples are very easily contaminated, and care needs to be taken in their analysis. Bulk samples will require a sampling strategy in order to produce a sub-sample from a larger seizure mainly for reasons of economy and practical ease. Sub-samples are then generally subjected to presumptive tests and TLC, followed by confirmatory chromatographic tests.

### Sampling

Sample integrity (in other words, being able to state that the analytical result obtained pertains to the collected and analysed sample) is the first important issue to be addressed in drug analysis. If the integrity of the sample is in doubt, then the relevance of the subsequent analytical results may also be doubtful. Information regarding the sample is paramount, such as whether it has been gathered at the scene and transferred to the laboratory for analysis or if it has been generated *in situ* in the laboratory.

Sampling, either at a crime scene or thereafter, has obvious consequences for any subsequent investigation. Choosing the right sample is critical. Incorrect sampling may result in unusable data and/or potentially incorrect and improper conclusions. The basis of sampling is that the composition found in the selected sub-samples reflects, in principle, the composition of the whole lot. The sampling strategy applied is fully dependent on the question being asked. Common questions include:

a) Is a drug present? In this case minimal sampling of a drug seizure may be required. It may be sufficient to analyse one item (e.g. one tablet, or one portion of a larger amount of powder), in order to arrive at a positive result. This is the simplest type of sampling strategy.

b) How much controlled substance is present in a seizure? In this case, either the whole sample is analysed, which in most cases is impractical, or a sampling strategy is adopted to remove a portion of a larger sample for analysis.

c) Is there a chemical link between a set of samples? In this case each sample under investigation may need to be examined.

When selecting the type of sampling protocol, a balance should be struck between the loss of completeness, time saving and the intention for each sample to produce new, useful information. Whichever scenario is encountered, there are a few universal objectives:

• the sample should be representative of the material in question;
• the sample should be randomly chosen;
• the sample should be of adequate size for the analysis to be performed and to allow subsequent analysis to take place if required.

*Random sampling and representative sampling*
A random sample is a selection of some members of a larger group of samples such that each member has an equal probability of independently being chosen. Random samples can be with or without replacement. Sampling without replacement (SWOR) means that once an item/unit is removed from the larger group it is not put back and can only ever be chosen once. Sampling with replacement (SWR) involves replacing items/units into the larger group after sampling. When sampling, two principles are assumed:

• the properties of the sample are a true reflection of the properties of the whole group from which the samples were taken; and
• each sample within the group has an equal chance of being selected.

Control samples are also analysed. Generally, both positive controls (standards) and negative controls (solvents used to prepare the samples and control samples) are used. These are then analysed with the case samples.

*Sampling protocols*
Many laboratories have developed their own sampling protocol for drug samples. In all cases, samples should be taken from items which have the same morphology (this concept is also called 'sampling by attributes'). If a seizure is found to contain different types of materials, then each type is sampled separately. This is particularly true for samples containing tablets with different logos or of different colours. Blocks of resin should be sampled, away from the edges of the block so as to preserve the potential for a physical fit with other blocks. In cases where samples of powder are seized, it is necessary to ensure that the powder is homogeneous and of the same morphology.

Sampling protocols will also be dictated by the nature of the analysis, (identification/quantification, profiling or sampling at clandestine laboratories). The UNODC suggested the sampling strategy below, which has been adopted by many laboratories worldwide.

*Powders, tablets and packages*

For a single package of material, the material should be removed from all packaging and weighed to a constant dry weight. The sample is then homogenised and a portion removed.

For more than one package, the material in each package should be examined visually for colour differences. The contents of each package should be weighed (cleaning the balance in between each weighing) and tested using a colour spot test or TLC. If all packages appear to contain the same material, then:

- if less than 10 packages are present, all should be tested;
- if 10–100 packages are present, 10 should be tested at random;
- if more than 100 packages are present, the square root of the total number of packages should be tested at random.

*Liquids*

If the liquid contains one phase only, then a sample of the liquid should be removed for testing. If more than one phase is present, then a sample of each phase should be removed for testing.

**The ENFSI drug working group recommended sampling methods**
The European Network of Forensic Science Institutes Drugs Working Group (ENFSI DWG) has also produced a guideline relating to sampling methodology for drug seizures. There are two recognised approaches suggested, a frequentist or statistical approach and a Bayesian approach.

*Frequentist approach*

The frequentist approach is based around the assumption that a fixed but unknown proportion of the seizure contains illicit drugs. The proportion of drugs in the sub-sample can therefore be used to estimate the proportion of drugs in the whole seizure. The frequentist method provides a level of confidence that within a given sample proportion chosen from the whole group of submitted samples a defined number of samples analysed will be positive.

*Bayesian approach*

The assumption behind a Bayesian approach is that the proportion of illicit drugs within the sample is known and fixed. This proportion is used to calculate probabilities on certain values of the unknown proportion of drug in the seizure. With this approach, it is possible to incorporate some knowledge about the seizure based on the analyst's experience. These various forms of 'prior information' result in different mathematical models to estimate a desired sample size. The assumption is made that, although the proportion of illicit drugs in the population is not known, the analyst may have some idea about the size of this proportion through experience. This idea is represented by a probability distribution which is the 'prior distribution' of the proportion. The uncertain knowledge is combined with information provided by analysis of the sample to give the 'posterior distribution'. With this posterior distribution, it is possible to calculate the probability that the proportion of units containing illicit drugs is greater than some value without using tests or confidence intervals.

### Trace samples

In the case of trace samples, swabbing is used to recover the sample. A clean sterile swab is usually rubbed over the surface of the item thought to contain the trace drug and then extracted with solvent and analysed.

## Presumptive tests

Presumptive tests are carried out on a sample to give an indication of the type of drug which may be present. The most common type of presumptive test involves the addition of various reagents to the sample to produce a colour. Other tests involve the use of microscopy to identify trichomes in suspected cannabis samples, or microcrystalline tests where the formation of specific crystals is indicative of the class of drug present. In all cases, appropriate positive and negative control samples must be used.

Most presumptive tests are carried out on porcelain tiles. There are a number of advantages to tests of this nature: they are cheap, quick and easy to use. They also have the advantage of being portable if required, and various 'roadside' test kits have been developed on the basis of colour tests. The main disadvantages are that the colours formed are subjective, may change over time, may be produced by more than one drug compound, or may be produced by non-controlled substances. These tests are also of limited sensitivity and are usually not suitable for the analysis of trace samples.

## Thin layer chromatography (TLC)

Having tentatively identified the class to which the drug belongs using presumptive testing, the next stage in drug identification is to examine which specific drug from the identified class is present. One way of doing this is by using a technique called thin layer chromatography (TLC) which separates the components of a drug mixture. The separation process depends on the relative strength of interaction of the sample components with a 'stationary phase', a plate coated with silica. The mobile phase, a solvent or mixture of solvents, is also required to move the components along the plate.

The sample and positive and negative (solvent only) controls are spotted on to the same TLC plate and developed in the same conditions. After development, the plate is viewed under UV light and any fluorescent spots marked. Other visualisation techniques are commonly used, and different classes of drugs require different techniques usually involving spraying the plates with various reagents. Rf values (the ratio of the distance a spot has travelled to the distance the solvent has travelled) are determined and compared with the controls run on the same plate.

Despite being relatively cheap, rapid and easy to interpret, TLC has a number of disadvantages which include:

- lack of resolution;
- lack of specificity of spray reagents, that is giving similar colour reactions for some compounds of the same class;
- edge effects on the TLC plate;
- variable Rf values;
- relatively low sensitivity.

### Chromatographic methods

Instrumental techniques utilising chromatography or spectroscopy, for instance, provide much stronger evidence than non-instrumental techniques. They may be used to determine the presence or identity of a drug (qualitative analysis), as well as the concentration of the drug in the sample (quantitative analysis).

Chromatographic techniques identify drugs through the physical and chemical properties of the molecule as a whole, such as structure and size; spectroscopic techniques tend to identify compounds on the basis of certain chemical bonds present within the chemical structure of the molecules.

#### High performance liquid chromatography (HPLC)

HPLC is a technique used commonly to identify and quantify drugs of abuse; however, difficulties may arise in complex mixtures of street drugs in which reaction by-products and impurities, as well as additives, can cause complications within the resulting chromatogram. Drug compounds are identified on the basis of retention time and direct comparison with known standards. Calibration standards and samples are generally interspersed by blank (solvent only) injections to ensure the instrument is free of carryover from previous injections. There are a number of detection systems available in HPLC analysis. By far the most common detector used for drug analysis is a UV detector which either monitors the output of the instrument at a single UV wavelength or across a range of UV wavelengths (diode array detector). The generation of UV absorption spectra using diode array detection (DAD) can help provide an identification of a drug in HPLC analysis, though many compounds can have similar UV spectra.

The technique has a number of advantages and disadvantages specific to drug analysis. Advantages include the following:

- it is non-destructive so samples can be recovered if required;
- the analyte does not need to be volatile;
- the sample generally does not require pre-treatment;
- the analysis can be automated;
- quantification can be achieved without the necessity of an internal standard.

Disadvantages include the following:

- the analyte needs to have properties which can be detected in a liquid stream;
- in most cases the detector is a UV or diode array detector (DAD) and so the sample must possess chromophores;
- the sample needs to be soluble in a wide range of solvents;
- quantification can be slow;
- large volumes of solvents are necessary.

### Gas chromatography (GC)

Gas chromatography (GC) has generally greater resolving power than HPLC systems and does not have the same problems associated with mobile phase choice. However, GC does require the compound to be thermally stable, volatile and exhibit good chromatographic qualities. This can sometimes require derivatisation or chemical modification of the compounds. The choice of derivatisation reagent depends upon the structure of the molecules in the compound of interest.

Many drugs can be chromatographed using GC directly; however, a number of compounds may give rise to problems such as:

- thermal decomposition (cannabinoids and cocaine alkaloids);
- reactions occurring within the instrument between compounds in the injected mixture (morphine and diamorphine with paracetamol in heroin); and
- co-elution of components.

GC and HPLC provide a means of separating the components of a complex mixture, but neither technique can definitively identify any component. For this reason, it is generally accepted that two (preferably three) independent techniques are required for identification of compounds present.

There are a variety of detection systems available in GC analysis. The most widely used detector for drug analysis is a flame ionisation detector (FID), though mass spectrometers (MS) are increasingly common. The mass spectrometer produces mass fragmentation patterns for each separated compound which, together with the chromatographic data, can be used for identification. Quantification can be carried out using a GC-MS (or a GCFID) usually by using an internal standard and direct comparison of retention times and mass fragmentation patterns of known standards.

### Fourier transform infrared spectroscopy (FTIR)

FTIR is an extremely useful technique for confirming the identity of pure compounds, but it has limited value for mixtures of compounds. The technique is based upon the identification of functional groups within molecules. A region of the FTIR spectrum, called the 'fingerprint region', is characteristic of the compound under test and is useful for comparison between two samples. Unfortunately, the majority of seized samples are mixtures of compounds;

thus, FTIR has limited practical use in the analysis of street samples of drugs of abuse.

### Ultraviolet-visible spectroscopy (UV-vis)

UV-vis, like FTIR, is a technique useful for the identification of pure drug compounds. Compounds containing specific chemical groups (chromophores) absorb specific wavelengths of ultraviolet or visible light, which is directly related to the concentration of the sample (this is the basis of the UV detector systems used in HPLC). Normally, UV and UV-vis spectra are recorded at high and low pH and the results of both compared with known standards for the sample under question.

UV-vis is a cheap and easy technique which allows sample recovery and good discrimination between pure compounds. It has less application for street samples involving complex mixtures.

### Choosing an instrumental technique

The instrumental technique chosen for any analysis depends upon the reason for the analysis and the nature of the sample. For example, large compounds such as the cannabinoids are not particularly thermally labile and therefore benefit from derivatisation if the analytical method chosen is GC. This has implications in drug profiling as derivatisation alters chemical structure. Samples thought to contain diamorphine may require derivatisation to help resolve some of the components if analysed by GC. Amphetamine compounds are generally easily analysed using either GC or HPLC and are profiled using a GC-MS system. HPLC is useful for quantification; however, a common diluent, caffeine, has a significantly different molar extinction coefficient than the amphetamines and can cause complications in the resultant chromatography. There may also be co-elution problems with structurally similar compounds.

## Drug profiling

In order to successfully counter the worldwide drug problem, there is a need to identify drug sources and trafficking routes. Drug characterisation and impurity profiling may assist in the identification of output from new illicit laboratories and in the monitoring of common methods used for drug manufacture. This, in turn, may provide information helpful to the maintenance of other intelligence gathering tools, such as precursor monitoring programmes. Drug characterisation and impurity profiling may also provide supporting evidence in cases where illicitly manufactured drugs need to be differentiated from those diverted from licit sources.

The ENFSI European Drugs Working Group have defined drug profiling as:

> The use of the methods to define the chemical and/or physical properties of a drug seizure for comparing seizures for intelligence (strategic and tactical) and evidential purposes (2006).

The forensic chemist, carrying out such characterisation/profiling studies, largely relies on physical and chemical information derived from the sample. Visual inspection of the physical characteristics of samples, such as colour or general appearance, can provide information at a relatively simple level. The packaging of seized samples may provide useful information to assist in connecting samples. DNA, fingerprints, the method of packaging, the materials used or any characteristic marks may also provide useful information which can be combined with chemical profiling.

Whether 'plant-based' (such as heroin, cocaine or cannabis), or synthetic compounds (such as the various amphetamines), illicit drugs are normally complex mixtures which rarely contain the drug alone. As a consequence of the often crude clandestine laboratory conditions under which these substances are produced, their chemical composition can show large variability. Variation will occur in the impurity content of final products from the same source; that is different batches from the same clandestine source can have different chemical characteristics which result in inter-batch sample variation. In addition, illicit products are generally non-homogeneous; thus, differences in impurity content may be observed in a single batch of drug, giving rise to intra-batch variation. Under normal circumstances, it is reasonable to assume that inter- (between) batch variations will be greater than intra- (within) batch variations.

As well as containing the drug itself, samples may contain one or more of three different types of components specifically: natural components, impurities and cutting agents.

- Natural components present in the raw materials (such as coca leaf or raw opium) may be present in the final product.

- Impurities are generated during drug synthesis and are related to the method of manufacture. They may not be completely removed during purification.

- Cutting agents may be added at any point in the distribution chain and may be pharmacologically inactive diluents (flour or sugar) or pharmacologically active adulterants (caffeine, paracetamol).

By identifying similarities and differences between drug samples, the information generated by drug profiling studies can be used to help answer the following questions:

- Are two or more drug samples connected?

- Does this relationship provide a link between, for example, a drug dealer and a user?

- Does the relationship between samples provide any useful information relating to local, national, regional or international drug supply and distribution networks or any information as to the extent of such networks?

- Where does the sample come from (e.g. geographic origin or laboratory source)?

- What is the method of clandestine drug production?

- Which specific chemicals are employed in the manufacturing process?

### Organic impurity profiling

The basis of organic impurity profiling of drugs is that illicit drugs (synthetic and semi-synthetic) contain extracted and synthetic impurities that have the potential to indicate the synthetic pathway used for manufacture or allow classification of seized samples into batches of common origin.

Impurities, often in very low quantities, can be present for a number of reasons. They may be generated as by-products in a particular manufacturing process, they may be introduced during synthesis due to unclean equipment, or they may be present in starting materials, reagents or solvents. Impurities may be carried through the synthesis and remain unchanged in the final product, or they may be transformed during the process (Gimeno *et al.* 2002). Impurity profiling research has been directed at all of the major drugs of abuse (van Deursen *et al.* 2006; Gimeno *et al.* 2005; Swist *et al.* 2005a; Swist *et al.* 2005b; Swist *et al.* 2003; Gimeno *et al.* 2002; Ballany *et al.* 2001).

The identification of 'route specific' impurities (that is, one or more impurities which, when present, indicate that a particular synthetic route was used) has been the focus of much research in recent years (Swist *et al.* 2005a; Swist *et al.* 2005b; Gimeno *et al.* 2002; King *et al.* 1994; Verweij 1989). Even without the identification of route specific impurities, however, the presence (or absence) and relative amounts of impurities can allow comparison between samples. Unfortunately, difficulties with this type of profiling have been identified. For instance, the clandestine laboratory may produce substances of high purity such that very few (if any) impurities remain (Swist *et al.* 2005b; Hays *et al.* 2000; Mas *et al.* 1995). Secondly, comparisons based on impurity profiling were often not conclusive enough due to difficulty in achieving reproducible chromatograms as a result of low level impurities. It has also been noted that chromatograms are often time and machine dependent (Besacier *et al.* 1997). For this reason, research has been directed at the development of harmonised methods (van Deursen *et al.* 2006; Ballany *et al.* 2001; Stromberg *et al.* 2000) in order to facilitate the exchange and comparison of information at national and international level.

### Inorganic impurity profiling

Since 1980, inductively coupled plasma mass spectrometry (ICP-MS) has emerged as a major and powerful technique in the area of elemental analysis. It offers extremely low detection limits, ranging from parts per billion to parts per trillion. In addition, these detection limits are broadly achieved for almost all the elements across the periodic table. The simple nature of the mass spectra of the elements makes this technique a quick tool for automated qualitative, semi-quantitative and quantitative elemental analysis.

Metal content of bulk drug substances may originate from different sources such as the plant from which the drug is extracted, from catalysts, reagents and solvents used in the extraction and/or synthesis or from exposure to airborne particles. A potential exists for the use of this technique in relation to drug profiling. Moreover, easy sample preparation and quick analysis time make this technique very attractive. However, both inter- and intra-batch variation can be very large within illicit drug samples. This, combined with the costs and accessibility of the equipment, limits the usefulness of the application of the technique for drug profiling.

### Isotope profiling

Isotope profiling is an emerging tool for drug profiling. Stable isotope analysis is based on the fact that all but 12 elements exist as one or more isotopes. For instance, carbon exists most abundantly with six protons and six neutrons ($^{12}C$), but it also exists in small quantities with six protons and seven neutrons ($^{13}C$). In theory, two samples synthesised within the same chemical batch should exhibit the same isotope abundances. One advantage of stable isotope analysis is that isotope ratios are intrinsic parameters of the drug molecule; therefore, they are not modified by partial degradation or addition of foreign materials during the distribution process.

An isotope ratio mass spectrometer (IRMS) measures the ratio of heavy to light isotopes ($^{13}C/^{12}C$ for instance) relative to a standard. Of particular interest are the ratios of $^{2}H/^{1}H$, $^{13}C/^{12}C$, $^{15}N/^{14}N$, $^{18}O/^{16}O$. In natural products, these abundances depend not only on the biosynthetic pathway of the plant, but also on environmental conditions such as humidity or temperature. Consequently, it is possible to use such isotopic analyses to determine the geographical origin of natural products. IRMS is routinely used by many food control laboratories to detect, for instance, the addition of foreign sugar in pure fruit juices or the authenticity of wines.

For synthetic substances, the isotope ratios of a substance are linked to the synthetic conditions used (such as synthetic pathway, reagents, reaction conditions, etc.) and to the purification processes. It should therefore be possible to discriminate between batches of synthetic substances. For instance, analgesic drugs such as aspirin, despite manufacture following precise protocols, are significantly heterogeneous in isotopic composition such that batches can be discriminated by isotopic profiling.

Current research is ongoing in this area (Buchanan et al. 2008; de Korompay et al. 2008; Nic Daéid and Meier-Augenstein 2008; Billault et al. 2007; Sewenig et al. 2007; Benson et al. 2006; Idoine et al. 2005; Palhol et al. 2003), and the usefulness of stable isotope analysis of precursors and illicit drugs is being explored.

### Evaluating impurity profiles

The challenge of suggesting sample linkages, either case-to-case linkages, or linkages for intelligence purposes, revolves around the issue of recognising differences accounted for by inter- and intra-batch variation as opposed to those due to the samples originating from different sources. The potential for batch variation is high because of the often crude laboratory conditions associated with their illicit production. Similarly, as precursors are increasingly controlled, their clandestine synthesis using pre-precursors is becoming more common, thereby introducing another level of chemical variation into the final sample matrix.

In most circumstances, the forensic chemist will be involved in the analysis of street level drugs, i.e. drugs which are seized at the end (or user) level of the supply chain. Comparison of diluents and adulterants and concentration of illicit substance may also be used in assigning linkage, though this must be evaluated in light of case circumstances.

Comparisons of chromatographic analytical results are often carried out by pattern recognition, in which direct comparison of the resultant analytical traces are made. In many cases the raw chromatographic data undergo data pretreatment in order to reduce the effect of high concentration components in the subsequent statistical comparisons and data correlation.

### Chemometric analysis

Increasingly, drug profiling makes use of chemometric techniques such as principal component analysis (PCA) and hierarchical cluster analysis (HCA). Both of these techniques examine analytical results and compare them mathematically for similarities. Samples which are similar are clustered or grouped together as illustrated in Figures 5.14 and 5.15.

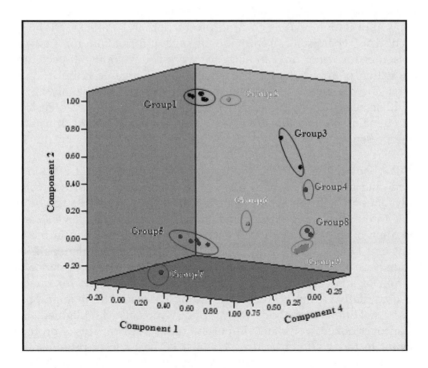

**Figure 5.14** A 3-D plot of principal components mathematically extracted from a data set for heroin seized in Glasgow

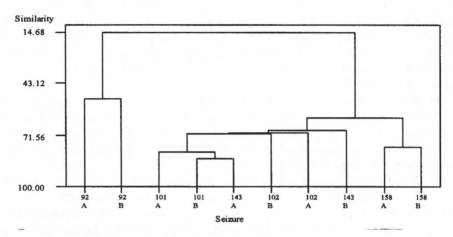

**Figure 5.15** HCA analysis in which samples are linked by the bracket shape. Above, 92A and 92B form a cluster separate from the remainder. Samples 101B and 143A are the most similar.

## Summary

The analysis of controlled drugs is one of the main areas of casework where forensic chemists are involved. In many forensic laboratories, the drugs section is one of the largest and busiest. As a consequence of developments in forensic drug chemistry, scientists are increasingly becoming involved in providing information relating to drug production and trafficking. The extent to which drug chemists can provide linkage information for case-to-case comparison or for wider drug intelligence work is developing at pace through the production of robust harmonised methods for organic impurity analysis and increasing research in promising methods such as IRMS analysis.

Notwithstanding these developments, the main focus of forensic drug chemists remains the identification and quantification of seized drug samples and the presentation of analytical results in robust forms for the justice system.

In this chapter, the global situation of drug abuse and trafficking was discussed, and an overview was given of the main types of drugs which are currently abused: natural, semi-synthetic, and synthetic. Particular attention was paid to the three main drug conventions set out by the UNODC and the incorporation of these conventions into national drug legislation in the UK as the Misuse of Drugs Act 1971 and the Misuse of Drugs Regulations 2001.

The analysis of drugs of abuse was discussed, from the importance of the preparation of analytical space through to the methods used for qualitative and/or quantitative analysis, such as presumptive tests, chromatography, and spectroscopy. Different methods of sampling were also highlighted, as this can be an overlooked, yet vitally important, area in the analyst's protocol.

Relevant to today's forensic drug chemist is the issue of profiling. In this chapter, both organic and inorganic profiling were discussed, including the foundations on which they are based. The newly emerging field of isotope profiling was also addressed, as this technique is attracting much research in forensic science. Lastly, the evaluation of impurity profiles was considered, with importance laid upon the assessment of intra- and inter-batch variation before conclusions are drawn about the relation of samples.

## Notes

1 Opiates is a term used in UNODC reports to denote opium, morphine and the final product heroin.
2 The term 'ecstasy' is used in the UNODC reports to denote MDMA, MDA, and MDEA.

## References

Ballany, J., Caddy, B., Cole, M. (2001) 'Development of a harmonised pan-European method for the profiling of amphetamines', *Science and Justice*, 41 (3): 193–196.

Benson, S., Lennard, C., Maynard, P. (2006) 'Forensic applications of isotope ratio mass spectrometry – A review. *Forensic Science International*, 157 (1): 1–22.

Besacier, F., Chaudron-Thozet, H., Rousseau-Tsangaris, M. *et al.* (1997) 'Comparative chemical analyses of drug samples: General approach and application to heroin', *Forensic Science International*, 85 (2): 113–125.

Billault, I., Courant, F., Pasquereau, L. (2007) 'Correlation between the synthetic origin of methamphetamine samples and their $^{15}$N and $^{13}$C stable isotope ratios', *Analytica Chimica Acta*, 593 (1): 20–29.

Buchanan, H.A.S., Nic Daéid, N., Meier-Augenstein, W. (2008) 'Emerging use of isotope ratio mass spectrometry as a tool for discrimination of 3,4-methylenedioxymethamphetamine by synthetic route', *Analytical Chemistry*, 80 (9): 3350–3356.

de Korompay, A., Hill, J.C., Carter, J.F. (2008) 'Supported liquidliquid extraction of the active ingredient (3,4-methylenedioxymethylamphetamine) from ecstasy tablets for isotopic analysis', *Journal of Chromatography A*, 1178 1–8.

European Network of Forensic Science Institutes (2006) 'Definition of drug profiling at *Drugs Working Group Annual Meeting*. Krakow, Poland.

EUROPOL (2006) *Drugs 2006*. Available from: http://www.europol.europa.eu/publications/Serious_Crime_Overviews/drugs2005.pdf [11/08/08].

Gimeno, P., Besacier, F., Bottex, A. (2005) 'A study of impurities in intermediates and 3,4-methylenedioxymethamphetamine (MDMA) samples produced via reductive amination routes', *Forensic Science International*, 155 (2–3): 141–157.

Gimeno, P., Besacier, F., Chaudron-Thozet, H. (2002) 'A contribution to the chemical profiling of 3,4-methylenedioxymethamphetamine (MDMA) tablets', *Forensic Science International*, 127 (1–2): 1–44.

Hays, P.A., Remaud, G.S., Jamin, E. (2000) 'Geographic origin determination of heroin and cocaine using site-specific isotopic ratio deuterium NM', *Journal of Forensic Sciences*, 45 (3): 552–562.

Home Office (2006) *Drug Laws and Licensing*. Available from: http://drugs.homeoffice.gov.uk/drugs-laws/misuse-of-drugs-act/ [06/11/06].

Idoine, F.A., Carter, J.F., Sleeman, R. (2005) 'Bulk and compound-specific isotopic characterisation of illicit heroin and cling film', *Rapid Communications in Mass Spectrometry*, 19 (22): 3207–3215.

International Narcotics Control Board (2004) *2004 Substantive Session of the Economic and Social Council*. Available from: http://www.incb.org/incb/speeches/ecosoc_ 04.html [20/12/06].

International Narcotics Control Board (2005) *Annual Report (E/INCB/2005/1)*. Available from: http://www.incb.org/incb/annual_report_2005.html [11/08/08].

Interpol (2005) *Heroin*. Available from: http://www.interpol.int/Public/Drugs/heroin/ default.asp [24/11/06].

King, L. (2003) *The Misuse of Drugs Act – A Guide for Forensic Scientists*. Cambridge: RSC.

King, L.A., Clarke, K., Orpet, A.J. (1994) 'Amphetamine profiling in the UK', *Forensic Science International*, 69 (1): 65–75.

Mas, F., Beemsterboer, B., Veltkamp, A.C. (1995) 'Determination of common-batch members in a set of confiscated 3,4-(methylendioxy)methylamphetamine samples by measuring the natural isotope abundances – A preliminary study', *Forensic Science International*, 71 (3): 225–231.

Nic Daéid, N., Meier-Augenstein, W. (2008) 'Feasibility of source identification of seized street drug samples by exploiting differences in isotopic composition at natural abundance level by GC/MS as compared to isotope ratio mass spectrometry (IRMS)', *Forensic Science International*, 174: 259–261.

Office of Public Sector Information (2003) *Statutory Instrument 2003 No. 3201*. Available from: http://www.opsi.gov.uk/si/si2003/20033201.htm [11/08/08].

Office of Public Sector Information (2006) *Statutory Instrument 2006 No. 3331*. Available from: http://www.opsi.gov.uk/si/si2006/20063331.htm [06/02/07].

Palhol, F., Lamoureux, C., Naulet, N. (2003) '$^{15}$N isotopic analyses: a powerful tool to establish links between seized 3,4-methylenedioxymethamphetamine (MDMA) tablets', *Analytical and Bioanalytical Chemistry*, 376 (4): 486–490.

Sewenig, S., Fichtner, S., Holdermann, T. (2007) 'Determination of $\delta^{13}$C(V-PDB) and $\delta^{15}$N(AIR) values of cocaine from a big seizure in Germany by stable isotope ratio mass spectrometry', *Isotopes in Environmental and Health Studies*, 43: 275–280.

Strathclyde Police (2006) *Drugs Section FAQ*. Available from: http://www.strathclyde. police.uk/index.asp?docID=213 [11/08/08].

Stromberg, L., Lundberg, L., Neumann, H. (2000) 'Heroin impurity profiling – A harmonization study for retrospective comparisons', *Forensic Science International*, 114 (2): 67–88.

Swist, M., Wilamowski, J., Parczewski, A. (2005a) 'Determination of synthesis method of ecstasy based on the basic impurities', *Forensic Science International*, 152 (2–3): 175–184.

Swist, M., Wilamowski, J., Zuba, D. (2005b) 'Determination of synthesis route of 1-(3,4-methylenedioxyphenyl)-2-propanone (MDP-2-P) based on impurity profiles of MDMA', *Forensic Science International*, 149 (2–3): 181–192.

Swist, M., Zuba, D., Stanaszek, R. (2003) 'The synthetic route specific impurities in 3,4-methylenedioxyphenylpropanone and 3,4-methylenedioksymethamphetamine prepared from isosafrole and piperonal', *Forensic Science International*, 136: 102–103.

United Nations (1961) *Single Convention on Narcotic Drugs, 1961*. Available from: http://www.incb.org/pdf/e/conv/convention_1961_en.pdf [11/08/08].

United Nations (1971) *Convention on Psychotropic Substances, 1971*. Available from: http://www.incb.org/pdf/e/conv/convention_1971_en.pdf [11/08/08].

United Nations (1988) *Convention Against the Illicit Traffic in Narcotic Drugs and Psychotropic Substances, 1988*. Available from: http://www.unodc.org/pdf/ convention_1988_en.pdf [11/08/08].

United Nations (2005) *2005 World Drug Report, Vol 1: Analysis*. Available from: http:// www.unodc.org/pdf/WDR_2005/volume_1_web.pdf [11/08/08].

United Nations Office on Drugs and Crime (2006a) *2006 World Drug Report, Volume 1: Analysis*. Available from: http://www.unodc.org/pdf/WDR_2006/wdr2006_volume1.pdf [11/08/08].

United Nations Office on Drugs and Crime (2006b) *UN Crime and Drug Conventions*. Available from: http://www.unodc.org/unodc/drug_and_crime_conventions.html [07/11/06].

van Deursen, M.M., Lock, E., Poortman-van der Meer, A.J. (2006) 'Organic impurity profiling of 3,4-methylenedioxymethamphetamine (MDMA) tablets seized in the Netherlands', *Science and Justice*, 46 (3): 135–152.

Verweij, A.M.A. (1989) 'Impurities in illicit drug preparations: amphetamine and methamphetamine', *Forensic Science Review*, 1 (1): 1–11.

# Chapter 6

# Body fluids in sexual offences

*Julie Allard*

## Introduction

The forensic examination of a sexual offence has many facets and it must necessarily begin with the police investigator establishing the relevant issues to be addressed in the case and where a forensic scientist can assist with them. For many cases this will be straightforward; where it is more complex, the police officer may enlist the assistance of forensic advisers within the force to devise a forensic strategy or contact a forensic supplier for more specialist advice. In England and Wales, the next stage is for the police investigator to gain authorisation from the forensic budget holders prior to submitting the work to a forensic provider.

Most sexual offence cases require an examination of intimate swabs, clothing and often scene items for body fluids – mostly semen – but may often involve examinations for damage to clothing, other trace evidence such as saliva, fibre transfer evidence, lubricants or a toxicological examination. It is essential that a holistic approach is taken to the setting of a forensic examination strategy so that all of the relevant evidence types are considered and those most likely to assist in addressing the case issues are prioritised. For example, to assist the investigative stage of a case, the detection of body fluids such as semen and DNA profiling to identify the perpetrator will be necessary. However, if the aim is to address claims that sexual intercourse took place with consent, rather than to identify a suspect, then a focus on the presence of semen and a matching DNA profile will not be probative, whereas the finding of forceful damage to clothing may be evidentially significant. Some forensic providers now have specialist teams for sexual offence cases which provide a tailored service encompassing all aspects of the forensic examination.

The forensic practitioner assigned to a case should also ensure that all relevant evidence types other than those in their own specialty are considered and discussed where appropriate with the investigator, even if they have not been requested at the time of the laboratory submission. In terms of body fluids, sexual offences will usually necessitate an examination for semen, frequently for saliva, blood and cellular material (such as from vaginal secretions) and occasionally for faeces and urine.

This chapter will describe and discuss two main aspects of forensic interest in relation to the collection and analysis of body fluids in support of the investigation of sexual offences. Firstly an outline of the assessment and evaluation processes in relation to sexual offences and secondly a description of the methods for the location, identification and recovery of body fluids. An overview of the forensic examination in the context of a criminal prosecution is summarised below (Figure 6.1). This process is not a straight route from incident to trial and at several stages further information may be provided that necessitates a revisiting of a previous stage and a review of the strategy and further examinations.

## Case assessment and evaluation

When a case is submitted to a forensic laboratory for examination, it is vital that the forensic biologist is provided with the relevant background information alongside the items so that an appropriate examination strategy and subsequent interpretation can be made. A standard submission form will list the police investigator, complainant and suspect details together with an outline of the case circumstances and the type of forensic examinations required. For sexual offences it is especially important that the forensic scientist is given detailed information of the acts that are alleged to have taken place and their order. Information on any actions (such as washing) that have taken place since the incident and might affect the persistence of body fluids is also important. This is best achieved by provision of a copy of the complainant's statement and information from their medical examination. It is also necessary to have information about the account given by any suspects, although in practice, a clear account from the accused person is rarely provided at this early stage and in many instances the suspect will respond with 'no comment' on arrest. More rarely witnesses' statements are relevant for some cases.

It is also important the scientist receives copies of any forms completed during medical examinations as these provide extra information from the person about when samples have been taken, washing, defecation and any sexual acts with partners prior to the incident.

In many instances the scientist will also speak to the police investigator to obtain further details and to clarify their request, since police requests are frequently very general in nature – 'examine items for semen', 'examine for accused's DNA' – and are not specific about the real issue to be addressed. The provision of this information enables the scientist to formulate an examination strategy tailored to address the pertinent issues in the case.

In cases in which no suspect has been apprehended, the scientist will be acting in 'investigative' mode initially (Jackson et al. 2006), for example examining items for scientific evidence such as semen to help address whether sexual intercourse has taken place and carrying out DNA profiling tests to address the source of the semen. Once an arrest has been made an

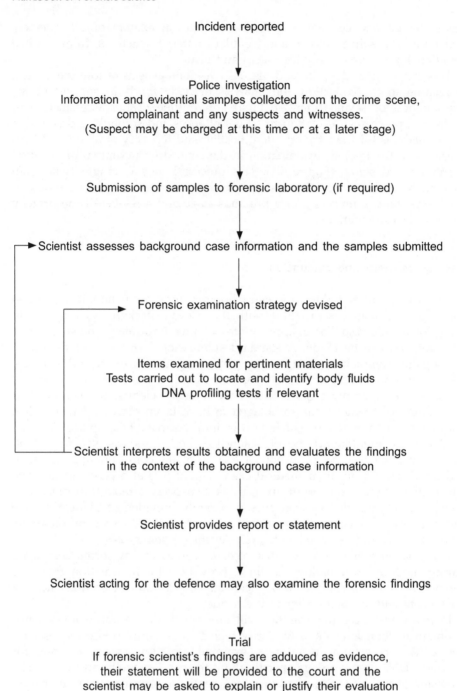

**Figure 6.1** Overview of the forensic examination process

alternative account may be provided by the accused person and the scientist should progress to 'evaluative' mode and assess their findings in relation to each account so that they can provide an expert opinion on the weight of the forensic evidence.

A schematic (Figure 6.2) showing these stages in the context of the prosecution of a case is shown below:

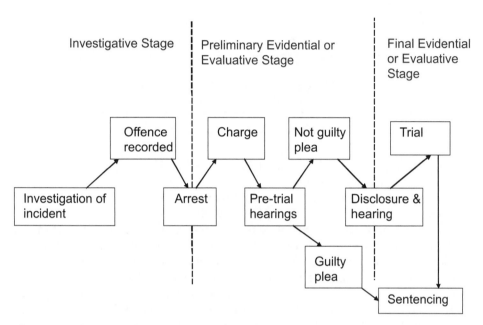

**Figure 6.2** Stages in the prosecution of a case

Consideration in terms of the hierarchy of questions or propositions (Cook *et al.* 1998; see also Chapter 16 of this Handbook) greatly helps to clarify the issues to be addressed.

For a sexual offence at the evaluative stage the levels in the hierarchy might be as shown in Table 6.1.

Evaluation of many sexual offences will require assessment and interpretation at activity level. Consideration of the offence level propositions is the remit of the jury and the forensic scientist will rarely evaluate their findings in relation to this level.

Prior to any arrests in a rape investigation, the police investigator may be assisted by the reporting of findings at source level, for example 'semen has been found on the internal vaginal swab and a DNA profile obtained'. This would assist by enabling a search of the National DNA Database and if a match is obtained, nomination of a suspect or another linked case. However, post arrest and the provision of the suspect's account, the presence of semen matching his DNA profile may not be probative in itself, whereas the amount and distribution of the semen might provide additional information, enabling an interpretation at activity level. For example it may be possible to use the

**Table 6.1** Hierarchy of propositions

| Level | Prosecution proposition | Defence proposition |
|---|---|---|
| Offence | Mr X raped Miss Y | Mr X did not rape Miss Y |
| Activity | Mr X had vaginal intercourse with Miss Y | Mr X did not have vaginal intercourse with Miss Y, but ejaculated on her groin |
| Source | Semen from Mr X is present in Miss Y's vaginal sample | Semen from someone else is present in Miss Y's vaginal sample |
| Sub-source | DNA from Mr X is present in Miss Y's vaginal sample | DNA from someone else is present in Miss Y's vaginal sample |

*Note*: Each level in this example relates to a different defence scenario.

findings to address whether sexual intercourse had taken place rather than another act causing a transfer of semen.

Current practice by some UK practitioners and by many outside the UK is to provide a factual report, sometimes with some additional interpretative comment and to deal with the activity level issues if called to give testimony. However, it is concerning that the scientist may not be called to give evidence in many cases where such a discussion is appropriate. Barristers and the court may be unaware that their lay interpretation of factual scientific findings is not giving the full picture and there may be further value if the findings are fully evaluated and opinion given by the forensic expert with full knowledge of, and in the context of, the prosecution and defence accounts.

Having gathered the requisite background information, the scientist will begin to formulate their thoughts, either formally or implicitly, about what they expect to find given the account(s) provided. This enables the construction of an examination strategy tailored to address the pertinent issues in the case. If done more formally, it also aids the evaluative stage by providing documented expectations prior to any results being obtained in order to avoid any tendency to be 'findings led'.

For example, consider a case where a woman has alleged that she was vaginally raped by a man she met in a club and she thinks that the perpetrator probably ejaculated inside her. She was medically examined six hours later and vaginal swabs were taken. No suspect has been arrested. At this 'investigative phase', the scientist will use their knowledge about the persistence of semen in the vagina, gleaned from their own experience and various publications, to assign a high probability or expectation to the finding of a large amount of semen on the vaginal swabs. However, if no semen was found, this would be surprising and suggest that either intercourse has not taken place or that intercourse with no ejaculation had occurred. In another situation where the swabs had been taken eight days after the alleged intercourse, then the expectations would be very different. There would be an extremely low likelihood of finding semen on them whether the incident took place as alleged or not, and the most effective initial strategy in this situation would be to examine underwear worn after the incident. This will enable the best means of detecting semen and obtaining a DNA profile to help this investigative stage of the case.

Let us now consider the situation where a suspect has been arrested for this case several days later and he denies that vaginal intercourse took place, but says that he had masturbated himself and then digitally penetrated the woman's vagina with her consent. This is the evaluative stage of the case and the scientist must now formulate their expectations in relation to his account as well as the woman's, considering the likelihood of semen present on his hands being transferred into her vagina by his fingers and if transferred, what amount might be expected to be found on an internal vaginal swab. Although there is limited published information about such transfer and persistence issues, the scientist can formulate some expectations based on the available literature and using their forensic knowledge and experience. The finding of a large amount of semen on the high vaginal swab is likely to be considered evidentially significant whereas a small amount would be equivocal. It is vital that such a case is reported by the scientist with an opinion at activity level as factual reporting of the presence of semen and matching DNA will not help the court to establish the truth.

### Evaluation at activity level – addressing sexual intercourse

The most likely explanation for the presence of semen on an internal swab is that the subject had recent sexual intercourse; however, the forensic expert should always consider other relevant scenarios. For example, consider the situation where a young girl (Miss A) alleges that she was forced to have vaginal intercourse. Her account is confused and she is unclear about whether the man ejaculated. The accused (Mr B) admits that he ejaculated externally on her groin and knickers during a consensual act, but says he did not penetrate her. Intimate swabs and underwear were taken from Miss A within a few hours and have been submitted to the forensic scientist with a request to establish which account the findings support. Firstly, let us consider what our expectations are in relation to each account:

- If the complainant's account were true, the expectations regarding the presence of semen hinge on whether there had been ejaculation. If vaginal ejaculation had taken place, the forensic biologist would give an opinion that there is a very high likelihood that semen would be found on the internal vaginal swabs. This would be dramatically different if no ejaculation had occurred when there would be a high expectation of no semen or, perhaps a very few sperm if transferred via the surface of the penis. Significant deposits of semen would be expected in the underwear only if ejaculation had occurred.

- If the accused's account were true, there would be a very high expectation of large amounts of semen on the external genital area and gusset of underwear and none on the internal vaginal swabs.

Abbreviations are used to denote these two accounts – Hp for the prosecution proposition and Hd for the defence proposition.

Although this assessment of expectations prior to an examination of the items can be done intuitively by the experienced forensic biologist, best practice would be to document this more formally, with the relevant propositions being clearly defined and all possible outcomes considered. This will facilitate the provision of sound advice as to whether it is worthwhile to proceed with the examination and the likelihood of a probative outcome in favour of either account. It also forms the basis for the evaluative stage after the examinations have been carried out and provides a record for the case file for any scientific examination on behalf of the defence. The following illustrates a means of formal assessment for this case example:

Propositions are defined

Hp:    Mr B had vaginal intercourse with Miss A

Hd:    Mr B did not have vaginal intercourse with Miss A, but ejaculated on her groin and knickers

Expectations are recorded (Table 6.2).

**Table 6.2**   Formal assessment of expectations

| Possible outcomes for internal high vaginal swab | Pr E/Hp, I* | Pr E/Hd,I* | Likelihood ratio | Finding would support |
|---|---|---|---|---|
| No semen | 0.49 | 0.95 | ~0.5 | Hd or inconclusive |
| Small amount of semen | 0.17 | 0.05 | 3 | Hp or inconclusive |
| Some semen | 0.17 | ~0 | Very large | Hp |
| Lots of semen | 0.17 | ~0 | Very large | Hp |

*Probability (Pr) of the evidence (E) given the hypothesis (Hp/Hd) and the background information (I)

Most biologists are likely to consider that these likelihood ratios are roughly estimated and therefore too close to one (inconclusive) for the first two outcomes and might report such findings as inconclusive in helping to address which of the accounts is true. However, the high likelihood ratio with the finding of larger amounts of semen would be very significant evidentially. If there is no dispute about the complainant having had any other sexual partners, DNA profiling may be considered unnecessary, although in practice this is generally requested given the serious nature of the offence.

The layperson might wonder why there is any expectation of semen internally if no intercourse has taken place. Some doctors quote cases of Somalian women becoming pregnant despite their labia having been fused to prevent penetration; others take the view that spermatozoa can swim fast and far enough on their own in their natural direction into the vagina so that deposition at the periphery of the vagina without penetration provides opportunity for spermatozoa to be found in the upper vaginal areas. There is currently no published research to investigate this issue so the scientist must be cautious in their evaluation of such cases.

A similar assessment can be carried out for the underwear and would show that there is a high expectation of finding a lot of semen if the suspect's account were true or if the girl's account were true and ejaculation occurred, whilst an absence of semen would not be expected given his account but might be given hers if no ejaculation occurred.

The examination strategy for this case might thus be staged, initially examining the vaginal swabs for semen and if a large amount of semen is present proposing that no further examinations are necessary. If a small amount of semen or no semen is found on the internal swabs, the underwear should be examined for semen.

Following the examination, the scientist can apply the findings to the assessment made at the start of the case and integrate the previously estimated likelihood ratios into an evaluation contained within their report.

### Evaluation at activity level – the time of sexual intercourse

Estimation of the concentration of acid phosphatase (AP – an enzyme found in high concentrations in semen) and spermatozoa on intimate swabs are established indicators of the time that has elapsed between sexual intercourse and sampling. All UK and Irish laboratories routinely broadly grade the relative concentration of spermatozoa on their microscopic preparations (under × 400 magnification) as follows:

+       Spermatozoa are hard to find
++      Some spermatozoa in some microscopic fields, easy to find
+++     Many or some spermatozoa in most fields
++++    Many spermatozoa in every field
T       Complete spermatozoa with tails present

Collections of data from previous cases and donor samples (Davies and Wilson 1974; Allard 1997) have enabled an evaluative approach when there is a dispute over when (rather than with whom) sexual intercourse has occurred, as is commonly seen in cases involving alleged rape by previous sexual partners. Seminal AP is unlikely to persist much longer than two days after vaginal intercourse and spermatozoa a week, although some workers cite the presence of spermatozoa for much longer, especially on cervical swabs (Willott and Allard 1982; Wilson 1982).

For example, in a case where there is a dispute about whether intercourse took place five hours prior to sampling rather than three days, the finding on a high vaginal swab of a strong AP positive reaction and numerous complete spermatozoa would support the contention that intercourse had occurred five hours previously rather than three days previously. A Bayesian approach by a trained forensic scientist with use of published data would enable an estimation of the strength of this support via a likelihood ratio and hence the weight of the evidence. Many UK laboratories currently use a verbal scale (limited support through to very strong support) to describe the weight of the evidence (Evett *et al.* 2000). The application of this multi-point scale can cause difficulties where limited data is available and it is now under debate in the UK by a quality standards specialist group working with the Forensic Regulator.

Initial data collection (Norton 2002) suggests that the level of prostate specific antigen (PSA) may also be useful as an indicator of the amount of semen present on an intimate swab and a broad relationship with estimation of the time since intercourse. The limited data available so far suggests that strong PSA reactions (using the Seratec® test) are only obtained from swabs taken up to 20 hours after intercourse and a weak PSA result up to 30 hours. Further data collection is planned to substantiate these indications.

## The location, identification and recovery of body fluids

Having assessed the likelihood of various body fluids stains being present and which are relevant to the investigation, the forensic scientist must set about the examination of the pertinent items in order to locate and identify the body fluids and retrieve them for further testing such as DNA profiling.

The effectiveness of this process is dependent on the body fluids not having deteriorated due to poor storage conditions since their deposition, which can cause difficulties in locating the stains and a degradation of the DNA. The scientist must also have available to them sensitive and specific tests to locate and identify which type of body fluid is present and they must also utilise effective methods to recover any staining from swabs and fabrics.

Detailed guidance (FFLM 2008) is available to police forces and medical practitioners regarding the optimum storage conditions and packaging materials for forensic items such as clothing, scene items and medical samples.

The following sections describe, firstly, the various facets of the medical examination of individuals in relation to the retrieval of forensic evidence in a sexual assault and, secondly, the nature and effectiveness of the tests used to locate and identify body fluids of different types.

### The medical examination

With sexual offences the complainant is effectively the prime 'crime scene' and therefore there will generally be a need for an extensive medical examination and collection of evidence from their person. An arrested person will also have to undergo a detailed medical examination in most instances. However, if the offence is not reported or the complainant not examined for several days, most of the evidence will have been lost from orifices and body surfaces and the examination of clothing and bedding will be more pertinent. In the UK, a national working group comprising representatives from medical, law enforcement and forensic science committees was set up in 1998 and provides guidance on best practice for the examination and collection of evidence. This group is led by the Faculty of Forensic and Legal Medicine (FFLM). They have endorsed a modular sexual offence kit (Newton 2004) produced by Scenesafe® which provides the relevant sampling materials to retrieve and preserve forensic evidence together with guidance and documents to record background information relevant to the forensic biologist. The kits contain sealed disposable instruments, sterile water, sampling swabs and containers, all monitored to scientific standards so that they have no detectable DNA. Other suppliers have also applied to the Faculty for endorsement of their kits.

Police can utilise elements of the kit to collect non-intimate samples before the medical practitioner arrives. Intimate samples should be collected by specialist doctors and nurses who have been trained to undertake forensic medical examinations. The guidance provided with the kits recommends that intimate swabs are taken from the female up to a week after vaginal intercourse and up to two days afterwards from the male; that anal swabs are taken up to three days after alleged anal intercourse and mouth samples up to two days after fellatio. These are specified as general guidelines which may need to be adjusted in certain cases. The vagina, vulva and perineum should also be sampled even when only anal intercourse is alleged so that the scientist can comment on whether any semen in the anal area is present as a result of vaginal leakage (Enos and Beyer 1978; Davies 1979). Each kit contains a disposable speculum and proctoscope to enable sampling of the high internal vaginal and rectal areas respectively. It is important that the medical practitioner uses disposable speculae to ensure that accidental transfer or contamination of other areas being sampled does not take place. The kit also contains materials to enable the sampling of fingernails which may often be pertinent in sexual offence if the offender was scratched or inserted fingers into an orifice of the victim.

### Semen

The identification of the presence and source of semen on intimate swabs, clothing and bedding is key in the investigation of most sexual assaults. However, with offences involving children, the presence of semen alone may be highly significant even if its source cannot be addressed.

Semen usually consists of a fluid containing many spermatozoa – the average human ejaculate of 3 ml contains approximately 300 million spermatozoa in seminal plasma. Some individuals may have a zero or low sperm count resulting from a vasectomy, clinical condition, therapeutic or other drugs or due to natural causes, and this can be permanent or transitory depending on the underlying cause. Low and zero sperm counts are described medically as oligozoospermia and azoospermia respectively. Confusingly, the term aspermia is also used to describe a lack of spermatozoa and also for the condition where no ejaculate is produced. In the medical context, these terms would only be applied if the whole of the ejaculate had been analysed. Since the forensic scientist is only looking at part of the ejaculate, the failure to detect spermatozoa could be due to azoospermia or oligozoospermia. The forensic biologist should therefore report such findings factually using a phrase such as 'seminal fluid containing no spermatozoa was detected'. If this is an important issue in a case it is advisable to provide some further background information in any report and also to recommend that the investigator additionally obtains a medical opinion about any clinical condition.

Seminal fluid contains high levels of phosphoryl choline and the enzyme acid phosphatase (AP) and on ejaculation phosphoryl choline is dephosphorylated by acid phosphatase to free choline and orthophosphate.

Seminal staining is generally detected and its distribution assessed by the presence of acid phosphatase, and identified by the presence of spermatozoa. In the absence of spermatozoa, the identification of prostate specific antigen (PSA) together with high levels of AP, or the presence of choline, are used as confirmatory tests. Although acid phosphatase and phosphoryl choline are present in biological materials other than semen, the richest source of these compounds is semen. Use of the PSA test is becoming more widespread as a replacement for the choline test (and also the occasionally used Laurell Rocket test), due to its greater sensitivity.

The first stage when examining an item of clothing or bedding is a visual search for the presence of whitish staining and/or a stiffening of the fabric. The visual search may be augmented by the use of different wavelengths of light. Admixture with blood, faeces or lubricants may cause discolouration and the adherence of pubic hairs and other materials that may be of evidential significance.

Stained areas located by eye or specialist light sources or areas where semen staining is suspected due to its position (for example, the gusset of a pair of knickers) are spot tested for the presence of AP. Such testing minimises the loss of staining compared to a general screening method. However, if no AP is detected using a spot test or the total distribution of semen is evidentially significant, a general screen may be necessary. Spermatozoa have been found to persist following washing of fabrics, even after a machine wash (Kafarowski et al. 1996; Joshi et al. 1981; Crowe et al. 2000; Jobin and Gouffe 2003) and therefore it is important to consider their relevance in the gusset of underwear since they may be due to a previous consensual act of intercourse. AP is water soluble and unlikely to persist after a thorough wash.

Areas giving a positive reaction to the AP test are further investigated by extracting or swabbing the stained area and carrying out a microscopic examination for spermatozoa.

Intimate swabs (vaginal, anal, oral etc.) taken from individuals are treated in a similar manner, using the AP test to give an initial indication of the possible presence and quantity of semen, followed by the microscopic confirmation of spermatozoa and in some instances use of the PSA, choline or Laurell techniques.

In cases of alleged oral intercourse it may be necessary to examine a liquid saliva sample or mouth rinse from the complainant, in addition to or in the place of any oral swabs. In some instances the likelihood of detecting spermatozoa in the saliva or mouth rinse is greater than on the swabs (Willott and Crosse 1986). Because spermatozoa are rapidly lost from the oral cavity within the first few hours, police forces can use 'early evidence kits' to enable the taking of mouth samples at the time of first complaint so that a delay of sample collection is avoided while a medical examination is arranged. Early evidence kits also allow for collection of urine for toxicological analysis where delaying just a few hours could adversely affect the findings.

The presence of even a single spermatozoon should be declared and then interpreted carefully in the context of the case. The presence of spermatozoa with an absence of AP may suggest that the item has been washed and the spermatozoa have persisted from a previous event. Alternatively there may have been an indirect transfer of small numbers of spermatozoa or the AP or PSA activity may have been lost. The indirect transfer of small amounts of semen is particularly pertinent to cases involving the sexual assault of children as spermatozoa could be present on their clothing due to its contact with semen-stained surfaces or items from adults within their household.

In the absence of spermatozoa, the detection of PSA may be of significance, especially in combination with high levels of AP. PSA is present in high levels in seminal fluid; however, male urine (but not female urine) also contains appreciable levels of PSA. Other issues that need consideration in the interpretation of PSA results include the presence of blood, which may give a false positive (Carter 2003). It has also been reported (Denison *et al.* 2004) that anti-depressant drug treatment in a female led to the detection of PSA in the vaginal secretion of that individual and liquid urine from the same donor also tested positive. Prostate cancer and benign prostatic hyperplasia can also elevate the level of PSA in the blood serum, although the effect on semen levels is unreported. Drug therapy for these conditions can reduce the PSA levels in the serum. The same drug type is being marketed to reduce the effects of male pattern baldness, and this can also reduce serum PSA levels; again the effect on semen levels is unreported (Pannek *et al.* 1998; Overstreet *et al.* 1999).

The following describes the various semen identification tests in more detail:

### Acid phosphatase

The Brentamine test is widely used for the detection and location of AP in semen staining (Kaye 1949; Kind 1965). Acid phosphatase catalyses the liberation of naphthol from the substrate sodium $\alpha$-naphthyl phosphate, which then forms a complex with buffered Brentamine fast black K salt to form a purple azo-dye. Brentamine fast blue B salt had been the preferred test for many years as the colour change is easier to assess. However, its use is diminishing as it appears to have greater associated health risks than the fast black salt. Sensitivity of the two salts is roughly comparable.

AP is highly soluble in water and this facilitates application of this method to a screening test to determine the distribution of semen on surfaces and fabrics such as clothing and bedding. A sheet of filter paper is dampened with distilled water and pressed on to the item in question so that the AP in any seminal staining transfers into the corresponding area on the paper. Application of the Brentamine reagent to the paper produces a purple colouration indicating the location of any AP present. Careful replacement of the paper into its original position over the garment enables the scientist to map the staining on the fabric. Spot testing of an extract from a sample containing potential semen can be carried out by direct application of a small drop of the extract or its supernatant to a filter paper which is then treated with the reagent. The strength, colour and speed of reaction provide an indication of the amount of AP and hence semen present. Formation of a clear purple colour within two minutes of spraying is a good indication of the presence of seminal AP, although weaker stains may not react for much longer. If the coloured product has a pinkish appearance, this may be an indication that the AP is from vaginal secretions; faeces can also give a pink-brown colouration with the test. Vaginal secretions are also reputed to give occasional fast purple colour reactions due to the presence of bacterial AP.

Since the use of Brentamine is hazardous, the test must be carried out in an appropriate safety cabinet and the papers safely disposed of. Despite this, the test can be used at crime scenes with care, provided appropriate masks and protective clothing are worn and a coarse spray (rather than a gas-generated aerosol) is used in a well-ventilated area. However, in this situation it is preferable to locate semen by visual means (including specialist lighting if necessary) and spot AP testing as this reduces the application of hazardous chemicals and any possible dilution of stains due to wetting. Some laboratories prefer to screen for AP at scenes by the use of the methyl umbelliferyl phosphate reagent (MUP) and then confirm using Brentamine.

### Prostate Specific Antigen

PSA is a glycoprotein secreted into seminal plasma by the prostate gland; it aids the liquefaction of semen post ejaculation. It is one of a group of prostaglandins and is also known as P30 and Prostaglandin. It is normally present in low levels in serum, and at much higher levels in seminal plasma where it is present independently of spermatozoa and acid phosphatase.

Numerous test kits are marketed for the assessment of serum levels of PSA and have been variously applied for the detection of seminal PSA (Yokoto et al. 2001). The membrane tests available are based on an immunoassay, and utilise mobile monoclonal anti-human PSA antibodies, which are conjugated to dye particles. The antibodies bind human PSA and the resulting Ag-Ab complexes migrate on the test membrane to a reaction zone which contains immobilised polyclonal antihuman PSA antibodies. Here an Ag-Ab-Ag sandwich concentrates the dye particles resulting in the formation of a coloured line which indicates the presence of human PSA. Unbound monoclonal anti-human PSA antibodies migrate further to a control zone, containing immobilised anti-Ig antibodies. These components complex to form further lines; a second line gives a reaction equivalent to 4 ng/ml of PSA, and a third line is used to validate the test.

### Choline

Choline is detected using the Florence test reagent (iodine and potassium iodide in water), when it forms characteristic brown choline periodide crystals (Florence 1896a and b; Dawson et al. 1957). The test lacks sensitivity and requires concentration of a dried extract on to a microscope slide and then the introduction of the reagent from one side of the coverslip to further concentrate the reaction.

### Laurell

The Laurell technique (Laurell 1972) has been applied to aid the identification of semen (Baxter 1972). It utilises an agar plate containing anti-human semen serum into which an extract from the potential stain is electrophoresed. Any semen antigens in the extract react with the antibodies in the serum and form a rocket-shaped antigen-antibody complex which is visualised by staining with Brentamine reagent for AP. The size and colour of any peaks can be diagnostic of semen. Vaginal secretions can also produce peaks but these are smaller and stain differently.

### Spermatozoa

The identification of spermatozoa is facilitated by the microscopic examination of a small portion of an extract of the suspected stain, which is dried on to a microscope slide and stained, generally using haematoxylin and eosin (Christmas tree stain is also favoured by some scientists). Human spermatozoa are identified as being ovoid in shape with a clear acrosomal cap and a darker staining base and sometimes the tails can be seen, particularly in stronger samples. Complete spermatozoa with tails may help assess the amount of semen and its likely persistence time in body orifices. Spermatozoa from other animal species will have a different morphology.

In many cases, epithelial cells are also visible in microscopic preparations since semen is invariably mixed with other body fluids such as vaginal secretions or saliva. When dense cell populations render the search for spermatozoa difficult, an aliquot of the extract can be treated with Proteinase K to disrupt epithelial cell membranes (Chapman et al. 1989). Thiol-rich proteins in the outer membrane of spermatozoa are resistant to this treatment; however, care must still be taken as overdigestion can affect their morphology. This treatment also enables a larger proportion of an extract to be quickly searched for spermatozoa or it can be used as the initial stage of a preferential extraction of semen for DNA profiling.

Another stain, acridine orange, is used very occasionally if the initial microscopic examination is difficult because of high numbers of fungal bodies. Using this method, spermatozoa stain yellow (as they contain DNA) and fungal bodies stain red (as they contain RNA – a different type of nuclear material). Observations of potential spermatozoa with this method are confirmed by subsequent treatment of the slide with haematoxylin and eosin.

### Vaginal secretions

There are many opportunities for the transfer of vaginal secretions during sexual assaults. However detection is problematical as there is currently no specific test to categorically identify its presence. Nevertheless an evaluative approach taking into account cell populations may be helpful. Vaginal secretions contain numerous squamous epithelial cells from the superficial, intermediate and occasionally parabasal layers of the vagina (and also usually bacterial populations and small numbers of leucocoytes). Cells cannot be identified as vaginal in origin; however, at certain stages in the menstrual cycle glycogen-rich intermediate cells are produced which stain characteristically chocolate brown with the Lugol's iodine reagent (Merkel 1924; Thomas and van Hecke 1963; Hausmann et al. 1994; Hausmann and Schellman 1994). In some circumstances the presence of numerous such cells can be taken as an indication that they are of vaginal origin, although such an interpretation must also take into account that similarly staining cells can be produced in the male urethra (Rothwell and Harvey 1978). Tests which will in the near future identify vaginal and other cell types (by the presence of a specific type of messenger RNA (Juusola and Ballantyne 2005)) sound promising. However the method is likely to be lengthy and expensive and for specialist rather than routine use.

Blood is also often mixed with vaginal secretions and may be menstrual in origin or venous caused by injury to the vagina. No tests are available to identify blood as menstrual in origin.

The location of potential stains of vaginal fluid on clothing, such as the accused person's underwear, is usually achieved by searching for associated semen, saliva or blood. The presence of a pink or reddish reaction colour with the AP reagent may help locate potential stains containing vaginal secretions. Otherwise speculative sampling for DNA in relevant areas may also assist.

### Saliva

The detection of saliva is often of relevance in the investigation of sexual offences, on breast or skin swabs due to kissing or biting, on vulval swabs in cases of cunnilingus and penile swabs in cases of fellatio. Identification of its presence can be problematical since detection relies on the presence of $\alpha$-amylase which can also be present in other body fluids. Varying low levels of amylase are present in sweat, nasal secretions, semen, urine and tears, whereas faeces and vaginal secretions can show similar levels to saliva (Willott 1974; Newton 1992). The absence of detectable amylase must also be treated with caution since some individuals produce little or no $\alpha$-amylase activity or the amylase may have become denatured. Reporting findings of a strong amylase reaction must take into account the possibility of other body fluids, but in certain instances the forensic biologist is able to justify an opinion that a stain is saliva.

The Phadebas® test is commonly used to detect amylase and utilises a Cibacron dye cross-linked to starch, which is hydrolysed by amylase causing release of the dye. Phadebas® tablets are dissolved in water and than applied to sheets of filter paper using an aerosol spray so that a fairly dense speckled blue layer is present (Willott 1974; Willott and Griffiths 1980). The paper is placed with the sprayed face down on to the garment to be tested, dampened and left for up to 40 minutes. Positive reactions are indicated by the appearance of clear blue areas which can be mapped back on to the garment. A spot test can also be carried out on stain extracts by the incubation of an aliquot of the extract with a tablet in water, when amylase causes the release of blue dye into solution. This method also enables the quantification of amylase, although since the amount of staining tested cannot be standardised, the expert must use their judgement as to the significance of any positive results. If the co-location of semen and saliva is of relevance in a particular case (for example if semen deposited in the mouth has been spat out on to clothing or bedding), Brentamine reagent can be subsequently applied to the Phadebas® paper to detect acid phosphatase in any semen staining and assess if it is coincident with the amylase detected from potential saliva.

Recently a test originally developed in the 1970s (Whitehead and Kipps 1975), utilising starch cross-linked to a Procion red dye, has been revitalised by the reappearance of Procion red dye on the market (Watson 2004 and Martin et al. 2006). The production of this 'red starch' paper is much quicker, cheaper and more consistent than that of Phadebas® and also slightly more sensitive. However, visualisation of amylase reactions requires rinsing of the paper which can be messy and the assessment of the strength of the reaction can be more difficult than with Phadebas®.

Identification of the presence of epithelial cells from saliva is not generally helpful as they cannot be attributed to saliva. However, the Lugols test may assist an interpretation by helping to evaluate whether vaginal cells are present. The presence of many glycogen-rich cells together with a mediocre or weak amylase reaction would suggest the presence of vaginal secretions rather than saliva.

### Blood

In sexual offences, blood examinations are pertinent where a physical assault has also taken place or it may have been transferred due to the complainant menstruating or receiving internal injury due to forceful penetration. Consideration must also be given to whether the perpetrator bled due to injury or more rarely whether blood is coincident with semen and suggesting haematospermia – the condition where blood is present in the ejaculate. With a physical assault such as punching or kicking the distribution of any blood transferred to the accused's clothing and its pattern may be of significance in addressing the events that have taken place (see Chapter 9).

In many cases locating blood is relatively straightforward as stains have a very characteristic appearance and an experienced forensic practitioner will often feel confident to offer a view that a stain is blood even without carrying out any tests. In practice, however, a presumptive chemical test will be carried out and a positive result to a peroxidase test together with a characteristic appearance will enable the reporting that 'blood is present'.

In other situations, the blood may be weak or dilute or on a dark-coloured surface and so less readily distinguished by appearance, whereupon the use of presumptive tests becomes a requisite to locate potential bloodstains and the need for a general screen of the item for blood necessary.

Consideration must also be given to whether the appearance or position of a stain suggests that the blood is mixed with other body fluids such as semen, saliva or mucus. Stains which give a presumptive test result but do not have a typical appearance of blood will be reported with caution as possible blood or indicative of blood.

Presumptive tests are defined as those which give an indication of the nature of a body fluid but do not provide absolute identification in isolation. Currently, for blood, these usually comprise a test for peroxidase-like activity which is associated with haemoglobin, a constituent of red blood cells, using the Kastle Meyer (KM) or Leucomalachite Green (LMG) tests (Kastle 1909; Glaister 1926; Grodsky *et al.* 1951). More detail about these is given below. Kits for presumptive testing and species identification of body fluids are now appearing on the market and can provide a quick and easy means of testing potential stains at a crime scene. However, the specificity and sensitivity of these are variable.

Crystal tests (Takayama 1912; Wagenaar 1935) are occasionally used to confirm the presence of blood. Both are based upon the formation of haemoglobin derivative crystals which can be readily identified using a microscope. They can be useful if a stain is weak or old, although their sensitivity is limited and they perform best when dried blood flakes are present.

The presence of a DNA profile specific for higher primates may also confirm the presence of blood, as can the precipitin test (which detects human antigens). However, consideration must be given to whether other body fluids may be coincident and contributing to the DNA or human reactions.

*Presumptive peroxidase tests*

These entail the addition of either a KM or LMG reagent to a small sample which has been collected by rubbing a piece of filter paper over the stain. Hydrogen peroxide is then added to the paper and a positive test result indicated by the immediate formation of a pink or green colour (respectively) on the filter paper. The test relies on the peroxidase-like activity associated with haemoglobin in the red blood cells. Reduction of hydrogen peroxide (catalysed by haemoglobin) releases oxygen which reacts with the reduced (colourless) form of either leucomalachite green or phenolphthalein (KM reagent), to produce a colour change. Both tests are sensitive but not specific for blood, KM detecting blood to a dilution of 1:100 with fresh stains and LMG to 1:250 (Gillbard 2001).

If a stain is weak, a damp filter paper can be used to increase sensitivity or the reagents can be added directly to a small portion of the stain. Where stains are not readily visible by eye or with appropriate lighting or magnification, a general screen can be done by dividing the garment into smaller areas and rubbing a piece of filter paper over each area and testing these with LMG or KM. If a positive reaction is obtained, the area can be subdivided or searched more closely with a low magnification microscope to help locate specific stains.

False positives are occasionally obtained due to the presence of chemical oxidants and are recognised by the development of a colour before the addition of peroxide. The KM, LMG and peroxide reagents can oxidise in air so care has to be taken that these are not producing a false positive. The most likely materials other than blood to give a positive result are plant peroxidases. However, these are rapidly inactivated at high temperature and with time and so are rarely an issue in the forensic context.

## Faeces

Faecal staining is of relevance in cases of anal intercourse where there is the potential for transfer to the perpetrator's penis or underwear, or more rarely where complete stools are left at a crime scene. The identification of large amounts is straightforward as appearance and smell are distinctive; however, smaller amounts can be difficult to identify. Use is made of a chemical test which detects urobilinogen, which is derived from bilirubin by degradation in the intestine and causes faeces to have their brown colour. Infant faeces tend to be yellow in colour due to unchanged bilirubin and for the first few days after birth, a dark green meconium is produced. Microscopy for food products such as plant cells, muscle fibres, starch grains and for bacteria, yeast or internal parasites can sometimes be helpful.

The Edelman's test detects urobilinogen by producing a green fluorescent complex in the presence of a reagent containing ethanol, chloroform, pyridine and zinc acetate (Price 1984). Distinction of omnivore/carnivore versus herbivore faeces is by use of a thin layer chromatography technique which produces distinctive band patterns (Waldron 1982). Thin layer chromatography has also been found to have good sensitivity when small amounts of faeces are present.

## Urine

Stains of urine are often found on items of clothing, but are only occasionally of evidential significance. Identification is based on the chemical constituents such as urea and creatinine whose concentration vary quite considerably depending on fluid intake and may fall so low that they may not be detectable in urine stains. The smell of urine is considered so characteristic that its presence amounts to the virtual identification and can be accentuated by warming the item after dampening the stain and may be ammoniacal if the item has been kept wet. Stains may be colourless to pale yellow in visible light due to the presence of urinary pigments.

Various chemical tests are in use to detect urea which is present in high concentration in urine as it is the main route for the excretion of nitrogenous wastes. The DMAC (p-dimethylaminocinnamaldehyde) test (Rhodes and Thornton 1976) is commonly used and in a strongly acidic solution it is a sensitive reagent for the detection of amides and amines. DMAC forms a Schiffs base with these substances to give a magenta-coloured product. In practice however the test has limited sensitivity to urine and old or weak stains may not give a reaction. Furthermore, prior treatment with a paper screening test, such as AP or Phadebas, can lead to loss of the urine solutes into the paper and a false negative result when the stain is tested. With the Nessler's and Azostix® tests urease, a hydrolase, converts urea into carbon dioxide and ammonia which is detected by the Nessler's reagent forming a brown precipitate or the production of a blue colouration on the Azostix®. Creatinine, a normal constituent of urine, can be detected by the Jaffe reaction (Taussky 1961) – the formation of a deep orange-coloured creatinine picrate in the presence of alkaline picrate solution. This reaction is not specific for creatinine, and therefore it is preferable to combine it with a chromatographic technique which is diagnostic.

Semen, milk and sweat also contain urea, and may give a positive reaction to the urea tests, although careful application of the method and assessment of results can assist here.

## DNA

Spermatozoa are a rich source of DNA and therefore DNA profiling techniques work well even with small amounts of semen. Obtaining profiles from blood is similarly successful but rates for saliva are variable.

When a small aliquot of an extract from a pertinent sample has been examined microscopically, there can be difficulty in locating spermatozoa at extremely low levels. However, a much larger sample is usually extracted for DNA processing and there are some reports of male DNA profiles being obtained from vaginal swabs when the biologist has been unable to detect spermatozoa in their microscopic preparation. In some such instances non-sperm DNA may have been detected.

When extremely small numbers of spermatozoa or cells are present, specialist tests such as laser microdissection (Elliott *et al.* 2003) and fluorescent *in situ* hybridisation (Collins *et al.* 1994) can be used to effectively pinpoint them and provide a sample for the very sensitive low copy number (LCN) DNA techniques (Gill *et al.* 2000). These techniques can also assist with cold case reviews when small samples or microscope slides are the only retained materials. The Y-STR technique (Johnson *et al.* 2005) can also be useful to provide information about the number of male contributors. It is also valuable when the male DNA is at much lower levels compared to female DNA, for example traces transferred via digital penetration of the vagina. As well as a transfer of defined body fluids, cells and DNA may be transferred by contact (Lowe *et al.* 2002), either directly by people or surfaces touching (primary contact), or indirectly via an intermediary (secondary contact). In these situations, it is especially important that full and detailed information about the incident and any subsequent activities (as alleged by both the complainant and the accused person) is provided by the investigator to the forensic scientist. This will enable an assessment of the likelihood of DNA being transferred and persisting, and help to establish likely contact areas so that they can be targeted for the retrieval of any DNA present. DNA transferred by touch is generally at very low levels and is best detected by the use of specialist DNA techniques (see Chapter 2). Such cases necessitate a consideration of the chance of DNA transfer by legitimate contact prior to conducting the tests and in any interpretation of results. The use of sensitive DNA techniques also highlights the need for sound contamination checks to be in place so that DNA transferred inadvertently during processing is detected. Such checks should include provision of DNA elimination samples from staff involved in both the collection and examination of forensic samples and the manufacture of consumable materials used during processing, together with environmental monitoring of forensic medical examination facilities and laboratory work areas.

Following the detection of a specific body fluid and the preparation of a DNA profile from the stained area, it is necessary for the scientist to consider whether the DNA profile can be safely attributed to the body fluid detected (Evett *et al.* 2002). For example a weak bloodstain overlying an area containing DNA from a cellular contact may give a profile originating from the cellular component whilst the blood failed to produce a profile.

## Conclusion

Best practice for the scientific investigation of a sexual offence utilising body fluid evidence begins with the forensic biologist devising a sound examination strategy based on information provided by the police investigator and the medical examiner. Ideally he or she will document their expectations taking into account pre- and post-offence activities and consider evidence-based sampling persistence data. This is a crucial stage in establishing a solid foundation for the subsequent forensic examination; however, it can be complex and requires consideration of many issues, evidence types and potential outcomes. It therefore must be done by skilled practitioners and ideally be peer reviewed before the examination begins. Application of the case assessment and interpretation model at this stage, including the hierarchy of propositions, elicits a logical and clear progression of thinking and is highly recommended.

Some police forces have set up service level agreements with forensic providers which have led to them having a greater appreciation of this process. These forces have also benefited from ready access to advice for specific cases, information about wider issues such as performance across a range of cases and bespoke training. As a consequence they are better able to manage the investigation process and this has resulted in an improvement in the quality of evidence submitted to the forensic provider and better timeliness of results to the police. The setting up of sexual assault referral centres (SARCs) in recent years has led to an improved service for patients referred by the police and is also available to those who self refer because they do not wish to involve the police. These provide a one-stop location for medical care, counselling and forensic investigation. Progress in important areas such as these should ultimately increase public confidence in the handling of sexual assaults, increasing the proportion of rapes that are reported to the police (currently an estimated 15 per cent).

In recent years, there have been few advances in the field of body fluid identification since most developments in relation to biological evidence types have been centred on DNA. The enormous development in DNA profiling techniques has resulted in huge advances for the sensitivity and discriminating power of such tests. This has enabled reinvestigation and prosecution in many old sexual offence cases where this had not been scientifically possible previously. In the body fluid arena we have benefited recently from the introduction of kits to detect PSA in seminal fluid and the introduction of the red starch test for amylase. However, there is much scope to improve aspects of body fluid evidence and there are frequently encountered areas needing development. Tests which would specifically identify the presence of saliva, vaginal cells and menstrual blood, and be able to provide information to aid the attribution of DNA profiles to these body fluids, would be of great value. Although the mRNA tests may hold promise with respect to the latter, these will be for specialist use due to their complexity and cost. Various commercial kits are currently being marketed as quick specific tests for body fluid identification, although their efficacy is variable.

When DNA profiling was first introduced to the courts, the DNA results, and hence the source of the body fluids detected, were heavily challenged by defence experts and lawyers. DNA profiling withstood this challenge and has remained powerful probative evidence, although paradoxically conviction rates remain low (6 per cent of those reported to police). In 20–25 per cent of the cases submitted to the Forensic Science Service® in 2006, the accused person stated that sexual intercourse had taken place with consent and hence there would be no challenge to any DNA match. This may well be an underestimate of the true figure since 54 per cent of rapes are committed by current or former partners and 55 per cent take place in the complainant's home. Many such cases also involve use of alcohol or drugs by one or both parties and thus the issue of consent is a complex one. Hence the trial hinges on the jury's view of the accounts of the complainant and accused, not surprisingly resulting in high attrition rates.

Where there are challenges to the body fluid evidence, these centre on how and when the body fluid was deposited rather than from whom it originated. This necessitates an appreciation of the transfer and persistence mechanisms in relation to body fluids and an evaluation of the findings in relation to the different activities or sexual acts that are said to have occurred according to the prosecution and defence accounts.

The forensic biologist currently approaches this by applying data from available publications (or using in-house work), together with their forensic expertise to estimate the probability that body fluid or DNA would be transferred, persist and be detectable. In some instances the lack of background data means that a robust evaluation cannot be made and the findings must be reported as inconclusive or unsuitable for evaluation. There is a real need for an increase in the collection and analysis of relevant transfer and persistence data in many instances. Although much data exists in individual forensic case files, its collection and collation will be time-consuming, costly and complex until a system of electronic case files and data extraction is well established. Although data from live casework may appear most relevant to inform expectations of what would be found following a particular event, caution is required as the accuracy of the events described is often unknown and sample types are limited. Data collected from samples from known sources, donors or mock scenarios can be very useful, especially in helping assess background levels of a body fluid or DNA profile, but may not truly mimic live casework situations. In practice a combination of both is probably most helpful.

In cases where there is a challenge to the scientific evidence, it is vital that the forensic scientist is provided with detailed accounts from *both* the complainant and the suspect so that they can assist the court by providing a scientific evaluation of the body fluid findings at the relevant activity level of the hierarchy. This will result in the Criminal Justice System being best served by a balanced and robust scientific evaluation of the findings against both the prosecution and defence accounts.

## References

Allard, J.E. (1997) 'The collection of data from findings in cases of sexual assault and the significance of spermatozoa on vaginal, anal and oral swabs', *Sci and Just*, 37 (2): 99–108.

Baxter, S.J. (1972) Personal communication.

Carter, G. (2003) Personal communication.

Chapman, R.L., Brown, N.M. and Keating, S.M. (1989) 'The isolation of spermatozoa from sexual assault swabs using Proteinase K', *J For Sci Soc*, 29: 207–212.

Collins, K.A., Rao, P.N., Hayworth, R., Schnell, S., Tap, M.P., Lantz, P.E., Geisinger, K.R. and Pettenati, M.J. (1994) 'Identification of sperm and non-sperm male cells in cervicovaginal smears using fluorescence in situ hybridization: applications in alleged sexual assault cases', *J Forensic Sci*, 39 (6) 1347–1355.

Cook, R., Evett, I.W., Jackson, G., Jones, P.J. and Lambert, J.A. (1998) 'A hierarchy of propositions: deciding which level to address in casework', *Sci and Just*, 38 (4): 231–240.

Crowe, G., Moss, D. and Elliot, D. (2000) 'Effect of laundering on AP and sperm detection', *Canadian Soc Forens Sci J*, 33: 1–5.

Davies, A. (1979) 'Letter in response to spermatozoa in the anal canal and rectum and the oral cavity of female rape victims', *J For Sci*, 24: 541–2.

Davies, A. and Wilson, E. (1974) 'The persistence of seminal constituents in the human vagina', *J For Sci*, 3: 45–55.

Dawson, R.M.C., Mann, T. and White, I.G. (1957) 'Glyceryl phosphorylcholine and phosphoryl choline in semen and their relation to choline', *Biochem J*, 65: 627–634

Denison, S.J., Lopes, E.M., D'Costa, L. and Newman, J.C. (2004) 'Positive prostate-specific antigen (PSA) results in semen-free sample', *J Can Soc For Sci*, 37 (4): 197–206.

Elliott, K., Hill, H.S., Lambert, C., Burroughs, T.R. and Gill, P. (2003) 'Use of Laser Microdissection greatly improves the recovery of DNA from sperm on microscope slides', *For Sci Int*, 137 (1): 28–36.

Enos, W.F. and Beyer, J.C. (1978) 'Spermatozoa in the anal canal and rectum and the oral cavity of female rape victims', *J For Sci*, 23: 231–3.

Evett, I.W., Gill, P.D., Jackson, G., Whitaker, J. and Champod, C. (2002) 'Interpreting small quantities of DNA: the hierarchy of propositions and the use of Bayesian networks', *J For Sci*, 47 (3): 520–530.

Evett, I.W., Jackson, G., Lambert, J.A. and McCrossan, S. (2000) 'The impact of the principles of evidence interpretation on the structure and content of statements', *Sci and Just*, 40 (4): 233–239.

FFLM (2008) *Guidelines for good practice. Guidelines for the collection of forensic specimens from complainants and suspects*. Faculty of Forensic and Legal Medicine.

Florence, A. (1896a) 'Du sperme et des taches de sperme en médecine légale', *Archives d'Anthropololgie Criminelle*, 11: 37, 146, 249.

Florence, A. (1896b) *Arch Exp Path Pharmakol*, 67: 275.

Gill, P., Whitaker, J., Flaxman, C., Brown N. and Buckleton, J. (2000) An investigation of the rigor of interpretation rules for STRs derived from less than 100pg DNA', *For Sci Int*, 112 (1): 17–40.

Gillbard, S. (2001) Personal communication.

Glaister, J. (1926) 'The Kastle-Meyer test for the detection of blood', *BMJ*, 650.

Grodsky, M., Wright, K. and Kirk, P.L. (1951) 'Simplified Preliminary Blood Testing-an Improved Technique and a Comparative Study of Methods', *Journal of Criminal Law, Criminology and Police Science*, 42: 95–104.

Hausmann, R., Pregler, C. and Schellmann, B. (1994) 'The value of the Lugol's iodine staining technique for the identification of vaginal epithelial cells', *Int J Leg Med*, 106: 298–301.

Hausmann, R. and Schellmann B. (1994) 'Forensic value of the Lugol's staining method – further studies on glycogenated epithelium in the male urinary tract', *Int J Leg Med*, 107: 147–151.

Jackson, G., Jones, S., Booth, G., Champod, C. and Evett, I.W. (2006) 'The nature of forensic science opinion – a possible framework to guide thinking and practice in investigations and in court proceedings', *Sci and Just*, 46 (1): 33–44.

Jobin, R.M. and Gouffe, M. (2003) 'The persistence of seminal constituents on panties after laundering. Significance to investigations of sexual assault', *J Can Soc For Sci*, 36 (1): 1–10.

Johnson, C.L., Giles, R.C., Warren, J.H., Flloyd, J.I. and Staub, R. (2005) 'Analysis of non-suspect samples lacking visually identifiable sperm using a Y-STR 10-plex', *J For Sci*, 50: 1116–8.

Joshi, U.N., Subhedar, S.K. and Saraf, D.K. (1981) 'Effect of water immersion on seminal stains on cotton cloth', *For Sci Int*, 17: 9–11.

Juusola, J. and Ballantyne, J. (2005) 'Multiplex mRNA Profiling for the Identification of Body Fluids', *For Sci Int*, 152 (1); 1–12.

Kafarowski, E., Lyon, A.M. and Sloan, M.M. (1996) 'The retention and transfer of spermatozoa in clothing by machine washing', *Can Soc Forens Sci J*, 29 (1): 7–11.

Kastle, J.H (1909) 'Chemical Tests for blood', *U.S Hygienic Laboratory Bulletin No. 51*. Washington, DC: US Government Printing Office.

Kaye, S. (1949) 'Acid phosphatase test for Identification of seminal stains', *J of Lab and Clin Med*, 34: 728.

Kind, S.S. (1965) 'The Acid Phosphatase Test', pp. 267–288, in A.F. Curry (ed.), *Methods of Forensic Science*, Vol. 3. London: Interscience Publishers.

Kipps, A.E. and Whitehead, P.H. (1975) 'The significance of amylase in forensic investigations of body fluids', *For Sci*, 6: 137–144.

Laurell, C.B. (1972) 'Electroimunoassay', *Scand J Clin Lab Invest*, 29 (suppl 124): 21–37.

Lowe, A., Murray, C., Whitaker, J., Tully, G. and Gill, P. (2002) 'The propensity of individuals to deposit DNA and the secondary transfer of low levels of DNA from individuals to inert surfaces', *For Sci Int*, 129 (1): 25–34.

Martin, N.C., Clayson, N.J. and Scrimger, D.G. (2006) 'The sensitivity and specificity of Red-starch paper for the detection of saliv', *Sci and Just*, 46 (2): 97–105.

Merkel, H. (1924) 'The glycogen content of the vaginal epithelium, its diagnostic significance and its critical evaluation', *Deutsch Zeitschrift für die gesamte Gerichtliche Medizin*, 4: 1–8.

Newton, M.A. (1992) Personal communication.

Newton, M.A. (2004) 'The sexual assault medical examination kit', pp. 105–134, in M. Dalton (ed.), *Forensic Gynaecology*. London: RCOG Press.

Norton, C. (2002) Personal communication.

Overstreet, J., Fuh, V.L., Gould, J., Howards, S.S., Lieber, M.M., Hellstrom, W., Shapiro, S., Carroll, P., Corfman, R.S., Petrou, S., Lewis, R., Toth, P., Shown, T., Roy, J., Jarrow, J.P., Bonilla, J., Jacobsen, C.A., Wang, D.Z. and Kaufman, K.D. (1999) 'Chronic treatment with Finasteride daily does not affect spermatogenesis or semen production in young men', *J Urology*, 162: 1295–1300.

Pannek, J., Marks, L.S., Pearson, J.D., Rittanhouse, H.G., Chan, D.W., Shery, E.D., Gormely, G.J., Subong, E.N.P., Kelley, C.A., Stoner, E. and Partin, A.W. (1998) 'Influence of Finasteride on free and total serum prostate specific antigen levels in men with benign prostatic hyperplasia', *J Urology*, 159: 449–453.

Price, C. (1984) Personal communication.

Rhodes, E.F. and Thornton, J.J. (1976) 'DMAC test for urine stains', *J Pol Sci and Admin*, 4 (1): 88–89.

Rothwell, T.J. and Harvey K.J. (1978) 'The limitations of the Lugol's iodine staining technique for the identification of vaginal epithelial cells', *J For Sci Soc*, 18: 181–184.

Takayama (1912) *Kokka Igakkai Zasshi*, no. 306: 15.

Taussky, H.H. (1961) 'Jaffe reaction', in D. Seligson (ed.), *Standard Methods of Clinical Chemistry*, Vol. 3, p. 99. New York, London: Academic Press.

Thomas, F. and Van Hecke, W. (1963) 'The demonstration of recent sexual intercourse in the male by the Lugol method', *Med Sci Law*, 3: 169–171.

Wagenaar, M. (1935)' Uber ein neues krystallinisches Blutfarstoffderivat', *Z Anal Chem*, 103: 417.

Waldron, S.J. (1982) Personal communication.

Watson (2004) Personal communication.

Whitehead, P.H. and Kipps, A.E. (1975) 'A test paper for detecting saliva stains', *J For Sc Soc*, 15 (1): 39–45.

Willott, G. (1974) 'An improved test for the detection of salivary amylase in stains', *J For Sci Soc*, 14: 341–344.

Willott, G. and Griffiths, M. (1980) 'A new method for locating saliva stains – spotty paper for spotting spit', *For Sci Int*, 15: 79–83.

Willott, G.M. and Allard, J.E. (1982) 'Spermatozoa – Their persistence after sexual intercourse', *For Sci Int*, 19: 135–154.

Willott, G.M. and Crosse, M.A. (1986) 'The Detection of Spermatozoa in the Mouth', *J For Sci Soc*, 26: 125–128.

Wilson, E.M. (1982) 'A comparison of the persistence of seminal constituents in the human vagina and cervix', *Police Surgeon*, 22: 44–45.

Yokota, M., Mitani, T., Tsujita, H., Kobayashi, T., Higuchi, T., Akane, A. and Nasu, M. (2001) 'Evaluation of prostate-specific antigen (PSA) membrane test for forensic examination of semen', *Legal Medicine*, 3: 171–176.

# Chapter 7

# Trace evidence

*Max M. Houck*

## Introduction

Trace evidence is a category of evidence that is characterised by the analysis of materials that, because of their size or texture, are easily transferred from one location to another. Once transferred, they persist for some period of time until they are collected as evidence, lost through activities, or ignored as insignificant. A characteristic of trace evidence is that it is gradually lost following transfer. Given this transience, the forensic scientist usually only recovers remnants of the transaction. The forensic analysis of trace evidence can reveal associations between people, places and things involved in criminal activity. The category 'trace evidence' encompasses a variety of materials, both natural and manufactured; they include, but are not limited to, glass, soils, hairs, fibres, paint, pollen, wood, feathers, dust and other detritus of things that surround us in our lives (Figure 7.1). Normally microscopy will be required to identify and analyse them, and additional instrumentation (which may have microscopes attached to assist in the location and analysis of these minute mute witnesses) may also be employed. Given the wide variety of material and substances involved, this chapter will focus on glass, paint, and hair as examples to illustrate the characteristics that trace evidence exhibits, the circumstances in which they are encountered, and how individual types of evidence are interpreted.

## Evidence

Most evidence is 'real', that is, it is generated as a part of the crime and recovered at the scene or at a place where the suspect or victim had been before or after the crime. However, not all evidence is created equal – some items of evidence may be accorded more significance than others: the context of the crime and the type, amount and quality of the evidence will dictate what can be determined and interpreted. Most of the items in our daily lives

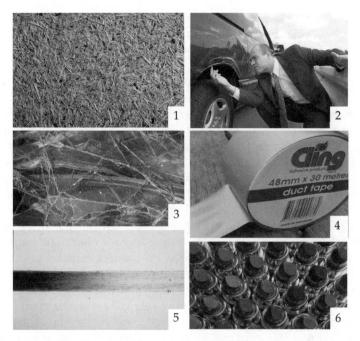

**Figure 7.1** Examples of *trace evidence*. Trace evidence occurs in a wide variety of forms and modes; for example, (1) fibres, (2) automotive paint, (3) glass, (4) duct tape, (5) hairs, and (6) cosmetics

are produced or manufactured *en masse*, including biological materials (the average person has about two million hair follicles, for example), and this has implications for what can be said about the relationships between people, places and things involved in a crime.

## The basis of evidence: transfer and persistence

When two things come into contact, information is exchanged by the physical transfer of trace material: this is one of the guiding principles of forensic science. Developed by Edmond Locard, a French forensic scientist in the early part of the twentieth century, it posits that such an exchange occurs, even if the results are not identifiable or are too small to be found. Forensic science uses this principle to demonstrate associations between people, places and things involved in criminal actions through the analysis of evidence.

The conditions that affect the amounts of material transferred in a variety of exchanges of the type that are considered here include:

- the pressure applied during contact (10 pounds of pressure should transfer more material than one);
- the number of contacts (six contacts between two objects should result in more transferred material than one contact);
- how easily the item transfers material (mud transfers more readily than does concrete);

- the form of the evidence (solid/particulate, liquid, or gas/aerosol);
- how much of the item is involved in the contact (a square centimetre should transfer less than a square metre of the same material).

Evidence that is transferred from a source to a location with no intermediaries is said to have undergone *direct transfer*; it has transferred from A to B. In contrast, *indirect transfer* involves one or more intermediate objects: the evidence transfers from A to B to C. Indirect transfer can become complicated and poses potential limits on interpretation. For example, suppose that you own a cat and before you go to the bar to meet some friends, you pet the cat. At this point, you have experienced a direct transfer of your cat's hairs to your trousers. Once at the bar, you sit in a lounge chair and sip your cocktail. The chair will probably have received an indirect transfer of your cat's hairs – your cat has never sat in the bar chair. You get up to go to the bathroom, and when you come back, someone is sitting in your chair. The person who is sitting in your chair has also experienced an indirect transfer of anything on the chair, except for any fibres originating from the chair's upholstery (which have been directly transferred). How would you interpret finding your cat's hairs on the bar patron if you didn't know she had sat in the chair? What this simple example shows is that, whilst direct transfer may be straightforward to interpret, indirect transfers can be complicated and potentially misleading.

**Figure 7.2** *Direct and indirect transfer.* A pair of muddy shoes is a good visual for the two types of transfer, direct and indirect. Walking in the mud transfers that material to the shoes (direct transfer); walking with those shoes on a clean floor transfers the mud to the floor (indirect transfer, with the shoes as a vehicle or intermediary for transfer). Some materials transfer better than others and persist longer; some types of activity result in more or less transferred evidence as well, so the forensic scientist must be careful of their interpretations. It may be better to speak of direct and indirect *sources* rather than transfers

Moreover, rarely, if ever, can a forensic scientist tell the difference between secondary (one intermediary) and tertiary (two intermediaries) transfer. It may be more accurate to speak of direct and indirect *sources*, referring to the originating source and not the mode of transfer (Figure 7.2). The 'transfer' terminology is more or less standard, however.

The flipside of the transfer coin is persistence. Once the evidence transfers, it will remain, or persist, in that location until it is further transferred, degrades until it is unusable or unrecognisable, collected as evidence, or is lost. The persistence of evidence depends on:

- the kind of evidence (such as, hairs, glass, paint, etc.);
- the location of the evidence (open to the environment or protected from the elements);
- the environment around the evidence (raining, dry, sunny indoors, etc.);
- time from transfer to collection (shorter elapsed time usually means more evidence);
- 'activity' on or around the evidence location (less activity leads to greater retention of evidence).

Studies suggest that transferred evidence is lost with normal activity (Pounds and Smalldon 1975; Robertson and Roux 1999), yet the very transience of trace evidence makes it both valuable as evidence and vulnerable to loss or contamination.

## Contamination

Once the activity surrounding the crime has ended, any transfers that take place may be considered contamination, defined as an 'unwanted transfer of material between items of evidence'. A wet, bloody pair of trousers from a victim must not be packaged with clothing from a suspect; the post-crime transfers might obscure the criminal evidence. Every item of evidence (where practical) should be packaged separately. Contamination is itself a kind of evidence – at least evidence of sloppy or careless forensic work, and whilst it is impossible wholly to prevent contamination, properly designed facilities, adequate protective clothing and quality-oriented protocols that specify the handling and packaging of evidence can help to minimise it.

## Classification and individualisation

All things are unique in space and time. No two (or more) objects are absolutely identical. Take, for example, a mass-produced product like a tennis shoe. Thousands of shoes of a particular type may be produced in any one year. The manufacturer's goal is to make them all appear and perform the same – consumers demand consistency. This is a bane and a boon to forensic scientists because it makes it easy to separate one item from another (this red tennis shoe is different from this white one) but these same characteristics make it difficult to separate items with many of the same characteristics (two red tennis shoes). How could two white tennis shoes off a production line one after the other be discriminated? You might say, 'this one' and 'that one' but if they were mixed up, you probably couldn't sort them again. They would have to be labelled somehow, perhaps by numbering them '1' and '2'. But what if the two shoes are the same except for colour: one is white and the other is red? The difference is obvious but do they belong in the same category? Compared with a brown dress shoe, the two tennis shoes would have more in common with each other than with the dress shoe. All the shoes, however, are more like one another than they are like other objects, for example, a cricket bat. Forensic scientists have developed terminology to clarify their communication about these issues.

Identification is the examination of the chemical and physical properties of an object and the use of such findings to categorise it as a member of a group. What is the object made of? What is its colour, mass and volume? All of the characteristics used to identify an object help to refine that object's identity (Thornton 1986). Identification is therefore a process of classification based on those physical and chemical properties of the object that are shared with other members of the set (or class) in which it can be placed. These properties can be observed by a combination of microscopy and chemical analysis. Accordingly, analysing a white powder and concluding that it is heroin is an example of identification; determining that a small translucent chip is container glass through elemental analysis is also identification. Likewise, the microscopic examination of debris from clothing at a crime scene and determining it contains hairs from an English Setter is identification. The analysis may or may not require particular instruments for its successful accomplishment. In this last example, the visibly fibrous nature of the material restricts what they could be: they are hairs or fibres rather than bullets or wood. The microscopic characteristics indicate that some of the fibrous objects are hairs, specifically dog hairs, and most like those from a specific breed of dog. This description places the hairs into a group of objects with similar characteristics, called a class. All English Setter hairs would fall into a class; these belong to a larger class of items called dog hairs. Further, all dog hairs can be included in the class of non-human hairs and, ultimately, into a more inclusive class called hairs. Going in the other direction, as the process of identification of evidence becomes more specific it permits the analyst to classify the evidence into successively smaller classes of objects.

'Class' is a movable definition – it may not be necessary to classify the evidence beyond dog hairs if you are looking for human hairs or textile fibres. Although it is possible to define the dog hairs more completely, you may not need to do so in the case at hand. Multiple items can be classified differently, depending on what questions need to be asked. For example, a grapefruit, a grape, a tennis ball, an axe handle and a banana could be classified as fruit versus non-fruit, round things versus non-round things and organic versus inorganic (Figure 7.3).

Stating that two objects share a class identity may indicate they come from a common source, but what is meant by a 'common source' depends on the material in question, the supply chain of production for manufactured goods,

**Figure 7.3** Classification. Identification and classification are key concepts in forensic science as they provide an infrastructure for making sense out of what a thing or a part of a thing might be. Unlike biological taxonomy, however, forensic classifications are flexible and relate to what characteristics are needed for sorting. For example, these objects could be classified in a variety of ways, such as food/non-food, sporting/non-sporting, small/large, organic/inorganic, or even fruit/sporting goods/cosmetic use

and the precision of the examinations used to classify the object. The potential complexity of what constitutes a common source can be extensive; this is, in part, determined and limited by the methods used in the analysis. Going back to the example of the two white tennis shoes: what is their common source – the factory, the owner, or where they are found? Because shoes come in pairs, finding one at a crime scene and another in the suspect's apartment could be considered useful to the investigation. The forensic examination of such objects may seek to find characteristics that will help determine if the two shoes were owned by the same person (the 'common source'), and if the question centred on identifying the production source of the shoes, then the factory would be the 'common source.'

Another simple example may involve fibres found on a body left in a ditch that are determined to be from automotive carpeting. The investigation identifies a suspect and fibres from his car are found to be analytically indistinguishable in all tested traits from the crime scene fibres. The suspect's car should be considered the 'common source' for investigative and legal purposes, but it is not the only car with that carpeting since other models from that car manufacturer or even other car manufacturers may have used that carpeting, and the carpeting may not be the only product that contains those fibres. Given the circumstances of the case, it is reasonable to conclude that the most logical source for the fibres is the suspect's car. If the fibres were found on the body but there was no suspect, part of the investigation may be to determine what company made the fibres and track what products those fibres went into in an effort to find who owns those products. In that instance, the 'common source' could be the fibre manufacturer, the carpet manufacturer, or the potential suspect's car, depending on what question is being asked.

If an object can be classified into a group with only one member (itself), it has been individualised. An individualised object is associated with one, and only one, source: it is unique. The traits that allow for individualisation depend, in large part but not exclusively, on the raw materials, natural variation, manufacturing methods and history of use. Trace evidence is almost never individualised. Because of the limitations of time, space and the sheer number of things in the world that could potentially become evidence, far more evidence is at the class level than individual level. The fact that every single item of a specific make, model and type cannot be accounted for in an analysis (think of the number of golf balls in existence, for example) means that most interpretations of forensic trace evidence are statistical interpretations.

## Relationships and context

The relationships between the people, places and things involved in crimes are central to deciding what items to examine and how to interpret the results. For example, if a sexual assault occurs and the perpetrator and victim are strangers, trace evidence may be more relevant than if they live together or are sexual partners. Strangers are not expected to have ever met before and, therefore, would not have transferred evidence before the crime. People who live together would have some opportunities to transfer certain types of evidence (head hairs and carpet fibres from the living room, for example) but not necessarily others (semen or vaginal secretions). Spouses or sexual partners, being the most intimate relationship of the three examples, would share a good deal more traces (Figure 7.4).

Stranger-on-stranger crimes beg the question of coincidental associations, that is, two things, which previously have never been in contact with each other, have items on them that are analytically indistinguishable at a certain class level, for example fibres. Advocates in cross-examination may ask, 'Could not [insert evidence type here] really have come from anywhere? Are not [generic class level evidence] very common?' It has been proven for a wide variety of evidence that coincidental matches are extremely rare (Houck 2003a; Koons and Buscaglia 2002; Ryland *et al.* 1981; Ryland and Houck 2001). The enormous variety of mass-produced goods, consumer choices, economic factors, biological and natural diversity, and other traits creates a nearly infinite combination of comparable characteristics for the items involved in any one situation. Some kinds of evidence, however, are either quite common, such as white cotton fibres, or have few distinguishing characteristics, such as indigo-dyed cotton from denim fabric. Despite the form of the trace evidence, the concepts of transfer and persistence predominate its interpretation. The mechanics, however, of transfer and persistence do depend on the form, as do its identification and comparison. The main types of trace evidence are detailed in the rest of this chapter, providing a background for better understanding of its collection, analysis and interpretation.

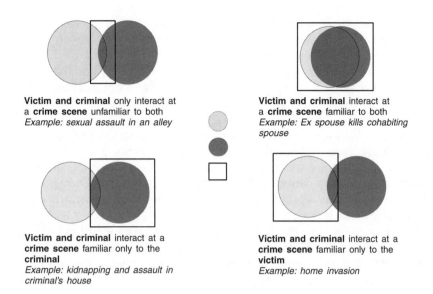

Victim and criminal only interact at a **crime scene** unfamiliar to both
*Example: sexual assault in an alley*

Victim and criminal interact at a **crime scene** familiar to both
*Example: Ex spouse kills cohabiting spouse*

Victim and criminal interact at a **crime scene** familiar only to the **criminal**
*Example: kidnapping and assault in criminal's house*

Victim and criminal interact at a **crime scene** familiar only to the **victim**
*Example: home invasion*

**Figure 7.4** *Relationship graphic.* The context of the crime is key to understanding the probative value of evidence. The evidence collected in a stranger-on-stranger crime where neither victim nor perpetrator has been before will be quite different from what is collected in a similar crime involving two cohabiting spouses

## Hairs

*Hairs* are a fibrous structure originating from the skin of mammals. Non-mammalian animals and plants have structures that may appear to be hairs (and erroneously named thus) but they are not: only mammals have hairs. Hairs grow from the *epidermis* of the body. The *follicle* is the structure within which hairs grow; hairs grow from the base of the follicle upwards. Hair is made of *keratin*, a protein-based material also found in nails and horns. In the follicle, the hair is still soft; as the hair proceeds up the follicle, it dries out and hardens and this process is called *keratinisation*.

Hairs have three growth phases. In the *anagen* (active) phase, the follicle produces new cells and pushes them up the hair shaft becoming incorporated into the hair. Specialised cells (*melanocytes*) in the follicle produce small coloured granules, called *melanin* or *pigment*, which give hairs their colour. The combination, density and distribution of these granules produce the range of hair colours seen in humans and animals. Hairs stay in the anagen phase for a length of time related to their body area; scalp hairs may stay in anagen for several years, for example. Head hairs grow an average of 1.3 cm per month. After the anagen phase, the hair transitions into the *catagen* (resting) phase. During the catagen phase, the follicle shuts down production of cells, which begin to shrink, and the root condenses into a bulb-shaped structure, called a *root bulb* or a *club root*. The hair now enters *telogen* or resting phase of the follicle – cell production has ceased, the root is condensed and is held in place mechanically. When the hair falls out, the follicle is triggered into anagen phase again and the cycle renews. On a healthy human head, about

80 per cent to 90 per cent of the hairs are in the anagen phase, about 2 per cent in the catagen phase and about 10 per cent to 18 per cent in the telogen phase. Humans, on average, lose about 100 scalp hairs a day.

A single hair on a macro-scale has a root, a shaft and a tip. The *root* is that portion that resided in the follicle. The *shaft* is the main portion of the hair and the *tip* is the portion furthest from the scalp. Internally, the three main structural elements in a hair are the cuticle, the cortex and the medulla (Figure 7.5). The *cuticle* of a hair is a series of overlapping layers of *scales* that form a protective covering. Animal hairs have *scale patterns* that vary by species and these patterns are a useful diagnostic tool for identifying animal hairs. Humans have a scale pattern called *imbricate* (Brunner and Coman 1974); this pattern does not vary significantly between people and is generally not useful in forensic examinations.

The *cortex* makes up the bulk of the hair and consists of spindle-shaped cells that contain or constrain other structures. *Pigment granules* are found in the cortex and they are dispersed variably throughout. The granules vary in size, shape, aggregation and distribution – all excellent characteristics for forensic comparisons.

It is easy to determine if a hair is human or non-human by a microscopic examination. Determining the species of the non-human hair takes effort, skill and a good reference collection. Animal hairs have macroscopic and microscopic characteristics that distinguish them from those of humans.

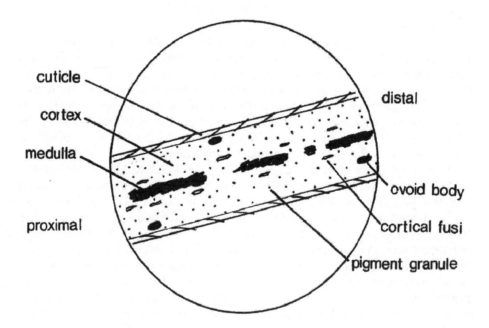

**Figure 7.5** *Hair diagram.* Hair is a complex biological structure consisting of an outer layer of overlapping scales (the cuticle), the main pigment-containing mass of the hair (the cortex) and a variably expressed series of air chambers that run through the centre of the hair (the medulla). *Source*: Adapted from Hicks (1977)

Unlike other animals, humans exhibit a wide variety of hairs on their bodies. The characteristics of these hairs may allow for an estimation of body area origin. The typical body areas that can be determined are:

- head (or scalp);
- pubic;
- facial;
- chest;
- axillary (armpits);
- eyelash/eyebrow; and
- limbs.

Typically, only head and pubic hairs are suitable for microscopic comparison; facial hairs may also be useful. Hairs that do not fit into these categories may be called *transitional hairs*, such as those on the stomach. It may be difficult to make a decision as to the body area of origin; it may not matter to the circumstances of the crime. Labelling the hair as a 'body hair' is sufficient and may be the most accurate conclusion given the quality and nature of the hair. Doing so, however, may preclude that hair from further microscopic examination.

Attempts to establish the ethnicity or ancestry of an individual from his or her hairs can only result in an estimate. The morphology and colour of a hair may give an indication of a person's ancestry but humans are more variable from one to another in their hair morphology than any other primate. This variation tends to correlate with a person's ancestry although it is not exact. For simplicity and accuracy, three main ancestral groups are used: Europeans, Africans and Asians. In the older anthropological and forensic literature, these groups were referred to as Caucasoids, Negroids and Mongoloids respectively; these terms are archaic now and should not be used. If an examiner estimates a hair to be from a person of a certain ancestry it does not mean that is how that person identifies themselves racially.

Misconceptions abound about hairs and what can be derived from their examination. Age and sex cannot be determined from examining hairs; grey hairs may occur from a person's twenties onwards. Hairs do not grow after you die (skin shrinks from loss of water) and, although there are some studies to the contrary, shaving does not stimulate hair growth.

The goal of most forensic hair examinations is the microscopic comparison of a questioned hair or hairs with a known hair sample. A known hair sample consists of between 50 and 100 hairs from all areas of interest, typically the head or pubic area. The hairs must be combed and pulled to collect both telogen and anagen hairs. A known sample must be representative of the collection area to be suitable for comparison purposes (Bisbing 2002).

A comparison microscope is used for the examination. This is composed of two transmitted light microscopes joined by an optical bridge to produce a split image. This side-by-side, point-by-point comparison is key to the effectiveness and accuracy of a forensic hair comparison: Hairs (and fibres) cannot be compared properly otherwise. The hairs are examined from root to tip, at magnifications of 40X to 250X. Hairs are mounted on glass microscope slides with a mounting medium of an appropriate refractive index, about 1.5. All of the characteristics visible are used; no set list exists for hair traits. The known sample is characterised and described to record its variety. The questioned hairs are then described individually. These descriptions cover the root, the microanatomy of the shaft, and the tip. Like must be compared to like: pubic hairs to pubic hairs and head hairs to head hairs only (Houck *et al.* 2004).

Three conclusions can be drawn from a forensic microscopic hair comparison. If the questioned hair exhibits the same microscopic characteristics as the known hairs, then it could have come from the same person who provided the known sample. Hair comparisons are not a form of positive identification, however. If the questioned hair exhibits similarities but slight differences to the known hair sample, then no conclusion can be drawn as to whether the questioned hair could have come from the known source. Finally, if the questioned hair exhibits different microscopic characteristics from the known hair sample, then it can be concluded that the questioned hair did not come from the known source. This evaluation and balancing of microscopic traits within and between samples is central to the comparison process.

It might appear that hairs could be coded, entered into a database, and statistics calculated in a similar manner to some other types of forensic evidence. If this were possible it would be of immense help in determining the significance of hairs as evidence. But the complex nature of the microanatomy, the subjective evaluation of the objective traits, and the natural variance in hair as a biological material make coding for a database all but impossible.

In an early paper on the coding and significance of hairs, the late Barry Gaudette, a hair examiner with the Royal Canadian Mounted Police, carried out a study to assess the specificity of microscopic hair examinations (Gaudette and Keeping 1974). Gaudette's work involved brown head hairs of European ancestry, coded and inter-compared. The study determined that only nine pairs of hairs were indistinguishable, resulting in a frequency of 1 in 4,500. He did further work with pubic hairs which resulted in a frequency of 1 in 1,600. Although critics considered that the study was flawed and the frequencies were not valid for any other sample, it was the first systematic study of its kind. Some examiners quoted these frequencies in their testimony to quantify the significance of their findings – a statistically unjustified and erroneous application of the study. A later paper by Gaudette's colleagues (Wickenheiser and Hepworth 1990) elaborated on his study and refined the frequencies. Other studies provided additional insights into the potential specificity of microscopic hair examinations but to date, no universal approach for calculating significance has been published, and probably none will be. While a computer could be used to analyse digital images and categorise the hairs, a human could do it much faster and just as accurately. And now that DNA analysis is more accessible, this approach is hardly justified.

Unless tissue from the follicle is attached to the root of a hair, the hair will not be suitable for nuclear (that is, traditional) DNA testing. The advent of forensic mitochondrial DNA (mtDNA) in the mid 1990s heralded a new era of biological analysis in law enforcement (Figure 7.6). This was especially true for hairs, as it offered a way to add information to microscopic hair examinations.

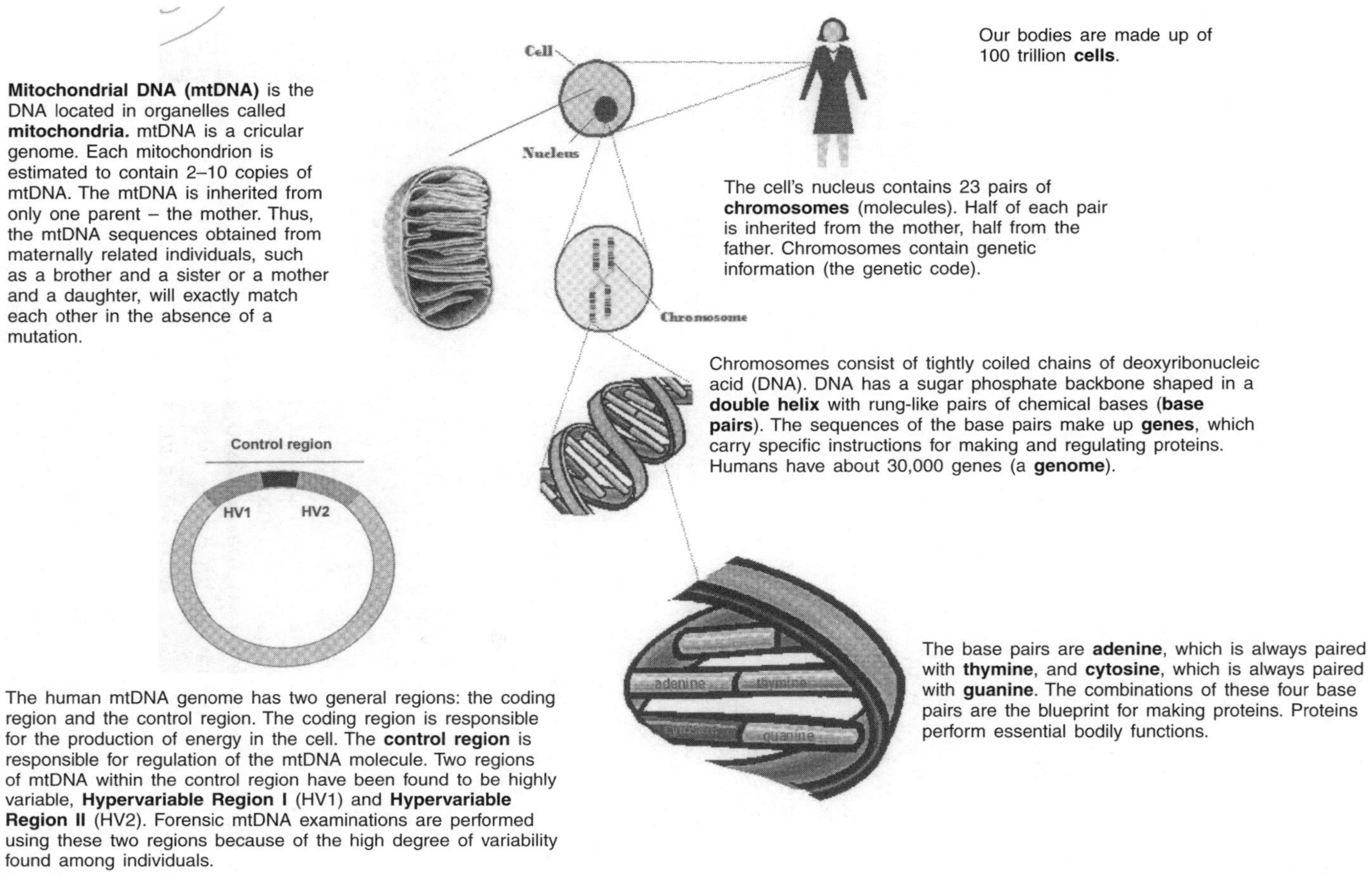

Our bodies are made up of 100 trillion **cells.**

The cell's nucleus contains 23 pairs of **chromosomes** (molecules). Half of each pair is inherited from the mother, half from the father. Chromosomes contain genetic information (the genetic code).

Chromosomes consist of tightly coiled chains of deoxyribonucleic acid (DNA). DNA has a sugar phosphate backbone shaped in a **double helix** with rung-like pairs of chemical bases (**base pairs**). The sequences of the base pairs make up **genes,** which carry specific instructions for making and regulating proteins. Humans have about 30,000 genes (a **genome**).

The base pairs are **adenine,** which is always paired with **thymine,** and **cytosine,** which is always paired with **guanine.** The combinations of these four base pairs are the blueprint for making proteins. Proteins perform essential bodily functions.

**Mitochondrial DNA (mtDNA)** is the DNA located in organelles called **mitochondria.** mtDNA is a cirucular genome. Each mitochondrion is estimated to contain 2–10 copies of mtDNA. The mtDNA is inherited from only one parent – the mother. Thus, the mtDNA sequences obtained from maternally related individuals, such as a brother and a sister or a mother and a daughter, will exactly match each other in the absence of a mutation.

The human mtDNA genome has two general regions: the coding region and the control region. The coding region is responsible for the production of energy in the cell. The **control region** is responsible for regulation of the mtDNA molecule. Two regions of mtDNA within the control region have been found to be highly variable, **Hypervariable Region I** (HV1) and **Hypervariable Region II** (HV2). Forensic mtDNA examinations are performed using these two regions because of the high degree of variability found among individuals.

Cell

Nucleus

Chromosome

adenine    thymine    guanine

Control region

HV1    HV2

**Figure 7.6** *Nuclear and mitochondrial DNA. Although the two molecules have very different structures, both nuclear and mitochondrial DNA have become indispensable forensic tools*

177

The microscopic comparison of human hairs has been accepted scientifically and legally for decades. Mitochondrial DNA sequencing added another test for assessing the significance of attributing a hair to an individual. Neither the microscopic nor molecular analysis alone, or together, provides positive identification. The two methods complement each other in the information they provide. For example, mtDNA typing can often distinguish between hairs from different sources although they have similar, microscopic characteristics. Hair comparisons with a microscope, however, can often distinguish between samples from maternally related individuals where mtDNA analysis is 'blind' (for example, see Bisbing and Wolner 1984).

In the first study of its kind (Houck and Budowle 2001), the results of microscopic and mitochondrial examinations of human hairs submitted to the FBI Laboratory for analysis were reviewed. Of 170 hair examinations, there were 80 microscopic associations; importantly, only nine were excluded by mtDNA. Also, 66 hairs that were considered either unsuitable for microscopic examinations or yielded inconclusive microscopic associations could be analysed with mtDNA. Only six of these hairs did not provide enough mtDNA and another three yielded inconclusive results. This study demonstrates the strength of combining the two techniques. It is important to realise that microscopy is not a 'screening test' and mtDNA analysis is not a 'confirmatory test', Both methods can provide important information to an investigation. The data in this study support the usefulness of both methods – and this is echoed in the expanding use of both microscopical and mitochondrial DNA examinations of hairs in forensic cases (Ryland and Houck 2001).

### Interpretations

What, then, can be determined from a forensic hair examination? Generally, these questions can be answered:

- Is the item a hair?
- Is it a human or animal (non-human) hair?
- If it is an animal hair, what kind (possibly to species or breed)?
- If it is human,
  - can the ethnicity or race be estimated?
  - from which body area did it originate?
  - is any damage, disease, or cosmetic treatment present?
  - is the hair suitable for comparison with a known sample?
- If so, can it be included with or excluded from the source of the known sample? If it cannot, then the result is inconclusive.

If the hair is included microscopically, that is, the questioned hair exhibits the same microscopic characteristics as hairs in the known sample, then it should be subjected to mtDNA analysis (assuming no tissue is present that would allow nuclear DNA analysis) to provide the most reliable statement possible (Houck *et al.* 2004; Robertson 1999).

# Fibres

Textile fibres are 'common' in the sense that textiles surround us in our homes, offices and vehicles. People are in constant contact with a dazzling diversity of textiles and they move through a personal environment of clothing, cars, upholstery and other people. Textile fibres are also neglected and undervalued as forensic evidence. Fibres possess many qualitative and quantitative traits for comparison. The production of textile fibres is complex, variable and polymer-specific (see Figure 7.7). Textile fibres are often produced with specific products in mind (underwear made from carpet fibres would be very uncomfortable) and these end-uses lead to a variety of traits designed into the fibres. Colour is a powerful discriminating characteristic. About 7,000 commercial dyes and pigments are used to colour textiles and no one manufactured dye is used to create any one colour. Millions of shades of colours are possible in textiles (Aspland 1981). It is rare to find two fibres at random that exhibit the same microscopic characteristics and optical properties (Houck 2003a).

A competent and properly equipped forensic fibre examiner, using established and modern methods of analysis, will be able to identify a fibre as natural (animal, vegetable or mineral) or manufactured; if manufactured, its generic (e.g. nylon) and sub-generic class (e.g. nylon 6) can also be identified. The analysis will also determine whether or not a questioned fibre sample is consistent with originating from a known textile source. A forensic fibre examiner must employ a comparison microscope and a compound light microscope equipped with polarised light capability; these may be the same instrument. A complete study of fibres is aided by knowledge of chemistry, physics, biology, microscopy, manufacturing, business and the textile industry. In daily work, the forensic fibre examiner may use only a few of these skills, but a working knowledge of them is desirable.

The types of crime in which fibres may play a role are almost limitless. However, there are a few types in which fibres are especially important. These include crimes of violent contact, including homicide and sexual assault. In the latter, fibres are frequently accompanied by hair evidence. Hit-and-run cases in which a pedestrian is involved often result in the transfer of fibres from the pedestrian's clothing to a surface on the vehicle. Transfer of fibres may also be expected whenever a vehicle is involved in transportation of the victim or perpetrator. A classic example of the importance of fibres in a murder case is the Atlanta child murders involving Wayne Williams (Deadman 1984a and 1984b). In this case, much of the crucial evidence linking the defendant to 12 of 28 murders of children over a two-year period was obtained by comparison of 62 fibres obtained from the bodies and their clothing to fibres in the defendant's environment, including his body, his home and his cars. This case also demonstrated the use of statistics in estimating the frequency of occurrence of a particular type of carpet fibre found in the Williams home. Another example is that of the fibre evidence in the O.J. Simpson case; regrettably, the evidence, although strong, went largely unheeded (Deedrick 1998). Other examples of the utility of fibre evidence abound (Houck 2001; 2003b).

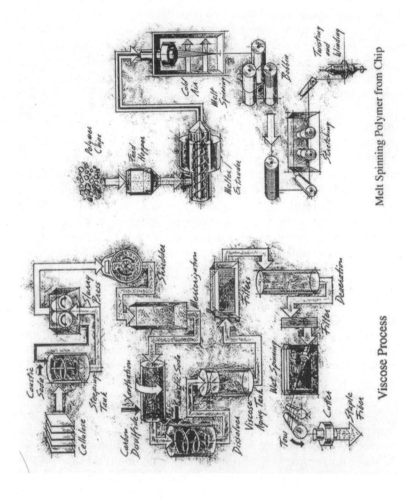

**Figure 7.7** *Fibre production*. The production of manufactured fibres is a complicated process, far removed from the romantic notions of a card of wool and a spinning wheel – it is large-scaled industrial chemistry. Each step in the process offers a chance for variation both in intended and unintentional traits which can be exploited by the forensic scientist to distinguish between otherwise similar products. *Source:* www.fibersource.com

### Textile fibres

A textile fibre, either natural or manufactured, forms the basic element of fabrics and other textile structures. Specifically, a textile fibre is characterised as having a length at least 100 times its diameter and a form that allows it to be spun into a yarn or made into a fabric by various methods. Fibres differ from each other in physical properties, chemical structure, cross-sectional shape, surface contour, colour, as well as length and width; these traits are used routinely to compare and include or exclude questioned fibres from a putative source.

The diameter of textile fibres is small, generally 11 to 50 micrometres (μm). Their length varies from about 2.2 centimetres (cm) to many miles. Based on length, fibres are classified as either filament or staple fibre. Filaments are a type of fibre having indefinite or extreme length, such as synthetic fibres which can be made to any length; silk is the only naturally occurring filament. Staple fibres are natural fibres or cut lengths of filament, typically being 3.75 to 28.5 cm in length.

Fibres themselves are classified into two major classes: natural and manufactured. A natural fibre is any fibre that exists as such in the natural state, such as cotton, wool or silk. Manufactured fibres are made by processing natural or synthetic organic polymers into a fibre-forming substance; they can be classified as cellulosic or synthetic. Cellulosic fibres are either made from regenerated or derivative cellulosic (fibrous) polymers, such as wool or cotton. Synthetic fibres are formed from non-fibrous precursors and include nylon, polyester and saran which are formed from melted polymer chips. No nylon or polyester fibres exist in nature and they are made of chemicals put through reactions to produce the fibre-forming substance. The generic names for manufactured and synthetic fibres were established as part of the Textile Fibre Products Identification Act enacted by the US Congress in 1954 (Table 7.1); this list is commensurate with the ISO standard with some minor name changes (such as viscose instead of rayon, for example).

*Manufactured fibres* are the various families of fibres produced from fibre-forming substances, which may be synthesised polymers, modified or transformed natural polymers, or glass. *Synthetic fibres* are those manufactured fibres which are synthesised from chemical compounds (e.g. nylon, polyester). Therefore, all synthetic fibres are manufactured, but not all manufactured fibres are synthetic. Manufactured fibres are formed by extruding a fibre-forming substance, called *spinning dope*, through a hole or holes in a shower head-like device called a *spinneret*; this process is called *spinning*. The spinning dope is created by rendering solid monomeric material into a liquid or semi-liquid form with a solvent or heat. The microscopic characteristics of manufactured fibres are the basic features used to distinguish them. Manufactured fibres differ in their optical and chemical properties.

### Optical properties

Fibres vary in shape but are almost always thicker in the centre than near the edges. Thus they act as crude lenses, either concentrating or dispersing the light that passes through them. This phenomenon is used to determine

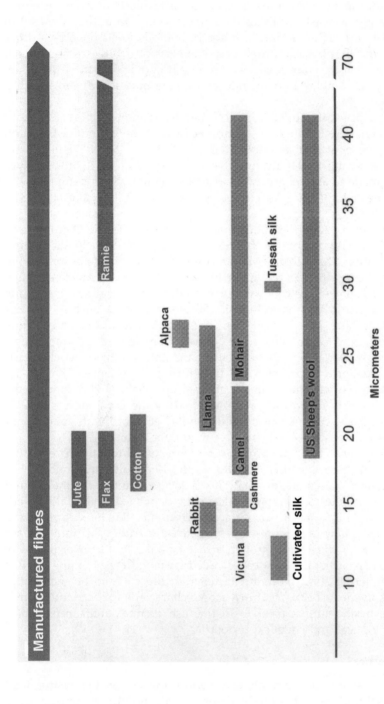

**Figure 7.8** *Fibre diameter.* The width of a fibre is a major trait for determining end use of a fibre; fibres that are too wide will not work well for a top-weight fabric (shirting, for example). The morphology of natural fibres is the main way they are identified. Note that manufactured fibres can, in theory, be of any diameter, from nanofibres to fishing monofilament

**Table 7.1** Examples of textile fibre definitions in the USA

| | |
|---|---|
| acetate | A manufactured fibre in which the fibre-forming substance is cellulose acetate. Where not less than 92% of the hydroxyl groups are acetylated the term triacetate may be used as a generic description of the fibre. |
| acrylic | A manufactured fibre in which the fibre-forming substance is any long-chain synthetic polymer composed of at least 85% by weight of acrylonitrile units. |
| glass | A manufactured fibre in which the fibre-forming substance is glass. |
| nylon | A manufactured fibre in which the fibre-forming substance is any long-chain synthetic polyamide in which less than 85% of the amide linkages are attached directly to two aromatic rings. |
| metallic | A manufactured fibre composed of metal, plastic-coated metal, metal-coated plastic, or a core completely covered by metal. |
| Modacrylic | A manufactured fibre in which the fibre-forming substance is any long-chain synthetic polymer composed of less than 85% but at least 35% by weight of acrylonitrile units. |
| olefin | A manufactured fibre in which the fibre-forming substance is any long-chain synthetic polymer composed of at least 85% by weight of ethylene, propylene, or other olefin units. |
| Polyester | A manufactured fibre in which the fibre-forming substance is any long-chain synthetic polymer composed of at least 85% by weight of an ester or a substituted aromatic carboxylic acid, including but not restricted to substituted terephthalate units and parasubstituted hydroxybenzoate units. |
| rayon | A manufactured fibre composed of regenerated cellulose, as well as manufactured fibres composed of regenerated cellulose in which substituents have replaced not more than 15% of the hydrogens of the hydroxyl groups. |
| saran | A manufactured fibre in which the fibre-forming substance is any long-chain synthetic polymer composed of at least 80% by weight of vinylidene chloride units. |
| spandex | A manufactured fibre in which the fibre-forming substance is any long-chain synthetic polymer composed of at least 85% of a segmented polyurethane. |

the fibre's refractive index: the ratio of the speed of light in a vacuum to the speed of light in a medium, in this case a fibre. Refractive indices for fibres range from 1.46 to over 2.0 for very optically dense fibres like Kevlar. Another useful trait of a manufactured fibre is its birefringence. Fibres have two optical axes and, because the fibres have an internal orientation (analogous to the grain in wood), each has a different refractive index. Birefringence is the difference between the two indices and ranges from 0.001 to 0.2 or more. Because manufactured fibres vary in their optical density, refractive index and birefringence are useful traits in fibre identification.

Colour is one of the most critical characteristics in a fibre comparison. Almost all manufacturing industries are concerned with product appearance. Everything that is manufactured has a colour to it and often these colours are imparted to the end product. Particular colours are chosen for some products rather than others (it's difficult to find 'safety orange' carpeting, for example) and these colours may indicate the end-product. A *dye* is an organic chemical that is able to absorb and reflect certain wavelengths of visible light. *Pigments* are microscopic, water insoluble particles that are either incorporated into the fibre at the time of production or are bonded to the surface of the fibre by a resin. Some fibre types, such as olefins, are not easily dyed and therefore are often pigmented. Over 80 dyers worldwide are registered with the American Association of Textile Chemists and Colorists (AATCC) and almost 350 trademarked dyes are registered with them (AATCC 1998). Some trademarked dyes have as many as 40 variants. Over 7,000 dyes and pigments are currently produced worldwide. Natural dyes, such as indigo, have been known since before history while synthetic dyes have gained prominence largely since the First World War. Very few textiles are coloured with only one dye and even a simple dye may be put through eight to ten processing steps to achieve a final dye form, shade and strength. When all of these factors are considered, it becomes apparent that it is virtually impossible to dye textiles in a continuous method; that is, dyeing separate batches of fibres or textiles is the rule rather than the exception. This colour variability has the potential to be significant in forensic fibre comparisons. The number of producible colours is nearly infinite and colour is an easy discriminator.

The most basic method of colour analysis is visual examination of single fibres with a comparison microscope. Visual examination and comparison is a quick and excellent screening technique. Because it is a subjective method visual examination must be used in conjunction with an objective method.

Chemical analysis involves extracting the dye and characterising or identifying its chemistry. Chemical analysis addresses the type of dye(s) used to colour the fibre and may help to sort out metameric colour pairs (colour pairs that appear the same in one lighting condition but appear different in another). It can be difficult to extract the dye from the fibre, however, as forensic samples typically are small and textile dyers take great pains to ensure that the dye stays in the fibre. Dye analysis is also a destructive method, rendering the fibre useless for further colour analysis. Yet some fibres have colours so similar that chemical analysis is required to distinguish them.

Instrumental analysis, typically microspectrophotometry, offers the best combinations of strengths and the fewest weaknesses of the three methods outlined. Microspectrophotometry measures colours in the visible and ultra-violet ranges of the electromagnetic spectrum by absorbance or transmission. Instrumental readings are objective and repeatable, the results are quantitative and the methods can be standardised. Importantly, the method is not destructive and the analysis may be repeated. Again, very pale fibres may present a problem with weak results and natural fibres may exhibit high variations due to uneven dye uptake.

While microscopy offers an accurate method of fibre examination, it is necessary to confirm these observations. Analysing the fibres chemically may provide additional information about the specific polymer type or types that make up the fibre. For most of the generic polymer classes, various sub-classes exist which can assist in discriminating between optically similar fibres. Fourier-transform spectroscopy (FTIR) and pyrolysis-gas chromatography

(PGC) are both methods of assessing the chemical structure of polymers. FTIR is the preferred method because it is non-destructive.

### Interpretations

In evaluating the significance of matching fibres most examiners would take into account:

- the number of fibres;
- the number of fibre types;
- colours and dye types or classifications;
- the discriminating power of the analytical techniques used;
- how common or rare the fibres are;
- the presence of one-way or two-way transfer;
- the circumstances of the case including the degree of contact between items and the time difference between deposition of the fibres and the recovery of items for examination.

It is rare to find unrelated fibres on a particular item and the probability of chance occurrence decreases rapidly as the number of different matching fibre types increases (Roux and Margot 1997a). Frequency studies add to the foundation of fibre transfer interpretation data. For example, one study has calculated the frequency of finding at least one red woollen fibre on a car seat is 5.1 per cent; if more than five are found, however, the relative frequency plummets to 1.4 per cent. The authors of that study determined that except for blue denim or grey/black cotton, no fibre should be considered as common (Roux and Margot 1997b). One study cross-checked fibres from 20 unrelated cases, looking for incidental positive associations; in over 2 million comparisons, no incidental positive associations were found (Houck 2003a). This makes fibre evidence very powerful in demonstrating associations.

### Paint

The forensic analysis of surface *coatings*, intended to protect, aesthetically improve, or provide some special quality, is one of the most complex topics in the forensic laboratory. Paint is one type of coating, and the most popular, but other coatings are encountered at crimes, including varnishes, stains, lacquers and the like. The manufacture and application of paints and coatings is one of the most complicated areas in industrial chemistry. Even if a forensic paint examiner specialised in analysing only coatings and paints, they could not be conversant with the entire range of goods manufactured worldwide. Oddly though, the complexity of the coatings industry works in the forensic scientist's favour because variety enables a more specific categorisation of evidence. The more specific the examiner's results, the greater potential for evidentiary significance in an investigation or court. This section will focus on paints, as the most frequently encountered type of coatings evidence.

A *paint* is a suspension of pigments and additives intended to colour or protect a surface. A *pigment* is a finely ground insoluble powder whose granules remain intact but are dispersed evenly across a surface. Pigments may be organic, inorganic, or a combination of these. The additives in paint are many and varied but the most common are binders, vehicles and solvents. The *binder* distributes the pigment evenly across the surface. The term *vehicle* refers to the solvents, resins and other additives that form a continuous film, binding the pigment to the surface. Depending on the application, the terms binder and vehicle are sometimes used interchangeably. *Solvents* dissolve the binder and give the paint a suitable consistency for application (brushing, spraying, etc.). Once the paint has been applied, the solvent and many of the additives evaporate and a hard polymer film (the binder) containing the dispersed pigment remains, covering and sealing the surface.

Paints can be divided into four major categories. *Architectural paints* are found in residences and businesses. *Product coatings*, those applied in the manufacture of products including automobiles, are the second major category. Because automobiles play a central role in society and in crime, much of this section will focus on automotive paints and coatings. *Special-purpose coatings* fulfil specific needs beyond protection or aesthetics, such as skid-resistance, waterproofing, or luminescence (as on the dials of wristwatches). Finally, *art paints* are encountered in forgery cases. Modern art paints are similar in many respects to architectural paints but many artists formulate their own paints, leading to potentially very specific sources.

### Automotive paints

The automotive finishing process consists of at least four separate coatings. The first is a *pre-treatment* (which often contains zinc) applied to the steel body of the vehicle to inhibit rust. The steel is then washed, rinsed, treated again, and then washed again. The forensic paint analyst should be aware that any zinc found during elemental analysis may come from this coating and not necessarily the paint itself.

The second coating is a *primer*, usually an epoxy resin with corrosion-resistant pigments; the colour of the primer is coordinated with the final vehicle colour to minimise contrast and 'bleed through'. The steel body of the vehicle is dipped in a large bath of the liquid primer which is plated on by electrical conduction. The primer coating is finished with a powder 'primer surfacer' that smoothes the surface of the metal and provides better adhesion for the next coating.

The *topcoat* is the third coating applied to the vehicle and may be in the form of a single-colour layer coat, a multilayer coat, or a metallic colour coat; this last layer is the one that most people associate with a vehicle's colour. Topcoat chemistry is moving towards water-based chemistries to provide a healthier environment for factory workers and the public; for example, heavy metals, such as lead or chrome, are no longer used in topcoats. Metallic pigments, including zinc, nickel, steel and gold-bronze, give a glittering finish to a vehicle's colour while pearlescent pigments, mica chips coated with titanium dioxide and ferric oxide, try to replicate the glowing lustre of pearls. The topcoat is applied, partially cured, and then finished with the clearcoat. *Clearcoats* are unpigmented coatings applied to improve gloss and durability of a vehicle's coating. Historically, clearcoats were acrylic-based in their chemistry but nearly half of the automotive manufacturers have moved to two-component urethanes.

Vehicle bodies are no longer made exclusively of steel and various plastics are now commonly used. Bumpers may be nylon, polymer blends or polyurethane resins; door panels and bonnets may be of thermosetting polymers; front grills and bumper strips have long been plastic or polymer but now may be coloured to match the vehicle. Braking systems, chassis, and even entire cars are now constructed from plastics. Automotive bodies are truly multi-component, composite constructions and multiple coatings, coating systems and polymers may be encountered.

### Analysis of paint samples

As with any trace evidence examination, the first step in forensic paint analysis is to visually examine the sample. This first step may be the last: if significant differences are apparent in the known and questioned samples, the analysis is complete and the paints are excluded. The paint samples are described and their condition, weathering characteristics, size, shape, exterior colours and major layers present in each sample are noted and recorded. The examiner's notes should include written descriptions, photographs and drawings, as necessary. Because significant changes can be made to a portion of a sample in the process of preparation and examination, it is crucial to document how that sample was received.

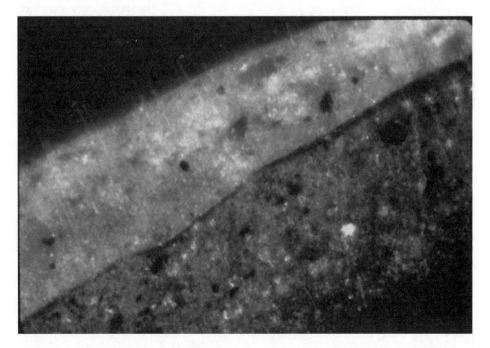

**Figure 7.9** *Paint layers*. Paints and coatings are some of the most complicated forms of trace evidence, from their chemistry and application to their final form on the surface they protect. Shown here are two paint layers with the pigments easily seen as small specks within the layers

Microscopical comparisons of paint layers can reveal slight variations between samples in colour, pigment appearance, flake size and distribution, surface details, inclusions and layer defects (Figure 7.9). Any visual comparisons must be done with the samples side by side in the same field of view (or with a comparison microscope), typically at the same magnification. Polarised light microscopy (PLM) is appropriate for the examination of layer structure as well as the comparison and/or identification of particles in a paint film including, but not limited to, pigments, extenders, additives and contaminants.

Many instrumental methods are available to analyse the complex chemistry of paints. Rarely will all of the instruments listed below appear in one laboratory – even if they did, the laboratory's analytical scheme would probably not include all of them – and the order of examination will be determined by the instrumentation available.

Infrared spectroscopy (IR) can identify binders, pigments and additives used in paints and coatings. Most IRs used in forensic science laboratories employ a microscopical bench to magnify the image of the sample and focus the beam on the sample. The bench is a microscope stage attached to the instrument chassis with optics to route the beam through the microscope and back to the detector. Most modern IRs will also be Fourier transform infrared (FT-IR) spectrometers, which employ a mathematical transformation (the fast Fourier transform) which translates the spectral frequency into wavelength.

Pyrolysis gas chromatography (PGC or PyGC) disassembles molecules through heat. It is a destructive technique that uses the breakdown products for comparison of paints and identification of the binder type. PGC is influenced by the size and shape of the samples and instrument parameters, such as rate of heating, the final temperature, the type of column, and gas flow rates. The conditions from one analysis to the next should be the same and should be run very close in time to each other. If the instrumentation is available, pyrolysis products may be identified by pyrolysis gas chromatography-mass spectrometry (PGC-MS). The resulting reconstructed total ion chromatogram may help to identify additives, organic pigments and impurities in addition to binder components.

One of the most generally useful instruments in forensic paint analysis is the scanning electron microscope fitted with an energy dispersive X-ray spectrometer (SEM/EDS). SEM/EDS can be used to characterise the structure and elemental composition of paint layers. The SEM uses an electron beam rather than a light beam and changes the nature of the information received from the paint. The primary reason for analysing paint samples with an SEM/EDS system is to determine the elemental composition of the paint and its layers.

### Interpretations

Evaluating trace evidence, including paint, is difficult. A consensus of forensic paint examiners agrees that the following factors strengthen an association between two analytically indistinguishable paint samples:

- the number of layers;
- the sequence of layers;
- the colour of each layer;
- cross-transfer of paint between items.

Scott Ryland of the Florida Department of Law Enforcement forensic laboratory in Orlando, and his colleagues have stated that an association between two paint samples with six or more correlating layers indicates that the chance that the samples originated from two different sources is extremely remote (Ryland *et al.* 1981). In cases with evidence this strong, merely stating that the two samples 'could have had a common origin' is not enough – that level of statement undermines the strength of a six-layer-plus association. Despite it not being a statistical or mathematical answer, this does not mean the statement is not accurate, valid and sound.

The significance of architectural paints varies and is in general not as well documented in the literature. This is most likely due to the enormous variability in colours, application styles and the application of the paint itself (not all brush strokes are equal, resulting in highly variable layers *between* samples). The situation is similar with spray paints, about which even less is known.

Generating statistics to assess the evidentiary value of paint has been attempted in both the research literature and in casework. These instances are based, as are most manufacturing inquiries, on the concept of a *batch lot*, a unit of production and sampling that contains a set of analytically indistinguishable products. For example, a batch tank of automotive paint of a given colour may hold 500 to 10,000 gallons, which would colour between 170 to 1,600 vehicles. This would then be the unit of comparison for the significance of an automotive paint comparison – the manufacturing batch lot. If analytically identifiable differences can be determined between batch lots, then the base population is set for any other analytically indistinguishable paint samples. The final significance will be determined by the number of vehicles in the area at the time of the crime and other characteristics that set that sample apart (very rare or very common makes or models). By comparison, a batch lot of architectural paint may be from 100 to 4,500 gallons.

## Glass

Glass is defined as an amorphous solid, a hard, brittle, usually transparent material without the molecular organisation (a crystal lattice) found in most other solids. Glass consists of doped oxides of silicon: the silicon oxides come from sand, the doping comes from other materials that provide useful properties. The sand is melted with the other desired ingredients and then allowed to cool without crystallising. The glass may be cooled in a mould or through a process that allows the glass to become flat.

There are three major types of glass encountered as forensic evidence: sheet or flat glass, container glass and glass fibres. Flat glass is used to make windows and windscreens; it can also be shaped into various forms, such as light bulbs. Container glass is used to make bottles and drinking glasses. Glass fibres are found in fibreglass and fibre-optic cables as well as composite materials. Speciality glass, like optical glass used to make eyeglass lenses, may be encountered in forensic cases although less frequently. More than 700 types of glass are in use today in the USA and the frequency of occurrence relates to the prevalence of specific products (Koons *et al.* 2002). For example, more bottle or window glass, on average, would be encountered than optical or speciality glass. Unless a fracture or physical is possible, small pieces of glass are considered to be class evidence (Figure 7.10).

### Types of glass

Float glass is made by mixing sand, limestone, soda ash, dolomite, iron oxide and salt cake and melting them in a large furnace. Pure silicon glass is rarely used as such. Instead, specific amounts of various impurities are added (called doping) to the melted glass that alters the final properties in a predictable fashion. For instance, sodium carbonate ($Na_2CO_3$, or soda) is added to make the glass melt at a lower temperature and viscosity, making it more malleable. Calcium oxide (CaO, or lime), as another example, stabilises the glass and makes it less soluble. If both calcium oxide and sodium carbonate are added, the glass is called soda-lime glass. Boron oxide ($B_2O_3$) makes glass highly heat-resistant; the result is borosilicate glass, better known through one of its product names as Pyrex©. Borosilicate glass appears in cookware, thermometers and laboratory glassware.

The molten glass is fed on to a bath of molten tin through a controlled gate, called a tweel. A pressurised atmosphere of nitrogen and hydrogen is maintained to eliminate oxygen and prevent oxidation of the tin. The nitrogen and hydrogen keeps the tin from oxidising. Some tin is absorbed into the glass and, under ultraviolet light, the tin side can be differentiated from the non-tin side. As the glass flows down the tin bath, the temperature is slowly reduced so that it anneals without internal strain or visible cracks. The glass is cut by machines into manageable-sized pieces. Surface tension, flow, and the tin bath cause the glass to form with an even thickness and a smooth glossy surface on both sides.

Glass may be strengthened by tempering or annealing, where the glass surface is intentionally stressed through heating and rapid cooling. Tempered glass breaks into many small solid pieces, instead of sharp shards; tempered glass is used in car windows for this reason. Windscreens in the USA are not tempered glass but are two layers of glass that sandwich a layer of plastic. When the windscreen breaks, the plastic keeps the glass from spraying the passenger compartment.

It is generally accepted that glass can be individualised when it breaks into pieces that have at least one intact edge that can be fitted to the edge of another piece; this is called a physical or fracture match, for obvious reasons. Glass is hard and brittle, so it doesn't deform when broken; glass is also amorphous, so no molecular 'grain' exists along which the glass may preferentially fracture. Therefore, glass fractures are random events and no two pieces of similar glass would be expected to break in exactly the same

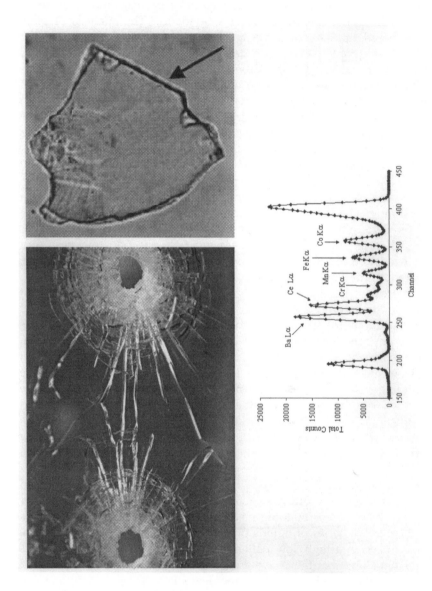

**Figure 7.10** *Forensic glass analysis.* Glass is a valuable type of evidence through all scales of its physicality, from fractures of whole pieces, to the optical properties of those individual pieces, and their elemental content. The spectrum is the microfluorescence from a 15-micrometer Sphere Multicomponent NIST Glass K919

pattern. If two pieces of glass have a mechanical fit, the conclusion is made that they were once part of the same piece of glass. This conclusion is often strengthened by stress marks along the face of the broken glass edge. Stress marks are microscopic lines randomly generated by the propagation of force along a breaking fracture.

The majority of forensic glass samples consist of particles too small to be physically matched and, therefore, are class evidence. The analysis of glass fragments is based on the optical properties and elemental content of the material. The first step, however, is to determine that the fragments are glass and not some other material. Glass is differentiated from other similar materials by its hardness, structure and behaviour when exposed to polarised light. Glass can be differentiated from translucent plastic, for example, by pressing it with a needle point: most plastics are indented by the needle but glass is not. Table salt, as another example, exhibits cubic crystals; glass is amorphous and does not. Glass is isotropic, meaning it has the same properties in all directions; most translucent minerals are anisotropic (think of them as having an optical 'grain', much like a wood grain). Anisotropic materials display birefringence, or double refraction, because their 'grain' changes the properties of the light that passes through it. Glass, being isotropic, has no birefringence.

Once it is determined that the material is glass, preliminary tests for similarity, including colour, surface characteristics, flatness, thickness and fluorescence, must be conducted. If the two samples are different at any stage, then they are excluded as having come from the same piece of glass.

Refraction occurs when light passes through a transparent medium: the light is bent away from its original path and is impeded by the medium's optical density. Glass exhibits refraction. The amount of refraction caused by glass is an important physical property for the comparison of known and unknown exhibits. The range of refractive indices for glass is between 1.4 and 1.7 and different glasses have different refractive indices, making this property valuable in distinguishing between glass fragments. It is not possible to measure the refractive index of glass directly; rather it must be indirectly determined through a phenomenon called the Becke line. The glass fragment acts as a crude lens and, when the piece of glass is taken out of focus (by increasing the distance from the bottom of the lens to the top of the fragment), light will either be focused out of or into the fragment depending on the refractive index of the surrounding medium. The band of light – the Becke line – thus focused moves towards the medium of higher refractive index; if the glass has a higher refractive index than the surrounding medium, for example, the Becke line will move *into* the glass. A series of liquids of known refractive index (to 3 decimal places) can be used in a high/low pattern until the glass fragment disappears in the liquid signalling that they have the same refractive index (the glass and the liquid are bending the light to the same degree).

The amounts of specific elements in glass can assist in characterising its source. Manufacturers control the concentrations of certain elements so that a particular glass product has the intended end-use properties. Depending on the elements and quality controls in manufacturing, these concentrations can help to identify the product type of a glass fragment. Glass manufacturers typically do not control for trace element concentrations, however, unless these would adversely affect the physical or optical properties of the glass. The differences in concentrations of manufacturer-controlled elements or uncontrolled trace elements may be used to differentiate sources when the variation among objects exceeds the variation within each object. Element concentrations may be used to differentiate among:

- glasses made by different manufacturers;
- glasses from different production lines of a single manufacturer;
- specific production runs of glass from a single manufacturer; and
- (occasionally) individual glass objects produced at the same production facility.

These distinctions relate to the manufacturing characteristics inherent in the desired properties of the final product.

### Interpretations

Similar to other types of trace evidence assessment of the significance of glass traces involves subjective and objective information and requires skill and judgement by the examiner. Factors typically taken into consideration in evaluating glass evidence include:

- where the glass was found;
- the number and size of fragments;
- the type of glass (window, container etc.);
- chemical and physical properties of the fragments;
- information on the frequency and distribution of the control glass;
- information and frequency of glass fragments in the general environment;
- the circumstances of the case, particularly the time between the incident (when the glass was broken) and recovery traces (e.g. from clothing).

## Conclusion

Trace evidence is a key component of many forensic investigations. Because it is characterised by microscopic fragments of a range of materials, trace evidence can be central to an investigation but only if it is recognised, collected and analysed properly. A characteristic of trace evidence is that it is gradually lost following transfer. Consequently it also has the potential to contaminate items and scenes and has to be recovered using suitable precautions. The particular precautions will depend on the type of trace material and case circumstances.

The methods of analysis of trace evidence vary widely depending on the evidence type but given the size range of the materials involved, microscopy and instruments that utilise microscopes are commonly used. The process of comparison involves analysis of physical and chemical characteristics, for example, composition, colour and refractive index. Colour, natural or man-made, is a central theme in trace evidence examination. Although naturally occurring trace materials such as hairs and certain fibres differ fundamentally from manufactured materials, the analytical approach and instrumentation involved is broadly similar. Evaluation of trace evidence is also dependent on the type. Factors frequently taken into account are the number of fragments recovered, the quality of the analytical match, the discriminating power of the analytical techniques used, information on the frequency (how rare or common) of the traces and the specific circumstances and stage of the investigation. Transfers of trace evidence are the indicators of association in a criminal activity. Although DNA can tell investigators 'who', it cannot tell 'what', 'where', 'when', or 'how'. Trace evidence is uniquely suited to provide answers to these questions. Sourcing, production locations, time series of events, production dates and manufacturing distribution, and the physical and chemical properties of materials all offer fertile possibilities to yield significant clues for guilt or exoneration.

## References

American Association of Textile Chemists and Colorists (1998) *Colour Technology in the Textile Industry*. Research Triangle Park, North Carolina: American Association of Textile Chemists and Colorists.

Aspland, J.R. (1981) 'What Are Dyes? What Is Dyeing?' in *AATCC Dyeing Primer*. Research Triangle Park, North Carolina: American Association of Textile Chemists and Colorists.

Bisbing, R. (2002) 'Forensic Hair Comparisons', in R. Saferstein (ed.) *Forensic Science Handbook*. Englewood Cliffs, NJ: Prentice-Hall.

Bisbing, R. and Wolner, M. (1984) 'Microscopical discrimination of twins' head hair', *Journal of Forensic Sciences*, 29 (3): 780–786.

Brunner, H. and Coman, B. (1974) *The Identification of Mammalian Hair*. Melbourne: Inkata Press.

Deadman, H.A. (1984a) 'Fiber evidence and the Wayne Williams trial: Part I', *FBI Law Enforcement Bulletin*, 53 (3): 12–20.

Deadman, H.A. (1984b) 'Fiber evidence and the Wayne Williams trials: Part II', *FBI Law Enforcement Bulletin*, 53 (5): 10–19.

Deedrick, D.W. (1998) 'Searching for the source: Car carpet fibres in the O.J. Simpson case', *Contact*, 26: 14–16.

Gaudette, B.D. and Keeping, E.D. (1974) 'An attempt at determining probabilities in human scalp hair comparison', *Journal of Forensic Sciences*, 19: 599–606.

Hicks, J.W. (1977) 'Microscopy of Hairs', Federal Bureau of Investigation. Washington, DC: Federal Bureau of Investigation.

Houck, M.M. (2001) *Mute Witnesses*. San Diego, CA: Elsevier Academic Press.

Houck, M.M. (2003a) 'Intercomparison of unrelated fiber evidence', *Forensic Science International*, 135: 146–149.

Houck, M.M. (2003b) *Trace Evidence Analysis*. San Diego, CA: Elsevier Academic Press.

Houck, M.M., Bisbing, R.E., Watkins, T. and Harman, R.E. (2004) 'The science of forensic hair comparisons and the admissibility of hair comparison evidence: *Frye* and *Daubert* Reconsidered', online at www.modernmicroscopy.com, 02 March 2004.

Houck, M.M. and Budowle, B. (2001) 'Correlation of microscopic and mitochondrial DNA analysis of hairs', *Journal of Forensic Sciences*, 45 (5): 1–4.

Koons, R.D. and Buscaglia, J. (2002) 'Interpretation of glass composition measurements. The effects of match criteria on discrimination capability', *Journal of Forensic Sciences*, 47 (3): 505–512.

Koons, R.D., Buscaglia, J., Bottrell, M. and Muller, E.T. (2002) 'Forensic glass comparisons', pp. 161–213, in R. Saferstein (ed.), *Forensic Science Handbook*. Upper Saddle River, NJ: Prentice-Hall.

Pounds, C.A. and Smalldon, K.W. (1975) 'The transfer of fibres between clothing materials during simulated contacts and their persistence during wear. Part II: Fibre persistence', *Journal of the Forensic Science Society*, 15: 29–37.

Robertson, J. (1999) *Forensic Examination of Hair*. London: Taylor and Francis.

Robertson, J. and Roux, C. (1999) 'Persistence and recovery of fibres', pp. 89–100, in J. Robertson and M.C. Grieve (eds), *Forensic Examination of Fibers*. London: Taylor and Francis.

Roux, C. and Margot, P. (1997a) 'The population of textile fibers on car seats', *Science and Justice*, 37 (10): 25–30.

Roux, C. and Margot, P. (1997b) 'An attempt to assess the relevance of textile fibers recovered from car seats', *Science and Justice*, 37: 225–230.

Ryland, S. and Houck, M.M. (2001) 'Only Circumstantial Evidence', pp. 117–138, in M.M. Houck, *Mute Witnesses*. San Diego, CA: Elsevier Academic Press.

Ryland, S., Kopec, R.J. *et al.* (1981) 'The evidential value of automobile paint. Part II: Frequency of occurrence of topcoat colours', *Journal of Forensic Sciences*, 26(1): 1–11.

Thornton, J. (1986) 'Ensembles of class characteristics in physical evidence examination', *Journal of Forensic Sciences*, 31(2): 501–503.

Wickenheiser, R.A. and Hepworth, D.G. (1990) 'Further evaluation of probabilities in human scalp hair comparisons', *Journal of Forensic Sciences*, 35: 1323–1329.

# Chapter 8

# Marks

*Terrence Napier*

## Introduction

Examination of marks left by objects in connection with a criminal investigation is one of the cornerstones of forensic science. Marks can originate from a wide range of sources such as shoes, tools, tyres and from parts of the body, for example finger marks. Some areas of mark examination have become disciplines in their own right, particularly in the fields of document and finger mark examination, and have specialists that deal in these areas alone. Marks, also commonly referred to as impressions, feature extensively in forensic investigation and can be used to predict the properties of an object or associate a specific object with a crime scene or victim. In some cases they may also indicate certain actions that could assist in the investigation of an incident.

Despite the huge variety of objects that can leave marks the principles involved in their examinations are very similar. This chapter will consider the distinctive characteristics of marks routinely encountered in forensic casework, how they are examined, their potential as evidence and intelligence and how their significance is evaluated. Since finger mark examinations are covered in detail elsewhere in this volume, they will be presented in more general terms in this chapter.

The most commonly encountered marks in crime investigation tend to be instrument marks, footwear marks and manufacturing marks such as printing defects and extrusion marks on plastic bags. Other marks are regularly encountered which do not fall neatly into any particular category. Examples are shown in Figures 8.1 and 8.2 below of marks and the suspect objects. One is a fabric impression and the other would be generally described as a glove mark although they could be regarded as essentially both fabric marks.

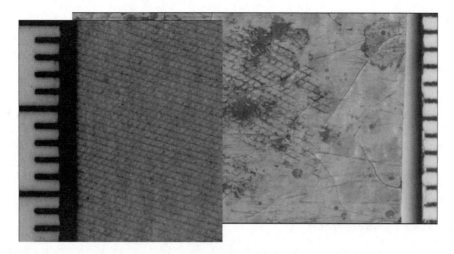

**Figure 8.1** Typical fabric impressions. The spliced photographs show the similarity of the dimensions and pattern of the suspect fabric (left) with the mark from the scene (right)

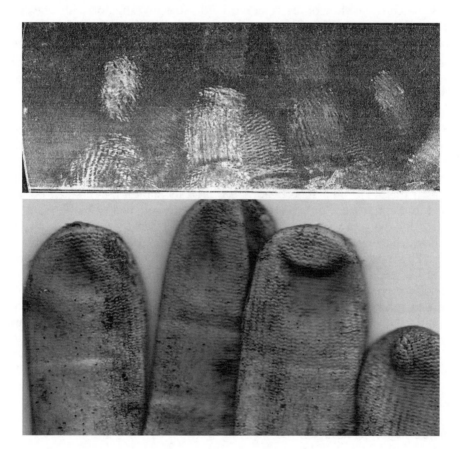

**Figure 8.2** Typical glove marks. The marks and the 'creases' where the finger joints would be suggest a glove. The suspect gloves show the same texture and creases

## What is a mark?

A mark could be considered as an image created by the interaction of one object with another. The word 'image' is a crucial one as the similarity between a single frame on a CCTV camera and an impression left by a crow bar is not immediately obvious. However, they are essentially the same thing – a visual record of an interaction. One of these images is made by light falling on a sensor, the other, in the case of a tool mark for example, by the compression of paint and wood caused by a metal blade. This comparison highlights a defining feature of marks: that they do not necessarily require the transfer of materials. This immediately differentiates marks from contact traces where transfer of material must take place.

### Marks and contact traces

Marks and contact trace materials are often associated in forensic investigations. A footwear mark in blood is a good example. In such a case the material in which the mark is made is as important as the features of the mark. A mark found in blood at a crime scene where the blood matches the victim and the mark matches the shoe of a suspect, provides the investigator with powerful evidence connecting the footwear and the crime. In order to provide the most compelling evidence both the mark and the blood must be considered together, not in isolation.

### Transfer of materials

A mark is made by this mechanism when it is formed by a net transfer of material. This can be directional, such as when one object leaves an impression in material transferred from it to another object. Alternatively, an impression may be caused by one object removing material from another. A commonly encountered example of this process is footwear marks in blood at a crime scene. If the blood on a shoe tread is acquired by standing in a small pool of blood, there may be a primary mark made by the removal of blood from the surface by the footwear tread. Subsequent marks can then be made by the tread transferring blood to other surfaces. Footwear examiners record marks formed by transfer of material as either 'positive' or 'negative'. 'Positive marks' generally refers to marks left by transfer of material from the footwear to the surface on which the marks have been found. 'Negative marks' generally refers to marks that have been formed by footwear acquiring material from the surface on which the marks were made. It is also possible for positive and negative marks to be made in the same contact. A wet footwear tread making contact with a dusty floor may well deposit moisture on the floor at the same time as acquiring dust from the floor. Although this has little relevance for any subsequent examination of the mark it has an important bearing on the choice of recovery or enhancement method.

### Compression of a surface

The application of pressure to a surface by an object often leaves marks if the material of the surface retains the characteristics of the object. Typical examples of this include impressions left due to impact or levering actions of tools and footwear marks in soil. One of the defining features of such marks is that they are three-dimensional. This property has implications for visualising or optimising the marks. Certain impressed marks have another interesting quality in that they originate from what is referred to as dynamic interaction. This refers to the movement of the object making the mark across the surface during deposition. A common example of this type of mark is 'striation' detail left by tool edges such as screwdrivers and drill bits. Striations are also found in firearms examinations (on cartridge cases) and on drugs packaging such as mass-produced plastic bags. In most cases striations are the result of imperfections or damage features in the object making contact, e.g. a blade, die or firing pin, being dragged across a surface and leaving a pattern of lines that reflects the spacing and size of each feature. These striations are not necessarily a direct 'image' of the object that made them in the sense that we have discussed previously. A 'static' impressed mark can often appear adjacent to a 'dynamic' impression as the starting or stopping point of the movement that made the dynamic mark.

### Other mechanisms

The vast majority of marks are made by the mechanisms described above. It is also quite possible in certain types of case for marks to be made without the transfer of material or permanent deformation of a surface. Bruises are a form of mark that do not require either of these mechanisms but will often contain features representative of the object that made the mark. By definition bruises are confined to injuries in living subjects but these can arise from a wide range of objects including weapons, footwear, teeth and vehicle bodywork (in road traffic accidents). Marks can also be made by altering surface features of an object without leaving a permanent impression. For example the pile of a carpet or fabric can retain a shoe impression. Such marks are often difficult to photograph and as they do not necessarily involve the transfer of materials the number of recovery options tends to be limited.

### Visualising marks

Finding marks is often a simple process of visual inspection. However, it is possible to see marks without recognising them as originating from a particular type of object or recognising their potential evidential significance. To increase the likelihood of discovering useful marks, it is necessary to reveal as much visual information as possible. A number of processes are available to achieve this. Some methods are particular to certain types of mark such as the Electrostatic Detection Apparatus (ESDA) used in handwriting cases. This chapter will be limited to the most common methods rather than an exhaustive review. In principle most methods could be used for most types of marks but there are strong associations between methods and types of marks due to practicality and utility.

Casting is a simple process for three-dimensional marks but tool marks and footwear marks generally involve using different casting materials selected for their particular physical properties. Three-dimensional footwear marks will generally require a bulky free-flowing liquid casting material that is relatively robust when set. Tool marks casting materials require greater adhesion and viscosity as the marks may be in a vertical surface.

Some methods can be used in combination but others may interfere with each other or are destructive. For this reason a sequential approach is used that takes into account other potential evidence types, as well as the optimisation of the marks themselves.

### Lighting

Effective lighting is an important means of revealing marks and is often used in combination with suitable physical and chemical methods. Directional lighting at a low angle is often used on three-dimensional marks, such as indented handwriting, tool marks, dust marks, footwear and tyre marks. Specialist lighting can also be used, such as high-intensity light sources with appropriate filtering. The main advantage of lighting methods is that they do not affect the mark or other evidence types.

### Visualisation by physical methods

These methods depend on the physical characteristics of the marks and generally involve transfer of the mark. Casting involves applying a liquid material which then sets to form a permanent record of the mark. The cast can then be removed and inspected as an inverted version of the mark. Marks in dust, commonly encountered in footwear and tyre marks examination, can be revealed by methods that transfer the mark to a contrasting background. The main methods, electrostatic lifting and gelatin lifting, both involve the transfer of marks on to black gloss film. In the case of electrostatic lifting, the dust forming the mark is attracted to a plastic laminate film using an electrical charge. Gelatin lifting uses a weakly adhesive rubber-like material to which the marks adhere following light pressure. As well as increasing the contrast (and therefore visibility) these methods allow recovery of the marks.

Powders are often used to visualise marks, particularly finger marks and footwear marks. Very fine inert powders are applied by brush to areas where marks may be present or are partially visible. Powder may adhere to either the mark or the background, revealing the image. Powders tend to be very dark, such as carbon, or bright, such as aluminium, but can also be fluorescent, in order to develop maximum contrast with the surface. Metal deposition, a facility often found in fingerprint development laboratories, works on a similar principle to powders but uses a gaseous metal, typically zinc. Metal deposition is very sensitive to slight chemical or physical differences on a surface and can reveal marks that may otherwise remain invisible using other methods. It is limited in use, being only suitable for smooth surfaces and small items as the equipment has a relatively small vacuum chamber.

One useful aspect of visualisation by physical methods (with the exception of metal deposition) is that the process often allows removal of the marks from the crime scene.

## Visualisation by chemical methods

Chemical methods as the name suggests feature the reaction of one or more components of the material in which the mark has been made with a chemical reagent. This limits the use of chemical methods to circumstances where the composition of the mark is known. This approach is commonly used with blood, whose composition is well known, and presence can be established by presumptive testing. There are a number of reagents used with blood marks that vary in practicality and effectiveness at the crime scene and in the laboratory. Most chemical methods used to reveal marks are confined to finger mark detection although these could also be applied to other marks if the material in which the mark was made was known.

## Identification of the object that made the mark

Although marks can originate from almost any object they tend to fall into well-defined categories in forensic casework. Most have characteristics that reveal their origins from their general appearance. It is also important to consider the context of the marks. Regular patterns found on a vehicle body following a suspected hit-and-run collision would strongly suggest fabric impressions. In most cases it is relatively straightforward to identify the type of mark from its appearance or from a consideration of the context. One of the most difficult areas of examination is bodily injury. It may be straightforward to attribute cuts and stab wounds to implements used in an attack but examination of bruises is more difficult. The random nature of interactions in violent crime often results in bruises caused by footwear, clothing and jewellery, and objects the victim may collide with, as well as blunt weapons. Injuries that have no clear indicators of the type of object that made them must be viewed with caution. Attributing bruises to footwear or objects used as weapons could be critical to the direction of an investigation as it would strongly suggest that the injuries had arisen from criminal activity.

## Information from marks

An essential quality of a mark is that its very appearance immediately provides information about the object that made it such as a finger, shoe or chisel. However, marks can also provide other information about the particular object, such as the make and model of a shoe or the width of a chisel. This enables the examiner to provide the investigator with information about the object and this is a routine part of the forensic process. In some cases the descriptive properties of a mark can support the use of a database, for example footwear, firearms and tool marks. Any match of properties between the marks at one scene and the marks at another could indicate an association between the two scenes. This is useful in investigating volume crimes such as burglary where there may be particularly active individuals.

## Marks databases

Fingerprint databases are now well established and routinely used in crime investigation. Other types of database have met with varying degrees of success. A common problem tends to be the volume and quality of material available to form such databases. Marks databases require particular types of data for them to function effectively. The properties of objects need to be straightforward in order to recognise and assign a value to them. They also need to be relatively long-lived (or permanent) and show sufficient variation to allow discrimination between different objects. Another issue which is difficult to resolve is the subjectivity of any classification system. Examiners may describe the properties of the same mark in different ways. This tends to be more of an issue when examining marks for inclusion on an index or database where the available information may be incomplete or ambiguous. Storing information about known shoes, firearms, tools etc. taken from arrested individuals is more straightforward as all of the properties of the original objects are immediately evident and can be classified with more precision.

## Comparison of marks

Irrespective of the type of mark the comparison process is essentially the same and considers the following question: 'Do the mark and the object share the properties of size, shape and arrangement?' If an object has made a mark there must be at least a similarity of the properties if not an exact match. The quality of the mark, i.e. the extent of information and detail present is crucial to this assessment. The 'best' quality marks can be regarded as those that contain the most information about the attributes of the object that made them, particularly the fine characteristics or individual detail. Conversely a 'poor' quality mark is one that contains the least information. The best marks are not necessarily those that are the most obvious on initial examination. It is also important to consider the context of the examination. An incomplete tool mark may contain sufficient fine detail to associate it conclusively with a given tool. However, the same mark may provide little information about the nature of the object that made it, such as the type of tool or blade width. In the early stages of an investigation this information may be more useful as it could be used to target a specific tool. The marks examiner should always consider other objects that may be similar to the item under investigation that may provide a better match and which suggest that the questioned item is not the one that truly made the marks. For example, a footwear pattern in a mark may be similar to a shoe tread but there may be information in the mark that suggests another similar but different pattern to the shoe. This information may not be immediately obvious even to the examiner. It is only when presented with an object during the investigation that provides a better match that it becomes apparent that there is more information in the mark than was originally considered.

### How individual are the matching properties?

The properties of an individual object can be shared with other similar objects. The shape and size of a blade or a shoe size are not unique. However, some features may be unique, such as wear and damage on shoes and blades, or mechanical defects etc. Eliminating those that are clearly different in some way can reduce the number of potential objects that could make a mark. This raises a crucial issue for all types of marks examination. That is, whether there are sufficient features in a mark such that it can be deemed to be unique to the object that made it. With most types of marks this is done on the basis that the possibility of any other object of the same type sharing these properties can be practically excluded. This is generally inferred on the basis of mathematical models or calculations that result in a near zero probability of the match being accidental. If this cannot be demonstrated it is still possible to assess the strength of an association of a match in terms of probability or likelihood ratios using Bayesian methods. In doing this, as in most forensic comparisons, some background information is valuable although this is not always available. In a similar sense to contact trace evidence, the 'commonness' (i.e. frequency) of the various properties needs to known and demonstrated. For glass particles one can measure a range of properties and compare these to samples previously analysed. In the same way footwear types can be recorded in footwear databases that can then be used to estimate their frequency of occurrence. The issue of a defined measurable value is important and it should be applied to those properties evident in the mark. Some objects do not lend themselves to collecting data as the available number of samples is very small or they do not have gross properties that can be categorised.

### Are there any differences?

Another critical consideration is how to evaluate differences that may persist between the mark and the item it is being compared with. There may be an explanation for such differences that requires the judgement of the examiner. If there is no reasonable explanation for a difference the object must be eliminated as the source. As this may be a critical conclusion in an investigation it is important that the examiner considers all of the issues that might explain any difference. Objects whose properties change with time, such as shoes that become worn, tools that also wear and may also be subject to corrosion, would not be expected to show identical properties if there was substantial time between the recovery of the mark and the recovery of the object. A subjective but informed assessment of the amount of wear to a tool or item of footwear is required. Exactly how much change through wear or other mechanisms would occur cannot be known definitively. For an object to be excluded, therefore, there must be demonstrable and significant difference in properties.

**Footwear marks**

Footwear marks are found in a wide variety of investigations including volume and serious crime. They offer the possibility of pre-emptive information and can contribute to crime intelligence prior to the arrest of an offender as well as useful comparative evidence following arrest and subsequent prosecution.

### Finding and recovering footwear marks

It is frequently suggested that footwear marks must be present at every location where an individual has walked. Even if this were true, the real issue tends to be whether they can be detected and recovered. The relevance and potential value of footwear marks to an investigation have practical implications for how a scene should be examined. The scene examiner needs to consider the issues below.

### Location of footwear marks

Footwear marks can indicate the position of individuals in a scene and their movements. Location and movement of individuals may be important to investigators and courts in evaluating the various accounts in a case. In some instances the position of marks may be sufficient to discount certain assertions and support or prove others. It is important therefore that detailed records are kept of where each mark was found before it is recovered. This process may include photography of visible marks that is generally the first step in the recovery process.

### Can the marks be related to the offence?

Marks found in critical positions, such as those at a point of entry or near a body, may support the inference that they have originated from an offender. In assessing which marks may be relevant in a scene the examiner can take a number of approaches. Marks on a windowsill or 'kicked in' door would be considered highly relevant. Marks in a substance related to an offence, such as blood, would also be obvious for selection. The objects on which marks are found, such as damaged door panels, disturbed paperwork or bedding, can also indicate the relevance of marks. If disturbed paperwork is dated it may allow marks to be given a maximum age of deposition.

Careful selection of marks is particularly important if they are to be searched against seized footwear from offenders using databases. Crime scene marks included in databases or indices can result in large numbers of evidential checks against offenders' footwear. This is usually due to the fact that tread patterns may match more than one shoe. Database searches may also increase the amount of unnecessary work if the marks are not directly related to an offence. Marks not relevant to offences become 'noise' in any footwear mark database or indexing system, reducing its efficiency and effectiveness, and should be screened out if possible. The examiner can do some elimination, particularly if examining a 'closed' scene or one with limited access. Inspection of footwear from the victim, police officers or any other innocent parties who had access to a scene may allow the elimination of marks of the same pattern which have been left by these individuals. This is a reasonable and practical approach in many circumstances but carries a risk of a false elimination if the offender and individuals with legitimate access to the scene have footwear of the same pattern. A more conservative but time-consuming option would be to obtain elimination prints from the individuals. This latter approach is more likely to be reserved for major investigations.

### Selection of marks for recovery

Even if the scene examiner has taken into account the locations and relevance of the marks there may still be a large number for recovery. Given that time and material resources will always be an issue, further selection may still be required. There is no single method of selecting marks that will guarantee a significant evidential outcome but some steps can be taken to optimise the likelihood of success. The first is to identify the number of different patterns present. Having identified the number of patterns, selecting marks corresponding to left and right feet will allow a comparison to be made on both shoes of a pair. This can be useful as the properties of both treads can be compared as a whole and this may enhance the strength of the evidence. If left and right shoes are represented and corresponding marks detected and recovered, it is also desirable to have more than one mark made by each shoe. It may be that different areas of the tread are represented in individual marks and these can be considered in combination. It is unlikely that every mark will be of the same quality or show all of the same features. The greater the total tread area of the footwear represented in the marks, the greater the confidence that can be attached to a match or exclusion. If the multiple marks show the same wear and damage features this also allows the examiner to be more confident that the features in the mark are genuine and derive from the footwear that made the marks. Good comparative evidence will depend on fine detail in the marks. If predictive information is required in an investigation, such as make, model or size, this will need marks that represent a substantial part of the tread.

To summarise, an appropriate selection strategy would be:

- Identify the number of distinct patterns present.
- Consider the relevance of marks, location, deposition material (e.g. blood).
- Select marks of each pattern if considered relevant.
- Select marks corresponding to each foot.
- Select multiple marks from the same foot.
- Select marks that give most information about the footwear.

The process is only necessary when there is a large choice of marks. More often than not a small number of fragmentary marks is available, most of which can be readily recorded or recovered.

### Recovery and enhancement of the marks

Having selected the marks the scene examiner then needs to consider the appropriate method of recovery. Footwear marks are subject to some peculiarities not shared with other marks. When footwear marks are first made they contain a certain amount of information about the tread. No enhancement or recovery method can increase the amount of information present: it can only reveal what is already there. Enhancement, a term frequently used in relation to marks, refers to various techniques used to increase visible information. Recovery methods allow the removal or lifting of the mark and transfer from the crime scene to the laboratory but do not enhance the mark. For footwear marks, recovery also includes photography although strictly speaking this is a recording process which does not physically remove the mark in its original form. For this reason. in common with other marks it is essential that footwear marks recorded by photography can be restored to their original size, referred to as 'life' or 'actual' size. This is essential in cases where the dimensions of the footwear tread are under consideration both in comparison and predictive examinations.

Generally speaking marks should be recovered and enhanced using a sequential approach using the least destructive techniques first. Ideally, if a mark and surface can be removed intact to a laboratory this should be done.

### Footwear comparison evidence

The comparison process routinely carried out in forensic laboratories follows the general procedure for most marks examinations. This addresses the following questions:

- What are the significant attributes of the footwear?
- Can they be observed in the mark or marks?
- Do the attributes observed in the mark match those on the questioned footwear?
- Do any attributes appear to be different?
- How significant are the matching attributes?
- Can any differences be reasonably explained (or should the mark be eliminated)?
- How significant is the match or elimination?

This process follows the sequence of most forensic examinations of observation, interpretation and conclusion.

This sequence illustrates the importance of determining the useful attributes of footwear at the outset of the comparison process. This approach can identify attributes or properties that can be used at an early stage to exclude the possibility that a given item of footwear made a given mark. It is important that such exclusions are made on the basis of significant differences.

### Footwear attributes

One would expect a mark made by an item of footwear to share many, if not all, of the properties of the footwear. The attributes that tend to be most useful in examinations are:

- tread pattern;
- pattern dimensions;
- manufacturing features;
- progressive wear;
- specific damage.

Although marks generally originate from the tread it is possible for them to originate from an upper. The upper will have properties that will fall into some of the above categories and these can be compared in a similar manner to the tread. The construction features of the upper can be considered as analogous to the tread pattern.

All of the above properties can be used individually or in combination to exclude the possibility of a footwear item making a mark and are useful for this reason. One of the most commonly encountered problems with footwear mark comparisons is that the appearance of the tread and the marks are greatly influenced by progressive wear. Wear is an attribute of the tread but it also influences the appearance of the tread pattern and can modify the appearance of damage to the tread. Damage and manufacturing detail such as mould texture and defects tend to be relatively small and will eventually disappear. New manufacturing detail can sometimes be revealed by ongoing wear. Defects such as air bubbles can appear to grow larger or smaller and then disappear as the tread wears. Even the tread pattern will be removed eventually. It is therefore not just the attributes of the tread that are important at any given moment in time but also how much time has elapsed between the deposition of the marks and the recovery of the shoes. Very fine features could be removed in a matter of days, more significant features in a matter of weeks or months.

### Comparison of marks

The comparison of a mark with an item of footwear is a simple process and little sophisticated equipment is required. Most of the detail present in footwear marks can be examined with a magnifying glass or low-power microscope. What is important is that the examiner recognises the attributes present, as these are not always immediately obvious in small or fragmentary marks. Once the presence of a viable mark has been established this can be enhanced or recorded, and produced in a suitable form for comparison. Marks recovered as casts need little more than thorough cleaning to reveal the detail present.

It is a common practice to produce a test or controlled impression of the tread of footwear for comparison with two-dimensional marks. Numerous methods can be used for this depending on available materials and local practice. Most of these result in the production of an impression on a transparent background. The test impression can then be overlaid (hence the commonly used term 'overlays') on the mark and that allows the examiner to compare the positions and spatial arrangements of the features of the tread. During this process similarities or differences in the manufacturing detail, wear and damage can be identified. Gross differences or similarities in overall tread pattern can usually be ascertained without the need for test impressions. If casts or other three-dimensional marks are being compared, it is also common practice to make a simple side-by-side comparison of the shoe and the mark. Most two-dimensional marks are mirror images of the tread and this is one of the reasons why test impressions are useful for comparisons. Test impressions also reveal details that are difficult to perceive when viewing the tread directly as they represent the contact area of the tread only. Very small or shallow indentations can appear in marks and test impressions that have no obvious feature on the tread when it is first examined.

### Assessing the comparison

Having compared the marks to the footwear or test impression the examiner will need to consider the features that are clearly visible in the marks and take a view on others that are partly reproduced. Marks are encountered in a very wide range of definitions, contrast and size. The larger the area of the tread represented and the better the definition, the more information is available and therefore the greater the chance of a conclusive association or exclusion. It should be noted however that conclusive associations and exclusions could be made from what initially appear to be relatively poor marks. And some complete and well-defined marks result in little more than a pattern and size match. This is because a conclusive association or exclusion also depends on the condition of the shoe. It follows that judging the potential of a scene mark before any comparison can be a precarious matter and generally should be avoided.

### Non-matching features

Once the matching features have been determined any non-matching features must be taken into account. Differences that do not have a reasonable explanation should result in the examiner excluding the footwear from having made the mark. A difference in pattern would exclude the shoe immediately. Even patterns that appear similar on first inspection could show critical differences. Examples of similar but different pattern are shown in Figures 8.3 and 8.4 below.

The patterns in Figures 8.3 and 8.4 show a high degree of similarity and have essentially the same general structure. In some marks these differences may not be obvious but if apparent they can exclude treads of a similar pattern.

Differences in pattern detail and degree of wear that do not necessarily eliminate the mark can be caused by a number of factors. Subsequent wear affects the general appearance of the tread and may even change the appearance of specific pattern detail. Square profile features will change little with progressive wear but tapered or angled profile pattern features will

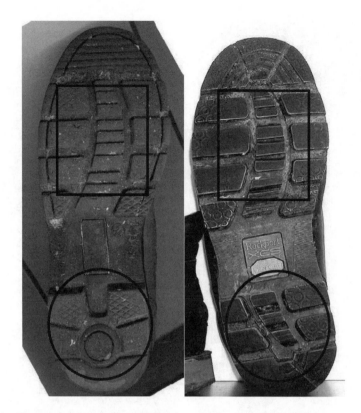

**Figure 8.3** Boot treads of similar design but with appreciable differences. Marks left by the tread area (boxes) would be indistinguishable if the fine texture was not visible. Marks left by the heel area (circles) would be clearly different

change shape and size and may even appear to move position. The appearance of characteristic damage features can be influenced in the same way. These changes are represented diagrammatically in Figure 8.5 below.

The examiner will assess the pattern features and decide what the likely effect of subsequent wear would be. In doing so the examiner refers to known samples of wear. If there were obvious differences in the pattern detail or wear and the time between the recovery of the shoes and marks was very short this would normally result in a conclusive exclusion. There are, however, other aspects of the way a mark was made that might affect its appearance. These include the following:

- the amount of pressure on the tread;
- the degree of movement of the tread when the mark was made;
- unstable surfaces;
- distortion of the mark when being recovered or recorded.

If all of the above can be discounted then any observed differences should result in exclusion. In practice most cannot be excluded because each will have had some effect on the formation of the mark. When differences are observed in a comparison that may be caused by one of the above the

**Figure 8.4** Two trainer treads of similar design but with appreciable differences. Marks left by the tread area would be clearly different but the heels would leave very similar marks

examiner will assess this by making test impressions on a similar surface in a similar material. These are often referred to as 'dynamic' impressions as they include some of the forces and movements to which footwear would be subjected in normal use and when the mark was made at a crime scene. However, it is difficult to ascertain exactly what the footwear was subjected to at a scene, for example how much force, or how soft or stable the surface was at the time the mark was made. The examiner can only show that there is a range of possibilities. Some examiners may assume that all of the above factors are at work for every mark and make an appropriate allowance. Some of the features may be obvious from the mark, particularly movement of the tread that often appears as a series of lines that follow the pattern in one or more directions. Differences in pattern detail and wear must be considered as critically different before they form the basis for a conclusive exclusion.

Figures 8.6 and 8.7 show readily visible differences in the pattern detail. Differences in damage or apparent damage are more difficult to deal with. If features appear in the marks that are not on the tread there are only two possibilities:

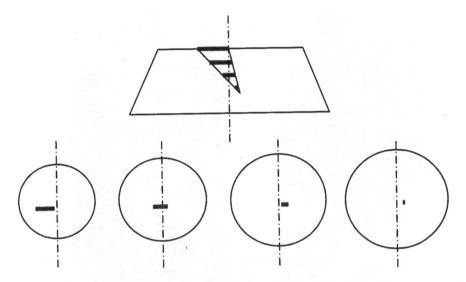

**Figure 8.5** This shows a cross-section of an angled profile circular stud with a damage feature that is straight in one plane but at an angle to surface of the tread. As the stud wears the cut diminishes in length and its position moves relative to the central axis of the stud. If the wear to the stud is even it will appear to increase in size as represented above. If the wear were uneven the appearance of the stud would become distinctly non-circular which would further change the position of the cut relative to parts of the stud boundary. This affects the spatial arrangement of components in the mark

- The features have not originated from damage on the tread of the footwear that made the mark.
- The features have originated from damage on the tread of the footwear that made the mark.

If the features in the mark have originated from damage then any footwear deemed to match should have the same features in the corresponding positions. Consideration needs to be given to the time between the recovery of the mark and the footwear. Damage features will be changed progressively by wear. If it could be shown that features in a mark did originate from damage and the damage was absent from an item that was recovered soon after the mark was made, the item could be conclusively excluded. If there was long delay between the recovery of the mark and the footwear it may not be possible to exclude the footwear. It should be noted that a feature in a mark that does not appear on a tread cannot be definitively attributed to damage regardless of time delay. If, however, a number of features appear in a mark and none of these is visible on the treads the examiner may consider that there is a strong possibility that at least some of these features are due to damage on the tread. If so and the time delay is very short they may then conclude that the footwear did not make the mark.

It is often the case that the reverse scenario is encountered and there are features on the tread that do not appear in the marks. Even with no significant

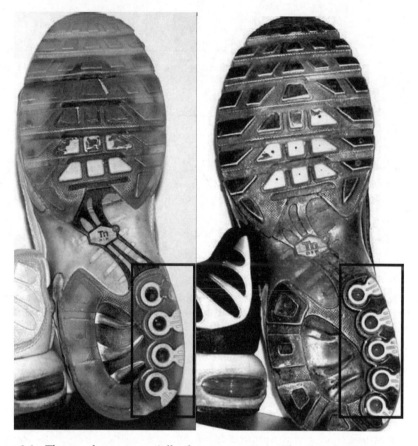

**Figure 8.6** The treads are essentially the same pattern. The shoe on the right has an extra circle in the heel design. In a well-defined mark from the heel area this design feature could provide definite exclusion of some shoes from having made the mark

time delays this should not be unexpected as damage features are usually small and easily obscured. This can be caused in a number of ways:

- pressure on the tread;
- movement of the tread;
- movement of the surface;
- uneven or grainy background;
- uneven distribution of material on tread;
- uneven or limited contrast.

It is reasonable to expect that gross damage on a tread should be present in a mark made shortly before the recovery of the shoes. In certain cases the examiner may take the view that the footwear could not have made the mark if there is gross damage on the tread and there are no similar features in the marks. It would also need to be established that the damage was present on the tread prior to the time when the marks were made. If the damage

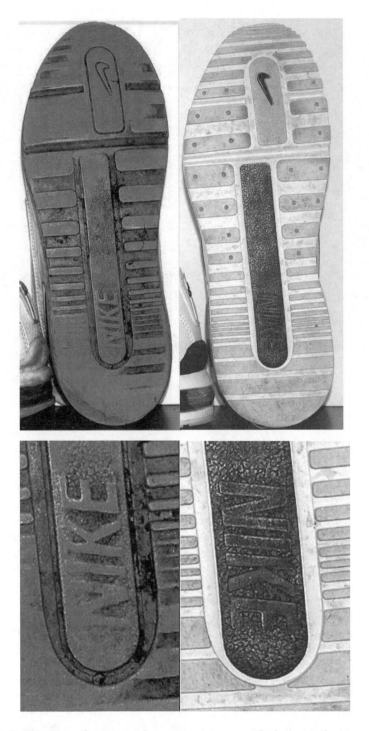

**Figure 8.7** The two shoes are the same pattern and designated size and both correspond to a right foot. The Nike logo in the heel area is inverted. Again if this area was clearly represented in a mark certain shoes of the same tread pattern could be excluded from having made the mark

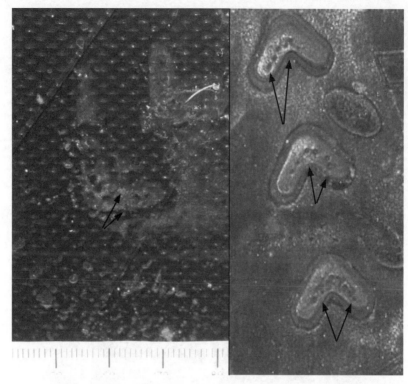

**Figure 8.8** Air bubbles trapped in tread (right) are revealed by wear and appear in marks made by the tread (left)

is particularly fresh in appearance some allowance may be made for the possibility that it has been recently acquired.

### Damage or design?

One of the difficulties faced by the footwear examiner is determining if a feature is due to damage (and therefore characteristic) or manufacturing and could be shared with other treads. Manufacturing features observed on a tread can form part of the pattern and therefore repeat on all treads made by the same machine. It is also the case that random defects happen during the manufacturing process. Defects can be shared by a small or large number of shoes of the same type, so it is important that the cause of a feature is identified as damage or manufacturing. For manufacturing features determination of whether it is likely to be unique or repeated is important. It is generally safe to assume that if a defect can happen once in a production run, it will almost certainly occur again and for certain types of feature, probably quite often. Differentiating damage and defects requires inspection of the feature on the footwear. Damage will often show fresh surfaces if recently acquired or microscopic striations where the damaging object has sheared the tread material. Manufacturing defects will generally not show striation detail. It is possible that some manufacturing detail will be revealed by wear, such as bubbles trapped in the tread. Bubbles have very smooth spherical surfaces and are generally easy to identify. Figure 8.8 shows an example of revealed air bubbles in a tread and their appearance in matching marks.

Some consideration should also be given to damage that has occurred in vulnerable areas of the tread. Constructional properties of tread may render it prone to being damaged in certain places. This would throw some doubt on the degree of character this confers to the tread. It may be possible in these cases to examine previously taken test impressions from treads of the same design to assess this.

### Quantifying matches

Quantifying matches is straightforward if suitable information is available but more complex if considering the context of the case. A match with no significant differences will include some or all of the following:

- the tread pattern;
- pattern or manufacturing detail;
- general and specific wear;
- characteristic features.

### Pattern

This is perhaps the simplest feature of the tread to quantify. In crude terms, if a certain footwear model (defined by pattern) is very popular there will be more in circulation and a greater chance of finding the pattern at a scene or on a suspect's shoe. Casework data from UK Laboratories indicates that the most common patterns at the time of publication represent up to 20 per cent of the marks and footwear recovered. There are, however, wide variations due to geography and time of year. It should also be noted that casework submissions are biased towards a certain population. Despite this, if such biases are taken into account, it should be possible to determine a representative population and the frequency of occurrence of a tread pattern. Table 8.1 shows a 'snapshot' of pattern frequency distribution in casework. It should be noted that the patterns in the table would change over time. Despite this, the shape of the distribution curve remains fairly constant. It is important that the examiner considers the number of footwear items that would leave marks of the same visible pattern and not the number of footwear items that share the same overall pattern. For partial marks the area of tread represented by the mark may be common to two or more distinct footwear models so the frequency for all models capable of leaving such a mark would need to be considered.

### Size

Pattern detail and general dimensions can provide an indication of the size of an item of footwear. It is straightforward to collate size data for the general population and the casework population. A mark may contain information that allows the examiner to differentiate this from a number of treads of the same pattern and nominal size. This is due to variations in

**Table 8.1** Typical pattern frequency distribution for footwear marks from a UK police force

| Make | Model | % Marks/footwear |
|---|---|---|
| Nike | Max Ltd | 10 |
| Nike | Max 95 | 8 |
| Adidas | Campus | 3 |
| Reebok | Classic 1 | 3 |
| Nike | Max 90 | 3 |
| Nike | Court tradition | 2 |
| Nike | Tuned 8 | 1.5 |
| Lacoste | Camden | 1.5 |
| Various | Ripple | 1.5 |
| Adidas | Country | 1.5 |
| Nike | Max Classic | 1.5 |
| | Other patterns | Less than 1% |

manufacture that result in two treads of the same pattern attached to shoes of the same designated size having clearly distinct features. To quantify the match precisely would require examples of all of the treads made by the manufacturers and information on distribution numbers. This is impractical so the examiner needs to make the reasonable assumption that the majority of shoes of differing sizes and/or point of manufacture would have different pattern detail. Some allowance must also be made for compression of the tread when worn that can affect the shape, size and spacing of the pattern elements. Most examiners are therefore relatively cautious in the level of significance they attach to a match of the dimensions and pattern detail. It is reasonable to assume that there will be one distinct tread unit or mould per size and for many current patterns there are a number for some sizes. For common shoe types, casework samples provide a good set of examples and give the examiner a reasonable idea of how many distinct moulds there are depending on manufacturing method, and the approximate distribution in the population represented by casework samples.

To complicate matters further the method of manufacture can result in variations in the tread that are random and may render the tread unique. Treads that are cut to shape or subject to finishing processes such as trimming, grinding or the application of further components can have distinctive or unique edge profiles. This is particularly so if the pattern is of uniform design. Figure 8.9 shows the minor but discernible variations that can occur in uniform tread designs caused by slight changes in the position of inserted features such as a logo or edges.

It is very difficult to quantify size in these instances without seeing every other example of the pattern. The examiner must also be certain that the mark actually contains the true edge of the tread that made the mark.

Assuming the pattern detail matches, the level of significance of this may be related exclusively to the size of the shoe. Casework samples can have frequencies of up to 1 in 1.6 if latitude of one size is allowed. The frequency

**Figure 8.9** Significant variations that can occur in uniform patterns even with shoes of the same nominal size. These variations can be detected in marks and be used to exclude a footwear item from having made a mark

may be less than 1 in 10 if it is considered that the pattern detail will show more variation than that related to the general size. If a very unusual size is being considered the frequency may also be considerably lower. It is interesting to note that the pattern gives a greater degree of discrimination even when considering the most popular models. The distribution of UK sizes encountered in UK casework is shown in Figure 8.10 below. The distribution implies this is an adult male population.

It should be noted that half sizes occur in a relatively small proportion of submissions. This may reflect a lack of availability or buying tendency in the population. The pattern detail on a prime size and its corresponding half size tend to be very similar.

### Wear and damage

These attributes either singly or in combination may make footwear tread unique. The older the tread the more damage it will accumulate and the more distinctive it becomes. Wear is progressive and its effect on the tread can vary. Fine design features will be removed relatively quickly but wear of the main pattern components will occur over a period of months. Some patterns will change their appearance progressively and others will change relatively little. For most designs the appearance of the wear changes very quickly when the tread is nearing the end of its useful life. Examiners will quantify wear by considering the general age of the tread based on its appearance but will also consider the specific degree and distribution if the marks are of sufficient quality to observe a match. The frequencies attached to matching wear can range from 1 in 2 for a general wear match to possibly 1 in 10 if the design of the tread results in a more progressive change to its appearance. The exact degree and distribution of wear is more difficult to assess precisely as the wearer of the shoes will influence this to some degree. If the wear has resulted in random profiles at wear boundaries the examiner may consider it to be unique. This wear pattern can appear when the tread is made up of layers and the outermost layer wears completely and a hole or edge appears.

Figure 8.11 shows the effect of progressive wear on two treads of different patterns and constructions.

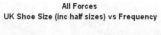

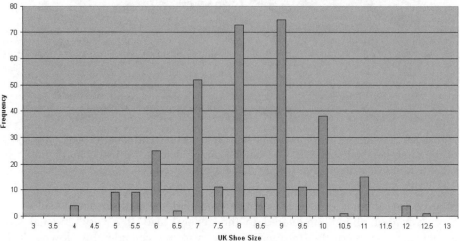

**Figure 8.10** Distribution of shoe sizes in casework submissions

Matching damage can be assessed in terms of quantity although this is difficult to evaluate precisely. However, even relatively crude models indicate that the likelihood of two items of footwear having a number of similar damage features in the same part of the tread is so small it can be practically discounted. This is a similar rationale to that used for fingerprints. Footwear requires more complex consideration when it comes to the character of a feature. A single feature may contain a number of distinct geometric properties and these could be reproduced in marks made by the item. The likelihood of another item of footwear having a similar feature anywhere on the tread would be very small and the likelihood of it being in exactly the same place on the tread could again be practically discounted. Figures 8.12 and 8.13 show typical matching damage features.

When considering character and location of damage the design and construction of the tread are important. Some tread designs render them prone to damage in particular places and sometimes in roughly the same shape. Thin bar patterns tend to show damage as breaks in the bars. Caution must be applied when assessing if such features should be considered as unique when observed in isolation.

Some manufacturing features can also be considered unique and can be quantified in the same way as damage. To do so the examiner needs to demonstrate that there is good reason to believe that the features in question are unique. This is not always practical as a relatively large sample of footwear items of the same type and size would be required for inspection.

Having considered all the matching attributes and assuming there are no critical differences in any of the attributes in the mark and on the footwear, the examiner would have enough information to estimate the potential pool of footwear capable of depositing the marks. Having made such an estimate

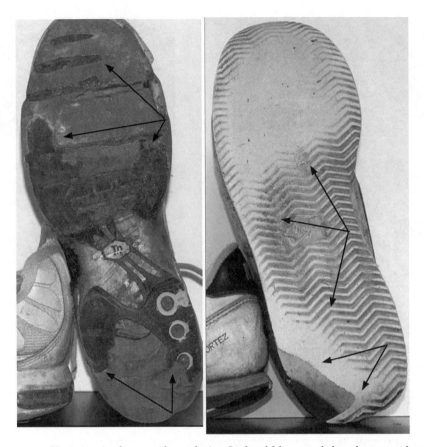

**Figure 8.11** Variation in the wear boundaries. It should be noted that the general wear pattern tends to conform to the main pressure points when walking or running as well as the shape of the foot but the exact pressure points will vary and the net effect on the tread will also depend to some degree on its design, manufacturing variation and the habits of the wearer. It is apparent that finer uniform designs such as the pattern on the right tend to be more sensitive indicators of the degree and distribution of wear. The multilayered construction of the tread on the right has resulted in very distinctive profiles on the worn edge of the outer layer of the tread

a conclusion can then be drawn as to the significance of the match. This can range from the opinion that footwear did make the marks in question, through various levels of support (from relatively weak to very strong) that the shoes could have made the mark.

### Footwear intelligence databases

Intelligence databases containing information on footwear have been in use for many years. Whatever the format, these databases have two principal aims: to link crime scenes and make associations between footwear from offenders and marks from crime scenes.

When organising large numbers of samples from crime scenes or prisoners in manual systems or computerised databases, the most useful variables need

**Figure 8.12** Three-dimensional damage features in a tread (top images) reproduced in marks cast from soil (bottom images)

to be selected. For attributes of footwear treads to be useful a number of criteria must be fulfilled. The attribute should

- be apparent in the majority of or all recovered marks;
- show a high degree of variation;
- be a permanent (or relatively permanent) feature of the tread;
- be easy to assign a fixed value.

Table 8.2 below shows how each of the footwear attributes fulfils these requirements.

The only attribute that fulfils all of these requirements is the tread pattern and most systems therefore work on this basis. Where systems vary is in the assignment of a value for the pattern. Some systems use specific classifications normally aligned to the make and model of the footwear, such as Reebok Classic 1 or Reebok 7, or a description such as 'straight bars' or 'circular studs'. These classification systems have the major advantage that only marks and shoes of exactly the same pattern will be potentially linked. The descriptive method could show potential links that are based on a pattern that is similar but is in fact different in pattern detail. In practice there are always a proportion of marks that contain insufficient information to assign to a particular pattern model. In such cases a descriptive code can be used on the basis of the most prominent pattern features in the mark. If the majority of marks on an index are classified as a particular pattern model and the remainder as descriptive codes the database will still work fairly efficiently. It follows that timely and precise classification of the pattern of a crime scene

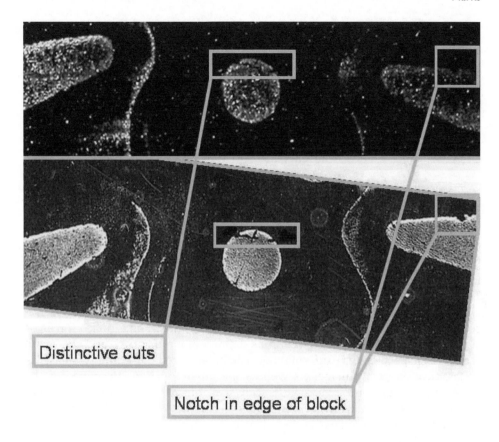

Distinctive cuts

Notch in edge of block

**Figure 8.13** More typical two-dimensional marks encountered in casework and the features that can appear and be matched to those on a tread. These images show the type and size of detail that can be used to form conclusive associations between footwear treads and marks

**Table 8.2** Footwear tread attributes

|                                                                 | Pattern       | Size      | Wear      | Damage                 |
| --------------------------------------------------------------- | ------------- | --------- | --------- | ---------------------- |
| Apparent in the majority of or all recovered marks              | Yes           | No        | No        | No                     |
| Show high degree of variation (useful discrimination)           | 1/10–1/500+   | 1/3–1/10  | 1/3–1/6   | Yes                    |
| Permanent feature of the tread                                  | Yes           | Yes       | No        | Major features only    |
| Can be assigned a fixed value                                   | Yes           | Yes       | No        | No                     |

mark is desirable and a footwear pattern reference collection is required. These are often referred to as footwear databases but it is important to define and differentiate their function. Often the marks index, suspect and reference collection are all part of the same software application. Some police forces or agencies use the reference collection as a stand-alone database and the crime scene or suspect pattern information is held in a general crime database as a classification or an image. As well as the other functions described in the following paragraphs, investigators can use this as predictive information about the footwear worn at the crime scene by the offender. Predictive information about footwear is described at the end of this chapter.

### Crime scene linking

One of the advantages of using a specific classification for footwear patterns is that it allows fast identification of multiple occurrences of a given pattern. If these occur over a short time period in a small area they may indicate a prolific offender. In numerical terms the recovery rates of most patterns at crime scenes is small. A typical marks database covering a three-month period for a UK police division or force area consists of only a few hundred marks. Even the most common patterns are found in small numbers. For most patterns therefore the normal occurrence rate is very low and multiple occurrences are readily visible. Even databases running over longer periods can be analysed effectively. Table 8.3 below shows the analysis of a specific pattern over a three-year period. (Some allowance must be made for the period over which the pattern has been on the market, in this case from August 2005 at the latest.)

It can be readily observed that pattern matches occasionally occur in clusters on the timeline, generally in the same approximate location and at the same type of offence. It can be seen that over 10 per cent of all occurrences (highlighted in red) from an entire police force are in one small area in a period of two weeks. These are very unlikely to be random and may indicate a persistent offender. Because the pattern classification is based on a specific model there is less 'noise' in the database. Attempting this type of collation

**Table 8.3** Long-term shoe mark pattern occurrence records for a typical UK police area

| Make | Model | Date of offence | Location code | Offence Type |
|------|-------|-----------------|---------------|--------------|
| K-Swiss | Classic Luxury | 08/03/2008 | BW | Non dwelling |
| K-Swiss | Classic luxury | 03/02/2008 | DB | Dwelling |
| K-Swiss | Classic luxury | 16/01/2008 | CC | Non dwelling |
| K-Swiss | Classic luxury | 06/01/2008 | BW | Non dwelling |
| K-Swiss | Classic luxury | 26/09/2007 | CY | Dwelling |
| K-Swiss | Classic Luxury | 14/09/2007 | BW | Theft |
| K-Swiss | Classic Luxury | 26/07/2007 | CC | Non dwelling |
| K-Swiss | Classic Luxury | 25/05/2007 | AH | Dwelling |
| K-Swiss | Classic Luxury | 24/05/2007 | CN | Damage |
| K-Swiss | Classic Luxury | 20/04/2007 | DA | Unknown |
| K-Swiss | Classic Luxury | 26/03/2007 | DA | Dwelling |
| K-Swiss | Classic Luxury | 14/03/2007 | AA | Dwelling |
| K-Swiss | Classic Luxury | 05/12/2006 | CC | Non dwelling |
| K-Swiss | Classic Luxury | 03/11/2006 | DA | Dwelling |
| K-Swiss | Classic Luxury | 29/09/2006 | CB | Dwelling |
| K-Swiss | Classic Luxury | 29/09/2006 | CB | Dwelling |
| K-Swiss | Classic Luxury | 04/09/2006 | CL | Dwelling |
| K-Swiss | Classic Luxury | 06/07/2006 | CC | Dwelling |
| K-Swiss | Classic Luxury | 23/06/2006 | CC | Dwelling |
| K-Swiss | Classic Luxury | 22/06/2006 | CC | Dwelling |
| K-Swiss | Classic Luxury | 21/06/2006 | CC | Dwelling |
| K-Swiss | Classic Luxury | 19/05/2006 | DW | Non dwelling |
| K-Swiss | Classic Luxury | 11/04/2006 | CO | Dwelling |
| K-Swiss | Classic Luxury | 03/04/2006 | DA | Dwelling |
| K-Swiss | Classic Luxury | 29/03/2006 | CO | Theft |
| K-Swiss | Classic Luxury | 14/03/2006 | BW | Non dwelling |
| K-Swiss | Classic Luxury | 03/03/2006 | DA | Dwelling |
| K-Swiss | Classic Luxury | 01/03/2006 | CS | Dwelling |
| K-Swiss | Classic Luxury | 15/02/2006 | DA | Dwelling |
| K-Swiss | Classic Luxury | 06/12/2005 | CL | Dwelling |
| K-Swiss | Classic Luxury | 22/11/2005 | DA | Dwelling |
| K-Swiss | Classic Luxury | 05/08/2005 | CY | Non dwelling |

and analysis with a database that uses descriptions rather than set values would result in much larger clusters that are not necessarily the same overall pattern.

Intelligence analysts can examine the specific geography to establish the theoretical centre of the crime cluster and other features of the offences. It is unlikely that such crimes will be the only offences committed by the person wearing the footwear and there will almost certainly be crimes where no marks are recovered but which are similar in other features. Should an offender routinely wear footwear of different patterns, two clusters would result and the patterns from these clusters would show a very close correlation and range.

If a cluster has been identified and analysis indicates that the patterns found are the result of a prolific offender the 'profile' of the offender now contains an additional piece of information: the footwear type. In this respect footwear marks can make a useful contribution to an investigation prior to arrest.

### Predictive information from footwear marks

Very often investigators will request information about the footwear that made a mark, prior to an arrest and seizure of footwear. While it would be desirable to provide precise information, the reality is that there are limits to what can be stated with confidence. This issue is considered below.

### Footwear type

The most useful feature of a footwear mark is the tread pattern since it can be used to predict the make and model of footwear. This gives an immediate and useful piece of information to an investigator. To assist in this process many examiners and analysts use reference collections, often computerised, and should be able to provide the investigator with an image of the tread pattern, an image of the upper and the make of the shoe. Upper images can often be of limited value, particularly if the exact make cannot be determined. A number of tread patterns are used on different brands with different uppers and it is important that examiner and investigators are aware of this

If a footwear make and model cannot be determined, which is often the case for marks of limited information, the examiner can provide the investigator with a copy of the mark and may be able to suggest the general footwear type rather than a specific make and model. The majority of marks can usually be attributed to a given make and model classification relatively easily. Some patterns can be difficult to identify even if there is an appreciable amount of available pattern information in the mark. This is largely due to the vast amount of different footwear tread patterns in the global footwear market and it is impossible for any forensic laboratory to have a comprehensive record of all of them in real time.

### Footwear size

Footwear examiners are often asked to determine the size of the footwear that left a mark. If there are no obvious clues, such as a recognisable number in the mark, this can be an involved process that requires identifying the manufacturer of the tread (not necessarily the brand), collating a range of sole units of known size and eliminating all but one size. If this is achieved with a reasonable degree of confidence the investigator can be provided with an estimate of the size. For most marks and footwear found in casework, however, the range of sizes is narrow and the value of such information is limited compared to pattern type. In practice accurate sizing is often difficult to achieve with a high degree of certainty.

### Condition of the tread

Predicting the age or condition of the shoe requires knowledge of the footwear type and examples of treads of the same type in various degrees of wear.

Patterns familiar to the examiner will be encountered in various degrees of wear. Depending on the pattern and the quality of the marks the examiner may be able to predict the condition of the tread with a high degree of confidence. Some tread designs, however, change little with wear and accordingly it is more difficult to assess the potential condition. Some allowance also needs to be made for the age of the mark. If a mark was made by a relatively new item of footwear its tread will be quickly modified by wear and as time elapses predicting its condition becomes more difficult. It may be that the footwear is not worn frequently by an individual, in which case it will still appear relatively new. Alternatively, it could be worn constantly and the tread will show substantial modification and additional damage. The more time passes, the less certain the prediction will be about its condition. This information is of limited value for screening footwear for further comparison.

## Conclusion

It is clear that marks evidence will feature in a range of criminal investigations. Marks are made by a variety of mechanisms but always involve the creation of visual representation of the object that produced them and their physical properties. These properties can be shared with other similar objects or be unique to a single object. Shared and unique properties are useful in investigations. Unique properties can establish conclusive associations in comparisons whereas shared properties can establish target objects and inform the investigator what to look for. Examination and comparison of marks rely mainly on visual observation and pattern or feature recognition.

Footwear marks are the most routinely recovered marks at crime scenes after finger marks and are therefore considered a valuable source of intelligence and evidence. Their evidential value is well established and footwear mark comparisons regularly yield conclusive matches as well as corroborative evidence. The current diversity of the footwear market and wide variety of tread patterns assists the implementation of viable pattern-based intelligence systems. These allow the relatively simple identification of associated offences, efficient selection of marks for comparison with an offender's footwear and the prediction of the type of footwear that made a given mark. It is important, however, that the limitations of any information provided in relation to footwear mark intelligence are understood. Despite these limitations it is possible to establish efficient and effective footwear intelligence systems to support the investigation of crime.

## Further reading

Bodziak, W.J. (1990) *Footwear Impression Evidence*. Elsevier Ltd.
Cassidy M.J. (1980) *Footwear Identification*. Canadian Government Printing Centre.
Aitken, C.G.G. and Taroni, F. (2004) *Statistics and the Evaluation of Evidence for Forensic Scientists* (2nd edn). Chichester: John Wiley and Sons.

## References

Champod, C., Evett, I. and Jackson, G. (2004) 'Establishing the most appropriate databases for addressing source level propositions', *Science and Justice*, 44 (3): 153–164.

Davis, Roger J. (1981) 'An intelligence approach to footwear marks and toolmarks', *Journal of the Forensic Science Society*, 21: 183–193.

Evett, I.W., Lambert, J.A. and Buckleton, J.S (1998) 'A Bayesian approach to interpreting footwear marks in Forensic Casework', *Science and Justice*, 38 (4): 241–247.

Geradts, Z. and Bijhold, J. (2001) 'New developments in forensic image processing and pattern recognition', *Science and Justice*, 41 (3): 159–166.

Girod, A. (1996) 'Computerized classification of the shoeprints of burglars shoes', *Forensic Science International*, 82 (1): 59–65.

Hannigan, T.J., Fleury, L.M., Reilly, B.A., O'Mullane, B. and deChazal, P. (2006) 'Survey of 1276 shoeprint impressions and development of an automatic shoeprint matching facility', *Science and Justice*, 46 (2): 79–89.

Milne, R. (2001) 'Operation Bigfoot – a volume crime database project', *Science and Justice*, 41 (3): 215–217.

Napier, T. (2002) 'Scene Linking using footwear mark databases', *Science and Justice*, 42 (1): 39–43.

Ribaux, O. and Margot, P. (2003) 'Case based reasoning in criminal intelligence using forensic case data', *Science and Justice*, 43 (3): 135–143.

**Section 3**

# Reconstructing events

# Chapter 9

# Bloodstain pattern analysis

*Adrian Wain and Adrian Linacre*

## Introduction

With any violent crime involving bloodshed there is the possibility of analysis of the resultant bloodstains in terms of both whom such stains could have come from and how such staining could have been caused. With the development of DNA profiling into an ever more sensitive and highly discriminating identifier the emphasis for investigation and later cross-examination has shifted from the 'whom' to the 'how'. DNA effectively answers the question from whom did the blood arise, and as such addresses the source level in forensic science, but blood pattern analysis can address how the blood may have been transferred and as such addresses the activity level[1] in forensic science (Cook *et al.* 1998). Bloodstain pattern analysis is the examination and interpretation of bloodstains in an attempt to establish the potential mechanisms that caused such staining.

In the UK bloodstain pattern analysis has traditionally been carried out by forensic scientists working from one of the forensic science laboratories allied to a forensic science supplier. This was true whether at the crime scene or examining bloodstains on items submitted to a forensic science laboratory. A recent trend in some parts of the UK is to have the analysis of bloodstain patterns at scenes of crime carried out by personnel within the police force dealing with the investigation of the crime. The examination of blood patterns and their interpretation has historically been performed by those trained in the further analyses of body fluids and hence these examiners come from a biological background. This is the case with the authors of this chapter, and knowledge of blood and the circulatory system is of value in understanding some methods by which blood is shed and transferred. However, much of bloodstain interpretation relies upon knowledge of physics and fluid dynamics (Wonder 2001).

The examination of blood patterns either at a scene or on items submitted to the laboratory does not require complex equipment; rather it is based upon visual observation and measurement of the bloodstains, analysing their shape and relative positions. This is in stark contrast to DNA profiling which requires a range of specialist equipment in a laboratory setting. Further, the terminology used in blood pattern analysis is based upon phrases and terms used in everyday English that describe the type of patterns seen. Again, this is in contrast to DNA profiling where there is an extensive technical vocabulary.

With an understanding of the mechanism that caused a bloodstain comes an opportunity to reconstruct events that may have happened during the commission of a violent crime. Examples of the questions that are frequently asked of the bloodstain pattern analyst are:

- Where did the assault happen?
- Has the deceased moved, or been moved, from the site of the original attack?
- What type of weapon was used?
- What amount of blood staining should we expect to see on the assailant?
- Could the blood staining found on an accused person's clothing have occurred if they were an innocent bystander?
- Has an assault happened here?
- In which direction was a bleeding person travelling?
- What were the relative positions of the assailant and the victim?
- Has any attempt been made to hide the crime and clean up the scene?
- Is all the blood present from the victim or has the assailant bled?
- What degree of force has the assailant used?

Such questions are often asked in the very early stages of an investigation and the answers can provide the investigator with a greater understanding of the nature of the incident. All of these questions are capable of being answered but whether it is possible to do so is very much circumstance specific. For example, a question frequently asked at the scene of a fatal stabbing, perhaps in response to conflicting accounts given by witnesses, is in what room did the assault start? If there are bloodstains in several rooms, each pattern of staining may be interpreted as to its causative mechanism but it may not be possible to put each pattern into a chronological sequence. It may have been possible for the injured party to be stabbed in one room and quickly move to another without leaving any bloodstains in the first room or en route between the two. Bloodstain pattern analysis therefore has its limitations. It may be that these limitations can be overcome, or at least supplemented, by other disciplines such as analysis of the wounds by the pathologist or identification of fingerprints or footwear marks in blood. Interpretation of bloodstain patterns is rarely reported in isolation and almost always requires the integration of information from medical examiners or pathologists with their comments and conclusions upon the nature of any injuries.

When blood leaves the body it obeys the basic laws of physics (discussed in more detail in Bevel and Gardner 1997; Wonder 2001; James et al. 2005). These include gravity, surface tension, cohesion between blood components and air resistance. This permits limited laboratory reconstructions which attempt to recreate stain patterns either produced at the scene or on clothing. Such reconstructions of blood patterns under laboratory conditions can illustrate that the findings are more likely given one hypothesis rather than another. However, crime scenes rarely produce stain patterns exactly matching those produced under laboratory conditions.

## The nature of blood

To understand how blood will behave when subjected to forces it is necessary to be aware of its composition. Blood is primarily water and has a mass close to that of water (1 litre of blood is just greater than 1 kg). In 1 mL of blood there are around 4.5 million red blood cells (4.5 billion in 1 litre) and around 7,000 white blood cells (the primary source of DNA in blood) in a healthy individual. If blood cells are removed from blood the resulting fluid is plasma, and it is in this fluid that proteins are dissolved.

The physical forces that affect liquids apply to blood. However, the constituents of blood make it a non-Newtonian fluid, meaning that it behaves differently from water and other liquids. Viscosity, surface tension and cohesion between cells all play their part in how blood behaves outside of the body. The constituents and therefore the nature of blood can vary between individuals and over time within a bleeding individual. The behaviour of blood is therefore not always predictable (Wonder 2001).

## Bloodstain patterns

There follows an overview of the bloodstain patterns encountered frequently in violent assaults and the information that an analysis of such stains may reveal. However, it should be borne in mind that bloodstain patterns are variable and this classification system describes ideals that may be infrequently encountered.

## Terminology

The different types of bloodstain patterns typically encountered are listed below:

1 Drip patterns
2 Impact spatter
3 Cast off stains
4 Expired (or exhaled) blood
5 Stains resulting from arterial damage
6 Altered bloodstains
7 Contact stains
8 Large volume stains
9 Complex stains

The terminology varies from country to country as currently there is no international nomenclature. The International Association of Blood Pattern Analysts (IABPA) (www.iaba.org) has published a recommended terminology list; however, this is not yet universally accepted.

### Drip patterns

Bloodstain patterns described under the classification of drip patterns are due to blood falling from an object under the influence of no external force other than gravity. In certain texts (e.g. James *et al.* 2005) this type of stain would be described as a passive stain, as no force other than gravity is acting on the blood. Blood dripping from wounds or weapons, often producing trails, would come under this category. Absence of any external force (other than gravity) is actually a rare event since blood dripping from a wound or weapon is likely to be subject to movement from the person bleeding or holding the weapon.

A drop of blood results when liquid blood leaves a source following some action or force applied to it. When the blood impacts upon a surface it will create a stain. The size and shape of a blood stain resulting from dripping blood is determined by: the volume of the drop; the height from which it drips; the angle at which it impacts upon the surface and the nature of the surface on which it lands. Figure 9.1 illustrates the typical shape of stain formed when blood falls on to a smooth surface from directly above.

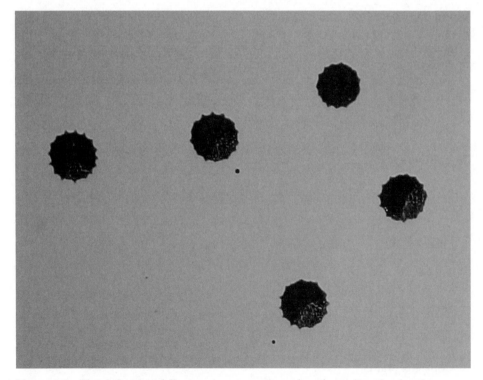

**Figure 9.1** Blood that has fallen on to a smooth surface from directly above

It is possible to demonstrate the relationship between the size (or volume more accurately) of a blood drop and the stain it produces under laboratory conditions. Figure 9.2(A) shows a blood drop about to be formed. It is still attached to the source of wet blood by surface tension, a physical force between molecules and the cohesive properties of the blood cells. When the force of gravity is greater than the surface tension and cohesion the drop will fall downwards, and it does so as a sphere.

The size, or volume, of blood drops varies; this will be determined by the nature of the item the blood is dripping from. For example, blood dripping from the point or tip of a knife has only a small area in which to collect before gravity overcomes surface tension and internal cohesion and a drop falls away. Blood collecting under a person's chin, perhaps from some facial injury, has a much larger surface area in which to collect and the resultant drop will be larger.

A blood drop will travel through the air as a sphere because of the cohesive properties of red blood cells and its surface tension (Wonder 2001 and James *et al.* 2005). This is shown in Figure 9.2(B). It is important to realise that a blood drop is spherical as this has a direct relationship on the shape of the stain produced when the drop lands on a surface. If the drop hits a hard flat surface, generally speaking, the resultant spot will increase in diameter as the height increases. A drop landing on a smooth hard surface at 90 degrees, such as blood dripping directly downwards, should create a round stain. The approximate diameter of the stain is a reflection of the volume of the blood drop. The diameter will increase marginally if the height increases. This is

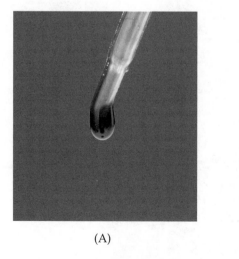

(A)                                        (B)

**Figure 9.2** (A) shows a blood spot about to drop from a pipette. The spot is held in place by surface tension and cohesion until gravity overcomes these forces and the spot falls to the ground. (B) shows a blood spot travelling downwards under gravitational force only. The blood drop is spherical as it travels

true up to a height of 7 metres for a 50 microlitres[2] drop, at which point the drop reaches its terminal velocity and no increase in stain diameter should result. It is rare to find blood dripping from more than 1.5 metres, such as dripping from a wound or a weapon.

If the blood drop lands on anything other than a hard, flat surface, such as fabric or carpet, the drop will elongate as it penetrates the surface and the visible spot at the surface may have a smaller diameter than its originating drop (see Figure 9.3). This can be seen most readily when a blood trail moves from the hard floor of, for example, a kitchen or hallway, to a carpeted floor of an adjacent room. Without knowing the volume of the originating drop it is not possible to say how high off the ground the source of dripping blood was.

Blood drops landing on a surface at an angle other than 90 degrees will show an elongated shape, hence it is possible to determine the direction of travel of the blood spot from the shape of the stain (see Figure 9.4). Blood impacting on a surface will make a stain on the surface but some of the wet blood will be thrown forward in the direction of travel due to the momentum of the drop. The resulting stain is elliptical in shape. As the angle of impact becomes more acute, so the stain will become longer and thinner, resulting

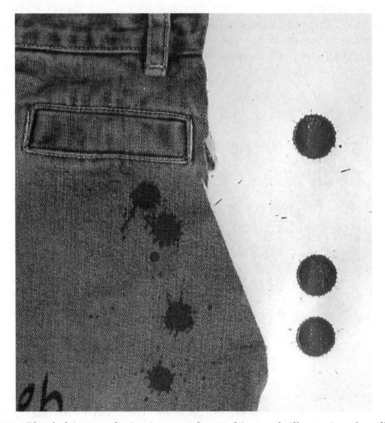

**Figure 9.3** Blood drips on denim jeans and on white card, illustrating the effect of surface on stain size

**Figure 9.4**   Blood drips on white card at 15 degrees

in a relationship between the length and width of a stain and the angle of impact. A satellite stain may be produced when part of the original is projected forward with the motion of the blood drop. Determination of the direction of travel and an approximation of the angle of impact are standard methods for the interpretation of bloodstain patterns. Such stain patterns as shown in Figure 9.4 require that the substrate upon which the blood impacts is flat and hard. At crime scenes therefore this type of analysis is most often carried out on walls and hard floors.

Trail patterns are encountered frequently at a crime scene when blood drips from a wound or a weapon. It may be possible, based upon the shape of the stain and the presence of satellite stains, to determine the direction of travel of a bleeding person. However, there are problems with this approach as blood dripping from a swinging hand, for example, may produce stains indicating two opposing directions.

A single drop of blood falling and landing on a surface can break up on impact causing secondary spatter (or satellite stains), often in the form of very small spots (see Figure 9.5) of blood (less than 1 mm). Such secondary spatter may become extensive if blood continues to drip into the blood pool.

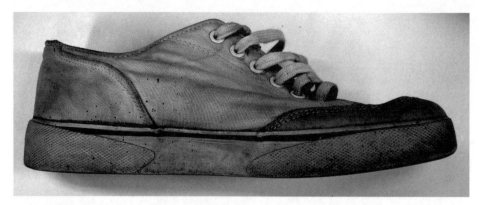

**Figure 9.5** Shoe with secondary spatter

It is possible for secondary spatter to travel up to a metre horizontally and 0.5 metres vertically. Secondary spatter is often seen on the footwear of injured people or people standing near to a source of dripping blood. Care is needed to differentiate these small spots from other types of spatter such as impact spatter (see below); secondary spatter will be uniformly small and at low level.

### Impact spatter

When a force causes blood to break up into drops and travel through the air it produces a pattern described as impact spatter. Blunt trauma assaults, kicking, stamping and punching can all produce impact spatter providing the site of impact has a source of wet blood already at the surface. Gunshot or invasive blunt trauma may produce spatter at the moment of impact. Generally, the greater the force the smaller the drops will be, as with increasing force there is more energy to overcome the surface tension and cohesive forces of blood resulting in the formation of smaller blood droplets. At the point of impact blood is subjected to force as it is squeezed between the weapon and the bloody surface. The weight and geometry of the weapon; the speed and angle with which it impacts; the nature of the surface it is hitting and the relative amounts of blood over the surface will all affect the amount; distance; direction and spot size distribution of the resultant spatter. The drops within the spatter will vary in size because the forces acting on the blood in the area of impact are not equal. The blood drops will radiate from the area of impact taking a path of least resistance.

At a given velocity and trajectory (or take-off angle) into still air the larger drops will travel further than the smaller ones. This is because larger drops have a greater mass and therefore a greater momentum and so are less susceptible to the effects of air resistance. Consider a grain of sand and a small pebble both thrown with the same force; the grain of sand will travel only a short distance before dropping to the ground, travelling less distance than the small pebble. It should be expected that blood spots forming an impact spatter pattern will decrease in number and increase in size as the distance from the impact site increases.

Blood spatter generated from an impact or series of impacts will rarely be symmetrical because the forces at the area of impact are not equal. Impact spatter will travel away from the source of the impact and often away from the assailant and the victim. A result of this is that whilst there may be an abundance of blood spatter at the scene, the assailant may not be so bloodstained. The absence of blood staining on a person's clothing may not necessarily support their lack of an involvement in an assault (MacDonnell 1993).

A common question asked of bloodstain pattern analysts is how far will impact spatter travel in a given situation. Blood staining of varying sizes may be found on the clothing of persons accused of an assault, although the accused may state that they were in close proximity to, but played no part in, an assault. MacDonnell (1971) measured the size of spots and distance travelled from the origin for what he described as medium to high velocity impact. Medium to high velocity impact could be achieved with blows from a weapon such as a hammer or steel bar. The initial velocity of the resulting blood spots was measured at about 9 metres per second. Spots of 0.1 mm diameter travelled 50 cm whilst the furthest travelling spot had a diameter of 4.4 mm and travelled a distance of 3.4 metres. Bear in mind this is spot size and not drop size; the spot diameter will be larger than that of the drop. These data did not incorporate a measure of trajectory, which was probably impossible to measure at the time.

Attempts have been made over many years to further classify bloodstains within a spatter pattern by relating them to the force that produced them. Paul Kirk (1963) suggested a classification based on the velocity of the blood drops when they hit their target. He classified stains as high, medium and low velocity impact by observing their morphology. MacDonnell (1971) suggested a scheme of classification based on the velocity of the impact (of the weapon) that caused the spatter. The problems with the latter classification system were that firstly 'velocity' only told part of the story; a length of foam pipe insulation travelling at high velocity will have a markedly different effect from a steel bar travelling at the same velocity. Secondly, any spatter rarely exhibits a uniform appearance. Whilst a spatter produced by a high velocity event such as a gunshot will exhibit some characteristics of this (very small, mist-like blood stains) close to the impact site, at distances away from the site the pattern may look more like a medium velocity event. It should be considered that during any examination of a blood spatter pattern the whole pattern may be incomplete; for example, you may be looking at the scene in isolation from the assailant or at an assailant's clothes in isolation from the scene. Latterly, Laber proposed a classification in 1985 that classified a spatter pattern by its predominant stain size and suggested mechanisms by which such staining could be produced (Laber 1985). Laber classified the stain sizes as follows:

*Mist* – a bloodstain pattern consisting of finely divided individual stains that are predominantly smaller than 0.1 mm in diameter. A high velocity impact such as a gunshot typically causes mist patterns. Due to the aerosol nature of this spatter, it will only travel a very short distance in flight and is affected by wind.

*Fine or tiny* – a bloodstain pattern consisting of individual stains that are predominantly 2 mm or smaller in diameter. Kicking, punching or stamping into wet blood typically causes this size of blood stain. These droplets are capable of travelling further than the mist aerosol and their presence on clothing is typical of the wearer being in very close proximity to the source of wet blood when force was applied.

*Medium* – a bloodstain pattern consisting of individual stains that are predominantly 2 mm to 6 mm in diameter. Cast off blood staining is characteristic of spatter of this type.

*Large* – a bloodstain pattern consisting of individual stains that are predominantly 6 mm or larger. Blood dripping from objects typically shows spatter in this size range.

Using a description of the predominant stain size within a pattern and giving a possible cause for this type of spatter avoids drawing categoric conclusions about what caused the spatter when all the information (including the entire spatter pattern) may not be available.

As blood spatter radiates from the area of impact and the shape of a bloodstain is proportional to the angle with which it impacts on a surface, it is possible to work back from a selection of stains within an impact spatter pattern to establish their area of origin. Traditionally, the approach involved selecting stains, using lengths of string to find an area of convergence and then application of relatively simple trigonometry to calculate the angle of impact for each stain to establish the origin of the stains. Such calculations need to be treated with caution however and at best are estimates. An experienced blood pattern analyst can usually carry out such estimates by eye. In our experience, in the UK, this stringing technique is rarely used. That is not to say that it does not have its uses, but that use is limited. It may help determine whether a victim was standing or sitting, for example; but this may well be obvious by eye or there may well be other aspects of the blood spatter evidence that make this clear, such as spatter on the chair in which the victim was sitting. There have been improvements in the technology used to make these reconstructions of point of origin by using digital images and computer manipulation. Whilst these programmes have been evaluated within the UK they have yet to be used widely.

### Cast off stains

When a bloodstained object is swung through the air, the forces produced by the swinging action can cause blood to be flung from its surface; the resulting blood pattern is known as swing cast off. When a bloodied object comes to an abrupt halt, such as when it hits something or at the full extent of a back swing, blood can also be flung from its surface; this is known as cessation cast off. Anything that becomes wet with blood can produce cast off, provided there is sufficient blood on it and sufficient movement of it. Therefore cast off is not confined to beatings with weapons; as long as there is a source of blood then cast off can occur from a wide range of items. Hands, hair and weapons of all dimensions are common sources of cast off and each can produce complex patterns.

Swing cast off will occur when blood is flung from a swinging weapon when the force produced by the swing is enough to release a blood drop from the pool of blood that has accumulated on the weapon. This will happen throughout the arc of the swing, provided there is sufficient blood, and so each drop will have a different origin in time and space. The effect is that the resultant stain pattern is often a linear series of blood spots on walls and ceilings. Such a linear pattern would be deemed characteristic of a cast off pattern and may yield information about where a weapon was swung and the number of swings once it became sufficiently bloody to produce cast off. Cast off may not produce a series of in line stains if there is insufficient blood; it could be that a single drop is cast off and will appear on its own some way from other staining.

Cast off staining can result from the backstroke of a weapon or the forward stroke, or both. Although there will be more blood available on the backstroke, having just been replenished from its source, it may be that the forward stroke is made with greater force since this is usually the striking blow.

Generally, long and relatively light weapons (such as a metal tubular broom handle) will produce greater amounts of cast off provided sufficient blood is available and picked up by the weapon. This is because these weapons tend to be swung faster and with a greater arc in order to produce the desired damage to the surface they are hitting. Short, heavy weapons (such as a hammer) only need to be swung a short distance and at relatively low velocities to produce the desired effect. Swing cast off staining, by definition, travels away from the arc of travel and therefore the blood drops will tend to be flung away from the assailant, unless the assailant, or part of him, is outside the arc. An exception is the presence of small bloodspots on the back of clothing running in a line from the shoulder region; these can be produced by swinging a short weapon wet with blood over the shoulder. However, such patterns are rarely observed in reality, presumably because such weapons are not swung in a manner that brings the assailant within the arc.

Cessation cast off occurs when a bloodied object comes to an abrupt halt. The obvious example of this is the bloody weapon hitting its intended victim or another surface. Blood will be forced along the weapon as with swing cast off when the weapon is swung but will be subjected to a rapid change in direction when the weapon strikes causing blood to be flung from it. This can also produce characteristic feathered type staining on the item itself (see Figure 9.6) and is often an indication that an item has been used as a weapon. This type of staining is termed percussive staining.

### Expirated (or exhaled) blood

When blood enters the upper respiratory tract it is a powerful irritant and will elicit a coughing reflex. Blood may enter the lungs via inhalation during an attack or due to an injury that has caused bleeding within the lungs or upper chest. Reproduction of such events in a laboratory environment is difficult if not impossible to achieve. The few experiments that have taken

**Figure 9.6** Shoe heel showing feathered type of staining

place have involved blood being taken into the mouth or nose and coughed, sneezed, spat or snorted out over a target rather than exhaled from within the lungs. Exhaled spatter patterns (see Figure 9.7) can exhibit a predominance of large blood spots (6 mm or larger), a mixture of large, medium and fine spots, through to those with a predominance of fine spots (2 mm or less). The overall shape of the pattern can be round or oval but of course this can vary with the angle of impact with the target and the nature of the target surface. Different amounts of blood present, differences in the force applied from within the chest and different configurations of the mouth, tongue, teeth, lips and nose will create different patterns.

As the blood in these patterns has passed through the mouth or nose it may have saliva and/or mucus mixed with it. If the blood has come from within the lungs it may also have surfactant mixed with it. Surfactant is a substance in the lungs that prevents the lung tissue from sticking together during normal breathing. These additional body fluids can make the resultant blood spatter appear frothy or at least contain air bubbles and be stringy or bead-like with mucus. However, exhaled blood spatter may not always have such characteristics.

In recent years this type of bloodstaining has come to prominence amongst blood pattern analysts in the UK, largely through the circumstances of the case of *R v. Jenkins* and largely through the work of scientists working for the defence. This case will be described in more detail later in the chapter.

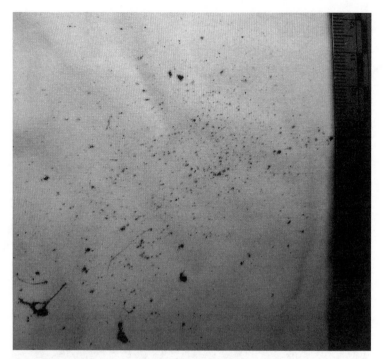

**Figure 9.7**  Image of exhaled blood on white T-shirt

## Stains resulting from arterial damage

The arteries carry blood under pressure provided by the pumping of the heart. Apart from the arteries supplying oxygenated blood from the lungs, blood is being pumped away from the heart to supply oxygen to the brain and the rest of the body. This is in contrast with the blood in the veins, which carry blood back to the heart. This distinction is important in that only arterial damage will produce gushing and spurting of blood away from the body; damage to veins may produce large volume pooling but will not produce the characteristic patterns possible from arterial damage.

Cutting or slashing type injuries can damage arteries, they can be damaged by gunshot and by crushing through blunt trauma beating; the result is that arterial damage may be encountered at almost any scene of violent injury. Those arteries closer to the surface are obviously more prone to damage than others deeper within the body and once breached any blood flow from them may be unimpeded by overlying tissue or clothing from leaving the body. Thus common sites of injury that may lead to arterial blood patterns are: the head and neck where the temporal (either side of the forehead) and carotid (either side of the neck) arteries lie; the arms where the brachial arteries lie along the inner aspect of each arm; the wrists where the radial artery lies near the surface on the inner aspect of each wrist and the groin where the femoral artery lies between the groin and each knee.

The patterns that result from arterial damage (see Figure 9.8) are often very characteristic but can also vary widely with movement of the injured person or interruption of the blood flow by, for example, clothing. Breaching

**Figure 9.8**  Image of arterial spurting on white wall

a muscular arterial wall is rather like puncturing a pipe or tube that has a liquid flowing along it under pressure. Indeed arterial damage blood patterns have been very successfully simulated by just such a set-up, some with sophisticated pumps simulating the rhythmic beating of the heart (Wonder 2001 and Emes and Price 2004).

Blood will leave a breached artery in a stream that will break up into drops of approximately equal size soon after exiting the body. These drops are typically large and as a result will fall quickly due to gravity, producing stains with a downward direction and forming runs on vertical surfaces. The beating of the heart causes the blood to flow in a series of spurts and this can lead to 'S', 'V' or 'W' shapes on surrounding surfaces formed as the injured person moves.

If the arterial spurting is near vertical and is not interrupted by impact with a surrounding surface the resultant drops of blood can fall back to the ground producing a stain pattern termed 'arterial rain'. This can produce a very large number of drips of blood covering a wide area and anything, or anyone, within it.

Arterial gush is a term used to describe a stream of blood hitting a surface causing a large round stain with resultant secondary spatter around it. This stain may then run if it is on a vertical surface and if the injured person does not move this may be all that is evident of arterial damage.

Stephen Lawrence, the 18-year-old stabbed while on his way home in south-east London in 1993, suffered two stab wounds, one to his right collarbone area and the other through his left biceps into his chest. The brachial artery on each side of his body was severed. However, his multi-layered upper clothing probably prevented any blood spurting over his attackers. All that was evident at the scene were a few drips and some pooling where he lay waiting for medical assistance (Macpherson 1999).

## Altered bloodstains

This type of staining is also referred to as physiologically altered bloodstains (PABS). Blood will clot or coagulate once it leaves the body and it can also become mixed with other body fluids such as saliva, mucus or cerebral-spinal fluid or stomach contents, all of which can produce characteristic blood patterns. Non-physiological admixtures are often found associated with bloodstaining. These include beverages such as tea, coffee, beer or wine, and cleaning fluids used to remove blood such as bleach or disinfectant.

The clotting process is a complex physiological and biochemical cascade of interactions between substances in the blood when it is exposed following damage to blood vessels. The physiological purpose of clotting is to form a plug in the wound and prevent further blood loss. The clotting process will begin within seconds of the blood vessel being damaged. However, the time taken to complete the clotting process to a stage where the red blood cells and other proteins have formed a dense plug and retracted away from the serum can vary hugely, and can be a matter of hours. The final clot when seen outside the body can resemble a piece of liver sitting in a yellowish pool of liquid.

Clotted blood is sometimes seen as part of a spatter pattern. The blood cells will stick together as clumps such that stains on absorbent surfaces can have a pale outer stain with a dark lumpy or irregular centre. This can occur when blood has started to clot during the assault or if the assailant has returned to the scene some time after the initial assault and continued the attack. Since clotting times can vary enormously, drawing conclusions about how long an assault has lasted or whether an assailant has returned some time later needs to be undertaken with caution.

If blood is swallowed or enters the stomach through abdominal injury it will mix with the stomach acid giving any resulting vomit a dark brown or black appearance with a granular texture.

Flies and other insects are inevitable visitors to bloodstained scenes and deceased persons, even shortly after death. Flies will feed on blood and lay their eggs on a suitable meat source or bloodstained item. Flies also regurgitate blood that they have been feeding on mixed with their own body fluids and their faeces can also contain undigested blood. The resulting stains are referred to as flyspeck and can be seen as small (1–2 mm) round spots often around windows. The round stains can sometimes have tails to them if the fly has moved while making its deposit. They are usually brown to dark red-brown in colour. To an untrained observer flyspeck can be mistaken for impact spatter (Benecke and Barksdale 2003).

Attempts to clean blood from a scene with cleaning products and water will rarely remove all traces if the staining was extensive. Wipe marks, dilute blood drips, runs around sinks and taps, footwear marks in dilute blood and bloodstained cleaning materials such as sponges and mops are all indicators that the scene was at one time more extensively stained. Chemical enhancement of blood and searching using variable wavelengths of light is discussed later in this chapter.

### Contact stains

A contact stain is caused when two items come into contact and at least one of them is wet with blood and transfers some blood to the other. These stains are also known as transfer stains. Sometimes such stains can be of immense value if a distinctive pattern (see Figure 9.8) is produced such as fingerprints, or footwear marks in blood at the scene, or a bloody knife impression on an item of clothing. Frequently there is no pattern to the contact stain, normally this type of stain is termed a smear, and little further interpretation can be made. It may be possible to determine the direction of movement of one of the items based upon the smear pattern. Drag marks where something, such as a body, has been dragged along a surface are also important contact stains.

### Large volume stains

The average volume of blood within the human adult is about 70 ml per kg of body weight. A person weighing 70 kg would have approximately 4.9 litres of blood. If more than 30 per cent of the total blood volume of a person is lost the person will go into shock and almost certainly collapse (James et al. 2005). Rarely, a blood pattern analyst may be asked to calculate the volume of blood in a pooled area of stain or several pools combined, perhaps to aid a pathologist in commenting on a possible sequence of events or timeline leading to death. Various methods have been formulated based around calculating the area of staining and/or its dry weight. These calculations can only be estimates since the depth of the pool, and whether the blood is mixed with some other body fluid or non body fluid, is often unknown.

### Complex stains

This classification system merely provides a framework for the analyst to work within. Many stain patterns encountered will not fit into one of these categories and many stains will consist of a combination of categories (so-called complex stains). For example imagine the scene where someone had been severely beaten about the head whilst sitting in a chair causing extensive blood spatter over walls, ceiling and floor. At some point the injured person stood up and walked over to a sink on the opposite side of the room dripping

**Figure 9.9**  Contact pattern made by hair

blood from his head and smearing the spatter on the floor with his feet in socks. The extensive blood staining on the floor consisted of a mixture of spatter from multiple blows, drips, contact smears and sock transfers.

Sometimes, identification of a particular type of stain will be obvious such as a large volume stain emanating from a deceased person or exhaled blood a few feet away from the deceased with noticeable frothing around the mouth. At other times it will be far from obvious, may well be ambiguous and will need to be interpreted with caution.

It is rare to see one of the stain types described in isolation, rather it is more common to note a number of stain patterns. A simple case may be in an allegation of kicking into wet blood. The classic stain pattern will include impact spatter on the upper and front areas of the shoe, due to the back spatter caused by the forceful impact, combined with a contact smear on the front of the shoe made by the direct contact with the wet blood. The combination of a number of stain types can assist with interpretation of different hypotheses. Consider the above allegation: if the wearer claimed that they were present at the time of an assault but were not actively involved in it, this may account for the spatter patterns, but may not account for the contact smear.

Whilst this chapter discusses blood stain patterns, consideration also needs to be given to the absence of blood staining. If a bloodstained object (or person) is removed from a scene then it may leave a 'void' area within a particular pattern. Such voids can be an indicator that something has been moved to a different location or removed from the scene altogether. The blood pattern analyst must also consider an absence of blood staining on the clothing of an alleged assailant. If the expectations of the analyst are that the offender would be stained with blood then the absence of such blood could be a very powerful piece of evidence in defence of the accused.

## Search methods

There are many tools available to aid the scene examiner in his search for blood. Typically, a search for blood will involve a visual examination aided by a bright source of white light and possibly a magnifying aid. Any stains considered to look like blood will be tested with what is known as a presumptive chemical test for blood. The two most commonly used presumptive tests are the Kastle-Meyer (KM) test and the Leucomalachite green (LMG) test (Cox 1991). These tests rely on a colour change in an indicator chemical in the presence of an oxidising agent. The oxidising agent comes in the form of oxygen, produced by the breakdown of hydrogen peroxide in the presence of haemoglobin in blood. These tests are called presumptive because the presence of blood is 'presumed' if a positive reaction is obtained with the test. Positive reactions can be obtained with material other than blood such as some plant material or bacteria. Generally, the presence of blood is confirmed if a stain has the appearance of blood and gives a positive presumptive test. The KM and LMG tests are not human specific and will give a positive reaction with blood from animals.

The OBTI blood testing kit (www.bluestar-forensic.com) is a more recent test that has become available, for scene examiners in particular. This is a hand-held, field useable, immunochromatographic technique which is specific for human (and primate, ferret and skunk) haemoglobin. This test is most useful in determining if a source of blood is most likely to be of human origin and therefore a crime is likely to have been committed. It is not a replacement for the routine use of LMG and KM tests.

At many scenes of violent crime the bloodstain patterns will be obvious and will take little searching for other than careful observation. This might not be possible in cases where the scene is examined many years after the alleged event or where efforts have been made to clean away the blood. White light sources, methodical searching by eye and presumptive chemical tests of potential bloodstains form the mainstay of any examination for blood. Light sources with variable wavelength can also be useful, particularly on dark surfaces; blood will absorb ultraviolet light and will appear black whereas the surface on which it lies may fluoresce. There are a variety of chemical reagents that can be used in spray form to detect even the most diluted of blood; Leucomalachite Green and Luminol are two examples.

Luminol has been in use as a blood-detecting agent for many years (Poescher and Moody 1939). Luminol is a chemical that gives off a blue light in the presence of an oxidising agent. The generation of light from a chemical reaction is known as chemiluminescence. It has been regularly and widely used worldwide for many years. In the UK, whilst Luminol was known about, there was a reluctance to use it because of concerns over its safety. It is currently listed as a respiratory irritant on its materials safety data sheet with, significantly, no information about its potential carcinogenic, mutagenic or teratogenic effects. In other words its toxicological effects have not been fully investigated. Luminol is also used in strongly alkaline solution, which also comes with its own hazards. However, providing a risk assessment has been carried out and adequate precautions are applied, then there is no reason not to use Luminol.

Unfortunately, Luminol is not specific for blood. It will produce chemiluminescence in the presence of other substances. These substances include metals, bleach and other cleaning agents and plant materials. Its sensitivity with metals means that it can react with substances containing traces of metals such as paint. Before Luminol is sprayed a thorough search should be made and any potential bloodstains should be tested with KM or LMG reagent and any positive stains sampled for DNA profiling. Any Luminol positive areas subsequently found should also be tested with KM or LMG and likewise sampled for DNA profiling. Whilst KM and LMG reagents are not specific for blood they are less prone to false positives than Luminol.

It should also be borne in mind that there are alternatives to spraying Luminol. LMG has been available in a formulation that can be sprayed for some time. These sprays have differing advantages and disadvantages. For example, Luminol is sprayed in an aqueous (or water-based) solution, which means that it can make bloodstains diffuse on porous surfaces or even run on non-porous surfaces. Testing with Luminol must be performed in the dark and recording of the chemiluminescence can require specialist photographic skills and equipment. LMG on the other hand, whilst not being as sensitive as Luminol, can be applied in a non-aqueous solution and so is much more suitable for non-porous surfaces such as might be found in bathrooms and kitchens. LMG also has the advantage of not requiring a darkened environment to view the colour change in the presence of blood but has the disadvantage of a pale green colour that is impossible to see on anything other than white or very pale surfaces. Both Luminol and LMG spray formulations have their health and safety issues and careful, situation specific risk assessments need to be made with each. There are also other specialist chemical treatments for the enhancement of fingerprints and footwear marks made in blood. Any chemical agent needs to be carefully considered as part of an overall strategy of examination.

## Bloodstains on clothing

Blood pattern analysis is applied to scenes of crime and to items from the scene such as weapons and clothing from witnesses and the accused. The same care with interpretation needs to be used when examining bloodstains on clothing as for those at scenes. Interpretation must take into account the presence or absence of the whole bloodstain pattern across a set of clothes attributed to an individual. For example, in a kicking type assault where blows have been made with footwear into a bloody head, the expectation would be that blood spatter would be present on the shoes and at least the lower part of the trousers. In the absence of either the shoes or the trousers any interpretation and the strength of any subsequent conclusion will be weakened. The analyst should be given the opportunity to examine the whole set of clothing where possible. Submissions for analysis should not be curtailed just because there is obvious blood staining on the shoes but not on the trousers. Further, it is necessary to examine clothing in the manner in which it was worn, rather than as laid flat on the examination bench.

Whether analysing blood patterns on items in a laboratory or at a crime scene the purpose is to provide information about what may have caused such patterns. In the early part of an investigation the blood pattern analyst can provide information about what happened at the scene, how blood stained he might expect the assailant to be, what sort of weapon may have been used or what samples to take for further analysis in an attempt to identify an injured assailant. This would be as part of the investigative stage of the case.

Bloodstains can be transferred to clothing either by direct contact with a bloodstained object or as airborne drops. These two types of stains can be very different in appearance. However, any forensic interpretation should evaluate two conflicting propositions, one from the prosecution and one from the defence (Cook et al. 1998). The prosecution proposition will be known, but that for the defence is often either absent or unknown. In the absence of a defence proposition it may be possible for this to be inferred. Consider an instance of an assault, the defence proposition if not stated may be that they were present at, but not active in, the assault. The presence of a few blood spots that have originated from airborne drops can be enough to conclude that the wearer of these clothes has been close enough to the 'action' to intercept such drops of blood. In such situations, in order to be balanced in his conclusions the blood pattern analyst may be required to give examples of situations that can generate such airborne spatter. This should not be confused by the commissioning authority with providing the wearer of the clothes with an explanation or excuse; forensic scientists ought to take an objective view.

## Bloodstaining on the deceased

In the case of a suspicious death, the blood pattern analyst should attend the scene whilst the body is *in situ* as it is an integral part of the scene. While blood pattern analysts are rarely medically trained, an external examination of the body *in situ* may reveal the presence of drips of blood on the exposed parts of the body that clearly could not have originated from the deceased. An analyst may then request that this blood is sampled before the body is removed or that clothing is carefully taken before the body is transported to the mortuary. If a deceased person has invasive injuries, wrapping a body in a plastic sheet and transporting it to the mortuary can result in lost evidence. Despite this the procedure is common practice. A blood pattern analyst will rarely attend a post-mortem, particularly if they have seen the body at the scene, but they will need to be informed of the injuries and whether there was any blood found in the upper airways.

Some patterns are so characteristic that their cause can be established with great confidence. An example of this may be a series of linear spots in a cast off stain or even an area of impact spatter. Analysing the stains in isolation (of any other information) and providing explanations for their cause could be considered as objective. However, blood pattern analysts, like any other forensic scientists, need to interpret their findings within the context of the case. To evaluate any evidence the scientist will need to know in particular about the injuries that were received, what witnesses have said about what happened and whether any first aid was carried out on the injured party.

## Personnel

A recent trend is to have the blood pattern analysis carried out by police personnel rather than scientists called in from an external forensic science provider. Any person making interpretations of blood patterns at the scene should be competent. Further, there needs to be a framework in which to work that allows time to consider the findings comprehensively and if necessary discuss their findings with similarly trained colleagues before making significant conclusions. The Forensic Science Service has quality assurance procedures in place including competency standards and tests and declared and blind trials. It also operates a system of debriefing after the scene is attended which acts as a peer review of the interpretation and conclusions made at the scene as soon as possible after the scene visit. Consideration should also be made of having an analyst's competence ratified by an outside body such as the Council for the Registration of Forensic Practitioners (CRFP). CRFP have a sub-specialty of blood pattern analysis within the specialty of Human Contact Traces.

## Case illustration: *R v. Sion David Charles Jenkins*

Sion Jenkins returned from a trip to a local DIY store in the late afternoon of 15 February 1997, to find his foster daughter (Billie-Jo Jenkins) lying on the patio at the rear of his house with severe head injuries. Due largely to the finding of blood spatter on his clothes he was accused of Billie-Jo's murder. This was a widely publicised case that had three trials and two appeals over nine years. It illustrates the power and the limitations of blood pattern analysis and demonstrates the need for integration of blood pattern evidence with other disciplines, in this case with medical experts and others. It also illustrates how two sets of experts can provide conflicting evidence on the possible causation of bloodstain patterns.

Sion Jenkins was convicted of murder in 1998 but was granted a retrial by the Court of Appeal in 2004 and he was acquitted in 2006 following two separate juries failing to reach a verdict.

Much of the scientific evidence related to the blood patterns found at the scene and on the defendant's clothing. The Crown and the defence called many experts from a wide variety of backgrounds. The case exemplifies some of the types of bloodstaining described earlier in this chapter and how the interpretation put on these findings can be challenged.

When Sion Jenkins returned from the trip to the DIY store Billie-Jo was lying face down with her head on its left side and her face looking away from the house. Her head was lying on a black plastic bin liner that contained leaves, twigs and other debris, swept from the patio earlier in the day. Sion Jenkins called for an ambulance and attended Billie-Jo along with a neighbour while waiting for medical attention. It would appear that Sion Jenkins had very little contact with Billie-Jo other than to push and/or pull her shoulder to enable a better view of her face; he said in interview, 'her face came up'. The neighbour similarly had little direct contact with Billie-Jo. Two paramedics arrived, turned Billie-Jo over on to her back and pronounced her dead at the scene. Near to Billie-Jo's body was a metal spike approximately 46 cm in length, 1.5 cm in diameter and 800 grams in weight. There was no dispute that this had been the weapon used by Billie-Jo's attacker. The neighbour was later to describe in court how she had gone to move the bin liner away from Billie-Jo's face to find that part of it was up her left nostril.

A blood pattern analyst made an examination of the scene on the following day. By that time a tent had been erected over part of the patio to protect it from rain. Inevitably, the tent restricted the area of examination by the analyst. Outdoor scenes can be difficult to manage, especially in winter, and no criticism is made here of the management of this scene.

Sion Jenkins's clothes were submitted to the Forensic Science Service laboratory in London along with the metal spike and other items a few days later. His trousers had approximately 70 spots of blood on the lower right leg and two spots on the mid left leg. His jacket had 48 spots on the upper mid chest, 21 spots on the left sleeve and three spots on the lower right sleeve. There were a few spots of blood on his shoes. The majority of the blood spots were fine spatter with a few larger spots on the trousers and jacket. No blood was found on the back of the clothing.

The blood patterns at the scene mostly consisted of spatter radiating out from the site of impacts where Billie-Jo's head had been on the bin liner. The blood spatter was on the adjacent wall, the inner surface of the patio door and the dining room floor. The blood pattern analyst working on behalf of the prosecution concluded that the attacker had been facing the house and as a result would have had very little spatter on his or her clothes since most of the spatter was travelling away from the attacker.

Clearly, a key question here was – was the fine spatter on Sion Jenkins's clothing part of the impact spatter found at the scene or did he acquire it when he found the body? In interview Sion Jenkins said that he had got blood on his hands and had shaken it off before going to a washroom to wash his hands. He said that he had seen blood on his shoes. He also said that he had seen a bubble come from Billie-Jo's nose and disappear. The blood pattern analyst's conclusion, given a number of days after the murder, was that the blood on Sion Jenkins's clothes was what he would expect to see if Sion Jenkins was the attacker; however, he could not rule out some other explanation that was yet to be considered. Experiments were carried out by scientists working for the prosecution producing and bursting bubbles of blood from plastic pipettes. This demonstrated that whilst fine spatter could be produced in this way the spatter had little or no vertical component but fell to the ground with a horizontal spread of some 50 cm.

The prosecution analysts also carried out some beating experiments using an identical metal spike on a bloodstained leg of pork and a pig's head. These types of experiment form the mainstay of training in blood pattern analysis;

learning through seeing blood patterns being produced and reflecting on these in the light of theoretical knowledge. The aim of such experiments is to see whether similar blood patterns to those observed in casework can be reproduced experimentally. Importantly, such experiments should attempt to examine two conflicting hypotheses, the prosecution view of events and the defence view. In the Forensic Science Service the leg of pork has become a commonly used medium for simulating human flesh and bone. Various other media have been tried over the years, including polystyrene heads and blood-soaked sponges. All have their limitations; the blood soaked sponges for example would disintegrate and any spatter can contain fragments of sponge as well as blood spots. One obvious limitation of any beating medium is an absence of a circulatory system. In *R v. Jenkins* blood was applied to slits in the skin of the pork in an attempt to provide a reservoir of blood. The medium was beaten a number of times and the overalls of the beater were examined after each exercise. A fine spatter was observed on the front of the overalls with no staining found on the back.

At the post-mortem examination it had been observed that Billie-Jo had blood in her airways and that her lungs were 'hyperinflated', i.e. something was preventing the residual air from being released. This was originally explained by the presence of blood blocking the *lower* airways. Some time prior to the first trial a blood pattern expert working for the defence raised the possibility of the fine spatter on Sion Jenkins's clothes having been produced by an exhalation from Billie-Jo. The defence analyst carried out some demonstrations by putting some of his own blood in his nose and exhaling it over a white paper target about an arm's length away. His snorts did produce a fine blood spatter.

At the trial in 1998 the prosecution presented the view that Billie-Jo was dead when Sion Jenkins found her and that she was therefore incapable of making a breath. The blood pattern analyst employed by the Crown was asked by the defence to demonstrate in the courtroom how he thought Sion Jenkins could have intercepted the spatter he had on his clothes. The analyst demonstrated how the attacker would have needed to be quite close to Billie-Jo as she lay on the ground and with a short heavy weapon would need to lean over her to beat her head. In these circumstances most of the blood spatters away from the assailant and very little comes back. Given the weight of the weapon the analyst believed it was quite possible to generate the fine spatter seen on Sion Jenkins's clothes. He also made the point that Billie-Jo's face was lying on a black bin liner, which witnesses described as partially enclosing her face, and her nostrils and mouth were pointing down into her chest or into the bin liner. The two blood pattern analysts for the defence agreed that the blood spatter found on Sion Jenkins' clothes could be impact spatter. Medical experts for the defence said that Billie-Jo could have survived long enough to make the exhalation over Sion Jenkins. Sion Jenkins was convicted.

At the appeal in 2004 more evidence was heard about the state of Billie-Jo's lungs; the samples taken at post-mortem having been variously examined. It was accepted by the Crown's pathologist that there must have been a blockage in the *upper* airways to create the interstitial emphysema (air that was trapped having been forced into the tissue forming the lungs) that experts for the defence said was visible on the lung sections. The defence argued that Billie-Jo could have exhaled over Sion Jenkins by a sudden release of the blockage and thereby releasing trapped air in her lungs, whether she was dead or alive. The conviction was quashed and a retrial ordered.

In preparation for the retrial two experts for the defence carried out their own blood pattern experiments. Whilst these defence experts were eminent in their own fields they were not trained blood pattern analysts or forensic scientists. They carried out beating experiments similar to the earlier ones carried out by the Crown's expert, if more extensive. More significantly, they also demonstrated that spitting and snorting blood from the mouth or nose could produce a fine spatter over someone kneeling in front of the spray. They also carried out some experiments that concluded that someone wielding this weapon would have a high probability of cast off staining on their back.

The Crown argued that the defence beating experiments confirmed their own expert's findings, that the spits and snorts bore no resemblance to the real situation on the patio and that the conclusions drawn from the cast off experiments applied only to their own hitter and to no one else. On the cast off experiments, since the weapon was short and heavy, it would not need to be swung right over the back to produce a lot of damage to the victim. If there was any cast off generated during the attack on Billie-Jo, it was the view of the Crown expert that it was more likely to have gone away from the attacker i.e. the attacker would have been inside the arc. A video of a defence scientist swinging the weapon right over her back was shown to the jury.

The size of the blood spots on Sion Jenkins's clothes became an issue at the retrials. One defence scientist argued that the drops that created these spots were too small to have travelled from the impact site on to Sion Jenkins's clothes if he were the attacker. However, he argued that if these spots had been exhaled then they could have been carried on the air currents of the exhalation and/or the inevitable natural eddy currents swirling around the patio. The Crown argued that the scientist did not know the size of the drops that created the fine spatter on Sion Jenkins's clothes; some measurements of the spots had been made by the Crown blood pattern analyst and he pointed out that the clothing fabric was not a smooth flat surface but a relatively deep pile of corduroy trousers and fleece jacket. Indeed a few of the spots were large enough to be described as medium spatter rather than fine.

These arguments were rehearsed at two retrials, both of which ended with an undecided jury. The Crown chose not to pursue the case further and Sion Jenkins was formally acquitted.

## Conclusion

Blood pattern analysis is a very powerful tool in a modern forensic setting. It is capable of building on source level conclusions by extending into the activity level. However, whilst the observation and measurement of blood patterns can be objective, the interpretation of blood patterns remains subjective and conclusions need to be very carefully considered. Second opinions must be sought and discussed where necessary and both defence and prosecution propositions carefully and equally considered. The limitation of an analyst's work by restricting the items he is allowed to see, or by limiting the number of stains tested to determine the source, can seriously undermine any conclusions he may give for either prosecution or defence. The value of case specific experimental work cannot be overemphasised. More research into areas such as the distances travelled by airborne blood spots in different situations would add value to many interpretations of everyday findings.

## Notes

1  See Aitken and Jackson, Chapters 15 and 16 in this volume.
2  1 microlitre equals $10^{-6}$ litres.

## References

Benecke M. and Barksdale, L. (2003) 'Distinction of blood stain patterns from fly artefacts', *Forensic Science International*, 137: 152–159.

Bevel, T. and Gardner, R.M. (1997) *Blood Pattern Analysis*. Florida, USA: CRC Press.

Cook, R., Evett, I.W., Jackson, G., Jones, P.J. and Lambert, J.A. (1998) 'A hierarchy of propositions: deciding which level to address in casework', *Science and Justice*, 38 (4): 231–239.

Cox, M. (1991) 'A study of the sensitivity and specificity of four presumptive tests for blood', *J Forensic Sci*, 36: 1503–11.

Emes, A. and Price, C. (2004) 'Blood Stain Pattern Analysis', in P.C. White (ed.), *Crime Scene to Court Essentials of Forensic Science* (2nd edn). London: Royal Society of Chemistry.

James, S.H., Kish, P.E. and Sutton, T.P. (2005) *Principles of Blood Pattern Analysis – Theory and Practice*. Florida, USA: CRC Press.

Kirk, P.L. (1963) *Crime Investigation*, p. 105. New York: Interscience Publishers, Inc.

Laber, T.L. (1985) 'Diameter of bloodstain as a function of origin, distance fallen, and volume of drop', *IABPA Newsletter*, 2 (1): 12–16.

MacDonnell, H.L. (1971) *Flight Characteristics and stain patterns of human blood*. USA: Dept of Justice.

MacDonnell, H.L. (1993) *Blood stain patterns*. New York: Golos Printing.

Macpherson, Sir William (Sir William of Cluny) *et al.* (1999) The Stephen Lawrence Inquiry. London: HM Stationery Office.

Poescher, F. and Moody, A.M. (1939) 'Detection of blood by means of chemiluminescence', *J Lab Clin Med*, 24: 1183.

Wonder, A.Y. (2001) *Blood Dynamics*. Oxford: Academic Press.

www.iabpa.org (accessed 28 October 2008).

www.bluestar-forensic.com (accessed 28 October 2008).

# Chapter 10

# Fire investigation policies and practices in the UK

*James Munday and Mick Gardiner*

## Introduction

Fire is a devastating force which kills, injures and causes extensive damage to properties and contents. Fire and explosion scenes present exceptional challenges to investigators in that much of the physical evidence may be destroyed or displaced during the incident and then disturbed or contaminated during rescue and fire suppression activities. The start of the investigation can be like viewing a charred and dampened jigsaw puzzle where the first responders, victims and other witnesses all hold pieces but where no individual has the overall picture. Therefore it is crucial that investigators methodically gather and properly assemble all of the pieces of the puzzle in order that an accurate picture of what happened before, during and after the event can be reconstructed.

The investigation of fires in the United Kingdom involves a variety of organisations including various roles from within the fire service, police officers, crime scene examiners, forensic scientists and representatives of the insurance industry. Whilst each may have different roles and responsibilities they should adopt the same systematic methodology and share the common goals of accurately identifying where the fire originated; what item was ignited first; what was the ignition source; how and why the fire spread; and what were the circumstances leading up to the outbreak and discovery of fire. There is also a need to evaluate the behaviour of people involved in fire; identify who is responsible and in what way; establish the effectiveness of fire safety/prevention measures; assess the damage to structures and contents; calculate the financial and indirect losses; and learn lessons which may support effective future preventative measures.

When suspicion is aroused, an incident is considered to be of non-accidental origin or when a fatality or serious injury occurs, the police should lead the ensuing investigation. If a fire is considered to be of accidental origin then responsibility for the initial investigation generally remains with the fire service, although further investigation may be carried out for insurers.

If an explosion occurs and is considered to be the result of an accident, for example involving an escape of natural gas, an appliance or an aerosol, then other agencies such as the Health and Safety Executive or utility companies may take responsibility for the investigation.

In practice, most non-terrorist explosions result from ignition of dispersed-phase fuels such as flammable vapours (e.g. petrol, paint thinners), gas escapes or ignition of dusts or mists in industrial settings. These often include fire damage within the chain of events and many aspects of explosion investigation are similar in approach to the investigation of fires. Consequently there is a high degree of overlap in both training and application between the knowledge and techniques required. Condensed-phase explosions, such as high explosives often encountered in military or terrorist situations, require a somewhat different approach and are outside the scope of this chapter.

The key to success in undertaking fire or explosion investigations is to adopt a coordinated 'team' approach where all parties understand each other's roles and responsibilities, acknowledge their limitations and recognise the potential value of their combined contributions.

This chapter will discuss why fires and, to some extent, dispersed-phase explosions are investigated and by whom, together with the education, training and accreditation needed to ascertain that individuals are knowledgeable, skilled and competent in their roles. It will describe the development of policies and practices that have led to this multi-agency approach. We will then discuss the methods and some of the practicalities of fire and explosion scene investigation, including the identification, recording, gathering and interpretation of physical and other evidence which can assist the investigator in the development and testing of competing hypotheses and the final evaluation of cause.

### Fire statistics

Over recent years the total number of fires attended by UK Fire and Rescue Services has dropped and the number of fire casualties and fatalities has reduced (DCLG 2000–05). This suggests that community fire safety strategies, such as the fitting of domestic smoke alarms, have had the desired effect. These data and valuable lessons learned from the investigation of fire scenes provide a springboard for further research and support both fire- and crime-related reduction strategies. Since the mid 1980s, when the fire service began directing more resources towards fire investigation, the number of fire data reports recording an 'unknown' cause has reduced. Whilst the statistics might not be entirely reliable it is noticeable that, over the same period of time, the percentage of investigations recorded by the fire service as suspicious or deliberate in origin has increased.

### Crime statistics

The improved response by the police to fire-related incidents has featured in a series of Home Office reports and Circulars dating back to 1980. Yet the number of arsons recorded by the police still only represents 61 per cent of primary fires identified by the fire service as non-accidental. Furthermore, only 9 per cent of the police cases were cleared up with a person charged, summonsed or cautioned (ODPM 2006). Notwithstanding, recent fire statistics suggest that the upward trend in the number of deliberate fires may have peaked. Some categories of deliberate fires, such as abandoned vehicles, now appear to be on the decline (DCLG 2000–05).

### The cost of arson

The *Safer Communities* report (Home Office 1999) estimated that in England and Wales in an average week arson resulted in 3,500 deliberately started fires, 50 injuries and two deaths, and a cost to society of at least £25 million. In 2006 this financial estimate was amended to £45 million a week with the annual cost of arson to the economy put at £2.53 billion. Although arson is recorded as only 1 per cent of total crime, its financial cost has increased by 32 per cent since 2000 (DCLG Good Practice Conference 2005).

The majority of deliberate fires start from a naked flame applied to readily ignitable materials. This explains why they are likely to spread more quickly and why the average cost of damage from such fires is much higher than from accidental fires, which often have a much slower rate of development. The location, time of day or night and whether or not a deliberately set fire is reported have a bearing on the likelihood of its developing into a major incident.

## Roles and responsibilities

### Fire service

The Fire and Rescue Services Act (2004) and The Fire (Scotland) Act 2005 provide fire and rescue authorities with formal powers to carry out investigations. These acts also contain provisions which, in the case of fires of accidental origin, allow a fire service representative to remove evidence, for example an electrical appliance, for further examination where a defect is suspected. Fire service first responders play a key role in an investigation as they are normally the first professionals on the scene. In addition to their primary role of carrying out rescues and extinguishing fires, they also gather information for completion of fire data and other reports. The fire service are in an ideal position to recognise and record fire phenomena, observe and preserve evidence and make crucial observations of evidential value. The vast majority of UK fire and rescue services now have in place some form of fire investigation support structure consisting of experienced officers who are trained to carry out detailed scene investigations and provide comprehensive reports.

### Police

The police service is responsible for the prevention and detection of crime and for reporting to the Coroner (Procurator Fiscal in Scotland) any death that results from a fire. In criminal investigations, the police are responsible for securing evidence and apprehending responsible individuals.

Notwithstanding, such investigations require a team approach so that all parties involved can contribute and fulfil their roles and responsibilities. The Senior Investigating Officer (SIO) should consult crime scene examiners and fire officers to establish how best to identify, preserve and retrieve evidence, decide if a 'Forensic Management Team' should be formed and if a forensic scientist should attend. As with all crime scenes, effective scene management is crucial to success.

### Crime scene examiner (CSE)

The CSE is trained to observe, record, interpret and recover physical evidence from a wide variety of incident types, including fires. Increasingly, there is an emphasis on the interpretation of the scene observations by CSEs to assist and advise the police investigators. In some instances, in recognition of the investigative aspects of the role, CSE has been redesignated as Crime Scene Investigator (CSI). Almost all CSEs will have some basic training in fire investigation techniques and most work closely with local fire service investigators. Their experience of dealing with other evidence types can be invaluable in establishing the circumstances surrounding the fire. There is a growing number of CSEs who are more highly trained in fire investigation and hold appropriate professional qualifications.

### Forensic scientists

In the UK there is a tradition of laboratory-based forensic scientists attending fire scenes to carry out the investigation or to assist the fire officer and CSE with additional expertise. In some organisations this has led to the formation of full-time specialist teams who would also carry out the laboratory examination of fire-related physical evidence. In other instances, fire scene investigation remains an occasional activity for forensic scientists. The move away from the traditional 'public service' forensic laboratory to a range of private service providers, combined with an increasing number of specialist CSE fire investigators, may change this pattern in the future.

There is also a significant private sector provision, which historically offered consultancy services mainly to insurers (see below). Police now increasingly consults these providers. Fire investigation is carried out by a range of specialists from varying backgrounds including science and engineering. Analysis and interpretation of recovered materials may involve use of methods from disciplines such as chemistry, materials science or electrical engineering.

### Insurance companies

Insurance representatives such as claims managers, loss assessors and scientific consultants become involved when a claim is made against an insurance policy. These individuals will investigate potential fraud, negligence, and liability or recovery issues. For this reason a private consultant may carry out a more detailed examination of a specific aspect of a fire than would normally be done by public sector investigators.

### Other agencies

Other parties such as the Health and Safety Executive (HSE), utility companies and fire and crime research establishments may become involved in incidents of fire and/or explosions depending on the specific circumstances.

## The development of an inter-agency team approach

The development of a team approach to fire investigation can be traced over three decades in a series of circulars and reports, referenced below. This change has led to the introduction of joint Memoranda of Understanding, a greater understanding of roles and responsibilities, improved working practices, the formulation of more effective fire and arson reduction strategies and inter-agency training programmes. While this concept evolved primarily within the public sector (fire and police services and their contracted forensic science support organisations), private sector investigators representing commercial interests (mainly insurers) have also been involved.

The *Prevention of Arson Report* (Home Office 1988) led to the establishment of the Arson Prevention Bureau (APB) and formulation of a National Arson Control Programme with aims such as improving national statistics and liaison between the police, fire and forensic services.

The *Safer Communities* report (Home Office 1999) led to the establishment of the Arson Control Forum (ACF) and identified the need to: establish working protocols and share information; improve the quality of fire scene investigations; increase detections and prosecutions; create national accreditation standards; and encourage inter-agency training programmes. The Chief and Assistant Chief Fire Officers Association Report (CACFOA 1999) argued that the fire service should develop an effective and comprehensive approach to fire investigation and take a stance on an arson strategy. The *Fire Investigation in Scotland Report* (Arson Prevention Bureau 2004) recommended that solid links should be established with the Arson Control Forum in England and Wales.

### Home Office Circulars 1980 to 2000

Home Office Circulars between 1980 and 2000 focused on investigations which regularly brought the fire service, police and forensic scientists together. These circulars were in response to a number of high-profile cases in which it had been recognised that investigators had failed to work as a coordinated team (Home Office 1980–2000).

A Fire Service Circular (ODPM 2006) acknowledged that: 'the successful investigation of a suspicious fire, including the prosecution of any suspected offenders, requires close co-operation and mutual assistance between the police and fire and rescue service. This requires not only an awareness of the legal responsibilities of the respective services but also an appreciation of the special qualities and different skills, experience and support facilities that are available to them'. The report recommended that 'the fullest possible liaison between police and fire and rescue services is essential in the course of any fire investigation' and should include:

- passing to the fire and rescue service any relevant information for recording purposes or other appropriate action;
- the opportunity for an appropriate fire service representative and other invited experts to participate in briefings and conferences held by the SIO;
- close cooperation in the management of information and handling of media interest.

Since the turn of the century inter-service protocols, Memoranda of Understanding between fire and police services and regional initiatives have become commonplace. An investigative framework first piloted in Bedfordshire and Derbyshire during the late 1990s subsequently became a National Model (ODPM 2003). In its simplest form this implements a tiered response framework with the following levels of investigation:

**Level One:** routine (FDR1)[1] carried out by operational fire service personnel;

**Level Two:** more complex investigations led by fire service support personnel;

**Level Three:** complex inter-agency investigations, usually led by the police.

This framework has led to improved inter-agency relationships in most local areas. An equivalent framework at regional level now appears possible. This would involve support for investigating fires of high profile or resource demand, for example multiple fire casualties and public buildings such as schools. On such occasions the local SIO could draw upon the additional experience of investigators from neighbouring counties who currently carry out Level Two and Level Three investigations. Inter-agency Arson Task Forces (ATF) operating in areas of England and Wales have assisted in reducing the incidence of arson and detecting offenders (Arson Control Forum 2003). The Crime and Disorder Act 1998 has provided an ideal opportunity for fire services, police, councils and other stakeholders to develop local initiatives in relation to the investigation and prevention of arson.

## Education, training, standards and accreditation

### Academic and vocational qualifications

For many years universities have offered study paths via Fire Engineering and Science degrees and at least two English universities currently offer an MSc in fire investigation. Other vocational training programmes leading to qualifications such as Membership of the Institution of Fire Engineers (and potentially to chartered engineer status) also offer continuing professional development (CPD).

### Training

Fire Service Circular 1-2006 (ODPM 2006) states that 'sound training in fire investigation methodology and techniques is crucial to the long-term prospects of reducing the number of fires regardless of the cause'. Over the past decade the number of public sector practitioners attending formal training programmes has increased dramatically and it is now commonplace for fire and explosion investigators from a range of backgrounds and organisations to be trained together and develop their skills in realistic environments.

The major UK training providers have responded to the need for sound basic knowledge by updating theory course materials to meet the Institution of Fire Engineers (IFE) knowledge-based examination syllabus and cross-matching professional role maps. At a time when the Fire Service in the UK has tended to move away from traditional written promotional examinations, the IFE examination syllabus materials have been updated and expanded to include a wider range of source material and reflect the current level of scientific and technical knowledge.

This is supported by the development of structured personal development systems and professional competency frameworks that provide the basis for practitioner assessment in the training and work environments. Practical and professional development programmes have also been developed which assess competency and are cross-referenced to National Occupational Standard (NOS) components (Local Government Employers 2006).

### Standards and accreditation

The question of whether an individual investigator's knowledge, training and application of skills are adequate for a specific role can be addressed by a range of assessment tools, leading to various forms of accreditation. Ideally an individual's performance and competency should be internally and externally assessed throughout their career. Assessments should be made against common benchmarks which are identifiable in training and workplace environments.

### National occupational standards (NOS)

The UK fire investigation NOS (Local Government Employers 2006), first published in July 2005, was designed to provide a set of essential components for fire officers, crime scene examiners and others who carry out detailed technical investigations at Levels Two and Three but who do not conform to the generic description of forensic scientists.

### The Council for the Registration of Forensic Practitioners (CRFP)

CRFP has taken a new approach to regulation, dealing with a wide range of professional groups using a common process (CRFP 1999–2006). Registration is intended to be a guide to the court that the individual is suitably competent to offer evidence within their field of expertise. Such evidence may include both factual and interpretative (opinion) testimony at the discretion of the court. The CRFP process does not itself assess how an individual performs as an expert witness but aims to ensure that the person has adequate professional knowledge, understanding and skills to support the opinions expressed.

In developing the assessment process for investigators of Level Two and Three incidents, initially from a crime scene background, CRFP drew upon the fire investigation NOS materials. These processes have also proved applicable to fire service investigators and others. Forensic scientists who evaluate laboratory-based evidence as well as investigating scenes follow a slightly different route to registration from fire scene examiners.

### The International Association of Arson Investigators Certified Fire Investigator (CFI) Programme

The International Association of Arson Investigators (IAAI) is a US-based practitioner-run organisation with branches or 'chapters' in many countries worldwide, including the UK. The IAAI administers a certification programme based on a core syllabus common to all countries, with appropriate allowance made for local variations in legal systems, technical issues etc. Individual members must provide evidence of relevant education, training and experience before being permitted to take a written examination. On passing, they are invited to an oral assessment conducted by suitably qualified fire investigators. Discussions continue as to how the CFI qualification might articulate with the NOS and CRFP schemes in the UK.

### The Forensic Science Society Diploma

The Forensic Science Society awards diplomas in a range of disciplines, including fire investigation, which is at postgraduate level. The diplomas combine examination of theoretical knowledge with practical testing of its application by the candidate, either in realistic scenarios or in case portfolios presented to an expert panel. The standard of the diploma is assured by the involvement of a leading UK university which validates the awards.

### The status of witnesses

In relation to expert witnesses in the UK, FSC 1-2006 (ODPM 2006) acknowledges the level of qualifications and scientific expertise of the forensic scientist. For non-specialist fire or police officers, FSC 1-2006 confirms that their evidence is normally restricted to facts but it is a matter for the courts to determine if they should provide opinion evidence based on professional knowledge and experience. There is a growing number of fire investigators who fall between the two, who conduct the Level Two/Three investigations referred to above. These investigators mainly comprise fire officers and crime scene examiners who fulfil the NOS requirements, are CRFP registered or moving towards registration, and may hold relevant academic or vocational qualifications. As such they are likely to be accepted by the courts as credible experts. The evidential role of the laboratory-based forensic scientist (other than the relatively few who actively specialise in on-site fire and explosion investigation) may, in turn, become more restricted to those areas in which highly specialised scientific knowledge and techniques are required. This would be similar to the situation in many other parts of the world, including North America, Australia and much of Europe.

## Summary

In recent years many advances have been made in providing sound education and training for persons involved in the investigation of fires, dispersed-phase explosions and related incidents. This has been coupled with more rigorous mechanisms for assessment of an individual's expertise and performance. Strategies aimed at improving the knowledge, understanding, skill and experience of fire investigators continue to be developed. The methodical and systematic multi-agency team approach to fire investigation continues to be a common theme.

## Methodology

### The scientific method

Forensic science can be described as the use of scientific methods to identify and evaluate evidence to assist the legal and investigative process. In practice, in a fire investigation context, this involves the use of scientific and engineering facts and concepts to inform a rational problem-solving model of the type used in many other areas of human endeavour. This is often described as a 'scientific method' and involves a number of steps in which the problem is defined, data collected and analysed and one or more competing hypotheses developed. Further data is then sought, including by experimentation if required, to enable the hypotheses to be tested and evaluated. If a hypothesis fails such testing, it is modified or discarded, taking into account the additional data. This procedure continues in an 'iterative loop' until, ultimately, a single hypothesis capable of withstanding any reasonable challenge is developed and all the realistic alternatives have been tested and rejected. A summary of this process is set out diagrammatically in the 2001 and 2004 editions of the *Guide for Fire and Explosion Investigations* (NFPA 2001–04)) and a similar description is given at pp. 7–8 of *Kirk's Fire Investigation* (DeHaan 2007). Please see Figure 10.1.

The key tests of whether the correct conclusion has been reached are predictability (if the same circumstances are repeated, the same result ought to be obtained) and whether input of fresh data gathered subsequently alters the conclusion. In practice it is rarely possible to test the predictability of a fire investigator's conclusion completely, because the precise set of circumstances at the start of the fire cannot usually be reproduced, but full or scaled reconstructions and mathematical models can assist. The introduction of new data requires a return to the iterative loop testing process. If it does not produce the same outcome, the data should not be dismissed as an aberration and the conclusion must be reviewed.

There is often a view that an individual has to be trained or qualified as a 'scientist' to use the 'scientific method'. This is not the case. Many occupational groups with a variety of training and knowledge carry out investigations using scientific methods. In the field of fires and explosions, examples include fire officers, crime scene examiners, loss adjusters, engineers and health and safety specialists.The methodology of fire investigation went

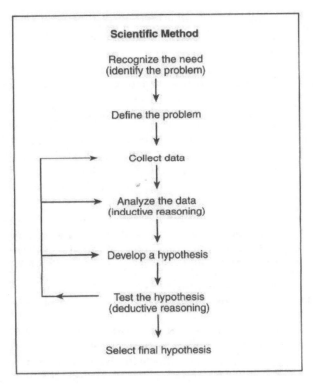

**Figure 10.1** The Scientific Method of fire investigation
*Source:* Reproduced from NFPA 921 (2001), p. 11, Figure 2.3

through a period of dramatic change from the early 1980s to the late 1990s. Prior to this period, it was often regarded as a 'black art' and the main training method was *ad hoc* apprenticeship. This led to the promulgation of many 'myths and legends', especially relating to some of the post-fire indicators which were heavily relied upon to resolve an investigation. This issue will be discussed later in the chapter. The work of a few pioneers led to a much better understanding of fire behaviour that has arisen from more and higher quality research and improved information sharing between investigators and researchers. The greater involvement in fire investigation of personnel with a scientific background who were prepared to question accepted wisdom was also of significance. Some of the publications from this period proved vital in changing the approach to a more scientifically rigorous process (e.g. DeHaan 1983; Cooke and Ide 1985).

The aim of the NFPA 921 methodology is to classify fires as 'accidental' (with subsequent breakdown of the causative factors as required), 'incendiary' (i.e. deliberate in UK terminology) or 'undetermined'. In practice, it may not always be possible to arrive at a definite solution and it may be necessary to report a range of possibilities that can be ranked on the basis of the available information. Unlike many other areas of forensic science, such as DNA and trace evidence, at the current state of knowledge of fire causes, it is rarely possible to evaluate competing alternatives statistically. In comparison to these other areas the opinion of the fire investigator is arguably more subjective.

However, by following the scientific method outlined above it is possible to describe and justify the reasoning processes involved in reaching such an opinion.

### Recognise and define the problem – objectives

The most common reason for carrying out a fire or explosion investigation is to determine the cause of the incident. The purpose of this is generally to prevent a recurrence and/or to identify criminal activity. There may be other objectives, including assessment of fire development, structure response, human behaviour or determination of liability. These different aims may modify the approach to data gathering and interpretation. It is rarely possible to specify the cause of a fire unless the point or area of ignition can be determined. Once the origin has been located, identifying the cause may involve interpretation of physical evidence and witness evidence using a process of elimination, if more than one potential ignition source and/or fuel was present. This may require consideration of fuel and ignition source characteristics, heat transfer mechanisms and possibly direct experimentation. In some cases, the way in which a fire has developed and spread from the initial area of origin to affect other materials or parts of a structure may be of greater importance to the investigator. In these cases it may be necessary to evaluate the interactions between initial and subsequent fuel packages, the influence of building construction and/or failure, fire fighting activities and numerous other factors. Identifying reasons for unusual fire development may be essential to understanding how to limit damage in future incidents and prevent financial loss.

Structural response to fire can also be a key issue. For many years the building industry in the UK has been closely regulated to prevent loss of life caused by fire. Much of this prevention historically depended upon the passive fire resistance of structures and materials. Regulations were continually reformed as changes in materials and building styles evolved; feedback from fire investigations has long been recognised as an essential part of this process. In recent years, there has been a trend away from prescriptive regulation towards 'engineering based solutions'. Building designers are now permitted to demonstrate that their design will achieve the same outcome by different means, usually derived from predictive modelling. The investigator has a major role to play in validating (or otherwise) these predictive techniques, by supplying data from real incidents to inform the future design processes. For example, the investigation of the building collapse which followed the terrorist attack on the World Trade Centre on 11 September 2001 has revealed a great deal of information about the behaviour of certain construction elements when exposed to prolonged high levels of heat flux (NIST 2006). It is generally accepted that such information will impact greatly on future building design and construction throughout the world.

In other investigations, the key issue may be the combustion behaviour of the structure contents. The contribution of materials such as fittings and furnishings, household items, commercial stock etc. is highly dependent upon their interactions with each other. An example of this was the 'Stardust' disco fire which occurred in Dublin in 1981. Detailed investigation found that none of the available fuels within the building was capable of burning on its own in such a way as to cause the catastrophic fire spread that took place. However, the particular combination of materials and the way in which they were arranged behaved in a hitherto unpredictable way (Republic of Ireland Government 1982). Knowledge derived from this and other similar investigations has enabled investigators and designers to take such effects into account.

Human behaviour in relation to fires has been one of the most active areas of research in recent years. It has been recognised for some time that individuals confronted by a fire do not always behave in a predictable manner. Investigators will therefore try to determine how they reacted and if they have had an influence on the initiation and/or progress of the fire. Understanding how people respond to fire alarms, use means of escape etc. in real incidents gives essential information to designers of buildings and systems.

Whatever the initial objective of the investigation, there is always potential for the findings to be used in subsequent legal proceedings such as criminal prosecutions, civil litigation or employment tribunals. Major incidents may also result in public inquiries. Every investigator therefore has a duty to ensure the proper conduct of his or her facet of the investigation.

The remainder of this chapter includes some technical terminology relating to fire ignition and development, and investigative findings. Space precludes a detailed discussion of these terms as they arise. Useful definitions and an overview of fire behaviour are contained in the current version of the NFPA 921 *Guide for Fire and Explosion Investigations*.

## Scene examination practice

### Gathering initial data – preliminary assessment

Most fire investigators now agree that it is essential to base investigations upon a systematic approach to the incident scene taking other available information into account. Agencies in many countries use the current edition of the USA-formulated *NFPA 921: Guide for Fire and Explosion Investigation* (NFPA 2004) or a local derivative as their basis for this approach. Other respected texts, such as *Kirk's Fire Investigation* (DeHaan 2007) also recommend and describe similar approaches. In the UK and Eire, the *Pocket Guide to Fire and Arson Investigation* (Gardiner 2000) is a useful summary for practitioners and supervisors which covers the methodology and basic technical information required in a locally relevant format.

Fire and explosion scenes are amongst the most dangerous to investigate. The possible hazards are too numerous to list here, but each of them poses a risk to the investigator and to others involved. Potential risks should be identified and reduced to acceptable levels using appropriate published guidance (e.g. Munday 1994; Lacy 1995). The starting point for all fire investigations should be the maxim in *Kirk's Fire Investigation* (5th edn), p. 3 that 'every fire scene is a *possible* crime scene' (DeHaan 2001) from which it follows that every fatal or serious injury fire is also a potential murder. If the scene is managed from the outset in accordance with crime scene investigation principles, the possibility of loss or contamination of evidence can be minimised. As any experienced detective will confirm, it is much easier and more productive to begin with a thorough investigation which can be scaled down if necessary, than to try to make up lost ground some time later. If there has been a presumption of accidental cause in the early stages, and crime scene management procedures are not employed, it may be impossible to effectively pursue any suspicious findings because the evidence has been compromised. A discussion of crime scene management in general is outside the scope of this chapter but the principles can be applied to all types of incident, including fires and explosions.

In order to manage a scene adequately it is necessary to define what the incident comprises. A fire or explosion may involve any or all of the following: structures and their environs; areas of open land; vehicles; people (dead and alive); other linked locations; displaced materials such as projected debris which lands some distance away. Key initial decisions include the size and perimeter of the scene. This will lead to consideration of approach routes, debris zone, preservation/contamination issues, casualties, consequential damage and pre-fire activity. The usual estimate for explosion incidents is that the radius of the scene should be set at 1.5 times the distance of the farthest piece of material observed. Fire debris is usually less widely dispersed and it could appear that the perimeter would not have to be set much wider than the zone of burning. However there may be related evidence farther away, for example items dropped or thrown away by persons leaving the area. The scene may be a single building or include a complex mixture of structures, surrounding areas and access routes. Linked scenes may include the location of casualties (hospital, mortuary) and the transportation used to move them. They will also include any other persons, items or materials removed from the main site and their transport mechanisms. All of these issues need to be taken into account when deciding how best to preserve evidence in the initial stages of the investigation.

One of the most important ways in which early control and management of the scene contributes to a subsequent investigation is by the provision of information. Detailed records should be made using photography, notes, sketches and video if available. Records of the early stages of the fire and initial fire fighting activities can be extremely useful to the investigator. The increasing prevalence of mobile phones with cameras is thus of great assistance. Media from other equipment that may have recorded the incident, e.g. CCTV surveillance or plant monitoring, should be secured as soon as possible. Recording transient information during the search and rescue or casualty handling stage is also valuable. Essential immediate observations of first responders and early-arriving investigators include descriptions of physical evidence, persons in the area, pre-incident activities (if apparent) and movements of vehicles and people. Names and contact details of witnesses should be recorded and brief accounts may be taken from them at an early stage. In general, first responders should not carry out formal interviews. Specialists from the appropriate agencies, who can assess whether cautions should be administered or if other constraints apply to the interview, best undertake these. All personnel should be aware of the procedures and problems involved in recording and transfer of information, witness contamination and the potential for introducing investigator bias. The term 'witness contamination' refers to the inadvertent provision of information to a witness of which they would otherwise be unaware.

The investigator should carry out a preliminary visual examination of the exterior and environs of the incident. Opinions vary as to best practice in this respect; some investigators prefer to take their first look at the incident scene before receiving any witness information so as to avoid unconscious bias, whereas others find it useful to have a general level of information available when first assessing the fire damage. If two or more fire scene examiners are involved in the investigation it is often helpful for the preliminary information gathering to be shared, one person deals with witnesses and another with the scene. The preliminary scene inspection informs the risk assessment and gathers initial data about the nature of the incident, fire spread and development, potential area(s) of origin, structural response and associated physical evidence. It also enables the team members to agree on a common approach path, and to identify and implement other crime scene management methods. Once a suitable approach path has been identified, a similar visual assessment is carried out of the interior. Again, this has a safety function as well as gathering data about the fire. The information gained at this stage includes gross damage and directional fire spread patterns, material and structure responses, occupancy and use factors, processes in use etc.

### Forming an initial hypothesis

The observations derived from the preliminary physical assessment will be combined with the initial witness accounts and other available information to form a preliminary or working hypothesis concerning the incident, for example where the fire began and how it spread. This point of the investigation is critical because the planning of the work to be carried out will depend upon the preliminary hypothesis. For example, identifying a room or area of origin within a building at an early stage will focus subsequent detailed examination on that location and may involve destructive activities in other areas. If the room of origin has been incorrectly identified at the preliminary stage, vital evidence could then be lost from other parts of the building during clearance of debris. The initial evidence will probably be incomplete or could be explained in a number of ways. The investigator must always bear in mind that the testing of hypotheses requires actively searching for evidence which opposes them.

### Gathering additional data – the detailed scene examination

This should start with the exterior of the structure and its surroundings. Unburnt or partially burnt elements of a structure can reveal information about pre-fire conditions including security, state of repair, utilities and services, ventilation effects and external fire spread. It is also possible that the area of fire origin is outside the building or that other evidential material (such as fuel containers, clothing, ignition sources) has been left there. In the case of an explosion, the direction and travel distance of projectiles and displacement of structures should be noted. Plotting out this information on a sketch plan often indicates very clearly the source of the over-pressure, allowing the investigator to concentrate on the fuels and ignition sources in that area.

The detailed interior examination of a fire-damaged building generally proceeds from areas of least to greatest damage. Parts of the building that have not been severely damaged by fire may reveal information about the pre-fire conditions. Examples of such information include the level of 'housekeeping', nature and condition of equipment and fittings, stock levels, presence or absence of articles of value, nature and location of fuels, and legitimate ignition sources. The fire patterns produced by flames, buoyant hot gases and smoke staining are then followed back towards the area(s) from which the flames and hot gases originate. The effects of building construction and ventilation on flow patterns of hot gases and smoke can be very complex and a thorough understanding of fire dynamics is needed to interpret these patterns correctly.

Once the general area of origin has been established from the fire patterns and other considerations, the zone of interest is usually excavated to remove the superficial layer of debris which has accumulated during the fire progression from the failure of decorative or structural elements. The process is somewhat analogous to that of archaeology. The extraneous material often covers, preserves and protects items and burning patterns of evidential value. The investigator will therefore remove this material before carefully excavating the stratified debris beneath. This stratification often reveals the sequence of events which occurred before or during the fire and the arrangement or disturbance of items in the room. In addition to the stratification evidence, uncovering remains of items such as furniture frames, wall studs, fixtures and fittings can reveal directional charring or other heat damage indicators which may help to locate the area of origin.

During the fire and subsequent fire fighting activities, furnishings are often disturbed or broken. Reconstructing the scene by replacing the furnishings in their original positions and orientations enables the investigator to study the fire progression patterns, for example from one item of furniture to another, compare the relative damage and narrow down the area of origin. It also clarifies pre-fire activities and may verify or refute witness accounts of the conditions prior to the incident.

Excavation and reconstruction can be physically demanding and time-consuming activities at many scenes, especially where damage is extensive. In large fires it may be necessary to use machinery for the initial phase of extraneous debris removal. However, the quantity and value of the information revealed is often the key to successfully resolving an investigation.

Locating the area of origin of the fire is relatively straightforward in some cases but is often complicated by a variety of factors. The most common of these are uneven fire loads within compartments or buildings, and the presence of certain fuel types which have very high heat release rates which distort the overall fire patterns. Sustained post-flashover burning, and ventilation changes which take place as the fire progresses and during fire fighting, also add complications. Accurately locating the origin of a fire is therefore more complex than might be supposed.

There are several basic techniques that can be applied in many situations to determine the area of origin of a fire. One of the most common is the comparison of heat exposure effects on structures and materials. Put simply, in many cases the place where the fire has been burning longest is where it started. The investigator therefore looks for evidence of the longest exposure to the greatest amount of heat. This may be reflected in structural failure, destruction of contents and/or different degrees of damage to items of similar construction such as furnishings. This situation is often complicated by differences in the type and amounts of fuel, ventilation and other factors such as re-radiation from nearby surfaces. These phenomena could result in the fire developing more rapidly or burning more intensely in locations other than the area of origin.

In general, flaming fires burn upwards and outwards at a much greater rate than they burn downwards. Therefore the investigator will also often search for the lowest area of burning within the structure. This can be complicated by falling materials, structural collapse or by the effects of smouldering, including 'hot spots' left after fire fighting. The investigator must also be aware of the effects of compartment geometry (such as room shape and dimensions) on fire development, for example the 'corner effect' in which some fires involving similar fuels develop much more rapidly and to a greater degree in the corner of a compartment than in the centre. This phenomenon is described in *Introduction to Fire Dynamics* (2nd edn, pp. 136–144 (Drysdale 1998) and *Kirk's Fire Investigation* (6th edn), pp. 42–45 (DeHaan 2007).

Local electrical failures, for example arcing on trailing leads and flexes, combined with the operation of protection devices, can enable the investigator to determine the directional progress of the fire through a compartment. On a larger scale, this can be applied to building circuits where the various points of arcing as the cable insulation fails, followed by the operation of circuit protection, can be used to help locate the first area of major flaming (Carey 2002). This process, known as arc mapping, is often very time-consuming but may be the only method available in a major structure fire.

Witness observations can be of great assistance, if the fire has been seen in its early stages by one or more independent observers. Care is needed in interpreting these observations, since the vantage point, illumination, presence of obstructions, distractions and cognitive processes may influence the account. Witnesses may be affected by shock, other psychological factors, the desire to mislead or their imagination. Where the witness first saw the fire break out may not be the actual origin of the fire and some witnesses are far from accurate in their descriptions.

Interpreting the damage to determine the area of origin relies heavily on good knowledge of fire science and engineering principles. Variables to be considered may include assisted ventilation, fire load discrepancies, geometry-affected plume movements, unusual thermal behaviour of structures and materials, and the effects of fire fighting activities or equipment. It may also be possible to interrogate fire and/or intruder alarm systems to determine sequential operations, or interpret operation of fixed fire extinguishing equipment.

The so-called 'fire patterns' which the investigator uses to assess the intensity and direction of the fire progression and thus to help determine the point of origin are more correctly described as post-fire indicators, i.e. physical effects as a consequence of heat, flame and smoke on materials such as parts of a structure or its contents. Typical post-fire indicators used include the degree and distribution of charring to timber surfaces, spalling of plaster and masonry surfaces, fracture and failure of glass (glazing, containers etc.), oxidation and melting of metals and the shapes of fire plumes as demonstrated by smoke deposition or heat damage on walls and ceilings.

Some older texts contained information suggesting that the rate of exposure to fire phenomena could be determined from these indicators but this is now known to be misleading or incorrect. In other words, it was considered possible to state from specific types of damage whether the fire had built up slowly or rapidly. On this basis decisions were often made as to whether a fire had been artificially accelerated, for example by the use of flammable liquids.

As a result of much more intensive study of fire behaviour over the past 20 years or so, it is now known that many of these indicators do not demonstrate rates of exposure reliably. Some examples are given in *Kirk's Fire Investigation* (DeHaan 2007: 291–3). It is also now clearly understood by most investigators that no single indicator should be used in isolation to affirm or refute a specific hypothesis. This is especially important is assessing post-flashover burning in which ventilation effects play a major part in the formation of burn patterns.

Modern interpretations of these post-fire indicators are quite different from those presented in some older publications and training courses. For example, many glass fractures and most plaster spalling are due to rapid cooling, mainly from the impact of fire fighting water, and therefore rarely yield useful information about the early development stages of the fire. Metal annealing is now understood to be more directly associated with total heat flux, thus a prolonged low temperature exposure may have a similar effect to a shorter period of very high temperature gases.

The presence of so-called 'hard-edged' or 'pool-shaped' burns at low level and fast flame development were commonly held to be indicators that ignitable liquid had been used to assist the fire. Better understanding of the phenomena of flashover and backdraught in compartments, combined with knowledge of the different properties of modern synthetic furnishings compared with natural materials, has radically redefined the way investigators interpret rapid fire development and low level burning. It is now widely understood that these phenomena are almost inevitable consequences of flame ignition in a normally furnished modern room and do not necessarily indicate the presence of ignitable liquids. This issue is discussed at some length in *Kirk's Fire Investigation* (DeHaan 2007: 242–53).

In addition to fire damage, post-explosion indicators include the size, shape and extent of the debris field. The size and mass of typical debris fragments and their displacement can indicate the over-pressure achieved in the incident, which in turn can enable the investigator to deduce features of the fuel–air mix such as the nature and probable concentration of the fuel

(Harris 1989). Displacement and distortion of structural elements of buildings also contributes a great deal of information, which can help localise the origin of the explosive event and determine the forces involved. From this information, fuel volumes, concentrations and venting areas can be estimated. Heat or soot damage on displaced or projected items can help to determine whether the explosion preceded the fire or vice versa and hence indicate the mechanism responsible.

The older approach of relying upon one or two key indicators to localise the origin and determine the nature and development rate of the fire is inherently unsafe. Modern methodologies such as NFPA 921 stress the need for a much more holistic approach in which all the physical evidence features are considered together. This provides a more robust and reliable basis for conclusions.

Having located and excavated the area of origin of the fire, the investigator must determine what fuel first became ignited and the nature of the heat source responsible. The initial fuel could be part of a malfunctioning appliance, furnishings, building components near a heat source, materials involved in a production process, waste materials or a fuel such as an ignitable liquid. The physical characteristics of the fuel play a major part in whether it will ignite and sustain combustion, so the investigator must consider the quantity, nature, physical state, condition and orientation of the fuel, as well as its proximity to any heat source.

Ignition sources may be anything that can produce heat in sufficient quantities and transfer it at a high enough rate to ignite the fuel in question. There may be more than one potential ignition source within the area of origin and the investigator then has to determine if one or more can be eliminated.

Sometimes there will be direct physical evidence of the first fuel package, the ignition source or both within the area of origin. The presence of timber frame pieces with sinuous (S-shaped) wire springs, and possibly associated components such as castors, might indicate to the investigator that the first item involved was a foam-upholstered chair. This is valuable information because the ways in which such items can be ignited and the associated rates of fire development are well understood. Similarly, there may be an obvious ignition source such as an overturned radiant heater or the hot surface of some industrial process. In some cases, however, the ignition source is destroyed in the fire; cigarette ends and matches rarely survive significant amounts of burning and their presence at the origin may have to be inferred from other evidence such as witness accounts or their presence in other areas of the building. In some deliberately set fires, both the fuel package and ignition source may become apparent after excavation. For example, the remains of a broken glass bottle with a burnt rag in the neck and surrounded by petrol residues provides good evidence of fuel, heat source and mechanism of ignition in one simple device – a 'petrol bomb'.

If there is direct evidence of only one potential fuel and ignition source combination in the area of origin the investigator's task is made much simpler. More commonly, the fire has destroyed the fuel package, ignition source or both, or several potential heat sources can be identified in the relevant area. If all the fuel has been consumed, it may yet be possible to identify what fuel was present by other means. These may be simple enquiries, such as asking persons familiar with the area what was stored or kept there prior to the fire, or may involve theoretical considerations. For example, from the burn patterns and witness descriptions it may be possible to estimate the initial heat release rate of a fire and this could help to differentiate between, for example, boxed paper goods or synthetic padded jackets as the first fuel.

Where more than one heat source is present, the nature of the interaction between it and the fuel must be considered to determine its viability; ignition is not simply a matter of temperature but of energy transfer. The heat source must be capable of providing sufficient energy for long enough to heat the fuel, while the physical and thermal characteristics of the fuel must permit adequate transfer of that energy if ignition is to result.

During the detailed scene examination phase of the investigation, the investigator should seek and record other physical evidence. It may not be clear at this stage how observations affect the final outcome but it is essential that they are noted. The security of the building is of major importance. It may be apparent that a door or window has been forced, or that some other illegal entry has occurred, but such evidence can be masked by fire fighting activities. These indicators are not confined to the building entrances; there may be evidence of forcing to internal doors, drawers, cupboards, safes etc. to indicate pre-fire activities. If the building security does not appear to have been compromised, keyholder activities should be considered. Interrogation of electronic alarm systems can provide useful information of when and by whom they were set or disarmed and which zones were enabled or activated. In an occupied building where external security is not an issue, internal access may be of considerable importance. Any access control systems, CCTV monitoring and physical locks will need to be checked in detail.

The investigator will also need to consider and examine aspects of the building systems that may have contributed to the cause or spread of the fire. These include fire protection systems, utilities, air handling systems, production processes etc. In many cases, a fire investigator will need to call on experts from other disciplines to complete this part of the work. This is especially so where complex electrical or alarm systems are installed.

The levels of stock and/or other contents at the time of the fire should be compared with what would normally be expected or is alleged. In commercial premises the quantity and quality of contents can be significant, as is the absence of specific items of value or their substitution by lower value alternatives. In domestic settings, valuable items that are frequently removed or substituted prior to a deliberately started fire include cash, jewellery, consumer electronics, sporting and fitness equipment etc. Absence of items of emotional value such as family photographs, heirlooms etc. and pets or livestock may also be significant.

The detailed examination of the building and its surroundings provides information concerning the state of repair and maintenance, lifestyle or housekeeping issues; any associated criminality (vandalism, graffiti, theft etc.) may also be relevant. In the case of deliberately started fires, factors such as the area of origin, method of ignition, access routes and any indication of targeting may help other specialists to indicate the offender's motivation and psychology, as well as linking incidents through *modus operandi* (MO). Linking MO information with other evidence of local trends and criminal activity may in some instances be the only way to identify the perpetrator of a fire if it is not someone directly connected with the premises.

### Forming interim hypotheses – reconstructing the sequence of events

Following the more detailed scene examination, the investigator is usually in a position to refine or discard the preliminary hypothesis and formulate one or more interim scenarios. Establishing the cause of a fire or explosion is not limited to identifying the fuel and ignition source. Arguably the most important part of the investigator's task is to establish how they came together, which usually involves determination of the probable sequence of events. A combination of physical evidence, witness accounts, documentation and background information can be used to establish a sequence of events and a reliable chronology. Occasionally witness accounts conflict with physical evidence. This could be due to a genuine mistake or may be an attempt to mislead the investigator. This does not necessarily imply that the fire was deliberately started; it may be that the individual feels at risk of blame or under pressure. Witness perceptions of time are often distorted during an incident. Wherever possible specific events should be corroborated by other information.

In fatal and serious injury incidents, the primary witnesses are rarely available for interview. Reconstructing the sequence of events is likely to rely heavily on physical evidence, such as burn distribution and pathological evidence, or other indirect evidence.

### Gathering additional data – other sources of information

If further witness canvassing is to be carried out, it is often helpful for the fire investigator to assist detectives or other specialist interviewers in preparing question plans to elicit specific information. Questions should be formulated so as to test specific areas of the interim hypotheses. Other valuable sources of information in some instances may include delivery notes, process and equipment details, maintenance and repair records, or instruction and service manuals for domestic or commercial appliances.

Information of value to the investigator may come from laboratory examination of materials recovered from the scene, or from professionals in other disciplines. In the case of fatal and serious injury incidents, information from pathologists and/or other medical specialists includes the nature and distribution of burns and other thermal injuries, levels of toxic gases and alcohol and drug concentrations in the body. Evidence may come from a range of other professionals including accountants, engineers, fire protection specialists, psychologists/psychiatrists, and even veterinary surgeons. Their contribution is usually made after the scene investigation has been completed but it is essential that all parties are kept fully informed, since the findings may modify the final scenario.

Laboratory examination in fire-related incidents includes analysis of debris for ignitable liquid residues, inspection of appliances and equipment, ignition and combustion testing of materials and interpretation of burn distribution on clothing. This information is often essential in evaluating the scene observations and testing the interim hypotheses. Historically, there has been little emphasis on examination of the types of trace evidence typically associated with other crime scenes, due to a widespread and long-standing perception that the fire and heat damage would render them unsuitable. However, it has been demonstrated recently that useable fingerprint and DNA evidence can often be recovered after fires and this should be taken into account during the scene investigation (Larkin 2003; Mann et al. 2003; Deans 2006; Stow and McGurry 2006). Other work reported more recently (Nic Daéid 2005) confirms that data may be recovered from heat-damaged digital memory devices. The fire scene examiner should be aware of these possibilities. Many modern security CCTV systems record images direct to a computer hard drive, which can be a valuable source of information about the early stages of the fire.

### Information recording

All aspects of the investigation must be recorded in sufficient detail and in a legally acceptable manner. There are many methods by which this can be achieved, including written notes and diagrams, photography and video. It is rare for any one technique to be sufficient on its own. Scene examination and witness interview records must be made contemporaneously and cannot safely or justifiably be prepared long after the event. Other records, such as equipment monitoring logs, CCTV tapes etc. should indicate clearly when they were made and/or copied. All records must be safely preserved and protected in such a way that they can be readily produced when needed. Legal requirements relating to 'best evidence' often mean that, although such formats as CD-ROM can be used for ease of reference, preservation and production of originals will still be required. All digital images and photographic negatives must be preserved in their original condition.

### Evaluation and final scenario

Having gathered all the available information concerning the incident, both physical and other evidence, the investigator will collate and interpret the findings using the iterative testing process previously described. As each hypothesis is developed, it is tested against all the available information. Any incongruence is identified and the hypothesis either discarded or refined to take it into account.

In practice, a series of interim hypotheses will usually have been refined during the scene examination. The final interpretation will then be a matter of reviewing and fine-tuning the last of the interim hypotheses. This version will often be a refinement of the original preliminary scenario, especially when experienced investigators are involved who are adept at assessing the initial scene. However, it is important to record clearly what other possibilities have been considered and on what basis they were ruled out. It is essential then to consider ways in which the final hypothesis from the scene and witness information could be further tested and refined. This involves consideration of any potential fresh data sources which have not yet been explored including an assessment of their relevance and reliability. Such information may include laboratory examinations and analysis, computer simulations or physical re-enactments of the event. The investigator must be sure that the results are meaningful. This involves setting appropriate parameters for test variables, being aware of analysis sensitivity and, above all, being open-minded and ready to consider alternative scenarios that are amenable to testing.

Investigators or other professionals may construct mathematical computer models to test scenarios. Typical fire safety engineering models are designed to predict fire development from a given origin and growth rate, and cannot be 'run backwards' to arrive at an origin by inputting the final damage details. However, they can be run with a number of different input variables to simulate different hypothetical ignition and growth scenarios and a 'best fit' to the observed facts obtained. *Kirk's Fire Investigation* gives a useful overview of the current state of computer modelling as applied to fire investigation (DeHaan 2007: 641–8).

## Conclusion

Ultimately, the fire investigator (or the lead investigator of a multi-agency team) should be able to combine the results of all of the above considerations into an objective overview, stating the most probable sequence of events and whether there are any limiting factors or unproven assumptions. As NFPA 921 (2001) states: 'A fire or explosion investigation is a complex endeavour involving skill, technology, knowledge and science. The compilation of factual data, as well as an analysis of those facts, should be accomplished objectively and truthfully.' Historically, the artisan/apprentice approach was often not based on sound scientific principles and objectively verifiable evidence. In addition, the approach to fire and dispersed-phase explosions was often unsystematic with great variability between both individual investigators and specific incidents. During the past 25 years or so, a combination of research and a more critical approach has improved the accuracy of interpretations while dispelling many previous beliefs which were found to have no reasonable basis. More recently, agencies involved in various aspects of fire investigation have reviewed their policies and practices in a largely successful attempt to improve the quality of service provided. This has involved changes in roles, education, training and competency assessment underpinned by modernisation of some of the relevant legislation.

As outlined in this chapter, the science and engineering concepts encountered within most fire investigations are complex and diverse. They are likely to include: energy sources and transfer through solids, liquids and gases; fuel behaviour and initial fire development; structural, electrical and mechanical engineering; analytical and testing methods. Other specialist knowledge and skills usually required include: crime scene management and examination techniques; fire fighting principles and application; interviewing and information gathering abilities; other forensic science and related disciplines (for example criminalistics, fingerprints).

In addition to the above, some fire and explosion investigations will involve consideration of medical or psychological evidence, financial information, design and execution of experimental scenarios, computer modelling, familiarity with plant, marine or aerospace machinery and a range of other subjects too diverse to predict. It would be a rare individual indeed who could claim sufficient expertise in all of these areas.

The authors therefore believe that these objectives are best achieved through the inter-agency team approach, in which individuals from a range of professional disciplines can bring their specialist knowledge and skills to bear on what are often complex and difficult investigations to resolve. This approach is now widely accepted as best practice in the UK and throughout many other developed countries. A properly constituted team with appropriate skills, following a systematic methodology of the type described in this chapter, provides the best opportunity of arriving at a correct decision as to the origin, cause, effects and circumstances of the fire or explosion incident under investigation.

## Notes

1  The FDR1 form is completed by attending firefighters in most cases of structure and vehicle fires. It is mainly used to compile statistics. Although a section relating to the area of origin, fuel involved and likely ignition source is included, it is not necessarily a definitive record of the origin and cause of the fire.

## References

Arson Control Forum (2003) *How to Set Up an Arson Task Force* (http://www.crimereduction.gov.uk/, accessed July 2007).

Arson Prevention Bureau (2004) *Fire Investigation in Scotland.* London: APB.

Carey, N. (2002) 'Powerful techniques: arc fault mapping', *Fire Prevention/Fire Engineers' Journal*, March: 42–50.

Chief and Assistant Chief Fire Officers Association (1999) *Report on Arson and Fire Investigation* (CACFOA).

Cooke, R. and Ide, R. (1985) *Principles of Fire Investigation.* Leicester: Institution of Fire Engineers.

Council for the Registration of Forensic Practitioners (www.crfp.co.uk 1999–2006, accessed July 2007).

Deans, J. (2006) 'Recovery of fingerprints from fire scenes and associated evidence', *Science and Justice*, 46 (3): 153–168.

DeHaan, J. (1983) *Kirk's Fire Investigation* (2nd edn). (out of print).

DeHaan, J. (2001) *Kirk's Fire Investigation* (5th edn). Upper Saddle River, New Jersey: Prentice Hall.

DeHaan, J. (2007) *Kirk's Fire Investigation* (6th edn). Upper Saddle River, New Jersey: Prentice Hall.

Department of Communities and Local Government (DCLG) (2000–05) *United Kingdom Annual Fire Statistics.* London: Her Majesty's Stationery Office.

Department of Communities and Local Government (2005) *Good Practice Conference* (http://www.communities.gov.uk/fire/arsonreduction/annualreports/goodpracticeconference/, accessed July 2007).

Drysdale, D. (1998) *Introduction to Fire Dynamics* (2nd edn). Chichester: John Wiley and Sons Ltd.

Gardiner, M. (2000) *Pocket Guide to Fire and Arson Investigation* (2nd edn). FM Global and Gardiner Associates.

Harris, R. (1989) *The Investigation and Control of Gas Explosions in Buildings and Heating Plant.* London: E. and F.N. Spon.

Home Office (1980 to 2000) *Home Office Circulars on Fire and Arson Investigation.* London: HMSO.

Home Office (1988) *Prevention of Arson Report.* London: HMSO.

Home Office (1999) *Safer Communities: Towards Effective Arson Control.* London: HMSO.

Lacy, H.B. (1995) *Safety on the Fire Scene.* National Fire and Arson Report, 13 (4): 1–5).

Larkin, T. (2003) *Recovery of DNA from fire scenes.* (Live Learn Pass It On conference, July 2003, Gardiner Associates, in Forensic Science Society Newsletter 'Interfaces', No. 36).

Local Government Employers (2006) *National Occupational Standards for Fire Investigation.* London: HMSO.

Mann, J., Nic Daiéd, N. and Linacre, A. (2003) *An investigation into the persistence of DNA on petrol bombs.* Proceedings of the European Academy of Forensic sciences, Istanbul.

Munday, J. (1994) *Safety at scenes of fire and related incidents.* Fire Protection Association.

National Fire Protection Association (2001–04) *NFPA 921 Guide for Fire and Explosion Investigations, 2001 and 2004 editions* (NFPA) – note new edition due 2008.

Nic Daéid, N. (2005) *Recovery of computer data from fire scenes.* Hong Kong: International Association of Forensic Sciences.

NIST (2006) *Federal Building and Fire Safety Investigation of the World Trade Center Disaster: Final Report of the National Construction Safety Team on the Collapses of the World Trade Center Tower* (http://wtc.nist.gov/pubs/, accessed July 2007).

Office of Deputy Prime Minister (2003) *Working Together: How to set up an Arson Task Force.* Arson Control Forum via www.arsoncontrolforum.gov.uk.

Office of Deputy Prime Minister (2006) *Fire Service Circular 1/2006.* London: HMSO.

Republic of Ireland Government (1982) *Report of the Tribunal of Inquiry on the Fire at the Stardust, Artane, Dublin.* Dublin: Stationery Office.

Stow, K. and McGurry, J. (2006) 'The recovery of fingerprints from soot-covered glass fire debris', *Science and Justice*, 46 (1): 3–14.

## Part 2

# Forensic Science as Investigative Support

# Introduction

## Jim Fraser and Robin Williams

> The research scientist will commonly repeat an experiment as many times as he wishes because he assumes that he is experimenting against a background of circumstances, or natural laws, which do not change with time. But the background against which the investigator operates is always changing with time, and often very quickly. Evidence which may be easily available today may be difficult to obtain tomorrow and have disappeared irrevocably the day after.
>
> (Kind 1999: 124)

Stuart Kind's comment reminds us that the effective use of forensic science in support of the investigation of crime – in helping to answer the 'who, what, when, where, why and how' questions that direct such investigations – depends upon and supports a number of organisational arrangements unrelated to the practical adequacy of the disciplinary techniques in use, let alone the scientific principles that underpin their authority. Whilst Kind focuses on the effort made by those who arrive at crime scenes to secure, preserve and interpret potentially relevant forensic evidence, there are many other factors which determine both the effectiveness of police uses of forensic resources and also the level of such resources available to them in the first place. Such matters are not normally the subject of forensic science textbooks or forensic science research reports, although they are sometimes dealt with in other policing and policy publications.

However, one of the distinctive features of this Handbook is that we have assembled a section of four chapters which seeks specifically to illuminate this area of forensic science policy and practice. Accordingly, the accounts that follow in Part 2 explicate the key expectations, strategies, frameworks and organisational arrangements that shape the way that various forensic science disciplines and resources contribute to investigative outcomes in contemporary criminal inquiries. The chapters largely focus on historical and recent developments in England and Wales, but reference is also sometimes made to other jurisdictions. In particular, Bramley's authoritative account of developments in DNA profile databasing (Chapter 12) draws a number of explicit comparisons with experiences in other European nation states and beyond. All the chapters give consideration to the overarching governmental strategies within which forensic science provision is located, the differing models used for the organisation of scientific support to 'serious' and 'volume' crime investigation, and the current state of knowledge about what works best – and why – when criminal investigators make use of the outcome of forensic analysis of evidence recovered from scenes of crime.

A number of themes recur across the chapters, and it is worth noting these, at least in outline, in this brief introduction. The first is the growing application of techniques of standardisation, or normalisation, to aspects of forensic science practice. Such techniques are used to encourage desired forms of conduct through a variety of rewards and punishments that are applied either to individuals or to collectives. Especially important in the field of forensic science and its uses by the police have been the introduction of key 'manuals' that guide investigators in their use of particular forensic technologies as well as the establishment of routinised ways in which expertise is channelled into police investigations.

Second, and underlying many of the efforts to establish 'best' or 'good' practice typical of such normalising processes, is the growing application of 'rational' models for the evaluation of forensic science effectiveness, where the meaning of 'rational' is often given an especially economic inflection. This has meant not only the introduction of market or market-like disciplines into forensic science decision-making, but also the application of (sometimes vaguely formulated) notions of efficiency and effectiveness drawn from the wider 'audit culture' that has been applied to UK public services for the past 30 years or so. Significant efforts of this kind have been made from 'inside' the criminal justice system by a number of key agencies including HMIC, the Police Standards Unit, and ACPO and from 'outside' by other agencies like the Audit Commission.

Third, is the significance of close attention paid to the contribution of forensic science to the prevention and detection of crime by legislators and other key policymakers concerned with the effectiveness of contemporary forms of crime control. It is impossible to think that the hugely important DNA Expansion Programme would have been possible without significant levels of interested optimism on the part of very senior members of several UK governments in the capacity of such a resource to contribute to wider efforts to detect offenders and reduce crime levels.

Finally, and importantly, all chapters draw our attention to the changing use of forensic science – from playing a largely corroborative to an increasingly inceptive role – and they way that this has impacted on the relationship between this technological resource and other aspects of police investigative expertise.

Chapters 11 and 14 in Part 2 (by Cooper and Mason and by Tilley and Townsley) focus on the ways in which these changes have become visible in the uses of various kinds of forensic science to support the investigation of volume crime, and Chapter 13 (by Barclay) is more concerned with how serious crime investigations have been reconfigured by changing understandings of forensic science. Each of these contributions, by prominent academics and leading practitioners, provides an exemplary and clear account of the major developments in the use of forensic science in a variety of investigative contexts as well as critical perspectives on the current state of knowledge about the effectiveness of these uses. Chapter 12 by Bramley, attends to one particular development in forensic science: the growing uses of DNA profiling by the police and the establishment and the expansion of State databases to enhance the utility of such forensic information. Many would argue that the growth of this kind of forensic science practice has provided an exemplary instance of the increasing power and significance of forensic science in general, and Bramley's detailed account bears out this argument. However, he, like the other contributors to Part 2, acknowledge that a number of operational and policy issues remain unresolved at the time of writing.

The most obvious commonality amongst all of these themes is that they are all aspects of underlying social and scientific changes, sometimes seemingly radical changes, that are modifying or supplanting older understandings of the meaning and use of forensic science in contemporary policing. Such changes are, by nature, continuous and unending. Accordingly, each of the contributors to this section has also offered comments on what future developments they hope and expect to see in the specific domains that they have chosen to describe. As editors, we will try to bring their comments together with those made by the authors of other chapters in a final reflection at the end of this book.

## References

Kind, S. (1999) *The Sceptical Witness*. Harrogate: The Forensic Science Society.

# Chapter 11

# Forensic resources and criminal investigations

*Amanda Cooper and Lucy Mason*

## Introduction

Over the past half century the use of forensic science in police investigations, like policing itself, has changed out of all recognition. The role of scientific support in police forces, and the level of resources given to it, has changed from a patchwork of fragmented local provision to a very substantial, integrated, national business utilising the very latest technology. This reflects and reinforces the wider changes in policing in England and Wales as it has moved away from small, autonomous, localised police forces towards larger forces supported by national provision in some key areas. It also exemplifies the increasing professionalisation of the police service, along with the broad recognition accorded to the importance of science and technology in policing.

Forensic science has proved increasingly useful to police forces. Since the middle of the last century forensic science has been ever more routinely called upon for a growing range of tasks, including identifying offenders, linking incidents to highlight serial offences, and to corroborate or dispute reported circumstances and witness testimony. In recent years the use of forensic science in major crime investigations has become so widespread that it is often a primary driver for police investigations, and can play a decisive role in the provision of dispositive evidence, for example through the use of increasingly sensitive DNA technology, or innovative applications of other forms of scientific knowledge.

Crime scene evidence is now routinely preserved for forensic analysis, and even evidence gathered long before the availability of new techniques for DNA analysis can provide valuable information through 'cold case' reviews. These reviews of past cases have notched up some impressive successes both in identifying offenders from decades-old offences, and in a few cases providing evidence for appeal, for example the many reviews of serious sexual assaults and rapes from the late 1980s and early 1990s which formed the Home Office-led Operation Advance in 2004,[1] and later Operation Advance II in 2005.[2]

This chapter explores the key trends in the development of forensic science as a police tool, the crucial role now played by DNA analysis in informing investigations and prosecutions, and the interplay between the government, forensic companies, and the police. We also consider how forensic science fits into the current police intelligence management model, and discuss briefly the future direction of police uses of forensic science.

## Trends in the use of forensic science

Because of the rather primitive nature of early performance data, it is hard to quantify the specific impact forensic science had historically, and early examples have to be cited with care. Even with current and much improved performance data, there are issues of quality, and it remains difficult to separate out the specific contribution of forensic science to the success of criminal investigations. However, key case studies can show the role of forensics even before the transformative advent of DNA technology. For example, forensic science was the primary tool used to link the attacks and murders attributed to the Yorkshire Ripper in the 1960s though to the early 1980s. In addition, in this case, forensic scientists and voice analysts were among the first to cast doubt on the theory that the offender was the individual responsible for the infamous 'Wearside Jack' letters and tapes, which had diverted the efforts of the investigation teams in the late 1970s. In 2006 routine DNA sampling for a minor offence matched a profile held on the national DNA database, and led to the identification and conviction of John Humble, the real author of the hoax letters in the Yorkshire Ripper case, who was sentenced to eight years in prison.[3]

Forensic services for police began as far back as the 1880s when the police began to call upon external specialists and doctors to provide useful information. The Metropolitan Police established a laboratory at Hendon Police College in 1934, and this was followed in the late 1930s by a series of regional laboratories (Fido and Skinner 2000). The Metropolitan Police laboratory moved to Lambeth in 1974. In 1991 the Forensic Science Service was established as an Executive Agency of the Home Office, and in 1996 it merged with the Metropolitan Police Forensic Science Laboratory to become a national service. The Forensic Science Service (FSS) is now the largest supplier of forensic science services in the UK[4] and in 2005 became a government-owned independent company, competing with a number of privately owned forensic services companies.

The increasingly widespread use of forensics in crime investigation is the result of a complex series of broader trends, which are explored in more detail later in this chapter. These include trends in applied science and computer technology, the introduction of new technologies, and the creation of national police investigation templates such as the *Murder Investigation Manual* (Association of Chief Police Officers (ACPO) 2000), the *Investigation of Volume Crime Manual* (ACPO 2001) and the *DNA Good Practice Manual* (ACPO 2005a). These templates have played a key role in driving up standards and embedding forensics within normal police practice, for example making evidence preservation routine. The creation of the National DNA Database in 1995 and other national forensic databases such as the automated national fingerprint database IDENT1 contributed to the increasing standardisation of the forensics process. The combined effect of these trends was to increase the pressure on police forces by the government and the public to make better use of science in crime investigation.

One of the most discernible trends in the use of forensic science techniques has been the move from expensive forensic techniques used rarely, and then only in the most serious cases, towards routine use of forensics in the support of the investigation of all levels of crime. This expanded utilisation has been supported by the increasing reliability, greater availability, reduced cost and increasing validation of many of the techniques that are now capable of providing evidence to the courts. Although there is undoubtedly variation in the performance of different police forces, forensic science has been an increasingly significant factor in both exceptional and routine investigations, affecting the choice of resources applied to an investigation and ultimately the outcome achieved. There is a useful analogy with the development of medical science over the past few decades, as drugs and treatments previously considered too expensive or unproven for use other than in extreme cases (such as prenatal diagnostic screening, keyhole surgery and HIV drug regimens) are now not only commonly used but are seen as the primary tool in treatments, impacting positively on prognoses and survival rates.

A significant development, especially in the UK, has been the use of forensic science in the investigation of volume crimes such as robbery, burglary and criminal damage. In 2000 the £1.2 million Pathfinder Project (Burrows *et al.* 2005) was set up as part of the government's Crime Reduction Programme, to measure the contribution of forensic science to the detection and reduction of burglary and vehicle crime. Lancashire and Greater Manchester Police were chosen to be pilot areas, in order to investigate the effect of enhancing scientific investigation in a large metropolitan force and a medium-sized rural force. The idea was to run the pilot in parts of two police forces which border each other, in order to investigate the impact on cross-border crime as one of the outcomes of the project. Morgan Harris Burrows consultancy and researchers from the University of Huddersfield collected data and evaluated the pilot, which ran from June 2000 until May 2001 with the evaluation completed in December 2001.

During the Pathfinder pilot forensic scientists worked closely with Scene of Crime Officers (SOCOs) to apply the new, much more sensitive, low copy number (LCN) DNA technology to volume crimes such as domestic burglary and vehicle crime. The LCN DNA findings were combined with other scientific information such as fingerprints, footwear marks and tool marks in order to identify any links between crime scenes. The evaluators measured the value of scientific information to officers in both detected and undetected cases. During the pilot, crime scene attendance increased by 9 per cent compared to the previous year, and DNA recovery increased by 73 per cent. In 25 per cent of cases a fingerprint identified a suspect, an increase of 2 per cent on the previous year. In 45 per cent of cases a forensic hit was the first link to a suspect.[5] However, the evaluation showed that the LCN technology was the most expensive element of Pathfinder, costing £1 million during the pilot, at a cost per 'hit' of £3,255 (Burrows *et al*. 2005: 56) and therefore LCN profiling is many times more expensive than the conventional SGM+ profiling system. Unfortunately, limited resources are one of the main constraints in volume crime investigation and so the present national guidance recommends that decisions to use LCN DNA analysis are considered on a case-by-case basis (ACPO 2005a).

Broadly, therefore, there have been two key trends in forensic science. Firstly, there was a shift from small-scale, expert use for certain serious crimes (mainly murders) towards large-scale and routine use at all levels of crime, by a variety of specialists within police forces and in external agencies such as the FSS, which is discussed in some detail later in this chapter. This routine use means that substantial sums are now spent from police force budgets on forensic services: for example in 2007/08 Thames Valley Police spent more than £5.2 million on forensic casework, pathologist fees, and crime scene samples. Secondly, a series of technological developments have meant that forensic findings have become increasingly reliable, proven in court and widely accepted in evidence. Forensic science now forms a core part of the police investigatory repertoire and can drive an investigation even in its early stages thanks to technological advances which make forensic science more rapid, more accessible, and more affordable. Forensic science has become embedded into police processes and Standard Operating Procedure, and is often indispensable even in routine police inquiries. Of course, one of the key technological developments which has made this possible is the forensic examination of DNA.

### DNA and the National DNA Database

The advent of DNA as a key forensic tool was seminal in transforming the role played by forensic science in police investigations. It is simply not possible to analyse the changes in the use of forensic resources without discussing the impact and influence of DNA technology, because of the effect it has had on the success rate of police investigations (Jobling and Gill 2004). Comparisons of DNA recovered from a crime scene and compared against the National DNA Database can provide important clues for an investigation – one study showed that a DNA hit actually provided the initial identification of a suspect in seven out of ten volume crime cases (Bradbury and Feist 2005). Some claim that the chances of detecting a crime are nearly doubled when DNA is available (Mennell and Shaw 2006).

In 1984 Jeffreys identified unique areas of the DNA in individuals that could be used to identify an individual (Zagorski 2006). The technique rapidly proved successful in both the United States and the UK. In 1986 this DNA technology proved decisive in the case of two schoolgirls who were murdered in the small town of Narborough in Leicestershire in 1983 and 1986 (Wambough 1989). Although the police were sure they had the right man in custody they could not prove a link to the first murder and asked for DNA analysis; the results showed that another man altogether was responsible for both murders, resulting in the first DNA-based murder hunt, which eventually resulted in the arrest and conviction of Colin Pitchfork, who was given a life sentence.[6] This well-known 'Pitchfork Murders' case was the first widely publicised use of the technology in a criminal investigation.

The success of DNA as an investigative technique for crime fuelled the emergence of commercial organisations in Britain to provide forensic services. As DNA analysis requires specialist equipment and expertise, it has largely been carried out in the UK by external companies rather than by police forces. The FSS pioneered the use of DNA profiling in forensic science using Jefferys's technology, and sells this service directly to police forces and Home Office laboratories.

Since the emergence of forensic DNA analysis, the techniques have been refined to improve the precision, sensitivity, and speed of results obtained (HMIC 2000; Jobling and Gill 2004). What once was a lengthy process, often resulting in a costly 12-week laboratory process which was used only in major and serious crimes, is today a rapid, relatively low cost (in comparison to the overall cost of investigations), automated process. Routine volume crime scene stains are now typically DNA-profiled within three days.

Together with the Association of Chief Police Officers (ACPO) and with political funding, the FSS developed the National DNA Database (NDNAD). This was made possible by the development of polymerase chain reaction (PCR)-based DNA tests. Current practice in DNA profiling is based on PCR amplification of a number of single tandem repeat (STR) alleles, changing the DNA profile from the approximate 'band' sizes attributed to a single locus allele to a specific numeric (Jackson and Jackson 2008: 159–63). This technique has had a huge impact on crime investigations across the world in general and the UK in particular. It allows accurate population databases to be created rapidly, so that a database of crime scene DNA profiles could be created which can then be directly compared with each other to identify links between records. It therefore became possible to compare DNA from a suspect in one case with DNA gathered from separate police investigations. The NDNAD was launched in 1995 by the Home Office and the FSS. Now DNA from any crime scene could be loaded to the DNA database, as could samples from identified offenders.

Demand for the NDNAD was immediate and already by December 1995 the NDNAD had a backlog of 130,000 samples, equivalent to two years' analytical capacity (Maguire and Hope 2006: 401). Between 1995 and 2000, approximately 750,000 DNA profiles from sampled individuals, and a further 65,000 from crime scenes, were loaded on to the NDNAD. Whilst this was seen by many as good progress, the absence of any national strategy for the collection of DNA from offenders and crime scenes, as well as a lack of financial resources available in police forces, meant that the build-up of the DNA database was partial and unsystematic. Initially there was little understanding of the demands being placed on individual police forces, which had extensive variations in structures and processes, and scant evidence basis to direct improvements. Nevertheless, as the numbers of profiles on the database grew, so did the number of matches and the variety in those matches. In particular, there were instances where DNA taken from offenders in low-level volume crime cases matched DNA profiles recovered from scenes of major crime. For example, in 2001 a shoplifter was arrested and his DNA was put on the NDNAD: this proved to match that of an offender who had raped and indecently assaulted two young girls in 1988. The offender pleaded guilty to the 1988 offences and was sentenced to 15 years imprisonment.[7] Cases such as this demonstrated that the DNA database would be a crucial intelligence tool for police forces, and provided the government with a strong case for greater investment.

### The DNA Expansion Programme

In 1999 the government announced additional funding to expand the National DNA Database. Between 2000 and 2005 more than £300 million was invested in the DNA Expansion Programme (about 7 per cent of the overall expenditure by police forces in England and Wales during this period). This includes £241 million from the government's DNA Expansion Programme funding and approximately £90 million from force budgets (Home Office 2005). The DNA Expansion Programme commenced in 2000.

By directly funding DNA collection and use through the DNA Expansion Programme, the government was able to influence how police forces implemented the use of DNA. The funding was aimed at the DNA sampling and profiling of known offenders, with further money provided to support the collection of DNA material from crime scenes, especially volume crime scenes which had previously been neglected because of the lack of police forensic resources. These funds were specifically allocated to the employment of more than 600 additional forensic staff and the vehicles and equipment associated with them. The aim of their deployment was to increase the number of crime scenes attended to improve forensic opportunities and aid investigation, and this was achieved. However, there were some concerns within police forces over the shift in focus towards DNA analysis to the exclusion of other types of analysis.

Because staff attended and examined scenes for any type of forensic evidence, such as finger marks and foot marks in addition to the collection of increasing numbers of DNA samples, the workloads within forces increased significantly. There was already a shortage of qualified fingerprint experts due to the long training period required, and the additional workload from the DNA Expansion Programme exacerbated this problem because the funds released to forces were only able to be spent on DNA-related staff. Unless a force could pay for additional fingerprint staff itself, anecdotal evidence from Scientific Support Managers showed that significant backlogs and pressures built up in Fingerprint Bureaus. These backlogs took some forces considerable time to shift and thus hindered the overall impact of the DNA Expansion Programme on improving force performance. Dealing with these backlogs, however, did create an opportunity to scrutinise and streamline functions within the Fingerprint Bureaus and to ensure closer engagement with investigators to establish actual work requirements and progression of case needs.

Despite these problems in implementation, the investment of millions of pounds into forensic science between 2000 and 2005 was probably the most significant factor in shaping how forensic science is used in criminal investigations today. The funding was supported by the necessary legislation in the Criminal Justice Act 2003 to sample and retain DNA from any person arrested. As a result of these measures, there were more than 3.8 million DNA profiles on the database in April 2006 – over 5 per cent of the UK population (Home Office 2006). A sizeable proportion of the crime scene profiles held on NDNAD are from volume crime, illustrating the significant rise in the use of forensic resources for volume crime. The DNA Expansion Programme seems to have improved the effectiveness of forensic science in the detection of volume crime (Bradbury and Feist 2005; Home Office 2005; Mennell and Shaw 2006) although some argue that the DNA Expansion Programme has not resulted in the level of improvement originally anticipated (McCartney 2006).

### DNA in major crime

As we have seen, DNA technology and the creation of the NDNAD together constitute a powerful tool for police investigations, and this has had a very significant impact on major crime investigations which, by their nature, are complex, high-profile investigations in which the reputation of individual police forces may be at risk. Notable cases in which DNA has provided crucial evidence in securing a conviction in the UK include those of Roy Whiting, found guilty for the murder of Sarah Payne in July 2000, and also Bradley Murdoch, convicted for the murder of Peter Falconi in July 2001.

DNA has also proved to be a crucial factor linking different offences, often separated by time or geography, and this enables police forces better to direct and combine investigation resources. DNA links first confirmed the series of rape offences in Operation Orb, the M25 'Trophy' rapes in 2002, and subsequently supported the identification and conviction of the offender, Antoni Imelia. Linking DNA collected from minor cases to identify more serious offenders has also proved fruitful, such as the arrest of Brian Lunn Field for a drink-drive offence in 1999, whose DNA profile matched a sample obtained from the clothing of 14-year-old Roy Tuthill, found dead in 1968.

At the same time, DNA analysis has been used in a number of high-profile cases in support of appeals against criminal convictions. Forensic science has been able to play a valuable role in bringing about justice by exonerating some convicted offenders, and can on occasion provide an independent witness compared to eyewitness and circumstantial evidence (Lee and Tirnady 2003).

In a number of cases it has been possible to charge and convict offenders for long-past criminal offences, where DNA evidence has been recovered from unsolved crime scenes through 'cold case' reviews. This has been successful even where the offender's own DNA is not held on the national database. For example, STR-based DNA techniques which had been unavailable at the time were used to re-examine the evidence from the 1988 murder of Lynette White. Three men had been convicted of her murder in 1990 but their conviction was found to be a miscarriage of justice. In 2000 a DNA profile was obtained, which was compared to the NDNAD. Whilst there was no direct match, there was a very similar linked profile, which subsequent investigation showed was from the nephew of the individual – Geoffrey Gafoor - who later admitted the murder. This was an early instance of successful 'familial searching' (Jackson and Jackson 2008: 169) where crime scene DNA profiles do not wholly match any profile on the NDNAD, but where partial matches may suggest that biological material may have come from a close relative. Such searches have provided a useful line of investigation which can then be used to direct other more traditional police methods.

DNA has therefore benefited traditional police investigative techniques in providing starting points for investigation, making savings in the time and effort of traditional investigations, and in some cases moving on an inquiry that would otherwise have been unsuccessful. The huge benefits that have been derived justify the very considerable investment by the government and police forces in forensic resources.

## Forensic science and government policy

There has been for decades a close relationship between government policy and the police use of forensic science. The Touche Ross (1987) Report, *Review of Scientific Support for the Police*, and the Home Office Report, *Forensic Science and Crime Investigation* (Tilley and Ford 1996) were among the first detailed reviews of the use of forensic science in the police service commissioned by the government. In 1997 the FSS and ACPO jointly published the seminal guidance book *Using Forensic Science Effectively* (Barclay *et al.* 1997).

### The Forensic Science Service

Before 1991 the FSS was funded by a combination of Home Office money and levies on police forces. Its services were, in effect, free at the point of use (Select Committee on Science and Technology 2005). From 1991 to 1995 the FSS was brought into the Home Office department as an executive agency as the primary forensic service provider for police forces in England and Wales. Although rival companies existed, such as Cellmark Diagnostics which was established in 1987, police forces had little finance available for spending on external companies, and the FSS custodianship of the NDNAD inhibited significant growth of competition in the provision of genetic forensic analysis to police forensic services and effectively gave the FSS a monopoly (Maguire and Hope 2006: 398).

There were no formal processes to manage supply and demand, and the FSS was very much the gatekeeper controlling what evidence was submitted and processed at its laboratories. This arrangement directly influenced the internal resourcing and management of forensic services within police forces, who primarily operated under the guidance and advice of the FSS which directly charged police forces for its services. The FSS was therefore able to develop its expertise but remained entirely separated from police force investigations. A Customer Satisfaction Survey in 2000 suggested that forensic science provision 'could almost be described as "reactive" and "bolted on" to the police investigation' (Maguire and Hope 2006: 400), which indicates that there was some way to go in integrating forensic science with police work. There was, however, some move towards integration with the secondment of members of individual police forces to the FSS through the normal Home Office secondment route in order to provide a link between the two organisations. These 'Forensic Liaison Officers' operated at a variety of levels including the management of submitted samples within the laboratory.

From 1995 the FSS was established as a separate government agency, and in 1999 acquired trading fund status. These changes had a significant effect upon the relationships between police forces and the FSS, along with the impact of the Local Government Act 1999 which required Police Authorities to obtain best value in local policing services (Select Committee on Science and Technology 2005). This required a change in procurement processes for forensic services as well as other external service provision for police forces to ensure open and fair competition and secure the best possible deal.

These factors, along with the increased need for DNA profiling, meant that demand began to outstrip supply and opened up a gap in the market for greater competition from companies such as Forensic Alliance and its associate DNA provider Cellmark Diagnostics, as well as LGC Plc, a forensic DNA and drugs analysis supplier. The creation of this new marketplace meant that a different approach by police forces to the management of forensic science resources was needed to match the more customer-focused approach of the new companies eager to gain and retain regular business from police forces. The FSS, which remained ACPO's preferred supplier until 2002, responded to the market competition with two new strategies: Operational Excellence and Service Leadership. These aimed to maximise the efficiency of the process and focus on timely delivery closely linked into a dynamic police operation (Maguire and Hope 2006: 401).

The McFarland Review (2003) of the FSS considered a number of potential organisational options for the FSS ranging from abolition to mergers, concluding that the balance of the argument was in favour of making the FSS a private-sector classified company with the government as minority shareholders – a Public Private Partnership (PPP) – thus relieving the government from having responsibility for a commercial enterprise. In the short term the FSS was to become a government-owned company (GovCo) as a precursor to evolution into a PPP. However, there was considerable opposition to this from those who feared that a PPP would have adverse consequences for the criminal justice system in the UK because of the profit-making factor and its potential to undermine public confidence in the impartiality of the FSS (Select Committee for Science and Technology 2005).

In December 2005 the FSS was made into a GovCo although there is some doubt about whether this will evolve into a PPP (Select Committee for Science and Technology 2005). However, the Home Office retains control over the NDNAD in terms of standard-setting and oversight, via a dedicated Home Office delivery unit, governed by a Board which now includes representatives of the Home Office, the Association of Chief Police Officers (ACPO), the Association of Police Authorities (APA), and the National Policing Improvement Agency (NPIA) as well as independent representatives from the Human Genetics Commission.[8]

The government has not only had a close interrelationship with the FSS and its funding, but has also introduced legislation to support DNA sampling and the NDNAD alongside a mandatory and stringent set of performance targets, which became the foundation of the Home Office Forensic Data Return. This is collected quarterly from police forces for benchmarking and comparison purposes (Bradbury and Feist 2005; Green 2007; Home Office 2005).

### Legislation

The government has further supported the growing usefulness of the NDNAD by enacting legislation to enable DNA samples to be taken from offenders in custody. Since 2001 suspects who have been charged with, or reported for, a crime have had their DNA sampled and held on the NDNAD even when they have not been convicted of any offence. This provision has been challenged as contrary to the European Convention on Human Rights, but so far English judges have decided that in this case the greater good of society takes precedence over individuals' rights because of the number of cases that would not have been detected otherwise, including a number of murders and rapes.[9] However, Chief Constables do have the power to request the removal of a DNA sample from the NDNAD in exceptional circumstances.

The Criminal Justice Act 2003 included a provision making it compulsory for the police to take DNA samples from any person arrested, and these powers were enacted in April 2004. Other provisions have also been made, such as in the Serious Organised Crime and Police Act 2005 which included amendments to the Police and Criminal Evidence Act (PACE) 1984 to allow the NDNAD to be used to try to identify a deceased person where the person has died of natural causes or as a result of a disaster (ACPO 2005a).

The police may now obtain samples from individuals who have been arrested, or charged, for a recordable offence, as well as individuals who agree to provide samples voluntarily to aid an investigation, for example by eliminating their DNA from a crime scene, because they were a victim of a crime where there was personal contact between the victim and suspect, or as part of an intelligence-led screen. For volunteers, written consent is needed and consent, once given, cannot be withdrawn. The general principle is that DNA, once placed on the NDNAD, cannot be removed without good reason, even following the death of the individual from whom it was taken.

### Performance management of forensic science

The performance management approach has been applied broadly to the public sector over the past few decades and in particular to the police service since the 1990s. In 2002 the Home Office established the Police Standards Unit and developed the Police Performance Framework to drive improvements in police performance designed, in the longer term, to reduce crime. Improving the use of forensic science is one way in which the police can improve detection rates and ensure more offenders are brought to justice by providing evidence to support the Criminal Justice System. The significant cost of forensic resources which, in their earlier stages, restricted their use to serious crime meant that performance statistics on forensic use were limited in nature; however, the increasingly large-scale use of forensics with improved returns on the investment enabled the inclusion of forensic utilisation data in performance measures.

The performance framework in the early years faced a significant challenge because many individual police forces were ill-prepared to collate and track such information accurately and unable to provide data comparable to other forces. The absence of any forensic IT system metadata collection meant that pulling data together was hugely time-consuming and the derived data were often inaccurate. Differences in approaches to crimes, definitions, and even the functions within forensic units meant that there were differences in the interpretation of the definitions informing the datasets. However, during the past five years, the investment of considerable time, money and energy has led to an improvement in this situation. ACPO led a review of the forensic indicators and together with the HMIC created a set of performance indicators for forensic science. These form part of the Police Performance Assessment Framework (PPAF) Baseline Assessment, *Improving Forensic Performance*.[10] The Specific Grading Criteria for this area range from the percentage of crime scenes attended and the percentage of fingerprint recovery from crime scenes, to the percentage of DNA matches from recovered evidence and whether the case resulted in detection.[11]

The inclusion of these data as part of force inspections and grading criteria meant that the issue began to be taken seriously by senior officers, as it could impact on the overall grading of the force and potentially lead to penalties or intervention by the Police Standards Unit. There was also increasing recognition of the need to track forensic cases to understand the effect on the outcome of a case, to match costs against cases to ensure forensic science was being used most efficiently for greatest effect, and to gear forensic work towards timelier end-to-end turnaround times to improve overall performance. This has resulted in more forces investing in software systems to support the functions of the forensic units; some of these directly link to, or were part of, force crime recording systems, while others are stand-alone systems with separate data warehousing.

The more standardised dataset required for performance management has enabled the use of comparison tools such as IQuanta in order to compare forces with one another, especially with those in their 'most similar' groups (Green 2007). Initial challenges about data integrity are mostly overcome or acknowledged, and this has now resulted in a more robust approach enabling forces to compare their own performance and seek out best practice. In many forces this has been implemented internally as well as externally, with many forensic staff having individual attendance and identification targets, and in some cases meeting these targets is directly linked to performance-related pay.

It has been recognised that these data, and the subsequent inter-force comparisons they enable, provide the most useful tools for acquiring investment, either from the force or from central funding. Finance is generally only provided if there is a commitment by the recipient to achieve a particular performance outcome within an agreed timescale. It is now possible to benchmark performance before and after, and demonstrate more convincingly the impact of forensic science.

In 2004 the Home Office's Police Standards Unit (PSU) introduced the Scientific Work Improvement Model (SWIM), a performance improvement work package for maximising the efficiency of forensic processes using computer simulation. This introduced the concept of process modelling by using an IT tool to enable the simulation of forensic processes, which enables the identification of bottlenecks and also the management of resources and timescales at each stage of the process. SWIM has achieved many real-life successes in increasing the levels of forensic identification and detections, maximising the investigative value of evidence, and increasing the cost-effectiveness of the process, and it is now rolled out nationally across 41 out of 43 police forces in England and Wales.[12] The resulting changes introduced range from investment in Scene of Crime (SOC) deployment and Tasking Units, amalgamations of SOC offices and stations, and changes to working practices and shift patterns in order to match demand. For example, Kent Police achieved significant improvements in forensic workload by realigning their fingerprint bureau shift pattern around peak times for custody.

## The forensic marketplace

Over the past decade police investment in forensics has become substantial, although remaining in percentage terms a small component of the police force budget. Spending has increased not only on forensics within police forces, with the expansion of in-house expertise and forensic staff, but also on external companies being contracted to provide specialist services. For example, Thames Valley Police spent in 2002/03 a total of £5.4 million on forensics, in 2003/04 £4.8 million, in 2004/05 £5.5 million, in 2005/06 £5.9 million, in 2006/07 £5.3 million, and in 2007/08 nearly £5.3 million – comprising between 1.5–2.0 per cent of the total annual budget.

External forensic providers have therefore also seen a huge rise in business from the police, thanks to the increased demand for forensics. To meet this new demand, existing forensic companies had to expand facilities to increase capacity. They have also capitalised on the changes to the status of the FSS which provided more opportunities for other companies to enter the market.

In 2003 the Metropolitan Police and Thames Valley Police for the first time undertook a competitive tendering process for their forensic custom, and the next year Surrey, Kent and Sussex police forces all followed suit. Formal tendering for forensic services has a significant implication for police resources, because of the need to establish beforehand technical specifications, ensure quality control and accreditation, and predict levels of demand to allow the bidding company to accurately cost and plan capacity. Security and vetting of external providers is a significant issue given that the services being procured end up as key evidential material in criminal courts.

Because of the exacting technical and security requirements the current UK forensic marketplace does not have a large number of suppliers. The barriers to entering the market are quite high, including the substantial set-up costs, the need to retain experienced specialists who are in high demand, the need to acquire accreditation and a good reputation among very risk-averse customers, and the fluctuating priorities and direction of the police forces themselves. This environment limits to some extent the real benefits to be gained from the ostensibly free-market approach.

The increasing reliance of the police on national forensic databases means that commercial forensic providers see the ownership of such databases as a crucial factor in making their services indispensable to police forces. The databases offer access to collated results which can provide a selling-point. Any move away from using these providers in the future could therefore potentially result in lost intelligence opportunities, which might be risky for a police force, whilst on the other hand a force may shift their custom to a provider with a larger customer base to maximise the forensic intelligence 'pool' available. Such issues have led to an ongoing debate over who 'owns' the forensic intelligence: the company which has obtained the forensic result, or the forces who have submitted the samples for analysis. This debate is still very current.

It is clearly beneficial for forces to collaborate together to tender for forensic services jointly. By operating within an umbrella of common terms and conditions, and mutual requirements, the lengthy tendering process can be made more efficient and effective for all parties, including the suppliers. This has proved to be a complex process as significant alignment of currently differing force practices needs to be achieved alongside close partnership working with suppliers to identify requirements that will meet force needs for transparency and financial control without compromising quality. This collaborative approach will be developed further with plans for a National Forensic Procurement process. However, collaborating creates a super-size customer which cannot always be accommodated by some smaller suppliers. This means that some forces will have to become more open to multiple suppliers rather than the more unilateral approach. If not, then smaller suppliers will not be able to stay within the market, and the shrinking number of providers will drive prices up, reversing all of the progress in service improvement and price reduction that has been achieved over the past five years. Collaboration amongst the suppliers could also be a potentially attractive strategy.

The relationships between external forensic suppliers and police forces are still very much developing and there are both risks and benefits for each side to take into account. The key tension for forensic providers is the need to maintain efficiency and a high quality of service for volume crime cases, balanced against the sometimes overwhelming pressure to achieve urgent forensic results, whatever the cost, for some key major crime cases. These can occur with short notice and severely disrupt laboratory planning and strategy. For example, the re-analysis of the forensic exhibits in the well-known Damilola Taylor case (Rawley and Caddy 2007) exposed several human failings resulting from the FSS being overwhelmed with urgent requests to analyse more than 400 items related to the case and a lack of clear communication between the FSS and police to manage the expectations of both parties: 'It is common ground that when the police want something done urgently they do not wish excellence to be compromised' (ibid: 3).

Such cases highlighted the need for a clear forensic strategy to be developed between forces and suppliers, with open sharing of results, progress and issues and good communication at the right levels. Such a partnership approach is essential to maintain public confidence in forensic evidence. In 2006 the Home Office announced that it intended to establish a Forensic Science Regulator to preserve the integrity and reputation of forensic science use in the Criminal Justice System, by ensuring that the expanding forensic market provides the right services, at the right price and delivered to an appropriate standard.[13] The Regulator post commenced officially in February 2008 and since that time significant progress has been made in raising the awareness of the Quality standards debate and achieving clarity and consistency across the various standards and competency-related agendas.

There are some tensions in police forces over the extent to which they wish to use the external forensic market rather than seek to establish internal service provision. Many police forces are now evaluating the potential benefits of shifting from external suppliers to in-house provision, partly due to issues over forensic provider service levels and increases in spending on external forensic services, compared to the cost of acquiring their own equipment and a desire to integrate all aspects of forensic processes. It may be more cost-effective to create facilities within the police for initial screening, for example, and for volume crime cases. Most police forces now undertake their own footwear screening and coding, only using the forensic provider for evidential work, and some forces are looking to extend into evidential work also. Lancashire Constabulary and some other forces have had their own 'forensic screening' facilities for some time. They are able to undertake basic forensic screening in order to reduce submissions to the laboratory, alongside forensic recovery such as swabbing or fibre taping. In March 2007 West Midlands Police opened a £5 million Forensic Unit which, in addition to co-locating all of their services under one roof, is to undertake similar kinds of forensic screening. Their drugs screening and firearms analysts work to the same accredited standards as those of the current forensic suppliers. However, a key issue for police forces will be to ensure that accreditation standards and quality are maintained; and there are also issues over continuing levels of funding in the future.

This shift on the part of police forces means that external forensic providers have to adapt to keep up, either to provide better deals and opportunities for working with forces that might reduce the level of force investment in their own units, or to realign their business strategies to avoid investing in areas which might later become a risk. However, there will remain a role for external forensic providers, because whilst there may be some aspects of the work that can be undertaken in-house, there will be an ongoing requirement for high-level technical skills for more complicated processes and the need for independent expertise, especially in high-profile cases, and also for evidential casework in court.

## Managing forensic resources in police forces

We have touched briefly on some of the changing aspects of managing forensic resources within police forces and it is worth discussing in more depth how new roles and management approaches have developed over time. The role of 'Scientific Support Manager' was established in all police forces in England and Wales in response to the Touche Ross (1987) Report. This role was responsible for the delivery of all internal force forensic provision, such as Scenes of Crime and Fingerprints, along with the task of managing the significant levels of budgets and spend required to support the forensic service provision by the external forensic suppliers. The Scientific Support Manager was also given responsibility for the provision of annual statistics returned to the Home Office, compiling data on force forensic resources as well as the numbers of internal and external forensic submissions and the subsequent outcome of such submission by crime type. This information, combined with the data from the DNA Expansion Programme, provided the evidential foundations for key reports such as Her Majesty's Inspectorate of Constabulary (2000) report *Under the Microscope* and later *Under the Microscope Refocused* (HMIC 2002).

*Under the Microscope* brought to general attention the potential benefits of a wider use of forensic science in criminal investigations, alongside a fairly damning exposure of the failure of police forces to use forensic resources effectively: 'It is regrettable that the inspection found not only that the advice of Using Forensic Science Effectively had frequently not been acted upon, but also that, even more regrettably, the failure to respond was a product of ignorance of its contents' (HMIC 2000). The far-reaching recommendations in the 2000 report heavily influenced the ACPO view of the use of forensics and the necessity for a 'forensic strategy' within forces. The recommendations were:

- ACPO and chief officers should ensure that their strategies and supporting policies on the use of forensic science to tackle volume crime are up to date and known and understood by operational officers;

- Chief officers should urgently review their systems to ensure that sampling policies are both clearly understood and implemented;

- Chief officers should make sure that systems are in place to comply with Home Office requirements on the National DNA database and Data Protection Act 1998. An audit of the National DNA database should be undertaken to help in this process;

- ACPO and the Home Office should develop and provide a list of approved technical equipment for use by forces and guidance on the procurement of such equipment.

The report ushered in a pivotal change in forensic management within police forces, and in some forces proved a turning-point by raising the profile of forensics to chief officer level, with increasing scrutiny and engagement at a senior level. However, the review of the 2000 report (HMIC 2002) based on self-assessment by forces concluded that there had been a mixed response and that there would need to be consistent attention given to the matter by HMIC at Force and Basic Command Unit (BCU) inspection level. This approach and concern continues today, with the 'effective management of forensic investigations' forming a significant section of the HMIC's Baseline Assessment process within the 'Investigation of Crime' domain.[14] Publishing these performance ratings results by the HMIC resulted in increased focus on the use and management of force forensic resources and added to the overall momentum for reform.

Projects such as Pathfinder and the DNA Expansion Programme demonstrated the advantages to be gained by introducing new forensic roles and expertise into police forces to work closely with external specialists. In the past the police input was fairly basic in terms of cordoning off the scene of crime and fingerprinting, with external specialists coming in as expert consultants. Current best practice is, in contrast, to have the roles of police and scientists working closely together within a team throughout the investigation process.

Thanks to the funding provided by the DNA Expansion Programme, which was ring-fenced for forensic science use, police forces began to acquire new staff and establish new forensic specialist roles, such as Volume Crime Scene Investigators. While it is difficult to quantify nationally the impact of the DNA Expansion Programme in increasing the numbers of SOCOs employed by police forces, in Thames Valley Police there was a 17 per cent increase in SOCOs and this is not to be seen as unusual: a national increase of between 15–20 per cent would be a reasonable conjecture.

The combined drivers of the HMIC and Home Office reviews of the use of forensic science, increased funding and increased numbers of specialist staff provided forensic managers with the increased visibility and broader awareness at senior levels which enabled them to secure additional funding and resources. In some forces forensic resources increased by some 20 per cent overall over a period of only a few years. Of course, such a rapid increase in recruitment resulted in high levels of demand for training, which soon outstripped supply, leading to something of a time-lag between increased resources from 2000 and improvements in the performance data. This is why it was only by 2002/03 that the data showed a sharp increase in crime scene attendance, DNA hits and fingerprint identifications.

The new roles that were created were able to develop in-house forensic strategy and expertise, and work operationally alongside external forensic scientists to ensure that the strategy reflects the investigative requirements (and that the level of expenditure is appropriate for a particular investigation). Increasing the availability of this forensic expertise also allows forensic techniques to be utilised at a much earlier stage of a police investigation, to provide intelligence and support the decision-making process. Alongside this development, Senior Investigating Officers themselves are now formally trained in the use of forensic science. This ensures that there is a good understanding at all levels of an investigation of the use being made of forensic science and the conclusions being drawn from the results.

These changes in the organisation of forensic science support for serious crime investigation are reflected in how resources are used in volume crime investigations. Police officers and support staff are the primary scene investigators, and in some forces they may actually be the only member of the force attending the scene in cases of burglary, car theft and criminal damage. The SOCO or Crime Scene Investigator will deal with the seizure and submission of all potential forensic evidence, typically including fibres, marks (such as tool or footwear) and trace evidence as well as any sources of DNA evidence and finger marks which could be used for identifying the suspect. In the UK, the processing of finger marks and sometimes footprints will be carried out by members of the police forces that recovered the material from scenes of crime, who will then recommend whether to submit material to external forensic providers for DNA and other forensic testing. This partnership approach is based on a sound knowledge of expected success rates of sample types matched against the crime type, and is designed to maximise the use of limited police resources.

This approach to volume crime is designed to manage the forensic investigation of high-frequency cases in a way that ensures resilience for the rarer, high-profile major crime investigations. Police forensic resources are monitored and controlled in order to ensure that sufficient resources are always available for these major crime investigations, which usually require lengthy and costly forensic inputs which may run to hundreds of thousands of pounds of forensic work. The forensic costs for the Soham murder investigation in Cambridgeshire, admittedly an unusual case, ran to many millions of pounds.

For volume crime cases, specialised forensic scientists from an external agency such as the FSS rarely attend the scene of crime, and are often only minimally involved during the investigation process. This means that such providers are able to manage their resources to develop expertise in major crime investigation. This is analogous to the modern provision of medical services in which nurses now attend to many patients in General Practice (GP) surgeries, with the authority to dispense and diagnose in certain cases, so that doctors' time is concentrated on seriously ill patients. Even minor operations can be carried out within community hospitals and GP surgeries.

This move towards in-house service provision was seen as an opportunity for many forces to broaden the skill base of the fingerprint staff, as new technologies in the fingerprint field created more capacity. Internal provision becomes more of an invisible cost, which means that forces begin to routinely check crimes for fingerprints to attempt to identify offenders before submitting evidence for DNA testing. DNA testing becomes one of a menu of options which can be applied if appropriate to the case.

### Forensic science and the National Intelligence Model

The police National Intelligence Model (NIM) is a business model which seeks to ensure that all types of information are fully researched, developed and analysed, provide intelligence that senior managers can use for strategic purposes, make tactical resourcing decisions about operational policing, and manage risk. The NIM was developed by the National Criminal Intelligence Service (NCIS) on behalf of ACPO and began to be implemented in 2000 (NCIS 2000). The *ACPO Code of Practice on the National Intelligence Model* was issued in 2005 as part of the Police Reform Act 2002, and provides a statutory basis for the NIM minimum standards which were originally published in 2003 and revised in November 2004 (ACPO 2005b: 8). The model's basic principle is that police forces should be intelligence-led in resource allocation and decision-making.

Forensic science is one of the 'source assets' which can contribute useful information as part of the NIM:

> Crime scene investigators should take an active role in intelligence and T&CG (Tasking and Co-ordination Group) processes to ensure that forensic information held at a local or force level is captured for intelligence analysis. Forensic evidence such as paint transfer, DNA, fingerprints, fibre transfer and tool marks are increasingly used to link scenes to each other as well as to suspects. These links are essential in identifying a crime series. To ensure the capture and management of intelligence, forensic information held at a national level should be subject to agreed protocols. (ACPO 2005b: 34)

The development outlined previously in the creation of the NDNAD and other national databases such as IDENT1 meant that forensic science is increasingly well adapted to contribute significant information as part of the NIM. National DNA database hits can link offences which occur across police force boundaries, thereby making it a particularly useful tool for intelligence and data-sharing on cross-border crime series. Database hits and matches across forces are circulated to all forces involved, leading to a more joined up response especially in identifying patterns in serial offences. West Midlands Police developed and promoted the use of the Forensic Led Intelligence System (FLINTS) to make more efficient use of the huge amounts of forensic intelligence gathered at crime scenes and from criminals, by compiling intelligence and forensic results and making it easier to spot links which otherwise might have gone unnoticed.[15] While the concept of linking forensic information had been recognised in the Pathfinder project, the FLINTS approach went much further, linking normal crime intelligence, potential offenders, their associates, and *modus operandi* information with forensic results. The types of forensic results included DNA, fingerprints, footwear, tool marks and contact trace evidence. FLINTS was successful in linking volume crime series, such as burglary and vehicle crime, and its success was a significant factor in promoting its use in other forces. Often the evidence in a single case would be unlikely to secure a conviction, but the association of offences by the use of such techniques has enabled conspiracy charges to be brought against potential offenders. In addition, the use of forensic linking enables the quicker identification of a series of offences likely to be by the same, unknown offender or offenders.

The use of the NIM requires resources throughout the police force to be 'intelligence-led', this includes forensic resources. For example, when a linked series is identified, it should be given a response priority as a successful investigation would have the greatest impact on reducing the crime rate by interrupting a prolific offender. Provided that the forensic staff responsible for resource management are present in local police Tasking and Co-ordination

Group meetings, the management of forensic resources and process can remain closely linked in to the intelligence picture, for example being flexible about the timing and delivery of forensic submission, and the subsequent response to the results. This approach is, to some degree, adopted by forensic units in all forces in England and Wales. Those with force-wide Forensic Resource Management units (SOCO Control Rooms) are able to adopt local policies and so appropriately direct resources out at the time of the crime being reported, in accordance with a NIM-developed forensic strategy, ensuring a much more rapid and dynamic response than had been achievable previously.

## Future trends for forensic science in police investigation

Forensic results are increasingly being required in very short time, as a fast-moving investigation develops, because the information it can provide could be crucial to the rapid resolution of a case. This is especially the case for high-profile situations or critical incidents, for example a suspected kidnap where a rapid forensic result could be a life-or-death factor in the outcome of the case. While this is an extreme instance, police investigations generally are now more rapid, dynamic, and fast-paced and limited resources need to be allocated according to the best available information.

Improvements in technology are making this sort of quick response more feasible, with developments such as Livescan, a system of capturing fingerprints electronically in the custody office, and 'Lab in a Van', a forensic response vehicle developed by the Forensic Science Service to provide some forensic services directly to a crime scene rather than removing samples for later analysis in the lab. Finger marks can now be lifted at the scene and transferred remotely to the database for analysis, giving the possibility of a virtually instant 'hit' on the name of a potential offender. Using the Livescan technology in custody units means that the identity of detainees can be confirmed, and their fingerprints be searched against the database to see whether there are links to other offences, before an interview even commences – giving a significant advantage to the interviewing officer. These sorts of improvements demonstrate the contribution that forensic science can make to the early stages of an investigation and provide opportunities for even greater use of forensics in policing (Mennell and Shaw 2006).

Apart from these technological developments, there are resource management issues to be addressed. The increasingly routine recovery of forensic evidence has had a significant impact in custody units where, previously, forensic recovery simply meant taking a wet set of fingerprints from detainees, but the introduction of new technology such as Livescan means that further investment is needed in staff, technological equipment, training and new custody building projects. Significant central funding was provided in 2006 alongside a national procurement process to enable all forces to install Livescan technology within their key custody sites, which means that Livescan has now become widespread. The new demands placed on custody units have coincided with a number of forces outsourcing custody services to private companies.

In addition to the use of the Livescan technology, custody staff must undertake DNA sampling of all arrestees who are not on the NDNAD, as well as seizing footwear for comparison against force databases. There is support for a national project to bring together all these aspects of detainees[1] forensic recovery into a manageable and efficient process. If this could be extended to using the 'Lab in a Van' technology, there is the potential for a suspect's DNA to be searched immediately against the NDNAD while they are still in custody, with obvious benefits for the police. The potential savings in police officer time further down the line are tremendous, in interviewing through to charging and case preparation for court. Whilst we are some way from achieving this today, it is necessary to put the foundations in place now in order to allow us to exploit the developments as soon as the technology gives us the opportunity.

Another key challenge for forces will be to manage increasing demand without substantially increasing the costs, by looking for potential efficiency savings. These might be in the form of in-house service provision, as discussed previously, and as many as 15 forces are planning to establish or expand their own forensic services over the next few years. The other main area for improvement is in gaining economies of scale by increasing collaboration and taking advantage of joint investment between police forces, perhaps up to a regional level.

### Increasing collaboration between police forces

We have drawn an analogy between the Health Service and developments in forensic science at various points in the argument. It is interesting that the latest government proposals for the amalgamation of large hospitals as 'centres of excellence' for serious conditions and illness types bear a striking similarity to the proposals made in 2005–2006 which aimed to merge some smaller police forces to create larger 'Strategic Forces'. In October 2005, following the Denis O'Connor (2005) report, *Closing the Gap*, the Home Secretary announced the Strategic Forces Programme and wrote to all forces directing them to review options for mergers within ACPO regions, or to justify that they were already a Strategic Force in their own right. A Strategic Force would be expected to have in-house capability to manage more serious and cross-border crime.

Despite a significant amount of work on the mergers plan by police forces, the proposals have for the moment been abandoned by the Home Office following a change of Home Secretary. In the wake of the failed mergers plan the focus for the Home Office and police forces has been on maximising efficiency and effectiveness by collaborating between forces where there are advantages to be gained.

Forensic services were identified very early on as an area with considerable potential for collaborative working. The increased development of remote and mobile technology, especially the use of digital technology, has meant that traditional services such as Fingerprint Bureaux, Imaging Units and Fingerprint Laboratories no longer have to be located within a force's geographical area. The use of technology such as Livescan has resulted in a requirement for round-the-clock routine fingerprint services that was not necessary before, and it would be difficult for each force to meet this demand individually without huge additional investment: however, a group of police forces, perhaps within a region, could achieve this with minimum additional costs and perhaps even some savings in the reduction of management roles.

In many ACPO regions this concept was embraced, with Scientific Support Managers often more keen to progress initiatives and proposals than their chief officers. This has resulted in a somewhat confused picture of development nationally that would benefit significantly from a level of cohesion and consistency. Although the benefits are clear, a steer is needed nationally towards achieving a common approach to the management of forensic service provisions – this would require some current programmes to be put on hold while other forces catch up, for example, by matching IT systems to ensure interoperability, which is an expensive process. Unfortunately the current financial climate militates against achieving this desirable outcome. Forces are increasingly under pressure to make significant savings at all levels, and police staff roles are being cut in order to maintain the numbers of frontline police officers. In such a climate, there is a risk that the best possible outcome for forensic services will drop off the agenda.

The National Police Improvement Agency (NPIA) commenced in April 2007 and is responsible for the modernisation and future direction of police services. Within this agency there will be a lead Forensic Role and it is hoped that this role will finally facilitate shared working across all police forces, with the aim of a cohesive framework for forensic service provision across the Criminal Justice System. Close partnership working is essential along with trust at all levels. This is also a challenging task; but provided there is support from the police forensic community much can be achieved through this structure. However difficult it might be, it has been recognised as vital to the future development of forensic science in policing.

## Conclusion

This chapter has examined the many complex factors that influence the use of forensic resources within criminal investigations, and considered the various ways in which the provision of forensic science support to policing has been shaped. However, what can be glimpsed are small parts of a continuously evolving picture. New structures in place such as the NPIA, the drive for collaboration between forces, and the desire to establish new forensic services within forces all mean that this picture will continue to change. With careful management these changes have the potential to produce further improvements in the quality and level of service, and the forensic contribution to criminal investigations.

Britain has long been established as one of the most effective users of forensic science in all levels of criminal investigation, with many other countries aspiring to set up processes which follow the model established in this country. The instigation of standards and processes, professional training and competency frameworks, government funding and support, alongside the services of credible and knowledgeable suppliers has served to support this. This high reputation must be maintained whatever the developments in the future.

## Notes

1  Home Office press release 26/07/04 '"Cold Cases" to be cracked in DNA clampdown', online at: http://press.homeoffice.gov.uk/press-releases/'Coldcases'_ To_Be_Cracked_In_Dna?version=1
2  Home Office press release 12/07/05 '"Cold Cases" Cracked – one year on', online at: http://police.homeoffice.gov.uk/news-and-events/news/pr-120705?version=1
3  Forensic Science Service press release 21/03/06 'Ripper Hoaxer trapped by DNA', online at: http://www.forensic.gov.uk/forensic_t/inside/news/list_press_release. php?case=48&y=2006
4  http://www.forensic.gov.uk/forensic_t/inside/FOI/class/documents/ Historyfactsheet.pdf
5  Dr Kathryn Mashiter, Lancashire Police, *Regional Seminar: Narrowing the Justice Gap* presentation, 10 December 2003, and personal communication.
6  http://www.forensic.gov.uk/forensic_t/inside/news/list_casefiles.php?case=1
7  http://www.homeoffice.gov.uk/science-research/using-science/dna-database/
8  Forensic Science Service press release 05/12/05 'Move to GovCo', online at: http://www.forensic.gov.uk/forensic_t/inside/news/list_press_release. php?case=44&y=2005
9  Lords of Appeal judgement in the case of *R v. Chief Constable of South Yorkshire Police (Respondent)* ex parte *Marper (FC) (Appellant)*, July 2004. Online at: http:// www.publications.parliament.uk/pa/ld200304/ldjudgmt/jd040722/york-1.htm
10  http://inspectorates.homeoffice.gov.uk/hmic/docs/ba2006frmwk/3d-fmwk- ba2006.pdf?view=Binary
11  http://inspectorates.homeoffice.gov.uk/hmic/docs/3e.pdf?view=Binary
12  http://police.homeoffice.gov.uk/operational-policing/technology-equipment/ forensic-science/
13  http://police.homeoffice.gov.uk/operational-policing/forensic-science-regulator/ about-the-regulator/
14  http://inspectorates.homeoffice.gov.uk/hmic/methodologies/baseline- introduction/
15  http://www.cwn.org.uk/999/west-midlands-police/2001/01/010126-flint-system. htm

## References

ACPO (Association of Chief Police Officers) (2000) *Murder Investigation Manual* (Restricted). Centrex, now NPIA.
ACPO (Association of Chief Police Officers) (2001) *Investigation of Volume Crime Manual*. Online at: http://www.acpo.police.uk/asp/policies/Data/volume_crime_manual. doc
ACPO (Association of Chief Police Officers) (2005a) *DNA Good Practice Manual* (2nd edn). Online at: http://www.acpo.police.uk/asp/policies/Data/dna_good_practice_ manual_2005.doc
ACPO (Association of Chief Police Officers) (2005b) *Guidance on the National Intelligence Model*. Joint Centrex and ACPO publication. Online at: http://www.acpo.police.uk/ asp/policies/Data/nim2005.pdf

Barclay, D., Leary, R. and Rankin, B. (1997) *Using Forensic Science Effectively*. Forensic Science Service, ACPO and Home Office.

Barnett, P.D. (2001) *Ethics in Forensic Science: Professional Standards for the Practice of Criminalistics*. London and New York: CRC Press.

Bradbury, S. and Feist, A. (2005) *The use of forensic science in volume crime investigations: a review of the research literature*. Home Office Online Report 43/05. Online at: http://www.homeoffice.gov.uk/rds/pdfs05/rdsolr4305.pdf

Burrows, J, Tarling, R., Mackie, A., Poole, H. and Hodgson, B. (2005) *Forensic Science Pathfinder Project: evaluating increased forensic activity in two English police forces*. Home Office Online Report 46/05. Online at: http://www.homeoffice.gov.uk/rds/pdfs05/rdsolr4605.pdf

Dale, W.M. and Becker, W.S. (2007) *The Crime Scene: How forensic science works*. New York: Kaplan.

Fido, M. and Skinner, K. (2000) *The Official Encyclopaedia of Scotland Yard: Behind the Scenes at Scotland Yard*. London: Virgin Books.

Green, R. (2007) 'Forensic investigation in the UK', in T. Newburn, T. Williamson and A. Wright (eds), *Handbook of Criminal Investigation*, Part 3, Chapter 13, pp. 338–356. Devon: Willan Publishing.

HMIC (Her Majesty's Inspectorate of Constabulary) (2000) *Under the Microscope: An HMIC Thematic Inspection Report on Scientific and Technical Support*. London: HMIC. Online at: http://inspectorates.homeoffice.gov.uk/hmic/inspections/thematic/utm/

HMIC (Her Majesty's Inspectorate of Constabulary) (2002) *Under the Microscope Refocused: A Revisit to the Thematic Inspection Report on Scientific and Technical Support*. London: HMIC. Online at: http://inspectorates.homeoffice.gov.uk/hmic/inspections/thematic/utm/microsco.pdf?view=Binary

HMIC (Her Majesty's Inspectorate of Constabulary (2005) *Closing the Gap: A review of the 'fitness for purpose' of the current structure of policing in England and Wales*. London: HMIC. Online at: http://police.homeoffice.gov.uk/publications/police-reform/ClosingtheGap 2005.pdf?view=Binary

Home Office (2005) *DNA Expansion Programme 2000 – 2005: Reporting achievement*. Forensic Science and Pathology Unit. Online at: http://police.homeoffice.gov.uk/news-and-publications/publication/operational-policing/DNAExpansion.pdf?view=Binary

Home Office (2006) National DNA Database Annual Report 2005/06. Online at: http://www.homeoffice.gov.uk/documents/DNA-report2005-06.pdf?view=Binary

Jackson, A. and Jackson, J. (2008) *Forensic Science: Second Edition*. London: Pearson Education Ltd.

Jobling, M. and Gill, P. (2004) 'Encoded evidence: DNA in forensic analysis', *Nature Reviews: Genetics*, Volume 5, October 2004: 739–752. Onlie at: http://www.le.ac.uk/ge/maj4/JoblingGill04.NRG.Forensics.pdf

Lee, H. and Tirnady, F. (2003) *Blood Evidence: How DNA is Revolutionizing the Way We Solve Crimes*. USA: Perseus Books.

McCartney, C. (2006) 'The DNA Expansion Programme and Criminal Investigation', *British Journal of Criminology*, 46 (2): 175–192.

McFarland, R. (2003) *Review of the Forensic Science Service*. London: Home Office.

Maguire, C.N. and Hope, C.A. (2006) 'DNA automation, expert systems, quality and productivity: the benefits to the FSS, the police forces and the community', *International Journal of Productivity and Quality Management* (IJPQM), 1 (4): 397–410. Buckinghamshire, England: Interscience Publishers.

Mennell, J. and Shaw, I. (2006) 'The Future of Forensic and Crime Scene Science Part I: A UK forensic science user and provider perspective', *Forensic Science International*, Vol. 157, Supplement 1: 7–12. Ireland: Elsevier.

NCIS (National Criminal Intelligence Service) (2000) *The National Intelligence Model*. Online at: http://police.homeoffice.gov.uk/news-and-publications/publication/operational-policing/nim-introduction?view=Binary

O'Connor, D. (2005), *Closing the Gap: A Review of the Fitness for Purpose of the Current Structure of Policing in England and Wales*. HMIC.

Rawley, A. and Caddy B. (2007) *Damilola Taylor: An Independent Review of Forensic Examination of evidence by the Forensic Science Service*. London: Home Office. Online at: http://www.homeoffice.gov.uk/documents/damilola-taylor-review-2007?view=Binary

Select Committee on Science and Technology (2005) *Seventh Report*. Online at: http://www.publications.parliament.uk/pa/cm200405/cmselect/cmsctech/96/9602.htm

Tilley, N. and Ford, A. (1996) *Forensic Science and Crime Investigation*. London: Home Office. Online at: http://www.nationalarchives.gov.uk/ERORecords/HO/415/1/prgpubs/fcdps73.pdf

Touche Ross (1987) *Review of Scientific Support for the Police*. Vols. 1–3. London: Home Office.

Wambough, J. (1989) *The Blooding: True Story of the Narborough Village Murders*. London: Bantam Press.

Zagorski, N. (2006) Profile of Alec J. Jeffreys. *Proceedings of the National Academy of Science of the United States of America*, Vol. 103, No. 22. Online at http://www.pnas.org/cgi/content/full/103/24/8918

# Chapter 12

# DNA databases

*Bob Bramley*

The United Kingdom has been at the forefront of developments in DNA profiling and has the most enabling legislation in the world for the taking, retention and use of DNA samples. It had the first DNA database for use in criminal investigations and still has, proportionately, per head of population, the largest in the world. This chapter sets out how the DNA technology developed in tandem with the legislation in the United Kingdom and how the National DNA Database (NDNAD) has grown and attracted considerable government investment because of its demonstrable impact. The governance arrangements for the NDNAD are described. Attention is drawn to the commensurate development of DNA databases in Scotland and Northern Ireland, and wider international comparisons are made with developments in Europe and the United States of America. The chapter concludes with a discussion of some of the contemporary issues being addressed.

## Development of DNA profiling in the United Kingdom

DNA 'fingerprinting' was developed by Dr Alec Jeffreys, a geneticist at the University of Leicester. He was able to demonstrate that he could achieve high levels of discrimination between blood samples from different individuals by restriction fragment length polymorphism (RFLP) analysis of the variable number of tandem repeat (VNTR) sections found in the non-coding part of their nuclear DNA (see Jeffreys, Wilson and Thein 1985a and 1985b). The application of DNA profiling to forensic science was first described by Gill, Jeffreys and Werrett (1985).

Early DNA profiling used the multilocus probe (MLP) RFLP approach which had a very high discriminating power of 1 in millions, but low sensitivity. It was also unsuitable for the analysis of mixtures of DNA from different individuals and very slow, taking several weeks to get a result. In 1990, there was a move to single locus probe (SLP) RFLP profiling. This was also highly discriminating, but slightly more sensitive and applicable to mixture analysis, although still very slow. In 1991, a technique employing the polymerase chain reaction (PCR) was introduced for the first time. PCR amplifies the DNA sections of interest by making many copies of them and PCR-based techniques are thus highly sensitive. PCR was first used for analysing the HLA DQ$\alpha$ gene and yielded results in days rather than weeks, but the match probability was very low, about 1 in 40. The main use of HLA DQ$\alpha$ profiling was therefore as an elimination tool.

A significant breakthrough in the use of DNA profiling for databasing purposes came in 1994, when Kimpton and others of the Forensic Science Service (FSS) developed the analysis of short tandem repeat (STR) loci, or microsatellites, using a multiplex PCR and polyacrylamide gel electrophoresis (see Kimpton *et al.* 1994). The STRs consisted of short repeating sequences of only 2–6 base pairs. The multiplex PCR technique gave increased sensitivity and speed of analysis; the use of polyacrylamide gel electrophoresis resulted in lower errors in measurement of the DNA fragment sizes and definitive designation of the allelic values; and the small size of the STRs enabled them to be recovered from old or degraded material as well as fresh samples. These attributes, and the relatively low cost of the analysis, were the essential requirements for databasing purposes.

At first, the FSS used a 'Quad' multiplex to test simultaneously for four STR loci (VWA, THO1, F13 and FES). This had a match probability of about 1 in 40,000 for full profiles from unrelated individuals. By early 1995, the FSS had developed the technique further and introduced a second generation multiplex, 'SGM' (see Sparkes *et al.* 1996). SGM tested for six STR loci (VWA, THO1, D8S1179, D18S51, D21S11 and FGA) and had a match probability of about 1 in 50 million. It also incorporated the amelogenin test for gender and became the technique on which the NDNAD was subsequently established. By 1999, however, it had become apparent that, given the size and anticipated growth of the NDNAD, the level of discrimination obtained using SGM would be insufficient to prevent an increasing number of adventitious or chance matches being obtained between profiles from crime scenes and profiles from persons unconnected with the offence. This led to the development by the FSS of a further multiplex, SGM Plus, which tested simultaneously for the six SGM markers, amelogenin and four new STR loci (D2S1338, D19S433, D3S1358 and D16S539), providing a reported match probability of less than 1 in 1 billion (1,000 million) (see Cotton *et al.* 2000). To date, and with almost 5 million persons now represented on the United Kingdom NDNAD, no adventitious matches between full SGM Plus profiles from unrelated individuals have been confirmed.

## Development and implementation of the legislative framework in England and Wales

*Police and Criminal Evidence Act 1984* Until the enactment of the Police and Criminal Evidence Act 1984 (PACE), the powers of the police to take samples from subjects were based on the common law and unclear. PACE differentiated between intimate samples (blood, semen or any other tissue fluid, urine, saliva or pubic hair, or a swab taken from a person's body orifice) and non-intimate samples (hair other than pubic hair, samples taken from a nail or under a nail, or swabs taken from any part of a person's body other than a body orifice).

Intimate samples (except urine) could only be taken by a registered medical practitioner and from a person who was in police detention, with their written consent and on the authority of a police officer of at least the rank of superintendent who had reasonable grounds for suspecting the involvement of the person in a serious arrestable offence and believed that the sample would tend to confirm or disprove the person's involvement. In any proceedings against that person where consent had been refused without good cause, the court or jury could draw such inferences from the refusal as appeared proper and treat the refusal as corroboration of any evidence against the person to which the refusal was material.

Non-intimate samples could be taken by a police officer. A person had to give written consent for the sample to be taken, unless they were in police detention, or held in custody by the police on the authority of a court, and an officer of at least the rank of superintendent had reasonable grounds for suspecting involvement of the person in a serious arrestable offence, believed that the sample would tend to confirm or disprove the person's involvement and authorised it to be taken without consent.

PACE required that any sample taken from a person suspected of having committed an offence had to be destroyed as soon as practicable after the conclusion of proceedings in which the person was cleared of the offence, or their discontinuance, or a decision was made not to prosecute and the person had admitted the offence and been dealt with by way of a caution. Any sample taken in connection with the investigation of an offence from a person not suspected of having committed an offence had to be destroyed as soon as practicable after it had fulfilled the purpose for which it was taken.

*Proposals for a National DNA Database*   The FSS had established the first DNA database for use in criminal investigations by the early 1990s. This was based on SLP profiles from convicted persons where DNA had been used to secure their conviction. It was used for checking against profiles from unsolved crimes and achieved some success, although comparisons were not very easy where the profiles had been generated in different laboratories.

In 1992, in partnership with the police, the FSS agreed to carry out research into the feasibility of creating a national DNA database that would better help them identify potential offenders and establish intelligence links between different offences. This required consideration of the most appropriate DNA technology to use, the IT implications, the mode of operation of such a database and, of course, the costs involved in obtaining samples, profiling them and running the database. The outcome of this feasibility study was presented to the Royal Commission on Criminal Justice in 1992/93.

*Royal Commission on Criminal Justice: Runciman Report.*   The Royal Commission on Criminal Justice (1993) made several important recommendations: first, that Parliament should introduce appropriate legislation for an extension of police powers to allow the police to take a sample of hair (other than pubic hair) or saliva as non-intimate samples without consent; second, that intimate samples should be taken not just for serious arrestable offences but for less serious crimes as well; and third, that the samples should be used to create DNA databases to assist with criminal investigations and to help establish the statistical probability of matched samples. They also recommended that when a person was not proceeded against or was acquitted, the samples should not be used subsequently for investigative purposes.

*Criminal Justice and Public Order Act 1994* The Royal Commission's recommendations were incorporated in the Criminal Justice and Public Order Act (CJPOA), which commenced on 3 November 1994. This Act made a series of changes to PACE that went further than the Commission's recommendations. It classified plucked hair (with roots), a swab taken from any part of a person's body (including the mouth but not any other body orifice) and saliva as non-intimate samples. It also empowered police officers to obtain such samples from anyone who had been arrested, charged, reported for summons or convicted of any *recordable* offence (except where the decision at the outset was to deal with the person by way of caution), whether or not the samples were required for evidence in the particular case. A recordable offence is broadly one for which there could be a term of imprisonment – see National Police (Recordable Offences) Regulations 2000.

The person was not required to give consent for the taking of such non-intimate samples, whether or not they were in police custody, provided that they were convicted after 10 April 1995 of a recordable offence, or charged with a recordable offence, and no non-intimate sample had been taken from them previously or, if such a sample had been taken, it had proved not suitable for the same means of analysis or insufficient for such analysis. However, an intimate sample could still only be taken, with the person's consent and by a registered medical practitioner, but now, with the appropriate authority, also from a person not in police detention where in the course of an investigation two or more non-intimate samples had been taken which had proved to be insufficient. The provision that refusal to provide an intimate sample could be taken as corroboration of other evidence against the person was repealed.

If an intimate sample was taken at a police station with consent, or a non-intimate sample was taken at a police station with or without consent, the suspect also had to be informed that it may be the subject of a speculative search against other records. This allowed, for the first time, a sample taken in the course of one investigation to be compared with a sample taken in another investigation relating to a completely different offence, and paved the way for establishment of the NDNAD.

*Home Office Circular 16/95* There was no mention of a national DNA database in the CJPOA, but details for the establishment, operation and use of a national DNA database for England and Wales were issued at the same time as its implementation, in Home Office Circular 16/95. The NDNAD eventually came into existence in April 1995.

*Criminal Evidence Act 1997*   The Criminal Evidence Act 1997 subsequently allowed samples to be obtained from certain classes of prisoner and persons detained under the Mental Health Act.

*R v. B; R v. Weir*   Under the CJPOA, if the case against a person was discontinued or the person was acquitted, the DNA sample and profile had to be destroyed as soon as practicable, except where they related to an investigation involving samples taken from more than one person, one of whom had been convicted. However, information derived from any samples that were retained could not then be used in evidence against the person or for the purposes of the investigation of an offence. This worked reasonably well, but resulted in wasteful repeated sampling of multiple offenders. There was also often a significant delay in the police requesting destruction of a DNA sample and profile, during which time matches with profiles from other crimes were sometimes obtained illegally.

This situation was highlighted in two very serious cases, *R v. B* and *R v. Weir*, where convictions for rape and murder respectively were overturned on appeal on this 'technicality', despite compelling DNA evidence that linked the defendants to the offences. In both cases, without the DNA links, there would have been insufficient other evidence to put either suspect on trial. As a result, in the one case (*R v. B*) the judge refused to admit the evidence and the prosecution was abandoned, and in the other (*R v. Weir*) the conviction was quashed by the Court of Appeal on the grounds that the DNA evidence should not have been admitted. The House of Lords subsequently ruled that it should be left to the discretion of the trial judge as to whether or not to admit evidence in these circumstances, but the convictions were not reinstated (Attorney General 2001).

*Criminal Justice and Police Act 2001*   These cases caused considerable public concern and on 11 May 2001 PACE was further amended by the Criminal Justice and Police Act 2001 (CJPA) to remove the obligation for the police to destroy DNA samples and profiles in the event of there being an acquittal or no prosecution, so long as the samples had been lawfully obtained in the first instance. The Act also had retrospective effect, so that any DNA samples and profiles that should have been destroyed under the previous legislation but had not been destroyed could also be retained. In both circumstances the legislation was permissive, not obligatory, with Chief Constables having discretion to decide whether or not samples and profiles should be retained in individual cases. The CJPA introduced another significant change, allowing persons who had provided samples voluntarily (such as victims of an offence or members of a target population selected for inclusion in an intelligence-led screen for example), which hitherto could only be used in relation to the specific offence, to provide additional written consent for the samples to be retained and their DNA profiles to be speculatively searched against the NDNAD. But once given, their consent could not then be withdrawn.

On 1 January 2003, the Criminal Justice and Police Act (Commencement No. 8) Order 2002 came into force. This allowed non-intimate DNA samples to be retaken where the first sample had proved insufficient, and widened the term 'insufficient' to include circumstances where the first sample was lost, destroyed, contaminated or damaged, and where the analysis of the sample had produced no results or unreliable results.

*R v. Chief Constable of South Yorkshire* ex parte *S and Marper*   The provisions of PACE which permit Chief Constables to retain the DNA samples and profiles of suspects who have not been prosecuted or have been acquitted were challenged by way of judicial review. In the case of S, the DNA sample and profile had been retained after he had been found not guilty of attempted robbery. In the case of Marper, the DNA sample and profile had been retained after a charge of harassment of his partner had been dropped. Both appellants argued that the Chief Constable's decision breached Articles 8 and 14 of the European Convention on Human Rights. The Court of Appeal found that, although there was some breach of Article 8, it was proportionate and justified, and there was no breach of Article 14. The cases were appealed further to the House of Lords, where the decision of the lower Court was upheld in a judgement given in July 2004 (House of Lords 2004). A further appeal to the European Court of Human Rights was heard in February 2008 (see page 327).

*Police Reform Act 2002*   The Police Reform Act 2002 (PRA) contained provisions that allowed non-intimate samples to be taken by an authorised civilian detention officer as well as a police officer and intimate samples to be taken by any registered health care professional.

*Criminal Justice Act 2003/ Home Office Circular 020/2004*   The Criminal Justice Act 2003 (CJA) came into force on 5 April 2004 and widened the scope of DNA sampling significantly by allowing a DNA sample to be taken from any person *arrested* for a recordable offence and detained in a police station, whether or not they are subsequently charged. The aim was to allow offenders to be detected at an earlier stage than would previously have been possible with corresponding savings in police time and costs. The Act also lowered, from Superintendent to Inspector, the level of authorisation required for taking intimate and non-intimate samples without consent from persons held in custody on the authority of a court.

   The provisions of PACE that allowed DNA samples and profiles to be retained when an individual is cleared of the offence for which they were taken, or a decision is made not to prosecute, were also extended by the CJA to cover samples and profiles from arrestees. However, if the samples and profiles are retained, the CJA specified that they may then only be used for the purposes of the prevention and detection of crime, the investigation of an offence or the conduct of a prosecution.

*Serious Organised Crime and Police Act (SOCA) 2005*   The strict constraints on use of samples and profiles taken under PACE meant that they could not be used to assist in the identification of a deceased person unless they were suspected of having died as a result of their involvement in a criminal offence, as the offender or victim. This precluded access to the NDNAD to help in the identification of victims who had died through natural causes or as a result of a mass disaster, such as the South-East Asian tsunami. The Act removed this constraint and extended access to the database in such circumstances. SOCA also revised the definition of an intimate sample to include a swab taken from any part of a person's genitals (including pubic hair), and the definition of a non-intimate sample to include a swab taken from any part of a person's body other than a part from which a swab taken would be an intimate sample.

### Summary

The law in England and Wales has not only kept pace with technological developments, but has also progressively widened the range of persons from whom the samples can be taken, eased the restrictions on who can take them, and allowed for the permanent retention and continued use of the samples and DNA profiles to facilitate the identification of repeat offenders through speculative searching of the NDNAD. This has received a large measure of public support, but not without some challenge. However, to date, the courts have taken note of the success of the Database in bringing offenders to justice and have come down on the side of the value to society outweighing any individual human rights infringements that may exist. The Home Office is currently reviewing the scope of PACE, but it is not anticipated that this will lead to a recommendation for further expansion of the current arrangements for DNA sampling or use of the NDNAD (see also page 327).

### Growth and impact of the NDNAD[1]

When the NDNAD was established in 1995, its use was restricted by the police to the investigation of serious crime, sexual offences and domestic burglary on grounds of cost. Despite the gradual easing of these restrictions, and technological developments that were helping to reduce the turnaround times for DNA analysis and reduce the cost, as well as offering innovative approaches for the police in tackling crime, the rate of growth of the Database remained quite slow. This was exacerbated by the legislation requiring subjects' profiles to be removed if the person was acquitted or not prosecuted. The result was that after five years the number of subject sample profiles retained on the Database had reached only 737,000, representing less than one-fifth of those who had committed qualifying offences.

Subsequent legislative changes allowing more suspects to be sampled and removing the need for profiles to be destroyed once they are on the Database helped improve the position. But the major initiative leading to the rapid growth and effectiveness of the Database was the development of a crime reduction model by the FSS which predicted greater success in dealing with volume crime as the Database increased in size. Acceptance of this model led to an announcement by the Prime Minister in the autumn of 1999 to provide additional funding to enable DNA profiles to be taken from all known offenders and more DNA material to be recovered from scenes of crime, particularly volume crime, where police clear-up rates were lower and resource limitations were preventing samples being taken.

*The Home Office DNA Expansion Programme*   The Home Office DNA Expansion Programme was the government's response to this commitment (see Home Office 2005). Over the next six years it provided £241 million on top of around £90 million from current police force budgets. £60 million of this was used to employ additional specialist staff, vehicles and equipment to increase the rate of sampling from crime scenes. Most of the remainder was used to pay for analysis of the samples, although some £3.6 million was also invested in developing the IT infrastructure and applications for the Database, and in ensuring that appropriate management information was available to monitor improvements in performance.

By March 2008, the NDNAD contained 4,920,703 profiles from some 4,264,251 individuals. This represents about 7 per cent of the population of the United Kingdom and about 14 per cent of the male population. The Database also contained some 323,466 profiles from undetected offences.

The information stored on the NDNAD about individuals is limited to their name, gender, date of birth, ethnic appearance (not ethnic origin), where and when the sample was taken and their DNA profile. The DNA profile itself is represented as a series of numbers. It is obtained from the non-coding part of the chromosomes and has very limited genetic predictive ability. As new DNA profiles from individuals and crime scenes are added to the NDNAD they are speculatively searched against all other profiles on the Database from persons and unsolved crimes. There is now a 59 per cent chance that a new crime scene sample profile will match immediately with a profile on the Database from a person and a 1.5 per cent chance that a newly added subject sample profile will match immediately with a profile from an unsolved crime. Further matches may also be obtained later, of course, as more new profiles are added to the Database.

The real impact of the Database on crime prevention and reduction, however, depends on the extent to which matches are turned into detections and successful prosecutions. For cases where a DNA profile was loaded to the NDNAD, it was shown that the detection rate was significantly improved compared with cases where no DNA evidence was available. For all recorded crime the improvement in detection rate rose from 26 per cent to 40 per cent, for domestic burglary from 16 per cent to 41 per cent and for theft from vehicles from 8 per cent to 63 per cent. It was also estimated that about 50 per cent of detections led to convictions and 25 per cent of convictions resulted in custodial sentences, each custodial sentence preventing a further 7.8 crimes from being committed. Research carried out in 2002/2003 on 620 cases in which there had been a Database match showed that 58 per cent of the matches led to detections and that for 58 per cent of these the DNA match was the first link to the offender. It also showed that, on average, each crime detected with DNA resulted in a further 0.8 crimes being detected.

## Oversight and operation of the UK National DNA Database

*Governance and Custodianship*   When the NDNAD was established in 1995, ACPO and the FSS shared oversight of its operation through joint chairmanship of the NDNAD User Board. The FSS was appointed Custodian of the Database for the next five years under a Memorandum of Understanding with ACPO and this arrangement was extended under a revised Memorandum of Understanding in 2000 and interim updates of the Memorandum of Understanding in 2003 and 2005 (see National DNA Database 2003 and 2006).

In 1995 the FSS was the only organisation doing the profiling, but from 1997 other organisations in both the public sector (Tayside and Strathclyde Police Forensic Science Laboratories, Forensic Science Northern Ireland) and private sector (Cellmark and the Laboratory of the Government Chemist) progressively gained approval as suppliers. In England and Wales, this resulted in a competitive commercial environment for the provision of DNA profiling services and even more organisations seeking accreditation. There are now nine UK-based organisations (25 separately accredited analysis units) supplying DNA profiles from samples from subjects and/or crime scenes to the Database. One overseas organisation has also shown interest.

The User Board evolved over time into the NDNAD Board. This was chaired by the ACPO portfolio holder for forensic science and included representatives of the police service in England and Wales, the Association of Chief Police Officers (Scotland) (ACPOS), the Home Office, the Custodian and the FSS. The NDNAD Board was responsible for the governance and oversight of the Database and its strategic development. The Custodian, under the terms of the Memorandum of Understanding, was responsible for its operation, for setting standards for the laboratories supplying profiles to the Database and for ensuring compliance with these standards. A Suppliers' Group was established fairly early on for discussion of quality standards in DNA profiling and other matters of a technical nature between the Custodian and representatives of the profiling laboratories. In 2003, a DNA Operations Group, chaired by an Assistant Chief Constable on the NDNAD Board, was also established to deal with the more detailed practical operational issues on behalf of the Board.

These governance arrangements drew criticism from a number of quarters. In March 2001, for example, the House of Lords Select Committee on Science and Technology (2001) recommended that the government should establish an independent body, including lay members, to oversee the workings of the NDNAD, to put beyond doubt that individuals' data are being properly used and protected. A year later, the Human Genetics Commission (2002) issued a report which made proposals for an independent body with lay membership to oversee the NDNAD, and a separate national ethical committee to approve all research projects involving the use of DNA samples. In 2003, the NDNAD Board responded to these concerns by inviting the Human Genetics Commission to nominate one of their Commissioners to sit on the Board to advise on ethical issues, and in 2003 the Board produced its first Annual Report as a further means of opening the way the Database was being managed to wider public scrutiny.

The position of the FSS as both a supplier of profiles to the NDNAD and as Custodian of the Database, regulating and overseeing the performance of all suppliers, also attracted criticism. The FSS responded to this by vesting the role of Custodian in its Chief Scientist, who had no commercial role in the FSS, and progressively erecting 'Chinese walls' between the Custodian and the FSS as a supplier. But high-level concerns about these arrangements continued to be raised.

In July 2002, Robert McFarland was asked by the Home Office to consider, in the context of the reports from the House of Lords' Select Committee on Science and Technology and the Human Genetics Commission, and any future organisational changes for the FSS, the need for independent oversight of the NDNAD and the role of the Chief Scientist of the FSS as Custodian of the Database.

In March 2003, McFarland recommended that the FSS be transformed into a private sector classified public-private partnership and also suggested a variety of different structures for the future governance and oversight of the NDNAD. These involved removal of the Custodianship of the Database from the FSS and the establishment of a national ethics committee, a concept put forward by the Human Genetics Commission. McFarland recognised, however, that none of the changes should jeopardise the robustness and integrity of the system developed by the FSS and ACPO.

In July 2003, a programme of work to implement McFarland's recommendations was established under the Forensic Science and Pathology Unit of the Home Office. With regard to the NDNAD, the overall management and Custodianship of the Database was removed from the FSS as it moved towards privatisation, retaining it within the public sector and developing a new governance structure to replace the NDNAD Board. Separation of the Custodianship of the NDNAD from the FSS was accomplished on 5 December 2005, when the FSS changed from being a Home Office Agency to a Government Owned Company with private sector classification and the Custodian, supported by a small team, transferred provisionally to the Home Office before moving to the National Policing Improvement Agency (NPIA).

A new NDNAD Strategy Board, providing oversight of the Custodian and strategic planning, first met in May 2005 and the new governance arrangements were formally adopted on 20 March 2006. The Board is still chaired by the ACPO portfolio holder for forensic science, but there is a tripartite membership of Board members involving ACPO, the Home Office and the Association of Police Authorities (APA). Two nominees of the Human Genetics Commission and representatives from the NPIA, ACPO (Scotland) and the Custodian are also invited to participate in Board meetings as non-voting members. There is no longer any representation from the police forces or the supplier laboratories, although the police and suppliers do continue to meet in the DNA Operations Group and Suppliers' Group structures.

An independent Ethics Group has also now been set up, as a Non-Departmental Public Body, under the authority of the Secretary of State for the Home Department, to advise Ministers on ethical issues concerning the NDNAD. The Chair is an *ex officio* member of the Strategy Board and there are up to 10 other members who are recruited through open competition via the public appointments process. The remit of the Ethics Group covers issues relating to the current services provided, and techniques employed, by approved suppliers of DNA profiles to the Database; proposals for new services and techniques; applications for research involving access to samples or data; and other matters relating to the management, operation and use of the Database. If so requested by Ministers, the Ethics Group may also conduct inquiries into other ethical issues relating to scientific services provided to the police service and other public bodies within the criminal justice system. At its second meeting in September 2007, it was agreed that its work should be as transparent as possible and notes of its meetings should be made available to the public, showing the background to an issue and the decision reached. Its first Annual Report was published in April 2008.

In February 2008 a Forensic Science Quality Regulator was appointed with the role of setting quality standards and monitoring performance against these standards for all suppliers of forensic science services, including those from the NDNAD. It is expected that the Regulator will work through existing structures where these are in place and effective, and he has joined the NDNAD Strategy Board to this end.

*Role of the Custodian*   The Custodian sets the analytical and performance standards for the profiling laboratories, accredits new laboratories and monitors compliance with the standards, to ensure as far as possible that all profiles added to the Database are reliable and compatible. All laboratories wishing to be accredited for providing profiles for the Database have first to be accredited by the United Kingdom Accreditation Service (UKAS) to the international quality standard for testing laboratories, ISO 17025, and agree to UKAS sharing with the Custodian the outcomes of their audits. They are also required to undertake various proficiency tests set by the Custodian and provide copies of their documented procedures for review, in order to demonstrate that they comply with the quality standards promulgated by the DNA Working Group of the European Network of Forensic Science Institutes (ENFSI) and any additional requirements specified by the Custodian (see UKAS 2001). These include, for example, that once accredited the laboratories have to duplicate a specified proportion of all their analysis for process monitoring purposes and participate in the Custodian's ongoing programme of proficiency tests. The aim is to prevent problems arising as far as possible, and to be able to deal with them as quickly and effectively as possible if they do arise.

The Custodian also maintains a link between the NDNAD and the Police National Computer (PNC), through which demographic data are added to the Database when the police take a sample under PACE for analysis and PNC is later updated once a profile from the sample has been added to the Database. This link has proved invaluable in reducing clerical data transcription errors and nugatory multiple sampling of suspects. Various checks on the integrity of the data from the profiling laboratories and PNC are carried out by the Custodian, both before and after they are added to the Database. Processes are also in place to ensure that any information shared with PNC is reconciled.

The actual maintenance and development of the NDNAD and the provision of operational services from the Database were contracted to the FSS, in December 2005, for a period of three years, to ensure continuity in supply of the operational services from the Database following the interim move of the Custodianship from the FSS to the Home Office. It also ensured more formal, transparent and legally binding control of the provision of Database services. The provision of Database services and Database development have now become the responsibility of the NPIA.

## Some international comparisons

Although many countries throughout the world are now developing or already have DNA databases, there are wide differences in national legislation concerning the taking, retention and use of the DNA samples and profiles. In some countries there are also issues regarding the sharing of the DNA profiling data, both internally between different jurisdictions and externally with other countries. The following examples have been selected to demonstrate these differences and the progress that is being made in dealing with them.

### Scotland[2]

In 1994, ACPO (Scotland) favoured all Scottish samples being analysed by the FSS and added to the NDNAD. But the FSS was unable to take on the extra work at that time so the Dundee Police laboratory developed the capability and by 1996 it was decided that Scotland should have its own DNA database. The Home Office supported this development of local DNA profiling, subject to the profiles also being fed into the NDNAD. On this basis the Scottish DNA database became operational in early 1997. It was managed from its inception by the Dundee Police laboratory. Under reorganisation in April 2007, this became part of Forensic Services – Scottish Police Service Authority (SPSA).

Like the NDNAD, the Scottish database was based initially on SGM before moving to SGM Plus. All subject samples taken in Scotland are analysed by staff at the DNA database in Dundee and added to both the Scottish DNA database and the NDNAD. Crime scene samples are analysed at the four SPSA laboratories at Aberdeen, Dundee, Edinburgh and Glasgow. The crime scene sample profiles are first checked against the Scottish database and only added to the NDNAD if no local match is obtained.

The population of Scotland is about 5 million. In February 2008, the Scottish DNA database held in excess of 230,000 profiles from subjects, representing about 220,093 individuals. Some 65 per cent of new crime scene sample profiles added to the database obtain an immediate match with a subject profile.

The DNA legislation in Scotland is broadly similar to that in England and Wales. Under the Criminal Procedure (Scotland) Act 1995, police officers could take a mouth swab, with the person's consent, from anyone arrested and lawfully detained, or within one month of their conviction. If the person refused to provide a mouth swab, a hair sample could be taken by force. In both circumstances, the prior authority of an Inspector or more senior officer was required. If the sample proved inadequate for profiling a further sample could be obtained.

At first, ACPO (Scotland) restricted the taking of samples to persons suspected of involvement in offences of a sexual or violent nature and theft by housebreaking, but also allowed an officer to take swabs whenever it was felt prudent to do so. However, profiles from a suspect could remain on the Scottish database (and the NDNAD) only for as long as the case for which the sample was taken remained active or a conviction had been obtained. Since a significant proportion of arrestable offences in Scotland do not attract court convictions, this resulted in the police taking large numbers of samples for minor crime (and repeat sampling of the same person since profiles were being removed from the databases after fairly short periods of time, sometimes only weeks).

The most notable difference between Scottish legislation and that in England and Wales relates to the retention of DNA samples and information. The CJPA 2001 amendment to PACE allowing retention of DNA samples and information obtained from persons acquitted or not prosecuted was not replicated in Scotland, so the requirement remained that such samples and information had to be destroyed following a decision not to institute criminal proceedings or on the conclusion of such proceedings otherwise than in a conviction or following an absolute discharge.

The Criminal Justice (Scotland) Act 2003 removed the requirement for an Inspector's authority where no force is involved in taking the sample. In most other respects it mirrored the CJA legislation in allowing samples to be taken from any person arrested and lawfully detained. However, it allowed persons who had volunteered samples for elimination purposes (and consented separately for their samples to be retained and their profiles to be added to the Scottish database and the NDNAD) subsequently to be able to withdraw their consent. Their sample then has to be destroyed and their profile has to be removed from both databases, so long as these actions do not conflict with their use for evidential purposes.

The Scottish Government have no intention of enacting a general retention policy like that in England and Wales, but the issue of retention is still under discussion. A review is also under way of the effectiveness of recent legislative changes which may identify further potential changes for consideration by Parliament, currently concentrating on the retention of DNA and information from juveniles. Persons aged 16 years of age make up 2 per cent of the database population but over the past 12 months have been responsible for just under 10 per cent of the intelligence matches.

The 2006 Act makes further provisions to allow the police to take a DNA sample from a sex offender who attends the station to notify; from any person who is subject to the sex offender notification requirements (i.e. on the sex offenders register) if they do not already hold their samples; and from those on Risk of Sexual Harm Orders (which can be retained for the duration of the Orders, after which they must be destroyed). These provisions were commenced on 1 September 2006.

There is currently no legislation in Scotland for the database to be used to aid the identification of deceased persons, other than those suspected of involvement in a criminal offence.

### Northern Ireland[3]

DNA legislation in Northern Ireland is essentially the same as that in operation in England and Wales, differing mainly in the timing of its implementation. Thus, the police in Northern Ireland have had the power to take non-intimate DNA samples, without consent if necessary, since implementation of the Police and Criminal Evidence (Northern Ireland) Order 1989 and the requirements for the taking, use and retention of DNA samples, equivalent to those in the CJPOA for England and Wales, were introduced under the Police (Amendment) (Northern Ireland) Order 1995. The CJPA 2001 extended to Northern Ireland and arrestee sampling was introduced under the Criminal Justice (Northern Ireland) Order 2004. Most recently, the Police and Criminal Evidence (Amendment) (Northern Ireland) Order 2007 was made which permits, *inter alia*, the use of the database to aid the identification of deceased persons.

From the outset it was decided that a provincial DNA database would be established for Northern Ireland. The first subject sample profiles obtained by the Northern Ireland Forensic Science Laboratory were added to the Northern Ireland database in mid 1996 and the first crime scene sample profiles in 1997. By March 2008, the Northern Ireland database held some 83,000 subject sample profiles and 12,000 crime scene sample profiles.

It was always intended that these profiles would also be added to the NDNAD. For a variety of reasons this was delayed, but a bulk transfer of some 36,000 subject sample profiles was eventually effected in 2005. Since then all new subject sample profiles have been routinely transferred. By March 2008 there were 44,700 such profiles from Northern Ireland on the NDNAD and it is anticipated that some 12,000 further subject sample profiles will be transferred annually. Since August 2007, 573 crime scene sample profiles have also been transferred.

Over 4,000 subject-to-scene matches have been reported since the provincial database was established. In 2007–2008, 594 such matches in 569 cases were reported, along with a further 33 scene-to-scene matches.

### Europe

In 2001, the European Commission recommended that all Members of the European Union should develop DNA databases for use in criminal investigations. The data from different sources is not entirely compatible, but a survey of the 25 EU Member States conducted in 2005 on behalf of the European Commission (Joannesse 2005) showed that, of the 20 countries that replied 15 (Austria, Belgium, Czech Republic, Estonia, Finland, France, Germany, Hungary, Latvia, Lithuania, The Netherlands, Slovakia, Slovenia, Sweden and the United Kingdom) had already established a national DNA database under the control of departments belonging to the Home Office/Ministry of Interior or the Ministry of Justice, with access to the information being strictly limited and controlled. Another five (Ireland, Italy, Portugal, Poland and Malta) were either in the process of creating one or drafting the required legislation. More recent data from the ENFSI DNA Working Group shows that, as at March 2008 25 countries in Europe now have national DNA databases (adding Bulgaria, Croatia, Denmark, Norway, Poland, Portugal, Romania, Spain, Switzerland and Ukraine to the 2005 survey list).

The criteria for addition of subject profiles to the national DNA databases vary greatly from country to country (see Asplen 2006). They may relate, for example, to whether the person has been convicted of an offence or is simply a suspect or arrestee; the type of offence (for example burglary or vehicle theft, or, more generally, serious violent crime); the length of sentence; or whether or not a specific court order is required. However, the general trend, as in the United Kingdom, is to amend current legislation to widen the scope of those from whom profiles might be obtained. Few countries impose any restrictions on the addition of crime scene sample profiles to the databases.

All European databases contain profiles from unsolved crimes. All but one (Portugal) contain profiles from suspects, either with or without their personal details. Searches are allowed within each database (except Portugal's) for subject-to-scene matches (sometimes subject to constraints related to the type of offence) and scene-to-scene matches, but only 12 of the countries in the 2005 survey allow suspect/suspect searching and fewer still allow access to the databases to assist with the identification of deceased persons or inquiries into missing persons.

Unlike the United Kingdom, most countries in Europe require the samples and DNA profiles to be destroyed if the person is acquitted or not prosecuted, either immediately or after a specified time interval.

Cross-border cooperation for exchange of DNA profiles and searching of other national DNA databases in Europe for Interpol member countries is facilitated through the National Crime Bureaux and Interpol, but is constrained by each country's own legislation (van der Beek 2006). To date 17 EU Member States have also signed up to the European Union Prüm Convention, which allows DNA profiles (but not personal information) to be shared via direct access to a view of the national DNA databases of the other participating countries through a national contact point on a 'match/no match' basis. And most recently, the Hague Programme on strengthening freedom, security and justice in the European Union requires that from 1 January 2008 the exchange of DNA information for law enforcement purposes should be governed by the principle of availability.

The United Kingdom and The Netherlands, between whom there is a high level of transit, have reached a bilateral agreement to allow exchange of DNA profiles directly. Any matches obtained in any of these exchanges are then followed up with a formal legal request for exchange of further details.

Joannesse (2005) showed that in the previous year a total of 510,000 subject sample profiles had been added to the United Kingdom DNA Database whereas only 185,000 profiles had been added to the other 14 European databases in the same period. The total number of subject profiles on the European databases at March 2008 was about 5.56 million, some 4.05 million being from the United Kingdom (van der Beek 2006). The European databases also held some 635,000 crime scene sample profiles, about half of which were from the United Kingdom. The latest Interpol survey, due to be published in June 2009, shows that after the United Kingdom, the largest national DNA databases are now held by Germany (with 505,000 records), France (304,112) and Austria (114,060).[4]

### United States of America[5]

Colorado was the first State to introduce DNA legislation in 1988, when it required samples to be taken from all convicted sex offenders. Individual States have since then gradually expanded their legislation, in the overwhelming majority of instances covering all felony offenders. Now all 50 States, the District of Columbia, and all federal jurisdictions have legislation relating to the taking of biological samples for DNA profiling. There is, however, significant variation as to what is authorised.

The primary federal legislation is The DNA Identification Act of 1994, which authorised the taking of samples from all convicted felons. The DNA Analysis Backlog Elimination Act (2000) further authorised the collection of DNA samples from federal offenders and from those who commit qualifying offences in the District of Columbia, the military and on tribal reservations. The USA Patriot Act (2001) expanded the list of offences for which offender samples could be taken to include acts of terrorism and crimes of violence, and The DNA Fingerprint Act of 2005 changed the scope of permitted sampling to include federal arrestees and detainees.

DNA analysis is carried out in the local, State and federal laboratories. The DNA Identification Act of 1994 created a DNA Advisory Board (DAB) to make recommendations for standards for quality assurance in DNA profiling. The Board's recommendations resulted in the issue of two publications by the Director of the Federal Bureau of Investigation (FBI): 'Quality Assurance Standards for Forensic DNA Testing Laboratories' (1998) and 'Quality Assurance Standards for Convicted Offender DNA Databasing Laboratories' (1999). The Act also authorised the FBI to set up a National DNA Index System (NDIS) for law enforcement based on the Combined DNA Index System (CODIS).

CODIS is configurable to support any RFLP or STR markers, but now the 13 core STR loci (CSF1PO, D13S317, D16S539, D18S51, D21S11, D3S1358, D5S818, D7S820, D8S1179, FGA, THO1, TPOX, VWA) and the amelogenin gender marker are used. It is claimed that this provides a match probability for full profiles from unrelated persons of about 1 in 100 trillion.

CODIS has been fully operational at local, State and national levels since 1998. The three-tiered system allows the local and State agencies to operate their individual databases within the confines of State laws, which vary from jurisdiction to jurisdiction. Data from the local laboratory systems (LDIS) are fed electronically into the State system (SDIS), which is maintained and operated by a designated State laboratory. The local laboratories cannot load directly to the national system, NDIS, but the State laboratories can if so permitted by State law and they have signed a memorandum of understanding to the effect that they are working in compliance with the FBI standards. NDIS is administered by the FBI and DNA profiles from samples analysed by the FBI laboratory are also added to NDIS. By April 2008 129 local laboratories, 50 State laboratories and two Federal agencies (the FBI and the Army) were participating in NDIS.

Originally, NDIS contained a Convicted Offender Index, containing unique identifiers (but no personal or criminal history information) and DNA profiles of individuals who have been convicted of various offences defined by State and/or Federal law, and a Forensic Index containing DNA profiles from scenes of crime samples. There were also databases of profiles from Unidentified Human Remains, Missing Persons and Relatives of Missing Persons. In 2006, three further indexes were added: an Indicted Persons Index (under the Justice for All Act, October 2004), an Arrestees Index (under the DNA Fingerprint Act 2005) and a Legal Index for profiles from lawfully obtained samples that do not fit into the other Indexes. The Indicted Persons profiles have since been included in the Arrestees Index.

Although federal government operated NDIS, individual States and local governments were required to fund most of the costs of DNA profiling. There was also a lack of training in the law enforcement area which significantly restricted development in understanding the power and value of the offender/suspect databases. This resulted in the analytical capability not keeping pace with the increasing demand for DNA analysis and significant backlogs developing. Over 500,000 casework samples were awaiting analysis at the time of the Attorney General's Backlog Report.

The DNA Backlog Elimination Act (2000) provided $140 million to States for DNA analysis. Further Federal appropriation was provided in 2003 and in 2005 the President authorised the provision of another $1 billion. Private laboratories are now being used to reduce the backlog for convicted offender samples. As of April 2008, NDIS contained over 5.68 million DNA profiles from offenders, representing about 1.8 per cent of the population, and almost 218,000 DNA profiles from crime scene samples.

The CODIS software checks for matches (or 'hits' as they are termed in the USA) in the Offender and Forensic Indexes. CODIS is set up to allow speculative searches to be carried out at different levels of stringency. At high stringency, all alleles must match and there must be no missing alleles, but most laboratories search at medium stringency, which returns matches with profiles that match at least one allele at each locus. Lower stringency searches are needed because the STR kits supplied by different manufacturers may have different primer binding regions for the same loci and thus yield different results. To prevent too many matches resulting from this approach, laboratories are required to enter data for all 13 CODIS STR loci for convicted offenders and at least 10 of the 13 CODIS loci for casework samples. Since its inception until March 2008, CODIS has produced 12,380 forensic hits, 47,061 intra-State offender hits and 7,030 inter-State offender hits. All samples identified as having matching DNA profiles are reanalysed by the submitting laboratories to either validate or refute the match.

## Summary

More and more countries are establishing national DNA databases, but the legislation varies widely on what samples can be taken, under what circumstances, how the DNA profiles can be compared with other profiles from persons or crime scenes, and what must happen to the samples and profiles thereafter. The situation is exacerbated where there are multi-jurisdictional states and this significantly impedes the growth, use and effectiveness of DNA profiling in those countries.

### Emerging issues

The NDNAD is undoubtedly an invaluable tool to assist the police in the fight against crime. It not only helps to identify offenders and links between offences, it also helps to eliminate individuals from suspicion and avoid unnecessary intrusion into their private lives. But alongside its success many policy and ethical issues have been raised, particularly in relation to individual data privacy and human rights. Some of these are discussed in the following section.

*Control of and access to the National DNA Database*  The view has been expressed by a number of bodies and individuals (for example the Science and Technology Committee of the House of Commons 2005; the Human Genetics Commission (HGC) 2002; GeneWatch 2005; Williams, Johnson and Martin 2004; the Nuffield Council on Bioethics 2007) that there should be independent and transparent oversight of the Database to assure the public that the information it holds is correct, and that it is held and used ethically and only in compliance with the relevant legislation.

Such calls for independence and transparency of oversight have not been made in respect of other police intelligence databases, however, and are undoubtedly influenced by the perception that the NDNAD contains sensitive genetic information about individuals, which it does not. The NDNAD in fact contains less personal information than the Police National Computer and some other police intelligence databases.

The NDNAD Strategy Board is charged with oversight of the operation of the Database through the office of the Custodian. It has independent members from the Home Office and the Association of Police Authorities. It is guided on ethical matters by these and by independent advisers nominated by the Human Genetics Commission as well as the recently appointed independent Ethics Group. There will also be wider scrutiny of its activities by the Forensic Science Regulator. Direct access to the database is restricted to the Custodian's staff, and the information retained and retrieved can only be used for the purposes specified by the legislation. The Strategy Board has now published four Annual Reports and proposes to provide even more information on its activities through a dedicated website; the Ethics Group has also made its discussions and conclusions publicly available. Because of all this, the NDNAD Strategy Board has indicated that it feels it has already gone a long way to assuaging the concerns raised.

*Whose profiles should be retained on the National DNA Database?*  The Human Genetics Commission (2002) showed that there is strong public support for the holding of profiles on the NDNAD from persons who have committed serious crimes such as murder and rape, and substantial support where offenders have committed less serious crimes. However, the Science and Technology Committee of the House of Commons (2005), reflecting concerns expressed elsewhere (for example by GeneWatch), commented that the legislation that allows permanent retention on the NDNAD of DNA profiles from persons who have not been prosecuted or have been acquitted was introduced without proper justification or meaningful public debate and is highly discriminatory.[6] More recently, a number of MPs have been expressing concern about the retention of profiles on the Database from minors and the disproportionate number of profiles retained from young black males. However, Lord Justice Sedley (2005) and others, including Sir Alec Jeffreys, have gone so far as to say that it would be less discriminatory to have everyone's profile on the Database.

It is accepted that the retention of profiles from persons who have not been prosecuted or have been acquitted for a given offence, but not from other groups of innocent persons (except volunteers), is discriminatory. However, it was estimated in December 2005 that of the 200,300 such individuals whose records had been retained on the Database at that time, some 8,493 (5 per cent) had since been identified as suspects for 13,964 other offences. These included 114 murders, 55 attempted murders, 116 rapes, 68 other sexual offences, 119 aggravated burglaries, 127 the supply of controlled drugs and a number of serious assaults. It is not known how many of these might otherwise have remained undetected.

The highest court of appeal in the United Kingdom has taken note of this in carefully weighing the value to society of retaining such profiles in helping to detect crime against any infringement of human rights of the individuals concerned, and has supported their retention. Whilst acknowledging that some persons who have not been convicted of an offence do sometimes feel aggrieved if their biometric information is retained, the Law Lords rejected the suggestion that this group of people are somehow stigmatised as a result. Persons who do not go on to commit an offence have no reason to fear the retention of this information. However, on December 13th 2008 (some time after this chapter was prepared) the European Court of Human Rights ruled that the retention of the profiles of individuals who had been acquitted of the offence for which they were charged, or against whom proceedings had been discontinued, was in breach of Article 8 of the European Convention on Human Rights. At the time of writing, the British Government is required to provide outline proposals on the implementation of the Judgement to the Council of Europe's Committee of Ministers in March 2009. It also seems likely that a public consultation process will inform these proposals, but as yet its form has not been determined.

The disproportionate representation of minors and young black males on the Database is a reflection of policing practice and the relatively high proportion of offences for which these groups are arrested, under-18s for example accounting for 23 per cent of all arrests in Britain. The United Kingdom Government has clearly stated that it has no plans to introduce a universal compulsory, or voluntary, NDNAD. Indeed, to do so would raise significant practical and ethical issues.

*Destruction of subject samples after a profile has been obtained*   It has been argued that although a DNA profile contains little genetic information, the sample itself could be used to generate such information about a person. It should therefore be destroyed once the DNA profile has been obtained (GeneWatch 2005; Williams, Johnson and Martin 2004). In fact there is currently no legal requirement for a sample to be retained or destroyed. It is solely at the discretion of the Chief Constable of the force that took the sample, although it is ACPO policy that the samples, and associated data, should only be destroyed in 'exceptional circumstances'. What constitutes 'exceptional circumstances' is not defined, but an advisory group has been established to collate all requests for destruction and help ensure consistency of approach. If the samples are retained, they can then only be used for purposes related to the prevention and detection of crime, the investigation of an offence, the conduct of a prosecution or the identification of a deceased person or a deceased person from whom a body part came.

For the benefit of the individuals concerned and the public at large, there are many good reasons for the samples to be retained after a profile has been obtained, the most important being to allow them to be reanalysed as technology develops in order to improve the effectiveness of the Database and minimise the risk of chance matches and the consequent implication of innocent persons as potential suspects. Such upgrading has already occurred once in the change from the 6 marker SGM profiling system to the 10 marker SGM Plus system in 1999. This gave an increase in the match probability for full profiles from unrelated individuals from 1 in 50 million to about 1 in 1,000 million. However, as at March 2008 11 per cent of the subject sample profiles and 11 per cent of the crime scene sample profiles on the NDNAD were still SGM profiles, so in order to minimise the risk of false inclusion these samples are retrieved for upgrading to SGM Plus as and when the SGM profile is involved in a match. It could be argued that all of the SGM profiles on the Database should be upgraded to SGM Plus by reanalysis of the retained samples which could then be destroyed, but in practice this would be very expensive and involve a lot of nugatory work. It will also be advisable within the next five years to change the profiling system once again, to increase the discriminating power even further as the size of the Database grows and to increase the possibility of obtaining fuller DNA profiles from crime scene samples (*vide infra*). Access to the retained samples will then be required again for similar upgrading purposes.

Retained samples are also valuable where other techniques such as Y-STR and mitochondrial DNA analysis need to be applied to reduce a pool of potential suspects; to facilitate the investigation of possible quality failures, where the validity of the DNA profile is in question or the profile is thought not to relate to the right person; and for their use in research to assist with the investigation of crime. It has been suggested that new samples could be obtained from suspects for reanalysis purposes and from volunteers for research but, unfortunately, this is not always possible or practicable and access to previously analysed samples is the only pragmatic approach.

With the ability to retain the samples, however, comes a responsibility to ensure that they are stored securely and accessed and used only for the permitted purposes. Until recently, samples in England and Wales were held on behalf of the police by the organisations that carried out the profiling. The NDNAD Board had to authorise their use for purposes other than routine quality assurance and the Custodian monitored their use for compliance. There is nothing to suggest that this arrangement led to any misuse of the samples, but McFarland (2003) recommended that accountability for the storage and access to the samples should pass to the Custodian, in order to be better able to demonstrate the required level of control. So consideration is now being given to their transfer to a central repository under the oversight and management of the Custodian.

*Are the profiles sufficiently discriminating to prevent innocent individuals falling under suspicion?* The House of Commons Science and Technology Committee (2005) questioned the adequacy of the current 10 marker profiling system to provide a sufficient level of discrimination to prevent an individual being wrongly identified with an offence on the basis of a chance match.

The probability of a match between full SGM Plus profiles from two unrelated individuals would be of the order 1 in a trillion (a million million) if the values of the markers were all independent. However, it has not yet been possible to carry out the required statistical testing to be able to quote this match probability and, in practice, in the United Kingdom, a conservative figure of 1 in 1,000 million is used. The match probability is much larger for related individuals, who share a larger proportion of their DNA than do individuals from the population at large, of the order 1 in 10,000 for full siblings.

The NDNAD now contains profiles of some 4.26 million individuals from our population of 60 million. Although there is a very small probability of a chance match occurring between full SGM Plus profiles from unrelated individuals, no such chance match has been confirmed to date. However, as the size of the NDNAD grows, or if international comparisons are being made with other countries' DNA profiles, the probability of a chance match, whilst still being small, will inevitably increase. The risk of a chance match will also increase if the crime scene sample profile is partial, and comparison of partial profiles from crime scene samples with full SGM Plus profiles from individuals on the NDNAD is thus more likely to result in 'matches' being found relating to more than one individual. The more partial the profile from the crime scene sample, the greater the number of such 'matches' that will be obtained. Partial profiles result from crime scene samples in approximately half of all cases. This is because the material recovered from crime scenes for DNA analysis can be quite degraded and limited in quantity, and the degradation process breaks the DNA molecules into very short fragments which are not amenable for DNA profiling using the multiplexes currently commercially available, which tend to detect only relatively undegraded DNA.

It would be possible to improve the discriminating power of the SGM Plus profiling system further by testing for more markers. These additional tests could be carried out sequentially or concurrently. Sequential testing could be accomplished using complementary commercially available multiplexes such as Cofiler (3 additional markers) or Profiler (5 additional markers). However, this approach would be more expensive and take longer, and would not be suitable where the amount of sample is limited. Concurrent testing could be carried out to improve the discriminating power using one of the large commercially available single multiplexes such as Powerplex 16 (15 markers) or Identifiler (15 markers) but, unfortunately, these larger multiplexes are primarily designed for the analysis of subject samples for databasing purposes, and are not as efficient or sensitive as the smaller multiplexes that are currently in use when it comes to crime sample analysis. In fact, the evidence suggests that the larger the multiplex in terms of the number of markers analysed, the less efficient it becomes. This means that even more partial profiles could result and it has been demonstrated that the success rate with crime samples would actually decrease if Identifiler were to be used to replace SGM Plus.

Recent extensive collaborative research studies by the European EDNAP and ENFSI groups have demonstrated that the success rate for analysis of degraded samples can, however, be substantially improved by employing tests for markers based on mini-STRs (shorter lengths of DNA) that have become available in the last year or so (Gill *et al.* 2006). The preferred way forward for the United Kingdom in the short term is therefore to incorporate tests for some of these mini-STRs into an enlarged SGM Plus multiplex. At the same time, work has been proposed to re-engineer the tests for the existing markers in SGM Plus to make them easier to detect in degraded DNA. In the longer term this should provide a single improved multiplex which could test for 13–16 markers. A 13-marker system would give match probabilities of about 1 in $10^{15}$ (compared to 1 in $10^{12}$ for the current SGM Plus). A 16-marker system would give match probabilities of the order of 1 in $10^{20}$. The rate of progress will be heavily dependent on commercial considerations.

In the meantime, it will be important to stress the limitations of DNA profiling for criminal investigations and that DNA evidence should not be used alone for prosecution purposes.

*Why not retain crime scene sample profiles on the NDNAD following a match with a subject sample profile to help identify any possible miscarriage of justice?* When a crime scene sample profile is found to match a profile on the NDNAD from one or more individuals, a match report is sent to the police. If the match involves full SGM Plus profiles the crime scene profile is immediately removed from the Database. In all other circumstances, the crime scene profile remains on the Database until the Custodian is notified by the police of a successful prosecution. Removal of the crime scene profile prevents subsequent match reports being issued for the same offence if the convicted individual is subsequently arrested as a suspect for another offence and another profile for that individual is added to the Database. However, it could be argued that this approach precludes alternative potential suspects for the crime being identified at a later stage, and hence the possibility of a miscarriage of justice is raised.

Where the crime scene sample profile is a full SGM Plus one, the risk of this is quite low, and in any event the retention of the original matching subject sample profile would provide a match with the new subject sample profile and highlight the need for any actions resulting from the previous match to be reconsidered. If the crime scene sample profile was a partial one, however, there could be subjects with different DNA profiles whom it would match, and if the crime scene profile had been removed following the initial match the subsequent additional potential suspect would not be identified.

For this reason the NDNAD Strategy Board are considering an alternative approach that will prevent the same match being reported repeatedly whilst at the same time leaving open the possibility of further suspects being identified.

*Use of samples and data for research purposes* Strong concerns have been expressed about the use of retained samples and profiles for research purposes without adequate authorisation and control. The House of Commons Science and Technology Committee (2005) reflected these concerns in calling for a national ethical committee to approve all research projects involving the use of DNA samples and data from the NDNAD, and for individuals to provide specific consent for their samples and data to be so used.

The law as it stands constrains the uses that can be made of samples and profiles obtained for the NDNAD to any purpose related to the prevention and detection of crime, the investigation of an offence, the conduct of a prosecution or the identification of a deceased person or a deceased person from whom a body part came. This provides a very wide remit and has been taken to cover the use of the samples and data for research purposes with relevant aims without the need for specific consent to be obtained for the samples and data to be so used. However, to assure the public that the law is being applied with due consideration and discretion, appropriate and transparent controls have been put in place and requests for access to samples or data from the Database for research purposes have always been considered very carefully by the NDNAD Board, taking due account of the legality of the purpose, the requirements of the criminal justice system and public interest. The Board has also taken into account any advice provided by the adviser nominated by the Human Genetics Commission and where necessary the Information Commissioner, as well as the requirements of the Data Protection Act 1998 when deciding what specific samples or information could be released.

The NDNAD Annual Report for 2005/06 records some 17 'research' requests having been approved to date. These included one for the provision of a copy of the Database with all personal identifiers removed to assist with the development of an expert system for designating the markers in profiles to be added to the Database. Another related to a police operational request for Database information to help evaluate the Pathfinder project (best practice in the collection and analysis of DNA samples in burglary/vehicle crime cases) and a third was to help identify persons on a force's dangerous offenders' register who did not have profiles on the NDNAD. A further six requests came from forensic providers who wished to conduct research in areas that may assist in future investigations. These involved the provision of anonymised samples for Y-chromosome analysis, to generate a Y-chromosome frequency database to help assess the significance of an individual having a specific Y-STR DNA profile; the provision of anonymised data on ethnic appearance (as perceived by the police, not ethnic origin) for the development of an ethnic inference database for predicting the likelihood of an undetected offender having one ethnic appearance as opposed to another; the provision of anonymised data for development of the familial searching approach for identifying potential relatives of an offender who are on the Database when the offender's profile is not on the Database; the provision of anonymised data for familial search applications in specific cases; the provision of data to assist with research into obtaining DNA profiles from fingerprints; and the provision of anonymised data for assessment of the use of rare alleles in geomapping/crime pattern analysis of offences.

Fuller information relating to research requests, the criteria for approval and the outcomes of any approved research are not widely available to the public and although the control mechanisms may have been operating effectively there remains a perception of lack of transparency. The independent Ethics Group will play an important role in future in helping the NDNAD Strategy Board consider the ethics of such research and make the whole process more open to public scrutiny. It would also be better practice if the police were to inform suspects and volunteers of the potential wider use of their samples at the same time that they are informed that their profiles may be compared with profiles from unsolved crime scenes.

Research into genetically controlled phenotypes, such as hair and eye colour, is also carried out by forensic science laboratories, aimed at providing the police with a 'Sherlock Holmes' type of genetic photofit of an offender from examination of traces left at the scene of crime. It is important to recognise that this research is not carried out on the samples taken for the Database, but on samples provided specifically for the purpose with informed consent from volunteers.

*Use of the samples and profiles in civil paternity cases*   The use of DNA samples obtained for the NDNAD for civil paternity purposes clearly falls outside the scope of permitted uses. The release of samples and use of profiles for this purpose has thus been resisted, notwithstanding some requests having been supported by a Court Order from a High Court Judge. The Home Office intervened in one such case, *London Borough of Lambeth v. S, C, V, and J (No. 3)*, in the Family Division of the High Court in order to clarify the legal position. In his judgement, overturning the High Court Order, Mr Justice Ryder said that 'The purposes to which samples may be put are ... specific and narrow' as described in PACE.

*Familial searching of the Database*   The House of Commons Science and Technology Committee (2005) expressed concern about the advent of familial searching of the NDNAD to identify potential relatives of offenders who themselves do not have profiles on the Database in the absence of any Parliamentary debate about the merits of this approach and its ethical implications.

The NDNAD Board felt that the proposed development fell clearly within the scope of PACE, but recognised the potential sensitivities involved so took advice from the Information Commissioner and its HGC representative before giving endorsement. In compliance with the advice received, familial searching was approved subject to strict guidelines setting out in detail under what circumstances the approach might be appropriate. A formal application process requiring Board approval was introduced and advice was developed on how best to conduct the investigation to minimise intrusion into the private lives of persons who are not themselves suspects. To date the approach has been used in only a limited number of the most serious cases and has helped identify suspects in several of these where other lines of enquiry had been less successful.

*Should volunteers be able to withdraw consent for their profiles to be retained on the NDNAD?* In England, Wales and Northern Ireland, the law does not allow a person providing a sample voluntarily for whatever purpose and giving consent for these to be retained for future comparison with other retained samples and profiles then to withdraw their consent. The law in Scotland differs in that volunteers can withdraw their consent and have their samples and profiles removed. The Custodian thus has to manage the NDNAD to reflect this requirement. The rationale for not permitting a volunteer to withdraw consent for their profile being retained on the NDNAD is to avoid a return to the situation prior to the Criminal Justice Act 2001, where consent had been given and then withdrawn, but for whatever reason the profile remained on the database and it was found to match that taken from a crime scene sample, leading to arguments as to the admissibility of such evidence in any subsequent criminal proceedings. A law-abiding person has nothing to fear from having their profile on the database and withdrawal of consent could be a precursor to future illegal activity.

However, although the information held on the Database is only used if a stored sample is matched with a sample recovered from a crime scene, as with individuals acquitted of an offence for which DNA was taken and those whose prosecutions are not proceeded with, there is a good case for treating volunteers differently. At the very least, they should be made more aware of the consequences of volunteering at the time the sample is taken and steps have been taken to ensure that this is the case.

*To what extent should there be transnational databases and international data sharing?* It is important with increasing organised cross-border crime and terrorism that investigators in one country have access to DNA information held by other countries in order to check crime scene profiles against profiles from other crimes and subjects on those countries' databases. The extent to which this is possible, however, is constrained by the compatibility of the profiling systems in use, national legislation and human rights considerations. England, Wales, Scotland, Northern Ireland, the Channel Islands and the Isle of Man are able to share and search one another's data via the NDNAD with no significant restrictions.

In Europe, DNA profiles can be exchanged between 17 of the EU member States under the Prüm Treaty. DNA profiles from subjects must contain at least 6 loci of the European Standard Set. DNA profiles from crime scene samples must contain at least 6 loci and must not already have matched a person in the national DNA database. Otherwise, the DNA profiles may contain any other locus which is used in the Interpol DNA database. One allele at one locus can be a wild card, but profiles derived from mixtures are not allowed. The information is exchanged via the European TESTA-II network. Personal information linked to the profile is usually only given where there are mutual legal assistance rules.

The Hague Programme on strengthening freedom, security and justice in the European Union now further requires that from 1 January 2008 the exchange of DNA information for law enforcement purposes should be governed by the principle of availability. This means that throughout the European Union a law enforcement officer in one Member State who needs the information in order to perform his duties should be able to obtain it from another Member State, and that the law enforcement agency in the other Member State which holds this information must make it available for the stated purpose, taking into account the requirements of any ongoing investigations in that State.

All EU Member States can also compare a profile from another country with their own database and vice versa via Interpol and/or via a rogatory letter from a magistrate, although there can be restrictions to this comparison, such as requiring authorisation to perform the comparison in the requested country, reciprocity of the offence, or risk assessment on the dissemination of the information.

Interpol also has a global database in Vienna with on-line access. In April 2008, the Interpol database contained 75,253 records from 47 member countries, but mainly Germany, France, Austria and the United Kingdom.

The DNA profiles on the Interpol database are anonymous and member countries retain ownership and control of how the data are used and accessed in accordance with their own national laws. Submitted profiles will either match or not match profiles on the Interpol database. By April 2008 151 transnational hits involving 16 different countries had been recorded. Further action is the responsibility of the relevant countries involved, subject to any restrictions imposed by their national laws.

### Conclusion

The United Kingdom DNA Database has proved to be an invaluable asset to the police in the investigation of crime. Its success has progressively led to an easing of the legislative constraints on its use whilst at the same time its governance has been strengthened and made more transparent. There is both considerable public support for its use and some concerns over its potential for misuse, some of which have been addressed here. Many other countries have followed suit, but none provides the same level of opportunity in support of criminal investigations and where there are multiple jurisdictions the growth and use of the databases has proved to be much slower. Nevertheless, the tendency overall is for DNA databases to become an integral and increasingly important tool of policing, both nationally and internationally.

### Notes

1 The most recent NDNAD statistical data for this section were provided by the Custodian and his staff.
2 Information for this section was provided by the Scottish Executive and by Tom Ross of the Scottish DNA Database.

3 Information for this section was provided by the Northern Ireland Office, Brian Irwin, Forensic Science Northern Ireland, and the Custodian of the NDNAD and his staff.

4 Personal communication from OIPC INTERPOL 10 April.

5 Information from this section was derived from a number of sources, including: FBI (2005), Department of Justice (2006), National Institute of Justice (2003), National Forensic Technology Centre (2005). Additional material was provided by Chris Asplen of Smith Alling Lane, Washington and Douglas Hares, NDNIS Custodian, FBI Lab, CODIS Unit.

6 Both the recent Human Genetics Commission sponsored Citizens Inquiry (2008) and the NDNAD Ethics Group have also discussed the current retention regime.

## References

Asplen, C.H. (2006) *Report on ENFSI Member Countries' DNA Database Legislation Survey*. The Hague: ENFSI.

Attorney General (2001) England and Wales Court of Appeal (2000) Reference No. 3 of 1999: 2 AC 1; *R v Michael Clive Joseph Weir* (2000) (Criminal Division) 43 (26 May 2000).

Cotton, E.A., Allsop, R.F., Guest, J.L., Frazier, R.R.E., Koumi, P., Callow, I.P., Seager, A. and Sparkes, R.L. (2000) 'Validation of the AmpflSTR SGM Plus system for use in forensic casework', *Forensic Science International*, 112: 151–161.

Department of Justice (2006) *Combined DNA Index System Operational and Laboratory Vulnerabilities: Audit Report 06-32*. Washington: Office of the Inspector General.

ENFSI DNA Working Group (2001) Quality Assurance Programme for DNA Laboratories. The Hague: ENFSI.

Federal Bureau of Investigation (2005) The FBI Laboratory Report Publication #0357. Washington: Federal Bureau of Investigation.

GeneWatch (2005) *The Police National DNA Database: Balancing Crime Detection, Human Rights and Privacy*. Buxton: Genewatch.

Gill, P., Fereday, L., Morling, N. and Schneider, P.M. (2006) 'New multiplexes for Europe – Amendments and clarification of strategic development', *Forensic Science International*, 163: 155–7.

Gill, P., Jeffreys, A.J. and Werrett, D.J. (1985) 'Forensic application of DNA fingerprints', *Nature*, 318: 577–579.

Home Office (2005) DNA Expansion Programme 2000–2005: Reporting achievement. London: Home Office Forensic Science and Pathology Unit.

House of Commons Science and Technology Committee (2005) *Forensic Science on Trial*. Seventh Report of Session 2004–2005. London: HMSO.

House of Lords (2004) R v. Chief Constable of South Yorkshire Police (Respondent) *ex parte* LS (by his mother and litigation friend JB) (FC) (Appellant); R v. Chief Constable of South Yorkshire Police (Respondent) *ex parte* Marper (FC) (Appellant) House of Lords 39.

House of Lords Select Committee on Science and Technology (2001) *Human Genetic Databases: challenges and opportunities*. London: HMSO.

Human Genetics Commission (2002) *Inside Information, Balancing interests in the use of personal genetic information*. London: Department of Health.

Human Genetics Commission (2008) *A Citizens' Inquiry into the Forensic Use of DNA and the National DNA Database*. London: The Human Genetics Commission.

INTERPOL (2001) *Handbook on DNA Data Exchange and Practice: Recommendations from the Interpol DNA Monitoring Expert Group*. Lyon: INTERPOL.

Jeffreys, A.J., Wilson, V. and Thein, S.L. (1985a) 'Hypervariable "minisatellite" regions in human DNA', *Nature*, 314: 67–73.

Jeffreys, A.J., Wilson, V. and Thein, S.L. (1985b) 'Individual-specific fingerprints of human DNA', *Nature*, 316: 76–79.

Joannesse, Y. (2005) *Synthesis of the Questionnaire on Legal Aspects of Searching National DNA Databases*. Brussels: European Commission.

Kimpton, C., Fisher, D., Watson, S., Adams, M., Urquhart, A., Lygo, J., and Gill, P. (1994) 'Evaluation of an automated DNA profiling system employing multiplex amplification at four tetrameric STR loci', *Int J. Leg. Med*, 106: 302–311.

McFarland, R. (2003) Review of the Forensic Science Service. London: The Home Office.

National DNA Database (2003) *Annual Report 2002/2003*. London: Forensic Science Service.

National DNA Database (2004) *Annual Report 2003/2004*. London: Forensic Science Service.

National DNA Database (2006) *Annual Report 2004/2005*. London: Forensic Science Service.

National DNA Database (2006) *Annual Report 2005/2006*. London: Forensic Science Service.

National DNA Database (2009) *Annual Report 2006/2007*. London: National Policing Improvement Agency.

National DNA Database Ethics Group (2008) *First Annual Report*. London: The Home Office.

National Forensic Science Technology Centre (2005) Principles of Forensic DNA for the Officers of the Court. Washington: National Institute of Justice.

National Institute of Justice (2003) Report for the Attorney General on Delays in Forensic DNA Analysis. Washington: National Institute of Justice.

National Police (Recordable Offences) Regulations (2000) London: The Home Office.

Nuffield Council on Bioethics (2007) *The forensic use of bioinformation: ethical issues*. London: The Nuffield Council.

Royal Commission on Criminal Justice (1993) London: HMSO.

Sedley, S. (2005) 'Editorial', *Science and Justice*, 45: 59–60.

Sparkes, R., Kimpton, C., Watson, S., Oldroyd, N., Clayton, T., Barnett, L., Arnold, J., Thompson, C., Hale, R., Chapman, J., Urquhart, A. and Gill, P. (1996) 'The validation of a 7-locus multiplex STR test for use in forensic casework (1)', *Int J Leg Med*, 186–194.

UKAS (2001) *LAB 32 – Accreditation for Suppliers to the UK National DNA Database*. London: UKAS.

van der Beek, C.P. (2006) Presentation to the European Academy of Forensic Sciences, Helsinki, 13–16 June.

Williams, R., Johnson, P. and Martin, P. (2004) *Genetic Information and Crime Investigation*. London: The Wellcome Trust.

# Chapter 13

# Using forensic science in major crime inquiries

*David Barclay*

Wherever he steps, whatever he touches, whatever he leaves, even unconsciously, will serve as a silent witness against him. Not only his fingerprints or his footprints, but his hair, the fibres from his clothes, the glass he breaks, the tool mark he leaves, the paint he scratches, the blood or semen he deposits or collects. All of these, and more, bear mute witness against him. This is evidence that does not forget. It is not confused by the excitement of the moment. It is not absent because human witnesses are. It is factual evidence. Physical evidence cannot be wrong, it cannot perjure itself, it cannot be wholly absent. Only human failure to find it, study and understand it, can diminish its value.

(Kirk: 1974)

## Introduction

Rather more eloquently put by Kirk than the summary I was taught – 'every contact leaves a trace' (Locard: 1918–1931) – this principle was the cornerstone of forensic science, or at least criminalistics, throughout the twentieth century. Nowadays investigators might add something about 'every action he takes and every motivation he has', because we now know that behavioural advice and crime reconstruction are synergistic in making sure that we do indeed 'find it, study and understand it' – at least in serious crimes of violence.

This chapter describes current investigative practice in the use of physical evidence in the UK, and suggests practical aids and processes to promote closer integration and mutual understanding of scientific and investigative systems.

Throughout the twentieth century forensic science worldwide progressed quietly through relatively uneventful decades where pathologists were the stars and advances were based on gradual improvement in scientific techniques to provide better discrimination and thus better evidence in courts. The pace of technological advance increased in the last three decades of the century – more robust blood grouping methods and polymorphic enzymes transformed forensic biology and the introduction of gas chromatography and then mass spectrometry had a tremendous influence on forensic toxicology and chemistry. There were even greater advances in fingerprint technology as various Automated Fingerprint Recognition (AFR) systems were implemented worldwide including across the UK, and the introduction of forensic DNA profiling to criminal casework in 1988 was a harbinger of what was to come.

However, serious concerns about the investigative process in 'stranger' murders or other serious crime began to surface in the 1960s and were brought to a head by the Black Panther murder and kidnap series (1974–5) and then crucially by the bungled Yorkshire Ripper serial murder investigation (1976–81). Both crimes were detected by a chance encounter with patrol officers, not by investigators. The subsequent report by one of Her Majesty's Inspectors of Constabulary (HMIC), Lawrence Byford (Byford 1982), made many recommendations, several aimed at closer integration of forensic science with the investigative process. At the same time changes caused by several miscarriages of justice (MOJ) and major changes of legislation (e.g. PACE[1]) in the 1980s began to move police investigative practice away from the 'nomination' approach, where evidence was sought against specific prime suspect(s), often chosen personally by the Senior Investigating Officer (SIO). This tactic had proved to be the root cause of many MOJs, because it was a closed process and work to reinforce the erroneous hypothesis tended to have higher priority. It is a natural but unfortunate human trait that once you think you know what has happened, there is a tendency to make everything fit that view.

Now for the first time the investigative process became focused on the *elimination* of suspects from a pool of possibles, until (ideally!) only one was left: Sherlock Holmes-like in its simplicity. This is a completely open process as the information is applied equally to all nominals, and no value judgement has to be made, although the elimination work is often prioritised against a matrix of factors.

The value of scientific evidence in securing convictions was now fully apparent, but difficulties were also emerging here. From 1990 onwards there were a series of investigations of the effectiveness of the processes police forces used to obtain scientific support. First a structural investigation (Saulsbury *et al.* 1992) and then reports outlining good practice and current difficulties in the effective use of forensic science (ACPO/FSS 1996), or reporting on the difficulties encountered (Police Research Group 1996) were produced. The body tasked to audit police forces in the UK, Her Majesty's Inspectorate of Constabulary (HMIC), also produced two excellent reports on the use of scientific support (HMIC 2000; HMIC 2002).

By the mid 1990s, police forces were becoming more aware of the value of physical intelligence, and the government had created the National DNA Database, an overt intelligence tool. However, almost all forensic scientists still regarded their primary role as providing evidence for use in court, and most investigators accepted this philosophy. But the increasing scientific organisation of forces and a parallel centralisation of investigative training was about to produce an unexpected paradigm shift in forensic science. As investigators became more professional, working to standard protocols for major incident rooms (ACPO Crime Committee 2000) and *The Murder Manual* (ACPO 1999), so parallel improvements in national support services were implemented. The National Crime Faculty (NCF), created in 1996 as a belated response to Byford, was designed to provide independent specialist support to investigators in the most serious crimes of violence, via a completely integrated approach with detectives, crime analysts, forensic scientists, pathologists and behavioural experts all part of the same team. It was outstandingly successful in concept and execution and from 1996 to 2001 doubled its workload every six months, so that by 2002 it was supporting virtually every complex murder in the UK. Although NCF evolved into National Crime and Operations Faculty (NCOF) and then National Centre for Policing Excellence (NCPE)[2] it is still known simply as 'Crime Faculty' to SIOs and provides the same support services across the UK, and indeed further abroad on request. From the inception of the 'Crime Faculty', investigators were able for the first time to attach an experienced forensic scientist to routine (albeit difficult) murder investigations, often as part of the management team. This was the start of a revolution in the use of forensic science.

As soon as NCF casework support started it became obvious to the NCF scientists that the real benefits of forensic science lay in the early stages of an inquiry during the investigative phase, and required the provision of physical intelligence, not hard evidence. It was also clear that this was simply not being done in most cases. Enormous numbers of observations, opinions and items of factual information were capable of being generated by the laboratory, pathology and scene work, but their potential significance was simply not appreciated by the scientists. This was because they were neither sufficiently aware of the circumstances, nor had they any knowledge of the lines of enquiry that the information might assist. The existing paradigm of forensic science actively discouraged the production of intelligence, because the focus was on evidence for court, confined to narrow areas of expertise and the need for rigorously justified interpretations. The provision of intelligence in a way which would match the investigative needs would require personal interpretations, soft facts and opinion expressed in shades of grey – the antithesis of what most forensic scientists wished to achieve.

The lessons derived from NCF casework support to serious crime were quickly learnt by the Forensic Science Service (FSS), which had seconded staff to support NCF, and from 1997 onwards the principles outlined below were being taught to SIOs on courses at the police training colleges across the UK, at seminars and ACPO meetings, and internally to scientists within the FSS. Over the succeeding years these principles have been developed into practical aids to maximise the impact and usefulness of physical evidence, and roles and responsibilities to support its provision, as well as being embodied in the national doctrine and manuals produced successively by NCF, NCOF and NCPE. NPIA now has overall responsibility for the design and accreditation of training to meet national requirements, and has recently subsumed many of the support bodies mentioned above, as well as some functions formerly carried out by the Home Office Police Standards Unit (PSU). PSU continues its role to measure performance within the police service, and provide intensive support where needed.

By 2005 the Parliamentary Select Committee on Forensic Science (House of Commons Science and Technology Committee 2005) was able to state as a given:

> Forensic science is critical to the efficiency and effectiveness of the criminal justice system. The main contribution that forensic science makes to the criminal justice system is the generation of intelligence to assist investigations: the provision of actual evidence to convict the guilty or exculpate the innocent represents a small, although very significant, part of its role.

At the time of writing, all the Police Agencies of the UK are working to the same National Intelligence Model (NIM) (National Criminal Intelligence Service 2000), and the primary role of forensic examinations in providing high-quality physical intelligence is recognised by forensic suppliers and investigators alike. However, a lack of understanding of investigative practice by experts, especially laboratory scientists, and an inevitable lack of detailed knowledge of all the circumstances remains a serious constraint.

By 1999 the FSS and NCF together had created a role to bridge that communication gap – the Specialist Adviser (SA) – and this role has been an outstanding success with SIOs and the ACPO Homicide Working Group, and was originally modelled on the investigative role of the Head of Physical Evidence at NCF. It was envisaged that the need for this role would gradually disappear as the paradigm shift became established and all reporting scientists thought primarily about intelligence, before concentrating on the evidential stage for court.

Although the paradigm has shifted irretrievably away from evidence and certainly towards intelligence and value judgements, this continues to be uncomfortable for many forensic scientists, and even some pathologists. The issue of investigative responsibilities was of such significance that it was specified in the new national contract for pathology introduced in 2006. However, physical evidence reviews by the author in the UK continue to uncover apparently obvious missed opportunities to assist the investigative phase of inquiries. Anecdotal and experiential evidence is that the situation is worse in other countries, whose problems are inevitably compounded by multiple agencies and a proliferation of small police forces and laboratories.

If we take 1990 as a benchmark (the start of the process of operational reviews of scientific support), the use of forensic science including fingermarks and pathology has been transformed in every aspect. There have been enormous improvements in organisation, control and management information accompanied by increases in utility and cost effectiveness exemplified by the National DNA Database. Investigators are better trained, to unified, national standards, with forensic science an integral part of that training. This more integrated relationship between investigators and forensic science has been supported at several levels by:

1 government funding of intelligence databases like the NDNAD and more recently the National Firearms database, as well as the National Automated Fingerprint Identification System (NAFIS);[3]

2 governmental organisations aimed at producing central support, doctrine and control of investigative activities NCOF, NCPE, PSU and HMIC respectively;

3 the production of investigative aids, aimed at clarifying the views of scientists and making physical intelligence explicit to investigators (sceneline, physical status reports, charting microsequence analysis);

4 the introduction of additional forensic services, funded directly or indirectly by the Government, in order to satisfy specific investigative needs – National Injuries Database (NCOF), Soilfit project (Macaulay Institute), Geographic Profiling (NCOF).

These changes have enabled forensic science to better serve the whole investigative process at a tactical level in serious crime, and the strategic level in volume crime, rather than simply being a useful add-on to produce evidence for a conviction.

Almost a hundred years after Locard's statement, it remains a foreign concept to some forensic scientists that the most important task they can do is to reconstruct the crime and clarify the fine detail – the microsequence of events at the scene(s). Understanding the scene, the victimology and the motivations of the offender provides the solid ground on which a successful investigation can be founded, and which allows additional physical evidence to be recovered. The microsequence of events is the key to uncovering additional contact points between offender and victim or scene. This is an iterative process; not only will each contact point, as Kirk states, provide an opportunity for the recovery of intelligence or evidence, but it will provide vital information for the Behavioural Adviser, from which further contact points can be postulated.

### Summary

In the recent past the primary focus of forensic science has moved away from the provision of evidence to a more active role in providing intelligence throughout an investigation. For the investigative process to use forensic science effectively and efficiently we need:

- shared understanding of roles;
- good forensic knowledge on the part of the police;
- good investigative knowledge on the part of scientists;
- systems to facilitate the recovery, analysis and scientific assessment of physical materials;
- scientific and investigative interpretation in the context of the case.

In the UK communication and interpretation have been improved by the role of 'forensic investigator' or Specialist Adviser (SA) which has become widely accepted in recent years. However, forensic knowledge of police investigators remains a concern, especially in volume crime (where decisions may be made at patrol level). This is despite attempts to address this issue by training videos such as *Think Forensic* (FSS Greater Manchester Police 1993) and DVDs produced specifically for new recruits.

## Police use of forensic science

In very serious offences, especially of violence, in addition to SOCOs, forensic scientists may be involved in recovery of evidence, and other more experienced scientists may act as advisers. Fingerprints found at scenes are checked against national databases directly by police forces, and information from a body is provided by a forensic pathologist.

Many aspects of the forensic analysis are subject to influence and constraints imposed by the police. Potential evidence is subjected to detailed laboratory examination and analysis using a range of techniques, some of which, for example shoe prints and presumptive testing for blood, may initially be examined 'in house' by the force. The choice of items to be submitted for testing, and the priority awarded to them, has a major impact on the benefit to the investigation that is derived from forensic analysis. The value of any forensic intelligence or evidence is also dependent not only on the scientific interpretation of the test result, but also the context of the item, necessitating an awareness and understanding of the particular circumstances of the case in question. Furthermore, appropriate action needs to be taken by the police once the forensic test results become available. The power of forensic science to facilitate the administration of justice is therefore entirely dependent on the ability of the police, and others, to use it effectively. It is of concern that there remain considerable variations in practice across forces, even when notionally working to the same doctrine, and the creation of PSU and its inclusion in the NPIA is a mark of how seriously the UK Government takes this issue.

Although there are a limited number of stakeholders in the UK (ACPO, ACPOS, SPSA, NPIA, FSS, LGC etc.) with significant influence on forensic issues, each force does have complete operational autonomy within national government guidelines and targets. This poses problems of compliance and definition for management statistics and monitoring of progress. Coupled with variations in practices and standards, this has the effect of making the performance measurement of scientific support activities less rigorous than would be desirable, which affects planning and cost effectiveness in volume crime.

A basic knowledge of the potential value of various types of physical evidence, and procedures for protecting and processing evidence is essential for all police officers. A lack of this 'forensic awareness' is a more important constraint in volume crime as availability of external support and advice is normally limited to specific operations, usually serious ones. Low forensic awareness may prevent cost effective physical evidential solutions and intelligence even getting on the agenda, especially since most items are submitted to laboratories through detective sergeants, whose knowledge has been found to be particularly poor

('Using Forensic Science Effectively' (USFE) 1996, and D. Barclay unpublished data 1998–2003). Although the FSS introduced volume crime SAs to assist in these areas the role was subsequently withdrawn.

## A changing environment

During the latter stages of the Yorkshire Ripper investigation (1976–81) a small advisory team was attached to the investigation. The team included the late Professor Stuart Kind, Director of the Home Office Central Research Establishment at Aldermaston, then the *éminence grise* of UK forensic science. Many of his recommendations were included in the subsequent report by Byford and Professor Kind himself wrote a classic account, 'The Scientific Investigation of Crime', now sadly out of print but notable for the first description and use of what became known as Geographical Profiling.

Two linked changes in the investigative process have occurred. First the investigative method itself changed from Nomination to Elimination for many reasons, including a substantial number of Miscarriages of Justice (MOJ) in the 1980s, and the realisation that eyewitness evidence, 'verbals' and 'prison informants' all provided extremely dubious evidence. This was accompanied by a much greater transparency across the whole of the investigative process driven by PACE (1984), and the Criminal Procedure and Investigations Act (1996) which was introduced in an attempt to make sure police and the Crown Prosecution Service (CPS) disclose to the defence everything which could be relevant to their case.

However, this meant that eyewitness and verbal evidence had to be replaced as investigative tools by forensic evidence, and this in turn led to a greater appreciation of the value of physical intelligence. This change was promulgated and nurtured by national investigative training developed by Centrex through NCF, SIO development training from the 1990s onwards and other courses such as MSSC (management of serious series crime) and MLSC (management of linked serious crime) which included inputs from experienced forensic scientists and in particular stressed the key role of physical intelligence in clarifying events and providing elimination criteria.

A further driver came from Her Majesty's Inspector of Constabulary, the central body which examines every aspect of operational policing. Each force is inspected regularly and Thematic Inspections target specific areas of concern. In recent years there have been a number of thematic inspections concerned with serious crime investigation, and scientific support including forensic science.

The Thematic Inspection Report, *Under the Microscope*, and its follow-up, *Under the Microscope Refocused* (HMIC 2000; 2002) identified a number of problems with the use of forensic science by police forces. As a result police forces put significant effort into improving policies on scene attendance by SOCOs. Models for costing this work and measuring performance were also developed. The reports made clear that scientific support staff are more effective when fully integrated into the whole intelligence and investigative process, an essential step in the intelligence-led approach to policing enshrined in the National Intelligence Model (NIM). The growing exploitation of forensic intelligence is a key factor in the effective operation of the National Intelligence Model.

The availability of the NDNAD clearly influenced the move to intelligence in volume crime and its use within police forces, but hardly impinged on the activities of most forensic scientists. In serious crime the provision of intelligence is immeasurably broader, across many lines of enquiry, requiring proactive thought and a change in mindset by the individual scientists.

Although NIM is based on proactive policing and is ideally suited to volume crime and offences, many elements of NIM may be used in reactive investigations, for example, to direct resources and establish a full picture of the crime. NIM ensures that information is fully researched, developed and analysed to provide intelligence that senior investigators can use to focus strategic direction, make tactical resourcing decisions, and manage risk.

The UK Government has not been slow to fund new sources of forensic intelligence, firstly through the establishment of the NDNAD and in 2007 the National Firearms Forensic Intelligence Database (NFFID) which is now fully operational, and is UK wide. The NFFID comprises two separate computer databases. The first allows information from weapons and ammunition to be collected, interrogated and interpreted in one central point. The second part is an automated system called Integrated Ballistics Identification System (IBIS), already in national use in the USA, that can compare striking pin marks and breech marks of fired ammunition from outstanding crimes and recovered weapons.

By 2005 the Parliamentary Select Committee stated, 'If used properly, forensic techniques can serve as vital intelligence tools to underpin the entire investigative process. Forensic science has a key role to play in enabling the intelligence-led approach to policing embodied by the National Intelligence Model. It is thus essential that police training in forensic science is delivered within the context of the National Intelligence Model.'

## Forensic science in the investigative process

### Investigative methods

There are two phases in any investigation – an investigative phase characterised by neutrality, crime reconstruction, gradual resolving of uncertainty, gathering of intelligence, provision of critical fact, and substantial policing activity across many lines of enquiry. The subsequent evidential phase is more focused on an individual suspect and has the obvious purpose of meeting the requirements of the criminal justice system. The vast majority of police resource is applied to the investigative phase and forensic science contributes in excess of 90 per cent of its value to this phase, as physical intelligence across many lines of enquiry. For example, one major line of enquiry is the victimology – what made her a target? This can be clarified by intelligence on victim movements (when did the victim last eat?), providing critical facts and enabling the determination of time of death.

## Science in context

Forensic science is the interpretation of results in the context of the case circumstances, not the tests themselves. It follows then that the scientist must be fully aware of the entire case context and therefore be either part of the investigation or have exceptionally good lines of communication to it. Historically this did happen in some extremely complex and high-profile cases, but very rarely. It was not generally accepted that large quantities of physical intelligence were being completely missed. It is no exaggeration to say that the author was horrified to find just how much practical information was being missed when he started casework for NCF in 1996. Each of the first three cases he reviewed was eventually detected using information known to the scientists, the significance of which had not been appreciated. It is not overstating the case to point out that failure to interpret such findings fully is an abdication of the responsibilities of the scientist.

As noted in the introduction, by 2005 it was recognised that the main contribution that forensic science makes to the criminal justice system is the generation of intelligence to assist investigations, and this principle is embodied in current investigative training, as well as in the marketing strategies of the suppliers.

In relation to evidence, the probative value of that evidence is a matter for the court and it follows that if either the test result or the context changes a new interpretation is required. This cannot be done unless the scientist is close to the inquiry and there are good lines of communication.

## Understanding and using physical intelligence

The most important aspect of the work of forensic scientists is the provision of physical intelligence during the investigative phase, before a specific suspect is identified. However, forensic scientists often consider their primary purpose to be the provision of evidence in court. Perhaps 90 per cent of their observations can best contribute to the investigative phase of an inquiry, a fact that is sadly lost on most scientists and many SIOs. In fact evidence, like intelligence, is more likely to be used to eliminate suspects or negate hypotheses than be of use in a court case against a named individual.

Forensic science can be used in an investigation to:

- clarify the sequence of events;
- identify critical facts (i.e. known only to the offender and the investigators);
- provide elimination factors;
- direct lines of enquiry such as targeting the house-to-house interviews;
- assist in interview strategies or crime scene examination strategies;
- prioritise and assist lines of enquiry.

It is vital then that the importance of integrating physical intelligence into the investigation is recognised and implemented fully. Physical intelligence has the unique attribute of being capable of conversion to physical evidence the availability of which is essential to effective prosecution nowadays. Intelligence detects cases but evidence is required for prosecution.

Much of the impetus for this improved appreciation by investigators of the usefulness of physical intelligence came from the wider use and spectacular success of the NDNAD in volume crime. However, it was in serious crime where the deficiencies of the existing systems first became obvious where role changes required to improve matters were devised and implemented. From 1997 onwards NCF and FSS together made great efforts to promulgate the principles of using physical items for intelligence and the FSS introduced a specific role, the 'Specialist Adviser', to assist the process. This role proved extremely popular with investigators and was endorsed by ACPO Homicide Working Group, although a full appreciation of the importance of 'intelligence not evidence' was slower to penetrate ordinary laboratory scientists, who had little knowledge of investigative lines of enquiry or the constraints of investigators.

We need to draw a distinction between crime scene reconstruction in the sense of Bloodstain Pattern Analysis (BPA) or ballistics to produce factual evidence suitable for court, and crime reconstruction or assessment. The latter requires consideration of more subjective factors such as motivation and victimology, to provide intelligence for the investigation to uncover fine details of the sequence of events, from which further physical evidence may be recovered. The ability to reconstruct crimes will require sufficient knowledge to understand and exploit the potential of BPA, pathology, criminal psychology, or finger marks, but not necessarily the expertise to perform any of these specialist roles. There is a need for an additional role requiring broad forensic and investigative knowledge, and a basic understanding of the scientific method and scientific reasoning. These attributes and knowledge are most likely to be found in experienced forensic scientists, such as the SAs, or some of the Scientific Support Managers.

Conclusions drawn regarding the actions and events on the basis of physical intelligence are of considerable utility and frequently result in tangible outcomes, in the sense of investigative options reduced, corroboration of witness statements, and the like. Intelligence which does not affect the investigation is of no value. However, powerful contradictory evidence may be produced by comparison of BPA findings with the alleged actions of the parties involved and the physical locations of witnesses or suspects at the scene.

The change to an elimination approach to investigation fully utilised for the first time the core strength of forensic science – its ability to provide absolute elimination of both suspects and circumstances. Whilst the strength of associative evidence must be carefully assessed and is rarely conclusive, physical intelligence can and usually does eliminate absolutely.

The value of this is obvious, at least to investigators, and one example will suffice.

*An elderly lady had been tied up, strangled and then stabbed. No overt sexual assault had taken place although this was clearly a sex crime. Good work by the laboratory identified that the engagement ring worn by the victim had been removed – the white band of protected skin was visible. DNA – in the time before Low Copy Number (LCN) – produced a partial profile showing only three very common alleles. Other circumstances made it certain that this partial profile was from the offender.*

*This would be classed as very weak associative evidence, as it produced a likelihood ratio of only 1:35, as opposed to the several billion that the courts now seem to expect. The SIO had assembled a pool of 830 nominals – active burglars and sex offenders etc. – which was too many to eliminate by alibi. Knowing that the offender possessed the three alleles reduced the pool to 22 at a stroke, as all those with even one allele missing could be absolutely eliminated. This led rapidly to the detection of the offence. Fortunately the offender had removed from the scene other items which gave a full DNA profile of the victim and these were recovered from his possession.*

### Influencing investigations

The need is for an advisory role, based on opinion not certainty, to assist the SIO in making his resource bets on the most cost effective lines of enquiry. For this to take place forensic scientists must be comfortable with uncertainty. There is still a tendency to restrict opinions to those which can later be proved in court, thus artificially constraining the impact of physical evidence on the investigative phase of an inquiry. One obvious reason for this behaviour is mistrust of police, who have a history of turning any 'grey' opinion into 'black and white'. This is also coupled with the desire of scientists to protect themselves during cross-examination in court. This situation is unedifying and unhelpful to criminal justice, but given human nature is probably an inevitable product of the UK adversarial system. The role of the SA, whose job is to champion physical intelligence and act on behalf of the SIO in maximising the physical evidence input, is partly recognition of these difficulties.

Forensic scientists need to know what the lines of enquiry being investigated are so they can see where the knowledge that they alone have may be significant. Examples of lines of enquiry are: establishing time of death (by phone calls, mail, newspapers, electricity meters, neighbours, sightings); investigating antecedents – what is the previous history of the victim; and house-to-house ('canvassing' in many parts of the world) to identify any witnesses; local burglaries; CCTV; cellsite analysis; bail hostels; media strategy etc.

To illustrate the importance of knowledge of the lines of enquiry we can consider the effect of one of the simplest scientific analyses currently in use – determination of blood and urine ethanol levels, routinely performed in every murder – on three lines of enquiry.

1 To take time of death as an example, most people would be aware that entomology can be useful in determining the date of death within a day or so, and the onset and relaxation of rigor mortis can set broad limits to 'hours since death'. However, most pathologists are honest enough to accept that their best estimate of the likely time of death is sometime between victim being last seen and victim's body found!

More useful, and much more precise than entomology, is a simple *back alcohol calculation*. This is based on the ratio between blood and urine ethanol levels at death, which are a function of the number of hours during which

347

the alcohol has been metabolised. In those rare cases when the amount of alcohol taken is known, the actual blood ethanol level remaining can act as a confirmatory factor. This calculation is a routine process in drink-driving cases, but is rarely considered in the different context of a murder, for reasons which are obscure to the author. This is perhaps yet another illustration of the importance and effect of context. Back alcohol calculation has been used many times at NCOF to clarify time of death, or to support or refute alleged movements of victims, and has proved invaluable – and correct in those cases later detected. A narrow window for time of death is very important as the opportunity for the offender to commit the crime must (obviously) fall within the same time window and this can thus provide an excellent elimination factor for other nominals.

2 Even the absence of alcohol in the body has proved vital in resolving a number of undetected or cold cases, by clarifying the movements of the victim. Sadly, in none of these did the scientists originally involved notice the significance. Clearly a negative result in one of the simplest scientific analyses carried out failed to impress the reporting scientist, who presumably had insufficient knowledge of the case to understand the context. Whilst understandable this is of course no excuse, since we have already defined the essence of *forensic* science as the interpretation of results in context.

3 One further example that may strike a chord with SIOs is the effect of an alcohol result on the media strategy, particularly for young female victims. Put simply, if the victim has been out clubbing and has a high level of alcohol, making her incapable of rational choices, and she is consequently separated from her friends, the media strategy would be to minimise her activities over the evening and stress her home life – that she is a good mother, etc. If on the other hand she has a low level or nil alcohol because she was the designated driver or simply did not drink, the strategy would be to make great play of this, how she did everything right on the night, was supporting her friends and yet still was attacked by this dangerous person in a particularly unlucky way. Both strategies are designed to maximise public concern for the victim, vital in the first few days, and are entirely dictated by the alcohol level. In my experience SIOs cannot understand why scientists do not appreciate the importance of this.

It is clear then that just as knowledge of context is vital for the interpretation of results, so is knowledge of the lines of enquiry to maximise the contribution of those interpretations to the investigation.

One of the main benefits of the role of SA is to bridge that gap between the investigation and its activities and the laboratory workers and their results.

This is complemented by the fact that SIO development training includes extensive input from scientists to a developing protocol devised by NPIA and ACPO Homicide Working Group, and reporting scientists are encouraged to attend the courses, and are attached to a Major Incident Room (MIR) to observe and understand the procedures. The experienced scientists acting as SAs provide a constant exemplar of the value of the process, as the resulting actions are fed back to the scientists working in the labs, complete with justification based on the investigative (rather than scientific) needs.

There are dangers, however. The police have in the past tended to 'run off' with tentative opinions, allowing every new fact to reinforce the conclusions they have already formed – sadly, a natural facet of human thinking – or transmuting carefully expressed shades of grey opinion into black and white. Consequently, intelligence opinions should be recorded and peer reviewed in the same way that we do for formal Criminal Justice Act statements.

If we are to convert intelligence to evidence we need to provide continuity and security of all samples taken to evidential standards. The changed paradigm therefore applies to selection of tests, observations and interpretations, including reconstruction of the detail of the crime and all its associated events, but *not* to the evidential chain – sample processing, security continuity or storage. However, this increased profile of physical intelligence does affect crime scene work. It will involve selection of additional crime scene items for intelligence testing alone, and conversely particular care in undertaking tests for intelligence purposes which might affect later substantive evidence.

This is an efficient use of resources as these items are now producing evidence, and many others will have already been useful in eliminating possibilities, or clarifying circumstances for the investigators. Often this physical evidence used in elimination could never have provided inculpatory evidence, but the exclusion of a possibility, or the redirection of resource may be highly significant. After all, one could accumulate conclusive physical and other evidence against an unknown offender, but if that person is never identified because of overlooked intelligence, then none of the evidence is of value to the criminal justice system.

### Case history – Ms Y physical intelligence

*The body of a teenage girl was found exposed amongst head-high thistles in scrubland alongside a road that lay on her normal route home from a social gathering in the centre of a small town in America. She had last been seen with her boyfriend leaving the gathering to walk home. The body was not found until it had been several days lying in the sun, during which time shade temperatures of over 35°C were recorded. The locus was examined as fully as possible given the delay in finding the body and the hot and damp conditions, but no foreign DNA profile was ever recovered from the body. Apart from the almost fully dressed body, no significant physical evidence was recovered from the scene.*

*After a year the investigation had essentially stalled, at least in respect of physical findings. However there were a number of findings incompatible with the original view that where the body was found was an attack site.*

1 *The mode of death was said to be suffocation by pressing the face into the ground, and this seemed unlikely since the ground was hard-baked earth.*
2 *There were fine parallel abrasions on the body which could not have been produced by anything at the scene.*
3 *The idea that the victim would have chosen to go into that area to have sex (with her boyfriend) was unlikely; her parents were not at home and an area with short grass and picnic tables was only 100 yards further down the road.*

*The fact that her panties were missing from the locus was also suggestive of another location.*

*These observations for intelligence purposes seemed in direct conflict with the views of investigators and initially with the pathologist. The importance to the investigation of course was that if this was a body deposition site, rather than attack site, then there were two more additional locations (attack site and transport vehicle) where evidence might be found. Further, the boyfriend had no obvious access to a vehicle, could not drive, and no one had ever seen him with a vehicle. If this was a deposition site then this would provide strongly exculpatory intelligence, and fit with his story of having left Ms Y in town.*

*Further discussion with the pathologist revealed that he had always thought it would be impossible to suffocate the girl in the proposed manner at the scene and that her face would have had to be pressed into something much softer. Although he had expressed this opinion at a review meeting, it had not overridden the initial police assessment of the scene.*

*An explanation for the fine scratches was postulated which pointed to her body being dragged over something such as the back bar of the tailgate of a pickup or similar vehicle which had been coated with anti-slip paint consisting of coarse sand in a rubberised matrix.*

*A number of suspects were identified, one of whom had sold the bed of his pickup truck in the period between the girl going missing and her body being found; as a consequence he was prioritised by the investigation team. Eventually a full DNA profile of the victim was recovered from the back tailgate bar of this truck bed (which had fortunately been stored in a barn by its new owner) and from a cushion from the settee at the offender's home and he made a full admission. Subsequently distinctive fibres matching the silk trim on a duplicate pair of panties were recovered from the side of the settee.*

Attaching a scientist to the investigation for the first few days will ensure that the opportunities to gain physical intelligence are maximised, and should ensure that the effect on prioritising lines of enquiry will be optimal. It is important that all advice, however informal, is recorded, together with the information on which it was based.

However, many category A murders (in which the link between offender and victim is not immediately obvious) will not be detected for some weeks or months. These cases, typically 'stranger' murders or murders of children, are often high profile with the media and with the officers involved. One method of maximising the input is for the scientist to undertake a formal physical evidence review, even in current ongoing murder investigations, as part of any investigative review. This review should have access to all the documentation of the inquiry and challenge even the most basic assumptions. In the UK there are three stages of formal review:

1  Internally by the force, but by officers outside the investigative team – after 28 days.

2  A full review after six months by a team from another force, but with local office support. The external review team will consist of experienced

detectives and often includes its own Crime Scene Investigator or Crime Scene Manager, crime analysts and other specialists.

3 By the force cold case team. This may be routine or following a significant event such as a failed prosecution, a successful appeal by the person convicted, or following media interest in a suspect convicted of other similar crimes.

### Specific practical outputs

There are three additional elements necessary to maximise the effect of any physical evidence review.

1 The processes and results must be integrated to include other experts since overall investigative significance of individual elements of specialist evidence requires a holistic interpretation, and the process of crime reconstruction is an iterative one.

2 The process and findings must be transparent to the investigative team; and conclusions and actions agreed, not imposed.

3 Where a solution to an investigative need is not immediately apparent, one must be researched.

In relation to point 3, NCOF provides a mechanism for coordinating the research to identify potential scientific solutions which may be unknown to the investigative team and forensic personnel.

Recent examples include:

- the National Injuries Database (NIDb) formerly based at Guy's Hospital and which now forms a core part of NCOF support for serious assaults and murders, providing intelligence as to the nature of an unknown weapon, and comparative evidence;

- 'soilfit' project to rationalise soil analysis techniques;

- geographical profiling. This was introduced and is nationally coordinated through NCOF.

At NCOF Behavioural Investigative Advisers (BIA), formerly called psychological profilers, and crime analysts were usually consulted immediately, as support to live cases. Physical evidence tended to become involved later, after force scientific support and forensic providers had explored the usual avenues. This meant that many reviews at NCOF were centred on physical evidence, but it was invariably necessary to check emerging findings with others such as pathologists and fingerprint experts. A particularly strong link emerged between BIAs and physical evidence. Many small observations from the scene or victim will greatly assist the BIA by clarifying the victimology, mode of attack and the detailed sequence of events during the attack phase or subsequently. This works both ways, since a prime purpose of the review is to uncover contact points between offender and victim, or offender and scene so that further analyses can be undertaken to produce additional evidence.

BIA views as to how the attack was likely to have proceeded, how the victim behaved and exactly where the victim was touched are extremely helpful in pointing us towards previously disregarded opportunities. This 'psychological profiling' and 'physical profiling' of the crime is synergistic. At NCOF it was found particularly beneficial to have an initial meeting of the 'experts' and perhaps the office manager of the investigation who would be aware of all the documentation available, to discuss the circumstances and difficulties and suggest an approach to be adopted. Each expert (BIA, geographical profiler, pathologist, forensic scientist etc.) would then work within their own speciality but in communication with the others and later present their initial findings at a meeting with the SIO and other members of the inquiry team. This ensures understanding of the circumstances and views of others and provides the opportunity for cross-checks and clarification.

Formal individual reports would follow, which referred explicitly to the work of other experts when it was relied on, and which suggested motivations and characteristics of the offender, and further investigative opportunities including interview strategies, factors for the prioritisation matrix and physical evidence actions.

However useful that process is in potential, much of its value will be lost if the resulting forensic intelligence is not made explicit to the SIO and the rest of his team. Several techniques were devised at NCOF to assist this:

- 'What we know' reports. This report sets out in strictly defined terms

  1 everything known for certain from physical evidence;
  2 scientific interpretations or intelligence; and
  3 things NOT known for certain (and which should therefore be avoided at interview if credibility is not to be lost).

The purpose is to provide a solid base for the inquiry and to ensure all members of the team, whether police officers or scientists, share a common understanding.

- Charting. Many forces worldwide use *Analysts Notebook* (Investigative analysis 2007) or similar software to produce timelines, charts with embedded hot links etc. and to analyse links between, for example, telephones or bank accounts. It is easy to use this software to produce detailed schematics of a crime scene with DNA or fingerprint symbols to identify items sent for such analysis. Items held by the force are labelled green; those sent for analysis change colour and are linked by an arrow heading out, and by an arrow returning when the result has been received. This is accompanied by a hotlink to the result and, if appropriate, further links to that nominal. The software will be familiar to most SIOs, and all crime analysts. The great advantage of this process is that items unexamined, still awaiting results, and links become instantly explicit even to less forensically adroit officers. This is because we are all much better at absorbing visual data than written. An entire forensic report can be expressed unequivocally on one side of A4, and items accidentally missed (on which no decision has been made) stand out.

- Sceneline. This is a simple 'timeline' of the alleged physical actions at the scene according to the investigative hypothesis, plotted against the actual known facts. All of the known facts *must* lie directly on the sceneline if the hypothesis is correct, or if they do not, must be capable of being connected to the sceneline by some verifiable fact or interpretation. It is particularly useful in challenging investigative assumptions, and uncovering anomalies. This is particularly useful in cold cases, where the search for anomalies is a key step to uncovering further forensic opportunities.

*Sceneline example*
*The body of a young girl was discovered at the back of some shops around 9 a.m. in February. She was naked and had bled extensively at the scene from facial injuries; she had been raped. She had last been seen around 10.15 p.m. the night before when she left a neighbour's house to set off into town to meet some friends at a local club; they then intended to go back to her house for a social gathering as her parents were away for the weekend. The lady who found the body felt she was alive when found but the police dismissed this as wishful thinking as the victim was certified dead at the scene and was very cold. The initial attack site was identified as near the side of the shop, which was about 10 minutes' walk from her home and on the direct route to the club. Some small items had been taken from her including a watch and money. The victim did not drink regularly and had only a small amount of alcohol in the blood.*

*Despite very extensive investigations this crime remained undetected for 18 months before NCOF became involved, although a full DNA profile was available.*

*The police hypothesis throughout that time was that the victim had been attacked in the street by a sex offender at around 10.30 p.m., knocked down by a blow to the head, raped at the side of the shop and left there. She had later crawled to the back of the shop to seek help, as there was a security light on inside the shop, and there died of head injuries. The police investigation focused on sex offenders and acquaintances.*

*Plotting the physical findings against this in a sceneline produced a number of anomalies:*

1 *The victim was a sturdy, attractive and physically fit girl, and the victimology did not fit the crime: why had she been selected out of the many young females out at that time?*
2 *She had numerous abrasions on the knees, but these were not parallel as would be expected from crawling on concrete, but arcuate.*
3 *There was no deliberate cause of death; she had not been stabbed or strangled and the head injuries were minimal.*
4 *There was no blood between the site of attack and the back of the shops where the body lay.*
5 *BIA advice was that the theft of small items of value is extremely unusual for a 'disorganised' rapist.*

*6 The witness who found the body believed that she responded to touch.*

*Having identified these findings that lay off the sceneline, an analysis was performed to try and bring them on to the sceneline either by providing an alternative hypothesis line, or a verifiable explanation of the anomalies. One previously overlooked analytical result proved to be the key.*

*The victim had a very small amount of alcohol in her blood, but over 130 mg per 100 ml in the urine. A routine back calculation indicated that she must have had a peak blood alcohol concentration over 2.5 times the driving limit in the UK, and had been metabolising alcohol for approximately 10 hours.*

*The victimology and the cause of death now made sense. Unused to alcohol she had been almost incapable of walking and became a target for that reason, and the effect of her minor head injuries was greatly exacerbated by the high level of alcohol in her blood. The abrasions on her legs and feet indicated that she had been raped from behind with one knee under her and one stretched out. The lack of blood between the initial attack site and the back of the shop was because there had been a two-phase attack. After an initial blow to the face the offender had picked her up and carried her to the rear of the shop in order to sexually assault her. She had indeed survived through the night as the witness said. The original pathologist later agreed these findings.*

*The new sceneline/hypothesis was that she had been drinking somewhere unknown, and had left to meet her friends and been assaulted probably much later than 10.30 p.m. She had been struck one heavy blow to the face, items stolen and then when the offender realised she was incapacitated she was taken to the back of the shops and raped. She had been left there and was overcome by a combination of alcohol, head injuries and hypothermia.*

*BIA advice was that the original motivation was very likely to be street robbery, and the sexual assault an opportunistic offence; the prime suspect group would therefore be street robbers, and those with convictions for violence, particularly domestic violence. Previous investigative work had concentrated on sexual offenders.*

*The offender later came to light after he committed an offence of public violence for which his DNA was taken. He had an offending history which included offences of street robbery and serious domestic violence, and had served prison terms for both offence types. He did not have any (known) history of sexual offences.*

One further analytical technique is useful in cases where the scientist/ reviewer suspects that an apparently well-supported hypothesis may still be wrong, and is particularly helpful in cases of alleged miscarriage of justice. That is to extend the search for anomalies into the consequential actions in addition to anomalies in the sceneline and direct evidence against the suspect. So, assuming the suspect did in fact commit the crime, what must he have obtained in advance, who should have seen him beforehand, how did he dispose of the weapon and who should have seen this? If the explanation is that he caught a train, was a ticket issued at that station, and at the right time? Whilst these may appear to be policing issues, here we are seeking independent physical confirmation.

In many jurisdictions once the police have sufficient evidence to put the alleged offender before the court they have no interest in these second and third levels of analysis. Indeed it could be argued that in an adversarial system this is a matter for the defence, so why should the police make a potential rod for their own backs? Consistent personal experience shows that it is dangerous to assume that defence lawyers will have any investigative ability, and in any event they tend to attack specific and detailed elements of the physical evidence (the value of DNA, paint, fibres etc.), so that both prosecution and defence often start their analysis from the same (wrong) assumptions about scene interpretations, timings etc.

## Malpractice

In those rare cases where it is suspected a miscarriage of justice has been deliberately manufactured by the police, analysis of dates and times of laboratory submissions and results against entries in the policy log (or equivalent) and other documentation showing location of officers (for example expenses claims) can prove most valuable. In the situation where a decision to charge or interview someone has been made on dubious grounds, it is likely that tidying up of decisions, items submitted for additional analysis may occur in the days immediately following. Since forensic scientists were and probably still are regarded as outside the investigative loop what are on the face of it consequential actions by the investigation can be out of step with the actual analytical results. Normally of course decisions by investigators would follow laboratory results, but it has been possible to demonstrate the converse in a number of cases, providing powerful evidence of malpractice.

Conversely, in one case officers continued to submit items for analysis which could not possibly help their case, and if negative should have undermined it. This provides a strong indication that they genuinely believed the suspect to be guilty, and thus expected the analysis to be positive.

Whatever the reason for selecting a case for cold case analysis, the reinvestigation, including a physical evidence review, should proceed utilising formal cold case protocols for both selection and process. In the UK examples were initially devised by NCOF and FSS and then implemented by many police forces, and have more recently been endorsed by PSU on a national basis. The UK process is very different from those often seen in other jurisdictions that rely more heavily on refreshing eyewitness evidence; this is undoubtedly because many gun crimes do not involve close contact and therefore not much transfer of physical evidence. In the UK such crimes are relatively rare and most 'cold cases' will be undetected stranger murders or sexual assault series.

## Cold case protocols

We can illustrate the process of physical evidence review by examining how this works in cold case investigations. These bear many similarities to a long-term active running murder investigation, with the addition of a front end initial assessment and recovery phase for both documents and physical items. It is important that we remember that physical analyses form only a very small part of the *investigative* actions, in any murder investigation, although physical evidence is likely to be essential for any successful prosecution.

In the UK, cold case reinvestigations involve a fresh start based on original witness statements and other primary documentation such as the pathologist's report. The expectation of progress is primarily based on physical evidence and increasingly on the reassessment of the crime in the light of behavioural and other information. Offences are typically close contact, sexually motivated homicide rather than gun crimes where there are obviously far fewer opportunities for physical evidence transfer. Although reinterviewing witnesses is essential for investigative purposes, it is primarily used to confirm or deny hypotheses as to the sequence of events rather than with an expectation of providing new eyewitness evidence.

What we are seeking in cold cases is to identify contact points between offender and scene(s) and victim. This is often achieved by reworking the original sequence of events in light of new behavioural, pathological or forensic observations. It is vital that the temptation to undertake a simple reworking of swabs and clothing for DNA should be resisted. Our current appreciation of offender behaviour and a detailed analysis of the microsequence of events will often lead to opportunities from items which have never been submitted to a laboratory or examined. Such items of course will be relatively uncontaminated and intact.

Forensic science is absolutely context dependent and it follows that if either the test result or the context changes a new interpretation is required. In cold cases, both the results and the context may have to be repeatedly revised as further work is undertaken. This cannot be done unless the scientist is close to the inquiry and there are good lines of communication, but is facilitated by the fact that all of the investigative team will at least initially be concentrating on intelligence rather than evidence. It is important that a new team undertakes the review to ensure that previous misconceptions are not reinforced.

A detailed account of cold case process in the UK has been published (Fraser 2005). This contains a useful account of a successful cold case reinvestigation of a miscarriage of justice, the 1988 murder of Lynette White in Cardiff. This led to the real offender being identified and pleading guilty in 2003.

### Managing exhibits and results

Exhibit tracking is an essential element of case reviews. There must be a common source of information, which describes the life history of all relevant items. Records must clearly illustrate what has been recovered, what has gone for analysis, when it went, why it went, when results were obtained and where the item is stored. This is not only an aid to the review process but an essential part of the criminal justice process, should the review result in a trial. A schematic approach is useful to show items which still await analysis or results or which have been overlooked, as you can identify them at a glance instead of ploughing through page after page of laboratory documentation. Any tracking system must be constantly refreshed and act as a definitive source of accurate information to the review team. Charting is useful for allowing the investigators to see the position at a glance.

The 'sceneline' technique has proved particularly powerful in cold cases where there may be a considerable feeling that investigators 'know' what happened, based on previous media coverage or work by the force. Often relatively small observations by the pathologist or overlooked laboratory results can completely disprove the initial hypothesis if it is tested in this way.

Effective cold case reviews are based on:

- a structured approach which uncovers overlooked opportunities and identifies new ones such as identification of contact points;
- information management tools such as 'what we know' reports; 'sceneline' and exhibit tracking software;
- integration of science with the investigative process;
- re-evaluation of previous findings such as sequences of events in a more rigorous and constructively critical manner;
- informed planning for key events such as interviews and searches.

Crucially, it is not just about science but science in context, focused clearly on investigative problems and the needs of the criminal justice system.

## Summary and conclusion

The recent history of major crime investigations has shown notable changes in practice as a consequence of interventions following a number of poorly handled investigations such as the Yorkshire Ripper inquiry. These changes have been driven by new legislation (PACE, CPIA) and supported by new developments in science and technology, notably the implementation of fingerprint and DNA databases. These databases have enabled the use of forensic science as an intelligence tool in investigations in direct support of major lines of inquiry in addition to its more traditional evidential role. The development of new roles such as Specialist Adviser and more extensive and standardised police investigative training have supported fundamental shifts in the use of forensic science (from evidence to intelligence) and in investigative process from 'nomination' (of suspects) to one of elimination.

The combination of forensic intelligence with behavioural information when applied to reinvestigation of unsolved cases has resulted in a number of spectacular successes and a more rigorous approach to ongoing and systematic review of major investigations.

Although considerable progress has been made in this area over several decades, continued education and training of police officers and forensic scientists is essential to maintain and develop this position in the interests of justice.

## Notes

1 Police and Criminal Evidence Act (1984).
2 This function is now part of the National Policing Improvement Agency (NPIA) created in April 2007.
3 Now IDENT1, see Champod and Chamberlain, Chapter 3 in this volume.

## Further reading

Nordby, Jon J. (2000) *Dead Reckoning – the art of forensic detection*. Boca Raton, Florida: CRC Press. ISBN 0-8493-8122-3.

## References

ACPO (1999) *The Murder Manual*. London: ACPO.

ACPO (2005) *Practice Advice on Core Investigative Doctrine*. London: ACPO/Centrex.

ACPO Crime Committee (2000) *Major Incident Room Standard Administrative Procedures*. London: ACPO.

ACPO/FSS (1996) *Using Forensic Science Effectively*. London: ACPO/Forensic Science Service.

Byford, L. (1982) *Review of the investigation of the 'Yorkshire Ripper' case*. Home Office unpublished – Cabinet Office papers.

Fraser J.G. (2005) 'Cold Case Investigations' in *Encyclopaedia of Forensic and Legal Medicine* edited by J. Payne-James, R.W. Byard, T.S. Cory and C. Henderson. Oxford: Elsevier Academic Press.

FSS/Greater Manchester Police (1993) *Think Forensic* video and 20 factsheets. Forensic Science Service.

Her Majesty's Inspector of Constabulary (2000) *Under the Microscope: Thematic Inspection Report on Scientific and Technical Support*. London: Home Office.

Her Majesty's Inspector of Constabulary (2002) *Under the Microscope Refocused*. London: Home Office.

House of Commons Science and Technology Committee (2005) *Forensic Science on Trial*. Seventh Report of Session 2004–2005. London: HMSO.

Investigative analysis (2007) *i2 Analysts Notebook 7*, http://www.i2.co.uk/

Kirk, P.L. (1974) *Crime Investigation* (2nd edn, p. 2). New York: Wiley.

Locard, E. (1918–1931) *Traité de Criminalistique (7 vols)*. J. Desvigne et ses fils (1931).

National Criminal Intelligence Service (2000) *The National Intelligence Model*.

Police Research Group (1996) *Forensic Science and Crime Investigation*. London: Home Office.

Saulsbury, W., Hibberd, M. and Irving, B. (1992) *Using Physical Evidence*. London: The Police Foundation.

# Chapter 14

# Forensic science in UK policing: strategies, tactics and effectiveness

*Nick Tilley and Michael Townsley*

This chapter will trace growing efforts to rationalise the use of forensic science in British policing, where rationalisation is understood to mean the creation of consistent patterns which also maximise overall efficiency and effectiveness. Factors inhibiting as well as encouraging rationalisation will be discussed. The last section of the chapter will make suggestions for further improvements. A distinction will be made at the start between the intensive use of forensic science techniques, amongst other investigative tools, in relation to major but relatively rare crimes, and their more routine use in relation to volume crimes. This chapter will have less to say about the use of forensic science in major crime investigations than its application to volume crimes. Though the use of new forensic tools, notably the National DNA Database (NDNAD), low copy number (LCN) DNA, and the National Automated Fingerprint Identification System (NAFIS), will be discussed, details of their development and debates over their statistical reliability lie outside the scope of this chapter. Rather, the focus here is on rationalisation in the ways in which science is mobilised to help achieve police objectives.

## The uses of forensic science

In major crime investigations, where detection of the individual case is deemed to be of critical importance, forensic science resources are drawn on relatively liberally according to specific needs as they are seen to arise. In particular, where other evidence to detect the case is not readily to hand, crime scene examiners (until recently called Scenes of Crime Officers or 'SOCOs') examine scenes thoroughly, and forensic scientists are brought in to play a major part in the investigation. 'Byford Scientists', who are experienced senior forensic practitioners, liaise with Senior Investigating Officers, oversee physical evidence collection and play an active part in ensuring that the various threads of evidence in the case are tied in and the inferences properly drawn. Byford scientists, named after Sir Lawrence Byford, were introduced following the 1982 HMIC inquiry into the failures of the Yorkshire Ripper investigation that eventually led to the conviction of Peter Sutcliffe but only after long delays where salient leads had been missed and false ones doggedly followed (Byford 1982). The emergence of Byford scientists describes a development in the interface between specialist advisers and crime investigators, bringing scientific techniques and reasoning to the collection and interpretation of physical evidence. The use of Byford scientists addresses a weakness in the way in which this interface had been working previously in major crime investigation. It represents, thus, one effort to rationalise the use of forensic science.

The main focus of this chapter, however, will be on the application of forensic science in the investigation of volume crimes, which are the bread-and-butter business of crime investigation and of most of those involved in delivering forensic science services. The sheer number of cases involved means that the case-by-case approach adopted in major crime investigation is not practicable. The speculative and thorough searches for possible physical evidence and analyses of items recovered, which can be undertaken where needed in major crime investigation, are not possible with the resources available. There are nowhere near enough senior forensic practitioners to allocate one to each case or sufficient crime scene examiners for every crime scene to be attended by one of them. Moreover, it is not conceivable that those resources will become available in the foreseeable future. The issue for volume crime investigation is, therefore, that of maximising the benefits from the limited resources available. The past 20 years have witnessed a series of efforts to address just this issue. There has been a succession of diagnoses of weaknesses in forensic processes followed by efforts to remedy them. At the same time there have been some major developments in technique and technology that have fed into the processes of rationalisation.

The assumptions behind processes of rationalisation in the use of forensic science in major and volume crime inquiries are rather different. In major crime inquiries, the emphasis is on making sure that relevant expertise is brought to bear in relation to the particulars of the specific case. Relevant expertise here refers less to the ability to follow standard procedures used in routine forensic work (though it is important still that they are still employed when applicable), than the capacity to look at the case and the inquiry to work through what value might be added and what inferences drawn from the collection and analysis of physical evidence. Rationalisation for major crime inquiry means making sure that forensic expertise is on hand and that conditions are created where proper attention is paid to it. In volume crime inquiries, on the other hand, rationalisation relates to the development of robust systems, rules, habits and standards that can be rolled out and routinely applied across many cases maximising the net benefit at minimum costs.

The classical sociologist, Max Weber, used the adjectives 'substantive' and 'formal' to describe two distinguishable types of rationality. The former refers to specific considerations over the particular merits of any individual case. The latter refers to consistency and predictability across any number of relevantly similar cases. Weber's view was that there was a secular trend towards increases in formal rationality to meet the needs of large-scale modern enterprises and government, where coordination, efficiency and consistency are *de rigeur*. This is a development that can be found in policing and forensic science over the past 20 years.

## Key players in forensic processes in volume crime investigation

Figure 14.1 shows who, for the most part, does what in the collection, analysis and use of physical evidence in volume crime case investigations. It will be helpful to have a general understanding of this process in looking at moves towards rationalisation. There have been significant developments throughout.

A volume crime may or may not be reported. Prior to the report, or after the report before the first officer attends, the scene may or may not be disturbed. The call handler taking the report may or may not advise the reporter that they should preserve the scene and how they should do so. The call handler may or may not despatch an officer to attend and they will allocate it a higher or lower level of urgency. They may also alert the crime scene examiner that the offence has taken place though this has more normally been left to the police officer attending. The police officer attending may arrive sooner or later. They may or may not collect some physical evidence themselves, but more normally they will determine whether to call a crime scene examiner to examine the scene for physical evidence. The crime scene examiner may

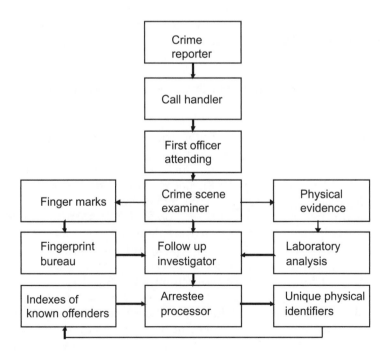

**Figure 14.1**  Volume crime investigation and physical evidence collection and use

or may not be briefed about the offence and what might most fruitfully be looked for in the course of the scene examination. The crime scene examiner will arrive sooner or later and will examine the scene for physical evidence of various sorts. They will collect the selected physical evidence, label it and package it for return to their base unit. A decision will then be taken as to what to do with the physical evidence.

Fingerprints may be sent to the in-force fingerprint bureau for comparison (either manually or through a computer database) with the collection of 'ten prints', the library of sets of prints taken from past offenders, and with marks collected from previous unsolved offences. Other physical evidence may be sent to a laboratory for further analysis. In most cases this will be external to the police though some processes, including fingerprint enhancement, may take place in-house. The analysis is done more or less quickly and results returned, where they will then be passed on to the officer in the case – whoever has assumed responsibility for the investigation, following up what has been done by the first officer attending. In cases where an arrest is made, whether with or without forensic evidence having played a part, unique physical identifiers for that arrestee are taken and forwarded for checks against and incorporation into a local and/or national database. Until quite recently the only unique identifier taken was the set of 'ten prints' (prints from the top parts of all fingers from both hands). 'CJ samples' that the police are entitled to collect (normally using 'buccal swabs') are now taken also from arrestees, for DNA profiling and entry on to the national DNA database (NDNAD).

There is a great deal of scope for error, inconsistency and inefficiency in this process. There are important strategic decisions to be made about the volume and disposition of resources to support these activities, as well as decisions about how the processes are to be managed and operated at a tactical level. The moves to rationalisation have related to just these issues.

### Rationalisation and the conversion of the Forensic Science Service into an agency

Early influential studies from the 1980s that found shortcomings in effectiveness and efficiency in the provisions for, activities relating to and use of forensic science in volume crime investigation include Ramsay (1987), Touche Ross (1987) and Audit Commission (1988). Each of these studies was conducted while the Forensic Science Service (FSS) remained part of the Home Office, when access was free at the point of use for police services. They found that the laboratories were unable to meet increasing demands deriving from growing crime levels and developments of more powerful forensic techniques. They also found very uneven crime scene attendance by SOCOs and apparently arbitrary levels of forensic service use within police forces.

Consistent with recommendations from Touche Ross (1987) and from a Home Affairs Select Committee Report in February 1989, which had also uncovered low morale, poor management and lack of direction in the FSS, agency status[1] was granted to it in April 1991, when direct charges were introduced for all customers including police services (the police accounting for about 95 per cent of FSS revenue). The Metropolitan Police Forensic Science Laboratory (MPFSL), serving the Metropolitan Police Service and the City of London Police, did not join the FSS until later. At the time agency status was granted there were 501 staff in the FSS and 226 in MPFSL. These provided almost all police forensic science needs, except for those met within police services and from a few specialist suppliers in niche areas, for example document examination. The level of provision was widely believed to be inadequate (see Home Affairs Select Committee 1989). By 1993 the number of staff in the Forensic Science Service had grown to 623 (Home Office 1993). And, by late 2005 the FSS were employing more than 2,600 staff (FSS 2005), in a context in which a range of other forensic services providers had also joined the market. Provision has, indeed, grown enormously.[2]

It was expected that the conversion of the FSS into an agency, paid for at the point of service by users of various sorts, principally non-metropolitan police services in the first instance, would introduce market discipline both to the provider and customer (Touche Ross 1987; Royal Commission on Criminal Justice 1993). The customer would learn to make use of services when worthwhile, to wit when the expected return matched the costs. The provider would attune services offered to what was actually needed or demanded by the customer. Alternative providers could compete for services ensuring that costs would be kept down, emerging needs met and innovations made as opportunities arose. The FSS would be free flexibly to pursue opportunities and to develop efficient working practices, less trammelled by subordination to the Home Office. The transformation into an agency represented a switch from a centrally managed and planned service to one shaped by market forces. The grounds were that the patterns of usage deriving from planned services were not in the event producing effective and efficient use or provision.

## Rationalisation of forensic provision and processes within police services

Studies in the 1980s and early 1990s, for example Touche Ross (1987) and the Audit Commission (1988, 1993), made suggestions for changes within the police to rationalise their collection of contact trace materials and submission for analysis, as well as for changes in the FSS as the major supplier. The Touche Ross report found the management of scientific support to be poor. It also found that there was insufficient understanding within the police of what forensic science could contribute to its work. It recommended the appointment of a Scientific Support Manager in each police service to oversee scientific support services, which included the work of SOCOs and fingerprint officers, the forensic science budget and the processes involved in the collection and preservation of physical evidence.

Touche Ross also noted wide variations in provision for scientific support by police forces. For example there was one SOCO in place for every 1,674 recorded crimes at one extreme and one per 5,226 at the other extreme. In addition the report found that numbers of crime scenes examined per annum by SOCOs also differed greatly, going from 331 to 1,476 cases per SOCO at an average of 705. Follow-up work by the Police Requirements Support Unit-Scientific Support Team (PRSU-SST) recommended 600 SOCO visits per annum. The Touche Ross report also noted diminishing resources relative to numbers of offences as crime levels increased. Continuing this theme, the Audit Commission (1993) noted the continuing slower rate at which numbers of SOCOs had grown when compared to numbers of crimes (up 16 per cent and 40 per cent respectively) between 1987 and 1991. It found an average of 800 crime scene visits per SOCO per annum, suggesting there was a growing shortfall in what was needed and a substantial number more visits than the 600 recommended by PRSU-SST. The Audit Commission again found wide variations between forces – from 450 to 1,350 visits per SOCO per annum.

In relation to the retrieval of contact trace material from crime scenes, both Touche Ross (1987) and the Audit Commission (1993) found substantial variations between police forces: for fingerprints respectively from 120 to 500 and 120 to 400 scenes per annum per SOCO, with no apparent explanation for why this should be the case. Further weaknesses identified included lack of minimum standards, lack of quality assurance, and inadequate communications between SOCOs and detectives.

Touche Ross and the Audit Commission were both trying to steer forces towards greater consistency of performance, a closer match of resource to need, improved quality standards in service delivery, and better liaison with investigating officers, all in the interests of rationalising the provision for scientific support within police services

In the mid 1990s a further detailed study of practices within police services was undertaken, looking at the ways in which forensic materials were collected, analysed and results used. An ambitious and wide-ranging study was co-sponsored by the Forensic Science Service, the Association of Chief Police Officers and the Home Office (ACPO/FSS 1996; Tilley and Ford 1996). It considered the entire forensic process, from scene preservation to presentation of evidence in court, though it concentrated in the main on police use of forensic science.

The main conclusions were that:

- though structural changes in the management of forensic science suggested by Touche Ross had generally been implemented in police services, little had been done to improve yields from forensic evidence;

- the use of forensic science in the investigation of serious crimes and series of serious crimes was generally informed and thorough, though this was not the case for volume crimes;

- in volume crime cases there was a great deal of discretion in decision-making about the collection and use of forensic material, though staff exercising this discretion knew very little about the nature or potential value of the analyses that might be undertaken;

- the process of investigation, the work of scientific support and the activities of external forensic science suppliers were managed separately and were poorly integrated;

- though there were quality assurance provisions within the FSS (and other public service laboratories) there were few for forensic science within police services or amongst other external suppliers;

- forensic science was mostly used reactively, individual case by individual case, with little contribution to intelligence and little orientation to prevention;

- training in the use of forensic science and communication between those involved in the forensic process (investigator, SOCO, fingerprint officer, investigating officer and external supplier) were both weak;

- there were substantial variations in force practices and investment in scientific support.

Table 14.1 goes through various stages in the forensic process as it relates to the investigation of individual cases, highlighting in the first column how in theory decisions would be made to maximise the potential investigative benefits from forensic science and in the second what was found to be happening in practice (Tilley and Ford 1996). The study found a consistent mismatch between what would be done if forensic science were to be used effectively and efficiently and what was actually done. This was especially marked in volume crime cases.

A large number of recommendations, published by ACPO and the Forensic Science Service as *Using Forensic Science Effectively*, emerged from the study. These aimed to rationalise the way forensic science was used in practice, and included specific suggestions for:

- an integrated team approach to investigation, where police officers, SOCOs, and forensic providers work together and communicate with one another, all focused on achieving outcomes;

- an intelligence-led proactive orientation to the investigation of volume crime, with an eye to strategic preventive use of forensic science rather than a focus only on detecting individual cases;

- performance indicators that emphasise outcomes, rather than processes;

- improvements in awareness of forensic science capabilities, so that informed decisions can be made about the collection, submission and analyses requested from forensic providers;

- the introduction of quality control techniques across the entire forensic process.

### Rationalisation following the ACPO, Forensic Science Service and Home Office review

Her Majesty's Inspectorate of Constabulary (HMIC) undertook an inspection to find out what progress had been made in implementing the recommendations

**Table 14.1**  The use of forensic science in crime investigation: a summary of findings

| The theory | The practice |
|---|---|
| 1 Scene well preserved by victim/ reporter of incident, then FOA* | Some evidence that evidence frequently disturbed/washed away |
| 2 FOA/IO* assesses scene accurately for scope for SOCO/forensic scientist collection of case-relevant CTM* | FOA ignorant about potential discriminative powers of forensic tests |
| 3 SOCO/forensic scientist examine scene adequately briefed by FOA/IO to look for CTM confirming/disconfirming and adding to original line of inquiry | In volume crime, little briefing about case. Generally routine scene examination without focus on details of case. In major crime more information on case, more verbal briefing, more directed examination |
| 4 SOCO/forensic scientist communicates useful findings to FOA/IO | In volume crime little direct communication: at best available on computer. Much more in major crime |
| 5 Cases selected for submission where there are prospects of evidence informing direction of inquiry and cost is warranted | Seriousness of case often more significant than prospects of usefulness. Little use for inceptive purposes. Corroboration rather than elimination orientation |
| 6 Items selected for submission which throw light on case, plus list of all other items collected which might be analysed | Lists of other items seldom provided. Selection on costs basis |
| 7 Items packaged appropriately with continuity assured | Some evidence of packaging problems |
| 8 Submissions provide full background information on case, enabling the forensic scientist to make a judgement about answerability and intelligibility of the question asked | Variable amounts and adequacy of information. Questions often poorly formulated |
| 9 Forensic scientists examine items that are likely to throw light on questions addressed and other issues germane to the inquiry | Some supplier examination of almost all materials sent to them and some failure to assess whether other forensic science examinations might be significant for inquiry |
| 10 IO and forensic scientists communicate verbally about question posed, proposed analysis and results | Some verbal communication |
| 11 Full QA*/QC* procedures for forensic analysis | Not all suppliers have QA/QC. In-force scientific procedures rarely have QA/QC |

*Table 14.1 continues opposite*

*Table 14.1 continued*

| The theory | The practice |
|---|---|
| 12 Forensic scientist writes clear, objective witness statement | Generally OK. Some police expectation of less equivocal reports |
| 13 CPS* grasps meaning and significance of forensic scientist witness statement in context of case and takes appropriate account in prosecution decisions | Infrequent informal contact/ consultation of CPS and forensic supplier pre-trial |
| 14 Court enables expert evidence to be presented clearly with agreed points of difference between prosecution and defence highlighted | Small number of pre-trial conferences involving counsel, prosecution and defence experts |

*Note*: *FOA refers to first officer attending; IO to investigating officer, CTM to contact trace material, QA to quality assurance, QC to quality control, and CPS to Crown Prosecution Service.

from *Using Forensic Science Effectively*, and also to look at progress in making good use of the DNA database and NAFIS, neither of which had been fully implemented at the time that the research for *Using Forensic Science Effectively* was conducted. The advent of the DNA database has had profound implications for the rational use of forensic science. It offered, as with fingerprints, a technique for establishing linkages with very high levels of confidence. A full DNA profile, as with a full fingerprint, could provide close-to-conclusive evidence linking a person to a scene or a scene to a scene in a way that is not matched by other forensic techniques, using for example, glass, fibres, shoe marks, or tool marks.

Collection of DNA stains at crime scenes in conjunction with a DNA database of known offenders promised the potential for mass forensic science use in relation to both volume and major crime. Fingerprinting had not been included at all in the ACPO/FSS/Home Office study. There were already automated fingerprint recognition (AFR) systems in many police services prior to NAFIS, though no national system. However, much fingerprint work had been of a craft nature. Fingerprint officers compared scene marks with those of known active offenders whose 'ten prints' were kept to hand in 'bundles'. They also made comparisons with marks of suspects nominated by investigating officers. Some had remarkable memories for finger marks and were quick to identify offenders. NAFIS, as a national system using common methods for all forces, offered new search possibilities, expanding the potential for wider-ranging linkages than those that were available in the craft work conducted within traditional police fingerprint departments, or with earlier AFR systems.

The HMIC inspection was published in summer 2000 as *Under the Microscope*, with a follow-up 18 months later published as *Under the Microscope Refocused*. Both reports aimed at stimulating rationalisation in the use of forensic science in police services. The first expressed disappointment at the progress in attending to the recommendations of the ACPO/Home Office/FSS study. It noted patchy implementation and very limited attention from ACPO level officers.

The section of the report dealing with policing and the DNA database was quite damning. The following shortcomings were identified.

- There was wide variation in the availability and use of IT.
- Most staff lacked formal training.
- There was little evidence of written guidance or policies to which staff could refer.
- There was poor monitoring of error rates.
- Little performance management information was collected.
- Administrative errors were not rectified.
- There were inadequate despatch and delivery service security arrangements.
- Storage arrangements for samples were inadequate.
- There were inadequate processes for the retaking of failed samples.

*Under the Microscope's* conclusions on fingerprinting uncovered problems of communication with members of the fingerprint bureau, lack of integration into the investigative processes, delays in process leading to identifications, and failures in performance management regimes to concentrate on outcomes rather than activities. It advocated the development of well-formulated Service Level Agreements delineating 'the reciprocal responsibilities and expectations between providers and customers [ensuring that] ... the parties know where they stand, what they can expect from each other, and have a joint foundation for improvement.' (paragraph 3.25)

*Under the Microscope Refocused* found only modest progress since the original report. Ten forces were included in the follow-up. The Executive Summary states that '[o]nly three of the ten forces enjoyed the active participation of an ACPO ranking officer in "championing" the scientific support function'. In terms of DNA it reported that '[i]t is clear from the responses that crime scene attendance and screening policies continue to present difficulty'; and for fingerprints '[o]nly one of the forces assessed had developed their use of Service Level Agreements'. Under 'Managing the Intelligence and the Identifications', it reported that '[m]any forces still have a great deal of difficulty in managing the process of turning identifications into detections and this is rooted in the paucity of quality performance management information'.

## Rationalisation since *Under the Microscope*

The Police Standards Unit (PSU) was set up within the Home Office in July 2001, as part of the government's police reform agenda for improving police performance and achieving reductions in crime (Police Standards Unit 2003). A Forensic Support Programme comprised one thread of PSU's work. PSU aimed to reduce disparities in performance and spread good practice by 'standardizing use of science and technology'. PSU focused in particular on

DNA and NAFIS. Special projects included 'Operation Cesare' in Lincolnshire, which attempted to improve SOCO performance, DNA and fingerprint processes and rates of capitalisation on DNA matches and fingerprint idents; and 'Safer Homes' in the West Midlands, which speeded up analysis of DNA stains recovered from burglary crime scenes. In the West Midlands case, of which more will be said later in this chapter, early claims for preventive success in relation to volume crime (Police Standards Unit 2003) were not supported in the subsequent systematic evaluation of achievements (Webb *et al.* 2005). Among other problems, weaknesses in feedback, variation in SOCO performance, and absence of arrests following matches were found even in this demonstration project. No independent evaluation could be found for the Lincolnshire project.

A 'Pathfinder project' assessing the effect of increased and improved forensic activity in relation to volume crime (burglary and vehicle crime) in two English police forces operated from May 2000 to April 2001, with results published in 2005 (Burrows *et al.* 2005b). The Pathfinder project was concerned to look at the use of new and improved forensic techniques, in particular low copy number (LCN) DNA, improved use of footwear and tool mark evidence, and improved linkages amongst and between offenders and scenes through a Force Led INTelligence System (FLINTS).[3] Special FSS employed Forensic Examiners were appointed to each of the seven divisions included in the Pathfinder project to help find (and train SOCOs to find) material for LCN DNA swabbing that might otherwise be missed from relevant crime scenes. The project was followed neither by improvements in detection nor falls in crime in the divisions where it operated in comparison to those where it did not operate. Notwithstanding this disappointing finding, overall use of LCN DNA techniques did result in a number of detections, notably of vehicle crimes, that would otherwise not have been achieved.

A seven-force study of the routine application of forensic science in volume crime cases published in 2004 found what should be by now familiar weaknesses in the management and use of forensic science within police services (Williams 2004). Across the seven forces included in the study findings included considerable variation

- in Scientific Support Unit (SSU) staff levels;

- in crime scene attendance rates (59 per cent to 89 per cent of domestic burglaries and 11 per cent to 33 per cent of vehicle crimes);

- in SOCO average numbers of scenes examined across the seven forces studied (348 to 575);

- in DNA hit and fingerprint ident rates (domestic burglary fingerprint 4 per cent to 19 per cent, domestic burglary DNA hits 2 per cent to 5 per cent, vehicle crime fingerprint idents 7 per cent to 23 per cent and vehicle crime DNA hits 4 per cent to 8 per cent); and

- in the level and type of integration of scientific support into wider investigative work.

Notwithstanding moves to increase provision of SOCOs/CSEs which are consistent with recommendations of earlier studies, huge differences in provision, workload and performance seem to have remained.

The most up-to-date substantial study (dealing with crimes committed in 2003–4) covering forensic processes, amongst other aspects of volume crime investigation, found continuing wide variations in practice and outcome by Basic Command Units (BCUs) across eight paired high and low detection rate BCUs (Burrows *et al.* 2005a). For example SOCO scene attendance varied from 63 per cent to 100 per cent for domestic burglary; from 27 per cent to 74 per cent for non-domestic burglary; from six per cent to 65 per cent for theft of motor vehicles; and from three per cent to 33 per cent for theft from motor vehicles. Combined fingerprint idents and DNA hits varied from 4.6 per cent to 8.1 per cent for domestic burglary; from 2.7 per cent to 8.7 per cent for non-domestic burglary; from nought per cent to 1.9 per cent for theft from motor vehicles; and from 1.9 per cent to 17.9 per cent for theft of motor vehicles. There was, unsurprisingly, a positive association between rates of attendance and DNA hits and fingerprint idents for non-domestic burglary, theft from motor vehicles and theft of motor vehicles, where attendance rates varied very widely. There was none, however, for domestic burglary where attendance rates were in all cases relatively high and where diminishing returns seemed to have set in.

It can be seen that for almost 20 years many similar problems in delivering on the promise of forensic science have persisted despite a series of efforts to address them, to improve outcomes and achieve consistently high levels of performance. Forensic science continues to appear technically impressive but making the most effective use of it in routine volume crime cases has proven remarkably tricky. Variation in levels of provision and inconsistency in achievement continue to be found, suggesting that benefits are not being optimised. Putting in place means of best exploiting the potential of the science continues to be a substantial challenge. The chapter turns now from efforts to rationalise the use of forensic science predominantly in its conventional role as an aide to detecting individual cases to examine its potential to inform crime preventive strategies.

## New directions in rationalising forensic science use

In the final section of this chapter we set out some ideas on how the use of forensic data could and should be developed in the future.[4] So far the main rationale for assembling forensic data has been to resolve single criminal cases. Apart from the obvious example where identical forensic data have been found at multiple scenes, relatively little attention has been paid to ways in which the voluminous quantities of forensic data that are collected routinely might be drawn on, in particular for crime reduction. We focus here on broadening the agenda for forensic science use, in particular by exploiting relatively recent national databases in fresh ways.

Two initial observations need to be made about limitations associated with the current type of use of national forensic databases. First, they do not assist immediately in situations in which the offender is not yet known to the criminal justice system (is not present in the database). The scenes data have to wait until matching offender data become available as and when this occurs. Some argue that there are very few perpetrators who have not come to the attention of police at some previous point, and they will certainly not be prolific offenders.[5] We will return to the issue of unknown offenders shortly. The second observation is that most forensic activity is reactive in nature, with the individual crime the unit of analysis.[6] By reactive we mean that the purpose is to identify a culprit (although of course along the way other suspects may also be eliminated). The goal is apprehension and ultimately conviction in court.

One of the major efforts so far to draw on forensic science in pursuit of crime prevention has involved widening and streamlining its application in order to improve the efficiency of conventional case detection in the hope that this will contribute to crime reduction through increased deterrence and incapacitation of active offenders. Unfortunately, simply populating national forensic databases more fully and streamlining their operation may not be enough to achieve significant crime reduction pay-offs. As noted earlier, the results of an evaluation by Webb *et al.* (2005) showed that 'fast-tracking' the recovery, matching and reporting of DNA material from burglary scenes and speeding up the apprehension of those individuals identified was, unfortunately, not associated with a reduction in the number of burglaries reported to the police. So, in the context of a much larger national DNA database and despite bringing burglars to book an average two months earlier than had previously been the case, no impact on levels of burglary was observed. Webb *et al.* suggest that there are various reasons why initiatives of this kind, which enjoy popular operational support, might nevertheless be found not to yield the anticipated benefits when examined independently. These include low collection rates of DNA, the offending patterns of those subject to swifter apprehension, the long-term decline in burglary in the area, and decision-making over remand and sentencing that cannot be controlled by those running pilot schemes.

A further important recent innovation in the use of national forensic databases has been the development of familial searching (Bieber *et al.* 2006). The technique exploits the fact that parents pass on genes to their offspring, which means that intra-family DNA will be more similar than inter-family DNA. The promise is that the NDNAD will become more useful as familial searching increases the proportion of the population who might be matched. In fact, the provision of familial searching underpins the Forensic Science Service's Forensic Intelligence Bureau.

What familial searching and fast tracking have in common is that they are primarily focused on improving the efficiency of finding offenders, the traditional main concern of forensic science. What these forensic innovations amount to, therefore, are efforts to improve the application of forensic science as currently envisaged. Their crime reduction effectiveness turns on catching committed offenders and incapacitating them through incarceration, or deterring them by perceived increases in chances of punishment via the criminal justice system. The following discussion speculates that the data collected may be put to rather different and more strategic crime control use.

Consider for a moment the types of non-forensic data collected at a single crime scene. These include victim characteristics, location information, time and date ranges of commission, generic *modus operandi*, property taken or damaged, suspect descriptions, witness statements and type of offence. Whilst ostensibly collected for the purposes of investigation, in the case of volume crime little is done from an investigative perspective with this information. However, the records can be combined with information from other similar crimes to identify and analyse crime patterns. These observed patterns then (ideally) inform prevention efforts. For example, if the majority of domestic burglary incidents share similar entry points then crime prevention advice on security measures might be disseminated throughout an estate. Goldstein (1990) explores this concept of problem orientation in greater depth.

Under the National Intelligence Model (NIM) in the United Kingdom it is relatively common that police-recorded crime data are subjected to analyses to understand features of crime in order to try to prevent further incidents. In fact, one of the four key intelligence products under the NIM exists for this very purpose (the problem profile). So far, forensic data have not been drawn on routinely for this purpose.

Part of the reason may be the perception of different types of information within police agencies and the purpose to which they might be put. Two broad functions of information and its interrogation can be identified: *intelligence* and *analysis*. *Intelligence* focuses mainly on individuals and their associates, is largely retrospective in scope, and the primary goal is usually conviction.[7] In this sense much data used for intelligence purposes could be described as yet to be verified evidence (in the legal meaning of the term). On the other hand, *analysis* (following Goldstein's ideas about problem-oriented policing) focuses on groups of events which are similar in some way. The goal is primarily preventative, and in this sense the purpose of the analysis is proactive.[8]

Forensic data are seldom used for *analysing* crime and criminality patterns with a strategic problem-solving purpose in mind. We think that this comprises a missed opportunity that has yet properly to be exploited. Let us see what might be attempted along these lines.

Even at the individual case level, the information yielded by the comparison of crime scene samples with other scene samples is relatively neglected. For the purposes of understanding offending patterns, scene-to-scene matches are at least as important as scene-to-person matches, since they could encompass the criminal careers of people who never come to official attention. This would offer insights into the active offender population that has previously gone unobserved. Importantly, forensic data are substantially free of the types of bias that plague conventional sources of data about offenders and offending, although they are inevitably subject to their own set of biases and operational filters. We limit our discussion to DNA in the main but there is no reason why other forensic material could not be used in the same manner outlined here. Looking at fingerprints and DNA together would be especially instructive, though difficult (since, for example, people have many fingers, so the prints of different digits of as yet unknown offenders would not be linked).

FLINTS (described briefly earlier) is probably the closest information system to what we have in mind. Data located in disparate datasets are linked by virtue of (for example) common spatial location, temporal range, associates, descriptions and biometric indicators so that patterns can be located efficiently. FLINTS provides the means by which separate elements can be linked, but it has the potential to provide forensic intelligence and forensic analysis.

From an analysis perspective, the strengths of forensic data are: (i) *complete environmental information*: each forensic sample could be matched with spatial, geographic and criminal data of the offence; (ii) *perfect linking*: forensic data are (virtually) unique to individuals, enabling the generation of scene-to-scene matches which would indicate how many offenders are leaving traces and their respective levels of offending; and (iii) *undetected crimes*: forensic data would be linked to all scene samples, not just those for which an offender has been found, leading to the identification of prolific unknowns – those offenders who are unknown to the criminal justice system but leave traces in many places. There are, however, two main weaknesses in using forensic data in the way set out below. First, offences are represented unequally – burglary, vehicle crime and sexual offences are represented in greater numbers than disorder, fraud or harassment. Second, none but the most reckless offender leaves traces at all their crime scenes.

So far, no one has systematically used forensic data to describe the active offending population. Wiles and Costello (2000) look at what DNA traces tell about offenders' travel-to-crime distances. Leary and Pease (2003) seek to establish 'proof of concept' by exploratory analysis of West Midlands data. By using forensic data in an *analytical* manner it should be possible better to understand the size, nature, structure and dynamics of the offender population. These patterns could then be used to enable more effective reduction and detection strategies to be developed. Further, this approach reorientates forensic science within the policing environment from servicing reactive investigations to informing organisational strategy.

Within the academic literature, criminal career research focuses on the active offender population. It explores a range of dimensions of offending patterns: *prevalence*, the proportion of individuals who participate in crime; *frequency*, the rate of activity of participating individuals; *duration*, the length of the criminal career; and *seriousness*, including both crimes committed and switching patterns. Its findings are central for policy- and decision-makers within and beyond the criminal justice system.[9] For example, knowing how many prolific offenders are active at any one time, how they switch between crime types, how many are unknown to the criminal justice system and how long average careers persist would all provide better strategic guidance for crime detection. The research is pretty consistent in concluding that:

1  demographic variables are closely associated with prevalence, but not frequency of offending;
2  the onset of criminal careers peaks in the late teenage years; desistance from criminality is common in early adulthood;
3  individual offending rates assume a highly skewed distribution – those with an early onset of criminality will have higher offending rates;

4  offenders are generally versatile, not exclusively specialising in one type of offence; and

5  because of the age–crime relationship, the duration of most criminal careers is very short.

Until recently, official records and self-report offending surveys were considered the only sources of data for criminal career research with researchers content to acknowledge the inherent data limitations.[10] Forensic data differ from both. Undoubtedly they do suffer from some form of bias. Compared to official data, however, they are collected earlier in the criminal justice process and therefore suffer less attrition (studies of prisoners will only include those arrested and convicted, a distinct subset of the offending population).

Forensic data are also exposed to different types of organisational filters than official crime data. For one, they are collected by a group with a different skill set and operational objective. Police collect details of volume crime incidents mainly for administrative purposes. Despite rhetoric to the contrary, most police officers do not actively engage in detecting criminal incidents. The incomplete and inconsistent recording practices of front-line police officers have been the bane of crime analysts who attempt to infer patterns from a fragmented data source.

Crime scene examiners perform a very different function from police officers at crime scenes. They scrutinise locations for clues as to how the incident occurred and the identities of individuals involved. This outlook generates data with biases of a different nature from officer-collected data. The bias introduced by the crime scene examiner process may be less severe than that associated with the police officer taking crime reports, given that the former has a scientific training which stresses consistent and accurate data collection.

Nonetheless, it is a fact that forensic data are collected at a minority of crime scenes, as shown in Williams (2004). To what extent could an accurate description of a population be based on such a small sample? Of themselves, small samples are not much of a problem if the sample is representative (consider the size [small] and accuracy [high] of pre-election polls). Moreover, potentially useful methods do exist for the analysis of information where large sample sizes are difficult to obtain.

*Capture–recapture* techniques are used in wildlife ecology to estimate population parameters when it is difficult, dangerous or costly to count every single organism (for example fish in the ocean). The simplest model involves capturing a cohort of a population of interest on two occasions. With three quantities – the number captured in the first sweep, the number captured in the second sweep and the number captured in both sweeps – it is possible to estimate the size of the population (Pollock *et al.* 1990). So, even if the sample size is proportionately small, it is still possible to generate an estimate of the population size.

Applying the technique to forensic data would mean that we would treat crime scene data as samples of 'captured' observations and by aggregating months of data into sweeps the capture–recapture technique could be employed to estimate the number of offenders active at a particular point in time. By taking observations at a number of points in time more complex (and realistic) models could be developed (Pollock 1982). For instance, closed population models assume no change in population size (for example no births, deaths, immigration, emigration), so are most suitable for sampling periods covering a relatively short period of time. Open population models allow births, deaths and migration to occur (that is to say, there may be gains or losses between sampling periods). Recent work has introduced a number of models which include temporary emigration (where subjects are unable to be captured during a sampling period) (Kendall *et al.* 1997). These models are likely to be relevant when considering members of the burglar population who become incarcerated or are transient and are therefore not present in the population being sampled but may return at some time in the future.

In this section, we have suggested that forensic data might be used in broader ways than hitherto, to generate an understanding of the criminal population and the criminal careers of offenders. This information would be of considerable operational relevance and could influence crime control strategies. It should be possible to investigate two of the four major dimensions of criminal careers (prevalence and offending rates) as well as estimate the size of the offender population.

## Conclusion

The major forms of rationalisation that have emerged to deal with major crime are very different in form, function and assumption from those that have developed in relation to volume crime. Both try to address the failure adequately to draw forensic science into the investigation of crime. The former mainly risks efficiency, by trying to minimise the chance that potential effectiveness is overlooked. The latter mainly risks effectiveness, by trying to minimise the chances that efforts are wasted where there is little scope of benefit. This may amount to horses for courses rationalisation, but leaves unresolved methods of minimising the costs of either rationalising strategy.

If we look a little more closely at the efforts at rationalisation in relation to volume crime, we find two models at work, whose workings have been identified by Williams (2004). These are shown in Table 14.2. They reflect more general variations between 'procedural' and 'discretionary' approaches to the investigation of volume crime using whatever means are available (Burrows *et al.* 2005a).

The technical assistance/procedural approach treats SOCOs (and other forensic science services, and by extension others involved in different aspects of the investigative process) as specialists with defined roles to be performed in relation to specified sets of cases in specified ways to specified standards with specified functions. Rationality and integration are achieved with clear division of labour and well defined decision rules aiming to produce consistency in the ways in which cases are processed. Net benefits are maximised to the degree to which the specified processes optimise trade-offs between missing opportunities and undertaking work which produces no benefits.

**Table 14.2** Two approaches to the routine integration of scientific support to crime investigation

| Technical assistance integrated into organisational structures | Expert collaboration integrated into the investigative process |
|---|---|
| Control | |
| External hierarchical supervision | Internal professional supervision |
| Attempt exhaustive attendance | Ensure informed attendance |
| Locally accountable | Locally co-accountable |
| CSEs as supervised specialists | CSEs as reflective practitioners |
| Reach | |
| BCU boundary governed | BCU and cross-border oriented |
| Reactive | Proactive |
| Contribute to intelligence | Define, contribute to, and use intelligence |
| Suspect identification orientation | Suspect targeting, identification and detection focus |

*Source*: Williams 2004: 24

The expert collaboration/discretionary approach treats SOCOs (and other forensic providers and others in the investigative process) as professionals exercising informed and collaborative case-by-case judgement to attempt to maximise overall outcome effectiveness in relation to the purposes of crime investigation and crime detection. Rationality is achieved through informed decision-making in relation to a particular offence or a specific crime problem. Net benefits are maximised to the degree to which those involved have the understanding, intelligence and commitment collectively to achieve targeted outcomes.

The ACPO/FSS/Home Office project tended to favour the expert collaboration/discretionary model (which comes closer to the Byford approach to major crime). *Under the Microscope* (albeit a follow-on to the ACPO/FSS/Home Office project), alongside the work of PSU has tended to favour the technical assistance/procedural approach. It is not clear yet which will prove the more useful.

This chapter shows that if forensic science is to contribute optimally to policing and criminal justice objectives – the reduction of volume crime, the quick elimination of the innocent and the conviction of the guilty – understanding and managing effectively the human, social side of the forensic process is absolutely critical. The series of findings showing recurrent weaknesses in the process indicates just how difficult it is to rationalise it. The difficulties are compounded by changes in the science, the legal framework within which forensic processes take place, the evolution of criminal practices, political priorities, and the understanding of criminal behaviour.

Scientific and technological developments, most obviously those that are increasing the potential of DNA profiling and improving the algorithms for and other functional capacities of AFR systems (MHB 2004), are creating new potential contributions of forensic science with likely implications for what should be done and delivered through the forensic process. The science and what it might offer does not sit still. Likewise, the legal framework alters. PACE, for example, increased the importance of forensic science as other routes to detection became more difficult to follow because of the risks they posed for justice. Alterations in the range of those for whom CJ DNA samples could be taken and kept have altered the size and potential from the DNA database. Criminal behaviour is thought to some degree to evolve with the tools available to the police for detection. Offenders adapt in their *modus operandi* (MO). For example they may torch cars stolen for joyriding rather than risk the recovery and analysis of finger marks or material open to DNA profiling. Political priorities partly affect the funding streams available to support DNA. They also shape policing priorities and through this the nature and extent that forensic processes might contribute. Improved criminological understanding may suggest strategies more effectively to disrupt criminal behaviour by focusing on identifying associations, patterns of offender recruitment, or prolific offenders. The preceding section has provided some pointers to what might be done in this regard.

In a context in which criminal behaviour, law, science, priorities and criminology are all in some flux it may be that rigid rules maximising consistency in patterns of outcome (which have never in practice yet been found) are less promising than an informed, professional model where informed reflective practitioners work together to forge evolving collaborative strategies.

## Notes

1 The Forensic Science Service became a Non-Departmental Public Board (NDPB), wholly owned by the Home Office but operating at arm's length.

2 The total number of recorded crimes (excluding violent crimes where counting rules make comparison across time meaningless) fell from 5 million in 1992 to 4.4 million in 2004–5. This means that the ratio of comparable crimes fell by over three-quarters from 6,900 to 1,700 per annum per member of the Forensic Science Service.

3 FLINTS uses forensic links provided by DNA, tools, footwear marks and fingerprints to draw out connections between scenes and people, for example people found at the same crime scene, and crime scenes linked to one another. The original acronym was Forensic Led INTelligence System.

4 The authors acknowledge their indebtedness to Ken Pease for insightful comments about the ideas contained in this section.

5 From countless discussions with police officers there seems to be a consensus that the size of the unknown offender population is very small.

6 Occasionally a series of scenes are linked but these are comparatively rare. Regardless, the endeavour focuses on an individual offender.

7 Obviously some variation exists, some intelligence can be used to prevent – but this is not its normal routine application. Regardless, individuals are the predominant focus of intelligence.

8  Like the intelligence definition, there will be some deviations in practice from our analysis definition, however the vast bulk of analysis that is routinely conducted in police agencies fits this pattern.

9  The literature on criminal careers is extensive. Interested readers are referred to Blumstein *et al.* (1986); Tarling (1993); Farrington *et al.* (1998); and Piquero and Mazerolle (2001).

10  Longitudinal data suffer from bias in offending patterns, but not the sample. Official data suffer from bias in the sample and probably in offending patterns.

## References

ACPO/FSS (1996) *Using Forensic Science Effectively*. London: ACPO/FSS.

Audit Commission (1988) *Improving the Performance of the Fingerprint Service*. London: HMSO.

Audit Commission (1993) *Helping with Inquiries*. London: HMSO.

Bieber, F.R., Brenner, C.H and Lazer, D. (2006) 'Finding Criminals Through DNA of Their Relatives', *Science*, (published online May 11).

Blumstein, A., Cohen, J., Roth, J.A. and Visher, C.A. (eds) (1986) *Criminal Careers and 'Career Criminals'*. Washington, DC: National Academy Press.

Burrows, J., Hopkins, M., Robinson, A., Speed, M. and Tilley, N. (2005a) *Understanding the attrition process in volume crime investigation*. Home Office Research Study 295. London: Home Office.

Burrows, J., Tarling, R., Mackie, A., Poole, H. and Hodgson, B. (2005b) *Forensic Science Pathfinder Project: Evaluating Increased Forensic Activity in Two English Police Services*. Home Office Online Report 46/05. London: Home Office.

Byford, L. (1982) *Report by Sir Lawrence Byford into the police handling of the Yorkshire Ripper case*. London: Home Office (released in June 2006, under the Freedom of Information Act).

Farrington, D.P., Lambert, S. and West, D.J. (1998) 'Criminal careers of two generations of family members in the Cambridge Study of Delinquent Development', *Studies on Crime and Crime Prevention*, 7: 85–106.

Forensic Science Service (2005) *Annual Report and Accounts 2004–5*. Norwich: The Stationery Office.

Goldstein, H. (1990) *Problem-Oriented Policing*. New York: McGraw-Hill.

Her Majesty's Inspector of Constabulary (HMIC) (2000) *Under the Microscope*. London: Home Office.

Her Majesty's Inspector of Constabulary (HMIC) (2002) *Under the Microscope Refocused*. London: Home Office.

Home Affairs Select Committee (1989) *Report on the Forensic Science Service*, 2 vols. London: Home Office.

Home Office (1993) *Report on Future Options for Home Office Forensic Science Service*, unpublished report jointly prepared by the Home Office Police Department and the Forensic Science Service.

Jeffreys, A.J., Wilson, V. and Thien, S.L. (1985) 'Hypervariable "minisatellite" regions in human DNA', *Nature*, 314: 67–73.

Kendall, W.L., Nichols, J.D. and Hines, J.E. (1997) 'Estimating temporary emigration using capture–recapture data with Pollock's Robust Design', *Ecology*, 78 (2): 563–78.

Leary, D. and Pease, K. (2003) 'DNA and the Active Criminal Population', *Crime Prevention and Community Safety: An International Journal*, 5: 7–12.

MHB (2004) *The Processing of Fingerprint Evidence after the Introduction of the National Automated Fingerprint Identification System (NAFIS)*. Home Office Online Report 23/04. London: Home Office.

Piquero, A.R. and Mazerolle, P. (2001) *Life-course Criminology: Classic and Contemporary Readings*. Belmont, CA: Wadsworth.

Police Standards Unit (2003) *Memorandum*, Minutes of Evidence submitted by the Police Standards Unit to Home Affairs Committee, 8 July 2003.

Pollock, K.H. (1982) 'A capture–recapture design robust to unequal probability of capture', *Journal of Wildlife Management*, 46: 757–760.

Pollock, K.H., Nichols, J.D., Brownie, C. and Hines, J.E. (1990) *Statistical Inference for Capture–Recapture Experiments*, Wildlife Monographs, No. 107.

Ramsay, M. (1987) *The Effectiveness of the Forensic Science Service*. Home Office Research Study 92. London: Home Office.

Royal Commission on Criminal Justice (1993) *Report*, Cm 2263 (Chairman Viscount Runciman). London: HMSO.

Tarling, R. (1993) *Analysing Offending*. London: Home Office.

Tilley, N. and Ford, A. (1996) *Forensic Science and Crime Investigation*. Crime Detection and Prevention Series Paper 73. London: Home Office.

Touche Ross (1987) *Review of Scientific Support for the Police*, 3 vols. London: Home Office.

Webb, B., Smith, C., Brock, A. and Townsley, M. (2005) 'DNA fast tracking', in M. Smith and N. Tilley (eds), *Crime science: New approaches to preventing and detecting crime*, Crime Science Series. Cullompton: Willan Publishing.

Wiles, P. and Costello, A. (2000) 'The "road to nowhere": the evidence for travelling criminals', *Home Office Research Study 207*. Research, Development and Statistics Directorate. London: Home Office.

Williams, R. (2004) *The management of crime scene examination in relation to the investigation of burglary and vehicle crime*. Home Office Online Report 24/04. London: Home Office.

## Part 3

# Forensic Reasoning and the Evaluation of Scientific Evidence

# Introduction

## Jim Fraser and Robin Williams

Throughout this Handbook, and elsewhere in contemporary accounts of the use of forensic science to support police investigations, it is usual for a distinction to be drawn between the use of forensic science to provide the police with investigative 'intelligence' and the use of forensic science to provide the courts with expert 'evidence'. Whilst there are clearly contexts in which this distinction is relatively straightforward (for example when information derived from forensic examinations is utilised to direct police inquiries but not deployed in the construction of a case against an accused person), the difference between 'intelligence' and 'evidence' is not always a simple or stable one. It is especially misleading to think of the former as requiring less robust science, or less clear reasoning. However, there may well be ways in which the distinctive orientations of investigators and the courts require forensic scientists to present the results of their analysis of evidence, as well as their opinions concerning their significance, in different ways.

The first section of this Handbook contains chapters which describe to readers the major features of a number of distinct domains of forensic science – including DNA, fingerprints, fire investigation, blood pattern analysis and so on – and in this sense mainly deal with the first desideratum listed above, i.e. the robustness of the procedures, science and technology. In this section, however, authors are concerned with the second desideratum, i.e. with the ways in which forensic science reasoning is and should be best constructed in the varying investigative and evaluative contexts of its use. They also seek to show how, and with what effects, such expert scientific reasoning may be deconstructed by legal practitioners when it is presented to the courts. Each chapter is written by an international expert in the relevant field, and together they bring to the topic of forensic reasoning and the evaluation of scientific evidence, extensive academic and operational authority in the domains of statistics, legal scholarship and investigative practice.

The critical survey offered in Aitken's chapter provides a clear historically informed introduction to the main approaches taken to forensic statistics in the twentieth and the early twenty first centuries. His account describes and explains how and why statistical methods based first on frequency counting, later on the concept of 'discriminating power' and then on the practice of significance testing, have subsequently been replaced by the provision of Bayesian likelihood ratios. In doing so he provides a sense of the complexity and contestability that underlies the ways in which relevant experts have used the varying mathematical resources on which forensic science reasoning is based. One of the remarkable things about this history is the speed at which understandings have changed within the expert scientific community, even though it is clear that the courts have not always found it easy to accommodate these changes. Furthermore, he reminds us that crucial logical errors in the statistical interpretation of forensic evidence (most obviously variants of the 'transposed conditional') continue to haunt both investigatory and judicial corridors as well as accounts of many factual and fictional cases in print and visual media.

The central feature of Aitken's historico-theoretical account is the increasing significance of Bayesianism as the paradigm of forensic science reasoning about probability in the domain of legal evidence. The sources, contours, and implications of this paradigmatic status are further explored in Jackson's detailed and well-illustrated treatment of the ways in which forensic science opinions – in both investigative and judicial contexts – are supported by principles of formal reasoning. Jackson's intimate and extensive experience as a forensic practitioner is also used to show how the Bayesian approach as a 'robust, logical means of inductive reasoning' provides a resource for clarifying the meaning of the routine but conceptually loose terminology used in many forensic scientists' reports of their findings. In addition, both writers explore and present to readers valuable accounts of the 'hierarchy of propositions' or 'hierarchy of issues' that are relevant to the robust application of Bayesian (or any other) reasoning to the assessment of the significance of forensic science findings and opinions in criminal investigations and prosecutions.

Both Aitken and Jackson discuss recent and contemporary forensic science reasoning against the background of the approaches taken to these issues by courts of England and Wales. However Roberts's chapter is concerned to foreground the significance of how, and according to what principles, the courts determine what kinds of forensic science evidence and reasoning are to count as sufficiently sound to be relied on by those concerned to assert or determine guilt or innocence in criminal cases. In accounting for the courts' view of the status and role of expert witnesses he provides a sense of the broader social and epistemic contexts in which these issues need to be placed. In addition he reminds us of the necessity to understand better the differences between scientific and legal priorities and the ways in which these priorities together shape the recurrent forms of contemporary forensic science custom and practice. Whilst forensic evidence and opinion provided to the court is determined by what has happened in earlier phases of the criminal process, participants in those early phases are required always to orient themselves to the possibility that the material evidence that they have collected, together with their interpretations of the significance of that evidence, may eventually fall under judicial scrutiny. In that sense, forensic science practice, whether assisting the police with their inquiries, or assisting the court to determine guilt or innocence is always and necessarily the product of the application of legal as well as scientific principles.

Finally, it is worth noting that, at many points in these chapters, their authors turn to the issue of DNA evidence and the ways in which the scientific innovations underlying the development of DNA profiling have challenged both the legal profession (by requiring an appreciation of a rapidly advancing technology, and the ways in which its results should be presented in court), and also the forensic science profession (by establishing new standards for the robustness of opinions relating to the 'identification' of individuals in the course of criminal proceedings and by casting a new light on the way in which more traditional forensic science disciplines have proceeded). These – largely unanticipated – consequences of the introduction of a new technology into forensic science serve to remind us that the forensic science enterprise is an essentially open one. This openness is something that requires exceptional alertness on the part of legislators, policymakers, academic researchers, the police and lawyers, as all such actors try to grasp the opportunities and control the risks associated with the constant restlessness of the application of science to the criminal justice process.

# Chapter 15

# Statistics and forensic science

*Colin Aitken*

## Introduction

The role of statistics in forensic science from the middle of the twentieth century to the beginning of the twenty-first century is covered, with a brief reference to the beginning of the twentieth century and the Dreyfus case. The emphasis is on the use of statistics for the evaluation of evidence.

In the 1960s, in a series of papers, Kingston and Kirk (1964a, 1964b) and Kingston alone (1965a, 1965b, 1966) discussed the role of statistics in forensic science (or criminalistics). These were predated by Kirk (1953) in which Kirk stated that '[p]robability is the very keynote of interpretation of all physical evidence'. A distinction was made then between *individualisation* and *identification*. The process of addressing the issue of whether or not a particular item came from a particular source was termed 'individualisation'. 'Criminalistics is the science of individualisation' (Kirk 1963). An 'identification' is, more correctly, defined as 'the determination of some set to which an object belongs or the determination as to whether an object belongs to a given set' (Kingston 1965a). However, established forensic and judicial practices have led to 'individualisation' being termed 'identification'. The establishment of an identification of a suspect or defendant with a criminal is an opinion on the issue of interest to the court and outwith the remit of the forensic scientist. The step from probabilities relating to evidence to probability relating to identity has been termed a 'leap of faith' (Stoney 1991).

The problems that may arise when numbers are introduced into a court of law are discussed at length in Tribe (1971), in response to an article by Finkelstein and Fairley (1970) with a response by these authors to the article by Tribe in Finkelstein and Fairley (1971). For example, in an issue which is still a matter of debate, Tribe raises the concern that a very low relative frequency for a characteristic may 'dwarf all efforts to put it into perspective'. This concern 'pervades all cases in which the trial use of mathematics is proposed'.

Current research and development on interpretation concentrates on ideas known as Bayesian, named after the nonconformist minister Reverend Thomas Bayes, FRS (1702–1761). The paper in which the principles of the reasoning that has come to be known as Bayesian inference was espoused was published posthumously in 1763 (Bayes 1764; Barnard 1958; Pearson and Kendall 1970).

The development of forensic statistics may be considered, roughly in chronological order, in the four stages of relative frequencies, discriminating power, significance probabilities, and likelihood ratios.

While sample frequencies are still being used in the courts (and will continue to be used where the rarity of particular characteristics is itself of interest), other ideas have been considered for the evaluation of evidence. The basic premise is that of a comparison between evidence found in association with a crime (victim or scene) and evidence found in association with a suspect. The question is whether these two pieces of evidence are similar and,  if so, whether the similarity is that of rare evidence or of common evidence. Amongst the earliest of these ideas were those of significance testing and discriminating power. The theory of significance testing was developed by statisticians in the 1920s and began to be applied in forensic science in the 1960s. However, the underlying statistical principle in significance testing is that of the assumption of a null hypothesis of common source (and its association with guilt in a forensic context). Evidence has to be accumulated against this null hypothesis. The strength of the evidence is represented by a significance probability. This philosophy does not sit easily with the legal principle of innocent until proven guilty. In the context of hypothesis testing the philosophy is akin to 'guilty until proven innocent'. A statistically significant result suggests different sources, a non-significant result suggests a common source. Also, it is difficult to determine the value of evidence which has been found non-significant. This is because of the need to assess the rarity of a similarity. Evidence which is not significant in the statistical sense may or may not be rare. A similarity in rare evidence may be thought to be more valuable than a similarity in common evidence but this thought is difficult to quantify using this approach.

Discriminating power is applicable as a general measure of the value of an evidential type (for example hairs, paint). It is a measure of the ability of an evidential type to discriminate between items of that type that come from different sources. Its value may be assessed empirically through a series of pairwise comparisons of items whose source is known. Thus a measure of the discriminating power is obtained by considering the number of comparisons which cannot be distinguished as coming from different sources amongst the total number of comparisons that have been made from items known to have come from different sources. Discriminating power is still being used and some of its advantages and disadvantages are described.

From the late 1970s onwards, the use of the likelihood ratio has become more established as the way in which evidence may be evaluated. Details of its development with illustrative examples are given. An excellent source of material for the statistical layman is Robertson and Vignaux (1995).

The use of Bayesian networks, an idea whose use in the legal area was first mooted in 1989, is becoming more prevalent in forensic science. These are diagrams with nodes and edges and associated conditional probability tables which may be used to provide an intuitively understandable presentation of the structure of evidence and its evaluation. A brief introduction to these networks with some examples is given. The chapter finishes with a section on sampling and quantity estimation.

## Terminology

There are certain words and phrases which are common in any discussion of the use of statistics in forensic science. It is helpful in understanding the underlying ideas to introduce these words and phrases at the start of the discussion.

In standard introductory courses and books on statistics, mention is made of the probability of an event. For example, this could be the probability of the toss of a fair six-sided die landing six uppermost. Note that a fair die is one in which every side has an equal probability of being the uppermost one, something which is very difficult to achieve in manufacture. The event is the outcome, a six, of a roll of a fair six-sided die. Reference is also made, occasionally, to the complement of an event. The complement of an event is, loosely speaking, the opposite of an event. The complement of an event is the set of possibilities of events such as when added to the original event gives the set of all possible events. Thus, for the event that the outcome of a throw of a six-sided die is a six, the complement is an outcome which is any number other than a six (i.e. a one, two, three, four or five). In forensic sciences, consideration is given to propositions and to evidence, both of which may be thought of as events.

Propositions may be proposed by prosecutors and defenders. Examples include:

- The defendant is guilty. This could be a proposition put forward by the prosecution. } *Crime level*
- The defendant is not guilty. This could be a proposition put forward by the defence.
- The defendant was at the scene of the crime. This could be a proposition put forward by the prosecution. } *Activity*
- The defendant was not at the scene of the crime. This could be a proposition put forward by the defence.
- Glass fragments found on clothing of a suspect came from the crime scene. This could be a proposition put forward by the prosecution. } *Source*
- Glass fragments found on clothing of a suspect did not come from the crime scene. This could be a proposition put forward by the defence.

In these examples, the defence proposition is the complement of the prosecution proposition though this need not always be the case. Evidence evaluation considers evidence at three possible levels, crime, activity and source (Cook et al. 1998b). The first two propositions above are at the crime level. They concern the identity of the criminal. The second two propositions are at the activity level. They concern an action of the defendant, that of presence at the crime scene. The third two propositions are at the source level. They concern the source of evidence found on a suspect and at the crime scene. In general notation, $H_p$ will denote the prosecution's proposition, $H_d$ will denote the defence proposition. Further discussion is given in the section on levels of proposition, p. 399.

Evidence will be denoted by $E$. Often, there will be a need to distinguish between two types of evidence. First, there is evidence, the source of which is known. This will be referred to as control evidence and denoted $E_c$. Second, there is evidence, the source of which is unknown. This will be referred to as recovered evidence and denoted $E_r$. For example, there may be a broken window at a crime scene with fragments of glass, considered to be from the window, on the floor beside it. These fragments of glass, and measurements of characteristics of the glass, such as the elemental composition, will be control evidence. A suspect is identified and he has fragments of glass on his clothing. The source of these fragments is not known. These fragments of glass, and measurements of characteristics of the glass, such as the elemental composition, will be recovered evidence.

Alternatively, there may be a crime scene where fibres, whose origin cannot be determined, are found at the scene. The fibres and characteristics of them, will be recovered evidence. A suspect is identified. Fibres of his clothing, and characteristics of these fibres, will be control evidence. Thus, control evidence may be evidence at the crime scene or it may be evidence associated with a suspect. Similarly, recovered evidence may be evidence associated with a suspect or it may be evidence at the crime scene.

Evidence may be of a material kind, such as the fragments of glass or fibres. It may also be measurements of characteristics of the material, such as the elemental composition of glass or the complementary chromaticity coordinates of fibres. The discussion in this chapter will be concerned solely with the measurements of the characteristics of the evidential material. Further details of the relationship between the type of evidence and the measurements on it are given in Aitken and Taroni (2004).

In the context of forensic science, evidence may be considered as an event. Thus, it is possible to discuss the probability of evidence, as one might talk of the probability of an event. For some readers, the concept of probability of evidence may be difficult to grasp. However, the concept formalises the idea of likelihood. Mention is often made of the likelihood of evidence. For example, 'how likely is it that there would be these similarities in the elemental compositions of the glass fragments from the crime scene and from the suspect's clothing if the fragments had a common source?' Note that mention is not made of the transposed phrase: 'how likely is it that the fragments would have a common source, given these similarities in the elemental compositions of the glass fragments'? This transposed phrase makes a comment on the source of the glass fragments, a matter which is properly the remit of the judge and jury and not of the forensic scientist. Its mistaken use gives rise to the idea of the fallacy of the transposed conditional.

A proposition may be also be thought of in a similar way to an event, if subjective probabilities are considered. A subjective probability, as the name suggests, is one which is determined in a subjective manner. This determination may be done by an expert witness or by a judge or by a member of a jury. The value attached to the probability of a particular event by different people may be different. For example, people may be asked for the probability that Scotland will win theWorld Cup of football in 2010. There will be many different answers, all of which, it is suspected, will be very small. Objective probabilities are ones for which everyone will agree. For example, everyone will (hopefully) agree that the probability of a six being the outcome of a throw of a fair, six-sided die is 1/6. Events may be measurements of characteristics of interest, such as concentrations of certain minerals within the traces. There may be a well-specified model representing the randomness in such measurements. However, the guilt or innocence of the suspect is something about which there is no well- specified model but about which it is perfectly reasonable for an individual to represent his state of uncertainty with a probability about the truth or otherwise of the propositions.

All probabilities are conditional. The probability of the event of interest will be conditioned on the background knowledge or information, $I$, about the rest of the world as known by the person who is determining the probability. The separation of an event for which the probability is wanted and the events on which it is conditioned will be denoted with a vertical bar $|$, the former coming to the left of, or before, the bar and the latter coming to the right of, or after, the bar. As examples of the associated notation, consider

- $Pr(H_p | I)$, which is read as the probability of the truth of the prosecution's proposition, given background information;
- $Pr(E | I)$, which is read as the probability of the evidence, given background information;
- $Pr(H_p | E, I)$, which is read as the probability of the truth of the prosecution's proposition given the evidence and background information.

Often $I$ will be omitted in the text for simplicity of notation but it should not be forgotten.

Knowledge of the basic laws of probability is assumed. Such laws include the multiplication law for the conjunction of two or more events and the addition law for the disjunction of two or more events. Readers uncertain of these laws are recommended to read the relevant chapter of Aitken and Taroni (2004). A summary of the notation used in this chapter is given in Appendix 1, p. 413, for ease of reference.

Now that certain terminology has been introduced, it is possible to discuss the various uses of statistics in forensic science.

## Relative frequencies

First, consider two misinterpretations of evidence, or fallacies, with which a probability may be associated, the probability usually being estimated by a relative frequency.

A small value for the probability of the evidence if the person on whom it is found is innocent does not imply a large value for the probability that a person is guilty if the evidence is found on them. The belief that these two probability statements, both apparently simple to understand, are equivalent is known as the prosecutor's fallacy (Thompson and Schumann 1987) or the fallacy of the transposed conditional. These two statements have been the source of much confusion in the interpretation of evidence in which probabilities have been mentioned.

A related fallacy is the defence fallacy (Thompson and Schumann 1987). Given a probability, $p$, of finding the evidence on an innocent person, the defender's fallacy then multiplies this probability, $p$, by the size of a relevant population (Coleman and Walls 1974), $N$ say, to obtain the expected number of people $Np$ with the evidence in that population. It is then argued that a large value of $Np$ renders the evidence meaningless as the accused is only one amongst $Np$ people. However, in rebuttal, before the evidence was presented, the accused was one of $N$ people. The evidence has reduced the pool of potential criminals from $N$ to $Np$ and is therefore of some worth.

Two examples (one real-life and one artificial) are given here of evidence interpretation using relative frequencies.

The relative frequency of a characteristic has been used as a measure of the strength of evidence for many years, since at least the mid nineteenth century. The relative frequency in a sample has been used as an estimate of the probability of the characteristic being present in a member of the population of which the sample is representative.

An early example of the use of a relative frequency in law was to query the authenticity of signatures on wills (Mode 1963; Meier and Zabell 1980). The use of probabilistic and statistical evidence in this case is probably the earliest instance of their use in American law. The evidence related to the agreement of 30 downstrokes in a contested signature with those of a genuine signature. It was argued that the probability of this agreement if the contested signature were genuine was extremely small; the probability of observing two spontaneous signatures with the number of overlaid strokes observed in those two signatures was estimated as $(1/5)^{30}$. Hence the contested signature was a forgery. This is an example of both a transposed conditional and a leap of faith.

Later examples in which the relative frequency of a characteristic in some background or relevant population was used as evidence include the Dreyfus case, the Collins case (Fairley and Mosteller 1977) and, in the present day, cases involving DNA profiling. In all examples, the smaller the frequency, the stronger the support provided by the evidence for the prosecution proposition.

### Artificial example

An artificial example to illustrate the difference between the probability statements

- the probability of the evidence, given the defence proposition is true and
- the probability that the defence proposition is true given the evidence

has been provided by Darroch (1987) (motivated by evidence he gave to a Royal Commission, Splatt 1984). Consider a town in which a rape has been committed. There are 10,000 men of suitable age in the town of whom 200 work underground at a mine. Evidence is found at the crime scene from which it is determined that the criminal is one of the 200 mineworkers. Such evidence may be traces of minerals which could only have come from the mine. A suspect is identified and traces of minerals, similar to those found at the crime scene, are found on some of his clothing. How might this evidence be assessed?

Denote the event that 'mineral traces have been found on clothing of the suspect which is similar to mineral traces found at the crime scene' as the evidence $E$. Denote the proposition that the suspect is guilty by $H_p$ and the proposition that he is innocent by $H_d$.

Assume that all people working underground at the mine will have mineral traces similar to those found at the crime scene on some of their clothing. This assumption is open to question but the point about conditional probabilities will still be valid. The probability of finding the evidence on an innocent person may then be determined as follows. See Table 15.1. There are 9,999 innocent men in the town, of whom 199 work underground at the mine, as shown in row 2. These 199 men will, as a result of their work, have this evidence on their clothing, under the above assumption. The ratio of 199/9,999 may be taken as an estimate of the probability of observing the evidence on a person when he is innocent; the notation for this is $Pr(E \mid H_d)$. Thus $Pr(E \mid H_d) = 199/9,999 \simeq 200/10,000 = 0.02$, a small number. However, there are 200 men in the town with the evidence ($E$) on them of whom 199 are innocent ($H_d$), as shown in column 1 of Table 15.1. The ratio of 199/200 may be taken as an estimate of the probability a person is innocent given he is associated with the evidence; the notation for this is $Pr(H_d \mid E)$. Thus $Pr(H_d \mid E) = 199/200 = 0.995$. This is a very different value from 0.02.

## Discriminating power

### Derivation

Two unrelated individuals are selected at random from some population. The probability that they are found to match with respect to some characteristic

Table 15.1 Numbers of men of a suitable age to have committed the crime in a town. Two hundred work in the mine and have evidence associated with the crime linked to them. One of the two hundred is guilty. Nine thousand, eight hundred men do not have the evidence associated with the crime linked to them; all are innocent.

| | Evidence ($E$) | No evidence | Total |
|---|---|---|---|
| Guilty ($H_p$) | 1 | 0 | 1 |
| Innocent ($H_d$) | 199 | 9,800 | 9,999 |
| Total | 200 | 9,800 | 10,000 |

(for example blood profile, paint fragments on clothing, head hairs) is known as the *probability of non-discrimination* or the *probability of a match, PM*. The probability they are found not to match with respect to this characteristic is known as the *probability of discrimination* (Jones 1972) or *discriminating power, DP* (Smalldon and Moffat 1973). Such a probability is known as a complementary probability in that it is the probability of the event which is complementary (or opposite) to the original event. Here, the original event is a match. The complementary (opposite) event is a non-match. The complementary probabilities are the probabilities of a match and a non-match.

Consider a population and a DNA locus in which there are $k$ genotypes, labelled $1,...,$ $k$ and in which the $j$-th genotype has relative frequency $p_j$, with $\sum_{j=1}^{k} p_j = 1$. Consider two unrelated people, $C$ and $D$ in this population. Let $Cj$ and $Dj$ be the event that they are of genotype $j$. This event has probability $p_j^2$. The probability of a match on *any* genotype is the disjunction of $k$ mutually exclusive events (i.e. one and only one of the events can happen), the matches on genotypes $1,...,k$, respectively. Let $Q$ be the probability $PM$ of a match in the genotype, without specification of the genotype on which they match. Then

$$Q = Pr(C_1D_1 \text{ or } C_2D_2 \text{ or } ... \text{ or } C_kD_k)$$
$$= Pr(C_1D_1) + Pr(C_2D_2) + ... + Pr(C_kD_k)$$

(because the events $C_1D_1,...,C_kD_k$ are mutually exclusive)

$$Q = p_1^2 + p_2^2 + ... + p_k^2.$$

The discriminating power, or probability of discrimination, is then $1 - Q$. The maximum value of $1 - Q$ is $1 - 1/k$ when all genotypes are equally likely. The minimum value of $1 - Q$ occurs when there is only one genotype. For example, if it is genotype 1, such that $p_1 = 1; p_2 = 0,...,p_k = 0$, then $Q = 1$ and $1 - Q = 0$. This result reflects the reasonable fact that if everyone has the same genotype then there is no discrimination at that locus.

Often, however, it is an empirical determination of $Q$ that is all that may be obtained. An example is given in an experiment described by Tippett *et al.* (1968). Tippett and his co-workers compared two thousand samples of paint fragments, pairwise. For various reasons, the number of samples was reduced to 1,969, all from different sources. These were examined by various tests and only two pairs of samples from different sources were found to be indistinguishable. The total number of pairs which can be picked out at random is $\frac{1}{2} \times 1969 \times 1968 = 1,937,496$. Two pairs of samples were found to agree with each other. The probability of picking a pair of fragments at random which were found to be indistinguishable was thus determined empirically as $2/1,937,496 = 1/968,478$.

This probability is an estimate of the probability of a match ($Q$). The method by which it was determined is extremely useful in situations such as the one described by Tippett *et al.* (1968) in which frequency probabilities are unavailable and, indeed, for which a classification system has not been devised. The extremely low value (1/968,748) of the $Q$ demonstrates the high evidential value of the methods used by the authors. The conclusion from this experiment is that these methods are very good at differentiating between paints from different sources. Low values of $Q$ were also obtained in work on head hairs (Gaudette and Keeping 1974) and footwear (Groom and Lawton 1987).

Discriminating power provides a measure of the general performance of an evidential type. It does not provide a measure for the evidential value in a particular case.


## Significance

A significance probability provides a measure of compatibility of an observation or observations with a proposition. As an example in forensic science consider continuous data, such as the refractive index of glass. The observations are the measurements of the refractive indices on fragments of glass for the control and recovered evidence. The proposition is that the control and recovered evidence come from the same source. The compatibility of the observations with the proposition is measured by considering the statistic formed from the difference in the mean measurements on the control and recovered evidence, relative to the estimated standard error of the difference. The larger the value of this statistic, the more incompatible the data are with the proposition that the control and recovered evidence come from the same source. The significance probability is the probability of obtaining a value of the statistic as large as that observed, if the proposition of a common source is true. This probability is sometimes denoted as $P$ and is then known as the $P$-value.

A common example of the statistic is that of the $t$-distribution, which arises when the data are normally distributed and the population variances for the control and recovered measurements are assumed to be equal, even when they come from different sources. The proposition of a common source is then equivalent to a proposition that the means of the populations from which the control and recovered evidence come from are equal.

A small value for the significance probability suggests that the observed difference is incompatible or inconsistent with a zero value for the difference in means of the distributions from which the control and recovered measurements have been assumed to come. Certain conventional values of the significance probability are taken to suggest that the proposition of zero difference is false. These conventional values include 0.10, 0.05. and 0.01. Thus, an observed difference, such that its value of $P$ lies between 0.05 and 0.01 is said to be *significant at the 5 per cent level*. It is not significant at the 1 per cent level. A difference with $P$ less than 1 per cent is significant at both the 5 per cent and 1 per cent levels. Occasionally, a result is said to be *significant*, with no mention of the level, when the result is such that the proposition of no difference in the means of the distributions is to be rejected.

It is a matter of subjective judgement as to when to decide to act as if the original proposition is false. It may be decided to do so if the significance probability is less than 0.05. If it is decided to act as if the original proposition is false, then that proposition is said to be rejected. If the decision is to do so if the significance probability is less than 0.05 then the proposition is said to be rejected at the 5 per cent level. Note that rejection at the 5 per cent level, say, is to reject a proposition because the statistic is such that the probability of a value as large as the observed value is less than 0.05, i.e. that value will occur less than 1 time in 20 that the experiment (of comparing two groups) is conducted. A corollary of this is that a value of the statistic as big as the one observed will occur, by chance alone, one in every 20 times, when the proposition is true. It is expected that about once in every 20 independent experiments that are done with this rejection rule, the proposition will be rejected when in fact it is true and thus rejected in error. Such a rejection is known as an error of the first kind or type 1 error. The alternative error is to fail to reject a proposition when in fact it is false. This error would be to decide to act as if the control evidence and the recovered evidence came from the same source when, in fact, they did not. Such an error is known as an error of the second kind or type 2 error.

There may be costs associated with a wrong decision and these may be influential in deciding when to reject or not a proposition. The above discussion is concerned with a proposition of common source for control and recovered evidence. A more serious proposition is one which proposes that a particular person is guilty of a certain crime. A proposition of common source suggests that the evidence associated with the suspect and the evidence associated with the crime have a common source. This is in turn supportive of a proposition that the suspect is guilty of the crime. It is a very serious error to decide that a person is guilty of a crime he did not commit. In many jurisdictions it is a much more serious error than the decision that he is not guilty of a crime he did commit. There are various judicial quotes that it is better that so many guilty men go free than that an innocent man is found guilty, that give some idea of judicial estimates of the probabilities of errors of the first and second kind.

Note that a significance probability is the probability of the value, or anything more extreme, of the observed statistic if a proposition is true. It is not the probability that the proposition is true, given the value of the associated statistic. However, the significance probability is often confused with this latter probability. A small value for the significance probability is often taken to mean a small value for the proposition of common source. This is an example of the prosecutor's fallacy or the fallacy of the transposed conditional, though in the converse of its usual interpretation. Here, a small value suggests different sources and hence innocence. The usual interpretation is that a small value for the probability of the evidence suggests a small value for the probability of innocence.

The significance probability is the output of the first part of a two-stage process (Parker and Holford 1968) which models some processes used by forensic scientists from before then until the present day. The first stage is a comparison stage. If the outcome of the comparison is significant then  the control and recovered evidence are deemed to have come from different sources. If the outcome is not significant then the control and recovered evidence are deemed perhaps to have come from the same source. It is only 'perhaps' since there may be an error of the second kind. This leads to an effect known as the 'fall- off-the-cliff' effect (credited in Evett 1991 to Smalldon). A comparison which is significant at the 4.9 per cent level leads to an exclusion of the evidence, one which is significant at the 5.1 per cent level leads to the continuation of the evidence in the investigative process.

The second stage is one of assessment of the rarity of the similarity. If the similarity is that of a rare characteristic then the evidence is stronger than if it is of a common characteristic. However, it is not obvious how such a strength of evidence may be assessed numerically and combined with other evidence.

Significance probabilities also *combine* in different way from the probabilities of events. For characteristics which are dependent, it is possible that the significance probability of the joint observation may be greater than either of the individual significance probabilities. For example, it is possible that the individual significance probabilities are both $< 0.05$ but the combined significance probability $> 0.05$.

Thus, the use of the significance probability to evaluate evidence may be criticised in two ways. First, there is the 'fall-off-the-cliff' effect. Second, there is the lack of an intuitive method of combining the evidential assessment with other evidence. Both of these criticisms are answered through the use of likelihood ratios.

## Likelihood ratios

From the late 1970s onwards, the use of the likelihood ratio has become more established as the way in which evidence should be evaluated. This approach to the evaluation of evidence has, as its fundamental assumption, the assumption that only two probabilities are of importance, the probability of the evidence if the prosecution's proposition is true and the probability of the evidence if the defence proposition is true. With this assumption, it can be shown that the only way that evidence may be evaluated is as a function of the ratio of these two probabilities, a ratio known as a likelihood ratio.

In the context of forensic science, consider two propositions, $H_p$ and $H_d$, and evidence $E$. It is desired to assign a value to $E$. The odds form of Bayes' Theorem states that

$$\frac{Pr(H_p|E)}{Pr(H_d|E)} = \frac{Pr(E|H_p)}{Pr(E|H_d)} \times \frac{Pr(H_p)}{Pr(H_d)}.$$

There are three ratios in this expression. Consider these one at a time. First, consider

$$\frac{Pr(H_p)}{Pr(H_d)}. \quad \textit{Prior odds}$$

This is the prior odds in favour of the prosecution's proposition, $H_p$, before the evidence $E$ is presented. In the situation in which it is the odds in favour of a proposition, $H_p$, that the defendant is guilty before any evidence is presented, the prior odds is the value associated with the dictum *innocent until proven guilty*. The next ratio

$$\frac{Pr(E|H_p)}{Pr(E|H_d)} \quad \textit{likelihood ratio}$$

is the ratio of the probability of the evidence if the prosecution's proposition is true to the probability of the evidence if the defence proposition is true. This ratio is known as the likelihood ratio as it is the ratio of the likelihoods (probabilities in this context) of the evidence under each of the two propositions.

The third ratio

$$\frac{Pr(H_p|E)}{Pr(H_d|E)} \quad \textit{Posterior}$$

is the posterior odds in favour of the prosecution's proposition after $E$ has been presented. These odds are associated with the burden of proof with which a court has to find in favour of the prosecution (in a criminal case) or a plaintiff (in a civil case).

Denote the likelihood ratio by $V$ (Aitken and Taroni 2004). The likelihood ratio is therefore the factor which converts the prior odds into the posterior odds. There are several points to note.

- The likelihood ratio takes values from 0 to infinity. This is in contrast to probabilities which take values between 0 and 1.

- A value of $V$ between 1 and infinity means that the posterior odds are greater than the prior odds. The evidence is said to support the prosecution's proposition.

- A value of $V$ between 0 and 1 means that the posterior odds are less than the prior odds. The evidence is said to support the defence proposition.

- The symmetry of the relationship between prior and posterior odds is better seen by considering logarithms. Thus

$$\log\frac{Pr(H_p|E)}{Pr(H_d|E)} = \log\frac{Pr(E|H_p)}{Pr(E|H_d)} + \log\frac{Pr(H_p|E)}{Pr(H_d|E)}.$$

The logarithm of the likelihood ratio, $V$, takes values between $-\infty$ and $\infty$. The values between $-\infty$ and 0 correspond to values of $V$ between 0 and 1 and the values between 0 and $\infty$ correspond to values of $V$ between 1 and $\infty$. This has an obvious analogy with the concept of *weight* where evidence can be added or subtracted to the scales of justice and the loglikelihood ratio is sometimes known as the weight of evidence (Good 1985).

- A value of $V$ close to 1 suggests the evidence is of little value (and hence of little relevance in the context of the US Federal Rule of Evidence 401, for example).

## Levels of proposition

A discussion of the interpretation of the evidence of the transfer of a single bloodstain from the victim to the criminal is given. The discussion is concerned with each of three levels of proposition: source, activity and crime. Consider a crime in which a victim has been assaulted. A suspect has been identified. There is a bloodstain on clothing of the suspect. The DNA profile of the stain (genotype $\Gamma$) matches that of the victim and does not match that of the suspect.

### Source level

The source level is concerned with the source of the stain on the clothing of the suspect. It is not concerned with how the stain reached there or whether a crime was committed or not. The two propositions to be compared are:

- $H_p$ : the stain on the suspect's clothing came from the victim;
- $H_d$ : the stain on the suspect's clothing did not come from the victim.

These are *source level* propositions. The scientist's results, denoted by E, may be divided into two parts $(E_c, E_r)$ as follows:

- $E_c$: the DNA profile, $\Gamma$, of the victim. This is the control profile with a known source, hence the subscript c.
- $E_r$: the DNA profile, $\Gamma$, of the stain on the suspect's clothing. This is the recovered profile, hence the subscript r, as its origin is unknown.

The frequency of $\Gamma$ in a relevant population is $\gamma$. Note that for $H_d$, the two pieces of evidence, $E_c$ and $E_r$, are independent. The probability that both are of type $\Gamma$ is $\gamma^2$. If $H_p$ is true, the victim and the source of the stain are the same person, and the probability this person is of type $\Gamma$ is $\gamma$. The likelihood ratio $V$ is then

$$V = \frac{\gamma}{\gamma^2} = \frac{1}{\gamma}. \tag{1}$$

The probability $\gamma$ is sometimes known as the *random match probability* or *random occurrence ratio*. It, or its reciprocal, is the figure often quoted in court.

### Activity level

This level is concerned with how the stain reached the suspect's clothing. It is not concerned with whether a crime was committed or not. The propositions are:

- $H_p$ : the suspect hit the victim;
- $H_d$ : some person other than the suspect hit the victim.

These are *activity level* propositions. They propose an activity, that of hitting the victim, but do not propose anything about the commission of a crime.

The bloodstain either came from some background source other than the crime scene or the bloodstain was transferred during the commission of the crime. The probability of the former event is denoted by $t_0$ where $t$ denotes transfer and the subscript 0 indicates zero stains transferred during the action. The probability of the latter event is denoted by $t_1$ where $t$ denotes transfer as before and the subscript 1 indicates one stain transferred during the action. The probabilities that a person from the relevant population will have no bloodstain or one bloodstain on his clothing from a background activity unrelated to the crime, are denoted $b_0$ and $b_1$, respectively, where $b$ denotes background and the subscript 0 indicates zero stains transferred from the background. The probability of the latter event is denoted by $b_1$ where $b$ denotes background and the subscript 1 indicates one stain transferred from the background.

In the numerator of the likelihood ratio, there are two mutually exclusive possibilities to consider: the bloodstain on the suspect's clothing came from some background source, and it is, coincidentally, of the same genotype as the victim, or the bloodstain was transferred during the act of hitting the victim. The first of these possibilities has probability $t_0 \gamma b_1$ and the second has probability $t_1 b_0$. There is no $\gamma$ term in the second probability because the assumption for the second term in the numerator is that the genotype of the victim is that of the stain on the suspect's clothing since the victim is assumed under the circumstances of the proposition for the numerator to be the source of the stain. As the possibilities are mutually exclusive, the probability of the evidence, assuming $H_p$ is true, is the sum of the two components, namely

$$t_0 \gamma b_1 + t_1 b_0.$$

In the denominator, the suspect and the victim are assumed not to have been in contact. The stain on the suspect's clothing came from some background source (with probability 1) and is, coincidentally, of type $\Gamma$. Thus the probability is

$$\gamma b_1$$

and hence

$$V = t_0 + \frac{t_1 b_0}{\gamma b_1} \qquad (2)$$

(Evett 1984). Note that, in general, $t_0$ is small in relation to $t_1 b_0/(b_1 \gamma)$ and may be considered negligible. An example in Aitken and Taroni (2004) shows circumstances in which the value for the activity level will be very different from $1/\gamma$ as given at the source level.

### Crime level

The propositions to be considered are

$H_p$ : the suspect committed the crime;

$H_d$ : the suspect did not commit the crime.

The concepts which have to be included at the crime level are those of innocent acquisition, $p$, and relevance, $r$. Innocent acquisition is a measure of belief that the evidence has been acquired in a manner unrelated to the crime. Relevance is the probability that the stain recovered from the suspect's clothing is connected with the crime; it has been left by the criminal.

The details of the derivation of $V$ in this context are not given here but may be found in Aitken and Taroni (2004). The value of the evidence is given by

$$V = \frac{r + \gamma'(1-r)}{[\gamma r + \{p + (1-p)\gamma'\}(1-r)]}.$$ (3)

A distinction is made between $\gamma$, the frequency of the crime stain profile $\Gamma$ amongst the population from which the offenders have come, and $\gamma'$, the frequency of the profile $\Gamma$ amongst the population of people who may have left the stain (which may not be the same population from which the criminal has come).

Notice that when $r = 1$ and $p = 1$, $V = 1/\gamma$ at the crime level. The result at the source level is a special case of the result at both the activity level, where transfer and background possibilities are considered, and the crime level where innocent acquisition and relevance are considered.

The results of these considerations of the value of the evidence at each of three levels is summarised in Table 15.2 with $\gamma = \gamma'$.

**Table 15.2**  Value, $V$, of the evidence for three levels of consideration. The frequency of the DNA profile in the relevant population is $\gamma$. The probability of transfer of a stain from the victim to the suspect is $t_1$. The probability of no transfer of a stain from the victim to the suspect is $t_0$. The probability a person from the relevant population will have no bloodstain on his clothing is $b_0$. The probability a person from the relevant population will have one stain transferred from the background is $b_1$. The probability that the evidence was acquired in a manner unrelated to the crime is $p$. The probability of relevance, that the stain recovered from the crime scene is connected with the crime, is $r$.

| Level | Value $V$ |
| --- | --- |
| Source | $1/\gamma$ |
| Activity | $t_0 + t_1 b_0 / \gamma b_1$ |
| Crime | $\{r + \gamma(1-r)\}/[\gamma r + \{p + (1-p)\gamma\}(1-r)]$ |

The transfer, background, relevance and innocent acquisition probabilities $t$, $b$, $r$ and $p$ are subjective probabilities. There can be considerable debate as to their value. However, the formulae given here have been determined rigorously. These formulae enable the implications of certain choices for the values of $t$, $b$, $r$ and $p$ to be thoroughly investigated.

## Measurements

Much evidence is of a form in which measurements may be taken and for which the data are continuous. Evidence $E = (E_c, E_r)$ can then be denoted by $(x, y)$ where $x$ are the measurements on the recovered evidence $E_c$ and $y$ are the measurements on the control evidence $E_r$. The two competing propositions are denoted by $H_p$ and $H_d$ and background information by $I$. The value $V$ of the evidence can be shown formally to be

$$V = \frac{f(x,y|H_p,I)}{f(x,y|H_d,I)} = \frac{f(x,y|H_p,I)}{f(x|H_d,I)f(y|H_d,I)}. \tag{4}$$

Continuous measurements are being considered so probabilities $Pr$ of the section on likelihood ratios are replaced by probability density functions $f$. Like probabilities, these functions may never be negative but, unlike probabilities, they can take values greater than 1.

The formulae for the likelihood ratio are developed for the situation in which there are two levels of variation. The first is for variation within a source and the second is for variation between sources. For example, with fragments of glass, there is variability between measurements of refractive index from fragments of glass from the same glass object and variability between measurements of elemental composition from fragments of glass from the same glass object, known as *within-source* variability. There is also variability between measurements of refractive index from fragments of glass from different glass objects and variability between measurements of elemental composition from fragments of glass from different glass objects, known as *between-source* variability.

The likelihood ratio provides a statistic which assesses both within and between-source variability. The model provides an assessment of similarity and of rarity within the one formula as is illustrated below in a simplistic example.

### Approximate derivation of the likelihood ratio

A simple example, given by Evett (1986) and repeated in Aitken and Taroni (2004), is given to illustrate the ability of the likelihood ratio to account for both rarity and similarity in its assessment of the value of the evidence, unlike the two-stage process of significance. Assume a crime has been committed and a window broken. It is assumed that a glass fragment from a single source has been found on the suspect.

Two propositions compared are

- $H_p$: the recovered fragment is from the crime scene window;
- $H_d$: the recovered fragment is not from the crime scene window.

The refractive index $(y)$ is measured from the recovered fragment and the refractive indexes of several fragments from the crime scene are measured. The mean of these crime scene measurements is $\bar{x}$.

The within-source (within-window) measurements are taken to be normally distributed with mean $\theta$ and variance $\sigma^2$. The distribution of refractive indexes between windows is the between-group distribution and is represented by a distribution for $\theta$. This is taken to be Normal with mean $\mu$ and variance $\tau^2$.

An approximate derivation of the likelihood ratio, that does not take account of the sampling variation in $\bar{x}$, the mean of the sample control measurements, is obtained by replacing $\theta$ by $\bar{x}$ in the distribution of $y$ so that $f(y|\theta, \sigma^2)$ becomes $f(y|\bar{x}, \sigma^2)$. Then it can be shown (Appendix 2) that

$$V = \frac{\tau}{\sigma}\exp\left\{\frac{(y-\mu)^2}{2\tau^2} - \frac{(y-\bar{x})^2}{2\sigma^2}\right\}, \tag{5}$$

the ratio of two Normal probability density functions. Values for $\tau$ equal to $4 \times 10^{-3}$ and for $\sigma$ equal to $4 \times 10^{-5}$ (a ratio $\tau/\sigma$ of 100) are given by Evett (1986). Values of $V$ for various values of the standardised distances of $y$ from the overall mean $\mu$ and the source mean, $\bar{x}$ of the crime window, are given in Table 15.3. The term $(y - \mu)/\tau$ provides a measure of rarity for the recovered measurement $y$. The larger it is, the further $y$ is from the overall mean $\mu$ and, for a normal distribution, the rarer $y$ is. The term $(y - \bar{x})/\sigma$ provides a measure of similarity of $y$ with $\bar{x}$, the significance of which is sometimes assessed by a significance probability, with no consideration of rarity as measured by $(y - \mu)/\tau$. The larger it is, the further $y$ is from $x$ and the more dissimilar $y$ and $\bar{x}$ are.

Appendix 2 gives mathematical details of the relationship between significance probabilities and likelihood ratios. In particular, an example is given of a result which is significant at the 5 per cent level in rejecting the proposition of a common source but which gives a likelihood ratio supportive of the proposition of a common source. Appendix 2, p. 413, also gives an approach which is more mathematically rigorous than the simplistic approach given in (5). This approach is outlined in Aitken and Taroni (2004) and given in detail in Lindley (1977).

**Table 15.3** Likelihood ratio values for varying values of $(y - \bar{x})/\sigma$ and $(y - \mu)/\tau$ when $\tau/\sigma = 100$.

| $(y - \bar{x})/\sigma$ | $(y - \mu)/\tau$ | | |
|:---:|:---:|:---:|:---:|
| | 0 | 1 | 2 |
| 0 | 100 | 165 | 739 |
| 1 | 61 | 100 | 448 |
| 2 | 14 | 22 | 100 |
| 3 | 1 | 2 | 8 |

## DNA profiling

There are certain features particular to DNA profiles for which a special section concerning the likelihood ratio of these is desirable. Hardy-Weinberg and linkage equilibrium are assumed throughout.

### Likelihood ratio

Consider the source level proposition. There is a DNA profile $E_r$ at a crime scene from the criminal (recovered evidence since the source, criminal, is not known) and a DNA profile $E_c$ of a suspect (control evidence since the source, suspect, is known). They are both of allelic type $A = A_iA_j$. The propositions are

$H_p$ : the suspect is the source of the stain at the crime scene;
$H_d$ : another person, unrelated to the suspect, is its source; i.e. the suspect is not the source of the stain.

The simplest form of the likelihood ratio in this context appears in random mating. In general, let $p_i$ and $p_j$ be the population proportions of alleles $A_i$ and $A_j$, respectively, for $i, j = 1,...,k$, where k is the number of alleles at the locus in question. The expected genotypic frequencies for A are $2p_ip_j$ for $i \neq j$ and $p_i^2$ for $i = j$. The value of DNA evidence is often determined using a likelihood ratio which is just the reciprocal of the profile frequency, say $1/(2p_ip_j)$ for a heterozygote suspect matching a bloodstain found on a crime scene.

The result $1/(2p_ip_j)$ is obtained by setting the numerator to 1 and the denominator to the genotypic frequency of $E_r$, assuming this to be independent of the genotypic frequency of $E_c$, corresponding to the result $1/\gamma$ at the source level.

However, it has been noted that the observation of one gene in the sub-population increases the chance of observing another of the same type. The conditional probability incorporates the effect of population structures or other dependencies between individuals (Balding 2005). If the expected value of the profile relative frequency is p ($2p_ip_j$ or $p_i^2$) and the variance about its expected value is $\sigma^2$ then the probability of a match between two individuals is $p + \frac{\sigma^2}{p}$ (Balding and Nichols 1994).

This is greater than p. The likelihood ratio decreases from $1/p$ to $1/(p + \sigma^2/p)$. Thus, to ignore $\sigma^2$ is prejudicial to the defence.

If relatives are considered, the match probability changes considerably. For example, if one is the father of the other, the match probability takes the value $(p_i + p_j)/2$. Further examples are given in Evett (1992) and Weir and Hill (1993).

### Variation in sub-population allele frequencies

Genetic correlations due to shared ancestry affect the likelihood ratio in a small, but important way (Balding 1997). There are three so-called F-statistics which provide a measure of relationship between a pair of alleles. One only, the *coancestry coefficient* denoted $F_{ST}$ is considered here. This compares the relationship between alleles of different individuals in one sub-population when compared to pairs of alleles in different subpopulations. Consider a typing AB with frequencies for A of $p_A$ and for B of $p_B$. It can be shown that

$$Pr(E_r = AB|E_c = AB) = 2\frac{\{F_{ST} + (1-F_{ST})p_A\}\{F_{ST} + (1-F_{ST})p_B\}}{(1+F_{ST})(1+2F_{ST})},$$

with the likelihood ratio as the reciprocal of this. Likelihood ratios are presented in Table 15.4 for various values of $F_{ST}$ to illustrate the effect of population substructure on forensic calculations. For example, with $F_{ST} = 0$, $p_A = p_B = p = 0.1$, the conditional match probability $= 2 \times 0.1 \times 0.1 = 0.02 = 1/50$ so the likelihood ratio equals 50. It can be seen that the effect of $F_{ST}$ decreases

**Table 15.4** Effects of population structure as represented by $F_{ST}$ the likelihood ratio, the reciprocal of the conditional match probability for heterozygotes between alleles with equal frequencies $p_A = p_B = p$.

| Allele frequency | $F_{ST}$ | | | |
| --- | --- | --- | --- | --- |
| | 0 | 0.001 | 0.01 | 0.05 |
| $p = 0.01$ | 5000 | 4152 | 1301 | 163 |
| $p = 0.05$ | 200 | 193 | 145 | 61 |
| $p = 0.1$ | 50 | 49 | 43 | 27 |

as allele frequencies increase and are not substantial when $p = 0.1$ even for $F_{ST}$ as high as 0.01 (Weir 1998).

Good reviews of the forensic interpretation of DNA evidence are given in Evett and Weir (1998) and in Buckleton *et al.* (2005).

## Bayesian networks

The use of graphical models, of which Bayesian networks (BN) are one kind, to represent legal issues is not new. Charting methods developed by Wigmore (1937) can be taken as a predecessor of modern graphical methods such as BNs. Wigmore charts are deterministic, Bayesian networks are probabilistic.

### Description

A Bayesian network is a collection of nodes, representing events or pieces of evidence, linked by arrows (also called arcs or edges) that either represent causal or evidential relationships. Each variable has a finite number of mutually exclusive states. Extensions to continuous variables are possible but not discussed here. A Bayesian network is a *directed acyclic graph (DAG)* that represents relationships amongst uncertain events. The nodes and arrows are combined to form the directed acyclic graph; i.e. one in which no loops or double-headed arrows are permitted so that there is no circularity in the evidence.

Nodes with no arrows entering them are known as source or *parent* nodes. An example of a source node may be the so-called ultimate probandum concerning the identity of an offender. Thus one may have a source node which indicates that A is the offender. This node could have two values, *innocent* or *guilty*.

Nodes with arrows which enter them are known as child nodes. A node, *E* say, for which another node, *A* say, is a parent, is known as a child of *A*. Thus one could have a child node of evidence, *E*, for the source (parent) node which indicates that *A* is the offender. The probabilistic association of *E* conditional on *A* could be written as $Pr(E|A)$. A table of probabilities for *E* will contain conditional probabilities. Thus, if *E* is a DNA profile of a crime stain, one could have a table of probabilities for the probability of that DNA profile given A is the offender and the probability of the DNA profile, given *A* is not the offender.

For a parent node $A$, a table of probabilities, or *node probability table*, containing unconditional probabilities $Pr(A)$ is required. (Note that there is a slight abuse of notation here. Symbol A denotes both the node and the proposition that person $A$ is the offender. It is hoped the context will make clear what is intended in any particular instance.) On the other hand, if $A$ is a *child* node with variables $B_1,...,B_n$ as parent nodes, the node probability table for $A$ will contain *conditional* node probabilities $Pr(A \mid B_1,...,B_n)$. A node which is a child of one or more nodes may also be a parent node of one or more nodes.

The combination of nodes and arrows constitute paths through the network. Attention is concentrated on Bayesian networks essentially because they are easy to develop as representations of evidential structure and uncertainties. A review of the use of Bayesian networks in forensic science is given by Taroni *et al.* (2006).

The use of Bayesian networks provides several benefits for both the investigation and the evaluation of evidence. The networks enable the structuring of inferential processes which, in time, permit the consideration of problems in a logical and sequential fashion. They ensure that all possible stories are evaluated. They enable the processes involved in the inferential problems to be communicated easily to others and the assumptions made at each node to be made clear. Discussion can then focus on the estimation of probability values and underlying assumptions.

### The construction of Bayesian networks

Each node represents a proposition or evidence which takes discrete values. For example, the discrete values for a proposition may be $H_p$ and $H_d$ where $H_p$ could be that the defendant is guilty and $H_d$ that the defendant is not guilty. A discrete value for evidence could be the DNA profile from the suspect.

There are three basic types of connections among nodes in a Bayes net: *serial, converging* and *diverging* connections. These are illustrated in Figure 15.1, as (a), (b) and (c), respectively.

In Figure 15.1 (a) the connection linking three nodes $A$, $B$, and $C$ with an arrow from $A$ to $B$, another one from $B$ to $C$ and no arrow from $A$ to $C$ is known as a serial connection. A serial connection is appropriate when it is judged that knowledge of $A$ provides information about the occurrence of $B$ and knowledge of $B$ provides in turn information about $C$ but, when $B$ is known, then knowledge of $A$ provides no more information about $C$. Similarly, knowledge of $C$, when $B$ is known, gives no additional information about the probability of $A$ occurring. For example, $A$ may be said to influence $C$ through $B$ but only $B$ directly influences $C$; $B$ is said to *screen off* $C$ from $A$. If the value of $B$ is known, then $A$ and $C$ are conditionally independent, i.e. $Pr(A \mid B, C) = Pr(A \mid B)$.

As an example, let A be the proposition that *the suspect is the offender*, B the proposition that *the bloodstain found on the crime scene comes from the suspect, and C that the suspect's blood sample and the bloodstain from the crime scene share the same DNA profile*. Then $A$ is relevant for $B$ and $B$ for $C$ but, given $B$, knowledge that the suspect's blood sample and the bloodstain from the crime

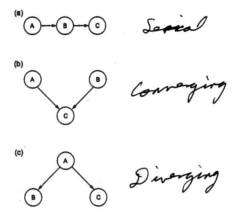

**Figure 15.1** Basic (a) serial (b) converging (c) diverging connections in Bayesian networks

scene share the same DNA profile (C) gives no additional information on the likelihood that the suspect is the offender (A).

In Figure 15.1 (b) there are arrows from A pointing to C and from B pointing to C, and no arrow between A and B. This is an example of a converging connection. It is said that A and B are probabilistically independent unless either the value of C or the value of any of the children (events or propositions) of C is known. Another way of expressing the same idea is to say that A and B are conditionally dependent given the value of C (Jensen 2001). Thus $Pr(AB) = Pr(A)Pr(B)$ but $Pr(AB|C)$ may not be equal to $Pr(A|C)Pr(B|C)$.

For example, let A be the proposition that *the suspect is the offender* and B that *the bloodstain found on the crime scene comes from the offender*. Knowledge that one of these events occurred would not provide information about the occurrence of the other, but if it is true that the *bloodstain found on the crime scene comes from the suspect* (proposition C), then A and B become related. Converging connections in BNs represent a very common pattern of reasoning known as conditional dependence.

In Figure 15.1 (c) there are two arrows originating from A and pointing to B and C, and no arrow between B and C. This is an example of a *diverging* connection. It is said that A *separates* B from C. If the value of A is known, then B and C are probabilistically independent, i.e. $Pr(B|A, C) = Pr(B|A)$ and $Pr(C|A, B) = Pr(C|A)$. A diverging connection is the graphical representation of what may be called a *spurious correlation*.

Nodes B and C are correlated because they both depend on a third factor, A. When A is fixed, the correlation vanishes. There are many examples of such spurious correlations. For example, a positive correlation may be shown between the number of doctors in a town and the number of deaths in a town. As the number of doctors (B) increases, so does the number of deaths (C). This does not mean that doctors are bad for one's health. Rather it is the case that both factors are correlated positively to the population of the town (A). Another example is given by the set of propositions A that *the suspect has been in contact with the victim*, B that *the bloodstain on the suspect's clothes comes from the victim and* C that *the bloodstain on the victim comes from the suspect.*

More complicated diagrams than presented in Figure 15.1 are able to be analysed using a procedure known as propagation, though the procedures of necessity become more complicated with the diagrams. Analysis may be done with software packages such as HUGIN (http://www.hugin.com/). See Taroni *et al.* (2006) for illustrations of the use of HUGIN.

## Sampling

One of the tasks of a forensic scientist may be to inspect a consignment of identical looking items and comment on the legality or otherwise of the consignment. Examples include a consignment of white tablets where the proportion that are illicit is of interest, a consignment of music CDs where the proportion that are pirated is of interest or a set of computer files where the proportion that contain child pornography is of interest. In all these examples it would be very helpful if it were not necessary to inspect all members of the consignment. Only part of the consignment is inspected, i.e. a sample. As only a sample is inspected, only a probabilistic inference can be made about the consignment as one will never be certain about the characteristics of the uninspected members of the consignment. Some ideas are given here concerning the choice of sample size and the inference that can be made from the results of the inspection of the sample.

Let the size of the consignment be N. An inspection of all N items in the consignment is known as a census. There are several disadvantages to a census, in addition to the issues of the resources of time and money.

- If N is large, inaccuracies inevitably occur in the inspection process because of constraints on the available resources so exact results cannot be guaranteed.
- If testing is destructive, no evidence would remain for any trial.
- Inspection of all items may expose the inspectors to potential health hazards, for example, from airborne dust, physical contact or mental stress.

It is often possible through appropriate use of samples to save valuable time and money with very little loss of inferential power relative to the results of a full census. When consideration is given to the possibilities of error and to the other work that could be done with the resources saved, the case for a sample over a census can be very compelling.

Various institutions issue guidelines on sample size choice. These include the United Nations (see the references for details), the European Network of Forensic Science Institutes (ENFSI) and the Scientific Working Group for the Analysis of Drugs (SWGDRUG) of the US Department of Justice Drug Enforcement Administration (2006). Various possibilities given by ENFSI (2004) are as follows for a population of size N, where m denotes the sample size.

- Sample all (census): advantage – 100 per cent certainty about the composition of the population.
- Proportion of $N$: advantage – simple.
- A function of $\sqrt{N}$: advantage – widely accepted; disadvantage – too small for small populations and little theoretical justification.
- $m = 20+10\%(N - 20)$ $(N > 20)$ : advantage – heterogeneous populations likely to be discovered before the analysis is complete.
- For $N < x$, $m = N$; for $x \leq N \leq y$, $m = z$; for $N > y$, $m = \sqrt{N}$; (where $x$, $y$ and $z$ are arbitrary numbers with $x \leq z < y$) With $x = 10$, $y = 100$, and $z = 10$ this is the United Nations Drug Control Programme recommended method.
- Sample one unit only: advantage – minimum amount of work; disadvantage – least amount of information on the characteristics of the seizure.

Apart from the last possibility, all the above have the disadvantage of possibly producing large sample sizes for large populations.

A Bayesian approach (Aitken 1999) is based on combining a binomial likelihood for the number $z$ of members of a sample of size $m$ that contain drugs with a so-called *beta* distribution which models the prior belief in the proportion of the super population that contains drugs of which the consignment is a subset. For example, assume a consignment of white tablets, homogeneous with regard to weight, colour, texture and logos, is picked up in circumstances such that it is thought to come from a certain part of the world. From previous experience, the variability in the proportion of consignments from that part of the world that are illicit is known. This variability may be modelled by a probability distribution and the result combined with the results from the sample to give a probabilistic statement about the proportion of illicit drugs in the consignment.

Consider as an example, a so-called *flat* prior, in which there is considerable uncertainty about the proportion of illicit drugs in the consignment, as may be the case where the origin of the consignment is not known. Then it can be shown (Aitken 1999) that if four tablets are examined and all are found to be illicit then the probability that at least 50 per cent of the consignment is illicit is 0.97. In other words, if four tablets are examined and all are found to be illicit then there is a 97 per cent probability that at least 50 per cent of the consignment is illicit. This result may be counter-intuitive. The sample size is independent of the consignment size and very small; it applies for consignments from 100 to 1 million tablets and beyond. However, the probabilistic statement only gives a result relating to a proportion of the consignment, not to an absolute number. A Bayesian approach using the hypergeometric distribution is described in Coulson *et al.* (2001).

There may be concerns that it is very difficult for a scientist to formalise his prior beliefs. However, if the prior beliefs are modelled with a distribution with large variance then large differences in the probabilities associated with the prior beliefs will not lead to large differences in the conclusions. This is not the case, however, if there is a probability of a misclassification error (Rahne *et al.* 2000). A frequentist approach using the hypergeometric distribution, with an adaptation to allow for false positives and false negatives is described in Faber *et al.* (1999).

## Conclusion

### *Value of statistics to forensic science*

Statisticians do not claim to have the right answers to the problems surrounding the evaluation of evidence. Law and statistics may be thought of as decision-making under uncertainty. Probability is the best measure of uncertainty so it is natural to consider how probability may help with decision-making in a court of law. It is reasonable to use probability to develop a method for the consideration of evidence about which there is uncertainty in such a way that the effect on the odds in favour of the ultimate issue can be measured on a continuous scale.

One of the criticisms of the Bayesian approach with the use of likelihood ratios is that the approach is subjective. Many forensic scientists use an approach based on the assessment of a significance probability in the belief that it is objective. However, there is subjectivity in this approach also in the choice of the level of significance (or the edge of the cliff) at which it will be determined to treat the control and recovered evidence as having different sources.

Bayesian ideas do not pretend to provide what some may think are the true probabilities. However, they do provide an effective method for the analysis and criticism of data. They also provide a check for the coherence of people's opinions and enable coherent revisions of these opinions as more evidence is presented or becomes available.

The Bayesian approach enables the correct combination of information from answers to two opposing and relevant questions. It helps to clarify exactly what questions need answering and how the questions should be phrased. It enables a coherent summary of an inconclusive result, ranging from very strong support for the prosecution's propositions through irrelevance to very strong support for the defence propositions.

There is an increasing awareness amongst jurists that professionals (including judges) working within the criminal justice system should acquire a minimum standard of understanding of statistics, particularly with regard to DNA evidence. There is also an argument that in all cases where evidence requiring probabilistic interpretation is considered, introductory information should be made available to jury members, to ensure some basic understanding of the capabilities, and also the limitations, of such evidence (Nuffield Council on Bioethics 2007).

In 1997, there was an Appeal Court ruling which illustrates a possible interpretation of DNA evidence.

> Members of the jury, if you accept the scientific evidence called by the Crown, this indicates that there are probably only four or five white males in the United Kingdom from whom that semen could have come.

The defendant is one of them. If that is the position, the decision you have to reach, on all the evidence, is whether you are sure that it was the defendant who left that stain or whether it is possible that it was one of the other small group of men who share the same DNA characteristics. (*Doheny* 1997 1 Cr App R 369, 375)

This ruling was used a few years later in two Appeal cases heard on the same day to assist in the achievement of two different results.

*Lashley* (8 February 2000). Lashley was convicted of robbery of a Liverpool post office. The only evidence against him was a DNA match. Following *Doheny* he was a suspect along with up to 10 other males in the UK. There was no evidence linking him to the Liverpool area. His conviction was quashed on appeal.

*Smith* (8 February 2000). Smith was convicted of a robbery in Hertfordshire. The principal evidence against him was a DNA match. Following *Doheny* he was a suspect along with 43 other males in the UK. His appeal was quashed because the DNA evidence 'did not stand alone because there was also quite clearly evidence of this man having been arrested some shortish distance away'.

However, with advances in DNA technology, the figures in many cases are now so small, of the order of 1 in a billion, that *Doheny* does not make very much sense in such cases, as it would be commenting that there would be about six people in the whole world with a matching profile.

In another Appeal Court case (*R v. Grey* 2003) concerning the interpretation of closed-circuit TV images, the court made some observations about the presentation of a numerical evaluation of evidence. Three factors were said to be necessary for such a presentation.

- Frequencies: evidence has to be given about frequencies in the general population of the characteristics in question.

- National database: there has to be a national database which is accepted generally and from which the frequencies may be derived.

- Accepted mathematical formula: the choice of technique used satisfies underlying scientific phenomena or principles; given such a formula, the probability of the occurrence of the characteristics of interest may be derived.

The last factor is of relevance to the Clark case (*R v. Clark* 2003, EWCA Crim 1020 2003, All ER (D) 223 (Apr), CA and 2000, All ER (D) 1219, CA). An assumption that the assignations of infant deaths to Sudden Infant Death Syndrome (SIDS) in the same family were independent could be said to fail to satisfy an 'underlying scientific ... principle' as there was ample evidence that this assumption was not true. The underlying principle is to assume dependence, not independence.

Earlier comments on the understanding of statistics by the law were expressed in an Appeal Court ruling in 1997 where the following remarks were made:

- It (probabilistic reasoning) trespasses on an area peculiarly and exclusively within the province of the jury.

- To introduce Bayes' Theorem or any similar method into a criminal trial plunges the jury into inappropriate and unnecessary realms of theory and complexity.

- The task of the jury was to evaluate evidence and reach a conclusion not by means of a formula, mathematical or otherwise, but by the joint application of their individual common sense and knowledge of the world to the evidence before them.

- In cases such as this, lacking special features absent here, expert evidence should not be admitted to induce juries to attach mathematical values to probabilities arising from non-scientific evidence adduced at the trial. (*R v. Adams, DJ*, 1997 2 Cr App Rep 4679; reported in Dawid (2002))

These remarks referred to the evaluation of non-scientific evidence (alibi and identification) and an attempt to combine evaluations of those with an evaluation of scientific evidence. Probability is the only way in which such a combination can be done coherently yet the Appeal Court has deemed the use of probability in such circumstances to trespass 'on an area peculiarly and exclusively within the province of the jury'. Common sense should be coherent but the application of what is thought to be common sense is not always so.

### The future

The role of statistical and probabilistic reasoning in the administration of justice is set to increase. There is a paradigm shift in forensic identification science (Saks and Koehler 2005). This is aided by the increasing ability to collect, analyse and interpret data of relevance to the forensic context.

The advent of DNA profiling in the 1980s acted as a catalyst for this shift. It illustrated to the courts the advantages of a rigorous probabilistic approach to evidence in which there was uncertainty. Identification by fingerprints, once thought of as the gold standard of identification though now replaced as such by DNA profiling, is coming under increasing scrutiny and there is considerable research on statistical models for fingerprint characteristics from which probabilities of matches will be able to be derived.

Developments of graphical and visual methods of analysing evidence are also far advanced. Networks are being developed, where nodes represent separate bits of evidence, edges represent links between bits of evidence and conditional probability tables represent the strength of the links. There is a branch of statistics known as decision theory in which the costs of decisions based on uncertain events are used to help make an optimal decision. The time is not far off when this theory will be able to offer assistance in the administration of justice through helping jurists consider more formally what the consequences of their decisions will be. There has already been some work in this area with the case, assessment and interpretation models developed by Cook *et al.* (1998a, 1998b, 1999) and Taroni and Bozza (2005).

## Appendix 1: Notation

| | |
|---|---|
| $E$ : | Evidence whose value is of interest. |
| $H_p$ : | Proposition brought forward by the prosecution. |
| $H_d$ : | Proposition brought forward by the defence. |
| $I$ : | Background information. |
| $Pr$ : | Probability; for example, the probability of the evidence $Pr(E)$ and the probability of the prosecution's proposition $Pr(H_p)$. |
| $f$ : | probability density function. |
| $\mid$ : | A conditioning bar; for example, $Pr(H_p \mid E)$, the probability of the truth of the prosecution's proposition given the evidence, and $Pr(E \mid H_p)$, the probability of the evidence given the truth of the prosecution's proposition. |
| $X \sim N(\theta, \sigma^2)$ : | The characteristic $X$ has a Normal distribution with mean $\theta$ and variance $\sigma^2$. |
| $\gg$ : | much greater than, as in $\tau^2 \gg \sigma^2$. |

## Appendix 2: Approximate derivation of the likelihood ratio

Consider equation (4) with $x$ replaced by $\bar{x}$.

$$V = \frac{f(\bar{x}, y \mid H_p, I)}{F(\bar{x} \mid H_d, I) f(y \mid H_d, I)} = \frac{f(y \mid \bar{x}, H_p, I) f(\bar{x} \mid H_p, I)}{f(\bar{x} \mid H_d, I) f(y \mid H_d, I)} = \frac{f(y \mid \bar{x}, H_p, I)}{f(y \mid H_d, I)}.$$

The approximate result for the numerator is that

$$(Y \mid \bar{x}, \sigma^2, H_p, I) \sim N(\bar{x}, \sigma^2). \tag{6}$$

Also, $f(y \mid H_d, I)$ is written as

$$(Y \mid \mu, \sigma^2, \tau^2, H_d, I) \sim N(\mu, \tau^2 + \sigma^2). \tag{7}$$

For $\tau^2 \gg \sigma^2$, $\tau^2 + \sigma^2$ can be approximated by $\tau^2$. The likelihood ratio is then

$$V = \left[ \frac{1}{\sigma\sqrt{(2\pi)}} \exp\left\{ -\frac{(y-\bar{x})^2}{2\sigma^2} \right\} \right] \Big/ \left[ \frac{1}{\tau\sqrt{(2\pi)}} \exp\left\{ -\frac{(y-\mu)^2}{2\tau^2} \right\} \right]$$

$$= \frac{\tau}{\sigma} \exp\left\{ \frac{(y-\mu)^2}{2\tau^2} - \frac{(y-\bar{x})^2}{2\sigma^2} \right\},$$

the ratio of two Normal probability density functions.

### Relationship of significance probabilities to likelihood ratio

Consider a measurement $X$ of interest (e.g. refractive index or elemental composition of glass). The prosecution and defence propositions are $H_p$ and $H_d$. The mean of the measurements over the source at the crime scene is $\theta_0$; the distribution of $X$ is $N(\theta_0, \sigma^2)$. For measurements from an unknown source, and hence of unknown $\theta$, assume that the unknown $\theta$ has a Normal distribution with mean $\theta_0$ and variance $\tau^2$, where, typically, $\tau^2 \gg \sigma^2$, as in Table 15.3. Then

$$f(x|H_d) = \int f(x|\theta) f(\theta) d\theta$$

and so

$$(X|H_d) \sim N(\theta_0, \sigma^2 + \tau^2).$$

With $\tau^2 \gg \sigma^2$, the distribution of $(X|H_d)$ is approximately $N(\theta_0, \tau^2)$. The likelihood ratio is, thus,

$$V = \frac{f(x|\theta_0, H_p)}{f(x|H_d)} = \frac{(2\pi\sigma^2)^{-1/2} \exp\{-(x-\theta_0)^2 / 2\sigma^2\}}{(2\pi\tau^2)^{-1/2} \exp\{-(x-\theta_0)^2 / 2\tau^2\}}.$$

Consider $\tau = 100\sigma$. Let $z^2 = (x-\theta_0)^2/\sigma^2$ be the square of the standardised distance between the observation $x$ and the mean specified by the null hypothesis, $\theta_0$. Then

$$V = 100 \exp\left(-\frac{z^2}{2} + \frac{z^2}{2 \times 10^4}\right)$$

$$\simeq 100 \exp(-z^2 / 2).$$

For example, for measurements of refractive indexes, consider $x = 1.518540$; $\theta_0 = 1.518458$; $\sigma = 4 \times 10^{-5}$, $\tau = 4 \times 10^{-3} = 100\sigma$. Then $z^2 = 2.05^2$ and the significance probability $P = 0.04$ which, at the 5 per cent level, would lead to rejection in a two-sided test of the hypothesis that the fragment of glass has the same refractive index as the window at the scene of the crime against the alternative that the refractive indexes are different. However,

$$V = 100 \exp(-2.05^2/2)$$

$$= 12.2,$$

a value for $V$ which is supportive of $H_p$ against $H_d$. Thus, the likelihood ratio approach leads to a different conclusion than the one based on significance testing. Such an apparent contradiction between the two approaches is not a new idea and has been graced by the name of Lindley's paradox (see, for example, Good 1956; Lindley 1957).

### Distribution for between-source data

Various formulae are given in the literature for the likelihood ratio for data in which the between-source distribution is Normal; see, for example, Aitken and Taroni (2004). If the between-group data are not Normally distributed it is possible to use a density estimation procedure, such as a kernel density model (Silverman 1986).

Consider a background data set $D = \{z_{ij}; i=1,\dots, k; j=1,\dots, l\}$ where there are $k$ groups and $l$ members of each group. Let

$$\bar{z}_i = \sum_{j=1}^{l} z_{ij} / l; \bar{z} = \sum_{i=1}^{k} \bar{z}_i / k$$

be the means of the groups ($i=1,\dots, k$) and the overall mean.

The within-group variance $\sigma^2$ is estimated by

$$\hat{\sigma}^2 = \sum_{i=1}^{k}\sum_{j=1}^{l}(z_{ij} - \bar{z}_i)^2 / (kl - k)$$

and the between-group variance is estimated by

$$s^2 = \sum_{i=1}^{k}(\bar{z}_i - \bar{z})^2 / (k-1) - \hat{\sigma}^2 / l.$$

The kernel density model procedure fits a Normal density function over each of the group means $\bar{z}_i$ of the background data set. It then takes the mean of these functions as the estimate of the underlying density function.

The sample standard deviation $s$ is then multiplied by a parameter, known as the *smoothing parameter*, denoted here by $\lambda$, which determines the smoothness of the density estimate. An estimate with too large a value of $s\lambda$ will provide an estimate which is very smooth and local variation in the density will be obscured. An estimate with too small a value of $s\lambda$ will provide an estimate which is very spiky and overall variation in the density will be obscured. There are various routines for the estimation of $\lambda$ and kernel density procedures are part of many statistical packages (e.g., R, http://www.r-project.org/).

The kernel density function $K(\theta|\bar{z}_i, \lambda)$ for a point $\bar{z}_i$ is taken to be a Normal distribution with mean $\bar{z}_i$ and variance $\lambda^2 s^2$,

$$K(\theta|\bar{z}_i, \lambda) = \frac{1}{\lambda s \sqrt{2\pi}} \exp\left[-\frac{(\theta - \bar{z}_i)^2}{2\lambda^2 s^2}\right].$$

The estimate $\hat{f}(\theta|\bar{z}_i, \lambda)$ of the probability density function between groups is then given by

$$\hat{f}(\theta|\bar{z}_i, \lambda) = \frac{1}{k}\sum_{i=1}^{k} K(\theta|\bar{z}_i, \lambda).$$

Work of Lindley (1977) for univariate data and of Stern *et al.* (2005) and of Aitken *et al.* (2006) for multivariate data incorporate a correlation term between the control and recovered data when they come from the same source. These authors assume that the within and between group distributions are both Normal, though Lindley (1977) has a section using a Taylor series expansion for $f(\theta)$ at the end of the paper.

### Lindley's formula for evidence evaluation

Let $\tau$ be the between-group standard deviation and $\sigma$ be the within-group standard deviation. The mean of $m$ control measurements is $\bar{x}$ and the mean of $n$ recovered measurements is $\bar{y}$. The overall mean of the measurements is $\mu$. The value $V$ of the evidence for comparing the propositions $H_p$, the control and recovered measurements come from the same source, and $H_d$, the control and recovered measurements come from different sources, is

$$V \simeq \frac{\tau}{a\sigma} \times \exp\left\{-\frac{(\bar{x}-\bar{y})^2}{2a^2\sigma^2}\right\} \times \exp\left\{-\frac{(w-\mu)^2}{2\tau^2}+\frac{(z-\mu)^2}{\tau^2}\right\}, \tag{8}$$

where $z = (\bar{x}+\bar{y})/2$, $w = (m\bar{x}+n\bar{y})/(m+n)$ and $a^2 = 1/m + 1/n$.

### References

Aitken, C.G.G. (1999) 'Sampling – how big a sample?', *Journal of Forensic Sciences*, 44: 750–760.

Aitken, C.G.G. and Taroni, F. (2004) *Statistics and the evaluation of evidence for forensic scientists*. Chichester: John Wiley and Sons Ltd.

Aitken, C.G.G., Lucy, D., Zadora, G. and Curran, J.M. (2006) 'Evaluation of trace evidence for three-level multivariate data with the use of graphical models', *Computational Statistics and Data Analysis*, 50: 2571–2588. doi:10.1016/j.csda.2005.04.005.

Balding, D.J. (1997) 'Errors and misunderstandings in the second NRC report', *Jurimetrics Journal*, 37: 469–476.

Balding, D.J. (2005) *Weight-of-evidence for forensic DNA profiles*. Chichester: John Wiley and Sons, Ltd.

Balding, D.J. and Nichols, R.A. (1994) 'DNA profile match probability calculation: how to allow for population stratification, relatedness, database selection and single bands', *Forensic Science International*, 64: 125–140.

Barnard, G.A. (1958) 'Thomas Bayes – a biographical note' (together with a reprinting of Bayes 1764), *Biometrika*, 45: 293–315. Reprinted in Pearson and Kendall (1970): 131–153.

Bayes, T. (1764) 'An essay towards solving a problem in the doctrine of chances', *Philosophical Transactions of the Royal Society of London for 1763*, 53: 370–418. Reprinted with Barnard (1958) in Pearson and Kendall (1970) 131–153.

Buckleton, J., Triggs, C.M. and Walsh, S. (eds) (2005) *Forensic DNA evidence interpretation*. Boca Raton, Florida, USA: CRC Press.

Coleman, R.F. and Walls, H.J. (1974) 'The evaluation of scientific evidence', *Criminal Law Review*, 276–287.

Cook, R., Evett, I.W., Jackson, G., Jones, P.J. and Lambert, J.A. (1998a) 'A model for case assessment and interpretation', *Science and Justice*, 38: 151–156.

Cook, R., Evett, I.W., Jackson, G., Jones, P.J. and Lambert, J.A. (1998b) 'A hierarchy of propositions: deciding which level to address in casework', *Science and Justice*, 38: 231–239.

Cook, R., Evett, I.W., Jackson, G., Jones, P.J. and Lambert, J.A. (1999) 'Case pre-assessment and review of a two-way transfer case', *Science and Justice*, 39: 103–122.

Coulson, S.A., Coxon, A. and Buckleton, J.S. (2001) 'How many samples from a drug seizure need to be analyzed?', *Journal of Forensic Sciences*, 46: 1456–1461.

Darroch, J. (1987) 'Probability and criminal trials; some comments prompted by the Splatt trial and The Royal Commission', *The Professional Statistician*, 6: 3–7.

Dawid, A.P. (2002) 'Bayes's Theorem and the weighing of evidence by juries', in R. Swinburne (ed.), *Proceedings of the British Academy*, 113: 71–90.

European Network of Forensic Institutes (2004) Guidelines on representative drug sampling. ENFSI DrugsWorking Group (available from http://www.enfsi.eu/page.php?uid=48, last accessed 21 April 2009).

Evett, I.W. (1984) 'A quantitative theory for interpreting transfer evidence in criminal cases', *Applied Statistics*, 33: 25–32.

Evett, I.W. (1986) 'A Bayesian approach to the problem of interpreting glass evidence in forensic science casework', *Journal of the Forensic Science Society*, 26: 3–18.

Evett, I.W. (1991) 'Interpretation: a personal odyssey', in C.G.G. Aitken, and D.A. Stoney, (eds), *The use of statistics in forensic science*. Chichester: Ellis Horwood.

Evett, I.W. (1992) 'Evaluating DNA profiles in the case where the defence is "It was my brother"', *Journal of the Forensic Science Society*, 32: 5–14.

Evett, I.W. and Weir, B.S. (1998) *Interpreting DNA evidence*. Sunderland, Massachusetts, USA: Sinauer Associates Inc.

Faber, N.M., Sjerps, M., Leijenhorst, H.A.L. and Maljaars, S.E. (1999) 'Determining the optimal sample size in forensic casework – with application to fibres', *Science and Justice*, 39: 113–122.

Fairley, W.B. and Mosteller, W. (1977) *Statistics and Public Policy*, pp. 355–379. London: Addison-Wesley.

Finkelstein, M.O. and Fairley, W.B. (1970) 'A Bayesian approach to identification evidence', *Harvard Law Review*, 83: 489–517.

Finkelstein, M.O. and Fairley, W.B. (1971) 'A comment on "Trial by mathematics" ', *Harvard Law Review*, 84: 1801–1809.

Gaudette, B.D. and Keeping, E.S. (1974) 'An attempt at determining probabilities in human scalp hair comparison', *Journal of Forensic Sciences*, 19: 599–606.

Good, I.J. (1956) 'Discussion of paper by G. Spencer Brown', in C. Cherry (ed.), *Information Theory: Third London Symposium 1955*: 13–14. London: Butterworths.

Good, I.J. (1985) 'Weight of evidence: a brief survey', in J.M. Bernardo, M.H. DeGroot, D.V. Lindley and A.F.M. Smith (eds), *Bayesian statistics, 2*. North Holland: Elsevier Science Publishers BV.

Groom, P.S. and Lawton, M.E. (1987) 'Are they a pair?', *Journal of the Forensic Science Society*, 27: 189–192.

Jensen, F.V. (2001) *Bayesian Networks and Decision Graphs*. New York, USA: Springer Verlag.

Jones, D.A. (1972) 'Blood samples: probability of discrimination', *Journal of the Forensic Science Society*, 12: 355–359.

Kingston, C.R. (1965a) 'Applications of probability theory in criminalistics', *Journal of the American Statistical Association*, 60: 70–80.

Kingston, C.R. (1965b) 'Applications of probability theory in criminalistics – II', *Journal of the American Statistical Association*, 60: 1028–1034.

Kingston, C.R. (1966) 'Probability and legal proceedings', *The Journal of Criminal Law, Criminology and Police Science*, 57: 93–98.

Kingston, C.R. and Kirk, P.L. (1964a) 'The use of statistics in criminalistics', *Journal of Criminal Law, Criminology and Police Science*, 55: 514–521.

Kingston, C.R. and Kirk, P.L. (1964b) 'Evidence evaluation and problems in general criminalistics', *Journal of Forensic Sciences*, 9: 434–444.

Kirk, P.L. (1953) *Crime Investigation*. New York: Interscience Publishers.

Kirk, P.L. (1963) 'The ontogeny of criminalistics', *The Journal of Criminal Law, Criminology and Police Science*, 54: 235–238.

Lindley, D.V. (1957) 'A statistical paradox', *Biometrika*, 44: 187–192.

Lindley, D.V. (1977) 'A problem in forensic science', *Biometrika*, 64: 207–213.

Meier, P. and Zabell, S. (1980) 'Benjamin Peirce and the Howland will', *Journal of the American Statistical Association*, 75: 497–506.

Mode, E.B. (1963) 'Probability and criminalistics', *Journal of the American Statistical Association*, 58: 628–640.

Nuffield Council on Bioethics (2007) 'The forensic use of bioinformation: ethical issues'.

Parker, J.B. and Holford, A. (1968) 'Optimum test statistics with particular reference to a forensic science problem', *Applied Statistics*, 17: 237–251.

Pearson, E.S. and Kendall, M.G. (eds) (1970) *Studies in the history of statistics and probability*. London: Charles Griffin.

Rahne, E., Joseph, L. and Gyorkos, T.W. (2000) 'Bayesian sample size determination for estimating binomial parameters from data subject to misclassification', *Applied Statistics*, 49: 119–128.

Robertson, B. and Vignaux, G.A. (1995) *Interpreting evidence: evaluating forensic science in the courtroom*. Chichester: John Wiley and Sons Limited.

Saks, M.J. and Koehler, J.J. (2005) 'The coming paradigm shift in forensic identification science', *Science*, 309: 892–895.

Silverman, B.W. (1986) *Density estimation*. London: Chapman and Hall.

Smalldon, K.W. and Moffat, A.C. (1973) 'The calculation of discriminating power for a series of correlated attributes', *Journal of the Forensic Science Society*, 13: 291–295.

Splatt, E.C., Royal Commission report concerning the conviction of (1984). By authority of D.J. Woolman, Government Printer, South Australia.

Stern, H.S, Carriquiry, A.L. and Daniels, M. (2005) 'Statistical analysis of bullet lead trace element concentrations', available from http://www.public.iastate.edu/alicia/Forensics.htm (last accessed 21 April 2009).

Stoney, D.A. (1991) 'What made us think we could individualise using statistics?', *Journal of the Forensic Science Society*, 31: 197–199.

Taroni, F. and Bozza, S. (2005) 'Decision analysis in forensic science', *Journal of Forensic Sciences*, 50: 894–905.

Taroni, F., Aitken, C.G.G., Garbolino, P. and Biedermann, A. (2006) *Bayesian networks and probabilistic inference in forensic science*. Chichester: John Wiley and Sons Ltd.

Thompson, W.C. and Schumann, E.L. (1987) 'Interpretation of statistical evidence in criminal trials. The prosecutor's fallacy and the defence attorney's fallacy', *Law and Human Behaviour*, 11: 167–187.

Tippett, C.F., Emerson, V.J., Fereday, M.J., Lawton, F. and Lampert, S.M. (1968) 'The evidential value of the comparison of paint flakes from sources other than vehicles', *Journal of the Forensic Science Society*, 8: 61–65.

Tribe, L. (1971) 'Trial by mathematics: precision and ritual in the legal process', *Harvard Law Review*, 84: 1329–1393.

United Nations Guidelines: Methaqualone (ST/NAR/15; December 1998); Lysergide (ST/NAR/17; January 1989); Cocaine (ST/NAR/7; February 1986); Benzodiazepine (ST/NAR/16; December 1988); Cannabis (ST/NAR/8; February 1987); Psilocybin (ST/NAR/19; December 1989); Mescaline (ST/NAR/19; December 1989); Opium, Morphine, Heroin (St/NAR/29/Rev.1; June 1998).

United States Department of Justice Drug Enforcement Administration (2006) The Scientific Working Group for the Analysis of Drugs (SWGDRUG). Recommendations.

Weir, B.S. (1998) The coancestry coefficient. *Proceedings of the 8th International Symposium on Human Identification*, Promega Corporation, 87–91.

Weir, B.S. and Hill, W.G. (1993) 'Population genetics of DNA profiles', *Journal of the Forensic Science Society*, 33: 218–225.

Wigmore, J. (1937) *The science of proof: as given by logic, psychology and general experience and illustrated in judicial trials* (3rd edn). Boston, USA: Little, Brown.

# Chapter 16

# Understanding forensic science opinions

*Graham Jackson*

## Introduction

Many chapters in this Handbook show how research into technological and analytical aspects of forensic science continues to provide significant improvements in the sensitivity, specificity, speed and cost of forensic scientific tests. However, despite these advances, the way in which forensic scientists form and express opinions based on the interpretation of the results of such tests has had much less attention in mainstream forensic scientific research.

While there is substantial scholarship dealing with reasoning and the logic of opinions, little of that material seems to have been assimilated by the forensic science community or to have influenced how opinions are formed and expressed in the course of everyday work. In this chapter I review the range of currently used expressions of opinion in an attempt to understand the logical processes used by forensic science practitioners. Following this, I propose a framework, based on Bayes Theorem, for categorising opinions. The framework encourages a shared understanding and a common language amongst the community of forensic practitioners and those who rely on their expertise. Finally, I look at some of the knowledge and skills required to present the different forms of opinion.

While this chapter draws on statistical theory, it is not written by a statistician; I am first and foremost a forensic science practitioner. Accordingly, the chapter is not a comprehensive or authoritative review of Bayes' Theorem and its application to forensic science problems. There are various books that serve that purpose well (see, for example, Robertson and Vignaux 1995; Evett and Weir 1998; Curran *et al.* 2000; Aitken and Taroni 2004; Lucy 2005; Taroni *et al.* 2006). The views and ideas I express in this chapter have been developed through my own experiences as a practitioner, through many workshops with colleagues across the majority of disciplines and through contacts with gifted and influential statisticians and forensic thinkers over the years.

Forensic science can be described as the application of scientific method to help answer questions that are of importance to participants in the criminal justice process. As forensic cases move from crime scene to court, numerous questions about aspects of the case may be asked at various times by investigators, lawyers, other professionals, members of the media, the general public and the jury. These questions relate to the issues that are uncertain within the case – aspects of the case that are not known, or not established as facts. In specific cases, these could include, for example, 'What was the cause of death?', 'Who left the finger mark on the door-frame?', 'Who handled the explosive material?' The forensic requirement is for these questions to be resolved by someone within the course of the investigation and subsequent court proceedings. But who will do this? Whether it is the forensic scientist who will provide answers to these questions will depend on various considerations, including:

- whether analytical and other techniques are available to address the question;
- whether the scientist has the necessary data and understanding about the evidence type involved;
- whether it is the scientist's role to answer the question.

In some jurisdictions, it is the accepted role of the scientist to provide an answer to some questions (Biedermann *et al.* 2007; ENFSI Expert Working Group Marks Conclusion Scale Committee 2006; Taroni and Biedermann 2005). But when that occurs, how robust and reliable was the answer and what reasoning process was used?

Generally, the role of the expert witness is seen as that of providing expert opinion that helps answer the questions that are important in a case. Expert opinion is the result of interpretation of factual observations and is seen as being beyond the knowledge and skill of the triers of fact. To understand how robust and reliable any one particular opinion might be, it would seem helpful to have some kind of framework with which to categorise opinions.

By way of explanation, I will use the words 'questions' and 'issues' interchangeably, although there may be difference in their meaning in the legal field.

## Expression of opinion

Forensic scientists use a wide range of words and expressions to convey their answers to investigators, the courts and other interested parties. Until the introduction by some providers of corporate templates for reports and statements, scientists used their own personal preferences for expressing opinion. Accordingly the range of expressions seen within any one group, or any one forensic provider, could be surprisingly large. Satterthwaite and Lambert (1989) reviewed 100 case files from one laboratory and, leaving aside case reports that contained categorical findings, they found 33 different expressions used to convey evidential strength. Some of this range could be explained by differences in the strength of evidence being reported but, even allowing for this, there were personal and group preferences for certain words and phrases. Importantly, there was also variation in the perceived strength of the expressions within the group of laboratory scientists and between these scientists and the lawyers/police officers group. This is an old study and there has since been movement towards a common structure and language for reports (Evett *et al.* 2000c). However, more recent, international, collaborative studies by Grieve (2000) and Krauß and Simmerlein (2004) of the European Fibres Group (EFG), European Network of Forensic Science Institutes (ENFSI), found a range of expressions used by different laboratories to report their findings from the same set of provided material.

A selection of phrases described in these studies is listed below and has been augmented by phrases from my own work in reviewing reports of scientists from forensic science providers in the UK and in Europe. It is by no means an exhaustive list.

- *'... match ...'*
- *'... could have come from ...'*
- *'... consistent with ...'*
- *'... entirely consistent with ...'*
- *'... cannot exclude ...'*
- *'... provides evidence of contact ...'*
- *'... suggests contact ...'*
- *'... points towards ...'*
- *'... indicates ...'*
- *'... there is an association between ...'*
- *'... provides strong evidence of a link between ...'*
- *'... very likely came from ...'*
- *'... likely to have been caused by ...'*
- *'... has come from ...'*
- *'... has been made by ...'*
- *'... supports an assertion that ...'*
- *'... the findings are what I would expect if (proposition H) were true.'*
- *'... the findings are very likely to be seen if (proposition H) were true.'*
- *'... provides strong support for the view that ...'*
- *'... no support for ...'*

I will look at each of these phrases and explore their strengths and limitations.

1) *'... match ...'*
A simple-looking word that conveys what may appear to be a purely factual observation and therefore would not seem to comprise an opinion as such. When two sets of measurements or observations correspond, then most people could deduce that the two samples *'match'*. For example, if we take two sets of numbers, <3, 6, 7, 15, 21> and <3, 6, 7, 15, 21>, nearly everyone would agree that these sets *'match'*. However, forensic science is not often as straightforward as comparing two sets of simple numbers. Often the *'matching'* procedure involves the comparison of sets of shapes, colours,

spatial patterns or complex numbers derived from the output of an analytical technology. While there may be a good degree of correspondence, there may be some differences. How does the examiner deal with difference? If the examiner is experienced and knowledgeable, she may be of the view that the difference is explicable and therefore an acceptable variation. The decision that two samples '*match*' has required expert judgement and, as such, could be seen as expert opinion as opposed to factual observation.

Work by Champod *et al.* (2004) has explored the meaning of the opinion of a '*match*' and has demonstrated the usefulness of replacing the word '*match*' with a description of two sets of measurements or observations – one set from the questioned (or suspect) sample and the other from the reference (or known) sample. In this way, a probabilistic approach can be applied to the measurements and observations in order to help address the issue of whether or not two samples share the same origin. In this chapter, I intend to use the word '*match*' as shorthand to mean the result of expert judgement on the comparison of two sets of measured or observed attributes but always bearing in mind that '*match*' may well be an expression of an opinion and a shorthand way of summarising the results of a complex '*matching*' procedure.

Finally, recipients of an opinion expressed as a '*match*' may translate that into meaning that the two '*matching*' samples share the same origin. This would be different from the meaning that the scientist would want to convey, namely that the samples share the same attributes. So, even when scientists and laypeople use the same word, the meaning to these two sets of people can be quite different.

2) '*... could have come from ...*'
This type of phrase appears relatively straightforward and easy to understand. Given there is a match declared between the observed attributes of a questioned sample and a reference sample, it seems obvious to draw an inference that the questioned sample '*could have come from*' the same source as the reference sample. Consider another example involving fibres. Imagine a case in which fibres recovered from pieces of adhesive tape fixing an explosive device in place in a vehicle are compared with those in a pair of gloves worn by a suspect. If fibres from the device are found to match the fibres comprising the gloves, then it may seem to be a logical deduction that the fibres '*could have come from*' the gloves. Indeed, it could be argued that this is a deductive inference (see Nordby (2000) for a description of inferential methods) and, as such, there is no need for expert opinion. However, as we have seen when we considered the word '*match*', the comparison process may well reveal both differences and correspondences between the measured or observed attributes. Assessment of the factors affecting the similarity and difference of attributes may enable a scientist to form the expert opinion of '*... could have come from ...*' As such, this would not be a deductive conclusion but rather an opinion formed through inductive inference using relevant data, knowledge and understanding. And it is not just trace, particulate evidence to which this applies; the same considerations apply to evidence supplied by marks and striations, by chemical analysis, by document examination, or any other comparative technique.

A major limitation of this type of phrase is the lack of assessment of the evidential value of the material. The phrase *'could have come from'* can be applied to materials that are common as well as rare. So, while it may be a useful first-stage opinion, it requires more qualification in order that its true evidential worth can be communicated. I have seen courtroom prosecutors putting great emphasis on the words '... *could have come from* ...' in an apparent attempt to embellish the opinion and persuade the judge or jury of the value of the match. On the other hand, for the same scientific evidence, I have seen defence lawyers attempting to diminish the opinion by asking the scientist a question along the lines of 'Well, you say it could have come from this source but isn't it the case that it could have come from any one of many other similar sources?' The opinion '... *could have come from* ...' can therefore be used by prosecution or defence lawyers to try to advance their own argument. A defence lawyer could even argue that a prosecution-commissioned scientist who gives such an opinion is tendering biased, misleading evidence as she is giving only one explanation to suit the prosecution's case. The skill of the scientist lies in being able to handle these two types of question in a balanced way that assists the court.

3) '... *consistent with* ...'
This is another, simple-looking phrase that deserves closer inspection. It is akin to the '... *could have come from* ...' phrase but it may be one that requires the expert to have greater knowledge than would be required to say simply '... *could have come from* ...' In order to conclude '... *consistent with* ...' the expert needs knowledge of the features that would be expected if the proposed conjecture were true. She would also need knowledge of what other conjectures would offer alternative explanations. And that is the limitation, since without that knowledge, the expert may be tempted to offer, or to agree with, just one conjecture that she has in mind or that is put to her. An example from blood pattern analysis may illustrate this point. Assume a scientist observes a pattern of very small bloodstains on a suspect's trousers. The scientist's opinion may be expressed along the lines of '... *the findings are consistent with the wearer of the trousers having hit the victim repeatedly with the iron bar found at the scene.'* That may be a reasonable opinion, based on the observation of expected findings, but there may be other, perhaps better, conjectures to explain the observations. As with the phrase '... *could have come from* ...', the phrase '... *consistent with* ...' usually implies no assessment of the weight of the observations or of the probability of the conjecture being true. It also leaves the scientist open to a criticism of bias, offering only the conjecture that fits a particular argument.

4) '... *entirely consistent with* ...'
The use of the qualifier *'entirely'* in this phrase may be an attempt to lend more weight, or greater probability, to the conjecture. However, without an explanation by the scientist of the rationale for arriving at this opinion, there is a risk of providing misleading or biased opinion. Take, for example, the opinion *'These findings are entirely consistent with the suspect having written the words on the ransom note.'* This could be portrayed by the prosecution as very

powerful evidence and could be seen as such by the judge or jury. However, the defence could ask the scientist, 'Are your findings entirely consistent with someone else, about whom you have no knowledge, having written the note?' The scientist may have to concede that there may, indeed, be someone else whose handwriting would also be entirely consistent with that on the note. The scientist may then have to go on to justify the strength of evidence that they implied by use of such a phrase. If they do not concede the point, then the defence may be able to challenge the impartiality of the opinion.

5) '... *cannot exclude* ...'

I have seen this phrase used when the scientist observes that the results have not eliminated a hypothesis that a questioned sample has come from a particular reference source, or that a suggested event had happened. Sometimes this seems a reasonable way of phrasing an opinion, particularly when there is a continuing series of samples or possible events to be tested. An example of this would be a case where police conduct a 'screen' of the shoes of a large number of possible suspects for a crime. Assume that the footwear mark at the scene were of such poor quality that only the pattern type of the offender's shoe could be deduced. Assume also that the police have little information or clues about the offender and they resort to a mass screen of a large number of potential suspects. It would seem reasonable for the scientist to say, when she has found a match on pattern type, that she '*cannot exclude*' this pair of shoes from having made the scene mark. This is reasonable, as far as it goes, but the scientist has not conveyed any impression of the weight of that match.

Furthermore, in other instances, the scientist may use the phrase '... *cannot exclude* ...' when they feel the suggestion or hypothesis is a poor explanation for the findings but cannot exclude it as a possibility. Used in this context, a receiver of the opinion may assume the suggestion or hypothesis to be a good one despite the scientist's own feelings. An example would be a situation in which the scientist has observed a pattern of bloodstaining at a scene. The question put to the scientist from the defence may be '*Has this been caused by someone flicking a towel that is wet with blood?*' The scientist may feel the findings are not very likely to have been observed if this were true but she '*cannot exclude*' the suggestion as a possibility. Without qualification or further explanation by the scientist, the lawyer and the judge/jury may have the impression that the suggested explanation is a good one whereas the scientist may think otherwise.

6) '... *provides evidence of contact* ...'

I believe this phrase is open to wide interpretation. On hearing or reading this type of opinion, some people may think that 'contact' between two items has been established; others may think that this just *points towards* contact having occurred. Another major difficulty with the phrase, as pointed out by Evett *et al.* (2000b), is the potential variation in the interpretation of what 'contact' means. For example, in a case of burglary by means of 'breaking and entering' a window, '*contact*' could mean:

- contact with fragments of glass as they showered over the person breaking the window;
- contact with fragments of glass as they showered over people in the vicinity of the breaking window;
- contact with broken glass as a person walked through the fragments on the floor;
- contact with the broken edges of the window as a person climbed through;
- contact through lifting property that was covered in fragments from the broken window;

or any one of a long list of other types of 'contact' that could be imagined.

*7) '… suggests contact …'*
This seems to be a combination of the opinions '… *could have been in contact* …' and '… *provides evidence of contact* …' but with perhaps more strength, or more direction, to the opinion. However, there is still a problem with the definition of '*contact*', and in addition, we would have to ask whether the scientist considered other explanations. If so, which alternatives were eliminated or reduced in probability? As there is no assessment of how likely it is that '*contact*' has occurred, it begs the question of how the receiver of this opinion evaluates the probability of the suggestion. It could well be that the scientist thinks that '*contact*' is likely, but has not explicitly stated that as an opinion, yet the receiver takes '*contact*' only as a possibility.

An example would be a case in which firearms discharge residues (FDR), 'matching' those from a discharged weapon used to kill a person, are found on the hand swabs of a suspect. The scientist offers the opinion that the findings '*suggest contact*' between the suspect and the fired gun. Prosecution could put this forward as very powerful evidence that the suspect was the person who fired the fatal shot; defence could suggest that '*contact*' could mean simply touching the weapon after it had been discharged, or shaking hands with the person who had discharged the weapon, or any one of a number of other conjectures over the word 'contact'.

*8) '… points towards …' or '… indicates …'*
These two phrases appear similar in their intent, and similar to the '… *suggests contact* …' opinion. The scientist may be trying to direct the receiver of the opinion towards a suggestion or hypothesis that, in the scientist's mind, is a good or likely one. A problem with this type of opinion is the lack of transparency as to how the scientist arrived at the opinion. What other suggestions or hypotheses were considered? Why were those not offered? What caused the scientist to offer only the one hypothesis?

*9) '… there is an association between …'*
This phrase is open to wide interpretation. It could convey a very persuasive, close connection between two samples, for example, that they share the same origin or that, in another context, they have been touching. However, it could also be taken to indicate some sort of looser connection, for example, that the

two items were from the same large production batch or that the two items have been in the same vicinity at some time in the past. Without clarification of what the scientist means by '*association*', at best the opinion is confusing and, at worst, it is potentially misleading. Perhaps the scientist does not know herself what her findings mean and so uses the word '*association*' to imply her uncertainty. Whether this is what a receiver would take away is unclear. There is a similarity of this phrase to that of '*... contact with ...*'.

10) '*... provides strong evidence of a link between ...*'
This may be seen by some as a strong inference. However, there is a similar, if not a more serious, problem with the word '*link*' to the one we saw with the words '*contact*' and '*association*'. We have to think carefully about the meaning of the word. We may all use '*link*' quite successfully in everyday language but, in a scientific and logical context, it is open to wide interpretation. Take the example of two bombings committed within a short time of each other. Assume that one man has been found guilty of committing the first one. A second man is arrested on suspicion of having committed the second crime. It is reported in the media that there is a '*link*' between the two men. That may be interpreted by some as strong evidence to point towards the second man having committed the second crime. However, what is the nature of the '*link*'? Towards one end of the spectrum, that '*link*' could be that they lived very close to each other, had the same extreme political views, purchased similar quantities of bomb-making materials at similar times from the same supplier, had the same documents about bomb-making in their possession and were tracked in each other's company on many occasions. At the other end of the spectrum, the '*link*' could be that they were both male, of the same age and ethnic group, and both lived in the south-east of England. Without definition of what is meant by the word '*link*', there is a risk of the receiver of the opinion misinterpreting that opinion. Furthermore, to then go on and say that there is '*... strong evidence of a link ...*' is potentially, and seriously, misleading. Without defining what is meant by the word '*link*' there is no point in assessing and communicating the strength of that '*link*'. Indeed, it could be argued that a person giving this type of opinion may be trying to mislead the receivers in situations in which the evidence against a defendant may be weak.

11) '*... very likely came from ...*', '*... likely to have been caused by ...*'
On first sight, these appear good expressions of opinion. They seem relatively clear and they address the probability of a suggestion or hypothesis – something that is of obvious importance to the triers of fact. However, a potential limitation may be the lack of transparency of how the scientist arrived at a probability for the suggestion. Unless the receiver of the opinion understands the prior, non-scientific information that influenced the scientist, there can be no assessment of the reliability and fairness of the opinion. Take, for example, a case of burglary in which the scientist has been asked to examine and compare the cast of a tool mark from the point of entry with a recovered screwdriver. On examination, the scientist observes good correspondence in size and shape between the cast and a test mark made

with the screwdriver. As there is very little recording of fine detail in the mark, no further comparison can be achieved. If the screwdriver is one of a large number of screwdrivers that have been recovered in a trawl through the possessions of a large number of suspects, then the scientist may be inclined to say *'The screwdriver could have made the mark'* or *'The screwdriver cannot be eliminated from having made the mark.'* However, if the scientist were to be given the information that the screwdriver had been found below the point of entry, and the householder says it does not belong to her, then the scientist may be tempted to give the opinion *'The mark was very likely made by the screwdriver.'* The scientist could therefore give two very different forms of opinion based on exactly the same outcome of the comparison. The only difference in the two situations would be the prior information. In the second scenario, the scientist may be influenced by the information that the screwdriver was at the scene and, therefore, the prior probability that this was the 'right' screwdriver may be seen as high. The second form of opinion (*'... very likely made by ...'*) is not necessarily a poor one provided that the scientist makes explicit her use of the prior information and that prior position is open to challenge and testing.

12) *'... has come from... '; '... has been made by ...'*
These two opinions are of the same broad form: they are categorical in nature. In the scientist's mind, there is only one conclusion that can be drawn from the observations; no other explanation is possible. Logically, to form such an opinion, the conclusion must be arrived at through a deductive process. The strength of this type of opinion lies in its clarity and its certainty, but its limitation is whether or not the basis of the opinion is truly deductive in nature. It has been argued that very few questions in forensic science are amenable to such deductive inferences. When a scientist gives such an opinion, then its deductive underpinning will be open to question. If the opinion were not truly deductive, then it may be an opinion based on the scientist's personal conviction of the truth of the assertion. The opinion has been formed not through a logical transparent process but a process more akin to an acquired skill. During the process of examination and comparison, the expert applies her knowledge and experience to become convinced that no other explanation is possible. In the fingerprint world, such application has been the source of much debate (see, for example, Champod and Evett 2001). More importantly, this type of opinion has led to misleading evidence being given (Cole 2005) and to miscarriages of justice. However, the problem of such categorical opinions does not lie solely with fingerprint evidence; it applies to all forms of evidence where this type of opinion is given.

13) *'... supports an assertion that ...'*
This is a phrase that has grown in popularity among scientists, particularly among those who are adopting a Bayesian approach to forming opinions (see later and Chapter 15 of this book). The phrase does seem to be an attempt to convey the evidential direction of the scientific findings and, in that sense, it is similar to phrases such as *'... suggests ...'*, *'... indicates ...'* and *'... points towards ...'* But, as with these other phrases, its weakness lies in its lack of

expression of evidential weight and a possible lack of transparency about what other assertions were considered.

14) *'... the findings are what I would expect if (proposition H) were true'* and *'... the findings are very likely to be seen if (proposition H) were true.'*
This form of phrase is a popular expression and focuses on the likelihood of the examination results given that a particular proposition were true; it does not focus on the probability of the proposition itself being true. In that sense, it is focusing on those areas that are truly in the scientist's domain and competence. However, it could be criticised for a lack of balance if there is no mention of the likelihood of the findings if an alternative were true.

15) *'... provides strong support for the view that ...'*
This is a currently recommended format for an expression of a Bayesian likelihood ratio (LR) (see, for example, Evett *et al.* 2000c). Many commentators recommend assessment and communication of a likelihood ratio as a logical, balanced way of providing opinion, and Kaye and Koehler (2003), referring to one specific case example, provide a very persuasive argument for why the use of an LR will mitigate against misleading evidence. In my view, while the strength of an LR approach is beyond doubt, a limitation is the question of whether or not the approach is understood by the recipients of such an opinion. Early studies (Taroni and Aitken 1998a, 1998b and Sjerps and Biesheuvel 1999) reported confusion and inconsistency amongst the receivers of forensic science opinions expressed as LRs. More recently, however, Bierdermann *et al.* (2007) report a study (Tentori *et al.* 2007) that suggested:

> ... the best predictor of the felt impact of an isolated item of evidence on 'philosophically naïve' people is the logarithm of the likelihood ratio.

The challenge for all involved in forensic science is to develop effective and efficient ways in which forensic scientists communicate the logical approach of Bayes' Theorem and the use of a likelihood ratio to police, lawyers and laypeople.

16) *'... no support for ...'*
This is a popular phrase among some practitioners and maybe among some receivers. In my experience, many scientists use this phrase to suggest or imply the assertion is implausible or not likely. Mostly it is used when the findings are not what would have been expected if the assertion were true. The use of the word *'support'* in this context is confused with use of the word *'support'* to convey the magnitude of a likelihood ratio, as in example 15). I would suggest that the word *'support'* should be used solely to convey the magnitude of the LR and should not be confused with low probability for the findings if the proposition were true.

## Categorisation of opinions

Bayesian inference is widely recognised as a robust, logical means of inductive reasoning. It provides a way by which new pieces of evidence, for example the results of scientific tests, observations made at scenes, or new information from other sources, can be incorporated to help modify a personal view on the probability that an uncertain event actually took place. Previous work by this author and colleagues (Jackson *et al.* 2006) attempted to apply a Bayesian framework to forensic science opinions. A scheme was presented that helped categorise opinions according to whether they were 'investigative' or 'evaluative' in nature and according to their position in the 'hierarchy of issues'. Using the examples given earlier in this chapter, I intend here to review and extend that scheme. I will deal firstly with categorisation according to a Bayesian framework and then consider categorisation following the hierarchy of issues.

### *Bayesian framework*

I refer readers to Chapter 15 for a detailed description of Bayes Theorem. Here I explain the general terminology used in the following section of this chapter.

When 'evidence' is mentioned, this is the set of observations made by the scientist during the course of her examination of the case material. Such observations can take the form of:

- shapes, sizes and conditions of items both from the suspect and from the crime scene/victim;
- the presence of any extraneous material on the items;
- the sizes, shapes and condition of these (extraneous) materials;
- the results of any analyses of the materials;
- any other observations within the scientist's domain of expertise.

I will denote all these observations with the letter $E$. The letter $H$ will be used to denote the uncertain event that is being investigated or judged. The convention has been to use the term 'proposition' for this uncertain event but the word accommodates other expressions such as 'view', 'assertion', 'allegation', 'suggestion', 'hypothesis' etc. $Pr$ stands simply for 'probability of'. The letter $I$ represents all the background information that conditions, or influences, a person's assessment of a probability.

Jackson *et al.* (2006) considered the distinction between prior probabilities for hypotheses, likelihoods for scientific observations, posterior probabilities for hypotheses and explanations for evidence. Using the notation, and keeping Bayes' Theorem in mind, I shall attempt to assign the various forms of opinion listed earlier to the following categories:

*Prior probability* of a proposition (H), given some background information (I) but before any scientific evidence (E) is presented: $Pr[H/I]$

*Explanations* put forward after the scientific evidence (E) has been acquired, and given some conditioning background information (I): $H_{1...n} | E, I$

*Likelihoods* – probability of obtaining the scientific evidence (E) given that a proposition (H) is true, and given some background information (I): $Pr[E | H, I]$

*Likelihood ratio* – the ratio of the probability of the scientific evidence (E) given that a prosecution proposition ($H_p$) were true and the probability of the evidence given its complementary, alternative (defence) proposition ($H_D$), were true, and given some background information (I): $Pr[E | H_p, I]/Pr[E | H_D, I]$

*Posterior probability* of a proposition (H), given some background information (I) and given the scientific evidence (E): $Pr[H | E, I]$

1) *Prior probability:* $Pr[H, I]$
The earlier discussion on expression of opinion assumed the opinions were given after the scientist had obtained some test results or had made some observations. In that sense, we should describe them as 'posterior opinions' – those given *after* the evidence has been obtained. Therefore, none of the opinions listed earlier would fit into this category of *prior* probabilities. However, some of the phrases could still be used to express prior probabilities if the scientist were basing her opinion on, for example, some data that revealed underlying frequencies of occurrence of an event in a relevant population. For example, before a court hears the specific findings of a post-mortem examination, the pathologist could express an opinion that the probability of this sudden infant death being a murder is x%, based on the relative frequency of occurrence of such incidents among sudden infant deaths in a specific, relevant population. Her opinion should be uninfluenced by her post-mortem examination findings. Once the scientific findings are presented, the court (or the pathologist) will form a new judgement on the posterior probability of the death being a murder.

In judicial settings, where the issues are about the guilt or innocence of the defendant, prior probabilities are generally seen as the domain of the judge or, in a jury trial, of the jury. These are the people who have heard and assessed all the non-scientific evidence so far presented in the case. They will have formed a view on the probability of the truth of the propositions, taking into account all of this prior information. The scientist does not generally hear all the prior evidence that the judge/jury hear and is therefore in no position to assess a robust prior. To do so would risk usurping the function of the court and of providing potentially misleading opinion. This was the spirit of the guidance from the Appeal Court in *R v. Doheny and Adams* (*Doheny and Adams* [1997] 1 Cr App R 369). However, in some jurisdictions, and with some forms of scientific evidence, the court will allow the scientist to offer such an opinion. Examples include footwear mark comparisons and DNA profiling. In some European jurisdictions the scientist is allowed to adopt a prior, usually of 50:50, for footwear mark opinions and so can give a posterior probability (ENFSI Expert Working Group Marks Conclusion Scale Committee 2006). Whether or not adopting 50:50 as fair and reasonable prior odds in all cases is open to debate (Biedermann *et al.* 2007), but one view would be that 50:50 is, generally, highly prejudicial to the defendant. A fairer prior would be based on the size of the potential suspect population of shoes. Additionally, in England and Wales, when the issue has been the source of the recovered DNA, some courts have suggested the size of a target population in order to provide an indication of a prior (Evett *et al.* 2000a).

In comparison, in investigative situations the scientist may knowingly, or unknowingly, adopt some prior probabilities. A very instructive example of the explicit use of such priors is given by Biedermann *et al.* (2005a, 2005b) in their work on the application of Bayesian thinking to the investigation of fires. Their groundbreaking work exposes how priors can, and should, be used when attempting to form an opinion on the cause of a fire. The same thinking can be applied to any other form of forensic investigative opinion, and Taroni *et al.* (2006) have explored this approach in greater depth.

2) *Explanations:* $H_{1 \ldots n} | E, I$
This category would include the following phrases:

- *'... could have come from ...'*
- *'... consistent with ...'*
- *'... entirely consistent with ...'*
- *'... cannot exclude ...'*

Note that there is no statement of probability associated with an explanation. Explanations are useful in that they provide options or possibilities for the investigator, or for the court, but the phrases contain no evaluation of the worth of the explanation proposed. Generation of such explanations could be viewed as the role of an investigator and may well require a very creative, imaginative approach. Some explanations may be very useful, practical options but, depending on the skill and knowledge of the scientist, they may be totally impractical, even whimsical, suggestions. A further problem with explanations is that there may be an unending list of potential explanations that the scientist has not even considered or offered.

3) *Likelihoods:* $Pr[E | H, I]$
*'... the findings are what I would expect if (proposition H) were true.'*

*'... the findings are very likely to be seen if (proposition H) were true.'*

In my experience, single likelihoods are rarely given as final opinions or conclusions but they may be seen within the 'Interpretation' section of reports and statements. In this context, they may be helpful to the court, but their limitation is that the weight of the findings is not assessed and, as mentioned earlier, the court may form the impression that the probability of the proposition is high – a subtle example of the transposed conditional or 'prosecutor's fallacy' (Evett 1995).

This form of opinion may increasingly be given in final conclusions in those cases in which the defendant has retained his right to silence. Where a defendant maintains a 'No comment' stance through to trial, it is possible that the scientist could offer an opinion about the degree to which the findings are likely to be seen if the prosecution proposition were true. As there would be no defence position, the scientist is unable to offer a likelihood ratio.

If a single likelihood opinion were to be given, it is important that the scientist makes very clear that this is not an evaluation of the weight or strength of her findings. In a Bayesian framework, no one can assess that weight unless an alternative proposition has been given and considered.

4) *Likelihood ratio: $Pr[E \mid H_p, I]/Pr[E \mid H_D, I]$*
These include the phrases:

- *'... supports an assertion that ...'*
- *'... provides strong support for the view that ...'*

The first phrase may be seen simply as a reflection of a likelihood ratio (LR) that is greater than 1 without expressing the magnitude of the LR. In such cases there are no grounds for criticism. However, instances arise where the scientist has not assessed an LR and has simply used the word 'support' to convey her view that the findings are possible if the proposition were true. That possibility may be a high probability or it may be a low probability. Without assessing an LR, it would be impossible to say whether the LR would be greater than 1 (supporting the prosecution), less than 1 (supporting the defence), or about 1 (not helping either way). Hence, the earlier comment (p. 428, example 16) about keeping the word 'support' to express the magnitude and the direction of the LR.

The second phrase is an expression of the magnitude of the LR using one form of a verbal scale to convey the log of the LR (Evett *et al.* 2000c). As mentioned earlier, there has been debate about how to communicate the LR, and that debate will continue for some time.

It should be noted that, in 'No comment' situations, there are several options available to the scientist, one of which is for the scientist to generate a defence proposition on behalf of the defendant. However, if a 'random man' alternative is adopted, that tends towards minimising the denominator likelihood and, thereby, maximising the LR.

5) *Posterior probability: $Pr[H \mid E, I]$*
I will include in this section all of the following phrases:

- *'... provides evidence of contact ...'*
- *'... suggests contact ...'*
- *'... points towards ...'*
- *'... indicates ...'*
- *'... there is an association between ...'*
- *'... provides strong evidence of a link between ...'*
- *'... very likely came from ...'*

- '... *likely to have been caused by* ...'
- '... *has come from* ...'
- '... *has been made by* ...'
- '... *no support for* ...'

At first glance, it may seem that these phrases have little in common. However, there is some pattern. Examine the subset:

- '... *very likely came from* ...'
- '... *likely to have been caused by* ...'

These and other similar phrases utilise words such as ' *likely*', '*very likely*', '*unlikely*', '*highly probable*' and convey the magnitude of the posterior probability of a proposition. Examples would include: '*Death was likely to have been caused by the high level of drug X detected in the blood sample*', '*The particle of firearms discharge residue very likely came from the gun that killed Ms A*'; and '*The DNA profile found on the swab is unlikely to have arisen by Mr A kissing the neck of Ms C.*'

To arrive at a posterior probability, the scientist should take into account prior probabilities as well as likelihoods of the observations. This may or may not be an explicit, or even a conscious, process. Even if the process were explicit, there will be questions about whether the priors were fair and reasonable in the context of the case.

A second subset of phrases would include:

- '... *has come from* ...'
- '... *has been made by* ...'

These phrases express a categorical, black-and-white opinion. Examples would include – '*The mark at the scene has been made by the suspect's shoe*', '*The fragments of glass have come from the same window as the reference glass sample*'. In Bayesian terms, to form such a conclusion requires a zero probability in the likelihood ratio. There are some instances where this may be justified, for example where clear, unexplainable differences have been seen, but there are other areas in which zero probabilities cannot be justified scientifically through the available data and knowledge.

A third subset of phrases includes:

- '... *provides evidence of contact* ...'
- '... *suggests contact* ...'
- '... *points towards* ...'
- '... *indicates* ...'

In Bayesian terms, this is a strange set of phrases. Each of them seems to imply, or convey, some sort of posterior probability for a proposition in that they could be interpreted as suggesting that one particular proposition is likely. If that is so, then they should rightfully be categorised as expressions of posterior probabilities and the same considerations as described earlier apply.

Finally, the last three phrases need individual attention.

- '... *there is an association between* ...'
- '... *provides strong evidence of a link between* ...'
- '... *no support for* ...'

The first phrase is difficult to categorise but is best seen as a form of posterior probability: the person giving this type of opinion probably intends to convey a view that the proposition in question is very likely. But it is not clear. The second phrase is commonly used, and often applied to interpretations that are not Bayesian. We have discussed this phrase earlier, and it can only be fitted into a Bayesian framework by assuming that it is intended to convey support for an alternative proposition. The final phrase is evidentially meaningless.

### Hierarchy of issues

Broeders (2007) has presented an analysis of the philosophy of forensic identification or 'individualisation'. Most practitioners would agree with the suggestion that individualising a questioned item or trace sample to one particular source is the central question in forensic science. Indeed, trying to arrive at an answer to the question of whether or not a trace shares the same source as a reference sample justifies efforts to improve analytical techniques to increase discrimination between samples. However, as Broeders argues, more analytical information may not necessarily provide more forensic value.

Forensic value has several aspects including an economic aspect – what does this technique cost; an operational aspect – how quickly would results be obtained; and an evidential aspect – what weight of evidence would the technique provide? From the point of view of weight of evidence, some cases will hinge almost solely on identifying the 'source' of a recovered sample. An example of a case of rape will illustrate this point. A woman reports she has been raped by an unknown man and says she has had no other intercourse or sexual activity in the previous six months. Vaginal swabs are taken from her within an hour of the offence. Police arrest a man on suspicion and he denies that he is the offender, saying that he does not know the woman and that he has not had any contact with her. A full SGMPlus DNA profile is obtained from the vaginal swab and is found to match that of the suspect. Whether or not the man is guilty of rape would seem to hinge on the key issue of whether or not the semen has originated from the suspect – an issue about 'identity of source'. However, this is the key issue only if certain assumptions are accepted:

1) the DNA profile obtained from the vaginal swabs has come from the semen on the swabs;
2) the semen on the swabs has originated from the man who had intercourse with the woman;
3) the woman did not consent to the intercourse.

If these are acceptable assumptions, then the central forensic issue will be that of identifying, beyond reasonable doubt, the source of the semen.

However, if there is uncertainty about any of these three assumptions, then consideration of guilt or innocence requires the tribunal to take into account additional aspects of the case, some of which may involve scientific evidence. If, for example, the suspect admits he did have sexual contact with the woman, then the issue of the identity of the source of the semen may not be of great importance. The issues of what sort of activity took place and whether or not there was consent would be the main considerations. If the suspect says that he did not have intercourse with the woman, but he did ejaculate over the woman's thighs, it would seem that the issue of guilt revolves around consideration of the probability that his semen would be found in a particular quantity on her vaginal swabs if his story were true. Cook *et al.* (1998b) have written about the requirement to appraise scientific evidence beyond simply issues of the identity of source. The authors provide a generic framework, the 'hierarchy of propositions', that reflects the interlinking of issues from the issue of the source of trace materials through to the ultimate issue of the offence. Jackson *et al.* (2006) developed the framework further to take into account the sensitivity of newer DNA technology, and also extended the framework into investigative work. These authors also introduced the concept of a 'hierarchy of issues', arguing that this is a necessary precursor to the 'hierarchy of propositions'. Before propositions can be defined, it is necessary for the scientist to consider and set out the issues, or questions, that are seen to be important in the case. These can be arranged in a hierarchical structure beginning with the 'sub-source' level and progressing through 'source' and 'activity' to 'offence' level.

The following case example may help to illustrate the hierarchy of issues and the subsequent hierarchy of propositions.

- A woman was asleep alone in her bedroom in the early hours
- She was woken by the sound of breaking glass
- A masked man confronted her in her bedroom and threatened her with a knife
- He took off his clothes and raped her; he re-dressed and left the scene
- The woman called the police, who attended quickly and arrested a man nearby
- He denied all knowledge of the attack and did not have a mask or knife
- Police noticed a fresh footwear mark in the garden below the broken window
- Crime Scene Examiners took a cast of the mark and a sample of the broken glass from the scene
- A medical examiner took vaginal and oral swabs from the woman
- The woman reported that she had had no prior intercourse or sexual activity for at least two months
- Clothing, shoes and penile and oral swabs were taken from the man

The first step for the scientist, through discussions with the police and/ or prosecution, is to capture all key issues in the case. These may well be numerous and at different 'levels' and could include (non-exhaustively):

- Is he the rapist?
- Did he tread in the garden?
- Did he have intercourse with her?
- Did he break the window?
- Is the footwear mark from his shoe?
- Is any soil on his shoe from the garden?
- Is any semen on her vaginal swabs from him?
- Are any epithelial cells on his penile swab from her?
- Is any glass on his clothing from the window?
- Is any non-self DNA on the vaginal swabs from him?
- Is any non-self DNA profile on his penile swabs from her?

The next step for the scientist is to arrange these into an interlinked network of a hierarchy of issues where the lower levels feed into, and inform, the next level of issue:

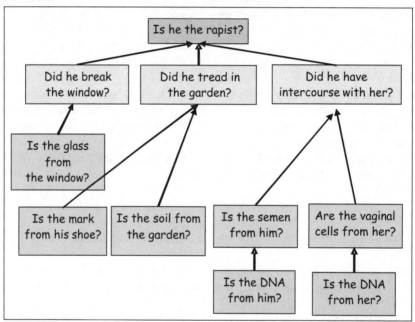

This structure may have the appearance of a Bayesian network (see, for example, Taroni *et al.* 2006), and there are some similarities, but it does not capture all the issues that a Bayesian network achieves. In addition, the arrows indicate a 'feed' of information rather than the direction of dependency as in Bayesian networks.

The next step is to convert the issues into pairs of competing propositions based on the prosecution and defence positions and agree with the police/ prosecution/defence/court which of these issues should be addressed. Addressing 'activity' level issues (i.e. what a suspect may or may not have 'done') offers better assistance to the court than the scientist simply staying at 'source' or 'sub-source'. If the scientist does not offer assistance at 'activity' level, then it is left to the lawyers to argue the weight of the 'source' or 'sub-source' opinion and advance that to 'activity' and 'offence'.

As described by Jackson *et al.* (2006), opinions offered in 'evaluative' situations, where there are prosecution and defence propositions, should take the form of likelihood ratios. Previous work (Evett *et al.* 2002) has shown that, while the LR provided by DNA evidence at 'sub-source' may be extremely powerful, when that evidence is considered at 'activity' level it may well not have as strong an LR. Therein lies the beguiling, but potentially misleading, view of a DNA match as powerful evidence of guilt in all cases.

The case just described involved a defendant and progression of the case to court; the hierarchy of issues can also be applied to suspect-less, 'investigative' situations. A similar generic structure can be applied to these situations, where issues take the form of *'What is the source of the recovered material?'*, *'What activity took place?'*, *'What offence took place?'*. Opinions expressed on 'investigative' issues generally take the form of 'explanations' or 'posterior probabilities'.

Using a Bayesian framework to categorise an opinion, together with a view of where that opinion sits in the hierarchy of issues, generates insight into the nature and basis of that opinion. This is useful not only in reviewing the scientist's own thinking and approach to cases but also in analysing and discussing cases with fellow practitioners.

## Knowledge and understanding required

If this categorisation using Bayesian language and the hierarchy of issues is a sensible analysis and a good model for the logical basis of opinion, it should help to determine what knowledge and understanding are required in order to give opinions that are robust and reliable.

### 1) *Prior probabilities, Pr[H/I]*

To give robust, reliable probabilities requires realistic datasets that reflect accurately the incidence of particular events in an appropriate population. A good example is given by Biedermann *et al.* (2005b) in relation to the cause of a fire. The authors use a dataset of fires of known causes in a particular area to estimate a prior probability for any one particular cause. Key considerations include whether the dataset is of a relevant population, is current and is of a sufficient size. So, for the fire example, a view would need to be taken on whether the distribution of fire types in the dataset is appropriate to the circumstances of the fire under investigation. Questions would need to be asked about when, and from which area, were the data collected and how many cases were included. If the data were collected from a few years prior to the incident, do the data still reflect fairly the current situation? If the data were collected from an area far away from the incident, do they reflect fairly the cause of fires in this location? Is the dataset of sufficient size to reflect the incidence of what may be unusual events? These questions require expert judgement and experience and, where necessary, some current sampling to validate the relevancy of the dataset.

2) *Explanations,* $H_{1...n} | E, I$

Generating explanations is a very open-ended, creative process. It should follow that experienced examiners will have better knowledge of possible explanations than inexperienced examiners. However, this may not be the case if experience is not also accompanied by good 'mental cataloguing' and recall of the experiences. There is also a risk of observer bias (Saks *et al.* 2003) – the scientist runs the risk of applying tunnel vision in seeing only those signs that further support her first explanation while ignoring, or not searching for, those signs that would point away from the first explanation. For example, at a scene of a suspicious fire, the examiner may quickly form a view that the cause of the fire was an electrical fault because of information she has been given at the scene. From that point on, she may look only for further signs of an electrical cause and not search for other signs, such as unusual patterns of burning, or unexpected traces in headspace analysis of debris, which would point away from an electrical cause.

3) *Likelihoods,* $Pr[E | H, I]$ *and* 4) *Likelihood ratios,* $Pr[E | H_p, I]/Pr[E | H_D, I]$

The first key skill required for opinions in the form of a likelihood or a likelihood ratio (LR) is the generation of a proposition and, for an LR, at least one alternative. This is by no means a trivial task and if done well will ease the course of the examination and the subsequent interpretation of observations. Generation of propositions and alternatives is driven by an understanding of the key issues in the case, based on the requirements of the police, prosecution, defence and the courts. It is key to good 'Case Assessment and Interpretation' (see Jackson *et al.* 2006; Cook *et al.* 1998a). The way in which the issues, propositions and alternatives are generated and agreed takes us into the heart of the Criminal Justice Process and exposes the role of the scientist within that process.

Generally, the proposition for the numerator of the LR is informed by the police/prosecution allegation or suspicion while the proposition for the denominator is informed by the defence submission. Probabilities of the scientific evidence given the truth of each of these propositions will be informed by what the scientist knows and understands about finding evidence, given the truth of different suggestions, and by whatever relevant data are available.

As with prior probabilities, assigning robust, reliable probabilities for scientific evidence requires intelligent, expert use of relevant, current datasets. These datasets may reside in the scientist's mind and the collective experiences of colleagues, in published papers, or in computerised, searchable databases. There will very rarely be a data set that is perfectly relevant to the proposition being considered, and so expert judgement must be applied in order to adjust the dataset to inform useful probabilities. Taroni *et al.* (2001) and Lucy (2005: 5, 6) offer useful comments on the essentially subjective nature of such probabilities.

Despite crime cases being individual events, and accepting that there is no single ideal data set for any individual case, some generalised propositions can be proposed in an attempt to drive the collection of data. Often, in the past, convenient data were collected and scientists then had to think how to use them. For example, during the 1970s and 1980s, some forensic science organisations collected samples of broken glass objects and analysed various parameters of the glass. Useful information was collected to help scientists understand the variability of glass but the collation of the data was of little use to inform probabilities of a likelihood ratio. It was only when scientists began to adopt a likelihood ratio approach to assessing value of evidence that more relevant data were collected. In some glass cases, a general form of alternative proposition along the lines of *'The suspect did not break the window; he had nothing to do with the crime'* would be appropriate. When the proposition is specified in that way, a relevant data set begins to be defined – it would be a set of people, from the environment like the suspect's, who also could be suspected of the crime but who did not actually break the window in question. The proposition defines the relevant population and so drives the collection of data. Curran *et al.* (2000) provides an authoritative work on glass interpretation for further exploration of this evidence type.

From a generic viewpoint, the 'hierarchy of issues' provides a structure that directs the scientist to appropriate data and knowledge. The following section sets out pairs of propositions that are generic in nature for the evaluation of LRs and illustrates these with specific examples based on the rape case described earlier.

### 1) 'Sub-source' issues

A generic pair of propositions for this level may be written as:

$H_P$ *'The test result (E) came from this source'*
$H_D$ *'The test result (E) came from some other source'*

In the example of the case of rape, this would translate as:

$H_P$ *'The DNA profile (E) came from the suspect'*
$H_D$ *'The DNA profile (E) came from some other person (unrelated to the suspect)'*

To assess a likelihood ratio, the scientist needs to assign probabilities for $E$ given the truth of each of $H_P$ and $H_D$, and given the background information $I$: $Pr[E \mid H_P, I]$ and $Pr[E \mid H_D, I]$.

For the numerator, $Pr[E \mid H_P, I]$, of the likelihood ratio, data are required on 'within-sample' variability. These data would inform the scientist's probability that she would have obtained the test result (the DNA profile) if the results had actually come from the same source as the reference sample (the suspect). Reliable, relevant information on the reproducibility of results from the same sample in the context of this case, and using the machinery and operators that were involved in generating the results, would inform this probability.

For the denominator, $Pr[E \mid H_D, I]$, of the likelihood ratio, data are required on 'between-sample' variability. These data would inform the probability that the scientist would have obtained the test result (the DNA profile) if the results had actually come from a source other than the reference sample (someone other than, and unrelated to, the suspect). Reliable information on the relative frequency of occurrence of the test result (the DNA profile) amongst a set of relevant, alternative samples (people other than the suspect and unrelated to him) is required. A key issue, however, is whether or not the set is of a relevant population. Champod *et al.* (2004) explored this question in relation to a variety of evidence types for 'source'/'sub-source' level and noted a requirement for information on three types of population – 'suspects', 'offenders' and 'crimes' (or 'scenes').

2) *'Source' issues*
A generic pair of propositions for this level may be written as:

$H_p$ *'The questioned sample (E) came from this source'*
$H_D$ *'The questioned sample (E) came from some other source'*

In the example of the case of rape, this would translate as:

$H_p$ *'The semen (E) came from the suspect'*
$H_D$ *'The semen (E) came from some other person (unrelated to the suspect)'*

As with 'sub-source', the scientist needs to assign probabilities for E given the truth of each of $H_p$ and $H_D$, and given the background information I: $Pr[E \mid H_p, I]$ and $Pr[E \mid H_D, I]$.

Because consideration of a 'source' likelihood ratio necessarily takes into account a 'sub-source' LR evaluation, then the 'sub-source' LR feeds into a 'source' LR. In effect, the LR assigned for 'sub-source' is subsumed within an evaluation of a 'source' LR. But, to assess a 'source' LR requires the additional consideration of the probability that the test result (the DNA profile) can be attributed to the actual material that has been tested (semen).

In the rape case, provided that

- semen had been identified on the vaginal swabs;
- the profile obtained from the preferential extract from the swabs gave a single, male profile of appropriate strength;
- it is accepted that the woman had had no previous sexual contact with a man for many weeks;

then it seems reasonable to assign a probability of approaching 1 for the probability that the DNA profile can be attributed to the semen on the swab. If this is so, then the LR for 'source' level will be of the same magnitude as the 'sub-source' LR.

Assumption of a value of 1 for the probability of attribution of a test result to a material is unlikely to be a reasonable or safe probability if

- the semen had been located on a soiled towel;
- the semen comprised a small area containing only a few spermatozoa of dubious appearance;
- other body fluids were detected on the towel;
- the profile was weak;
- the profile was a mixed profile from more than one person.

In this situation, the magnitude of the LR at 'source' will be smaller that that at 'sub-source'.

It may be that the scientist feels she can only offer an LR at 'sub-source' level. This begs the question of who would then be in a better position to move the evaluation to 'source' and then to 'activity'. This is a non-trivial problem in cases involving 'low copy number (LCN)', or 'low template, DNA'.

For the numerator and denominator of the likelihood ratio, $Pr[E \mid H_D, I]$ and $Pr[E \mid H_p, I]$, at 'source' level, provided we can attribute confidently the test result to the material under test, then we need no more data and knowledge than we have already at 'sub-source'. If attribution is uncertain, then data, knowledge and understanding about success rates of obtaining test results (DNA profiles), and on background levels of test results, in the specific circumstances of the case, are a necessity to inform robust, reliable probabilities. This may require some additional testing on the items in the case and maybe some experimentation to replicate the conditions as alleged. Use of Bayesian networks offers a good tool with which to explore and evaluate this aspect.

## 3) 'Activity' issues

A generic pair of propositions for this level may be written as:

$H_p$ 'The suspect did the activity in question'
$H_D$ 'The suspect did not do the activity'

In the example of the case of rape, this would translate as:

$H_p$ 'The suspect had sexual intercourse with the woman'
$H_D$ 'The suspect did not have intercourse with the woman'

As we saw when moving from 'sub-source' to 'source', the LR generated from the 'lower' level is subsumed in the next 'higher' level. Likewise with 'activity', the LR at 'source' is subsumed into the LR at 'activity'. To move from 'source' to 'activity', the quantity and distribution of the questioned material has to be considered.

For the numerator, $Pr[E \mid H_p, I]$, of the likelihood ratio at 'activity' level, data are required on transfer, persistence and distribution of the material on items like the recipient in the case. Reliable, relevant information is needed to inform the probability that, in the context of the case, the scientist would have obtained the quantity of material, in the position and form found, if the activity took place as alleged.

For the denominator, $Pr[E \mid H_D, I]$, of the likelihood ratio at 'activity' level, data are required to inform the probability that the scientist would have obtained the quantity of material, in the position and form found, if the alternative activity had taken place. However, the data required will depend critically on what the defence alternative will be. Generally, if we are considering material on a defendant and if the defendant alleges he had nothing to do with the crime or crime scene, then a dataset of innocent people, like the defendant, who could be suspected of the crime would provide good information to inform the probability. However, if the suspect says he did not do the alleged activity but did do some other activity, then the requirement is for knowledge and data about the transfer, persistence and detection given this alternative activity.

I make one note of caution. It is tempting to begin an evaluation of the LR of the findings at 'sub-source' or 'source' level and then proceed upwards to 'activity', thereby apparently subsuming the 'lower' level LRs. However, in so doing, there is the risk of losing some conditioning information. I recommend evaluation of an LR solely at 'activity' level. This automatically includes a consideration of 'sub-source' and 'source' LRs and will condition these LR values on what has actually been found during the examination. It is a logical, one-step process at 'activity' level instead of a disjointed, multi-step approach if 'sub-source', 'source' and 'activity' are considered as separate steps in evaluation. This concept is applicable generally throughout all forensic science interpretation.

### 4) Posterior probabilities, Pr[H | E, I]

These could be considered the ultimate form of opinion that a scientist could offer. A posterior probability is necessarily the outcome of considering the prior probabilities as well as the likelihoods (probabilities for the evidence). Key questions are, firstly, whether it is seen as the scientist's role to offer posterior probabilities and, secondly, whether the scientist has assigned robust, reliable prior probabilities and likelihoods.

Whether or not it is the scientist's role will depend primarily on the nature of the judicial process in the jurisdiction. Whether or not the priors and the likelihoods are robust and reliable will depend on the scientist's knowledge and skills, as discussed earlier. If the scientist has not made the priors and the likelihoods explicit, then it will be unclear how the scientist has arrived at the particular value for the posterior probability. If that is the case, then there is much scope for challenge of that opinion. Finally, in the special case of categorical opinions, the key question would be whether a probability of zero is justified.

## Closing comments

There is a very powerful, persuasive argument that the LR is a logical, balanced, robust way of assessing probative value of scientific evidence in courts of law. Furthermore, use of the LR is now being recognised by the courts in England and Wales as a robust way of presenting scientific findings. In their judgement in the second Appeal of Barry George (Barry George (Appelant) and R (Respondent) [2007] EWCA Crim 2722), convicted of the murder in 1999 of Jill Dando, the Court of Appeal accepted an earlier Criminal Cases Review Commission (CCRC) report recommendation that opinion on the strength of the findings in relation to firearms discharge residue (FDR) in this case was best expressed as a likelihood ratio at 'activity' level. It remains to be seen what will be the extent of the impact of this judgement on other cases involving forensic science evidence in England and Wales.

This chapter has offered an analysis of the nature of forensic science opinion and has suggested a framework to categorise opinion. If it is a robust and useful framework, then it reveals the knowledge, understanding, and some of the skills that are required to form robust, reliable opinions. It may provide the scientist with an *aide-mémoire* with which to check the validity of their opinions before they offer them to clients. It helps the scientist to assess whether they have appropriate data, knowledge and understanding to offer the opinion.

This framework also provides police, lawyers and laypeople with a similar checklist to test the robustness of the opinion being presented to them.

## Acknowledgements

I am very grateful to the many colleagues who have given freely of their time in discussions about their cases. I am indebted to my friend and colleague, Dr Ian Evett, who sparked my interest in interpretation and who has, over many years, guided and supported me.

## References

Aitken, C.G.C. and Taroni, F. (2004) *Statistics and the Evaluation of Evidence for Forensic Scientists*. Chichester: John Wiley and Sons Ltd.

Biedermann, A., Taroni, F., Delemont, O., Semadeni, C. and Davison, A.C. (2005a) 'The evaluation of evidence in the forensic investigation of fire incidents (Part I): an approach using Bayesian networks', *Forensic Science International*, 147: 49–57.

Biedermann, A., Taroni, F., Delemont, O., Semadeni, C. and Davison, A.C. (2005b) 'The evaluation of evidence in the forensic investigation of fire incidents (Part II): practical examples of the use of Bayesian networks', *Forensic Science International*, 147: 59–69.

Biedermann, A., Taroni, F. and Garbolino, P. (2007) 'Equal prior probabilities: can one do any better?', *Forensic Science International*, 172: 85–93.

Broeders, A.P.A. (2007) 'Principles of forensic identification science' in T. Newburn *et al.* (eds), *A Handbook of Criminal Investigation*. Cullompton: Willan Publishing.

Champod, C. and Evett, I.W. (2001) 'A probabilistic approach to fingerprint evidence', *Journal of Forensic Identification*, 51: 101–123.

Champod, C., Evett, I.W. and Jackson, G. (2004) 'Establishing the most appropriate databases for addressing source level propositions', *Science and Justice*, 44: 153–164.

Cole, S.A. (2005) 'More than zero: accounting for error in latent fingerprint identification', *The Journal of Criminal Law and Criminology*, 95: 985–1078.

Cook, R., Evett, I.W., Jackson, G., Jones, P.J. and Lambert, J.A. (1998a) 'A model for case assessment and interpretation', *Science and Justice*, 38: 151–156.

Cook, R., Evett, I.W., Jackson, G., Jones, P.J. and Lambert, J.A. (1998b) 'A hierarchy of propositions: deciding which level to address in casework', *Science and Justice*, 38: 231–240.

Curran, J.M., Hicks, T.N. and Buckleton, J.S. (2000) *Forensic Interpretation of Glass Evidence*. Boca Raton, Florida: CRC Press.

ENFSI Expert Working Group Marks Conclusion Scale Committee (2006) 'Conclusion Scale for Shoeprint and Toolmarks examinations', *Forensic Science International*, 172: 85–93.

Evett, I.W. (1995) 'Avoiding the transposed conditional', *Science and Justice*, 35: 127–131.

Evett, I.W. and Weir, B.S. (1998) *Interpreting DNA Evidence*. Sunderland, Massachusetts: Sinaur.

Evett, I.W., Foreman, L.A., Jackson, G. and Lambert, J.A. (2000a) 'DNA profiling: a discussion of issues relating to the reporting of very small match probabilities', *Criminal Law Review*, May: 341–355.

Evett, I.W., Gill, P.D., Jackson, G., Whitaker, J. and Champod, C. (2002) 'Interpreting small quantities of DNA: the hierarchy of propositions and the use of Bayesian networks', *Journal of Forensic Sciences*, 47: 520–530.

Evett, I.W., Jackson, G. and Lambert, J.A. (2000b) 'More on the hierarchy of propositions: exploring the distinction between explanations and propositions', *Science and Justice*, 40: 3–10.

Evett, I.W., Jackson, G., Lambert, J.A. and McCrossan, S. (2000c) 'The impact of the principles of evidence interpretation on the structure and content of statements', *Science and Justice*, 40: 233–239.

Grieve, M.C. (2000) 'A survey on the evidential value of fibres and the interpretation of the findings in fibre transfer cases. Part 2 – interpretation and reporting', *Science and Justice*, 40: 201–209.

Jackson, G., Jones, S., Booth, G., Champod, C. and Evett, I.W. (2006) 'The nature of forensic science opinion – a possible framework to guide thinking and practice in investigations and in court proceedings', *Science and Justice*, 46: 33–44.

Kaye, D.H. and Koehler, J.J. (2003) 'The misquantification of probative value', *Law and Human Behaviour*, 27: 645–659.

Krauß, W. and Simmerlein, N. (2004) 'Collaborative Exercise Trial 11, 2004', Forensic Science Institute, Landeskriminalant Baden-Wurttemberg, 70372 Stuttgart, Germany. Available at http://www.enfsi.org/ewg/efg/Coll.%20Exercise/document_view (Last accessed 17 January 2008).

Lucy, D. (2005) *Introduction to Statistics for Forensic Scientists*. Chichester: John Wiley and Sons Ltd.

Nordby, J.J. (2000) *Dead Reckoning: the Art of Forensic Detection*. Boca Raton, Florida: CRC Press.

Robertson, B. and Vignaux, G.A. (1995) *Interpreting Evidence: Evaluating Forensic Science Evidence in the Courtroom*. Chichester: John Wiley and Sons Ltd.

Satterthwaite, J. and Lambert, J.A. (1989) 'Interpreting the Interpretations. A survey to assess the effectiveness of conclusions in statements written by forensic scientists', *Home Office Forensic Science Service Technical Note 714*.

Saks, M.J., Risinger, D.M., Rosenthal, R. and Thompson, W.C. (2003) 'Context effects in forensic science: a review of the science of scene to crime laboratory practice in the US', *Science and Justice*, 43: 77–90.

Sjerps, M. and Biesheuvel, D.B. (1999) 'The interpretation of conventional and Bayesian verbal scales for expressing expert opinion: a small experiment among jurists', *Forensic Linguistics*, 6: 1350–1771.

Taroni, F. and Aitken, C.G.G. (1998a) 'Probabilistic reasoning in the law, part 1: assessment of probabilities and explanation of the value of DNA evidence', *Science and Justice*, 38: 165–177.

Taroni, F. and Aitken, C.G.G. (1998b) 'Probabilistic reasoning in the law, part 2: assessment of probabilities and explanation of the value of trace evidence other than DNA', *Science and Justice*, 38: 165–177.

Taroni, F. and Biedermann, A. (2005) 'Inadequacies of posterior probabilities for the assessment of scientific evidence', *Law, Probability and Risk*, 4: 89–114.

Taroni, F., Aitken, C.G.G. and Garbolino, P. (2001) 'DeFinetti's subjectivism, the assessment of probabilities and the evaluation of evidence: a commentary', *Science and Justice*, 41: 145–150.

Taroni, F., Aitken, C.G.G., Garbolino, P. and Biedermann, A. (2006) *Bayesian Networks and Probabilistic Inference in Forensic Science*. Chichester: John Wiley and Sons Ltd.

Tentori, K., Crupi, V., Bonini, N. and Osherson, D. (2007) 'Comparison of confirmation measures', *Cognition*, 103: 107–119.

431

# Chapter 17

# The science of proof: forensic science evidence in English criminal trials

*Paul Roberts*

Previous chapters of this Handbook have indicated the rapidly expanding contribution of forensic science to criminal investigations across a broad range of factual scenarios and types of criminality, employing an increasingly sophisticated array of scientific technologies and forensic techniques. This chapter takes as its central focus the criminal trial in England and Wales, in order to explore the translation of forensic science into admissible evidence capable of contributing to the conviction of the guilty and exoneration of the innocent. The courtroom is the crucible in which science and law confront each other most directly in the administration of justice, an interface typically mediated through the testimony of one or more expert witnesses. A central task for this chapter is accordingly to identify, explain and critically evaluate the legal rules of evidence and procedure which regulate the admissibility, presentation and interpretation of expert witness testimony in criminal trials. The impact of forensic science evidence on the course and outcome of criminal proceedings is often significant and sometimes dispositive. Yet forensic science evidence has also attracted its fair share of controversy in recent decades – on some occasions receiving plaudits for its impressive contributions to controlling crime and visiting offenders with their just deserts, at other times berated as a potent cause of miscarriages of justice.

This chapter's concentrated focus on the final courtroom drama of criminal proceedings should not be taken to imply a rigid separation between the trial and pre-trial (including investigative) phases of the criminal process. To the contrary, everything that takes place at trial is shaped, and sometimes even determined, by decisions that were taken at earlier points in the process. If perishable material with potential evidential value is not identified and preserved by investigators in a secure and timely fashion, the opportunity to adduce such material as evidence at trial may be lost for ever. More dramatically still, if the accused decides to admit the charges by pleading guilty there is no longer any need for a contested trial and the court will proceed directly to sentencing. Of course, in the earlier stages of a criminal investigation it is seldom possible to predict with much confidence how, if at all, a particular line of inquiry will develop into a criminal prosecution. Will a suspect be identified? If so, will there be sufficient evidence to bring formal charges? If so, will the Crown Prosecution Service (CPS) persevere with a prosecution? If so, will the accused contest the charges? If so, will the judge allow the case to go to the jury? If so, will the jury find the prosecution's evidence compelling? In view of these cumulative uncertainties, investigators and prosecutors must build each case on the assumption that it *might* result in a contested trial, even though in reality the vast majority of criminal investigations in England and Wales never get that far,[1] and most of the minority of cases that do proceed all the way to trial are resolved by the accused's plea of guilty.[2] The influence of the legal rules which regulate the admissibility and interpretation of forensic science evidence at trial consequently extends far beyond the confines of the courtroom. Indeed, it is no exaggeration to say that, from the very first moment of their inception, criminal investigations are conducted in the shadow of procedural law, which both specifies the nature and scope of investigative powers available to the police (Roberts 2007a) and determines the extent to which potentially incriminating objects or information obtained by investigators could be admissible as proof of guilt in the event of a trial. Forensic scientists involved in criminal investigations are subject to these legal strictures no less than any other professional investigator, and they therefore have equally powerful incentives to know the legal rules which apply to their situation and to strive at all times to conduct themselves in accordance with the law.

Many of the countries of continental Europe and elsewhere in the world have adopted comprehensive codes of criminal procedure, and this is said to make the law of criminal investigation, prosecution and trial relatively simple and accessible to all its professional users (as well as curious members of the public) in those jurisdictions. England and Wales has no such code (Spencer 2000). The English law of criminal evidence and procedure must, instead, be reconstructed from a chaotic jumble of statutes and case-law precedents handed down by judges over several centuries, and recently overlaid with a fast-developing quasi-constitutional human rights jurisprudence following the entry into force of the Human Rights Act 1998 on 2 October 2000. Partly in consequence of this lack of structure and piecemeal evolution, but also owing to its byzantine technicality, the English law of evidence has a (not entirely unmerited) reputation amongst lawyers for formidable complexity. Textbooks and professional manuals on the law of criminal evidence run to hundreds, if not thousands, of pages (Hooper and Ormerod 2008; Roberts and Zuckerman 2004). Fortunately, the basic tenets of English law as they apply to forensic science evidence can be summarised, and grasped in their essentials, without getting too bogged down in technical legal details. The beginners' guide to procedural law presented in this chapter will be situated within the broader institutional context of criminal adjudication in England and Wales.

The following exposition is divided into four parts. Section I outlines the basic adversarial structure of English criminal trials and explores the overriding objectives and values of criminal adjudication. The adversarial format for presenting and testing evidence at trial has important implications for forensic science evidence and expert witness testimony, which will emerge as the discussion proceeds. Section II then briefly reviews some general principles and doctrines of English law which regulate the admissibility of all evidence, including forensic science evidence, in criminal trials in England and Wales. Here we encounter the law of relevance, fair trial, hearsay and bad character evidence. Section III turns to consider bespoke rules of evidence which apply specifically to forensic science and other expert testimony. These rules govern both the threshold admissibility of scientific evidence, and also the way in which such evidence may be utilised by the fact-finder in the event that it is admissible and presented at trial. Finally, Section IV offers some speculations about future developments in law and process, particularly in relation to the practical challenges posed for criminal adjudication by scientific innovation and novel forensic techniques. These reflections prompt further questions about the susceptibility of the legal process to infiltration by 'junk science' and the associated risks of fact-finders being hoodwinked by charlatans or misled by incompetents. Whether judges should attempt to arbitrate in disputes over scientific validity, or can fairly be expected to shoulder the responsibility for expert witness accreditation, are further topics for discussion.

## I. The structure and values of adversarial criminal trial

English criminal procedure (as everybody knows) is 'adversarial', conforming to an 'Anglo-American' or 'common law' model shared with other English-speaking countries in North America, Australasia, Africa and South-East Asia. Adversarialism is conventionally contrasted with the 'inquisitorial' model of legal process favoured by most Continental European jurisdictions, and exported to their former colonies in South America and the Francophone parts of Africa and Asia (Glenn 2007; Vogler 2005). The essence of an adversarial trial process is that 'the parties' to the litigation – the Crown represented by the prosecutor, and the accused and his or her advocate and legal advisers – are primarily responsible for gathering, presenting and testing the evidence which each adduces at trial in support of its own partisan contentions. This solemn piece of public theatre is acted out in the presence of a neutral fact-finder, who watches and listens passively as the parties develop their respective cases (Frankel 1975), paradigmatically through oral witness testimony (Roberts and Zuckerman 2004: ch. 6).

Procedural rules of antique pedigree dictate that testimony is elicited first through examination-in-chief of the party's own witnesses, who are then cross-examined by the opposing party. At the close of proceedings the fact-finder delivers a verdict on the basis of its holistic assessment of all the evidence and arguments that have been presented to it. Adversarial trials thus proceed as a kind of contest or debate between two partisan factions, each urging a different conclusion on the fact-finder, who must somehow reconstruct an accurate portrayal of disputed events from the evidential debris of full-blooded forensic conflict. The fact-finder in English criminal proceedings is normally[3] a 'lay person', that is, somebody without legal qualifications. This will be either a lay jury of 12 randomly selected adults in Crown Court trials on indictment (the most serious cases), or a panel of three lay magistrates conducting summary trials in the magistrates' courts (for cases of medium or lesser gravity).

Adversarialism pervades the broader institutional structures and cultural milieu into which forensic scientists venture when they put themselves forward as expert witnesses. It is only stating the obvious to say that criminal courtrooms are an unfamiliar environment for scientists (as they are for most people), and it is hardly surprising that individual scientific experts report that the experience of testifying in court was disorientating, frustrating or disappointing, possibly – to them – unacceptably so (McEwan 1998: 158–165; Roberts and Willmore 1993: ch. 4; Gee 1987). At least in its own self-image and public persona (particular practices and individual practitioners sometimes fall a long way short of the ideal), science celebrates open, collaborative and above all disinterested, impartial inquiry. The objective in its impeccable 20/20 vision is the unvarnished truth, its currency hard facts, and its method trial and error until scientific theory has been demonstrably vindicated through robust experimentation (Haack 2003). Adversarial trial process, with its partisan witness testimony and fork-tongued advocates in search of a plausible story to advance their client's interests rather than anything necessarily resembling 'the truth', can easily be caricatured as the very antithesis of scientific method. Where scientists trade facts, lawyers construct narratives; where scientists pool their material and intellectual resources to facilitate a more efficient collaborative search for truth, the parties to adversarial litigation prefer to hold their cards close to their chest; and where scientific theory remains at a deep level contingent and open to refutation in its particulars or even wholesale 'paradigm shifts' precipitating extensive reconsideration of previously received wisdom, definitive closure is an essential characteristic of successful criminal adjudication: the verdict of the jury must be authoritative and final (subject only to the established system of criminal appeals and exceptional post-conviction review). With such ostensibly divergent epistemological commitments, methodological preferences, routine *modus operandi* and overarching objectives, small wonder that the 'marriage of opposites' (Wonder 1989) between science and law has been plagued by recurrent tensions, occasionally erupting into major rows accompanied by bitter public recriminations (Ward 2004: Dwyer 2003; Redmayne 1997; Hamer 1981). Happily, reconciliation invariably swiftly follows, as Punch and Judy patch things up and resume their stormy yet apparently durable relationship. As the ill-begotten offspring of this troubled union, forensic science was all too likely to grow up into a rather confused adolescent.

Caricature always contains half-truths, otherwise it would only amount to more or less defamatory abuse and misrepresentation. But half-truths never tell the whole story, which is why caricatures should never be taken too seriously. It is perfectly true to say that law and science conduct their routine business rather differently, and that these differences sometimes place individual scientists in uncomfortable, even *risky*, positions when they appear as expert witnesses in court. Perhaps the epistemological and methodological distances between law and science are truly unbridgeable in the final analysis, and it is certainly fair to say that not all scientists – irrespective of narrow technical competence – are temperamentally suited to forensic work, which involves presentational skills and ethical responsibilities (Sanders 2007) not normally associated with laboratory science. Be that as it may, however, the *apparent* distance between law and science can be reduced very substantially by cultivating a more nuanced understanding of criminal adjudication and the role of forensic science evidence within it. A first step on the road to enlightenment is to consider afresh, and without too many preconceptions, the most elementary questions about the relationship between law and science in the context of criminal proceedings.

Why does the law turn to science in the administration of criminal justice? The straightforward answer is that science can provide useful information not otherwise available to legal process, specifically in the form of technical expertise beyond the ordinary common-sense knowledge of lay fact-finders. The practice of resorting to expert advice on scientific and technical matters has been established in English law for many centuries.[4] Whilst the scope, sophistication and probative potential of scientific techniques have all dramatically increased in recent decades, English law has consistently maintained its characteristically receptive approach to scientific expertise.

On the face of it, the law's requests for technical information ought to be satisfied, without much scope for strife or controversy, by the expert witness's provision of hard scientific facts bearing on disputed questions in a criminal trial. This assumption implies what might be termed a 'juror deference' model of scientific expertise, according to which lay fact-finders – who by definition are manifestly ill-equipped to second-guess a properly qualified expert in matters requiring specialist knowledge – are effectively obliged to accept scientific evidence, at face value, as incontestable fact. It would be irrational, on this view, for lay jurors to substitute their own untutored surmises and intuitions for the authoritative pronouncements of an expert. Prepossessing and articulate forensic scientists with substantial experience of testifying in court as expert witnesses doubtless do, regularly, command this level of near-automatic deference from lay jurors and magistrates. Yet here lurks a first indication of unresolved tensions in the relationship between law and science. For, as a matter of legal principle, English law rejects the juror deference model of scientific expertise, in favour of a competing vision of 'juror education' (Allen 1994).

The classic judicial statement explaining the circumscribed role of scientific experts in legal proceedings was formulated by Lord President Cooper in the Scottish case of *Davie* v. *Edinburgh Magistrates*:

> Their duty is to furnish the judge or jury with the necessary scientific criteria for testing the accuracy of their conclusions, so as to enable the judge or jury to form their own independent judgment by the application of these criteria to the facts proved in evidence.[5]

The foundational premiss of this 'juror education' model is that expert testimony should supply information on specialist topics in a form readily comprehensible by the average lay person, so that jurors or magistrates themselves, as the designated fact-finders in contested criminal trials, will be able to arrive at their own independent conclusions of fact, even in relation to matters requiring scientific or technical expertise. Legal commentators differ on the extent to which 'juror education' is a practically feasible aspiration for legal proceedings (Imwinkelried 1997; Edmond 1998). Whilst relatively modest procedural reforms might conceivably improve the prospects for juror education (especially since certain aspects of current practice are almost perversely unhelpful in this regard: cf. Auld 2001: 518–22), it seems likely that deference rather than education will routinely characterise lay responses to expert testimony. The old canard (it is as old as Socrates) that any knowledge, no matter how abstruse, can be explained in common-sense language accessible to 'the ordinary intelligent reader' is simply false; and it is implausible to imagine for much of the territory of forensic science that a short, intensive course of juror education within the context of criminal trial proceedings could truly substitute for an expert's long years of education, training and practical experience.

The law's formal commitment to juror education, notwithstanding its dubious epistemological assumptions, reflects the pre-eminent status of lay adjudication in English criminal proceedings, and by extension reinforces the underlying values of substantive justice, procedural due process, democratic accountability, civic participation, liberty, security and public confidence in the administration of criminal justice, some or all of which lay adjudication arguably promotes (Roberts and Zuckerman 2004: 59–67; Clark 1999: cf. Hörnle 2006). Moreover, for those who take seriously the rationales informing lay adjudication, the naivety of juror education is more apparent than real. Some commentators advocate a principle of 'jury equity', according to which a lay jury is always entitled to acquit against the weight of evidence in order to do justice according to its conscience on the facts of the instant case.[6] On this view, common-sense justice must always ultimately prevail over scientific fact. Less radically, English criminal law contains normative standards of liability, such as the test for dishonesty in the law of theft[7] and the concept of 'substantially impaired mental responsibility' in the partial defence to murder of diminished responsibility,[8] which a lay juror is deemed uniquely well qualified to apply. Thus, in *Byrne* Lord Parker CJ said that the test of 'substantially impaired mental responsibility'

is a question of degree and essentially one for the jury. Medical evidence is, of course, relevant, but the question involves a decision not merely as to whether there was some impairment of the mental responsibility of the accused for his acts but whether such impairment can properly be called 'substantial', a matter upon which juries may quite legitimately differ from doctors … [M]edical evidence is no doubt of importance, but the jury are entitled to take into consideration all the evidence, including the acts or statements of the accused and his demeanour. They are not bound to accept the medical evidence if there is other material before them which, in their good judgment, conflicts with it and outweighs it.[9]

In these and similar instances, what might appear to be factual questions which are in principle amenable to scientific proof are actually, in significant measure, moral judgements expressly reserved in law to the fact-finder (Zuckerman 1986). For these, cumulative, reasons, English criminal courts will often insist that the jury must arrive at its own decision, even in relation to findings of fact on which the testimony of an expert might appear to be conclusive. This is perfectly consistent with a generalised judicial expectation that a presumptively reasonable jury will pay careful attention to expert scientific testimony, and will typically defer to an expert's uncontested conclusions in the exercise of its lay common sense.

Criminal adjudication pursues a complex objective – the conviction of the guilty, and only them, *according to law* – and simultaneously promotes and reflects a multitude of subsidiary objectives and constitutive and incidental values (Roberts 2006; Roberts and Zuckerman 2004: 18–25). These values often cohere in virtuous synergy, at their 'local' point of application in individual cases and globally with English criminal procedure's official overriding objective 'that criminal cases be dealt with justly'.[10] Sometimes, however, the objectives and values of criminal adjudication are in conflict, demanding sacrifices and trade-offs between competing legal principles and rival conceptions of justice. These fundamental precepts of jurisprudence and political morality supply the broader normative and institutional framework regulating the roles of forensic science evidence and expert witness testimony in English criminal trials.

### The role of the expert witness in adversarial criminal trials

In particular, it follows from the proceeding discussion that self-consciously *forensic* science, science applied to the administration of justice, is science on the law's terms, and expert witnesses must consequently dance to a legal tune. It is vital to appreciate what, precisely, this asserted priority of law over science entails. It does *not* imply that scientists should ever testify to anything other than what they regard in good faith as pertinent scientific facts. Still less should expert witnesses consciously bend their testimony to suit the litigation priorities of adversarial parties or in any way, including through sins of omission, deliberately mislead the court about the significance of their evidence for the matters in dispute at trial. To the contrary, a scientist who fails to uphold the highest standards of independence, objectivity and scientific rigour in the provision of forensic evidence is worse than useless in the courtroom, because a partisan witness appearing in the guise of a neutral expert testifying to unvarnished scientific facts is especially liable to mislead a jury and contribute to miscarriages of justice. To this extent, there is no conflict whatever between scientific methodology and forensic practice: the forensic expert's first professional ethical duty is to uphold the methodological integrity of his or her scientific discipline and to guarantee the validity of its technological and contextual applications in the instant case. The Court of Appeal has found it necessary to reiterate the fundamental importance of an expert witness's duties of objectivity, impartiality and candour in several recent cases,[11] and these duties are now enshrined in Rule 33.2 of the Criminal Procedure Rules (CrimPR) 2005. In practical terms, however, lawyers rather than scientists dictate the course and conduct of criminal litigation, and in this institutional context the values of the legal system will necessarily take ultimate priority over scientific concerns. In the final analysis, scientists must therefore defer to lawyers and courts on the significance of their evidence for criminal adjudication, whilst steadfastly holding the line on internal standards of scientific validity and the range and strength of factual inferences genuinely supported by their findings.

In a procedural system in which expert witnesses are instructed by adversarial parties, it is likely that experts will experience diffuse, and perhaps occasionally more concentrated, pressures to tailor their evidence to lawyers' expectations. However, as independent advisers to the administration of justice whose advice is valued precisely because it is assumed to be scientifically valid and non-partisan, there is only one type of advocacy that expert witnesses can afford to be drawn into, and that is advocacy promoting the integrity of their own, technical evidence. Scientists who are temperamentally unable to withstand a certain amount of institutional pressure to distort scientific facts so that they appear to support adversarial legal narratives would be well advised to stay clear of forensic work altogether.

This admonition is not intended to trivialise the delicate nature of the relationships between forensic scientists and the police and lawyers who instruct them, or to underestimate the legal and practical complexities of their forensic collaborations. Police and prosecutors are always trying to put together 'a case', just as defence lawyers are in the business of punching holes in the prosecution's allegations. These strategic objectives inform police and defence lawyers' calculations in deciding to turn to science for assistance in any particular case, and thereafter strongly influence selections of material submitted to the laboratory for analysis, the manner in which forensic scientists are instructed, the particular questions posed or lines of inquiry suggested for further scientific exploration, and so forth (Roberts 1994; Roberts and Willmore 1993). Forensic scientists are thus called upon to implement objective scientific protocols in the service of partisan objectives, and there is room within these complex institutional arrangements for negotiation and a measure of compromise with the demands of criminal investigation and legal proof. For example, a scientist might reasonably agree to run further, more discriminating, tests where police investigators are convinced of a particular suspect's involvement in a detected crime but which initial testing has failed to corroborate. The crucial point is that scientific validity must dictate the extent to which forensic scientists can be flexible and accommodating in negotiating their working relationships with police and lawyers. To the extent that the adversarial dynamic in criminal litigation tends to encourage lawyers to push factual plausibility to – and beyond – its outer limits, scientists must do their utmost to avoid becoming complicit in a corruption of their evidence. This will sometimes mean telling police or lawyers, in no uncertain terms, that science cannot provide what they want. On occasion it may even require complete withdrawal from further participation in particular criminal proceedings if the instructing lawyer is intent on utilising scientific evidence in a manner which the expert regards as scientifically invalid or otherwise unconscionably misleading.

### Adversarialism and court-appointed experts

Empowering judges to instruct expert witnesses, rather than ceding this important function to prosecution and defence lawyers, might appear at a stroke to resolve many of the problems traditionally associated with adversarial trial procedure. The scientific credentials of court-appointed experts can be vetted and approved in advance. As an independent adviser to the court, the judicial appointee is relatively insulated from adversarial partisanship, ensuring that distracting courtroom 'battles of expertise' which sometimes arise between party-instructed expert witnesses can be pre-empted. Rather than receiving confusing mixed messages about the evidential implications of scientific information, the fact-finder is presented with a single, authoritative expert witness, whose testimony comes pre-stamped with judicial approval.

The patent advantages for efficient fact-finding of court-appointed experts accounts for their widespread adoption in the 'inquisitorial' legal systems of Continental Europe (van Kampen 1998). Observing their apparent success abroad, several commentators advocated similar systems of court-appointed experts for England and Wales (Spencer 1992; Spencer 1991: cf. Howard 1991; Redmayne 2001: ch. 7), and they have now, in effect, become the default option in civil litigation (Zuckerman 2006: ch. 20). Although English judges notionally enjoy a general power at common law to instruct their own experts,[12] this power is hardly ever exercised in criminal trials, and never to the exclusion of party-instructed expert witnesses. Yet without exclusivity, many of the vaunted advantages of court-appointed experts evaporate (for example the fact-finder's task is not made any easier by being confronted with a concatenated three-cornered scientific dispute involving court-appointed as well as party-instructed experts, as opposed to the more familiar bilateral battles of expertise).

Why have court-appointed experts made so little headway in English criminal litigation? Part of the answer lies in pragmatic considerations, such as the practical difficulty of identifying best practice across the disparate disciplinary spectrum of forensic sciences in order to compile a credible, relatively uncontentious list of appropriately qualified court experts. There are also more principled concerns that court-appointed experts could detract from adversarial conceptions of due process. Depriving the accused of opportunities to develop the defence case by instructing scientific experts of his own choosing might be regarded as a source of procedural unfairness. Forcing the accused to accept the opinion of the state's scientist might erode the fundamental precept that justice 'must be seen to be done', just as it would be procedurally suspect to force the accused to accept the advice or assistance of the state's lawyer. Appearing to sanctify an expert's testimony with the imprimatur of the court might also be regarded as detracting from judicial impartiality and trenching on the constitutional province of lay fact-finding.

From a comparative perspective, Mirjan Damaška (1986, 1975) has suggested that countries with inquisitorial criminal procedures tend to be characterised by relatively high levels of social trust in state bureaucracies and professional expertise, whereas adversarial cultures are generally more suspicious of state officials and tend to place greater store by lay involvement in public decision-making, even if this entails contradicting expert opinion on occasion. Anglophone liberal political culture is strongly invested in personal autonomy, individual rights, economic *laissez-faire* and self-reliance, in criminal proceedings no less than in other major dimensions of the public sphere, whereas the comparatively corporatist states of Continental Europe, East and West, place a more pronounced accent on social responsibility and public welfare. These contrasts are admittedly drawn in sweeping and somewhat indistinct brush strokes, and they are consequently very difficult to substantiate empirically. Nonetheless, when read in conjunction with the normative features of criminal adjudication previously discussed, Damaška's suggestive parallels between a society's political culture and its design preferences for legal procedure provide a more than plausible explanation of the markedly contrasting fortunes of court-appointed experts on different sides of the English Channel. Court experts flourish where officials dominate legal process and authoritative expert pronouncements are seldom challenged (a theoretical hypothesis confirmed in practice by the deference typically extended to expert evidence by Continental fact-finders: van Kampen and Nijboer 1997). Where, by contrast, the parties develop their own cases and dictate the course of legal proceedings, whilst professionals, experts and officials of all kinds incite popular ambivalence and even a measure of suspicion, the court expert will not be held in comparably high esteem and is unlikely to be an acceptable surrogate for party-instructed expert witnesses.

## II. General principles and doctrines of the law of criminal evidence

Having provided a sketch of the enveloping institutional structures, basic procedural 'architecture' and animating values of English criminal trials, we now turn to consider the legal rules which regulate the presentation, interpretation and evaluation of forensic science evidence in the courtroom. A large chunk of the law of evidence is comprised of rules of admissibility, which perform the pivotal role of regulating the flow of information to the fact-finder. Scientific evidence cannot even be presented to the jury unless it is first deemed admissible by the judge, usually after hearing relevant legal argument from the parties where admissibility is contested. However, the law of evidence is not comprised exclusively of rules of admissibility. Additional 'forensic reasoning rules' (Roberts and Zuckerman 2004: ch. 10) direct *how* evidence which has already been admitted into the trial should, and should not, be utilised by the fact-finder. Evidence is frequently admissible for one purpose, but inadmissible for another, and where such multifunctional evidence is admitted at trial the judge must direct the jury to use it only for legally sanctioned purposes.

Rules of evidence pertaining specifically to forensic science will be examined in the next section. But before we look at bespoke legal doctrines, it is necessary to review general principles of admissibility in English law, because these legal standards apply to forensic science evidence *in addition* to the rules specifically formulated for scientific evidence. Consequently, expert evidence which is methodologically impeccable from a scientific perspective might still nonetheless be inadmissible at trial if it infringes one or more of the general legal principles of admissibility discussed in this section – relevance, fair trial, hearsay and character.

## Relevance

Only *relevant* evidence is admissible in criminal trials. This elementary qualification flows directly from the institutional context of adjudication as a mechanism for dispute resolution. Contested issues of fact must be resolved before justice can be done. Evidence is worthless to the legal process unless it might help to resolve the issues in dispute. Relevant evidence could still be inadmissible on other grounds, but irrelevant information falls at the first hurdle: it is categorically inadmissible. Evidence is 'relevant' if it tends to prove or disprove a 'fact in issue', these being the facts of allegations against the accused specified by the prosecution in the indictment and any countervailing defences. There is seemingly no quantum of relevance in law: whilst the weight or 'probative value' of any piece of evidence may vary, depending on how persuasively or conclusively it proves (or disproves) a fact in issue, evidence is relevant if it has *any* probative value whatsoever, and irrelevant if it has none.[13]

The low threshold of relevance mandated by English law is normally easily satisfied by forensic science evidence. A fingerprint or blood sample placing the accused at the scene of the crime is patently relevant; as are the results of drug tests, toxicological screens, questioned document analysis, pathology reports and so on, whenever such information tends to confirm (or disprove) that a crime has been committed or to identify particular perpetrators. Indeed, such evidence is not merely relevant, but often of immense and sometimes decisive probative value. There are, however, two types of situation in which scientific evidence might fail to surmount the relevance hurdle to admissibility. The first is where scientific evidence relates to matters no longer in dispute in the litigation. It often happens that the prosecution is prepared to prove facts which, when it comes to the day of trial, the defence is no longer contesting. For example, the accused in a rape case might concede the fact of intercourse, but claim that sex with the complainant was consensual. In these circumstances, DNA evidence establishing that the accused was the donor of semen recovered from the complainant is no longer strictly relevant to any contested fact (though in practice the DNA report might still be submitted to the court as agreed evidence).

A second potential relevancy deficit particularly concerns recent scientific discoveries and novel or idiosyncratic techniques. We will see in the next section that the law of evidence has struggled, not entirely successfully, to accommodate the uneven, unpredictable and often (at least temporarily) uncertain progress of science. Normally, this is a matter of adjudicating on plausible claims that a particular novel scientific theory or technique is valid and that its results can therefore safely be relied upon. However, relevance may become an issue at the extremities of (purported) scientific expertise. Since crackpot theories, untested hypotheses and unvalidated scientific techniques fail to satisfy even the threshold expectations of common-sense rationality, they are irrelevant in law, and consequently inadmissible in criminal trials.

### Fair trial

Criminal justice cannot be achieved unless criminal proceedings, including trials, are conducted fairly. Dispensing justice demands due process of law, and justice must be seen to be done in order to sustain the moral legitimacy of criminal verdicts and foster their popular acceptability. Ensuring a fair trial has always been regarded as one of the judge's most fundamental common law duties, but this traditional precept has been reinforced and greatly expanded in recent decades by judicial innovation against a backdrop of the growing influence of human rights law (Choo and Nash 2003; Roberts 2007b). Article 6 of the ECHR guarantees the right to a fair trial and elaborates a number of specific procedural rights for criminal suspects and the accused (Trechsel 2005). Crucially, the 'right to a fair trial' is not limited to what takes place *at trial*. It also regulates criminal investigations,[14] evidence-gathering[15] and pre-trial criminal procedure.[16]

It might be thought that rules regulating the fairness of trials have nothing to do with scientific evidence. After all, it is a category mistake to inquire after the *justice* of scientific facts. For example, it just is the case that things fall down rather than up under normal atmospheric conditions on Earth, and anybody who purported to challenge the 'justice' of gravity has simply failed to grasp the meaning of either 'justice' or 'gravity' (or is speaking metaphorically, etc.). Whilst this is all perfectly true as far as it goes, conceptual analysis cannot exempt scientific evidence from fair trial standards, which bear on the way in which evidentiary material is procured in the first instance, its handling and storage, and the access granted to scientific testing and data in the pre-trial process. Thus, irrespective of the scientific validity of a particular testing procedure, scientific results establishing – say – a suspected substance's chemical composition or the identity of a perpetrator may still be ruled inadmissible at trial if the trace material on which the tests were conducted was obtained or retained illegally, if a proper chain of custody cannot be demonstrated to rule out the risk of accidental contamination (Pattenden 2008), or if test results were not disclosed to the defence when they should have been (Crown Prosecution Service 2006).

Section 78 of the Police and Criminal Evidence Act (PACE) 1984 empowers trial judges to exclude prosecution evidence where its admission 'would have such an adverse effect on the fairness of the proceedings that the court ought not to admit it'. This is a broad exclusionary discretion, equally applicable to scientific evidence as to any other type of evidence.[17] Police impropriety or illegality in exceeding their lawful powers of investigation, interrogation, stop, search and seizure does not automatically lead to evidentiary exclusion.[18] However, where investigative improprieties were 'significant and substantial'[19] exclusion is a serious possibility, especially if the law was breached deliberately or otherwise in bad faith. Proactive investigative methods can easily result in evidentiary exclusion if they are not carefully planned and monitored in order to keep criminal investigations within the bounds of propriety and preserve the integrity of their evidential product. Police 'entrapment' is not a stand-alone defence in English criminal law,[20] but collusion by undercover officers or police informants which might be regarded as crossing the line into active incitement of criminality runs a serious risk that evidence of subsequent offending by a targeted suspect will be excluded under section 78.[21] In particularly egregious circumstances, the trial judge may effectively throw the case out of court by staying proceedings indefinitely as an abuse of process (Choo 2008: ch 5).

Collection of trace evidence for scientific testing will not present fair trial issues in the vast majority of cases. Fingerprints,[22] blood samples, footprints, tool marks, bite marks, ransom notes and the like are normally in plain view or can be recovered with the cooperation of the victim without employing questionable investigative techniques or breaching anyone's rights. Difficulties are more likely to arise in relation to material procured from suspects or the accused, or possibly from recalcitrant third parties. Contraband like drugs and drug-dealing paraphernalia, illegal weapons, or items connected to terrorism can be seized without any difficulty.[23] Serial amendments to PACE have empowered the police to take mouth swabs and pluck head hair from detainees in order to facilitate DNA testing to establish the identity of a person who has been arrested,[24] match known suspects to crime scenes and perform speculative searching[25] in the rapidly expanding National DNA Database (NDNAD 2006). These techniques may pose urgent questions for the future direction of public policy (Nuffield Council on Bioethics 2007; Williams and Johnson 2008), but in the meantime they make life considerably easier for police and prosecutors. Even when samples have been retained unlawfully, the courts have been so impressed by the reliability of DNA evidence that they have been prepared to condone flagrant official law-breaking in order to uphold convictions of serious offences.[26] The remarkably rapid proliferation of open street and 'mass private space'[27] CCTV schemes throughout the UK over the past two decades likewise raises urgent policy concerns (Crossman *et al.* 2007; von Hirsch *et al.* 2004), but poses few evidential dilemmas. Where available, CCTV images of crimes in progress or their precursors or immediate aftermath can readily be subjected to forensic analysis, and the tapes will often be admissible at trial.[28] Evidence procured through covert listening devices is also routinely admissible, even where the police trespass on private property and commit minor criminal damage in order to install a 'bug' on the exterior of residential premises.[29] However, there are greater restrictions on telephone tapping. The police can apply for a judicial warrant to eavesdrop on conversations conducted over a public telecommunications system,[30] but this information can be utilised for investigative purposes only. Telephone-tapping evidence is currently completely inadmissible in English criminal trials[31] (albeit that this blanket policy of exclusion, which is strongly advocated by the security services in order to preserve the secrecy of their investigative techniques, is almost constantly under review).

The highest level of legal protection is afforded to information procured by, or in consequence of, police interrogation of a suspect. The admissibility of confessions is regulated by section 76 of PACE 1984, which provides that a suspect's admissions cannot be adduced if they were, or might have been, procured by oppression or in circumstances conducive to their unreliability. Scientific evidence based on material discovered through an improperly obtained admission – as where the suspect is tricked into revealing the location of contraband or incriminating articles to an undercover agent posing as a prison cellmate – might by extension be excluded as tainted 'fruit of the poisoned tree', although exclusion is not the invariant consequence of such official illegality in England and Wales[32] (as it would be, for example, in the USA).[33]

Once scientific testing has been undertaken by the prosecution, the resulting evidence should be shared with the defence through timely pre-trial disclosure.[34] Trial by ambush is never desirable regardless of who is doing the ambushing, but the prosecution bears especial responsibility for comprehensive disclosure owing to its vastly disproportionate investigative resources and opportunities. Timely disclosure is an important facet of the prosecutor's dual status as a 'minister of justice', as well as an adversarial litigant, in English criminal proceedings.[35] The accused is entitled to know the case against him well in advance of trial in order to prepare an effective defence or plead guilty on an informed basis. Late or incomplete disclosure by the prosecution has been a major contributor to miscarriages of justice over the years. The extent of the prosecution's duty to disclose scientific evidence was clarified in R v. Ward, in which the accused, Judith Ward, was eventually cleared of the infamous M62 IRA coach-bombing, having served 17 years in prison for a crime she did not commit:

> An incident of a defendant's right to a fair trial is a right to timely disclosure by the prosecution of all material matters which affect the scientific case relied on by the prosecution, that is, whether such matters strengthen or weaken the prosecution case or assist the defence case. This duty exists whether or not a specific request for disclosure of details of scientific evidence is made by the defence. Moreover, this duty is continuous: it applies not only in the pre-trial period but also throughout the trial. The materiality of evidence on the scientific side of a case may sometimes be overlooked before a trial. If the significance of the evidence becomes clear during the trial there must be an immediate disclosure to the defence.[36]

In Ward itself, the Court of Appeal lambasted three forensic scientists instructed by the prosecution for failing to reveal the full extent of their testing procedures and results to their instructing lawyers. Negative test results seemingly contradicting the prosecution's case were consequently withheld from the defence and later suppressed at trial, an outcome which particularly infuriated the Court of Appeal because the jury had been kept in the dark about potentially significant information:

> The consequence is that in a criminal trial involving grave charges three senior government forensic scientists deliberately withheld material experimental data on the ground that it might damage the prosecution case. Moreover [in their testimony at trial, two of them] misled the court as to the state of their knowledge about the possibility of contamination

occurring from the debris of an explosion. No doubt they judged that the records of the firing cell tests would forever remain confidential. They were wrong. But the records were only disclosed about 17 years after Miss Ward's conviction and imprisonment.[37]

If it emerges at trial that the prosecution has failed to discharge the full extent of its disclosure duties in relation to scientific evidence, the proper course will normally be for the judge to consider granting an adjournment to allow the defence time to deal with new information. The defence would not necessarily require extra time in every case: it all depends on the precise nature of the evidence and the way in which the trial is being run by both sides. It is conceivable, however, that the evidence would have to be excluded altogether, as where the defence position has been irreparably damaged because the opportunity to conduct further testing on perishable samples has been lost. In the event that material non-disclosure of scientific evidence comes to light after the trial has been concluded, the Court of Appeal may determine that a conviction is no longer 'safe', in the words of the Criminal Appeal Act 1968, and must be quashed. Re-trial might be a practical option in some, but by no means all, such cases.

The unifying normative thread linking police illegality, unfair investigative tactics, and failures of prosecution disclosure is *procedural impropriety*. Justice demands due process and fair trial. Irrespective of internal standards of scientific validity and methodological rigour, scientific evidence tainted by procedural impropriety is flawed, from a legal perspective, and it is consequently vulnerable to being sacrificed – ruled inadmissible – at trial in order to preserve the procedural integrity of criminal adjudication.

### Hearsay

In the adversarial common law tradition, the oral testimony of witnesses speaking live, on oath and in the presence of the jury in the courtroom is regarded as the paradigm of judicial evidence. The rule against hearsay is the *alter ego* of this principle of orality. Witnesses must testify only to what they themselves have personally observed, heard or otherwise perceived through their senses, and on which sensory perceptions they may be cross-examined directly. Mere hearsay – information told to the witness by somebody else, other people's conversations overheard by the witness, and even the witness's own out-of-court statements – do not qualify as original evidence in a court of law.

English law's hearsay prohibition is complicated, and recent statutory reform has done nothing to reduce its complexity (Worthen 2008). The basic rule states that a statement other than one given by a witness in the current proceedings is not admissible in order to prove the truth of its contents. For our purposes, we can simplify somewhat by saying that the hearsay prohibition excludes out-of-court statements adduced for their truth.[38] Hearsay evidence thus has two, essential and irreducible, characteristics: (i) a geographical location (out-of-court); and (ii) a particular purpose in the trial (to prove the statement's truth).

The hearsay prohibition could, in theory, be a major irritant for forensic science evidence. A great deal of the informational content of expert witness testimony is technically hearsay. Scientific literature and experimental data are compiled over many decades, or even centuries, by countless scientists of every nationality working alone or in teams in government, industry and the universities scattered across the globe. Any individual scientist can, at best, only claim first-hand, personal knowledge of a tiny fraction of the theoretical underpinnings and experimental content of their courtroom testimony. Less dramatically but no less consequentially for this discussion, the generation of scientific evidence is typically a collaborative enterprise. Trace evidence is routinely collected by scenes of crime officers (SOCOs) or Crime Scene Investigators (CSIs) and submitted to the forensic laboratory where one scientist might undertake preliminary screening, subsequently distributing evidential material to a lab technician who prepares samples for a third colleague to undertake scientific testing, ultimately reporting to a fourth, more senior forensic scientist who interprets the test results in a final written report and will later testify to its contents in court if called upon to do so. Strictly speaking, however, most of this report is hearsay, because the testifying expert did not personally collect the samples, conduct the scientific testing, or record the data to which she testifies in court. With the exception of her own interpretations of the raw data, for which she can personally vouch, the scientist can only repeat what she has been told by her colleagues, and this is classically hearsay. The same objection theoretically applies to forensic databases of fingerprints, shoe prints, tool marks, firearms, glass composition, DNA profiles, and so forth, which are likewise compiled over extended periods of time, possibly in multiple locations, by scores or hundreds of individuals who may not even be identifiable at a later date, but at any rate will not be in court to testify to the integrity of the processes for collecting, testing and retaining relevant samples on the basis of their own first-hand, personal knowledge.

The hearsay rule has been characterised, with deliberate ambivalence, as a *theoretical* obstacle to the admissibility of forensic science evidence in criminal trials. In fact, the courts have pragmatically acknowledged the enormous probative potential of scientific evidence for criminal adjudication, and expert evidence has largely been exempted from the operation of the hearsay prohibition. Information derived from general scientific literature, reference works, experimental data and the common store of scientific knowledge is admissible in court provided that it is incorporated into, or subsumed within, the 'opinion' of an appropriately qualified expert witness.[39] Evidence of 'matches' between crime scene trace evidence and samples or data contained on large-scale criminal justice databases are also admissible.[40] It might be thought that any other conclusion would be idiotic, in view of the tried-and-tested probative value of scientific data. However, the hearsay rule is a doctrine of conceptual logic rather than common sense, and it sometimes leads to counter-intuitive results, including, in the past, the exclusion of apparently reliable database evidence which cannot be 'laundered' through expert testimony.[41] Section 127 of the Criminal Justice Act 2003 now formally empowers expert witnesses to testify to data, test results and other information supplied by their scientific colleagues, so long as each person who contributed to the final report is clearly identified and the court is satisfied that proceeding in this way without requiring every scientific collaborator to testify in person is consistent with the interests of justice.

Whilst core scientific knowledge and original experimental data and test results are now relatively insulated from legal challenge on hearsay grounds, forensic scientists must still be cautious about their use of second-hand information relating to the current proceedings when writing their reports and testifying in court. For example, case details divulged to a forensic scientist by an investigating police officer, no less than factual information provided to the doctor who examines an injured complainant or to a psychiatrist whilst interviewing the accused,[42] are all hearsay, and their legal status should be clearly flagged if experts make any reference to such alleged facts in their reports or testimony. Where an expert's conclusions are built upon particular factual assumptions, the expert's evidence is not even admissible, let alone persuasive, until the party calling the expert has laid an appropriate evidential foundation by proving the assumed facts through admissible, non-hearsay, evidence (Roberts 1996). If after the expert has already testified it turns out that these essential factual predicates cannot be established, the jury will be instructed to disregard the expert's evidence in its entirety. Scientific evidence which, although internally valid, has no legitimate factual connection to the matters disputed in the trial is legally irrelevant, and therefore inadmissible.

### Character evidence

English penal law aims to punish individuals for their criminal conduct: sin, rather than sinful personality, is the primary target of penal censure. This fundamental ideological commitment is clearly reflected in traditional common law doctrines. A criminal trial is an investigation into particularised allegations of wrongdoing, not a wide-ranging evaluation of the accused's whole life and moral character. To the extent that character may be probative of conduct, however, there is room for admitting general character evidence at trial as material proof of the instant charge(s). This inferential logic applies to witnesses and complainants, whose character might be thought to shed light both on the events currently in dispute and on individuals' testimonial credibility as witnesses in court. It also applies to the accused, who might, for example, have committed similar offences in the past or revealed distinctive criminal tendencies through his previous behaviour.

Routine reliance by the prosecution on evidence of the accused's previous convictions or other extraneous misconduct has generally been regarded throughout the common law world as unfairly prejudicial. Such evidence is not normally admissible unless its probative value is compelling.[43] The Criminal Justice Act 2003 has recently relaxed English law's traditional aversion to character-based proofs, but evidence of the accused's extraneous misconduct still remains subject to a special evidentiary regime requiring more than bare relevance to secure its admissibility at trial.[44]

Forensic science evidence limited to proving the accused's involvement in a particular crime will not normally stray onto bad character territory. Trace evidence tending to prove the accused's presence at the scene of the crime, for example, is direct proof of the current allegation, not an exposé of extraneous bad character. It is conceivable that scientific evidence might be employed to link the accused to uncharged – or even previously acquitted (Roberts 2000) – crimes in order to demonstrate the accused's propensity for committing the type of offence currently before the court, in which case the evidence must satisfy the additional admissibility criteria specified by ss. 101–106 of the Criminal Justice Act 2003. If the evidence is excluded, this will not reflect any inherent scientific defect, but rather the court's judgement that revelations of extraneous misconduct would be unfairly prejudicial and disproportionate to the probative value of the evidence.

Fingerprint evidence and DNA matches potentially engage the law of bad character in more subtle ways. If it emerges during the course of a trial that the accused was first identified from a fingerprint left at a crime scene, or by a DNA profile derived from the NDNAD, a savvy juror could easily infer that the accused must already have been 'known to the police'. In the past, only those who were convicted of criminal offences had their genetic information loaded on to the NDNAD and their fingerprints retained, so an individual's inclusion on these police databases was a reasonably reliable indicator of a criminal record. Retention of fingerprints and DNA profiles has rapidly expanded in recent, post 9/11 years, and now extends to people who have never been charged, let alone convicted or acquitted, of a criminal offence.[45] The inference from inclusion on the NDNAD to past criminality has consequently been considerably weakened: but that will not necessarily prevent individual jurors from jumping to the, possibly erroneous, conclusion that the accused must have 'form' because he was initially identified from a DNA profile. Its susceptibility to irregular disclosure of extraneous misconduct and prejudicially misleading impressions has not, thus far, affected the admissibility of identification evidence derived from the NDNAD, which is freely received in English criminal trials. The House of Lords considered, and rejected, a further argument that inclusion on the NDNAD represents a diminished civic status of perpetual suspicion which is incompatible with the right to respect for private and family life guaranteed by Article 8 of the ECHR.[46] In the latest twist in this unfolding saga, the European Court of Human Rights has decided that the indefinite retention of fingerprints and DNA samples from unconvicted suspects is a disproportionate measure which cannot be justified on grounds of crime prevention or public safety under Article 8(2).[47] The British government may be obliged to destroy some 1.6 million fingerprint records and DNA profiles currently held on the NDNAD in consequence of this ruling (Ford 2008).

Character can be good as well as bad. Just as the prosecution may attempt to show that the accused betrays a particular propensity for engaging in distinctive types of criminality, the defence might try to invoke the accused's character and previous conduct in order to persuade the fact-finder that the accused is 'not the sort of person' who would do what he is alleged to have done. Although the accused enjoys an antique dispensation to adduce evidence of good reputation,[48] however, the law has traditionally frowned on self-serving evidence of disposition,[49] which is normally regarded as easily manufactured and probatively inconsequential. Accordingly, the general rule is that a party is prohibited from leading self-serving character evidence to 'bolster the credit' of the party's own witness. This prohibition operates, for example, to prevent a psychiatrist or psychologist who has examined the accused from advising the court that the accused is not a person disposed to violence, or that the accused is a truthful witness.[50] Whether or not the accused was violent on the occasion in question, and whether his courtroom testimony should now be believed, are matters on which the jury is supposed to arrive at its own, common-sense, judgements. It would be different if the accused or another witness was suffering from a clinical condition making him a pathological liar: the jury can always be informed of such expert medical or psychological diagnoses.[51] In recent pronouncements, moreover, the Court of Appeal has indicated somewhat 'greater willingness to accept medical expert evidence on the issue of the credibility of a witness', in accordance with its professed general inclination to be 'more generous towards the admission of expert evidence than was once the case'.[52]

## III. Rules of law specifically regulating the admissibility and interpretation of forensic science evidence

The last section described the principal legal standards regulating the admissibility of all types of evidence in English criminal trials. It also hinted at several additional criteria of admissibility specifically applicable to forensic science evidence, which must now be made explicit. We have already established that, in order to secure its admissibility at trial, forensic science evidence must be relevant to the matters in dispute, consistent with fair trial norms and procedural due process, and compatible with complex legal doctrines pertaining to hearsay and character evidence. We can now add that admissible forensic science evidence must also be (i) helpful to the jury; and (ii) presented by a competent, properly qualified expert. English law, as this section will show, has adopted a notably liberal approach to formulating and applying both sets of criteria. Having completed our survey of admissibility standards, the final part of this section turns to consider the 'forensic reasoning rules' which have attempted, with varying degrees of success, to structure the ways in which lay fact-finders utilise scientific evidence in resolving contested factual issues and arriving at their ultimate verdict.

### Helpfulness – the only essential criterion

There is no comprehensive statutory framework to regulate the admissibility of expert testimony in England and Wales, nor any dedicated legislative provisions governing the admissibility of particular types of scientific evidence. The applicable rules are almost entirely derived from judge-made case law precedents. Whilst commentators have advanced competing interpretations of this expanding corpus, the one and only overriding desideratum consistently reiterated by the courts is that expert evidence should be helpful to the jury in resolving disputed questions of fact. Forensic science evidence, moreover, must render this practical assistance without usurping the jury's ultimate responsibility for fact-finding,[53] breaching other evidentiary standards (including the rules of admissibility surveyed in the last section), or otherwise turning out to be more trouble than it is worth in facilitating the administration of criminal justice.

In the leading case of *Turner*,[54] the question for the Court of Appeal was whether an accused charged with murdering his girlfriend could adduce psychiatric evidence to support a plea of provocation. In a passage which has subsequently attracted extensive critical commentary, Lawton LJ explained that the trial judge had correctly excluded psychiatric evidence tendered by the defence, on the grounds that it would not have assisted the jury's deliberations in this particular trial:

> An expert's opinion is admissible to furnish the court with scientific information which is likely to be outside the experience and knowledge of a judge or jury. If on the proven facts a judge or jury can form their own conclusions without help, then the opinion of an expert is unnecessary ... We all know that both men and women who are deeply in love can, and sometimes do, have outbursts of blind rage when discovering unexpected wantonness on the part of their loved ones; the wife taken in adultery is the classical example of the application of the defence of 'provocation': and when death or serious injury results, profound grief usually follows. Jurors do not need psychiatrists to tell them how ordinary folk who are not suffering from any mental illness are likely to react to the stresses and strains of life. It follows that the proposed evidence was not admissible to establish that the defendant was likely to have been provoked ... [W]e are firmly of the opinion that psychiatry has not yet become a satisfactory substitute for the common sense of juries or magistrates on matters within their experience of life.[55]

This passage has been taken as authority for the existence of a 'common knowledge' rule, according to which expert evidence cannot be admitted if it concerns matters within the knowledge and experience of 'ordinary folk' (Mackay and Colman 1991; Freckelton 1987: ch. 3). Alternatively, or in addition, *Turner* is said to imply that expert evidence must be confined to mental abnormality as opposed to normal mental or psychological processes – an 'abnormality rule' of admissibility (Sheldon and MacLeod 1991; Thornton 1995). More generally, Lawton LJ's observations are held up as a typical example of legal ignorance and hostility towards science in general, and mental health professionals in particular. As later decisions have tended to confirm, however, Lawton LJ probably meant to insist on nothing more tendentious than this banal proposition: expert evidence should only be admitted in criminal trials when, and to the extent that, it is likely to be genuinely helpful to the jury.

*Turner's* critics rightly insist that expert testimony might still be helpful even if it concerns matters within jurors' broad general knowledge or questions of normal human psychology. Jurors are unlikely to share an expert's detailed, systematic knowledge of specific aspects of normal psychological processes, for example. Where 'common sense' beliefs are a witches' brew of genuine knowledge, mangled half-truths, urban myth and popular invention, an expert might be able to help jurors disentangle fact from fiction so that they can evaluate the disputed evidence more objectively. It is for these sound reasons that the courts do *not* routinely insist on any 'common knowledge' or 'abnormality' criterion: such tests are rarely more than rough rules of thumb to guide the application of the helpfulness standard in particular cases.[56] A clear illustration is *Stockwell*,[57] which concerned expert 'facial mapping' evidence identifying the accused from security camera footage of a robbery. Having quoted from the relevant passage in *Turner*, Lord Taylor continued:

> It is to be noted that Lawton LJ there referred to a jury forming their own conclusions 'without help'. Where, for example, there is a clear photograph and no suggestion that the subject has changed his appearance, a jury could usually reach a conclusion without help. Where, as here, however, it is admitted that the appellant had grown a beard shortly before his arrest, and it is suggested further that the robber may have been wearing clear spectacles and a wig for disguise, a comparison of photograph and defendant may not be straightforward. In such circumstances we can see no reason why expert evidence, if it can provide the jury with information and assistance they would otherwise lack, should not be given. In each case it must be for the judge to decide whether the issue is one on which the jury could be assisted by expert evidence ...[58]

If English law really did propound a 'common knowledge' rule, expert evidence of identification from a photograph could not have been received in *Stockwell*. Looking at photographs is hardly an arcane activity, yet the Court of Appeal endorsed the reception of expert evidence where it was felt that jurors would benefit from further assistance in a matter well within their everyday experience. Nor is any supposed 'abnormality rule' consistently supported in the cases. Courts have received expert evidence of child psychology, for example, without any suggestion that children, as a class, are 'abnormal' or beyond the experience of ordinary people.[59] Helpfulness, however, is a composite standard incorporating negative as well as positive considerations, and this is something *Turner's* critics tend to overlook.

The historical record of miscarriages of justice (Nobles and Schiff 2004; Edmond 2002; Walker and Stockdale 1999; Jones 1994: ch. 10) should be a constant reminder that expert evidence imports risks, as well as major benefits, into criminal litigation. Beyond the diffuse background fear that charlatan experts or bogus science might infect particular proceedings (topics to which we will return in this chapter's concluding section), even authentic expert evidence may be misinterpreted or misunderstood, divert jurors' attention into collateral issues, or waste time with cumulative proof of points already well established by other evidence. Some forms of expert evidence may be especially prone to misinterpretation. It is widely held, for example, that lay jurors have a poor grasp of statistical evidence, though there is disagreement about whether fact-finders are overawed by statistics or more commonly underestimate their true value (Allen and Roberts 2007; Koehler 2001; Lempert 1991; Tribe 1971).

The judgement that proffered expert evidence is 'helpful' to the jury, and therefore admissible at trial, must arbitrate between numerous factors arguing for and against admissibility. It is understandable that the language in which judges sometimes choose to couch their admissibility determinations – 'common knowledge', 'abnormality', 'ordinary folk', etc. – should be seized on by commentators as expressing the full force of law. However, none of these catchphrases has ever really caught on, and they are not a reliable guide to judicial practice in future proceedings. Helpfulness is the only key necessary to unlock the logic of admissibility decisions. Whether expert evidence will actually be admitted on any particular occasion turns on a detailed evaluation of all the available evidence viewed in light of the parties' respective litigation strategies, a factual matrix which will necessarily vary enormously from one trial to the next. Appellate judges' highly context-sensitive assessments of the admissibility of expert evidence in the current proceedings may consequently be of limited value as legal precedents in subsequent cases.

### Expert qualification

English courts have demonstrated similar flexibility in their assessments of experts' scientific credentials. The legal test of competence for expert witnesses adds little if anything to the basic relevancy standard, and operates in practice to promote the reception of expert testimony.

There is no requirement of formal training or paper qualifications, professional practice, or even membership of a relevant organisation or learned society. The well-known case of *Silverlock*[60] decided that a witness's informal interest and study were sufficient to qualify him as an expert in handwriting analysis. As Lord Russell of Killowen CJ explained, the question is simply whether or not the witness possesses expert knowledge relevant to an issue before the tribunal, irrespective of how he or she might have acquired it:

> It is true that the witness who is called upon to give evidence founded on a comparison of handwritings must be *peritus*; he must be skilled in doing so; but we cannot say that he must have become *peritus* in the way of his business or in any definite way. The question is, is he *peritus*? Is he skilled? Has he an adequate knowledge? Looking at the matter practically, if a witness is not skilled the judge will tell the jury to disregard his evidence. There is no decision which requires that the evidence of a man who is skilled in comparing handwriting, and who has formed a reliable opinion from past experience, should be excluded because his experience had not been gained in the way of his business.[61]

It is not difficult to find case law illustrations of the courts' catholic conception of expertise. A drug user with no scientific training or knowledge has been permitted to identify a substance in his possession as cannabis,[62] whilst a police officer with experience in drug offences could testify as an expert on the street price of heroin.[63] In 1993 the Court of Appeal said that it was perfectly proper for an artist to give 'facial mapping' evidence, even though he had 'no scientific qualifications, no specific training, no professional body and no database'.[64] In another case, membership of the Inner Circle of Magic qualified a witness as 'a highly expert magician'.[65] Just about anybody who can provide the jury with specialist information relevant to the proceedings qualifies as an 'expert' in English law.

### Forensic reasoning rules interpreting scientific evidence

The law of evidence is not exhausted by questions of admissibility. It also aspires to regulate the ways in which fact-finders reason about evidence, chiefly through the mechanism of judicial directions to the jury given as part of the judge's 'summing-up' at the close of the trial. Some of these 'forensic reasoning rules' impose mandatory directions. For example, the trial judge is always obliged to direct the jury on the burden and standard of proof. Other rules empower the trial judge to give discretionary directions in appropriate cases. Forensic reasoning rules of this type have been proliferating in recent years (Roberts and Zuckerman 2004: ch. 10). They typically draw the jury's attention to the inherent infirmities of particular sorts of evidence, such as eye-witness identifications[66] or the incriminating testimony of an erstwhile accomplice,[67] or warn the jury to resist slipping into enticing reasoning fallacies, such as misinterpreting the probative significance of a lie and other forms of evidential 'double-counting'.[68]

We have already adverted to one forensic reasoning rule applicable to scientific evidence, namely, the judicial admonition in *Davie* v. *Edinburgh Magistrates* that jurors must decide all factual questions for themselves, even if they have heard uncontradicted expert testimony which appears to resolve the matter in question. This injunction cuts across the complex dynamic between juror education and juror deference in criminal adjudication.[69] Another long-running saga concerns the appropriate way of directing juries in relation to statistical evidence, an issue that has arisen most pointedly in recent years in relation to DNA profiling testimony.

DNA evidence is founded on the conjunction of two scientific specialisms, genetics and demography (or 'biometrics'). The properties of the DNA molecule, through which individuals can be identified from even the smallest amounts of their genetic material such as a few epithelial skin cells or a hair follicle, are biological. In order to assess the probative significance of DNA evidence, however, it is necessary to estimate the likelihood that a 'false positive' match between a crime stain sample and the accused's DNA profile might have identified the wrong person by a random fluke of chance. This is achieved by statistical forecasts estimating the number of individuals in the relevant suspect population who might be expected to share the same profile as the real culprit, bearing in mind that forensic DNA profiles are extracted from only a tiny fraction of a person's complete genetic code. Although – as far as we know – each person's DNA is unique to that individual (or shared only by identical twins), his or her selectively sampled forensic DNA profile may not be. DNA profiling has become increasingly refined and powerfully discriminating since its first forensic applications in the mid 1980s, so that the chances of an adventitious match are now said to be in the order of a billion to one against.[70] Assuming the reliability of such estimates, this still leaves unanswered the closely related questions of how best to present DNA evidence to the jury during the course of the trial, and what, if anything, trial judges should tell juries about DNA evidence when summing up at the close of proceedings. During the 1990s, the Court of Appeal was obliged to grapple with these issues in a trilogy of cases with defendants called Adams.

The 'Adams family' is best approached out of chronological sequence, starting with the conjoined appeals of *Doheny and Adams*[71] (which is actually the second case in the trilogy). In *Doheny* the Court of Appeal squarely confronted the issue of how DNA evidence should be presented to a jury, and a notably cautious approach was advocated. Experts should confine their testimony to DNA comparisons expressed in terms of 'the random occurrence ratio', which is the probability that the accused's DNA profile would match a crime stain sample purely by chance. Experts must of course avoid the solecism of expressing any opinion about the accused's guilt ('the ultimate issue'), which is a question for the jury, taking account of all the evidence in the case, not just DNA evidence. However, the Court of Appeal went considerably further in insisting that a scientist 'should not be asked his opinion on the likelihood that it was the defendant who left the crime stain, nor when giving evidence should he use terminology which may lead the jury to believe that he is expressing such an opinion'.[72] Expert testimony confined to the random occurrence (a.k.a. 'random match') ratio would enable the trial judge to direct the jury along the following lines:

> Members of the jury, if you accept the scientific evidence called by the Crown, this indicates that there are probably only four or five white males in the United Kingdom from whom that [crime] stain could have come. The defendant is one of them. If that is the position, the decision you have to reach, on all the evidence, is whether you are sure that it was the defendant who left that stain or whether it is possible that it was one of that other small group of men who share the same DNA characteristics.[73]

Why is the expert, on this studiously cautious approach, not even allowed to say that DNA evidence places the accused at the scene of the crime with a quantifiably very high degree of probability? The answer is that the courts are striving to protect jurors from drawing faulty inferences, and in particular to prevent them from slipping into the notorious 'prosecutor's fallacy'. The prosecutor's fallacy can be formulated in various ways. This is the version suggested by the Court of Appeal in *Doheny*:

1  Only one person in a million will have a DNA profile which matches that of the crime stain.
2  The defendant has a DNA profile which matches the crime stain.
3  Ergo there is a million to one probability that the defendant left the crime stain and is guilty of the crime.[74]

Attractive though this line of reasoning might at first sight appear to be, it is clearly fallacious. If the relevant potential suspect population includes, say, four million people, then fully four of these individuals would be expected to have DNA profiles matching the crime stain. Taken in isolation, this is only a 1-in-4 (25 per cent) chance of guilt, or odds of 1:3 – a very long way away from the one-in-a-million chance of *innocence* proposed by the prosecutor's fallacy. Furthermore, as the Court's hypothetical deduction (3) correctly implies, a random match probability should not even be equated with the probability that the accused left the crime stain, let alone that he is guilty of the crime charged. It is impossible to calculate the probability that the accused left the crime stain without first trying to estimate the size of the suspect population, which, taking account of all the other evidence in the case, could be just a handful of suspects, or might be more in the order of every male in a radius of 100 miles. Allowances should also be made for confounding factors such as the possibility of sample contamination or laboratory testing error (Donnelly and Friedman 1999).

The Court of Appeal found that versions of the prosecutor's fallacy had been committed by the forensic scientists, and then repeated by the judges in summing up their evidence to the jury, in the trials of both Doheny and Adams. However, in neither case was the error held to be fatal to the safety of the accused's conviction, principally because the mild version of the fallacy (equating the random occurrence ratio with the probability that the accused left the crime stain) is essentially harmless when the random occurrence ratio is very small. As the forensic scientist who testified at Adams's trial explained, 'there probably are only 27 million male people in the whole of the United Kingdom so a figure of 1 in 27 million does tend to imply that it is extremely likely there is only really one man in the whole of the United Kingdom who has this DNA profile'.[75] Doheny's appeal was still allowed, notwithstanding this convenient neutralisation of the prosecutor's fallacy, because the forensic scientist in his case had also illegitimately multiplied together two random occurrence ratios, to produce a composite ratio of 1 in 40 million, without first ensuring that the two ratios were truly independent of each other. This was an elementary statistical error,[76] which seriously undermined the sustainability of Doheny's conviction. On other occasions, however, it has been the complexity of proposed mathematical solutions rather than the simplicity of statistical fallacies that has exercised the Court of Appeal.

The other two *Adams* cases both involved the same defendant. Denis Adams was convicted of rape exclusively on the basis of DNA evidence. He successfully appealed against this conviction,[77] but was convicted again at a retrial, and then launched a second, this time unsuccessful, appeal.[78] At both trials a prosecution expert witness testified that Adams's DNA matched the assailant's, and that the odds against achieving such a match purely by chance were over 200 million to 1 against. In reply, the defence called its own expert statistician to demonstrate the salience of Bayes' Theorem (Redmayne 1998; Allen and Redmayne 1997; Robertson and Vignaux 1995) to the issues before the court. By assigning probability estimates to the hypothesis that the rapist would have been a local man and to the complainant's failure to pick out Adams at an identity parade, and making several other estimates and assumptions, the defence expert purported to demonstrate that the impact of the DNA evidence was far less dramatic than figures such as '200 million to 1' might suggest. On this expert's assumptions and calculations, for example, the prosecution's case favoured guilt by a ratio of 55 to 1, or to a probability of a little over 98 per cent. On the assumption that if Adams left the crime scene stain he was also guilty of rape, this is still, of course, a very high probability of guilt. Nonetheless a 2 per cent chance of innocence sounds, and is in fact, much better odds than one chance in 200 million, which equates to a 99.9999995 per cent probability of guilt.

With evident reluctance, the Court of Appeal allowed Adams's first appeal against conviction on the ground that the judge had failed to give an adequate direction to the jury on how they should go about evaluating the statistical evidence before them. But in the course of ordering a retrial, Lord Justice Rose dropped heavy hints that the Court was not at all impressed by Bayes' Theorem:

> [W]hatever the merits or demerits of the Bayes Theorem in mathematical or statistical assessments of probability, it seems to us that it is not appropriate for use in jury trials, or as a means to assist the jury in their task ... [T]he attempt to determine guilt or innocence on the basis of a mathematical formula, applied to each separate piece of evidence, is simply inappropriate to the jury's task. Jurors evaluate evidence and reach a conclusion not by means of a formula, mathematical or otherwise, but by the joint application of their individual common sense and knowledge of the world to the evidence before them.[79]

For all that, the defence evidently decided not to take the hint. At Adams's retrial, experts instructed by the defence team went even further than before, presenting a comprehensive Bayesian analysis of the evidence in meticulous detail. They even provided jurors with a questionnaire outlining each stage of the Bayesian approach so that, if jurors accepted defence counsel's invitation to adopt that style of reasoning, jurors could perform their own calculations in the jury room. Adams's second appeal against conviction once again complained of inadequacies in the judge's summing-up regarding statistical evidence. This time dismissing the appeal in *Adams (No. 2)*, the Court of Appeal reiterated its dissatisfaction with probabilistic approaches to non-statistical evidence, and spelt out the evidentiary consequences:

> [W]e regard the reliance on evidence of this kind ... as a recipe for confusion, misunderstanding and misjudgment, possibly even among counsel, but very probably among judges and, as we conclude, almost certainly among jurors. It would seem to us that this was a case properly approached by the jury along conventional lines ... We do not consider that [juries] will be assisted in their task by reference to a very complex approach which they are unlikely to understand fully and even more unlikely to apply accurately, which we judge to be likely to confuse them and distract them from their consideration of the real questions on which they should seek to reach a unanimous conclusion. We are

very clearly of opinion that in cases such as this, lacking special features absent here, expert evidence should not be admitted to induce juries to attach mathematical values to probabilities arising from non-scientific evidence adduced at the trial.[80]

The Court of Appeal's agitated response to the introduction of Bayes' Theorem in the *Adams* litigation epitomises the orthodox Anglo-American approach to forensic fact-finding. Juries and magistrates are expected to marshal relevant generalisations from their own knowledge and experience, which they then bring to bear on the matters in dispute (Anderson 1999). As autonomous fact-finders, presumed to have the resources of common-sense reasoning at their disposal, they are largely left to their own devices in drawing inferences about facts. Moreover, the 'ultimate issue' of determining the accused's guilt or innocence is always reserved to the fact-finder. Whilst expert testimony is received enthusiastically in appropriate cases, the courts are assiduous in ensuring that 'trial by expert', or even 'trial by science', is never allowed to usurp the constitutional functions of trial by judge and jury. As Lawton LJ memorably remarked in *Turner*, emphatically rejecting the suggestion that expert psychiatric assessments of ordinary human mental states and emotions should routinely be admitted in English criminal trials:

If any such rule was applied in our courts, trial by psychiatrists would be likely to take the place of trial by jury and magistrates. We do not find that prospect attractive and the law does not at present provide for it ... [W]e are firmly of the opinion that psychiatry has not yet become a satisfactory substitute for the common sense of juries or magistrates on matters within their experience of life.[81]

Although forensic science evidence plainly often exceeds 'the common sense of juries or magistrates on matters within their experience of life' it ultimately shares the same legal status as expert psychiatric testimony, inasmuch as science must defer to legal conceptions of due process and rational fact-finding in criminal adjudication.

## IV. Facing up to the future challenges of scientific innovation

What does the future hold for forensic science evidence in English criminal trials? How are the rules of evidence and procedure which regulate the admissibility and interpretation of scientific evidence likely to evolve in the comings years and decades? Prognostication is always perilous, the more so in relation to scientific and technological innovation, which is characteristically rapid and unpredictable. Still, the best guide to the future is often the past. Looking back over recent experience and its venerable historical antecedents, perhaps the most impressive feature of English law's approach to expert witness testimony has been its receptivity to scientific innovation, novel technological applications and new areas of expertise.

The basic common law tests for expert qualification and the admissibility of scientific evidence have barely altered in modern times. As the new forensic sciences were developed during the course of the twentieth century, culminating in the triumph of DNA profiling, they were quickly and easily incorporated into criminal adjudication through flexible applications of (what we know today as) the *Turner* helpfulness standard. Dedicated legislation was not required to facilitate their admissibility. Of course, there is a downside. The inevitable concomitant of such flexible, open-textured standards is a measure of inconsistency in their judicial application in individual cases, which also introduces an element of unpredictability into the process of instructing experts. A party might have been relying in good faith on particular scientific or other expert evidence, only to find it ruled inadmissible at trial. In addition, there will always be those who think that the law is too slow, and lawyers and judges too arrogant and ignorant, to appreciate the full forensic potential of scientific knowledge in all its various guises. (This attitude is particularly noticeable amongst psychiatrists, psychologists, and other behavioural and social scientists who have personally experienced judicial rejection.) Whatever merit such concerns and objections may have, they seem a small price to pay for English law's overwhelming success in utilising forensic science evidence of all kinds with minimum fuss and effort.

Conversely, it might be said that English law has been rather *too* liberal in receiving scientific evidence in criminal trials (Roberts 2008; Ormerod 2002). For the most part, this chapter has proceeded on the assumption that scientific evidence proffered at trial is theoretically valid and methodologically sound, so that the only real forensic challenge lies in successfully communicating its true meaning to lay judges and jurors in the 'noisy' institutional environment of an adversarial contest. But of course this is only part of the picture. Some purported science is only 'junk science' (Bernstein 1996; Huber 1991); not all forensic experts are properly qualified,[82] and some may be irresponsible charlatans. Even genuine experts may unknowingly propound false theories, make operational errors in their testing or calculations, or overstep the boundaries of their legitimate expertise. The question then arises as to whether criminal trial procedure is sufficiently well insulated from fake science and bogus experts, and capable of distinguishing between valid and invalid scientific claims. Given that the whole system of criminal adjudication is predicated on lay fact-finders utilising ordinary common-sense techniques – principally listening to the testimony and observing the demeanour of witnesses who appear before them in the courtroom – assessing scientific validity obviously poses a major design challenge for English criminal procedure. The House of Commons Science and Technology Committee (2005: [140], [142]) is only the latest in a long line of critics to express dissatisfaction with current arrangements:

During the course of this inquiry we heard much evidence to suggest that the weight ultimately attached to expert evidence by juries is determined in significant part by the way in which the evidence is presented ... We are disappointed to discover such widespread acknowledgement of the influence that the charisma of the expert can have over a jury's response to their testimony, without proportional action to address this problem. If key players in the criminal justice system, including the police and experienced expert witnesses, do not have faith in a jury's ability to distinguish between the strength of evidence and the personality of the expert witness presenting it, it is hard to see why anyone else should.

Recent developments in other common law jurisdictions may provide valuable comparative guidance to law reformers and other policymakers in meeting this challenge in England and Wales. In the Australian state of New South Wales, for example, the admissibility of expert evidence is now governed by statute as part of the comprehensive codification of the law of evidence undertaken in that jurisdiction in the mid 1990s.[83] For other Australian states, in which the common law still prevails, the High Court of Australia has elaborated on the basic *Turner* standard in an attempt to give more detailed guidance to trial judges called upon to determine the admissibility of expert evidence.[84] The Supreme Court of Canada has undertaken a similar exercise for the benefit of Canadian trial judges and legal practitioners.[85] However, the most spectacular doctrinal developments in this field have undoubtedly occurred in the federal courts of the United States.

*Frye* v. *US* was, for 70 years, the leading authority on the admission of novel scientific evidence in US federal and many state criminal proceedings. *Frye* proposed a 'general acceptance' standard:

> Just when a scientific principle or discovery crosses the line between the experimental and demonstrable stages is difficult to define. Somewhere in this twilight zone the evidential force of the principle must be recognized, and while courts will go a long way in admitting expert testimony deduced from a well-recognized scientific principle or discovery, the thing from which the deduction is made must be sufficiently established to have gained *general acceptance in the particular field* to which it belongs.[86]

In 1993, however, the US Supreme Court was invited to reconsider the status of *Frye's* 'general acceptance' test in the light of the Federal Rules of Evidence (FRE), which had come into force in 1976. In *Daubert* v. *Merrell Dow*,[87] a 7–2 majority of the Supreme Court (Rehnquist CJ and Stevens J dissenting in part) held that scientific evidence must be relevant *and reliable* in order to be admitted in legal proceedings. A trial judge should consequently pay particular regard to four criteria when determining the admissibility of novel scientific evidence: (1) whether the theory or technique underpinning the evidence has undergone testing and withstood the scientific process of falsifiability; (2) whether it has been subjected to peer review and publication in refereed journals; (3) its known or potential error rate; and (4) whether the theory or technique enjoys the support of some relevant scientific community or communities (a nod in the direction of *Frye*, which is preserved by incorporation to this extent). *Daubert* provoked extensive discussion and a deluge of academic commentary, much of it notably critical of the Court's reasoning and allegedly tenuous grasp of scientific methodology. The

Court was subsequently obliged to hear two further appeals in fairly quick succession in order to clarify the implications of its *Daubert* ruling.[88] Thereafter, the position seems to have stabilised at the Supreme Court level, and FRE Rule 702 was amended to take account of the impact of the *'Daubert* trilogy' (Berger 2000).[89]

English law has thus far experienced nothing comparable to the seismic impact of *Daubert* on the legal tests for admitting expert evidence. English authorities have not even traditionally insisted on a *Frye*-type standard, which would restrict the scope of expert testimony to recognised branches of scientific inquiry or institutionalised disciplines with supporting infrastructures and professionally conducted research. As Bingham LJ explained in *Robb*:

> The old-established, academically-based sciences such as medicine, geology or metallurgy, and the established professions such as architecture, quantity surveying or engineering, present no problem. The field will be regarded as one in which expertise may exist and any properly qualified member will be accepted without question as an expert. Expert evidence is not, however, limited to those core areas. Expert evidence of finger-prints, hand-writing and accident reconstruction is regularly given. Opinions may be given of the market value of land, ships, pictures or rights. Expert opinions may be given of the quality of commodities, or on the literary, artistic, scientific or other merit of works alleged to be obscene (Obscene Publications Act 1959, s. 4(2)). Some of these fields are far removed from anything which could be called a formal scientific discipline.[90]

The issue on appeal in *Robb* concerned evidence of voice identification. An expert instructed by the prosecution, Dr Baldwin, had listened to tape recordings of telephone calls containing ransom demands and concluded that there was a precise match between the accused's voice and the voice of the unknown blackmailer who made the calls. Albeit intimating that this was a borderline case, the Court of Appeal nonetheless endorsed the trial judge's decision to admit Dr Baldwin's evidence. Though apparently highly unorthodox, Dr Baldwin's exclusive reliance on auditory techniques – basically just careful repeated listening unaided by quantitative analysis of speech patterns – was no barrier to admissibility in this case:

> The great weight of informed opinion, including the world leaders in the field, was to the effect that auditory techniques unless supplemented and verified by acoustic analysis were an unreliable basis of speaker identification … A unit recently established in Germany under a respected director rejected identification based on auditory techniques alone. Other Western European countries did not receive such evidence. There were only a handful of others, and they were in this country, who shared Dr Baldwin's opinion. He had published no material which would allow his methods to be tested or his results checked. He had conducted no experiments or tests on the accuracy of his own conclusions. Despite all this, Dr Baldwin's opinion remained that acoustic analysis itself called

for interpretation. Voice identification was not an exact science. While accepting that he could be wrong, Dr Baldwin was led by his experience and training to believe that his conclusions were reliable. Acoustic analysis was a possible, but not in his view a necessary, supplement. If he thought otherwise he would adopt that technique also, but he did not. His opinion remained that the voice on the disputed tapes and the control tape was the same ... Dr Baldwin's reliance on the auditory technique must, on the evidence, be regarded as representing a minority view in his profession but he had reasons for his preference and on the facts of this case he was not shown to be wrong.[91]

It is unlikely that Dr Baldwin's evidence would have been admitted under a *Daubert* standard, and it might not even have satisfied the less stringent *Frye* test. The Northern Ireland Court of Appeal subsequently held that cases resting substantially on auditory voice identification should not generally be brought to trial,[92] but even though some judges might not be entirely comfortable with the specific holding in *Robb*, the English Court of Appeal has expressly declined to follow the Northern Irish courts' rejection of expert voice identification based on auditory techniques.[93] Lord Bingham's judgment in *Robb* still stands as an implicit rejection of any formal 'field of expertise' rule to regulate the admission of expert evidence in English criminal trials.

The suggestion has nonetheless been advanced that English law does, after all, apply a *Frye*-style 'general acceptance' standard to novel or disputed forms of scientific expertise (Roberts 2008). Lord Justice Rose has been the chief judicial proponent of this revisionist interpretation,[94] although English legal authority is suspiciously flimsy.[95] The question remains whether English law should in principle embrace a 'general acceptance' standard, or even possibly develop more detailed and demanding criteria to regulate the admissibility of scientific evidence in criminal proceedings. A further step might be to enact dedicated legislation akin to US FRE 702, to rationalise the law of expert evidence and place it on a more secure statutory footing. At the time of writing, the Law Commission is actively considering this option (LCCP No 190, 2009). Such radical reform of the rules of admissibility would need to be accompanied by appropriate judicial training and technical support to enable trial judges to make informed assessments of the scientific validity of contested theories and techniques. Procedural rules, such as those relating to pre-trial disclosure, might also need to be reconsidered, in order to ensure that litigants are adequately informed and properly equipped to debate the merits of contested scientific evidence within the context of an adversarial trial process.

The comparatively primitive condition of English law's rules of admissibility might induce one to believe that criminal adjudication cannot muddle along in this pragmatic fashion indefinitely, that '[s]omething has to give soon' (O'Brian 2003: 184). But this is to underestimate the resilience, and indeed the genuine strengths and advantages, of the common law's flexible approach to the reception of expert evidence in criminal trials, which has served the courts well enough, from a practical point of view, for several centuries. Moreover, trial judges may soon be deriving a previously unavailable level of assistance from renewed, officially sanctioned, efforts to develop robust systems of formal accreditation for expert witnesses. Prior to its sudden demise, the Council for the Registration of Forensic Practitioners (CRFP)[96] was aspiring to become a single point of reference, listing all the recognised forensic sciences and their appropriately qualified practitioners – a kind of 'bible' of forensic sciences for the benefit of all criminal justice professionals. This mantle is now expected to pass to the Forensic Science Regulator and the Forensic Science Advisory Council (FSAC). Effectively 'outsourcing' judgements of scientific validity and expert witness qualification to government-sponsored accreditation and self-regulatory peer review may prove to be an elegant and durable alternative to *Daubert*-style validity hearings. Even then, there are always going to be arcane sciences and dilettante or maverick experts who elude mainstream classification, leaving judges with an inescapable residual role in determining the boundaries of forensically legitimate scientific expertise. The extent to which the Court of Appeal will be inclined, or able, to provide general guidance to trial judges on making context-sensitive determinations of scientific validity (Beecher-Monas 2000) and assessing the competence of individual experts remains to be seen (cf. Risinger 2007).

Scientific innovation, in the immediate and longer-term future, is likely to continue to demand flexible legal thinking, normative development and imaginative institutional responses. However, the reform of law and legal institutions will not be dictated by an exclusively scientific agenda, implicitly equating justice with reliable evidence and factual proof. For as this chapter has laboured to explain, forensic science evidence must ultimately conform to the local procedural culture and official political morality of criminal adjudication. In England and Wales, criminal trials will continue to be characterised by party-dominated adversarial contests, commonsensical lay fact-finding and an ideological preference for oral witness testimony, at least for the foreseeable future. Forensic scientists who appear as expert witnesses in English criminal courts must recognise and learn to live within these normative commitments and their associated procedural conventions, even if the unflinchingly rationalist scientific mind is unwilling or incapable of growing to love them.

## Notes

1 The rate of 'attrition' in English criminal proceedings can be calculated in different ways, and varies by offence category. Overall, the clear-up rate for police recorded crime is about 28 per cent, or less than 14 per cent of crimes reported to the annual British Crime Survey (Kershaw *et al.* 2008). In 2007, a little over 8 per cent of police recorded crime (4 per cent of BCS-reported crimes) resulted in court proceedings (Ministry of Justice 2008).

2 In 2007, the guilty plea rate for indictable proceedings in the Crown Court was 68 per cent. The comparable figure for cases conducted by the Crown Prosecution Service in the magistrates' courts was 67 per cent (Ministry of Justice 2008: 12–13).

3 Some cases in the magistrates' courts are heard by a single professional judge.

4 *Buckley* v. *Rice Thomas* (1554) 1 Plowden 118, CB; *Folkes* v. *Chadd* (1782) 3 Doug KB 157.

5 *Davie* v. *Edinburgh Magistrates* [1953] SC 34, 40; endorsed, for example, in *R* v. *Gilfoyle* [2001] 2 Cr App R 57, CA, 67; *R* v. *JP* [1999] Crim LR 401 (Transcript on LEXIS).

6 *R* v. *Ponting* [1985] Crim LR 318, Central Criminal Court.

7 Theft Act 1968, s.2; *R* v. *Ghosh* [1982] QB 1053, CA.

8 Homicide Act 1957, s.2.

9 *R* v. *Byrne* [1960] 2 QB 396, 403–4; *R* v. *Dietschmann* [2003] 1 AC 1209, HL. But cf. *R* v. *Matheson* [1958] 1 WLR 474; *R* v. *Bailey* (1978) 66 Cr App R 31, 32 (suggesting that, although 'of course juries are not bound by what the medical witnesses say', yet 'at the same time they must act on evidence, and if there is nothing before them, no facts and no circumstances shown before them which throw doubt on the medical evidence, then that is all that they are left with, and the jury, in those circumstances, must accept it').

10 Criminal Procedure Rules (CrimPR) 2005, Rule 1.1.

11 *R* v. *Harris*; *R* v. *Rock*; *R* v. *Cherry*; *R* v. *Faulder* [2006] 1 Cr App R 5, [267]-[274]; *R* v. *B(T)* [2006] 2 Cr App R 3, [174]-[178].

12 This seemingly follows from the trial judge's general residual discretion to call any witness of fact in the interests of justice: *R* v. *Roberts* (1985) 80 Cr App R 89, CA; *R* v. *Cleghorn* [1967] 2 QB 584, CA. In former times court-appointed experts were the norm (Hand 1901), though modern authority for the continued existence of a residual judicial power to instruct court-appointed experts is admittedly sparse: e.g. *R* v. *Holden* (1838) 8 Car & P 606, 173 ER 638. Also see CrimPR 2005, Rule 33.7 (power of court to direct single joint expert).

13 '[T]o be relevant the evidence need merely have some tendency in logic and common sense to advance the proposition in issue': *R* v. *A (No. 2)* [2002] 1 AC 45, [31] (Lord Steyn).

14 *Ramanauskas* v. *Lithuania*, App No 74420/01, ECtHR Judgement 5 February 2008; *Teixeira de Castro* v. *Portugal* (1998) 28 EHRR 101, ECtHR.

15 *Jalloh* v. *Germany* (2007) 44 EHRR 32, ECtHR (Grand Chamber); *Allan* v. *United Kingdom* (2003) 36 EHRR 143, ECtHR; *Saunders* v. *UK* (1996) 23 EHRR 313, ECtHR.

16 *Edwards and Lewis* v. *UK* (2005) 40 EHRR 24, ECtHR (Grand Chamber); *Rowe and Davis* v. *UK* (2000) 30 EHRR 1, ECtHR; *Edwards* v. *UK* (1993) 15 EHRR 417, ECtHR.

17 *R* v. *Flynn and St John* [2008] 2 Cr App R 20, CA.

18 *Fox* v. *Chief Constable of Gwent* [1986] 1 AC 281, HL (Lord Fraser); *R* v. *Leatham* (1861) 8 Cox CC 498 (Crompton J.).

19 *R* v. *Keenan* [1990] 2 QB 54, CA.

20 *R* v. *Sang* [1980] AC 402, HL.

21 *R* v. *Looseley*; *Attorney General's Reference (No. 3 of 2000)* [2001] UKHL 53, [2001] 1 WLR 2060.

22 PACE 1984, s. 61; PACE Code of Practice D (2008 edition), Part 4(A).

23 PACE 1984, ss. 54–55; PACE Code of Practice B (2008 edition), Part 7.

24 PACE 1984, ss. 63 and 63A(2); PACE Code of Practice D (2008 edition), Part 6.

25 PACE 1984, s. 63A(1).

26 *Attorney General's Reference (No. 3 of 1999)* [2001] 2 AC 91, HL.

27 That is, privately owned land to which the public have general access, such as shopping centres, car parks and universities.

28 e.g. *R* v. *Lawson* [2007] 1 WLR 1191, CA; *R* v. *Clare and Peach* [1995] 2 Cr App R 333, CA.

29  *R v. Khan (Sultan)* [1997] AC 558, HL; *Khan v. UK* (2001) 31 EHRR 45, ECtHR.

30  Regulation of Investigatory Powers Act (RIPA) 2000, Part I. Unauthorised eavesdropping is itself a criminal offence: RIPA 2000, s.1.

31  RIPA 2000, s. 17.

32  cf. PACE 1984, s. 76(4).

33  *Mapp v. Ohio*, 367 US 643, 81 S.Ct. 1684 (US Supreme Court, 1961). But now see *Hudson v. Michigan*, 547 US 586, 126 S.Ct. 2159 (US Supreme Court, 2006).

34  Criminal Procedure and Investigations Act 1996, Part I (as amended); *Attorney General's Guidelines on Disclosure*, online at: www.attorneygeneral.gov.uk/attachments/disclosure.doc.

35  *R v. Preston* [1994] 2 AC 130, HL; CrimPR 2005, Part 24.

36  *R v. Ward* (1993) 96 Cr App R 1 CA, 50–51.

37  Ibid. 49.

38  Now see Criminal Justice Act 2003, ss.114 and 115.

39  *Davie v. Edinburgh Magistrates* [1953] SC 34; *R v. Harris; R v. Rock; R v. Cherry; R v. Faulder* [2006] 1 Cr App R 5, CA. Also see CJA 2003, s. 118(1) rules 1 and 8.

40  *R v. Abadom* [1983] 1 WLR 126, CA; *R v. Kempster (No. 2)* [2008] 2 Cr App R 19, CA.

41  *Myers v. DPP* [1965] AC 1001, HL.

42  *R v. Hurst* [1995] 1 Cr App R 82, CA.

43  *DPP v. Boardman* [1975] AC 421, HL; *Makin v. AG for New South Wales* [1894] AC 57, PC.

44  CJA 2003, ss. 101–106.

45  PACE 1984, s. 64, as amended by the Criminal Justice and Police Act 2001, s. 82.

46  *R (S) v. Chief Constable of South Yorkshire Police* [2004] 1 WLR 2196, HL.

47  *S and Marper v. UK*, App Nos 30562/04 and 30566/04, ECtHR (Grand Chamber) Judgement, 4 December 2008.

48  *R v. Rowton* (1865) 34 LJMC 57; 10 Cox CC 25, CCR.

49  *R v. Redgrave* (1982) 74 Cr App R 10, CA.

50  *R v. Robinson* (1994) 98 Cr App R 370, CA.

51  *Toohey v. Metropolitan Police Commissioner* [1965] AC 595, HL.

52  *R v. Pinfold and MacKenney* [2004] 2 Cr App R 32, [14]–[15], discussed in Roberts (2004).

53  This principle is sometimes elevated into a more formalised 'ultimate issue rule', which has some historical basis but today is virtually obsolete: *R v. Stockwell* (1993) 97 Cr App R 260, CA.

54  *R v. Turner* [1975] 1 QB 834, CA.

55  Ibid.: 841–2, 843.

56  There is one particular context in which the courts could be said to have adopted an uncharacteristically rigid and formalistic approach. An IQ of 69 is taken to be the absolute cut-off point for expert testimony of abnormal personality. If the individual in question has an IQ of 70 or above such testimony cannot generally be given: *R v. Masih* [1986] Crim LR 395, CA; *R v. Weightman* (1991) 92 Cr App R 291, CA. However, the courts are perfectly candid about this rule's pragmatic rationale. A line must be drawn somewhere. Setting the standard of normality at an IQ of 70 reflects psychological convention and is no more arbitrary than any other plausible cut-off point: *R v. Henry* [2006] 1 Cr App R 6, CA (also noting the marginal relevance of such evidence in many cases).

57  *R v. Stockwell* (1993) 97 Cr App R 260, CA.

58  Ibid.: 263–4.

59  *DPP v. A and BC Chewing Gum Ltd* [1968] 1 QB 159, DC.

60  *R v. Silverlock* [1894] 2 QB 766, CCR.

61  Ibid.: 771.

62  *R v. Chatwood* [1980] 1 WLR 874, CA, per Forbes J: 'these drug abusers were expressing an opinion, and an informed opinion, that, having so used the substance which they did use, it was indeed heroin, because they were experienced in the effects of heroin'.

63  *R v. Hodges* [2003] 2 Cr App R 247, CA.

64  *R v. Stockwell* (1993) 97 Cr App R 260, CA, 264. Also see *R v. Clare and Peach* [1995] 2 Cr App R 333, CA, but cf. *R v. Flynn and St John* [2008] 2 Cr App R 20, CA.

65  *Moore v. Medley, The Times*, 3 February 1955, cited by Smith (1995: 113).

66  *R v. Turnbull* [1977] QB 224, CA.

67  *R v. Beck* [1982] 1 WLR 461, CA.

68  *R v. Lucas* [1981] QB 720, CA.

69  See Section I, above.

70  *R v. Bates* [2006] EWCA Crim 1395, [22].

71  *R v. Doheny and Adams* [1997] 1 Cr App R 369, CA.

72  Ibid:. 374.

73  Ibid:. 375. There might be 'four or five white males in the United Kingdom from whom that [crime] stain could have come' because DNA profiling was less discriminating in 1997 than it is today.

74  Ibid:. 372–3.

75  Ibid:. 384.

76  The same error was exposed in *R v. Sally Clark* [2003] EWCA Crim 1020.

77  *R v. Adams* [1996] 2 Cr App R 467, CA.

78  *R v. Adams (No. 2)* [1998] 1 Cr App R 377, CA.

79  [1996] 2 Cr App R 467, 481.

80  [1998] 1 Cr App R 377, 384, 385.

81  *R v. Turner* [1975] 1 QB 834, CA, 842, 843.

82  cf. *R v. Luttrell* [2004] 2 Cr App R 31, CA.

83  Section 79 of the Evidence Act 1995 (NSW and Cth) provides that 'If a person has specialised knowledge based on the person's training, study or experience, the opinion rule does not apply to evidence of an opinion of that person that is wholly or substantially based on that knowledge.'

84  *Murphy v. R* (1989) 167 CLR 94, HCA, updating *Clark v. Ryan* (1960) 103 CLR 486, HCA.

85  *R v. Mohan* (1994) 114 DLR (4th) 419, SCC.

86  *Frye v. US* (1923) 54 App DC 46, at 47; 293 F 1013, 1014 (emphasis supplied).

87  *Daubert v. Merrell Dow* (1993) 125 L Ed 2d 469; 113 S Ct 2786.

88  *Kumho Tire Co v. Carmichael* (1999) 119 S.Ct. 1167; *General Electric v. Joiner* (1997) 118 S.Ct. 512.

89  FRE Rule 702 now states that scientific evidence may only be admitted: 'if (1) the testimony is based upon sufficient facts or data, (2) the testimony is the product of reliable principles and methods, and (3) the witness has applied the principles and methods reliably to the facts of the case.' Note that some state courts have explicitly rejected *Daubert*: see for example *Logerquist v. McVey* 1 P (3d) 113 (2000), Sup. Ct of Arizona.

90  (1991) 93 Cr App R 161, CA, 164.

91  (1991) 93 Cr App R 161, at 165, 166.

92  *R v. O'Doherty* [2002] Crim LR 761, CA(NI).

93  *R v. Flynn and St John* [2008] 2 Cr App R 20, CA, [62]-[64].

94  *R v. Luttrell* [2004] 2 Cr App R 31, CA; *R v. Gilfoyle* [2001] 2 Cr App R 57, CA.

95  Reliance has been placed on the South Australian case of *R v. Bonython* (1984) 38 SASR 45.

96  www.crfp.org.uk/.

## References

Allen, R.J. (1994) 'Expertise and the *Daubert* Decision', *Journal of Criminal Law and Criminology*, 84: 1157–1175.

Allen, R. and Redmayne, M. (eds) (1997) *Special Issue on Bayesianism and Juridical Proof*. *International Journal of Evidence and Proof*, 1(6): 253–360.

Allen, R. and Roberts, P. (eds) (2007) *Special Issue on the Reference Class Problem*, *International Journal of Evidence and Proof*, 11(4): 243–317.

Anderson, T.J. (1999). 'On Generalizations I: A Preliminary Exploration', *South Texas Law Review*, 40: 455–481.

Auld, Lord Justice (2001) *Review of the Criminal Courts of England and Wales – Report*. London: The Stationery Office.

Beecher-Monas, E. (2000) 'The Heuristics of Intellectual Due Process: A Primer for Triers of Science', *New York University Law Review*, 75: 1563–1657.

Berger, M.A. (2000) 'The Supreme Court's Trilogy on the Admissibility of Expert Testimony', pp. 9–38 in *Reference Manual on Scientific Evidence* (2nd edn). Federal Judicial Center. www.fjc.gov/public/pdf.nsf/lookup/sciman00.pdf/$file/sciman00.pdf

Bernstein, D.E. (1996) 'Junk Science in the United States and the Commonwealth', *Yale Journal of International Law*, 21: 123–182.

Choo, A.L.-T. (2008) *Abuse of Process and Judicial Stays of Criminal Proceedings* (2nd edn). Oxford: Oxford University Press.

Choo, A.L.-T. and Nash, S. (2003). 'Evidence Law in England and Wales: The Impact of the Human Rights Act 1998', *International Journal of Evidence and Proof*, 7: 31–61.

Clark, S.J. (1999) 'The Courage of Our Convictions', *Michigan Law Review*, 97: 2381–2447.

Crossman, G. with Kitchin, H., Kuna, R., Skrein, M. and Russell, J. (2007) *Overlooked: Surveillance and Personal Privacy in Modern Britain*. London: Liberty/Nuffield Foundation.

Crown Prosecution Service (2006) *Disclosure: Experts' Evidence and Unused Material – Guidance Booklet for Experts*. London: CPS Policy Directorate. www.cps.gov.uk/publications/docs/experts_guidance_booklet.pdf

Damaška, M.R. (1986) *The Faces of Justice and State Authority: A Comparative Approach to the Legal Process*. New Haven: Yale University Press.

Damaška, M.R. (1975) 'Structures of Authority and Comparative Criminal Procedure', *Yale Law Journal*, 84: 480–544.

Donnelly, P. and Friedman, R.D. (1999) 'DNA Database Searches and the Legal Consumption of Scientific Evidence', *Michigan Law Review*, 97: 931–984.

Dwyer, D. (2003) 'The Duties of Expert Witnesses of Fact and Opinion: *R v Clark (Sally)*', *International Journal of Evidence and Proof*, 7: 264–269.

Edmond, G. (2002) 'Constructing Miscarriages of Justice: Misunderstanding Scientific Evidence in High Profile Criminal Appeals', *Oxford Journal of Legal Studies*, 22: 53–89.

Edmond, G. (1998) 'The Next Step or Moonwalking? Expert Evidence, the Public Understanding of Science and the Case Against Imwinkelried's Didactic Trial Procedures', *International Journal of Evidence and Proof*, 2: 13–31.

Ford, R. (2008) 'Police are ordered to destroy all DNA samples taken from innocent people – Judges say databases stigmatise individuals', *The Times*, 5 December.

Frankel, M.E. (1975) 'The Search for the Truth: An Umpireal View', *University of Pennsylvania Law Review*, 123: 1031–1059.

Freckelton, I.R. (1987) *The Trial of the Expert*. Melbourne: Oxford University Press.

Gee, D.J. (1987) 'The Expert Witness in the Criminal Trial', *Criminal Law Review*, 307–314.

Glenn, H.P. (2007) *Legal Traditions of the World: Sustainable Diversity in Law* (3rd edn). Oxford: Oxford University Press.

Haack, S. (2003) *Defending Science – Within Reason: Between Scientism and Cynicism.* New York: Prometheus Books.

Hamer, M. (1981) 'How A Forensic Scientist Fell Foul of the Law', *New Scientist*, 91: 575.

Hand, L. (1901) 'Historical and Practical Considerations Regarding Expert Testimony', *Harvard Law Review*, 15: 40–58.

Hooper, Lord Justice and Ormerod, D. (eds) (2008) *Blackstone's Criminal Practice 2009.* Oxford: Oxford University Press.

Hörnle, T. (2006) 'Democratic Accountability and Lay Participation in Criminal Trials', pp. 135–153, in A. Duff, L. Farmer, S. Marshall and V. Tadros (eds), *The Trial on Trial Volume Two: Judgment and Calling to Account.* Oxford: Hart Publishing.

House of Commons Science and Technology Committee (2005) *Forensic Science on Trial – Seventh Report of Session 2004–05.* HC 96-I. London: TSO.

Howard, M.N. (1991) 'The Neutral Expert: A Plausible Threat to Justice', *Criminal Law Review*, 98–105.

Huber, P.W. (1991) *Galileo's Revenge: Junk Science in the Courtroom.* New York: Basic Books.

Imwinkelried, E.J. (1997) 'The Next Step in Conceptualizing the Presentation of Expert Evidence as Education: The Case for Didactic Trial Procedures', *International Journal of Evidence and Proof*, 1: 128–148.

Jones, C.A.G. (1994) *Expert Witnesses: Science, Medicine and the Practice of Law.* Oxford: Oxford University Press.

Kershaw, C., Nicholas, S. and Walker, A. (eds) (2008) *Crime in England and Wales 2007/08.* Home Office Statistical Bulletin 07/08. London: Home Office. www.homeoffice.gov.uk/rds/crimeew0708.html

Koehler, J.L. (2001) 'The Psychology of Numbers in the Courtroom: How to Make DNA-Match Statistics Seem Impressive or Insufficient', *Southern California Law Review*, 74: 1275–1305.

Law Commission (2009) *The Admissibility of Expert Evidence in Criminal Proceedings in England and Wales.* Consultation Paper No 190. London: TSO.

Lempert, R. (1991) 'Some Caveats Concerning DNA as Criminal Identification Evidence: With Thanks to the Reverend Bayes', *Cardozo Law Review*, 13: 303–341.

Mackay, R.D. and Colman, A.M. (1991) 'Excluding Expert Evidence: A Tale of Ordinary Folk and Common Experience', *Criminal Law Review*, 800–810.

McEwan, J. (1998) *Evidence and the Adversarial Process – The Modern Law* (2nd edn). Oxford: Hart Publishing.

Ministry of Justice (2008) *Criminal Statistics: England and Wales 2007.* London: Office for Criminal Justice Reform. www.justice.gov.uk/docs/crim-stats-2007-tag.pdf

NDNAD (2006) *The National DNA Database Annual Report 2005–2006.* www.homeoffice.gov.uk/science-research/using-science/dna-database/

Nobles, R. and Schiff, D. (2004) 'A Story of Miscarriage: Law in the Media', *Journal of Law and Society*, 31: 221–244.

Nuffield Council on Bioethics (2007) *The Forensic Use of Bioinformation: Ethical Issues.* London: Nuffield Council on Bioethics.

O'Brian Jr., W.E. (2003) 'Court Scrutiny of Expert Evidence: Recent Decisions Highlight the Tensions', *International Journal of Evidence and Proof*, 7: 172–184.

Ormerod, D. (2002) 'Sounding Out Expert Voice Identification', *Criminal Law Review*, 771–790.

Pattenden, R. (2008) 'Authenticating "Things" in English Law: Principles for Adducing Tangible Evidence in Common Law Jury Trials', *International Journal of Evidence and Proof*, 12: 273–302.

Redmayne, M. (2001) *Expert Evidence and Criminal Justice*. Oxford: Oxford University Press.

Redmayne, M. (1998) 'Bayesianism and Proof', in M. Freeman and H. Reece (eds), *Science in Court*. Aldershot: Ashgate.

Redmayne, M. (1997) 'Expert Evidence and Scientific Disagreement', *UC Davis Law Review*, 30: 1027–1080.

Risinger, D.M. (2007) 'Goodbye To All That, Or A Fool's Errand, By One of the Fools: How I Stopped Worrying about Court Responses to Handwriting Identification (and "Forensic Science" in General) and Learned to Love Misinterpretations of *Kumho Tire* v *Carmichael'*, *Tulsa Law Review*, 43: 447–475.

Roberts, A. (2008) 'Drawing on Expertise: Legal Decision-Making and the Reception of Expert Evidence', *Criminal Law Review*, 443–462.

Roberts, P. (2007a) 'Law and Criminal Investigation', pp. 92–145, in T. Newburn, T. Williamson and A. Wright (eds), *Handbook of Criminal Investigation*. Cullompton, Devon: Willan Publishing.

Roberts, P. (2007b) 'Criminal Procedure, the Presumption of Innocence and Judicial Reasoning under the Human Rights Act', pp. 377–423, in H. Fenwick, R. Masterman and G. Phillipson (eds), *Judicial Reasoning Under the UK Human Rights Act*. Cambridge: Cambridge University Press.

Roberts, P. (2006) 'Theorising Procedural Tradition: Subjects, Objects and Values in Criminal Adjudication', pp. 37–64, in A. Duff, L. Farmer, S. Marshall and V. Tadros (eds), *The Trial on Trial Volume Two: Judgment and Calling to Account*. Oxford: Hart Publishing.

Roberts, P. (2004) 'Towards the Principled Reception of Expert Evidence of Witness Credibility in Criminal Trials', *International Journal of Evidence and Proof*, 8: 215–232.

Roberts, P. (2000) 'Acquitted Misconduct Evidence and Double Jeopardy Principles, From *Sambasivam* to Z', *Criminal Law Review*, 952–970.

Roberts, P. (1996) 'Will You Stand Up in Court? On the Admissibility of Psychiatric and Psychological Evidence', *Journal of Forensic Psychiatry*, 7: 61–76.

Roberts, P. (1994) 'Science in the Criminal Process', *Oxford Journal of Legal Studies*, 14: 469–506.

Roberts, P. and Willmore, C. (1993) *The Role of Forensic Science Evidence in Criminal Proceedings*. Royal Commission on Criminal Justice Research Study No. 11. London: HMSO.

Roberts, P. and Zuckerman, A. (2004) *Criminal Evidence*. Oxford: Oxford University Press.

Robertson, B. and Vignaux, G.A. (1995) *Interpreting Evidence: Evaluating Forensic Science in the Courtroom*. Chichester: John Wiley and Sons Ltd.

Sanders, J. (2007) 'Expert Witness Ethics', *Fordham Law Review*, 76: 1539–1583.

Sheldon, D.H. and MacLeod, M.D. (1991) 'From Normative to Positive Data: Expert Psychological Evidence Re-Examined', *Criminal Law Review*, 811–820.

Smith, J.C. (1995) *Criminal Evidence*. London: Sweet and Maxwell.

Spencer, J.R. (2000) 'The Case for a Code of Criminal Procedure', *Criminal Law Review*, 519–531.

Spencer, J.R. (1992) 'Court Experts and Expert Witnesses: Have We A Lesson to Learn From the French?', *Current Legal Problems*, 45: 213–236.

Spencer, J.R. (1991) 'The Neutral Expert: An Implausible Bogey', *Criminal Law Review*, 106–110.

Thornton, P. (1995) 'The Admissibility of Expert Psychiatric and Psychological Evidence – Judicial Training', *Medicine, Science and the Law*, 35: 143–149.

Trechsel, S. with Summers, S.J. (2005) *Human Rights in Criminal Proceedings*. Oxford: Oxford University Press.

Tribe, L.H. (1971) 'Trial By Mathematics: Precision and Ritual in the Legal Process', *Harvard Law Review*, 84: 1329–1393.

van Kampen, P.T.C. (1998) *Expert Evidence Compared: Rules and Practices in the Dutch and American Criminal Justice System*. Antwerp: Intersentia.

van Kampen, P. and Nijboer, H. (1997) '*Daubert* in the Lowlands', *UC Davis Law Review*, 30: 951–995.

Vogler, R. (2005) *A World View of Criminal Justice*. Aldershot: Ashgate.

von Hirsch, A., Garland, D. and Wakefield, A. (eds) (2004) *Ethical and Social Perspectives on Situational Crime Prevention*. Oxford: Hart Publishing.

Walker, C. and Stockdale, R. (1999) 'Forensic Evidence', in C. Walker and K. Starmer (eds), *Miscarriages of Justice: A Review of Justice in Error*. London: Blackstone Press.

Ward, T. (2004), 'Experts, Juries, and Witch-hunts: From Fitzjames Stephen to Angela Cannings', *Journal of Law and Society*, 31: 369–386.

Williams, R. and Johnson, P. (2008) *Genetic Policing: The Use of DNA in Criminal Investigations*. Cullompton, Devon: Willan Publishing.

Wonder, A.K.Y. (1989) 'Science and Law, A Marriage of Opposites', *Journal of the Forensic Science Society*, 29: 75–76.

Worthen, T. (2008) 'The Hearsay Provisions of the Criminal Justice Act 2003: So Far, Not So Good?', *Criminal Law Review*, 431–442.

Zuckerman, A. (2006) *Zuckerman on Civil Procedure: Principles of Practice* (2nd edn). London: Sweet and Maxwell.

Zuckerman, A.A.S. (1986) 'Law, Fact or Justice?' *Boston University Law Review*, 66: 487–508.

**Part 4**

# Themes and Debates in Contemporary Forensic Science

# Introduction

## Jim Fraser and Robin Williams

... the umbrella term 'forensic science' embraces a set of intensely practical disciplines to which the paradigm of pure scientific enquiry cannot readily be applied. (Roberts and Willmore 1993)

In describing forensic science as they do, Roberts and Willmore identify three recurrent themes of this Handbook; themes that have also been addressed, in differing degrees of detail, by the contributors to this section. The first of these themes is the notion that forensic science is constituted by a loose assemblage of diverse activities that have (or may share) attributes of value to criminal legal inquiries. However, the quotation identifies a general association of entities rather than the relationship between them or the boundary surrounding them. The second theme is that the primary focus and value of forensic science derives from its utilitarian stance: forensic science deals with tangible issues of day-to-day significance rather than with theoretical speculation about their underlying properties. The final theme is the lack of conformity between forensic science and 'pure science' (however we seek to define the latter) – or at least the presence of notable differences between these spheres of activity.

Accordingly this description of forensic science resonates with the many concepts and routines described in previous chapters (for example those on fingerprint examination and bloodstain pattern analysis) where relevant knowledge and practice is not self-evidently 'scientific' and where claims to attain the objectivity or legitimacy of 'pure science' remain contested. Furthermore, even the extent to which such activities draw on the authority of science is increasingly challenged. But whatever this assemblage of activity comprises, an understanding of its individual elements, purposes and boundaries is fundamental to how we train and educate practitioners (scientists, other specialists, investigators), set standards (scientific, procedural, ethical), control behaviour (professional and personal), and manage cooperation across legal and international borders. All of these issues are explored in this section.

In considering the nature, current status and significance of ethical standards for expert witnesses, Willis notes the importance of defining knowledge and practice boundaries. Yet she also explains how the heterogeneity and variety of 'acceptable' practice from jurisdiction to jurisdiction ultimately 'adds to the ambiguity ... [of] the ethical use of science'. She contrasts this with the increasingly regulated scientific and procedural standards within laboratories by independent authorities, but questions the lack of such formal quality systems in the regulation of crime scene investigation.

Kershaw also identifies this inconsistency between laboratory-based practitioners and field personnel (as they are referred to by Roux and Robertson) as a matter of significance where he describes the rationale for the implementation of the Council for Registration of Forensic Practitioners (CRFP). The purpose of this body, which was implemented following a number of high-profile miscarriages of justice in which forensic science played a part, is to set standards and regulate the bewildering array of specialists who find their way into criminal investigations as witnesses, irrespective of whether they are expert witnesses (for example scientists) or witnesses to fact (for example crime scene investigators). One of the distinctive features of CRFP is the recognition that consistent standards ought to be applied throughout the entire chain of evidence (and therefore to all practitioners) on the basis that failure to deal effectively with evidence at a crime scene may have serious implications subsequently (a point which echoes Willis). Both Willis and Kershaw explore the nature and trajectory of professionalisation within forensic practice including issues of competence and integrity.

In the context of this variety and ambiguity of practice, Roux and Robertson consider the training and education of forensic practitioners from an international perspective. However, they also argue (citing Margot 1994) that, despite such seeming variability, forensic science 'has all the requirements for a true single scientific discipline ... [whose aim is] ... to ultimately answer the fundamental, essential question ... "What is the weight of the evidence?"' In describing the huge increase in forensic science education and training programmes throughout the world, it is perhaps unsurprising that they identify extensive variation in the structures and accreditation processes, and question the espoused rationales of some of these programmes. Notwithstanding, they recognise the potential benefits to forensic science of more structured and effective education and training, and potential growth in research activity.

Wilson's chapter also considers forensic science from an international perspective in relation to policing, particularly in light of the current and anticipated need for more coordinated and cooperative activities in the investigation of transnational crime. In doing so he describes how forensic science 'overlaps with more complex, inchoate, and less transparent or accountable areas of law and policy'. Numerous studies and cases (particularly in relation to DNA) are cited in arguing the potential benefits that might derive from more effective international cooperation, whilst the complexity of evaluating the contribution of forensic science is recognised. Arguing that these benefits can only arise as a corollary to substantial financial investment, Wilson expresses concerns about the feasibility and timescales of developing such a capability and capacity, particularly with regard to the differing attitudes to law, practices of data protection and legal use of bioinformation. He concludes that progress in this area is likely to be slow and may be overtaken by operational, economic or political developments.

Finally, it is interesting to contrast the slow rate of development in issues of transnational cooperation with the rapid developments in education and training which appear to have been driven more by operational and economic needs of universities and educational institutions than any identified benefit to forensic science practice or education. As in many other spheres of activity, major developments or changes are more likely to arise as a consequence of external events or contingencies than the internalised views or expectations of a 'profession'.

## References

Margot, P. (1994) Forensic Science Education ... or How Do We Foster Quality? Proceedings of the 3rd meeting of the European Network of Forensic Science Institutes. Linköping: 31–37.

Roberts, P. and Willmore, C. (1993) The Role of Forensic Science Evidence in Criminal Proceedings. Royal Commission on Criminal Justice Study 11. London: HMSO.

# Chapter 18

# Forensic science and the internationalisation of policing

*Tim Wilson*

## Introduction

> Disappearing national borders create the need for international compatibility of forensic methods and techniques …
>
> There will be an increase in the exchange of forensic data, and international forensic database networks need to be established, for example for fingerprints, DNA, drugs, firearms and explosive devices …
>
> In the coming years, there will be a trend from producing evidence to producing intelligence. In order to do this, there will be more emphasis on forensic intelligence, in a national as well as in an international context …
>
> (Koeleman 2005)

Albert Koeleman was formerly Director General of the Netherlands Forensic Institute and Chairman of the European Network of Forensic Science Institutions (ENFSI). His vision of forensic science's potential international role acknowledges the crucial importance of changing perceptions among police officers and other investigators. Disciplines originally shaped largely by 'forensic' (in the sense of evidential) or 'corroborative' (against already identified suspects) requirements, are increasingly gaining an additional inceptive role as a source of 'intelligence' (in the sense of obtaining investigative leads or the actual identification of suspects) (Bradbury and Feist 2005).

Will this vision be realised? There is now much more uncertainty about the future of forensic science. What would Albert Koeleman have said in 2009, as Deputy Secretary-General at the Dutch Ministry of Finance? Economics will determine what may be possible, even potentially (McCartney 2006) displacing normative considerations. 'Asymmetry of choice' (R. Rose 2006), even in fiscally easier times, favours expenditure on legacy spending against new or weakly established policy initiatives. Spending in real terms on forensic science, particularly biometrics for volume crime investigations,

491

might decline during a recession. The resources needed nationally and for international cooperation will only be provided if the case for forensic science can be justified persuasively, also overcoming insufficient forensic awareness among police, judicial and governmental decision-makers (Wilson 2008).

Funding is not the only issue. Joined-up thinking, together with common standards and processes need to be adopted across professional and departmental boundaries – police and investigating judges, ministries of the interior and justice (some with separate forensic establishments and parallel databases) – as well as national borders. As was explained recently, the newest forensic discipline – nuclear forensics – could harness science to identify the origin and perhaps the history of fissile material, but only if there are effective arrangements for sharing information internationally and ensuring standard crime scene practices (Royal Society 2008).

Cooperation also poses ethical and political questions. The increased use of bioinformation, especially the greater use of DNA analysis, raises questions about safeguarding civil rights, individual privacy and human dignity. How such issues and possible solutions are perceived – at least initially – in each state will mirror its political culture and recent history. Also, can we discuss transnational crime without adding to the casual fear of foreigners and stigmatisation of migrants, or reinforce the 'anxiety society' (Den Boer 2005) and a culture of 'social legitimacy' (Loader 2004) that threatens to emasculate political debate or transform democratically accountable policing into a tool of political control (Jenkins 2005)?

The concept of 'internationalisation' as used in the title of this chapter refers to 'high levels of international interaction and interdependence' in contrast to globalisation which implies that there are no longer distinct national economies in a position to interact (Baylis and Smith 2006: 775). Governance and authority can become fragmented (Sheptycki 2007) or, conversely, intelligence-sharing may favour centralisation. Either could weaken political accountability and transparency. Yet an effective response to transnational crime need not necessarily result in anonymous and unaccountable bureaucratic management and political direction via Europol and SOCA. The challenge, therefore, is for police authorities and more generally Parliament working with colleagues in Brussels – now Europol is more open to scrutiny by the European Parliament (Wilson and Williams 2008) – to assure honest governance and examine whether decisions are judicious and ethical.

The increasing use of DNA in law enforcement has engendered un-precedented scrutiny in the UK (House of Commons 2005 and 2007; House of Lords 2007a and 2007b) and independent enquiry (Nuffield 2007). This might prove to be the forensic science equivalent to the 'Pinochet moment' for international law (Sands 2006), but that was followed by Guantánamo Bay and quite possibly UK government complicity with extraordinary rendition. Nothing can be taken for granted, but analysis of and rational debate about the issues can help.

Even with the narrower focus of this chapter, it is possible only to lightly sketch the complex issues. It attempts to do this in three sections:

- How is transnational crime evolving in response to economic and social changes and can forensic science help us to understand what is happening and respond more effectively?

- What is the extent of existing cooperation and is there a case for more investment (more as a heuristic device than cost-benefit analysis) in forensic science to enhance this?

- Can the benefits that come from the effective use of forensic science be experienced globally and the risks controlled?

The analysis is focused primarily on 'bioinformation' (Nuffield 2007), especially DNA. The relative newness of this forensic science technique makes it possible to indicate (albeit imperfectly) the scope of the social learning – the accumulated experience of experts in a policy area (R. Rose 2006) – relevant to the subject of this chapter. The risk remains of falling into the trap (Newburn and Sparks 2004) of implying greater order and rationality than can possibly exist in the interplay of science, law enforcement and political culture with economics and the ghostly image on a radar screen that passes for knowledge of transnational crime.

## I Transnational crime

National boundaries are a boon to criminals and a block to law enforcement agencies. (Naím 2005)

The term 'transnational crime' is used here to designate crime undertaken within a single state and for all intents and purposes is a domestic crime, except for the fact that the offender is a citizen of another state. It may be unclear until the point of detection whether the offender was a resident or even held dual nationality of the state where the crime was committed, or was there temporarily either for the express purpose of committing crime, or for other reasons. Prior to detection it may not be possible to classify the offender within these three categories (i.e. resident, visiting for criminal purposes or for other reasons). In all three instances such crime is transnational because of the offender's ultimately foreign origin, and thus intelligence from abroad might help to detect the criminal.

While bearing in mind throughout this section the numerous caveats about measuring crime (Newburn 2007), it is generally accepted that transnational crimes have greatly increased over the past 20 years (Lewis 2007). However, there is also overwhelming and consistent evidence from the UK, North America and Australia indicating that most crime – as an immediate physical (not economic or cyber) manifestation – is local (i.e. most offenders and victims live within a few miles of each other). Variations tend to be the result of offender routines (holidays, shopping and family visits) rather than ranging further afield in search of targets. In this respect there has been little change over the past 60 years. Indeed, the most recent comprehensive UK study of crime mobility found little evidence for the presumption 'that various global forces are undermining traditional social structures and culture and this will ultimately affect crime patterns' (Wiles and Costello 2000). The details of this research and earlier work together with other later studies and forensic intelligence, however, reveal a more discrete process involving, in the UK at least, a small but growing element of crime manifested at particular localities and following specific changes in economic activity or mobility.

Analyses of NDNAD (National DNA Database) matches in 1996/97 indicated that 20 per cent involved more than one police force area (Porter 1996). This overall general pattern appears to have remained reasonably consistent. In 2003/04, 24 per cent of matches involved more than one force (Home Office 2005). Much of the 1996/97 inter-force area activity may not have reflected very great distances, with (when the data was available) half involving an adjoining force. A Dutch analysis of DNA data indicating the geographical extent of criminal collaborations (between two and 14 persons cooperating at one or more crime scenes) identified 34 per cent operating across police boundaries (van der Beek and Tullener 2004), but it is unclear whether this reflects greater mobility than the UK or smaller police areas.

An analysis of reasonably recent research (Porter 1996) has indicated how overall national patterns can disguise significant local variations:

- A study in 1989 of detections in four force areas had indicated that 2 per cent to 27 per cent of burglaries were by offenders from outside their area.

- A small sample of detections examined in 1994 in a non-metropolitan force sub-unit covering an affluent area, suggested that external offenders were responsible for more than 50 per cent of crimes.

- Other studies during this period indicated a low rate of external offending in metropolitan areas and twice the level of external offending among the non-metropolitan areas covered by the research when they adjoined a metropolitan area. One possible reason advanced for this was that more adventurous metropolitan criminals took advantage of the motorway network. It was also suggested that, despite affluent areas in metropolitan regions, outside criminals thought the opportunities less attractive and metropolitan criminal gangs had established effective barriers to entry.

More recent data from the UK force with the greatest out-of-area offending rate (including transnational offenders), Kent, indicated that this was in the order of 40 per cent (*Kent and Sussex Courier* 2006). This is for an area with a resident population of 1.6 million, but which is crossed annually by 36 million travellers using the Channel Tunnel and ferry ports.

Traditional crimes increased with the inflow of offenders from the other side of the border via the Channel Tunnel, but the effects may have been asymmetrical. In contrast, in two regions of Sweden and Denmark that were intended to become more integrated with the opening of the Øresund Bridge, there was no rise in the total number of offences in a short period prior to the bridge being opened and afterwards. Instead, there appear to have been shifts in location and changes in volume of certain offences in Sweden.

Improved rail access to Denmark may have increased the number of cars entering Malmö and parking near the main railway station. This resulted in increases – spatially and by volume – of local hot spots for vehicle offences (Ceccato and Haining 2004). This is reminiscent of observations about the relationship between crime and economic changes and transport infrastructure in Yorkshire. Sheffield's out-of-town shopping mall – 'the largest attractor of visitors to the city and also the main attractor of imported offenders' – displaced offending from the city centre, where it declined from 25 per cent in 1966 to 10 per cent in 1995. Outside offenders entering a rural area were attracted to a motorway service station because of the favourable conditions and high volume of opportunities that such a site presents for theft from motor vehicles (Wiles and Costello 2000). Similarly and over a larger area, the centripetal significance of commercial activities, particularly in Perth, on the distribution of robbery, property damage and theft within urban Western Australia (Morgan *et al.* 1999) has been noted and mapped for almost a decade (most recently Loh *et al.* 2007). Material from such studies suggests possible causal links between economics and transport in shaping the spatial occurrence of some criminal behaviour. Indeed, observations made about Chicago as a railway hub attracting national and international migrants and its transformational impact on crime gave rise to a school of criminology in the twentieth century, although today there would be less agreement with the Chicagoans' views about underlying causality (Valier 2003).

A study in 1994/95 indicated that only 1 per cent of detected serious crime was international compared with 94 per cent from within force areas (Porter 1996). Penal and arrest statistics have to be treated with caution, particularly in those countries, including the UK, where ethnic variations in official statistics may not be matched by similar differences in self-reported offending (de Maillard and Roché 2004), but English and Welsh prison statistics probably provide a more current, broader and reasonably reliable (at least the best available) indication of trends in transnational crime within the UK. Between 1996 and 2006 the percentage of foreign nationals in prison increased from 8 per cent to 14 per cent (the total prison population rose by 41 per cent) (National Statistics 2007). Slightly older data indicated that Europe was the main continent of origin, and within it Ireland, the Netherlands, Turkey, Germany, Italy and Cyprus. Jamaica, Nigeria, Pakistan and India were also significant (Home Office 2000; Prison Reform Trust 2004; HM Inspectorate of Prisons 2006).

There is an appreciable difference between the proportion of foreign citizens in the English and Welsh prison population and UK resident population (8.3 per cent) (Frith 2006). The nationalities that featured most in the prison data are far less prominent in the migration and labour force statistics. In contrast Germany, Ireland and the Netherlands were, respectively, the second, third and fourth most common country of origin of visitors in recent years (IPPR 2004 and National Statistics 2005). Some transnational crime has been linked by Europol analysts with settlement. Turkish transnational criminals are reported to be long-term residents within the host country. The same analysts place equal weight on the geographical and economic position of the country of origin, especially the Netherlands as the main EU point of entry for goods and Germany by virtue of its general importance for the European economy and logistics (Europol 2004 and 2005).

Transnational offending varies both in intensity, seriousness and transference of behaviour from the country of origin, and such behaviour may be atypical or fully integrated with the country of origin as two examples illustrate. In January 2007 some 80 per cent of pickpockets arrested on the London Underground were Bulgarian. This country, like most of the Balkans, has lower crime rates than Western Europe, even after taking lower reporting rates into account, with lower income and differences in demographic profiles to explain this (UNODC 2008). In contrast a feud originating in organised crime in Calabria resulted in multiple (six victims) murder in Nordrhein-Westfalen (Wischgoll 2007). Society, economics and institutions in the host country also shape the pattern of transnational crime. The Metropolitan Police estimated in 2006 that 180 gangs speaking 24 languages were responsible for one third of murders in London. The majority of these gangs were thought to be based on clan or country of origin, but almost half had formed from acquaintances made in London neighbourhoods or prison (Khan 2007; Wischgoll 2007; Leapman 2006). More generally Europol analysts have drawn attention to how a lack of integration of migrant communities and concentration within restricted areas makes them vulnerable to exploitation by organised crime groups (Europol 2007).

Forensic information adds to our understanding of patterns of transnational crime within and among countries. The Scottish DNA match rate in 2005–06 of (68 per cent) is higher than the overall rate for Great Britain (52 per cent) (NDNAD 2007). This probably reflects (at least partly) geography. Only 1.2 per cent of Scottish convicted prisoners in 2003 were foreign nationals compared with 10.6 per cent in England and Wales (European Sourcebook 2006) within penal systems with similar, high, imprisonment rates (respectively, 142 and 144 per 100,000 population) (Scottish Parliament 2007). This interpretation of different DNA match rates is consistent with the lower DNA match rate in Austria (39 per cent) (Prainsack 2008) and a much higher proportion of foreign citizen arrests (26 per cent) (European Sourcebook 2006) compared with the best available data for England and Wales (12–13 per cent) (Hannam 2008). (Prainsack and others (Nuffield 2007) place a greater emphasis – see Section 3 of this chapter – on retention rules. There is also a major impact from the efficiency with which changes in rules are implemented.)

Arrest data (Hannam 2008) provides a radar image at Figure 18.1 (albeit incomplete) of UK transnational offending. This can be compared with arrest, conviction and penal data (European Sourcebook 2006) at Figure 18.2 from many other countries of the European Union and its neighbours. These suggest a spatial zone experiencing a high level of transnational criminality that is broadly coterminous with a similar zone of economic activity. That is the core European economic and logistical corridor:[1] the EU point of entry or exit in 2006 for 40 per cent of air travellers, 74 per cent of air cargo or mail and 36 per cent of maritime cargo (European Commission 2008).

Migration data appears to be equally limited (BBC 2008b), but by comparing in Figure 18.3 cumulative work registration with the arrest information used for Figure 18.1, it appears that such recent movement within the EU may, with

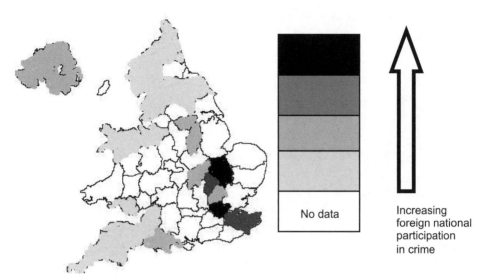

**Figure 18.1** Transnational offending in England, Wales and Northern Ireland, 2005 and 2006

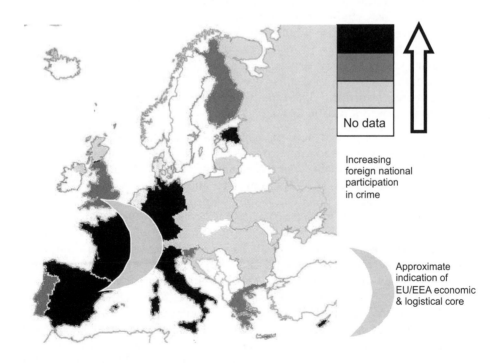

**Figure 18.2** Transnational offending in EU member states and neighbouring states, 2003

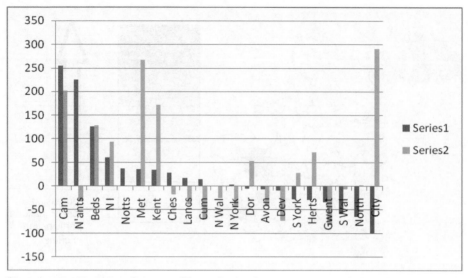

**Figure 18.3** Variation from median value – Series 1: in cumulative registrations at 04.12.07 and Series 2: arrests of foreign citizens in (depending on latest data) 04/05 or 05/06

the exception possibly of Cambridgeshire and Bedfordshire, have significantly less impact on crime than more general or transient mobility.

Individual case studies have long shown the harm that highly mobile violent offenders can cause within this zone:

- Volkhart Eckert, a lorry driver, was named as the suspect in 19 murder investigations relating to deaths between 1974 and 2006 in industrial areas of Germany, France and Spain mainly within the zone's core economic and logistical corridors (Castle 2007).

- Michel Fourniret moved from his native France to work in a Belgian school after completing a prison sentence for sex offences. In 2008 he was convicted of the murder of seven young women between 1987 and 2001 in the Franco-Belgian border area. There may be another three victims (BBC 2006 and 2008) and until a potential victim escaped from him these crimes were being investigated (if not closed) as separate offences (Lichfield 2008).

The way organised crime mimics the logistical processes of legitimate businesses is revealed by successful convictions, for example, that of a gang specialising in the theft of high-value cars in London freighted from Maastricht to the United Arab Emirates (Metropolitan Police 2008). Other patterns are more difficult to explain. Perhaps a lack of competitive advantage explains why in 2006 only 19 per cent of heroin dealers in Switzerland and 37 per cent of traffickers in Austria were citizens of those countries, but why was the equivalent trafficking figure for Italy 65 per cent (UNODC 2008)? Moreover, is the Swiss figure indicative of a particularly intense level of transnational crime? The proportion of non-nationals arrested there for rape between 1982 and 2002 rose from 40 per cent to almost 70 per cent (Eisner and Killias 2004).

Many of these faint radar images suggest that the centripetal effect of economic activity and transport nodes may be reshaping the spatial pattern of a small (at least in the UK), but significant proportion of offending behaviour. More extensive analysis may confirm what Figure 18.1 implies: that for many crimes location within an economic and logistical spatial zone may prove to be more significant than formal national borders. Dealing with the specific challenges to law enforcement posed by transnational offending in London and Kent may greater require cooperation with and learning from foreign colleagues in an arc stretching from Flanders to Catalonia than national colleagues in Edinburgh and Cardiff. Such cooperation cannot be restricted to the EU. What is believed to be the biggest police operation against the 'date-rape drug', GHB (gammahydroxybutyrate) covered Switzerland as well as Germany and Austria (Paterson (2008); AP 2008). Moreover, just as this transnational drug ring was identified by a forensic understanding of the significance of the purchase of a constituent chemical, a Belgian DNA analysis has linked a number of serious crimes or offenders at locations in France, Belgium, the Netherlands and Germany (Van Renterghem 2006), as Figure 18.4 shows.

### Conclusions to Section I

It is important not to exaggerate the significance of transnational crime. In some countries, including the UK, this is likely to account for a relatively small proportion of recorded crime and may be less of a challenge to investigators than criminal mobility within its borders. Geography, social influences in both

•A robbery in Amsterdam linked to similar crime in Belgium

•A robbery in Mill, North Brabant, with two separate crime stains linked to a convicted offender (robbery) and crime stains left by the second offender at a burglary in Belgium

•A murder in Cologne linked to arson in Belgium

•A robbery in Lille linked to a convicted offender in Belgium

**Figure 18.4** Using DNA to link transnational crime and identify offenders

home and host countries, economic activity and logistics all appear to have an impact. Changes in the use of forensic investigative techniques that evolved in response to increased criminal mobility within national borders are also likely to assist internationally, both in detecting and analysing the presence, volume and forms of transnational offending.

## 2 Existing levels of cooperation and the case for forensic investment

> Can the Prime Minister explain how such a catastrophic failure to protect the public took place?
>
> David Cameron MP (Hansard 2008)

Angry words in Parliament between the British Prime Minister and the Leader of the Opposition illustrated the potential of DNA to increase the political scrutiny of forensic science. An Anglo-Dutch initiative to seek intelligence relating to some 4,000 DNA crime stains from unsolved crimes in both countries (Lewis 2008) placed the issue of international cooperation centre stage. Unfortunately both politicians failed to acknowledge a key issue: this single exercise resulted in Dutch stains being matched with 15 persons (BBC 2008a) (11 of whom had meanwhile committed offences in the UK), equivalent to 70 per cent of all UK international matches in 2004–2005 (Wilson and Williams 2008). Even when cooperation takes place, it may be the result of chance rather than routine:

- A Spanish citizen, Francesco Arce Montes, the murderer in 1996 of English schoolgirl Caroline Dickinson, was responsible for a large number of sexual offences in many different countries over a period of more than 20 years. Following Caroline's murder in France, his path took him through Spain where he was arrested for an attempted rape at knifepoint. There he skipped bail and disappeared. He was finally located and identified as the suspect by DNA – by chance – in custody in Miami, Florida (Dickinson and Pierce 2006).

- Smail Tulia was convicted in 2007 of a 1990 New York murder because a detective on a training course noted similarities between this case and offences in Europe. Once this connection had been spotted Tulia was located in his home in Montenegro after an Interpol fingerprint search (Interpol 2007a).

With an effective business process, however, sharing such data can become routine, as indicated by the 710 matches of German crime scene stains (including 41 murders) with known individuals on the Austrian database achieved during Prüm technical trials (House of Lords 2007b: 16). This still begs the question: how regularly will there be information to share?

The power of DNA to transform criminal investigations was known by 1986 (Jeffreys 2004) and three years later the House of Commons Select Committee for Home Affairs advocated the creation of a national DNA database. This was finally provided in 1995, but was of limited value to investigators because very little data was uploaded. The analysis of DNA profiles had to be paid for in cash and such expenditure was vulnerable to cuts during frequent police budget crises (Blakey 2000).

Eventually the government provided £241 million from central funds over the five years ending March 2005, to increase the size of NDNAD in response to concerns about volume crimes such as burglary and theft of or from motor vehicles. These central payments were structured to lever significant but smaller contributions for DNA investment from local police budgets (£90 million over the same period) (Wilson 2006). By March 2005 DNA was having a major impact on volume crime detection rates when it could be recovered from the crime scene (see Table 18.1).

The increased use of DNA also transformed many serious crime investigations. In 1988, two young girls (aged 11 and nine) were raped and indecently assaulted in Canterbury. Thirteen years later and over 175 miles away (280 km) in Derby in 2001, a shoplifter was arrested and a DNA sample taken. His DNA was automatically uploaded to NDNAD and matched the 1988 crime scene samples (Home Office 2006a).

This investment has been questioned. One criticism is that DNA detections have constantly been below 4 per cent of recorded crime (Gene Watch 2007). The impact on recorded crime as a whole is not an issue. This term covers a wide range of conduct, including, for example, financial, drug possession, driving and planning law offences. The Expansion Programme's main targets were burglary together with theft of and from motor vehicles. These offences in 2005/06 accounted for fewer than 25 per cent (1.4 million crimes) of recorded crime (Walker et al. 2006). Moreover, not all of these offences are investigated forensically (or need to be). The assessment of benefits needs to focus on the outcomes derived from the forensic examination of 0.9 million crime scenes (not confined solely to volume crimes) resulting in the recovery of DNA relating to 0.1 million offences (Home Office 2006a: 9).

Assessing the benefits from this activity is a complex and contentious matter, not least because of a lack of confidence in recording and reporting nationally (Williams et al. 2004) and the wide range of factors, including crime mix, level of resources, organisational approaches and relationship with the community, that will affect the ability of the police to detect offenders (Tilley et al. 2007).

**Table 18.1** DNA and volume crime detections 2004/05 (England and Wales)

| Crime category | Overall detection rate (detected crime/ recorded crime) | DNA detection rate 2004/05 (detections/cases where scene sample loaded) |
|---|---|---|
| All recorded crime | 26% | 40% |
| Domestic burglary | 16% | 41% |
| Burglary (other than dwelling) | 11% | 50% |
| Theft of vehicle | 15% | 24% |
| Theft from vehicle | 8% | 63% |
| Criminal damage | 14% | 51% |

*Source*: Home Office (2006a: 16)

Any analysis needs also to touch upon fingerprints. Sometimes the impact of different techniques cannot be distinguished. Also Expansion Programme funding (in its final form) was intended to increase the recovery and use of all forensic material. Moreover, linking genetic profiles obtained from DNA to 'separately established and validated personal identities' (Williams and Johnson 2008) might sometimes only be possible (and then not always successfully) with the kind of fingerprint technology capable of searching 6 million profiles in less than 10 minutes after arrest (Wilson 2008).

The availability of evidence and volume of detections are directly affected by attendance and attrition rates. A study of 3,000 volume crimes in six BCUs (force geographical sub-units) indicated varied response rates. Police officers attended the scene of 89.4 per cent to 99 per cent of domestic burglaries, supplemented by SOCOs (forensic scene examiners) in 62.7 per cent to 100 per cent of those attendances. The comparable attendances for, respectively, theft from motor vehicles and theft of motor vehicles ranged from 38.9 per cent to 84.4 per cent and 2.5 per cent to 64.6 per cent, and 4.4 per cent to 80.4 per cent and 31.05 per cent to 55.1 per cent (Burrows *et al.* 2005a: 17). Nationally it can be estimated from Home Office statistics that in 2004/05 DNA was retrieved from 5.5 per cent of crime scenes attended by SOCOs (Home Office 2006a: 9). While adequate attendance and retrieval rates are essential these are likely to vary between localities. For reasons indicated later, 100 per cent attendance and retrieval is unlikely to be either necessary or cost-effective. The current attrition rates (erosion of potential value) for DNA material and fingerprints demonstrate that this is more important for technical efficiency than retrieval alone (see Table 18.2).

The contribution of forensic examinations generally is also given sharper relief by considering what other options are available to identify suspects. An analysis of the results of scene attendance from the six BCU study (3,000 cases) indicates the importance of physical evidence in obtaining detections. If offenders could not be caught at or close to the crime scene or identified from information provided by victims or witnesses (the initial investigation), despite the comparatively low level of SOCO attendance in some areas, physical evidence (also including CCTV images) was by far the next best means of initially identifying a suspect or suspects (see Figure 18.5).

**Table 18.2**  DNA and fingerprint attrition rates 2002/03

|  | Yield from crime scenes attended* | Identifications/ matches | Detections | Additional detections |
|---|---|---|---|---|
| Fingerprints | 330,840 | 64,534 | 33,450 | 15,915 |
| DNA | 102,722 | 49,913 | 21,082 | 12,717 |
| Ratio of fingerprints to DNA | 3.4 | 1.3 | 1.7 | 1.2 |

*There were just under 1 million crime scenes atttended (998,185) in 2002/03.

*Source*: Home Office (2006a) (Crown Copyright)

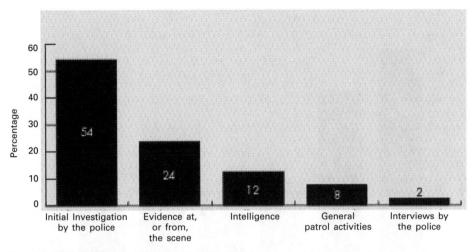

Unweighted. N = 950 cases (63 cases where the 'first link' was unclear were excluded)

**Figure 18.5**  Initial identification of suspects in detected offences
*Source*: Burrows *et al.* (2005a: 44) (Crown Copyright)

This 24 per cent contribution to direct detections in 2003/04 is a significant increase since the mid 1990s when earlier research suggested that forensic leads accounted for only 6 per cent of detections (Bradbury and Feist 2005). This would be consistent with a successful change in investigative strategy based on an inceptive role for forensic attendance and speculatively searching the DNA profiles or fingerprints recovered against national databases. Indeed, other research (seven BCUs) indicates that forensic science may have even greater potential to improve police effectiveness. Using Low Template DNA Analysis (also termed Low Copy Number or LCN) resulted in forensics providing the first link with the suspect in 45 per cent of detected cases. Also, in 75 per cent of successful prosecutions police officers reported that the forensic match contributed to building the case (Burrows *et al.* 2005b). Moreover, the comparative significance of forensic intelligence and evidence where there were multiple sources of information about the suspect may be clearer from research that has pinpointed the 'principal' evidence leading to a decision to prosecute (see Figure 18.6).

Detections directly resulting from crime scene attendance do not indicate the overall outcomes achieved as a result of the initial recovery of physical evidence. In 2004/05 each detection directly attributable to DNA resulted in a further 0.8 crimes being taken into account (Home Office 2006a: 15). This is probably an underestimate. The enhanced forensics pilot study resulted in an additional detections ratio of 1.5 (Burrows *et al.* 2005b). Moreover, given the tendency for offenders often to commit crimes with associates, the retrieval of DNA from a crime scene may result in criminal intelligence about, or the detection of, more than one offender. The tendency to commit crimes as a joint enterprise is reflected in official records of the average group size of 2.3 persons for each crime resulting in conviction (Farrington 2003: 20). The

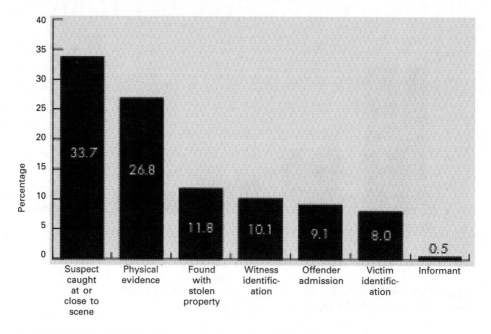

Unweighted. Base = 1,014 (excluding cases where principal information not known)

**Figure 18.6** Principal information used to identify suspects in detected offences
*Source*: Burrows *et al.* (2005a) (Crown Copyright)

detection of prolific offenders will be of even greater significance. Self-report and official data suggest that 3 per cent of 'chronic' offenders commit 22 per cent of crime (Farrington 2003: 4). Other studies suggest that as few as 5 per cent of offenders commit more than 70 per cent of all recorded crime and violent offences (D. Rose 2006).

A further question about the potential value of the benefits from forensic investment is that of longevity. While by 2002 there had been no sign of diminishing returns (and official data still demonstrate increasing match rates as the number of reference samples (identified profiles) on NDNAD gets bigger), it was recognised that at some point the churn rate might change this pattern. That is to say some offenders whose reference sample is on the database might cease to offend and for those offenders who are just embarking on a criminal career their reference sample is still to be uploaded. It is important also 'to remain realistic over the shortness of time for which most of those contributing criminal justice samples remain relevant for criminal justice purposes' (Leary and Pease 2002). Cohort studies of sets of offenders born in 1953 and 1958 indeed suggest that for over 40 per cent of the males and 60 per cent of the females a criminal career appears to have lasted less than five years, but for 17 per cent of males and 4 per cent of females their criminal career seems to have lasted 10 to 15 years or longer (Soothill *et al.* 2002).

Also, could the benefits from forensic investment decline if the volume of crimes falls or appears to fall? It has been interesting to see how the decline in DNA detections relating to these offences has been, generally, much slower than the reduction in the number of such crimes, as Figure 18.7 shows.

The DNA Expansion Programme has resulted in a demonstrable increase in the efficiency of criminal investigations. The overall outcomes have been significant and this has been achieved for a relatively low additional cost. Forensic science expenditure in England and Wales (including central government funding) has been estimated to amount to just 0.04 per cent of total (central and local) police expenditure (Home Office 2004). This could be an underestimate. The Metropolitan Police, albeit a force that may have exceptional requirements, spent 1.1 per cent of its operational budget on forensic services in 2005/06 (Metropolitan Police Authority 2006). It is clear, however, that a comparatively small additional investment has made an expensive police capacity much more efficient.

### Conclusions to Section 2

Assessing the technical efficiency of investments in forensic science is a complex matter and the benefits have been under-reported nationally. There is no doubt that the use of DNA in the UK has improved police effectiveness, but exactly how much is unclear (Williams and Johnson 2008). Research indicates that in contrast to a 6 per cent contribution to detections from a largely corroborative use of forensic science in the mid 1990s, an inceptive role for forensic science can result in initial links to suspects in 24–45 per cent of key volume crimes and a contribution to the outcome in up to 75 per cent of successful prosecutions of such crimes The overall impact may well

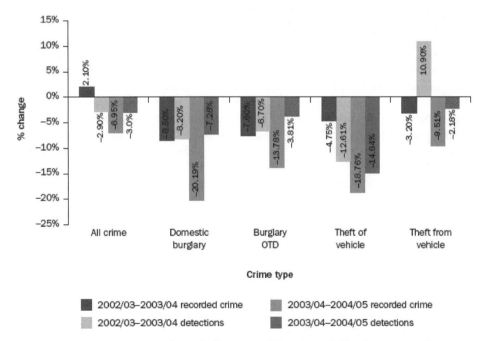

**Figure 18.7** Change in number of offences and detections, 2002/03 to 2003/04
*Source*: Home Office (2006a: 13) (Crown Copyright)

be higher than these figures suggest. A single investigative lead may result in multiple arrests, additional offences detected and the apprehension of chronic offenders. DNA has also transformed successfully many investigations into serious offences. Given the fluid nature criminologically of spatial boundaries demonstrated in Section 1 in contrast to national boundaries, it would seem foolish not to harness the potential of forensic biometrics to seek to repeat the improvement in detections experienced in the UK over a wider area. This argument is validated by both chance examples and the more systematic results of the Prüm technical trials.

## 3 Can the benefits of forensic science go global?

[DNA profiling is] a discovery that has benefited mostly the wealthiest of countries.

Ronald K. Noble, Secretary General of Interpol (Noble 2007)

In Portugal, wealthy in both EU and global terms, questions are being asked about whether the extensive use of DNA could be justified when resources are scarcer and criminality lower than in the UK (Machado and Silva 2008). Likewise, in Central and Eastern Europe (CEE), although the conviction statistics suggest superior attribution rates (29 per cent of crimes compared with 15 per cent in Western Europe) (Mayhew 2003: 111–12), public perceptions are comparatively unfavourable, as Table 18.3 demonstrates.

There is a more fundamental issue at stake. If it is accepted that good policing can help to provide 'the conditions that make human rights possible' (Sheptycki 2007) the contribution of forensic science may prove invaluable as a building block for greater professionalism and objectivity in criminal investigations. It has been noted how criticism of forensic science can arise from concerns about crime management overshadowing justice (Williams and Johnson 2008) and there are profound reasons for disquiet about some cases that have turned unduly on the 'hallowed' status of some experts and their evidence (McCartney 2006). The DNA community, however, has perhaps done more to expose the risk of undue inferences being drawn in court than many other forensic disciplines, particularly dactyloscopy (Broeders 2007; Cole 2008).

Progress in this area is faced with a resources conundrum:

Table 18.3  Satisfaction and technical efficiency comparators

|  | CEE | Western Europe |
|---|---|---|
| 1. Satisfied | 40% | 60% |
| 2. Dissatisfied | 49% | 26% |
| 3. Suspects/convictions per officer | 2/1.1 | 5/2.3 |

Sources: del Frate (2004: 70) and Mayhew (2003: 121)

- Even after making adjustments for purchasing power parity, the monetary value of law enforcement spending appears to be lower in poorer states (CEPEJ 2002: 59).

- Yet, possibly in line with an explanation of criminal justice expenditure as a necessity whereby such countries spend disproportionately more on criminal justice than richer countries (Farrell and Clark 2004), it appears to consume a much higher proportion of resources (CEPEJ 2002: 60).

As the UK Expansion Programme demonstrated, even in wealthy countries, the introduction of an inceptive forensic strategy is unlikely to happen unless much of the cost is met from outside normal investigative and policing budgets.

Estimates (Table 18.4) produced for the Home Office in 2005 put the cost of the new EU member states achieving the same DNA profile coverage as in the UK (4.8 per cent) and Austria (0.6 per cent) in the range of €14–427 million.

**Table 18.4**  Estimated cost of DNA expansion in the New EU member states

| Initial estimate of investment required in new EU states | | Total € millions | Per annum € millions | Per 1000,000 pop per annum €1,000s |
|---|---|---|---|---|
| **Minimum DNA Strategy (DNA I database investment only)** | | | | |
| Over 5 years | 0.6% of population | 14 | 2.7 | 4 |
| Over 7 years | 1.2% of population | 28 | 3.9 | 4 |
| Over 10 years | 4.8% of population | 110 | 11 | 6 |
| **Major forensic development programme (broader forensic capability building)** | | | | |
| Over 5 years | 0.6% of population | 53 | 10.7 | 15 |
| Over 7 years | 1.2% of population | 106 | 15.2 | 22 |
| Over 10 years | 4.8% of population | 427 | 42 | 58 |

*Source*: Home Office Seminar (2005, unpublished)

In addition to the size of databases the range in estimated cost is accounted for by two different approaches to estimating these costs. Both were based on current UK DNA Expansion costs adjusted by OECD purchasing power parities for the 10 new states. The first (Minimum Strategy) was based solely on the cost of analysing DNA samples and uploading them to a central database, together with database running costs. The second (Broad Strategy) reflected the approach funded by the DNA Expansion Programme: to increase the collection of all forensic material from crime scenes, and to employ analysts to ensure that forensic results were quickly actioned, including integration with other intelligence available to an investigation. Such an integrated strategy within the EU was endorsed by some 130 experts (from over 20 member states) in 2005 (Home Office 2006b: 57).

There is a means to overcome the economic barrier to effective international cooperation. This would be to apply the concept of the weakest link public good: the overall level of public protection internationally depends on the lowest level of control provided by any actor in the chain. The elimination of the vulnerability of American state and municipal airports to terrorist attacks was a major reason for creating the US Department of Home Security (DHS) in 2003. Post-9/11 investigations had identified vulnerability resulting from the diffusion of responsibility for US airline and airport security, weak communications and coordination between different public sector and private organisations, and differences in the level of incentives to achieve a sufficiently high level of security. DHS rapidly implemented a 'federalisation' process, by training and deploying professional screeners at all US airports. These federal employees had to meet higher standards than their private counterparts. In addition, improved equipment was installed at airports to screen passengers, hand baggage and checked baggage (Sandler 2006).

Within Europe a 'federalisation' process is not an option, but there are examples of wealthier countries pooling resources to augment security where it is weakest, yet critical (Sandler 2006) as well as the more general precedent of EU Structural Funds and specialist programmes. The 2003 Phare Programme included a project for 'a DNA profiling database for use in the identification of Romanian nationals perpetrating offences on the territory of EU member states' (Phare 2003). By July 2006 the Hungarian Police had trained 50 operative staff, 25 prosecutors and 10 laboratory staff. Legislation had been drafted and quality assurance preparations made. The Commission also provided some €0.75 million for equipment and consumables. It is intended to yield 25,000 DNA profiles (approximately equivalent to a maximum of 0.12 per cent of the population) (European Commission 2006). While valuable, funding of this order will never achieve the forensic strategy endorsed by the experts in 2005. What is needed is the level of pool funding available for initiatives, such as the Trans-European Transport Networks (TEN-T).

This will add 55,900 miles (89,500 kilometres) of high-speed roads and 58,800 miles (94,000 kilometres) of railways, including 12,500 miles (20,000 kilometres) of high-speed lines to European infrastructure by 2020. The cost of 30 'priority axes' will exceed €600 billion. This amounts to 0.16 per cent of European GDP, but it is estimated that the investment will result annually in 0.23 per cent additional growth (European Commission 2005a) from the improved movement of goods and people to and from countries neighbouring the EU and beyond via four major transnational axes. It is right that prosperity is enjoyed more widely and fairly within the EU, but TEN-T will undoubtedly also increase transnational crime.

It has long been recognised that transport projects cause technological externalities: damage to other people or the environment that does not have to be paid for by those who carry on the activity. Hitherto, the consideration of technological externalities resulting from TEN-T and related to law enforcement has been focused more or less exclusively on customs regimes and security of the infrastructure itself (European Commission 2005b) and not, for example, 'the evidence of crime clusters following transportation axes connecting the densest urbanized areas' (Ceccato 2007: 152). Each TEN-T link is funded by the member states whose territory it crosses, but Structural and Cohesion Funds are available in regions that are weaker economically. In addition, the European Investment Bank can assist in reducing the cost of capital for such projects (European Commission 2005a).

The amount of forensic investment required to assist new member states – even for the broad approach endorsed by EU experts – would be quite modest within the context of TEN-T expenditure, the UK counterterrorism budget or even the estimated additional security costs of the two-week 2012 Olympics (see Table 18.5).

The UK Government has already indicated support for pooled funding:

> In the future sharing of DNA information and other forensic data should become a routine investigative tool that is used to identify criminals and solve EU-wide crime. It is important that, as Europe moves forward, countries increasingly pool resources and sign up to a shared agenda on this matter. This will benefit all EU countries, and will give citizens throughout the EU greater security and peace of mind. (Burnham 2006)

Funding is an essential precondition, but is only one of five issues that regulates the impact of DNA on investigations. Three – sample acquisition, speculative searching, and profile or sample retention –are determined in the legal domain of each state. Permitted use is thus more extensive and, as a result, database size is likely to be greater where either there is higher legislative or public trust (probity) or confidence (competence) in the police or government (Scandinavia) or where trust or confidence may be lower but a greater percentage of GDP is devoted to public order and safety (Western Europe) (see Figure 18.8).

The impact of the three legal issues are illustrated in Table 18.6 by a (necessarily simplified) comparison of the main differences between the UK and Belgium.

The fourth issue – science capability and capacity – although often overlooked, can be equally significant. This relationship is illustrated at Figure 18.9.

Where the legal domain severely restricts use of DNA there may be symmetry. Operating on a small scale similar to other forensic disciplines DNA analysis is likely to be provided at an acceptable level of service. A change in the legal domain, for example, to allow sampling on arrest may not be matched by improvements and increases in capacity in the technical and economic domain. This will result in increased delays at laboratories and eventually work being turned away, nullifying the legal changes. Hence, any decisions to make use of DNA nationally or internationally need to be followed by an increase in laboratory capacity and capability to match the scale of forensic work envisaged in the legal domain. Unfortunately public sector forensic scientists may not have the commercial skills or interest to manage the transition to what is effectively industrial scale forensic science.

**Table 18.5** DNA investment in perspective

| Initial estimate of investment required in new EU states | Total as % of remaining expenditure on TEN-T (€600 billion) | Per annum cost as % of annual TEN-T budget + 05/06 New MS cohesion and Structural Fund budget (€5.6 billion) | Total as % of planned UK annual expenditure on counterterrorism measures (€2.9 billion) | Total as % of planned security expenditure for 2012 Olympics (€0.78 billion) |
|---|---|---|---|---|
| **Minimum DNA Strategy: DNA database investment only** | | | | |
| 0.6% of population | 0.002 | 0.048 | 0.483 | 7.865 |
| 1.2% of population | 0.005 | 0.070 | 0.966 | 16 |
| 4.8% of population | 0.018 | 0.196 | 3.793 | 62.857 |
| **Major forensic development programme** | | | | |
| 0.6% of population | 0.009 | 0.191 | 1.828 | 30.286 |
| 1.2% of population | 0.018 | 0.277 | 3.655 | 60.571 |
| 4.8% of population | 0.071 | 0.750 | 14.724 | 244 |

*Sources*: European Commission (2005a): Home Office (2007b) and *The Independent* (2008)

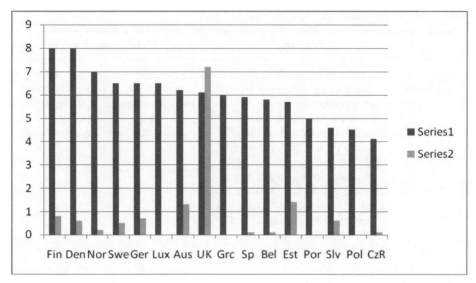

**Figure 18.8** Series 1: Trust measured on 10 point scale and Series 2: Personal Profiles on database as % of resident population
*Sources*: Kääriäinen (2007) and ENFSI (2008)

Public sector provision 'is almost universally characterised by backlogs' (Fraser 2006).

In 1997 the UK Forensic Science Service (FSS) – then a Home Office agency – had a backlog of 120,000 samples, no capacity to analyse Scottish samples and a 350-day turn around time (NAO 2003: 6 and 28). Competition between different forensic suppliers and the security for investment in automation created by predictability of demand with guaranteed ring-fenced funding under the DNA Expansion Programme for the police as purchasers of services now means that analyses, including those by the FSS, are completed and uploaded within days. Work is never turned away. The same problem persists, however, in the USA. $1 billion of federal funding during 2005–2009 was provided to reduce sampling backlogs (Zedlewski and Murphy 2006). As recently as 2008, however, the National Institute of Justice referred to a 500,000 backlog in 2002 in the publicly funded laboratories on which 95 per cent of prosecutors' offices rely. Laboratories are reported to have resorted to either limiting the inflow of samples, even returning them to the police on reaching full capacity (NIJ 2008 and Sourcebook: table 1.88.2005).

Competition among forensic providers and their separation from policy-making and standard setting, which should remain with government scientists, can also bring important benefits in terms of independence, quality assurance and governance. While even competitors acknowledged that the Damilola Taylor case did not reflect a systemic failure in the FSS (LGC 2007), the inquiry into this case highlighted the value of alternative sources of forensic expertise. The Northern Ireland state laboratory was suspended twice from NDNAD for failures during independent accreditation testing (more than a third of cases examined failed) (BBC 2008a). Above all, government proposals about taking DNA samples are now more independent of the FSS balance sheet and

**Table 18.6** Legal issues affecting the use of DNA

|  | Belgium | United Kingdom |
|---|---|---|
| 1 Sample acquisition | Unidentified crime scene stains can only be recovered by order of a prosecutor. Coercive sampling must be authorised by a prosecutor, and only if a prison sentence of five years or more may be imposed for the crime being investigated, there is already other evidence associating the suspect with the crime and DNA has been recovered from the crime scene | Resources are the only constraint on recovery at police discretion. Coercive sampling is permitted after arrest for any offence punishable with imprisonment |
| 2 Speculative searching | Only permitted if there is a match between the suspect's sample and that found at the crime scene | No restrictions |
| 3 Retention on a national database | After conviction for specified criminal offences (mainly severe traumatic assault, such as rape or murder) | No requirement to remove if not convicted or proceedings discontinued, except in Scotland where retention in such circumstances is permitted only when the arrest was for assault (including rape and murder), reckless conduct causing injury, and lewd and libidinous behaviour (at least 13 per cent of all arrests in 2003) |

*Sources*: Dierickx (2008), Nuffield (2007) and European Sourcebook (2006)

will be more so when it becomes a private company. It is not suggested here that there were any improper considerations in the past, but distancing FSS management from policymaking is vital for demonstrating integrity.

A critical governance issue for international cooperation is that norms established within the legal domain, particularly data protection rules, are not compromised when information is transferred between countries. The Data Protection Directive (46/1995) does not extend to the third pillar of the European Union (police and judicial information), but some member states implemented that directive in their national legislation so that it would apply to some aspects of the processing of criminal justice information (for example the Data Protection Act 1998). In June 2005 the European Parliament called for a data protection directive specifically for third-pillar data. What is required can be understood from two opinions published by the European Data Protection Supervisor (EDPS 2006a, 2006b). These are analysed and

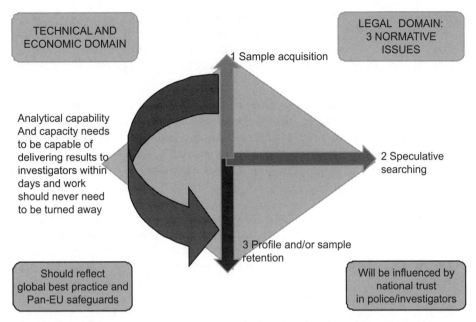

**Figure 18.9** Need for symmetry between the legal and technical/economic domains

interpreted here as a set of principles and specific safeguards that might govern such cooperation. It is clear from them that there is much common ground between data protection experts and investigators. The opinions are informed by recognition that harmonising the protection and processing of data can assist police and judicial investigations as this will result in more efficient cooperation (EDPS 2006a: Paragraph 8). More fundamentally this could make it easier to establish the crucial mutual trust between investigators from different countries (Den Boer 2002; Naím 2006).

There are what might be described as four general principles:

1 The third-pillar data processing regime should be consistent with ECtHR case law relating to Article 8 (Right to Privacy): the transfer of information must be adequate, relevant and not excessive. See especially *S(2) and Marper* v. *The United Kingdom* (30562/04 and 30566/04) (2008).

2 The rules for data protection in criminal matters should reflect the principles of data protection contained in Directive 46/1995, but should where necessary be expanded or modified to address specific considerations unique to criminal justice: hence where that directive has already been applied nationally to some aspects of criminal justice data the transition to a specific third-pillar regime would be much easier.

3 Police and judicial information should be treated as identical for the purposes of ensuring the protection of data both within the country of origin and when exchanged with another state: thus, the effectiveness of the safeguards would not be undermined by the considerable legal and organisational variations between member states, with frequently different

responsibilities for managing and rights to access information between the police and judicial bodies. This also takes into account that information will reach a judicial file at different stages in the investigation depending on how the chain of investigation and prosecution diverges between member states.

4 Permissible data processing should be 'necessary' rather than 'merely facilitate or accelerate the prevention, investigation, detection or prosecution of an offence': in practice, crime scene stains might be searched internationally in the absence of a national match, but reference profiles or information about them should not be shared until a crime scene match has occurred.

There are six specific safeguards. All are consistent with good investigative and prosecuting practice. None are barriers to international cooperation:

1 Lawful processing: a country requesting assistance and any state that may be able to help it must ensure that information has been lawfully collected, processed and stored and will not be used unlawfully (in respect of the legal regulations within the data providing country) following an exchange of information.

2 Quality of data and processing: not only should the accuracy of personal data be regularly and properly checked and different sources (e.g. crime scene, convicted offenders and volunteers) need to be distinguished, but also by extension in the DNA context, it is suggested here that the credibility of reported matches between different marker systems or with a partial sample should be subject to rigorous scientific scrutiny.

3 Purpose limitation: information should only be exchanged for internationally recognised law enforcement purposes.

4 Retention: information should only be retained for the period required for the purpose of the investigation giving rise to the exchange of information.

5 Audit arrangements: covering not only exchange of data, but also access, so that the data supervision authorities in the countries involved may be confident that this action has not compromised the data protection regime through individual unauthorised action and mistakes, as well as organisational or systems failures.

6 The rights of data subjects should be harmonised: for example, a person whose profile is on a national database should have the right to check the data and be told the circumstances in which it might be searched internationally.

Such an approach places great reliance on a state being able to refuse a request for cooperation should there not be confidence that these principles and safeguards will be observed and enforced. Despite being proposed by the Commission in 2005 the third-pillar Data Protection Framework appears to be making unacceptably slow progress. The UK government was criticised for not insisting that the implementation of Prüm should be conditional on the introduction of the third-pillar data protection framework (House of Lords 2007b).

There are currently three technical and organisational initiatives or models for cooperation involving DNA:

- A *global database*: Interpol's DNA Gateway where a single enquiry can result in data from (theoretically unlimited) multinational sources being searched. This is technically similar to the US CODIS system that also operates a four million plus profile database, against which crime scene stains that cannot be matched first at either local or state level databases are searched (FBI 2006).

- *'Peer to Peer' searching* of nominal indexes (shadow database) of all DNA crime scenes and individual profiles whereby member states can separately search the anonymous profiles held by each member state within the system: the 2005 Prüm Treaty (between initially Belgium, Germany, Spain, France, Luxembourg, the Netherlands and Austria, but since 2007 envisaged as the basis for routine law enforcement cooperation between all EU states) has adopted this model for DNA and fingerprint searches (Hager 2006).

- *'Peer to Peer' requests* to each member state within the system to search their national database (a Search Request Network): this would operate similarly to the previous model, but without a nominal index as all searches would remain under the direct control of and be undertaken by each national authority. Technically this would be the simplest model to establish and could operate efficiently as an e-mail system using highly standardised requests supplemented by information about each participating state's DNA legislation, data rules and technical standards. The latter feature would assist each member state to decide unilaterally which other state to cooperate with because of compatibility between national legislation and data protection arrangements, together with technical information that would enable its scientists to assess the credibility of any reported possible matches. It is well suited initially to bilateral cooperation or working within small groups of states. It might, thus, also help to overcome the way in which global police cooperation is so often 'crippled by lack of trust' between the member forces of Interpol, in a manner similar to the successful 'peer review' (demonstrated adherence to group norms) approach of the G8 Financial Action Task Force (FATF) (Naím 2006). A template for a SRN for exchanging information about DNA has been published on the ENFSI website (ENFSI 2007). The concept was successfully pilot tested between the UK, Canada and USA via Interpol's I 24/7 secure messaging service in June 2007 (Interpol 2007b).

All three options would replace informal police-to-police cooperation, which is unsuited to transparency and accountability and, as the Anglo-Dutch DNA disc initiative demonstrated, may not be secure or efficient; although the first – as a police and not a judicial database – cannot be used in some countries, including the Netherlands, for legal reasons (Lewis 2008). Indeed, the EU Council has indicated that an EU-wide DNA database is not seen as the way forward. It considered that data sensitivity and the quite different legal regulations in member states would pose legal as well as technical difficulties (European Parliament 2006). Globally all three options will be used depending on which states are engaged in cooperation and all share an important feature: searches are confined to anonymous DNA profiles. Personal information such as a name, age, appearance and criminal record etc. would not be exchanged unless the potential match of the anonymous profiles had been judged by forensic scientists to be sufficiently robust to initiate cooperation. Any subsequent cooperation would take the form of well-established arrangements for international cooperation permitted under national law by virtue of bilateral treaties and international conventions for mutual assistance in criminal and judicial matters.

The EU, if a data protection framework for the third pillar is introduced, potentially offers a strong comitological structure to protect rights as well as encourage cooperation; the right business processes could extend the necessary safeguards to cooperation with third countries. A normative regime cannot be taken for granted, however, especially as the role of forensic science in law enforcement overlaps with more complex, inchoate, and less transparent or accountable areas of law and policy:

- The UK Government has proposed legislation (Home Office 2007b and 2008) that would bring within the scope of the criminal law the taking and loading to NDNAD of bioinformation from a person detained under an anti-terrorism order, for sharing such data internationally with intelligence and security agencies and to place the hitherto secret counter-terrorist database on a similar statutory footing to NDNAD. The ACPO response (ACPO 2007) to this consultation indicates that some of this data is likely to have been covertly obtained. While many commentators have welcomed the Government's initiative, concern has been expressed that it seeks to regularise a quasi-judicial system for dealing with terrorism outside the criminal law and adds to the risks of misusing bioinformation. It clearly exposes a use of bioinformation beyond PACE (Police and Criminal Evidence Act 1984)-defined law enforcement purposes – the prevention and detection of a crime, the conduct of a prosecution or the identification of a dead body – and into the realm of national security. Fortunately, under the Human Rights Act 1998 the actions of the executive justified on grounds of national security are now justiciable if they are alleged to infringe human rights.

- The British Airports Authority (BAA) has claimed that it was complying with government requirements in fingerprinting passengers – including those for domestic flights – using Heathrow Terminal 5. The Home Office has denied this. The Information Commissioner is investigating a complaint that this initiative is solely to boost retail sales by fast tracking security checks, but has suggested that an effective facial recognition system would be preferable (EDRI 2008).

Another potential issue in future years may be the relationship between clinical bioinformation and criminal investigations. For example, a combination of the low-activity MAOA allele and early exposure to maltreatment has been linked by some research with a high correlation (85 per cent) to long-term and persistent antisocial behaviour (D. Rose 2006). If this wins acceptance clinically and ethically as the basis for clinical or social work intervention, both the genetic information and treatment would need to be protected by professional confidentiality and kept quite separate from the law enforcement use of DNA.

### Conclusions to Section 3

Substantial investment is essential if the citizens in all countries are to benefit from modern forensic science. Even if financial barriers can be overcome, a state monopoly of forensic analysis is unlikely to be capable of providing the capacity and performance required. Such considerations, however, are ultimately subordinate to decisions in each state about the legal usage of biometric information. The nature of the data protection principles and safeguards required so that international cooperation respects organisational and legal differences between states as well as fundamental human rights is clear. Developments within the EU indicate that a comitological structure that will most effectively encourage such cooperation might emerge. Regrettably, and for no good reason, progress with data protection and democratic accountability remains slower than operational, economic and political developments.

### Notes

1  The author is grateful to Benedict Wilson for drawing this to his attention.

### References

ACPO (2007) *Response to Possible measures for inclusion in a future CT Bill*. London: ACPO.

AP (2008) The Associated Press '600 Raids in Europe for Date-Rape Drug', published by ABC News on 10 July 2008 at www.abcnews.go.com

Baylis, J. and Smith S. (2006) *The Globalization of World Politics: an introduction to international relations*. Oxford: OUP.

BBC (2006 and 2008) 'Widening the EU's criminal justice net', 'Serial killer main murder suspect' and 'French "serial killer" on trial' news reports published on 5 October 2006, 3 November 2008 and 27 March 2008 at www.bbc.co.uk

BBC (2008a) *Fresh criticism of Omagh evidence*, 8 December 2008 and *Trial told of forensic 'errors'*, 11 December 2008, News reports published at www.bbc.co.uk

BBC (2008b) 'Mapping Migration from the new EU countries', news report published 30 April 2008 at www.bbc.co.uk

Blakey, D. (2000) *Under the Microscope: Thematic Inspection Report on Scientific and Technical Support*. London: Home Office.

Bradbury, S.A. and Feist, A. (2005) *The use of forensic science in volume crime investigations: a review of the literature*. London: Home Office.

Broeders, A.P.A. (2007) 'Principles of forensic identification science', in T. Newburn, T. Williamson and A. Wright (eds), *Handbook of Criminal Investigation*. Cullompton: Willan Publishing.

Burnham, A. (2006) 'Opening Speech', in *Maximising the Opportunities for Sharing DNA Information across Europe*. London: Home Office.

Burrows, J., Hopkins, M., Hubbard, R., Robinson, A., Speed, M. and Tilley, N. (2005a) *Understanding the attrition process in volume crime investigations*. London: Home Office.

Burrows, J., Tarling, R., Mackie, A., Poole, H. and Hodgson B. (2005b) *Forensic Science Pathfinder project: evaluating increased forensic activity in two English police forces*. London: Home Office.

Castle, S. (2007) 'Suspected serial killer thought to be behind 19 murders in Europe', *The Independent*, 20 March 2007.

Ceccato, V. (2007) 'Crime Dynamics at Lithuanian Borders', *European Journal of Criminology*, 4 (2): 131–160.

Ceccato, V. and Haining, R. (2004) 'Crime in Border Regions: The Scandinavian Case of Øresund, 1998–2001', *Annals of the American Geographers*, 94 (4): 807–826.

CEPEJ (2002) *European Judicial Systems 2002*. Strasbourg: Council of Europe.

Cole, S.A. (2008) 'The "Opinionization" of Fingerprint Evidence', in 'Forum on the Nuffield Report', *BioSocieties*, 3: 87–103.

de Maillard, J. and Roché, S. (2004) 'Crime and Justice in France', *European Journal of Criminology*, 1 (1): 111–151.

del Frate, A.A. (2004) 'Counting Crime in Europe: Survey trends 1996–2000', in K. Aromaa and S. Nevala (eds), *Crime and Crime Control in an Integrating Europe, Plenary Presentations held at the Third Annual Conference of the European Society of Criminology*. Helsinki: HUENI.

Den Boer, M. (2002) 'Intelligence Exchange and the Control of Organised Crime: From Europeanisation via Centralisation to Dehydration', *European Monographs*, Volume 40: 151–164. Kluwer: Alphen aan der Rijn.

Den Boer, M. (2005) 'Ins and Outs of an EU Integration Policy: The Position of Migrants in the Era of Security', Cicero Foundation website, www.cicerofoundation.org

Dickinson, J. and Pierce A. (2006) 'Why the international exchange of DNA information is important', in *Maximising the Opportunities for Sharing DNA Information across Europe*. London: Home Office.

Dierickx, K. (2008) 'A Belgian Perspective', in 'Forum on the Nuffield Report', *BioSocieties*, 3: 97–99.

EDPS (2006a) *Opinion of the European Data Protection Supervisor on the Proposals for a Council framework decision on the protection of personal data processed in framework of police and judicial cooperation in criminal matters, 19 December 2005*. Brussels: Official Journal of the European Union.

EDPS (2006b) *Opinion of the European Data Protection Supervisor on the exchange of information under the principle of availability, 28 February 2006*. Brussels: EDPS.

EDRI (2008) 'Information Commissioner Warns Against Fingerprinting At New UK Terminal', *Edrigram* 6, 26 March. Brussels: European Digital Rights, published on the web at www.edri.org

Eisner, M. and Killias, M. (2004) 'Country Survey: Switzerland', *European Journal of Criminology*, 1 (2): 257–293.

ENFSI (2007) ENFSI, Search Request Network Study: Final Report, 2007 www.enfsi. org/ewg/dnawg/documents/Annex/20F/20AGIS/Final/20Report, accessed on 15 April 2007.

ENFSI (2008) DNA databases, latest data at 11 February 2008 (private communication).

European Commission (2005a) *Trans European Transport Network*. Brussels: European Commission.

European Commission (2005b) *Networks for Peace and Development: extension of the major trans-European transport axes to the neighbouring countries and regions – report of the high level group chaired by Loyola de Palacio*. Brussels: European Commission.

European Commission (2006) Private communication.

European Commission (2008) Directorate General for Energy and Transport, Energy and Transport in Figures 2007, in *Statistical Pocketbook 2007*. Brussels: European Commission.

European Parliament (2006) Reply on 27 June 2006 to PQ E-0178/06 tabled by R. Kilroy-Silk on 24 January 2006.

European Sourcebook (2006) European Sourcebook of Crime and Criminal Justice Statistics – 2006. The Hague: Wetenschappeijk Onderzoek – en Documentaliecentrum.

Europol (2004) *European Union Organised Crime Report: Open Version*. Luxembourg: Office for Official publications of the European Communities.

Europol (2005) *2005 EU Organised Crime Report: Public Version*. Den Haag: Europol.

Europol (2007) *EU Organised Crime Threat assessment 2007: Public Version*. Den Haag: Europol.

Farrell, G. and Clark, K. (2004) 'What Does the World Spend on Criminal Justice?' HUENI Paper 20. Helsinki: HUENI.

Farrington, D.P. (2003) *What Has Been Learned from Self-Reports About Criminal Careers and the Causes of Offending?* London: Home Office.

FBI (2006) CODIS website http://www.fbi.gov/hq/lab/codis/index1.htm accessed November 2006

Fraser, J. (2006) 'The application of forensic science to criminal investigation', in T. Newburn, T. Williamson and A. Wright (eds), *Handbook of Criminal Investigation*. Cullompton: Willan Publishing.

Frith, M. (2006) 'The world city: one in three Londoners was born overseas', *The Independent*, 14 November.

Gene Watch (2007) 'The National DNA Database: an update', *Human Genetics Parliamentary Briefing*, 7. Buxton: Gene Watch.

Hager, K. (2006) 'The Prüm Treaty', in *Maximising the Opportunities for Sharing DNA Information across Europe*. London: Home Office.

Hannam, L. (2008) *New figures unearthed by Channel 4 News online show a huge increase in foreign arrests throughout the UK*, web article published on 28 January 2008 at www.channel4.com

Hansard (2008) House of Commons Hansard Debates, 20 February 2008, cols. 340–341.

HM Inspectorate of Prisons (2006) *Foreign nationals*. London: HM Inspectorate of Prisons.

Home Office (2000) *Prison Statistics England and Wales, 1999*. London: Home Office.

Home Office (2004) 'Memorandum of Evidence', in *House of Commons Science and Technology Committee, Seventh Report of Session 2004–05, 'Forensic Science on Trial', Volume II, Oral and Written Evidence*, HC 96-II, Ev 91-102. London: The Stationery Office Limited.

Home Office (2005) Private communication based on DNA Expansion Programme monitoring data.

Home Office (2006a) *DNA Expansion Programme 2000–2005: Reporting Achievement*. London: Home Office.

Home Office (2006b) *Maximising the Opportunities for Sharing DNA Information across Europe*. London: Home Office.

Home Office (2007a) RDS, chronological recorded crime statistics online at http://. home.office.gov.uk/rds/recordedcrime1.html (accessed January 2007).

Home Office (2007b) *Government Discussion Document Ahead of Proposed Counter Terror Bill 2007*. London: Home Office.

Home Office (2008) *Explanatory notes to The Counter-Terrorism Bill as introduced in the House of Commons on 24 January 2008*. London: The Stationery Office.

House of Commons (2005) *House of Commons Science and Technology Committee, Seventh Report of Session 2004–05, 'Forensic Science on Trial'*, HC 96-I. London: The Stationery Office Limited.

House of Commons (2007) Home Affairs Committee, *Committee Announces Inquiry into 'A Surveillance Society'*, Press Notice 13 March 2007.

House of Lords (2007a) *Lords Constitution Committee to Investigate Impact of Surveillance and Data Collection*, press notice 26 April 2007.

House of Lords (2007b) European Union Committee, 18th Report of Session 2006–07, *Prüm: an effective weapon against terrorism and crime?* HL Paper 90. London: The Stationery Office Limited.

*The Independent* (2008) 'Mobile fingerprint checks', 19 March.

Interpol (2007a) Press Notice: *Interpol fingerprint match assists US law enforcement in arrest of suspected serial killer in Europe*, 26 February 2007.

Interpol (2007b) Press Notice: *Interpol network links forensic laboratories in G8 countries*, 6 July 2007.

IPPR (2004) *Labour migration to the UK: an ippr Fact File*. London: Institute for Public Policy Research.

Jeffreys, A.J. (2004) 'Genetic Fingerprinting', in T. Krude (ed.), *DNA: Changing Science and Society*. Cambridge: Cambridge University Press.

Jenkins, S. (2005) 'It's not a Blair police state we need fear, it's his state police', *The Sunday Times*, 13 November.

Kääriäinen, J.T. (2007) 'Trust in the Police in 16 European Countries', *European Journal of Criminology*, 4 (4): 409–435.

*Kent and Sussex Courier* (2006) News report on 1 December (Tonbridge edition).

Khan, U. (2007) 'Bulgarian women gangs bring pickpocket crisis', *The Observer*, 18 February 2007.

Koeleman, A. (2005) Speech given in Madrid, published 23 May 2005 at www.ensfi. org

Leapman, B. (2006) 'London's criminal families replaced by ethnic gangs', *Daily Telegraph*, 23 April.

Leary, D. and Pease, K. (2002) *DNA and the active criminal population*. London: Jill Dando Institute of Crime Science, University College.

Lewis, C. (2007) 'International structures and transnational crime', in T. Newburn, T. Williamson and A. Wright (eds), *Handbook of Criminal Investigation*. Cullompton: Willan Publishing.

Lewis, P. (2008) *DNA Profiles Disk Inquiry*. London: Crown Prosecution Service.

LGC (2007) Home Office Review welcome but remit too narrow says leading forensics company, 18 May 2007, published as an LGC news release on www.lgc.co.uk

Lichfield, J. (2008) '"Ogre of Ardennes" stands trial for girls' murders', *The Independent*, 26 March, and '"Ogre of Ardennes" sentenced to life in prison after sexual reign of terror', *The Independent*, 29 May.

Loader, I. (2004) 'Policing, securitisation and democratisation in Europe', in T. Newburn and R. Sparks (eds), *National and International Dimensions of Crime Control*. Cullompton: Willan Publishing.

Loh, N.S.W., Maller, M.G., Fernandez, J.A. Ferrante, A.M. and Walsh, M.R.J. (2007) *Crime and Justice Statistics for Western Australia, 2005*. Perth: University of Western Australia Crime Research Centre.

McCartney, C. (2006) *Forensic Identification and Criminal Justice*. Cullompton: Willlan Publishing.

Machado, H. and Silva, S (2008) 'A Portuguese Perspective', in 'Forum on the Nuffield Report', *BioSocieties*, 3: 87–103.

Mayhew, P. (2003) 'The Operation of Criminal Justice Systems', pp. 84 –127, in K. Aromma, S. Leppä, S. Nevela and N. Ollus (eds), *Crime and Criminal Justice in Europe and North America 1995–1997: Report on the Sixth United Nations survey on Crime Trends and Criminal Justice Systems*. Helsinki: HEUNI.

Metropolitan Police Authority (2006) *Metropolitan Police Authority and Metropolitan Police Service Accounts 2005–06*. London: Metropolitan Police Authority.

Metropolitan Police (2008) 'Stolen Vehicle Unit on the right road', *The Job*, February 2008. London: Metropolitan Police.

Morgan, F., Fernandez, J. and Ferrante, A. (1999) *Mapping Crime, Offenders and Socio-Demographic Factors*. Perth: University of Western Australia Crime Research Centre.

Naím, M. (2006) *Illicit: How Smugglers, Traffickers and Copycats are Hijacking the Global Economy*. London: William Heinemann.

NAO (2003) *Improving Service Delivery: The Forensic Science Service*, HC 523 Session 2002–03. London: The Stationery Office Limited.

National Statistics (2005) *A Report on the International Passenger Survey 2005*. London: The Office for National Statistics, Table 2.09.

National Statistics (2007) *Statistical Bulletin: Offender Management Caseload Statistics 2006*. London: The Office for National Statistics.

NDNAD (2007) *The National DNA Database Annual Report 2005–2006*. London: ACPO.

Newburn, T. (2007) *Criminology*. Cullompton: Willan Publishing, pp. 50–80.

Newburn, T. and Sparks, R. (2004) 'Criminal justice and political cultures' in T. Newburn and R. Sparks (eds), *National and International Dimensions of Crime Control*. Cullompton: Willan Publishing.

NIJ (2008) *In Short – Towards Criminal Justice Solutions: Increasing Efficiency in Crime Laboratories*, January 2008. Washington DC: National Institute of Justice.

Noble, R.K. (2007) *Opening Remarks at 5th International DNA users' conference for investigative officers*, 14 November 2007. Lyon, Interpol, published at www.interpol.int

Nuffield Council on Bioethics (2007) *Forensic use of bioinformation: ethical issues*. London: Nuffield Council.

PACE (1984) *Police and Criminal Evidence Act 1984 (as amended)*.

Paterson, T. (2008) 'Labs making date-rape drug raided', *The Independent*, 10 July 2008.

Phare (2003) Tender reference Europe Aid/121255/D/SV/RO.

Porter, M. (1996) *Tackling Cross Border Crime, PRG Crime Detection and Prevention Series paper 79*. London: Home Office.

Prainsack, B. (2008) 'An Austrian Perspective', in 'Forum on the Nuffield Report, The Forensic Use of Bioinformation: Ethical Issues', *Biosciences*, 3: 92–96.

Prison Reform Trust (2004) *Forgotten Prisoners – The Plight of Foreign National Prisoners in England and Wales*. London: Prison Reform Trust.

*R v. Marper and S* (2004) UKHL 39. House of Lords (Appellate Committee).

Rose, D. (2006) 'Lives of Crime', *Prospect Magazine*, 125, August: 26–31.

Rose, R. (2006) 'Inheritance before choice in public policy', pp. 51–64 in L. Budd, J. Charlesworth and R. Paton (eds), *Making Policy Happen*. Abingdon and New York: Routledge.

Royal Society (2008) 'Detecting nuclear and radioactive materials', *RS policy document 07/08*. London: The Royal Society.

Sandler, T. (2006) 'Recognizing the Limits to Cooperation Behind National Borders: Financing the Control of Transnational Terrorism', pp. 194–216 in I. Kaul and P. Conceição (eds), *The New Public Finance: Responding To Global Challenges*. New York: OUP.

Sands, P. (2006) *Lawless World: Making and Breaking Global Rules*. London: Penguin Books, p. 23.

Scottish Parliament (2007) Prison Statistics Scotland, 2006/07, Table 37. Edinburgh: Scottish Parliament.

Sheptycki, J. (2007) 'The Constabulary Ethic and the Transnational Condition', in A. Goldsmith and J. Shetycki (eds), *Crafting Transnational Policing*. Oxford: Hart.

Soothill, K., Francis, B. and Fligelstone, R. (2002) *Findings 171*: 'Patterns of offending behaviour: a new approach'. London: Home Office.

Sourcebook, Albany University, *Sourcebook of criminal justice statistics Online*: table 1.88.2005 published at http//www.albany.educ/sourcebook/pdf/t1882005.pdf , accessed on 7 April 2008.

Tilley, N., Robinson, A. and Burrows, J. (2007) 'The investigation of high volume crime', in T. Newburn, T. Williamson and A. Wright (eds), *Handbook of Criminal Investigation*. Cullompton: Willan.

UNODC (2008) *Crime and its impact on the Balkans*. Vienna: UN Office on Drugs and Crime.

van der Beek, K. and Tullener, F. (2004) From a presentation, 'The Use of DNA Profiling for the Investigation of High-Volume Crime in the Netherlands', at the Home Office and ACPO Forensic Science Conference: Beyond DNA in the UK – Integration and Harmonisation, 17–19 May 2004, Newport (unpublished).

Van Renterghem, P. (2006) From a presentation entitled 'Belgium and International Exchanges of DNA Data', at a conference held by the Institut National de Criminalistique et de Criminologie Justice, 9 October 2006 (unpublished).

Valier, C. (2003) 'Foreigners, Crime and Changing Mobilities', *British Journal Criminology*, 43: 1–21.

Walker, A., Kershaw, C. and Nicholas, S. (2006) *Home Office Statistical Bulletin: Crime in England and Wales 2005/06*. London: Home Office.

Wiles, P. and Costello, A. (2000) *The 'road to nowhere': the evidence for travelling criminals, Home Office Research Study 207*. London: Home Office.

Williams, R., Johnson, P. and Martin P. (2004) *Genetic Information and Crime Investigation: Social, Ethical and Public Policy Aspects of the Establishment, Expansion and Police Use of the National DNA Database*. Durham: University of Durham.

Williams, R. and Johnson, P. (2008) *Genetic Policing*. Cullompton: Willlan Publishing.

Wilson, T. (2006) 'UK Perspective', in *Maximising the Opportunities for Sharing DNA Information across Europe*. London: Home Office.

Wilson, T. (2008) 'Applying the Science', in S. Brown (ed.), *Combating International Crime: The Longer Arm of the Law*. Abingdon: Routledge-Cavendish.

Wilson, T. and Williams, R. (2008) 'Memorandum to the House of Lords Select Committee on the European Union Sub-Committee F (Home Affairs) in response to its inquiry into Europol' and the author's oral evidence on 18 June 2008 to be published in the Sub-Committees Report (forthcoming). London: The Stationery Office Limited.

Wischgoll, P. (2007) *Six Italians shot in Germany in Mafia feud*. Reuters press report, 15 August 2007.

Zedlewski, E. and Murphy, M.B. (2006) 'DNA Analysis for "Minor" Crimes: A Major Benefit for Law Enforcement', NIJ Journal No. 253, January 2006. Washington DC: US Department of Justice.

# Chapter 19

# Forensic science, ethics and criminal justice

*Sheila Willis*

## Introduction

The aim of this chapter is to examine the main ethical issues that arise in the course of contemporary forensic science practice. Accordingly what constitutes forensic science and whether or not it is a sufficiently mature profession capable of endorsing and ensuring allegiance to a coherent set of ethical standards of conduct will be considered.

It is generally recognised that ethics are the principles or assumptions underpinning claims about how individuals or organisations ought to conduct themselves. Ethical principles may be drawn from a variety of traditions (including utilitarianism, right-based approaches and duty-based approaches), and all determinations of right and wrong conduct necessarily draw on such principles, regardless of their origins and whether or not they are clearly foregrounded. There is constant debate about the ethics of individual and collective conduct in contemporary society and the actions of forensic scientists, like those of any other citizen, can be interrogated for their ethical propriety as well as for their technical adequacy. However, there remain questions about the nature of the ethical principles that should matter most to forensic science professionals, about the extent to which communal ethical requirements should be applied to all such individuals, and also what mechanisms should exist to establish any such requirements, monitor their application and deal with those who fail to meet them.

Whilst it is relatively easy to arrive at an initial consensus of the nature of ethical issues and questions, it is more difficult to establish an agreed definition of the essential features of forensic science. Modern forensic science is often considered to owe its origins to Orfila, early in the nineteenth century. He studied poisons, developed tests for blood in a forensic context, and is also credited with attempting to use a microscope to assess blood and semen stains (Inman and Rudin 2001). However, there are also many earlier instances in which proto-scientific assumptions are recorded as having been used – for example, Stockdale (1982) reports that the first recorded case of forensic firearm examination occurred in 1784, when John Toms was convicted of murder on the basis of a torn newspaper from his pocket which physically matched the wad from the pistol taken from the wound of Edward Culshaw.

Interesting as they may be, however, such early instances do not always help in arriving at a definition of forensic science. It may be trivially true that the term refers to the use of science in criminal justice systems, but even here such systems are comprised of a number of different contexts and processes ranging from crime scenes through laboratories to judicial settings. The analytical services provided by forensic science laboratories are only useful if they address the questions raised by the examination of crime scenes, assist in the direction of investigations, and are capable of being explained in a transparent, logical and unbiased manner in subsequent court deliberations. Moreover, the detailed processes relevant to each of these contexts are structured differently in different criminal jurisdictions. Despite these differences, however, it may safely be asserted that there are sufficient common characteristics in the practice of forensic science – at least in modern democratic societies characterised by the rule of law – for forensic science to constitute an organised domain in which common ethical questions arise and standards or codes of conduct could be developed and applied. At the very least, forensic science practice is more than a casual occupation, and many have argued that it is best understood as professional, or even vocational in character.

Let us begin by commenting briefly on the significance of the use of the term 'science' in this context. Science can be considered a method of learning about the physical universe by applying the principles of the scientific method, which includes making empirical observations, proposing hypotheses to explain those observations, and testing those hypotheses in valid and reliable ways. Science can also be used to refer to the organised body of knowledge that results from scientific study. If we add the term 'forensic' to such general statements about a form of knowledge and its associated practices, then we easily arrive at an understanding of forensic science as an organised body of scientific knowledge used to address questions raised by criminal investigations and the examination of evidence with potential relevance to judicial deliberations of various kinds. However, there is much to debate on the very definition of science. Chalmers (1999) talks of the widely held common-sense view of science as that captured by the slogan 'science is derived from the facts' and goes on to critically discuss this. His more probing view of science offers a better lens with which to view the difficulties which arise when the disciplines of science and law meet as they do when forensic science is used in court. The view that science is a matter of the simple accumulation of naturally occurring facts is to miss the point raised by Chalmers that the acceptability of experimental results is theory dependent.

Most discussions in the professional literature of forensic science have given little attention to understandings of science itself; instead, a number of writers have provided a greater specification of the practical concerns of forensic science in order more clearly to demarcate it from other areas of applied scientific practice and to mark its distinctiveness. Whilst European scholars did much of the early work on this, a University of California academic, Paul Kirk, has been especially influential in defining the discipline in the English-speaking world. He defined 'criminalistics' as the 'science of identification' but also noted the absence of underlying principles governing this science.

Although the literature associated with forensic science has grown considerably in recent years, much of it focuses on 'how to' books and articles, whilst fundamental research and the enunciation of candidate underlying principles remains in scarce supply. Inman and Rudin's (2001) *Principles and Practice of Criminalistics* is a notable exception insofar as it attempts to define the necessary and sufficient features of forensic science and outlines its underlying principles.

In this book, the authors suggest that the nature of forensic science is captured in its orientation to six basic concepts outlined below:

1   Transfer: the Locard (1928; 1930) exchange principle is often paraphrased as 'every contact leaves a trace' and is the basis of the majority of scene and subsequent laboratory examinations.

2   Identification: defining the physico-chemical nature of the evidence as outlined by Saferstein (1998). However, the use of the word identification can be misleading as an equally acceptable interpretation of the word identification is to consider it to be a unique identification rather than to identify a type. The two meanings are interchangeable in forensic science. The comparison of fingerprints considered to be unique to an individual is referred to as the science of identification while chemical analysis to classify a drug is also referred to as identification. Recently, however, Champod (2008) has recommended a move away from the concept of unique identification even when examining finger marks and proposes a probabilistic approach to all comparisons.

3   Classification/Individualisation: attempting to determine the source of the evidence (Kirk 1953; DeForest *et al.* 1983).

4   Association: linking a person with a crime scene (Osterburg 1968).

5   Reconstruction: Understanding the sequence of past events (DeForest *et al.* 1983).

6   A largely unarticulated fundamental principle they call the 'divisibility of matter'. The authors comment that matter divides into smaller components when sufficient force is applied and from this propose three corollaries:

    • some characteristics retained by the smaller pieces are unique to the original item;
    • some characteristics retained by the smaller pieces are common to the original item as well as other items of similar manufacture;
    • some characteristics of the original item will be lost or changed by the division.

Whilst there is scope for debate about the adequacy of a number of the scientific principles described above, they remain useful for understanding the ambitions that lie behind the overwhelming types of practice that are carried out in forensic laboratories, used to advise investigators and inform opinions offered to assist courtroom decision-making. While they are a useful guide to the principles guiding the processes, they do not assist in the additional challenge for the forensic scientist in reporting findings. We will return to that later in the chapter, but before we consider the ethical correlates of such practice, we need to consider the significance of the term 'profession' in this context.

## Professionalism

The idea of a 'profession' originated historically around areas of human activity and experience which were uncertain and which required the application of specialised knowledge and expertise held by a distinct minority within social aggregations. Conspicuous examples of such specialisms include law, medicine, the military, science, and pedagogy. It is conventionally asserted that the rise of designated professions was driven by the desire of these specialists to tighten their control over their own particular area of expertise, by controlling access to, and authentification of, membership. The development of professional organisations (often taking the earlier form of 'Guilds') occurred in league with significant educational establishments and included efforts to establish and enforce standards of performance amongst group members. The retention of powers of regulation and admittance produced the *Walled Garden* syndrome producing 'gatekeeping' (regulation of access), and maintenance of the mystique of the specialisation, forcing society in general to accept and respect the professional's knowledge and expertise on trust (Jackson 1970). The formalisation of this process in society by using the universities and other educational institutions to grant degrees or licences governing admittance to and permission to practise the profession is still in operation. However, the *Walled Garden* is more difficult to maintain in the twenty-first century where near-universal access to university education and the ever increasing use of the internet to source information means that the aura of expertise within particular specialist groups is open to more scrutiny. Never has there been a greater attack on the specialised knowledge of the specialist, and Dr Johnson's (eighteenth-century) view that all 'professions are a conspiracy against the public!' is regularly invoked.

Nevertheless, contemporary claims for expert professional status are regularly made and usually rest on some or all of three specific arguments: that members are holders of unique knowledge; that membership involves a specific and highly technical area of practice; and that membership is formally regulated by reference to one or both of these properties. In other words the professions continue to have significant levels of protection through measures to define the boundary between the professionals and those outside. In this context, then, it is reasonable to pose two questions: 'Is there a profession of forensic science; and, if so, what boundaries separate the forensic scientist from others similar groups?'

First we need to note that the educational field that underpins forensic science is heterogeneous and confusing. Many practising forensic scientists hold degrees in the natural sciences though some take postgraduate specialisation in forensic applications. This means they are not separated from other scientists by their disciplinary background. More established professions such as medicine could equally well be considered to be applied science but they are so well established that they exist in their own right (Houck 2006). Whilst there is some indication of change in this area insofar as forensic science and/ or criminalistics are increasingly popular subjects in degree courses, there is little to suggest that these courses are working within frameworks that separate forensic science from other specialisms. A number of them deliver education in the basic sciences with some additional lectures and information on legal systems. The number of courses with forensic science in the title on offer greatly outnumbers the potential number of positions available for forensic science, and questions can be raised whether such courses are addressing needs in the field or satisfying an internal institutional need to attract students to otherwise unpopular science courses. The link between practising forensic scientists and such academic institutions is not universally strong and the flow of knowledge is often from practice to academia rather than the more traditional approach.

The claim to possess unique knowledge is difficult to sustain in a forensic science context. Forensic science consists of a body of knowledge on specific materials and the application of the laws of physics, chemistry and biology. So claims to unique knowledge usually rest on the basis of specific training in how and when to undertake these applications. Paul Kirk (1953) proposed that this expertise does require specialised training at a high educational level – perhaps at postgraduate level – and since then many educators (e.g. Siegel 1988; Stoney 1988) have written on what constitutes an appropriate education. Sensabaugh and Gaensslen (2003: 464) have proposed a set of standards for forensic science graduate programmes and suggest that they should 'promote interdisciplinary communication and foster the development of professional concepts and values'. In practice, however, most stakeholders will accept a primary training in the natural sciences as being appropriate. This is in keeping with the view that a 'trained mind' takes precedence over technical competence which it is assumed can be picked up when the formal education process is complete. Perhaps for this reason it is regularly asserted that the demarcation between education and training in forensic science is blurred, and in response to this, most operating laboratories have in-house training programmes and many also have competency testing. However, there remains little agreement on the education needs of the novice practitioner, including their needs for knowledge of ethical issues that relate to their practice.

If there are difficulties demarcating forensic science by reference to background education, consideration of the second element of contemporary professional status – a specific area of technical practice – may serve to distinguish the particularity of forensic science and support its claim for professional status. To understand forensic science as the application of scientific knowledge to questions of civil and criminal law characterises it not as elucidating fundamental questions of nature but, to paraphrase Sensabaugh (1998), as answering specific questions posed by particular case situations. Thus forensic scientists use the scientific method and the organised body of specialised knowledge they possess as a result of training to address questions raised in the course of criminal or civil investigations and subsequent court cases.

Despite this, control of membership is not well regulated in forensic science. This is partly due to the definitional and boundary issues raised above but also to the relative youth of the profession, and different approaches to professional control on either side of the Atlantic. In the US, professional control can be traced back to the establishment of the American Academy of Forensic Science (AAFS), and at its inception in 1984 R.B.H. Gradwohl declared: 'There is no fixed border for any forensic science, each has more than necessity to rely on the others. It would thus seem fitting that a central organisation be of extreme value in collating and disseminating the fundamentals of all forensic sciences.' The ultimate goal of the founding members became the establishment of a professional organisation to engender the confidence and the respect of the nation's courts and to see the ends of justice attained. The American Academy is devoted to 'the improvement, the administration, and the achievement of justice through the application of science to the process of law'.

It is a 'multi-disciplinary professional organisation that provides leadership to advance science and its application to the legal system. The objectives of the Academy are to promote education, foster research, improve practice, and encourage collaboration in the forensic sciences.'

The history of the control of membership of a recognised and organised group of forensic scientists was very different in the UK. In 1950, Stuart Kind wrote that half of the job of the forensic scientist lies in the communication of ideas to non-specialists, and this emphasis on forming and sustaining relationships beyond the expert group meant that the professionalisation of forensic scientists developed more slowly in the UK. Accordingly the Forensic Science Society did not formally institute professional membership until 2004, although many of the characteristics of a professional body (such as code of ethics and mechanisms to police it) already existed. The reluctance to formalise the process can be traced to the founding view that establishing understanding between constituent players in the criminal justice system was of overriding importance. Thus, unlike the American Academy, membership was not linked to academic qualifications.

The founding of the European Network of Forensic Science Institutes (ENFSI) in 1992 (along with other similar organisations throughout the world) reflects the growing need to organise such expert groups, but sheds little light on the more fundamental question of drawing the boundaries of legitimate membership in the continuing debate over the professionalism of forensic science.

## Professional ethics

Barber's (1963) list of the constitutive features of a profession included one other element which is especially central to the focus of this chapter: the existence of an 'internalised' code of ethics. It is certainly true that various relevant learned societies and professional bodies insist on a code of ethics to govern the activities of their members. However, it is important to note that there is no obligation on forensic scientists anywhere to be part of a professional body in order to practise as a forensic scientist.[1] Thus, although the American Academy of Forensic Sciences and the Forensic Science Society expect their members to abide by their code of ethics, court will accept a scientist who is not a member of either body. In this way forensic science is significantly different from the established professions. Professional bodies for medicine, for example, control the profession on behalf of the state in return for monopoly status within that state.

Other organisations of forensic scientists such as ENFSI and the Association of Crime Laboratory Directors (ASCLAD) also have a code of ethics to regulate the conduct of those who are involved in their work. The most recent regulatory body in the broad sense of the word is the Council for the Registration of Practitioners (CRFP) established in the UK in 1999 (now ceased trading). Despite this proliferation of professional organisations, however, with the exception of Barnett (2001) there remain few extended treatments of ethical issue in forensic science.

The American Academy of Forensic Sciences has the following brief description of ethics in their career advice section:

> The forensic scientist, no matter where or by whom he is employed, works only for truth. He must make sure that the examination is complete, the tests performed are done correctly, the interpretation of the data is thorough, the written report is correct and easily understood by a non-scientist, and the testimony is complete and truthful. Anything less is not acceptable.

This captures the core of ethical considerations for forensic scientists.[2] The European Network of Forensic Science Institute's code of conduct, however, gives a more complete outline of duties and responsibilities and also emphasises the need to be competent, to gain sufficient information to carry out the work required, and has specifications on reporting. In this section of the chapter I will expand on this very brief list by considering a number of its points in more detail and also by discussing barriers to compliance.

The first of these is to 'seek the truth and interpret it for stakeholders'. There are clear attractions in representing the forensic scientist as a seeker of truth. However, whilst the forensic scientist shares with other scientists this quest for truth, she also works under constraints that are not obvious for other scientists. The consequences of the work of the forensic scientist are considerable and therefore so are the responsibilities. The ability to communicate the significance of his or her findings to a lay audience is arguably the most onerous task of the forensic scientist. The scientist who confines their efforts to performing a series of tests is not acting ethically. Rather they have a responsibility to check the circumstances and ensure that the tests are relevant and the conclusions valid. Only then can they address the question of communication or reporting their findings. The forensic scientist needs to be sure that the police, court and other legal professionals understand the strength and weakness of their findings, and this means that they have a responsibility to ensure that the other players in the field (i.e. the police, lawyers and the public generally) have a clear understanding of the significance of their results. This responsibility to keep stakeholders informed is, I believe, what distinguishes the forensic scientist from scientists in various other disciplines. The research scientist must seek the truth but she reports, in the main, to her peers. The forensic scientist cannot afford to permit misinterpretations of her findings. He or she has a responsibility to ensure that the non-scientists in her environment have a clear understanding of her findings together with the associated uncertainty. This is difficult in the Anglo-American culture of today, where expectations of science are variable, and where there are significant differences between the epistemic cultures of science and the law. Accordingly, the advice that the forensic scientist need only communicate the truth to power is quite a challenge. In addition, forensic scientists have the drawback of operating in an environment in which they may be strangers. The court is the home of the legal world and the actors are those whose skill in verbal manipulation is supreme. Precedent is their God and truth the outcome from a very sophisticated game. It is in this arena that the forensic scientist must operate. It is agreed by all that the scientist must behave ethically but I believe it is less understood which factors may interfere with the scientist communicating the truth. The forensic scientist has a responsibility to deliver clear, unbiased truthful evidence but the profession is slow in defining how that should be accomplished, and the traditions of the courts do not always facilitate or support this responsibility.

I recall a situation where the forensic scientist was questioned at length about the absence of trace evidence. Everyone in the courtroom except the jury knew that the evidence that the clothing had been burned was ruled inadmissible. I have always found this example a clear one of the difference between the rules governing science and those governing a criminal trial. I have encountered many other examples since that early one and often they are more subtle but all return to the core finding that the evidence given in court is ultimately dependent on the court.

### Good science

A forensic scientist needs to use up-to-date knowledge based on valid science. This is implicit in the codes of conduct and generally accepted to be the minimum requirement of a forensic scientist. It puts an ethical responsibility on the scientist to keep his/her knowledge base up to date. The growth of knowledge and the ease of communication in today's world makes that an easier proposition than in earlier generations. Many modern laboratories maintain competency records updated on a regular basis but, in keeping with many other similar professions, few carry out examinations of the core knowledge base. Although the expert witness is regularly tested in court, it is important that the profession polices its own knowledge base. There is some evidence of this willingness in that the American Board of Criminalistics (ABC) in the US tests practitioners' knowledge and the Council for the Registration of Forensic Practitioners (CRFP) established in the UK serves a similar purpose. In addition, some state laboratories in the Scandinavian countries run their own in-house examinations. ENFSI as a body has agreed on the value of a competency assessment model but it remains at the planning stages for most members.

No competency schemes are compulsory, and it is usual for courts to decide whether or not the knowledge base of any particular expert witness is sufficient. This is not always a good solution but does begin to identify the complications that arise when science and law are mixed. In effect this means that the use of the forensic scientist is controlled by the rules of another profession, yet at the same time there have been a number of high-profile cases where the forensic science evidence has been held responsible for miscarriages of justice. I believe this is an oversimplification of the root problem. I have no doubt that in some cases the science was not valid. However, I believe the more common problem was one of omission on the part of both the scientist and the lawyers. The scientist has responsibility to ensure that the court has all relevant information but the lawyers have responsibility to probe the evidence. There are particular challenges for this process in our adversarial criminal justice system. When I followed the case of the Birmingham Six appeal closely in newspaper reports, I was struck by the realisation that the objections to Schuess's evidence raised during the appeals had, for the most part, all been raised in the original trial by Dr Black. I knew neither person but am prompted to ask what mechanisms could be instituted to ensure that Black's arguments would have been given more consideration at the original trial?

Starrs (1985) has written to the effect that the court has no obligation to accept scientific evidence any more than any other evidence. The jury is entitled to discard the finding if they consider that it lacks credibility. The professional forensic scientist is thus further challenged to ensure that in delivering their evidence in a clear, meaningful way, they are not so authoritative as to ignore all other views. This can lead to ethical issues where the scientist can be tempted to simplify the findings or fail to emphasise the shortcomings in the evidence in an effort to make findings more acceptable to courts or police.

The ethical scientist needs to be mindful of the boundaries of their knowledge and not be enticed into an area of which their knowledge is no greater than the man in the street. This can at times be difficult given that the forensic scientist also needs to have a good general knowledge base. I have seen expert witnesses prepared to give evidence on a range of areas so broad that it is very difficult to imagine how they can claim to be up to date and competent in the full range.

It is better that the scientist refuse to carry out work in which they are not competent, either at the stage of carrying out the primary work or at the delivery of evidence to the court. It can happen that the scientist, careful to confine their efforts to their area of expertise at the bench level, can be enticed out of their expertise by a lawyer at the trial stage.

## Scene examination

Most thinking forensic scientists will agree that their work is determined by the samples taken from the scene but many laboratory systems are operated with little connection between the scene and the laboratory. Such a system is unlikely always to communicate the truth. A system where an isolated laboratory carries out sophisticated analyses in complete isolation from the context of the case is unlikely ever to be in a position to ask all relevant questions and, in my opinion, can on occasion be said to be acting unethically. Let us consider some examples. A footprint may match the suspect's shoe but the evidence is of little value if the crime scene house contains a shoe with the same sole pattern. Matching DNA profiles may have less value in an investigation where the blood pattern analysis shows that the blood originated from smears rather than drops or sprays. Matching fibres at a point of entry will lose a lot of significance if there is a source of these fibres at the scene.

The scene examiner has responsibility to interrogate the scene as well as collect the correct samples. To carry out this function correctly the scene examiner needs a knowledge of how materials interact and the potential limitations of laboratory-based science. They also need to ask the relevant questions and, generally, cooperation with the police investigation is necessary to achieve this. It is my contention that the laboratory scientist has a responsibility to ensure that scene examiners are sufficiently trained, either by the scientist or to some approved standard. Anything less is unethical.

Whether working at the scene or receiving materials from the scene the scientist must satisfy him or herself that sufficient evidential materials have been collected to enable meaningful questions to be addressed by the analyses that follow. The role of the crime scene examiner is increasing in importance as forensic science itself develops. In Australia and in many areas of the UK, the examiner is a trained scientist. The Council for the Registration of Practioners (CRFP) in the UK have registered 1,000 crime scene examiners, thus making this group the largest number of specialists taking the route of exposing themselves to control mechanisms and sanction for violation of their code of ethics.

### Illegally obtained evidence

There are occasions when samples taken from a scene or from a person are later deemed to be taken illegally. This is another difficult area for the forensic scientist. In general he or she will not be aware of the legality as it generally will not be adjudicated on until the trial stage. The scientist may then rightfully leave the matter of the legality of the sample to the court. However, it is somewhat different if he or she has knowledge that the sample is compromised by the collection. Sample collection which may give rise to inadvertent contamination needs to be investigated. It is the responsibility of the forensic scientist to establish, as far as is reasonably practicable, whether any evidential materials may have been compromised before coming into his or her possession. There is no universal agreement concerning the covert taking of DNA samples from suspects; instead local legal considerations must govern the approach. A sample taken from a person spitting on the footpath may be an adequate reference sample in some jurisdictions but completely taboo in another.

## Quality

Quality assurance is increasingly seen as one of the safeguards of good science. It is sometimes mistakenly considered that quality systems guarantee good science and though this is definitely not the case, a quality system is vital in an organisational setting. From an ethical standpoint, it is necessary to know that the science being used is the accepted norm in the profession. This approach does not exclude innovation because a quality system is in fact a system of continuous improvement but I believe it is not ethical for novel science to be introduced into the forensic process without consideration and validation. The lack of consensus of what is acceptable from jurisdiction to jurisdiction adds to the ambiguity as to what is the ethical use of science. It is vital that courts have the benefit of new science but mechanisms to control its introduction are not well developed. It is a difficult area because if the courts confine their use to accepted norms they may lose the value of new science. However, if novel science that has been tested by few is used, a repeat of some miscarriages of justice is more likely. If the scientist is tasked ethically with communication of the truth of his/her findings, then quality systems must be in place, not only to ensure the validity of their analytical results but also to enable them to give some understanding of the reliability of the findings. This was one of the key criteria cited under Daubert.[3] The reality that the process from crime scene to court is important needs to be considered together with the realisation that judgements are subject to change as our scientific understanding develops (Chalmers 1999). Therefore the ethical forensic scientist needs to be aware of the history of the items he or she tests and conscious of the theories being tested.

Table 19.1 is a risk analysis of those aspects of the crime scene to court process that are not presently covered by laboratory accreditation schemes. In fact there are critical areas where, at the time of writing, no standards apply.

If we map the aspects that are difficult to control with those where the implications for mistakes are high or have ethical considerations, we can divide the discussion between the 'doing' and the 'reporting'. Quality systems are better controllers of the doing than the reporting because the standards tend to focus on the analytical chemistry or metrology approach, where the reporting is clear and has associated uncertainty of measurement figures to assist the reader in assessing the value of the findings.[4]

## Management

In approaching ethical issues that arise in the management of forensic science activity – especially in the management of forensic laboratories – we need to be mindful that the imprimatur of a governmental agency, laboratory, office or title does not automatically make either its results or the testimony of its staff inherently trustworthy, credible or reliable. A shocking and explosive example of inadequacies, misrepresentations, flawed science, doctored laboratory reports, posed evidence, woeful investigative work and false testimony was revealed in a report by the US Department of Justice, Office of the Inspector General, entitled *The FBI Laboratory: An Investigation into Laboratory Practices*

**Table 19.1** Aspects of the crime scene to court process not covered by laboratory accreditation schemes

| Part of process | Ease of control | Availability of standards | Implications |
|---|---|---|---|
| Scene | Difficult | Few – ISO 17020 proposed to Europe | Implications for mistakes high throughout the process |
| Transport | Easy | None | Implications for mistakes high |
| Prioritisation/ assessment | Interdependence needed for control | No written standards* | Mistakes reversible if detected in time |
| Testing | Controls available in some fields | Standards available in some fields | Implications for mistakes high – main focus of most discussions |
| Report writing/ interpretation | High interdependence for control | No written standards* | Reversible if detected – relevant to ethics discussion |
| Oral evidence in court | Difficult to control | No written standards* | Implications for mistakes high – relevant for ethics discussion |

* See note 4, page 543

*and Alleged Misconduct in Explosives-Related and Other Cases,* (Bromwich *et al.* 1997). The principal findings and recommendations of the Justice Department's report addressed 'significant instances of testimonial errors, substandard analytical work, and deficient practices', including policies by the Federal Bureau of Investigation Laboratory.

The managers of forensic laboratories (and those who manage the closely associated work of crime scene examination) are inceasingly forced to consider questions of the efficiency of their work, especially as the interest in technical solutions to crime investigation continues to grow. This has implications for forensic scientists. Ethical considerations may demand that more samples or additional testing are considered to clarify the signifance of available findings. Yet efficiency needs may sometimes override these considerations. In addition, an increasing number of professional managers are employed in forensic science laboratories which means that senior staff are not drawn from the cadre of experienced practising scientists. Both recruitment methods have their pros and cons, but we need to be mindful of the lack of tradition and the unavailability of clear standards with respect to the use of tacit knowledge in forensic science. The more established professions use a mentoring system to impart cultural values to more junior colleagues. A trend towards making forensic science into a commodity organised by managers with no background in the field could have the effect of undermining the ethical considerations. Alternative methods of promoting ethical norms are needed if the mentoring approach to scientists' development is substituted by other models.

Scientific curiosity is not a native human talent. It has to be shaped and directed by social situations, institutional arrangements and vested interests, which give certain inquiries their characteristic verve and momentum. A good mentoring system to ensure that ethical values will be passed on to each generation is important. The more regulated professions rely on the role of mentors who help to impart ethical principles. Codes and regulations will have no effect if they are not used in the correct environment. The leaders must foster the ethical norms of the organisation. Schein (2004) (has written extensively about the culture generated in an organisation by the leader. I submit that a leader who is immersed in the ethical considerations of the profession is needed within a laboratory even if such a person is not the overall manager.

Most forensic laboratories are divided into sections based on discipline, and the origin of this division is in keeping with the arguments proposed by Galbraith (1977) that organising arises from division of tasks and that an organising mode, therefore, is a pattern of relationships by which tasks can be accomplished through division of labour. However, I believe that forensic science can be divided into two streams. There are indeed situations where the test outcomes stand alone and where the most important considerations are accurate and timely results. This 'clinical' model can be delivered using any conventional management models. Yet in complex cases the questions of 'which test and when' are questions which can only be answered by the integration of the forensic science itself into the investigation process. This makes possible an iterative process in which clarity is established in that not only are the correct results obtained, but also that the correct questions are asked. High levels of accuracy and precision in the provision of answers to the incorrect question is more likely to lead to misunderstanding and miscarriage of justice than low accuracy answers to the correct question. Finally, it is important to remember the important effect that the quality of crime scene examination work has on the work of the laboratory itself. Most countries have staff with higher levels of qualifications at the testing stages than at the scene examination stages. This may be in keeping with the view that scene examination is primarily sample collection, but in fact the nature and quality of crime scene examination can determine the direction of the investigation – at least in some instances. In this context, an understanding of the whole forensic process begins at the crime scene when questions of the quality of forensic science support to investigations and prosecutions are considered.

Communication enters the arena again and raises even higher the responsibility of the forensic scientist to ensure that all the stakeholders in the system understand the potential and limitations of their science and the importance of addressing the correct question. The management decision-makers as well as external stakeholders need this knowledge. Confining ethical responsibilities to the bench workers is not a realistic model.

## The report

One could argue that the most critical aspect of forensic science is the production of a report. It is at this stage that the scientist is challenged with ensuring that the audience, whether the investigating police or the court, is fully aware of the value of the evidence including its limitations. All scientists make complex decisions relating to the data they collect and the interpretation of their findings. The heart of forensic science according to Evett (1996) is the 'interpretation' the scientist brings to a set of observations; however, what interpretation means or how opinions are derived is not agreed across the whole of the forensic science community.

### Measurement uncertainty

The question of measurement uncertainty is well elucidated in the field of analytical chemistry and in forensic science those areas where the main discipline is analytical chemistry are reasonably well served. However, other situations leave much to be desired and the result can be misleading to the ultimate user. This can result in a breach of ethics. The testing used and the level of reporting needs to be fit for purpose. Take a crime scene examination for example. Some idea of the scene needs to be conveyed to the laboratory scientist and later the court. Photographs and videos are common today but measurements continue to have a place. The danger is that the measurements will be made using precision without accuracy. D.H. Garrison (http://www. chem.vt.edu/chem-ed/ethics/garrison/precision.html) illustrates this well. He lampoons a crime scene diagram with a measurement of 99 feet 11.42 inches. He quite rightly suggests that the crime scene examiner would be more helpful, and I would subscribe more honest, if he said approximately 100 feet. The attempt to seduce the jury into thinking that the examination is of more value by using numbers that are not helpful and more particularly not verifiable is not ethical. This example may seem outlandish but there is a view that the use of any number will lull the listener into a false sense of certainty. There are varying views on the value of using probability figures in reporting matching DNA profiles. One side argues that this is the only manner to deliver the true value while the other considers that the high values of the figures are misleading.

Overall I believe positive measurements and the uncertainty associated are appropriately used where analytical results are available but much more difficult in the more traditional fields where qualitative results or comparisons based on observations are the relevant findings. However, the real difficulty arises when we consider negative findings. I suggest that the ethical dilemmas are at least as likely to be raised in the case of negative findings and this is discussed later in this section.

Jackson et al. (2006) differentiate between the scientist operating as an investigator and an evaluator. In the former role the scientist works in partnership with the investigator and uses his skills in the most imaginative way possible to assist the investigation.[5] A series of papers written by Evett and his colleagues (for example Evett *et al.* 2000) propose the use of Bayes' Theorem as a suitable framework to use for reporting the value of any evidence to investigators and to courts. This theory is an elegant method of distinguishing the contribution of the scientist to the court process and I encourage any reader interested in this area to read the papers.

This approach, the basis of the standard produced by the Association of Forensic Science Providers (AFSP) see note 4, page 543, is particularly suitable to evaluate the contribution of DNA comparisons where is it easy for the court to mistake the highly discriminating nature of DNA as equivalent to guilt rather than evaluate the significance of the finding in the particular circumstance. The reporting of DNA matches out of context is potentially more misleading than other evidence types because of the highly discriminating nature of DNA. The use of DNA as a tool in forensic science has been a paradigm shift and is having an effect on the use of science in a manner not fully developed. The highly discriminating nature of DNA and the fact that reliable evidence can be obtained from varying sources for long time periods makes it the most significant development in crime investigation since fingermarks. Fingerprint bureaux were set up some years after the early work in this area. They were in the main established as subsets of police departments. There is little evidence of DNA service following suit. In fact in some European countries and indeed in some US States the DNA laboratory is being set up as a specialised unit separated even from the traditional forensic laboratories. It is my contention that this development will mitigate against the forensic scientist carrying out their full responsibility in keeping the court informed of the true significance of their findings. The provision of DNA profiles with frequency figures seems an attractive option as opposed to having to offer interpretation in words to the court. The numerical accuracy appeals to the view that science is a black-and-white issue and that the findings are absolute. I strongly believe that the true place for DNA evidence is as a response to questions raised in investigations where there is a realistic option of a limited number of answers. I agree with the widespread view in the literature that this should be addressed by using probabilistic reasoning. It is somewhat disheartening that Bayes' Theorem has been found by legal authorities to be too complex for juries (*R* v. *Doheny and Adams* [1997] 1 Cr App R 369, CA). The scientist is thus handicapped in the proper use of the science and constrained to use the rules of the legal profession rather than the logic of their own. The result is the potential for misunderstanding and miscarriages of justice.

In some senses, what is true for DNA is also true of all trace evidence, and some examples may serve to illustrate this point. In cases involving glass, fragments of relevant glass are routinely measured in forensic laboratories and compared with reference or control samples thought to be the source of the fragments. The glass fragments may match the control and the significance of the match will be affected by the commonness of the glass but the significance in the context of a case will be affected to a much greater extent by the location of the fragments and what might be expected in a particular situation. Thus matching glass fragments embedded in the sole of a shoe will have little value while matching fragments on the uppers in an allegation of kicking will be more significant. It is much easier to standardise and control reports where the result is confined to the matching of a questioned and control sample. Evett *et al.* (2000) refer to this as the source level propositions and they are the least questioned reports and therefore favoured by a lot of people inside forensic science and by a lot of stakeholders. However, it can be argued that they are also the least useful and that the ethical forensic scientist has a responsibility to ensure that the audience, particularly at the court stage, understands that the significance of this finding in the context of the case can be quite different. Cook *et al.* (1998b) refer to the activity stage and an evaluation at this level is more difficult. I have personally encountered the situation where the evidence is discarded by the court because the level of discrimination at a source level proposition is low and an activity level is not accepted. Here again we can note the ways that the court governs forensic science. Thus standards to be accepted need unanimous support from within the profession before the wider range of stakeholders find them acceptable. In more established professions, academic training fed by research would be the vehicle for establishing these norms. Acceptances of court judgements are as likely to be the method of establishing norms in forensic science.

Unfortunately the use of many terms for different approaches to evidence evaluation doesn't help the situation. In a comparison of different approaches, Buckleton *et al.* (2005) describe three approaches as follows:

- The frequentist approach considers the probability of the evidence under one hypothesis;
- The logical approach considers the probability of the evidence under two competing hypotheses;
- The full Bayesian approach considers it under any number of hypotheses.

The lack of universal agreement as to the most appropriate approach can put significant pressure on an ethical forensic scientist. There is a danger that the path of least resistance will be taken and source results reported to court, a practice which will simply fail to serve the interests of justice.

### Positive v. negative findings – to report or not to report

When considering ethical conduct in forensic science, it is vital to consider the issue of the reporting of negative findings. To understand the problem, let us consider a trace evidence scenario, for example, fibre evidence. The results of finding matching fibres can be reported and interpreted using background information and studies generally resulting in some level of association between a person and a place or another person. The corollary of not finding fibres would lead to the expectation that no association took place. All trace examiners know that absence of evidence is not evidence of absence and that many factors can give rise to the negative finding. It is vital that the individual forensic scientist ensures that the investigating police and later the court understand this. Laboratory management have difficulties in relation to systems to check the validity of negative findings. The rational explanations of passage of time or unsuitable surfaces are easy in comparison with another possible explanation, i.e. incompetence in searching. Suitable competence tests are very difficult to set up in these situations. The detection of semen poses a similar dilemma. The absence may not be proof against the proposition and the searching is difficult to repeat in any efficient manner. In both cases re-examination is the only possible approach and this is extremely time-consuming.

Another ethical dilemma which is not well elucidated in forensic science is how to report positive results at baseline levels. A rule of thumb in many walks of life is expressed as 'if in doubt – leave out'. Would that it were so simple. The positive result at low level needs to be brought to the attention of police and court. How this is done is difficult. Reporting it gives it validity, yet it does not withstand the rigours of the criteria set for scientific acceptance. Take, for example, a trace explosive case. A slight indication of a positive result can support the suspicion that a person handled explosives yet the finding is not analytically valid. Should the scientist report the result or not? The advice to report with caveats may not overcome the difficulty. It is one of the situations where the scientist's communication skills are tested to the limit. An obvious answer may be to collaborate and agree standards. However, with the passage of time the sensitivity of the techniques increases and a sample that provides an inconclusive result today may be capable of clear detection even within the time frame of a case going to trial. A working forensic scientist encounters situations like this on a regular basis. Take for example a case of a suggested hit-and-run traffic accident. The victim's clothing is examined and compared with samples supplied from the suspect vehicle. In the absence of paint smears on the clothes and in an instance where no fibres from the clothes are recovered from the samples from the car, should the scientist report that the vehicle is not the one involved, seek more samples or report inconclusive findings? The critical consideration in this case is knowing what samples were taken from the vehicle, and considering the expectations in the totality of the findings. If the pathology report supports injury from being run over rather than struck when upright, the most appropriate samples from the vehicle may be those from underneath. Does the forensic scientist have an ethical responsibility to collate all relevant information before seeking additional samples or rely on his or her report? Codes of Conduct such as that from ENFSI says 'yes', but laboratory systems do not always support this approach.

Cook *et al.* (1998a) addressed this issue and proposed the case assessment and interpretation model where the expected findings for a particular scenario are identified before undertaking the examinations. If adapted this clearly puts a responsibility on the scientist to gather all relevant information before carrying out the work. This approach is enshrined in the ENFSI code of practice and is the basis of the AFSP standard for expert opinion. It is, however, difficult to achieve without a very close partnership relationship with the investigators and scene examiners. Yet in many instances only lip service is paid to the real need for integration of the forensic science into the investigation. In fact there is an alarming trend to consider that forensic science is in control so long as laboratory tests are controlled.

## Changing sensitivity

The sensitivity of the techniques increases with improvements in technology over time. At any one stage the amount of material present may not be sufficient to positively identify the source of the DNA. Should anything be reported? Take a case where a young girl is assaulted and a stain on her clothing is thought to be semen but is so slight as to prevent positive identification. DNA profiling produces ambiguous results including the possibility that the stain originated from the suspect. Should this result be reported? A report claiming that the result cannot be confirmed adds to the suspicion of the suspect; reporting a negative finding supports exoneration. As far as I can ascertain, the cause of most confusion and problems in cases involving forensic science in recent times revolves around the absence of expected evidence, or situations where the low level creates an ethical conundrum for practitioners. Such situations are made more difficult by the fact that improvement in technology may result in the provision of more conclusive results by the time the case is later tried.

The issue is not confined to chemical or biological evidence. Modern automatic fingerprint systems vary in discriminating power. It is possible that a mark searched on one system with negative results will produce a match at a later date. The profession has not tackled either situation well and it is clear that forensic scientists need mechanisms to deal with these dilemmas in an ethical manner. An additional issue arises when the sensitivity of the technology improves. Is the forensic scientist obliged to re-sample cases where no, or poor, results were obtained? Most other professions are not obliged to revisit their work in light of improving technology. Yet there is a tendency to reopen cases, particularly to check if DNA can be used to give greater certainty. The Innocence project in the US has used DNA to highlight many wrongful convictions. Legal oversight drives these investigations. How much responsibility does an individual scientist carry when and if they are aware of potential new evidence? It is an area which is not well debated, and questions both of what, and how to report are of major ethical concern. Finally, inadvertent contamination is a greater issue in instances where the sensitivity of the test increases. The increase in sensitivity of DNA testing suggests that transfer and persistence studies such as those carried out in the earlier days of trace evidence are needed to facilitate useful interpretation. Here again then the forensic scientist needs to be ever mindful and willing to report results only when the risk of inadvertent contamination is eliminated.

## The adversarial system

The above discussions focus on situations where the forensic scientist is concerned with producing primary evidence. This means dealing, for the most part, with organisations. Ethical forensic scientists will aim to offer fair and unbiased evidence, taking both prosecution and defence views into consideration. The adversarial system does not make this approach easy. Scientists working for the state will not always be aware of the explanations offered by the defence.

What are the ethical considerations for the scientist tasked with reviewing the evidence on behalf of the defence? The scientist employed by the defence is more likely to have information from the prosecution than the prosecution is to have re the defence. However, the defence operates at a much greater disadvantage in not having primary evidence generated at the scene. They can examine the prosecution work but may not get a chance to reproduce the original conditions at the scene. Are the obligations different for scientists depending on which side they work for? Both obviously need to carry out their work in an ethical manner. However, most codes of conduct stress the importance of client confidentiality as an ethical desideratum. In this scenario, the forensic scientist employed by the defence will have occasions when it will not be appropriate to fully disclose their findings to the court. Is client confidentiality the ultimate ethical test or is the greater good served by disclosing information? The lawyers operating in this system are on clearer ground because their duty is to their client and not necessarily to the truth. It is relatively easy to discuss the results of clear unambiguous tests. The real world of forensic science is the same as many others including modern medicine where many borderline results are open to interpretation through no fault of the scientist or the technology.

There is an additional consideration for the scientist whose main job is to review the work of others. They share the same responsibility of keeping their knowledge up to date. They differ from the producers of primary evidence in that they may never test themselves. It can be easy to set standards for others which are not attainable and not adhered to by oneself. The defence scientist operating in this manner is unethical. This chapter has argued that much science is grey rather than black and white. In this context it is possible for an unethical defence scientist to emphasise the least likely explanation for the findings to justify their fee. This is a very different approach from that of additional experiments to support the suspect's viewpoint. Organisations who offer a service to both sides are more likely to give rise to common ethical standards but the trend, although there are exceptions, is for separate organisations to operate for each side. The defence scientist who is not involved in testing himself needs to be careful not to fall into the trap of unethical behaviour mentioned above

### DNA profiling and databasing

Finally, it is worth noting that the development of DNA typing introduces additional considerations for the forensic scientist, over and above how the findings should be reported. Potentially phenotypic information is available for DNA samples. Forensic scientists today confine their examinations to areas of the genome which are not known to code for particular characteristics except the sex gene. In this rapidly changing field this may not always be the case.

The use of DNA in databases also raises further ethical issues. Arguably the storage of DNA profiles is an unjustifiable intrusion into an individual's right to privacy. Mechanisms to select the persons from whom samples are taken can also be considered to be discriminatory. However, most states in the developed world have taken a view that this approach is justifiable for the common good. This approach raises the important point that ethics do not respond to a rigid mathematical formula but rather are context dependent. For this reason they are constantly changing. Like justice itself they reflect what is acceptable in society. The wider ethical issues related to DNA databases need more in-depth discussion but it is noteworthy that the forensic scientist is well placed to keep society sufficiently well informed of the issues that need to be understood so that informed discussion can take place and consensus re ethical considerations be reached.

## Conclusions

In the course of this chapter, I have argued that forensic scientists need to

- be competent;
- keep up to date;
- inform themselves as to the most appropriate testing to carry out;
- communicate their findings to a range of stakeholders;
- remain mindful of the thresholds of reliability and the significance of their findings in the context of the case.

It would be easy to review the variety of existing documents on codes of conduct, but I have preferred to look at these issues at a more fundamental level.

I have argued that forensic science, although a profession, is not at a sufficiently well-developed stage to devise and govern its ethical guides in isolation. While accepting that the existing professional bodies have codes of ethics, much work is needed in defining the boundaries and establishing codes of practice for the practitioners in the whole process. To achieve consensus professional bodies need to be strengthened and mechanisms put in place to agree ethical norms. Ethics is central to scientific integrity and, accepting a requirement for ethical conduct, it is reasonable to say that the forensic scientist who acts ethically will carry out their work conscious of human dignity and the social impacts of forensic science work. The forensic scientist should be a guardian of the human rights charter but in the muddled manner in which the profession is developing, the forensic scientist is as likely to be portrayed as contravening human rights as protecting them.

Better understanding of what forensic science is; high-class academic programmes to support the science, backed up by research on the effects, as well as the changing nature, of forensic technology; the development of codes of ethics that are universal; and improved communication between scientists and the range of people they interact with; all of these features are necessary to the successful – and ethical – growth of forensic science.

The successful investigation of crime rests on strong partnerships between all of those involved in the criminal justice process, and a highly systemic approach to policing embracing forensic science knowledge and expertise as integral components of the broader policing processes was recommended by an EU conference in 2004 (see AGIS 2004). This meeting identified the ideal solution of working in partnership to investigate crime. It may be that this is the appropriate model for the scientist working as an investigator as described by Jackson *et al.* (2006). However, for much of the time, consideration of forensic science practice (including its ethical components) tends to be more focused on its uses in an evaluative mode. In this mode, expert opinion needs to be balanced, logical, robust and transparent. Much of the text above highlights the obstacles to achieving these standards. More collaboration and consensus building in forensic science is needed to ensure a properly ethical approach in this branch of science.

## Notes

1 This might be argued to be the result of the relative youthfulness of the profession.
2 The more formal code is focused towards actual membership of the Academy and does not greatly assist us in examination of ethics in a broad sense.
3 The Daubert standard for evaluating the admissibility of scientific evidence is based on 'reliability' where reliability is a matter of:
  1 whether the scientific theory can be (and has been) tested;
  2 whether the scientific theory has been subjected to peer review and publication;
  3 the known or potential rate of error of the scientific technique; and
  4 whether the theory has received 'general acceptance' in the scientific community.
  When determining relevance, trial courts must consider whether particular reasoning or methodlogy offered can be properly applied to the facts in issue, as determined by 'fit'. There must be a valid scientific connection and basis to the pertinent inquiry.
4 In recent times a newly formed Association (the Association of Forensic Science Providers) has developed a standard for the delivery of expert opinion. This standard addresses many of the ethical issues raised in this chapter and if it gains widespread acceptance will do much to fill the gaps caused by the lack of universal norms in reporting forensic science.
5 The distinction between the role of the scientist and that of the court is also outlined by Robertson and Vignaux (1995).

## References

AGIS (2004) *Conference Report on Integrated Evidence Management*. Dublin: AGIS.
Aitken, C.G.G. (1995) *Statistics and the Evaluation of Evidence for Forensic Scientists*. Chichester: John Wiley and Sons.
American Academy of Forensic Sciences (nd) *Code of Practice*. http://www.aafs.org
Barber, B. (1963) 'Some problems in the sociology of the professions', *Daedalus*, 92(4): 669–88.
Barnett, P.D. (2001) *Ethics in Forensic Science: Professional Standards for the Practice of Criminalistics*. London: CRC Press.
Bromwich, M.R. *et al.* (1997) *USDOJ/OIG Special Report, The FBI Laboratory; An Investigation into Laboratory Practices and Alleged Misconduct in Explosives-related and Other Cases*. http://www.usdoj.gov/oig/fblab1/fbil1toc.htm.

Buckleton, J. *et al.* (1995) 'Interpreting evidence: evaluating forensic science in the courtroom', *Nature*, 377: 300.

Buckleton, J., Triggs, C.M. and Walsh, J.A.K. (eds) (2005) *Forensic DNA Evidence Interpretation*. London: CRC Press.

Chalmers, A.F. (1999) *What is this thing called Science?* Milton Keynes: Open University Press.

Champod, C. (2008) From Statistics to Individualisation. Presentation at Forensic Science Society Annual General Meeting. Wyboston.

Cook R., Evett, I.W., Jackson, G., Jones, P.J. and Lambert, J.A. (1998a) 'A model for case assessment and interpretation', *Science and Justice*, 38: 151–156.

Cook, R., Evett, I.W., Jackson, G., Jones, P.J. and Lambert, J.A. (1998b) 'A hierarchy of propositions: deciding which level to address in casework', *Science and Justice*, 38: 231–239.

Cook R., Evett, I.W., Jackson, G., Jones, P.J. and Lambert J.A. (1999) 'Case pre-assessment and review in a two way transfer case', *Science and Justice*, 39: 103–111.

Criminal Appeal Reports (1997) Court of Appeal: Doheny and Adams, July 22, 23, 24, 31 1996.

*Daubert v. Merrell Dow Pharmaceuticals*, 509 US 579, 1993.

DeForest, P., Lee, H. and Gaensslen, R. (1983) *Forensic Science. An Introduction to Criminalistics*. New York: McGraw Hill.

European Network of Forensic Science Institutes (nd) *Code of Conduct*.

Evett, I. (1996) 'Expert evidence and forensic misconceptions of the nature of exact science', *Science and Justice*, 36: 118–122.

Evett, I.W, Jackson, G., Lambert, J.A. and McCrossan, S. (2000) 'The impact of the principles of evidence interpretation on the structure and content of statements', *Science and Justice*, 40(4): 233–239.

Galbraith, J.R. (1977) *Organisational Design*. Reading, MA: Addison Wesley.

Gradwohl, R.B.H. (1948) Quote on application form for American Academy of Forensic Sciences. http://www.chem.vt.edu/chem-ed/ethics/garrison/precision.html).

Houck. M. (2006) Presentation to EAFS Conference, Helsinki.

Inman, K. and Rudin, N. (2001) *Principles and Practice of Criminalistics: The Profession of Forensic Science*. London: CRC Press.

Jackson, G., Jones, S., Booth, G., Champod, C. and Evett, I.W. (2006) 'The nature of forensic science opinion – a possible framework to guide thinking and practice in investigations and in court proceedings', *Science and Justice*, 46: 33–44.

Jackson, J.A. (1970) *Professions and Professionalization*. Cambridge: Cambridge University Press.

Kind, S. (1960) 'Note from the editor', *The Forensic Science Society Journal*, 1: 1.

Kirk, P.L. (1953) *Crime Investigation*. New York: Wiley.

Locard, E. (1928) 'Dust and its analysis', *Police Journal*, 1: 177 [cited in Inman and Rudin (2001)].

Locard, E. (1930) 'The analysis of dust traces', Part 1–111, *Am J. Police Sci.* 1: 276, 401, 496 [cited in Inman and Rudin (2001)].

Osterburg, J.W. (1968) *The Crime Laboratory: Case Studies of Scientific Criminal Investigation*. Bloomington: Indiana University Press.

Robertson, B. and Vignaux, G.A. (1995) *Interpreting Evidence: Evaluating Forensic Science in the Courtroom*. Chichester: John Wiley and Sons.

Saferstein, R. (1998) *Criminalistics: An introduction to Forensic Science*. Englewood Cliffs, NJ: Prentice Hall.

Schein, E. (2004) *Organisational Culture and Leadership* (3rd edn). New York: John Wiley and Sons Ltd.

Sensabaugh , G.F. (1998) 'On the advancement of forensic science and the role of the university', *Science and Justice*, 38: 211–214.

Sensabaugh, G.F. and Gaensslen, R.E. (2003) 'Standards for Forensic Science Graduate Program Evaluation', *Journal of Forensic Sciences*, 48: 460–464.

Siegel, J.A. (1988) 'The appropriate educational background for entry level forensic scientists: a survey of practitioners', *Journal of Forensic Sciences*, 33: 1065–1068.

Starrs J. (1985) 'In the land of Agog: An allegory for the expert witness', *Journal of Forensic Sciences*, 30: 289–308.

Starrs J. (1982) 'A still-life watercolor: *Frye* v. *United States*', *Journal of Forensic Sciences*, 27: 684–694.

Stockdale R.E. (ed.) (1982) *Science against Crime*. London: Marshall Cavendish.

Stoney, D.A. (1988) 'A medical model for criminalistics education', *Journal of Forensic Sciences*, 33(4): 1086–1094.

Standard for expert opinion described at Forensic Science Society AGM 2008 – available on Society website: http://www.forensic-science-society.org.uk

# Chapter 20

# Professional standards, public protection and the administration of justice

*Alan Kershaw*

Q  Doctor, will you take a look at those X-rays and tell us something about the injury?
A  Let's see, which side am I testifying for?

> (From *Disorder in the Court*, a collection of verbatim transcripts from court proceedings in the USA, National Court Reporters' Association 1996)

That forensic practitioners and others called to provide professional evidence for court should be reliable and trustworthy is demonstrably a matter of public interest. This book has described the wide range of specialties in which forensic practitioners operate, most of them in areas of technicality considerably beyond what non-specialists can be expected to understand; and has discussed some of the issues around what can reasonably be expected of such practitioners.

This chapter addresses broader questions of standards, including how clients and the courts can be sure of what they are getting; ethics in professional practice; the nature of expertise and of expert evidence; and sources of guidance on who is qualified to provide such evidence. It goes on to describe the Council for the Registration of Forensic Practitioners (CRFP) – a UK experiment in the accreditation and regular revalidation of individuals offering forensic services.

Over the past generation the work of all professionals has become increasingly scrutinised, questioned and challenged. This is a general trend, related less to falling standards than to universal education, access to information – both reliable and unreliable – through mass media and the internet, and a general falling away of respect for authority.

Forensic practitioners are neither above nor immune from this trend. If court experts were ever regarded as above contradiction, this is certainly no longer the case. And yet the phenomenon documented by sociologists as the 'cult of the expert' proves remarkably resilient: in any group 'expert' status tends to be accorded to the person in the room who is least inexpert in the subject at hand. That this still happens in the courtroom should not surprise, but it is nonetheless remarkable how few questions are sometimes asked about the credentials of individuals holding themselves out to be experts in one or more specialties.

## Court experts in history

The long history of experts in court, and attitudes towards them, merits a study considerably beyond the scope of this chapter (Golan 2004). Some selective references, chosen to illustrate the issues under consideration here, must suffice.

The courts in England have allowed experts to give opinion evidence since at least the middle of the sixteenth century. In 1554, Saunders J. wrote:

> If matters arise in our law which concern other sciences or faculties we commonly apply for the aid of that science or faculty, which it concerns. Which is an honourable and commendable thing in our law. For thereby it appears we don't despise all other sciences but our own, but approve of them and encourage them, as things worthy of commendation.[1]

In allowing such opinion evidence the courts approved two exceptions from the principles that normally governed evidence: experts' opinions frequently would be hearsay; and their evidence would only coincidentally, if ever, qualify as that of an eyewitness. What has only recently been addressed – and then only in the civil courts, in limited circumstances – is the question of how far professionals should be called to act purely as the court's neutral adviser, rather than as an interpreter on behalf of one or other side.

In 1782 the celebrated Chief Justice Lord Mansfield confirmed the admissibility of opinion evidence, saying that 'in matters of science the reasoning of men of science can only be answered by men of science'.[2] The use of experts as witnesses called to support either side was by then well established. Whatever the rights and wrongs of this in legal principle, the perception that expert evidence can be tailored to fit a particular case is due at least in part to the adversarial nature of the proceedings in which experts become involved.

Judges have not been backward in expressing doubts about the manner in which expert evidence is handled. In 1877 Sir George Jessel, as Master of the Rolls, wrote in a patent case:

> ... the opinion of an expert may be honestly obtained, and it may be quite different from the opinion of another expert also honestly obtained. But the mode in which the evidence is obtained is such as not to give the fair result of scientific opinion to the Court. A man may go, and sometimes does go, to half a dozen experts ... he finds three in his favour and three against him; he says to the three in his favour: 'Will you be kind enough to give evidence?' And he pays the ones against him their fees and leaves them alone; the other side does the same ... I am sorry

to say the result is that the Court does not get the assistance from the experts which, if they were unbiased and fairly chosen, it would have a right to expect.[3]

A century later Sir Thomas (now Lord) Bingham, also as Master of the Rolls, expressed a similar view:

For whatever reason, and whether consciously or unconsciously, the fact is that expert witnesses instructed on behalf of parties to litigation often tend, if called as witnesses at all, to espouse the cause of those instructing them to a greater or lesser extent, on occasion becoming more partisan than the parties.[4]

Concerns about the way science has been used in court have not been confined to judges. In the mid nineteenth century the scientific community, concerned doubtless about the implications of scandals over court cases for their collective reputation, campaigned for reform of expert testimony. Dr Henry Letheby, Medical Officer for Health in the City of London, wrote to *The Times* in 1859 about the apparent contradiction of science in the courts:

... the seeming uncertainty of its results, and the conflicting testimony of its alumni, are such as to deprive it of that value which it ought to have in the estimation of the public ... (Letheby 1859)

R.A. Smith, a sanitary chemist, was so disturbed by his experience of giving expert evidence in 1857 that he swore never to appear in court again. Two years later, in an address to the Royal Society of Arts, he remarked that 'it is repugnant to our feelings to see great questions from nature played with, distorted and hidden for selfish purposes'; and commented on

... the partisan position men of science have come to occupy in the adversarial courtroom ... The scientific man ... simply becomes a barrister who knows science ... If we allow him or encourage him to become an advocate, we remove him from his sphere ... we teach them to study impartially and then tell them to practise with partiality. Such a division of the moral nature of man is extremely hurtful, both to the individual and to society. (Smith 1860)

This tension remains largely unresolved. Scientists' efforts to alter their status, to reflect more their independence and impartiality, foundered on the rock of the legal profession's characteristic resistance to change. The adversarial system persists; and, despite the introduction of single, court-appointed experts in some civil cases, no such change in the criminal courts is even in prospect.

## What is an expert?

The paradox is this: the court calls in the expert because the court lacks expertise in a particular subject – a medical or financial matter, a construction question, the interpretation of digital data. Legal practice requires the court to decide who is an expert on the subject. But how, having admitted that it lacks the appropriate expertise, is the court fitted to make that decision? It is a circle that needs to be broken.

'An expert', Mark Twain is supposed to have said, 'is some guy from out of town.' As usual he put his finger on a simple but profound truth. It is hard to avoid the impression that some part of an expert's standing can derive from a certain mystique, bringing something of the unknown or unfamiliar, a special knowledge that sets them apart from ordinary folk.

Few deny that the contribution of experts to court proceedings is both invaluable and irreplaceable. Few believe that the vast majority of forensic practitioners are less than sincere, hard-working, competent and fair-minded professionals. What needs puncturing is the myth that they should never have to prove their credentials beyond the catalogues of qualifications to which they habitually lay claim.

Different jurisdictions have sought to address the problem, in different ways and with some measure of success. None can, however, be said to have found a complete solution to the problem. In 1993 the Supreme Court of the USA established an important precedent regarding the admissibility of expert witnesses' testimony. The Court held that trial judges were the 'gatekeepers' of scientific evidence. Under what has become known as the *Daubert Standard*, judges must evaluate proposed expert witnesses to determine whether their testimony is both

- **relevant:** does it contribute to determining the facts of the case? For example, a meteorologist called to testify about the weather at the time of an incident would not be allowed to testify if the state of the weather had no bearing on the issue at hand;

and

- **reliable:** were the expert's conclusions derived from scientific method? For example, is the theory or technique repeatable, refutable, testable? Has it been subjected to peer review and publication? What is the known or potential error rate? What standards underpin its operation? Does the relevant scientific community generally accept it?[5]

The Daubert Standard was later extended to cover non-scientific expert testimony.[6] The effect of the ruling has probably been more to exclude evidence than to admit it; but it represents an honest attempt to address one of the key issues: what forms of science can reliably be admitted in court, as opposed to the untested and the speculative? As an approach, however, it still relies on individual judgements in individual courts, in matters where the judge may not be the person best placed to make the final decision; and it does not directly address the issue of the competence and ethicality of the aspirant expert.

## The duties of the expert

In English law the approach to managing experts has traditionally been based on a statement of their duties when providing evidence in the civil courts. These derive from case law[7] and are now set down in Part 35 of the Civil Procedure Rules and, most fully, in the Practice Direction which accompanies that part of the Rules (Civil Procedure Rules 1998). These texts set out the expert's paramount duty to the court, overriding any obligation to the person who instructed the expert; and emphasise the importance of staying within the boundaries of one's expertise, providing unbiased opinion, and so on. They are by way of a code of conduct, and are to an extent underpinned by the reform introduced following Lord Woolf's report on the civil justice system, for the use, in some civil cases, of a single court-appointed joint expert (Woolf 1996).

The duties are generally well understood among experts but, like the Daubert Standard, rely for their application on individual judgements in individual cases. Experts falling short of the expected standards will rarely be exposed to sanctions because their behaviour in particular cases will not generally be reported outside those proceedings; nor are there any arrangements in place to enforce remedial action, still less to prevent a thoroughly incompetent, unethical or unscrupulous practitioner from continuing to practise without restriction.

## Sources of information about experts

In the wider world of expert witnesses, where professionals offer their services in court work as a sideline to their mainstream activity, or as a retirement activity, there have for some years existed a small group of organisations which those calling themselves expert witnesses may join.

The Expert Witness Institute and the Academy of Experts are concerned with standards and aim to act as collective voices for expert witnesses, offering also forms of training and developmental conferences (EWI 2008; Academy of Experts 2008). Their membership requirements are similar, applicants being required to submit a CV, proof of a professional qualification and the names of solicitors or barristers to act as referees. Membership is granted subject to satisfactory references. There is no assessment of competence in a professional field. Both organisations have in recent years been moving to introduce higher levels of membership, assessing competence in expert witness skills but taking professional competence as read.

The Society of Expert Witnesses (SEW) is linked with the *UK Register of Expert Witnesses*, a commercial publication, membership being based on self-certification with no requirement for references even from satisfied customers (SEW 2008; UK Register of Expert Witnesses 2008). There are other publications in which those holding themselves out to be experts may pay to advertise their services. Such publications are more by way of catalogues than of registers, since their entry requirements are rudimentary; but they are commercially successful and are evidently consulted by lawyers and others proposing to commission the services of experts. Beyond them, lawyers tend to rely on word of mouth recommendation, personal experience and informal lists kept within the firm or, sometimes, within a court circuit.

Expert witness training is offered by a number of providers, predominantly lawyers who can teach aspirant experts about how to present themselves in court, prepare an effective report and stand up to rigorous cross-examination. Such training is worthwhile in itself, but as a measure of quality it is limited: the fact that an expert has undergone it is an input measure, but no indicator of competence in a professional field.

## Two cautionary tales

The limitations of these less than rigorous methods of identifying competence in court work are readily apparent, and are illustrated by some of the stories that emerge, from time to time, where a supposed expert has turned out to be a fraud, or at least has strayed beyond the boundaries of their professional competence.

I will confine myself to two recent examples, which perhaps illustrate how open the forensic market can be to individuals seeking to exploit the ignorance of others; and how unwary even sophisticated customers can be when commissioning 'expert' evidence.

### The 'psychiatrist'
Barian Baluchi is not a doctor. In the late 1990s he bought a PhD from the USA and stole the identity of a trainee doctor who had not moved on from provisional to full registration with the General Medical Council (GMC) (GMC 2008). He claimed to have studied at Harvard, Columbia, Newcastle, Leeds and Sussex Universities, and to have lectured in the UK and USA. He was a member of the Expert Witness Institute and he had an entry in the *UK Register of Expert Witnesses* (Lister 2005).

He was exposed as a fraud and convicted in January 2005, but not before he had produced, over some 15 years, 'psychiatric' reports on hundreds of asylum seekers.

### The 'psychologist'
Gene Morrison was not a psychologist. He obtained certificates for a BSc in Forensic Science, a Masters in Forensic Science and a Doctorate in Criminology, from a non-existent university via a website entitled 'affordable degrees'. Through the *Yellow Pages, Solicitors' Journal* and his own website he advertised services in blood and fingerprint analysis, polygraph testing, facial mapping and other specialties as well as the forensic psychology to which he claimed title. When a customer became suspicious – after he had practised for some 26 years and acted in over 700 cases – the police raided his premises and

found a laptop, a camera and a large magnifying glass. He was convicted in February 2007 of deception, perjury and perverting the course of justice (Bradshaw 2008).

## What are we getting?

It is essential that any member of the public, when in want of professional help of any kind, should have a reliable way of knowing what they are getting: what are this individual's credentials, what is the scope of their competence, how do we know they are up to date? The traditional means of providing such information is through an effective system of professional regulation. Typically this is centred on a published register of qualified people whose current competence may (up to a point) be inferred from their inclusion in the list.

All professionals should aspire to best practice, consistently deliver good practice and never fall below safe, competent practice. Professional registers are an attempt at defining safe, competent practice, putting a boundary around it and seeking to ensure that registered practitioners always practise above that threshold. To restrict registration to just the top practitioners – the ones who attend the conferences, deliver the addresses and publish the learned papers – is simply to talk to the wrong people.

An easy way to build a professional register is to identify the educational qualifications that can reasonably be expected to fit an individual for entry to a profession, and then admit any applicant holding such a qualification. For doctors, lawyers, accountants and others that is relatively straightforward.

Forensic practice is different. It is ill suited to a first degree (despite the proliferation of forensic science courses in many UK universities), since forensic science is applied science and demands firm foundations in a pure academic discipline. To be a forensic anthropologist one first needs to be an anthropologist – application comes later. It is well suited to a course at Masters level, but most forensic practitioners do not hold a Masters degree. Alternatively, forensic expertise may be gained through long years of practice. But there is at present no single qualification that could be said to denote current competence in a forensic specialty.

In attempting to identify experts the courts, acting on behalf of the public, similarly need to know what they are getting. They need authoritative, impartial indicators of the current competence of individuals, and of the scope of the forensic specialties in which they do their professional work. Without that, they lack any reliable means of negotiating their way through the forests of qualifications and experience claimed by those who want to be called experts – an obstacle course which to the non-specialist can be bewildering.

## Accrediting organisations or accrediting individuals?

Would the accreditation of organisations providing forensic services offer a way through? Organisational accreditation has been established for some time in the UK forensic world. Forensic suppliers have sought accreditation with an organisation offering quality assurance through the development of manuals formalising procedures and processes, with periodic inspection to ensure compliance with the standards the organisation has set for itself. The leading quality assurance organisation in this field is the United Kingdom Accreditation Service (UKAS 2008).

This form of accreditation is admirable in that it provides a formal framework that underpins providers' efforts to ensure that everything goes as it should. As regards the competence of the individuals providing the service, a quality system will typically seek to be satisfied that staff have been properly trained and understand their responsibilities. But quality assurance systems, in themselves, rarely use more than input measures in this respect. They omit the much more sensitive questions, pursuit of which can be painful and are therefore usually avoided: How good is this person at their job? Are they fit to practise, at least to the threshold standard? Are they fit to do that today?

Organisational quality systems need to address issues of places, processes and people. For the 'people' part, what is needed, but is rarely offered in traditional approaches, is a method of assuring the current competence of individual practitioners that seeks not to tick boxes but to assess the individual's approach to the sequence of thoughts and actions that make up the professional process. Professionalism is about a great deal more than the ability to complete a set series of tasks. It is about the ability to relate apparently unconnected facts, thoughts and concepts derived from different sources. It encompasses the willingness and the capacity to think beyond the immediate task in hand and outside received patterns. It is driven, above all, by a passion for the truth.

## Compulsory registration?

In most professions, some form of registration or professional membership is essential for successful practice. No sensible person would be likely to consult an accountant, architect, doctor, vet or pharmacist without the assurance that they are being policed in an effective way and that the profession's standards are being upheld in the public interest.

There are, however, significant differences with forensic practice compared to other professions. There will always be specialties too small, or too rarely needed in court, to make a registration scheme worthwhile. There will always be practitioners too early in their careers to have built a portfolio of casework which can be assessed, but who need to give evidence in court in order to develop that portfolio. And there are good reasons of principle why the courts must be free at any time to hear evidence from anyone they choose: no one, apart from the courts themselves, should seek to constrain them in this.

Despite this, calls for a system of compulsory accreditation for expert witnesses are not unusual in the wake of media coverage of cases where the work of a professional in court has had an undesirable outcome. But the old wartime saying 'Danger past, God forgotten' comes into play and the legal and scientific establishments settle back into familiar comfort zones:

practitioners continue to be selected by word of mouth, anecdote and the most cursory of quality checks.

The cautionary tales summarised above illustrate the inevitable problem. Somehow these individuals managed to persuade apparently well-informed lawyers, over a long period, that they could be trusted to do forensic work, and succeeded in making a good living before anyone spotted a flaw and blew the whistle. Such is the power of the cult of the expert – a power readily exploited by the unscrupulous in the face of ignorance, laziness or complacency.

## CRFP – an experiment in accreditation

Concern over the part played by forensic science in a series of high-profile miscarriages of justice in the 1970s, which came to light some considerable time later, led to calls for some form of regulation to assure the public that such events were less likely to occur in the future. The cases in question – the Birmingham Six, the Guildford Four, Stefan Kiszko, Judith Ward – resonate still in the public mind; and even less high-profile incidents, taken together, continue to knock public confidence in the reliability of science in the courtroom (Eddleston 2000).

The *House of Commons Home Affairs Committee First Report on the Forensic Science Service* concluded in 1989 that a statutory system of regulation was premature given that, outside the government's Forensic Science Service, forensic science was little developed (House of Commons Home Affairs Committee 1989). The absence of a diverse commercial market appeared sufficient to convince the Committee that a system of independent regulation could add little to the assurances offered by the fact that the large majority of forensic services were provided from within the public sector. This overlooked the question of how a virtual monopoly supplier was any better placed than others to guarantee the competence and ethicality of its individual employees, however much the 'public sector ethos' was prayed in aid.

In 1993 the Royal Commission on Criminal Justice recommended a Forensic Science Advisory Council (Royal Commission on Criminal Justice 1993). Earlier the same year the House of Lords Select Committee on Science and Technology had recommended the establishment of an Advisory Board and a register of forensic scientists. Calling for 'a system of individual registration of all forensic scientists', they said:

> Scientists should be registered according to specialty, and at one of two levels. Anyone should continue to be allowed to practise, but it should be an offence to purport to be registered when not, and expert evidence from unregistered persons should become exceptional. Registration should depend on qualifications, experience, references and a casebook; it should be subject to review and withdrawal. It should be administered by the Government, with the help of a small Board, and delegated to the appropriate professional body wherever possible. (House of Lords 1993)

Those recommendations, reinforced in 1996 by Professor Brian Caddy's report on contamination at the Forensic Explosives Laboratory at Fort Halstead led the government, with strong support from the forensic science community, to set up a Working Group to explore alternative means of ensuring and safeguarding standards in forensic practice (Caddy 1996). Chaired by Lord Lewis of Newnham, a distinguished scientist, and funded by the government, the Group reported in 1997 (Lewis 1997).

The Group considered alternative approaches including the establishment of a professional body or institute to encourage high standards; and the restriction of the scope of any new organisation to forensic scientists, as opposed to including all those involved in the forensic process. It decided that an independent regulatory council, with strong user involvement and a clear focus on accreditation through assessment of current competence, was more likely to achieve the desired result than a professional body that could influence but not enforce. And, responding to the vast majority of those from whom it heard evidence, the Group came down strongly in favour of an organisation 'encompassing the whole of the forensic process' (Lewis 1997).

The Group recommended a Registration Council for Forensic Practitioners, with four key features (non-statutory; self-financing; self-regulating; standard setting and safeguarding) and six objectives:

- serve justice;
- set and maintain high standards of competence, practice, discipline and ethics;
- build on and incorporate existing expertise and infrastructure and utilise the present experience of a wide range of existing professional bodies;
- be adequately flexible to evolve as required over time;
- be self-regulating and independent with input from users;
- be cost effective.

The government accepted the recommendation and in May 1998 the Rt Hon. Jack Straw MP, as Home Secretary, announced the setting up of CRFP:

> The setting up of the Registration Council will be a significant step forward in further raising quality and standards in the forensic science industry ... the Council will do much to enhance the standing of forensic science in the criminal justice process ... I am pleased that the proposals to establish the Council for the Registration of Forensic Practitioners have received the overwhelming support of the forensic science community as well as considerable backing from those in the wider criminal justice system.

A year later CRFP was established as a company limited by guarantee, governed by a Memorandum and Articles of Association which prescribed a Governing Council which, in core form, consisted of a Chairman – the recently retired Vice-Chancellor of Durham University – a circuit judge, a Chief Constable, a senior Home Office official and the General Secretary of the Royal Society of Chemistry. The Council later expanded to include lay members to represent the public interest, representatives of some leading forensic organisations, user representatives such as the Association of Chief Police Officers (ACPO), the Bar Council and Law Society and, once the register was open, practitioner representatives directly elected by registrants (ACPO 2008; Bar Council 2008; Law Society 2008).

### The model

Questions of professional regulation are not common talking points among the general public, or even among politicians or in the media, except when an unsatisfactory case comes to light. At that point calls for more rigorous discipline, tougher penalties or even reform of the regulator are not uncommon. But disciplinary work, while attractive to headline writers, is generally a small part of any regulator's work.

Sir Ian Kennedy QC eloquently enunciated the concept of modern professional regulation in the report of his public inquiry into doctors involved in paediatric heart surgery at Bristol Royal Infirmary (Kennedy 2001). Recognising that regulators typically – and rightly – took significant disciplinary action against only a tiny minority of registrants in any one year, whereas their work on professional education and standards directly affected every registrant, he reasoned that regulation should be about helping good practitioners to remain good and to improve throughout their professional careers.

This requires a holistic approach, with a number of elements in place for the regulatory system to be truly effective:

- a regulatory body – concerned above all with the public interest;
- one or more representative bodies – focused on the interests of the profession(s) concerned;
- centres of excellence – leading in professional education and training, providing professional leadership.

It can readily be seen that a regulatory body cannot do this in isolation: to be effective, regulation must be worked through as a partnership. CRFP was originally conceived, and only ever operated, as a regulatory body. The model was a relatively traditional one: a central council representing both professional and consumer interests; a published register of those deemed competent; a clear statement of professional ethics to which all registered practitioners subscribe; no trade union or representative function.

However, CRFP had some features which marked it out from longer established, and better known, regulatory bodies such as the GMC, the Royal College of Veterinary Surgeons (RCVS) and others (GMC 2008; RCVS 2008). These would require some creative thinking and a fresh approach in CRFP's early days: there was no 'off the peg' model that could readily be adapted for use. For example:

- Registration with CRFP was not compulsory for forensic practitioners: CRFP would have to convince individual practitioners and users of forensic services of the benefits of a purely voluntary system;

- There were no primary qualifications which, in themselves, could automatically qualify a practitioner for registration: CRFP would have to devise an entirely new method of assessing competence in order to determine who should be admitted to the register;

- Forensic practice covers a huge range of professional specialties, for many of which registration with another body is already compulsory: CRFP would need to adopt a lighter touch than statutory regulators, and complex arrangements for interlocking with other regulators' requirements;

- The diversity of the forensic sector meant that the partnership between the regulator and its stakeholders would, unavoidably, be extremely complex: there is no one representative body to deal with, or any single model for such bodies, and the enormous variety of routes into forensic work would make it impossible for CRFP to prescribe or, in the short term, even influence, particular educational requirements;

- Forensic work in some specialties constitutes a relatively small part of a practitioner's professional activity, while for others it is the entire purpose of their job: the CRFP system would have to be flexible enough to encompass all parts of the spectrum.

### Mapping the sector

When the idea of a regulatory system was being considered, there was no consistent 'map' of the forensic world. Professional groups such as the Forensic Science Society, the Fingerprint Society, the British Association of Forensic Odontologists (BAFO), the Institute of Traffic Accident Investigators (ITAI) and a heterogeneous range of associations for forensic medical practitioners provided some focus, but none functioned as a formal professional body which could act as the voice of forensic practice, and none could be the natural home for a register of forensic practitioners (Forensic Science Society 2008; Fingerprint Society 2008; BAFO 2008; ITAI 2008). Nor did any national or regional association represent some significant forensic groups, such as police scene examiners.

In addition to the specific forensic interest groups, several learned societies – including the Royal Society of Chemistry, the Institutes of Biology and Physics, and most of the medical royal colleges – included members doing varying amounts of court work; but the numbers were small relative to the whole membership, and again none of these organisations could act as the accreditor for the whole of forensic practice (RSC 2008, IOB 2008, IOP 2008).

Centres of excellence which trained forensic specialists – the police training colleges, major employers such as the Forensic Science Service and universities such as Strathclyde and King's College London, which offered Masters degrees in forensic science – were doing outstanding work but were in no position to transform themselves into a single professional institute which could guarantee not just the educational input but the *output* of working practitioners through their professional careers (Forensic Science Service 2008, Strathclyde University 2008, KCL 2008).

Forensic practice, particularly the investigative work of scene examiners and their specialist colleagues in fire and accident investigation, digital data capture and examination, image origination, fingerprint development and related specialties, needed to be put on the map. CRFP sought to recognise the essential unity of the forensic process, from the scene of an incident to the courtroom and beyond: all practitioners playing a part in that professional process had a vital (though not necessarily equal) contribution to make if a matter was to be properly investigated and resolved. A failure of competence, at any stage, could compromise the end result.

This opened up some sensitive issues. Should the register be confined, for example, to 'experts', or to 'scientists', or to graduates? Some powerful voices in the forensic world argued for exclusivity, believing that a more comprehensive approach would make registration unattractive to distinguished practitioners whose reputations were already generally secure. Others argued that the public interest demanded the assessment and registration of all professionals who play a direct part in the forensic process, believing that the public are less concerned with practitioners' status than with the integrity of all evidence given by specialists. This argument prevailed.

### Experts, professionals, facts and opinions

The technical categories of *opinion* evidence, delivered only by those designated as experts, and evidence of *fact*, delivered by others, are not quite subtle enough to describe the forensic situation. Leaving aside the philosophical question of whether there is such a thing as a pure fact – simply the stating of facts necessarily involves judgements on what to leave out, what order to place things in, where the emphasis lies, and so on – the courts habitually receive different grades of factual evidence.

A man falls from a window into the street. A passer-by witnesses this and, even though having no forensic (or any other relevant) expertise, could if asked testify in court that they saw him fall from a particular window into a certain place, at a certain time of day, etc. They might remember what the weather was like. Less reliably, they might remember what he was wearing.

A police crime scene examiner who examined the scene following the incident would similarly not be deemed an expert for the court's purposes. But they could expect to be asked in court questions whose answers might be all but indistinguishable from the opinions which the court would expect to hear only from an expert witness: were the findings consistent with various possible explanations? Was the fall voluntary? Were there signs of a struggle? Does the evidence indicate intent on the part of anyone else? And so on.

So there is factual evidence, opinion evidence and *professional evidence as to fact*. Any attempt to map the forensic world, and to assess the competence and integrity of individuals in forensic practice, must concern itself with the third of those categories as well as the second.

CRFP from the outset concerned itself not with *experts* (which would have implied a concern only with what the law technically terms opinion evidence) but with *expertise*, drawing inspiration from a ruling by Lord Widgery, in 1979, that a police officer – or, by implication, anyone else – could be regarded as an expert if they had sufficient expertise for the subject in question.

The scope of the Register of Forensic Practitioners (See Table 20.1 below) – which grew to over 3,000 in number and was freely accessible via CRFP's website – would therefore encompass all those in active practice, using professional skills to produce evidence for the court, and delivering evidence in their own name. In the first instance, it was concerned with the immediate issue CRFP was set up to address: standards of practice in the forensic mainstream – but could readily expand later to cover the wider expert witness world.

These specialties (the register could in principle grow to become a complete map of the practising forensic world) divided broadly – though not exclusively – into:

- those which *investigate* an incident – capturing, examining and preserving material from a scene (which may be a place, a body, a hard disk or any other source) and not speculating about explanations for scientific findings; and

**Table 20.1** Forensic specialties registered with CRFP (as at March 2008)

| |
|---|
| Anthropology<br>Archaeology<br>Computers<br>Drugs<br>Fingerprint development<br>Fingerprint examination |

| |
|---|
| Fire scene examination<br>Firearms<br>Human contact traces<br>Imaging<br>Incident evaluation<br>Marks |

| |
|---|
| Medical examination<br>Nursing<br>Odontology<br>Paediatrics<br>Particulates and other traces<br>Podiatry<br>Questioned documents<br>Radiography<br>Road transport investigation<br>Scene examination<br>Scene examination: volume crime<br>Telecoms<br>Toxicology<br>Veterinary science |

- those that evaluate such material and its evidential value – weighing alternative interpretations and preparing evidence that could serve to identify people, places, times and dates.

A central part of CRFP's purpose was to help the public, and especially those who commissioned forensic work, to understand what they could expect to receive from different types of practitioner. Indicative descriptors of each specialty were set out in CRFP's document *The Forensic Specialties* (CRFP 2008). This explained how the roles divide and also how they merge, making clear for example that some investigators (for example, scene examiners) do some evaluative work; and most evaluators, at some stage, do some straight investigation, often at the scene of an incident.

## Standards of conduct and ethics

Effective regulation is founded on the ability of a professional group to abide, in all normal circumstances, by an agreed, published code of conduct and ethics to which all registered practitioners sign up and against which all must be prepared to be judged if someone has cause for complaint.

CRFP took early steps to draw up such a code so that, as soon as the register opened, both forensic practitioners and the public could be in no doubt about what the new register stood for. It would not be fair to suggest that no such code existed before CRFP; but previous statements of ethics in forensic practice had tended to be generalised, specific to particular employers or focused on sectoral groups.

The CRFP code, devised through broad consultation and published as *Good practice for forensic practitioners*, set down unambiguous generic standards which would apply to practitioners across the whole forensic spectrum (CRFP 2008). First published in 2000 and changed only marginally since, the Code was never seriously questioned. Every applicant for registration had to sign a statement that they understood it, agreed to abide by it in their professional work, and were prepared to be judged against it if their fitness to practise was called in question.

The Code says that registered forensic practitioners must:

1 *Recognise that your overriding duty is to the court and to the administration of justice: it is your duty to present your findings and evidence, whether written or oral, in a fair and impartial manner.*

The emphasis on independence and the duty to put the needs of the court before the demands of the client – even if the client is your direct employer – underpined CRFP's entire philosophy. It reflected the courts' proper expectations of expert witnesses even if the perception of a 'hired gun' culture still bedevils the popular imagination.

2 *Act with honesty, integrity, objectivity and impartiality.*

This principle recognised the critical importance of an ethical approach to scientific and other professional work, again avoiding bias and partiality.

3 *Not discriminate on grounds of race, beliefs, gender, language, sexual orientation, social status, age, lifestyle or political persuasion.*

The key issue here was the avoidance of unreasonable assumptions, or any kind of stereotyping, which might distort opinions and compromise the interpretation of scientific findings.

4 *Comply with the code of conduct of any professional body of which you are a member.*

This recognised the fact that registered forensic practitioners are frequently members of professions which do more than purely forensic work, and so might well be answerable to other professional and regulatory bodies as well as to CRFP.

5 *Provide expert advice and evidence only within the limits of your professional competence and only when fit to do so.*

This is a central point in professional regulation: the temptation to stray beyond professional competence is one that professionals can face in everyday practice, let alone when being led subtly (and perhaps flatteringly) into unfamiliar territory by a highly skilled advocate.

6 *Inform a suitable person or authority, in confidence where appropriate, if you have good grounds for believing there is a situation that may result in a miscarriage of justice.*

This was not only the permission but also the *duty* to speak out if, for whatever reason, a practitioner became aware that, perhaps because of incompetence, cost cutting, management or client pressure or even malpractice, professional evidence might be skewed to the point where the quality of justice was at stake. It was intended to counterbalance the tendency – still, sadly, evident in some professional circles when a complaint is made – for ranks to close and a wall of silence to go up.

Other provisions of the Code emphasised the importance of continuing professional development, avoiding conflicts of interest, ensuring the integrity of evidential materials, maintaining full records, confidentiality, legal professional privilege, and working in accordance with the established principles of one's profession.

Such professional codes typically have the appearance of statements of the obvious; and indeed their provisions should be obvious to all right thinking professionals: the task of regulatory bodies would be quite different if they were not. But the provisions of this Code were not so obvious that CRFP did not find examples of practitioners:

- withholding certain results from a report, on the ground that they were adverse to the case and the commissioning solicitor would not offer further work if they were included;
- using careful language which, while true in itself, was designed to obscure a weak case by casting subtle doubt on the opinions of the opposition – a relatively easy task in highly technical, jargon-rich areas;
- holding themselves out as competent in specialties where they had little or no recent casework, or insufficient breadth of experience.

These are just examples.

## Assessing competence

Any regulatory body must control entry to its register. As noted above, no single indicator already existed which would reliably identify those practising safely and competently. CRFP therefore had to devise an entirely new assessment strategy. This would necessarily involve hard labour, but it offered significant advantages. First, every practitioner, however eminent and however long their experience, would need to jump the same hurdle so that CRFP could comfortably say that every registrant had reached the threshold standard. Secondly, registration would denote current competence rather than the achievement of a qualification perhaps many years previously. Thirdly, it would pave the way for a revalidation assessment at periodic intervals, enabling the register to stay up to date and indicate continuing competence, to the benefit of both practitioners and users.

Though CRFP regarded qualifications and references from colleagues and users as important, its assessment of an individual focused on actual cases that the applicant had handled over the past six to 12 months – longer for less common specialties such as odontology where forensic work is more sporadic. The assessment was by peer review.

For each forensic specialty, CRFP worked with leading practitioners, training institutions and employers to identify an agreed list of *essential elements of competence* – the things that any competent practitioner should be expected to do. Each element was fleshed out with guidance for those who would assess applicants for registration, and each list was pilot-tested with groups of practitioners, even in specialties where standards were already well established. An example of the registration criteria, and the associated assessor guidance, is given in the box below.

The inclusion of the 'softer' competences, such as communication and team-working skills, in addition to technical skills, was something of an innovation but essential, in CRFP's view, to the credibility of the scheme and the promotion of public confidence. The City and Guilds Institute particularly commended the feature when CRFP was granted Designated Authority status in 2007 (CRFP 2008). This opened the way for registered forensic practitioners

**Scene examination: essential elements of competence and guidance for assessors**

*Understanding the task, selecting the proper resources, getting priorities right*

Does the applicant start a case by getting a clear picture of the question they are addressing? What are their sources of information? Do they select and prioritise logically? Do they have a clear understanding of the difference between volume and major crime? Can they decide when a scene is not worth visiting, and do they know when to adjust their priorities as circumstances change?

*Gathering information, sorting out what the problem is, controlling and managing the scene*

Do they gather information from all appropriate sources, both at the scene and elsewhere? Do they use a logical thought process to identify and protect the scene, assess risk and establish safe working conditions? Do they make an effort to evaluate the scene and formulate a strategy that best fits the situation before them?

*Putting together theories to help the investigation and deciding which ones are most worth pursuing*

Can they identify the most important matters for examination, including for example items touched, moved or taken away by a suspected offender? Do they then turn their information into a logical line of enquiry, or at least use it logically to identify matters for which there is at present no obvious explanation?

*Identifying, selecting, recording and recovering physical material to test ideas*

Do they use reasoned thinking to decide what to recover, what to examine and which examinations are needed in order to advance the enquiry? Do they record and recover potential evidential material competently?

*Making sure everything that might provide evidence is handled, secured and labelled to comply with the needs of the law, the investigation and the organisation's quality assurance requirements*

Do they use proper procedures for this, protecting material against contamination? Do they make appropriate decisions about what to submit for analysis; and about the right analyses to request? Do they appreciate the possible consequences of wrong decisions in this respect? Are they also aware of the limitations of their own competence, showing an appreciation of when to seek advice or hand over to a colleague?

*Weighing up evidence and intelligence and discussing and interpreting results, and their meaning, with others involved in the investigation*

Do they demonstrate appropriate use of evidence and intelligence; and can they communicate information to others clearly and in a way that avoids misunderstanding? Do they have good working relationships with colleagues in the investigating team? Do they take steps to ensure that all relevant information is considered at each stage?

*Reconsidering theories in the light of new findings and information*

Are they ready to rethink an issue in the light of new or modified information, excluding and eliminating explanations, suspects or material? Are they flexible enough to adjust their thinking or their priorities as a situation develops? Do they take a critical approach to their work, learn from mistakes and avoid being bound by preconceived ideas?

*Reporting methods, findings and results, orally and in writing, clearly and accurately to colleagues, others in the investigation and the court*

Are they able to prepare clear, unambiguous written statements that can be relied on to give an accurate picture of the facts and findings in a case? Can they communicate just as well in private discussion? In court, do they present evidence confidently, concisely and in a way that non-specialists can understand? Do they communicate an understanding of the technical issues, processes and procedures involved?

*Keeping up to date with developments in the field and taking active steps to maintain competence*

Do they show appreciation of recently developed techniques, new scientific information and examples of good practice? Are they up to date with changes in legislation, including health and safety requirements? Do they take steps to review their work and learn from experience?

to achieve licentiateship with City and Guilds in the same process as their registration assessment.

Applications for registration were scrutinised individually by specialty assessors, all of whom were registered in the same specialty but who did not as a general rule assess applicants who work for the same organisation. The assessors were central to the process. They were appointed by CRFP on recommendation by leading employers, training institutions and practitioners, and formally trained by CRFP in the principles of assessment using a variety of sources. The first assessors in each specialty assessed each other's applications, after which new assessors were appointed only if they were already registered.

Registration was dependent on the assessor's recommendation. If it was refused, the applicant was entitled to a second opinion but more usually they withdrew and put right the deficiencies that had been identified before reapplying. Registration was granted for a fixed period of four years, towards the end of which the practitioner had to demonstrate that they had stayed up to date and maintained competence.

The whole process was quality assured by independent *process verifiers*. These were senior academics who scrutinised a sample of assessments to ensure that they were consistent with one another and that the process was operating fairly. From 2007 they were selected through a process of open advertisement and formally appointed by the Lord Chancellor, to whom CRFP was accountable.

## After registration

Historically, professional registers have been managed by exception. Once registered, a practitioner remains registered unless evidence emerges – as it does in a tiny minority of cases – that someone has committed misconduct to a degree that demands their removal. This is a serious weakness in the light of the demands now made of professionals. Steadily, professional registers are moving to a more modern and proactive approach, in which registrants are required to demonstrate continued competence at periodic intervals. This approach has not yet been seen through for any of the established professions.

CRFP started without the baggage of the traditional approach. Its declared aim was to create a register which reliably denoted *current* competence, so the argument for time-limited registration was made at the outset and was never questioned, even in the early stages. Practitioners and users alike readily saw the value of regular checks in a field where technological and other developments have been moving so rapidly and where up-to-date professional knowledge and expertise are vital to the delivery of a professional service on which the courts can rely. Other professional fields, such as medicine, nursing, pharmacy and the law, where current competence is equally vital, have begun to catch up with such thinking but formal revalidation schemes have still yet to be introduced.

CRFP registrants completed an annual return in which they summarised the developmental activity they had undertaken in the past year – new qualifications, assessed training, cases and professional experience (including mistakes) from which they had learned something, appraisal results, comments by judges and users. This built into a dossier on which they could draw in the fourth year of their registration, by the end of which they had to undergo a simplified form of assessment in which an assessor would again scrutinise recent casework against the essential elements of competence.

Generally speaking, registrants achieved a further period of registration without undue difficulty; but the process provided a valuable check which, as a by-product, enabled the registrant to reflect on the scope of their professional work and whether, for example, the time was right to seek registration in a new specialty or sub-specialty, change specialties altogether or leave one or more behind. For users, the process assured currency and enabled them to check whether a practitioner was genuinely up to date in the forensic services they offered.

## If something went wrong

Inevitably, there are times when a registered practitioner's fitness to practise is called in question. CRFP did not deny its responsibility to act in such situations, but it approached this aspect of its regulatory work cautiously. For one thing, many CRFP registrants were registered with other organisations, some of which (such as the General Dental Council (GDC) or the Nursing and Midwifery Council (NMC)) have statutory duties and so have primary responsibility for policing the professionals they register (GDC 2008, NMC 2008). In these specialties, a complaint received by CRFP would first be referred to the statutory body for consideration, CRFP acting later if action by them appeared to be appropriate.

Another potential difficulty arose from the forensic context itself. In any legal proceedings, at least one person will often be dissatisfied with the outcome, and seek redress by whatever means are available. This can lead to a tendency to play the man rather than the ball – aiming at any professional deemed to have some responsibility for the unsatisfactory result. The temptation to use CRFP as a vehicle for this proved too much for the earliest complainants; and CRFP had to be assiduous in distinguishing generalised dissatisfaction from genuine concerns about a registered practitioner's professional conduct or performance, or for that matter their state of health.

CRFP's fitness to practise procedures were in place from the outset, and were revised in 2007 to bring them into line with developments in modern regulatory law and practice. The focus was remedial rather than punitive; but inevitably there would be occasions when a practitioner has to be struck off the register. Formal proceedings would take place in public and any action taken against a practitioner would be a matter of public record.

## Was CRFP registration intended to become compulsory?

At the insistence of the Government, CRFP registration remained voluntary from the outset. But the difficulty of securing both universal take-up by practitioners and widespread use of the register by those commissioning their work caused thinking to develop; and there might have been ways through the difficulties with a voluntary scheme that were noted above.

The issue of small or rarely used specialties could have been overcome by a fast-track system for temporary registration. The question of the novice practitioner could have been tackled by adding arrangements for provisional registration, from which new practitioners could move to full registration once they had a case log of sufficient size to assess. And the issue of principle – that no one from outside the courts should seek to constrain them – could have been overcome if the courts themselves, led by the senior judiciary, had reached the point where they were prepared to say that unregistered practitioners should give expert or professional evidence only in exceptional circumstances.

In March 2005 the House of Commons Select Committee on Science and Technology, after enquiring in depth into standards in forensic practice, recommended:

> ... as the percentage of registered practitioners in the mainstream specialities increases, there will be a strong case for CRFP registration being made mandatory for experts in those specialities presenting evidence to the courts. This would not prevent the courts from hearing evidence from an expert in a speciality for which CRFP had not achieved a critical mass of registrants, or from experts based overseas. (House of Commons Select Committee on Science and Technology 2005).

It would be good to think that such thinking could have come together into a coherent policy; but change is frightening to everyone, not least to established and powerful professional groups who are used to controlling their environment and their ways of working. Most of the key voices in the forensic community accept the need for a system to describe, promote and maintain standards in court work. Special training is useful but it is not enough.

Sadly, continuing resistance to a compulsory system of registration, coupled with rapidly gathering constraints on public expenditure, caused the Government to withdraw financial support, forcing CRFP to cease trading on 31 March 2009. Standards work will be taken forward through a limited system of organisational accreditation which I cannot regard as anything but inferior to the comprehensive and widely respected system created by CRFP.

## Courtroom science in the future

The case for a regulatory system, independent of sectoral interests, with no axe to grind and with the public interest as its primary focus, has never been greater. In forensic science there is a particular reason for this. Over the past two decades the market for the delivery of forensic practice has expanded and diversified. Where once the overwhelming bulk of forensic work was done by the police or by government agencies, now the market – in England and Wales, at least – has fragmented and diversified. Independent providers such as LGC Forensics have grown out of the public sector and now tender freely for contracts with the police and other law enforcement agencies. Smaller independent concerns run increasingly sophisticated operations – a long way from the one-man band operating out of a garage with a white van.

The key development, though, is the steady move of the Forensic Science Service from an arm of government into the private sector. In principle this need not of itself lead to any lowering of standards; indeed, in many respects it should provide a powerful incentive to provide a consistent quality service. But the demands of a challenging, highly competitive business environment may be perceived as bearing down on quality in favour of cost cutting and a target culture.

This is by no means inevitable; but the developing situation needs to be watched carefully. Customers for forensic services should be, but are demonstrably not always, intelligent customers. Both the wary and the unwary need to be able to identify competent practice in areas where they are not expert themselves.

The future of what is steadily becoming an increasingly commercial market for forensic science in the UK is uncertain. The appointment of a government-sponsored Regulator, supported by an informed Advisory Council, to act as a public watchdog from the spring of 2008, was a useful development. This may be the right way not only to police organisational standards as the market diversifies; but also to secure robust guidance on the emergent specialties, scientific techniques and approaches that have proved themselves sufficiently reliable to be used in the courtroom – guidance for which there has been no definitive source hitherto – and which could be a significant step in the direction in which the Daubert Standard, described above, has sought to move in the USA.

I said above that a successful regulatory system needs three main components: a regulatory body, professional representative bodies, and centres of excellence. CRFP made a start as the first of these, aiming to regulate in the public interest by monitoring the professional competence, conduct and performance of individual practitioners. CRFP would have been well placed to complement the work of the Regulator by providing the 'people' element of the quality system that is developed. This is a wheel that no longer needs to be invented, though until those commissioning forensic work insist on having access to a definitive indicator of current competence, the ambitious project is as yet some way short of completion.

Alongside this the forensic community needs to secure the position of professional bodies that can act as the voice of practitioners. The Forensic Science Society has already taken steps in this direction but has yet, in my view, to fulfil its potential to become the strong, coherent and influential voice that the scientific community needs. Other groups – the British Associations for Human Identification and for Odontology, the Fingerprint Society and many others – need to get used to talking not just to themselves but to their users and to opinion formers at large. These organisations are potentially the engines to drive professional standards forward, providing the leadership that will otherwise be left to a handful of charismatic and media-friendly individuals (with which the forensic community has, admittedly, sometimes been well endowed).

As for centres of excellence, the universities that are prepared to take forensic science seriously may become the vehicles for delivering the high-quality teaching and research that will keep the UK at the forefront of forensic practice. This cannot come from the headlong rush towards undergraduate courses that include the word *forensic* in their title. Rather, it is in the Masters courses and those that ground students in a thorough foundation of pure science that excellence will be nurtured in the forensic practitioners of the future.

## In conclusion

Professional standards – their design, definition, promulgation and maintenance – in court work are key to public protection and the administration of justice. In this chapter I have sought to reflect on how assurance can be given that those standards are reliably maintained across the spectrum of forensic practice; how the public may be protected against bogus or poor practice in matters which may radically affect their lives; and how the courts can obtain reliable guidance on the forms of science which should be trusted, for the purposes of justice, and on whether those they accept as experts actually have the up-to-date expertise to which they lay claim.

I have indicated the limitations of historic approaches based on practitioners' qualifications or professional memberships alone; on the accreditation of organisations but not their individual employees; on assuring the science but not its practitioners; on published catalogues of those holding themselves out as experts; on training in court skills without summative assessment of competence; on individual judgements in individual courts; and on word of mouth recommendation or, bluntly, guesswork.

I have argued for a method which addresses directly the question whether individual practitioners are currently fit to do their job, basing assessment of that on nationally agreed standards of competence and conduct. CRFP represented an honest attempt to follow through such an approach. It was unable to prove itself without the ability to make registration, in practice, compulsory; and so was unable to fulfil its complete potential. Whether new approaches will emerge which can stand on CRFP's shoulders, and produce the complete solution the courts so obviously require, remains to be seen; but the foundations have been laid and there are good reasons to build on them.

It is a truism that effective use will be made of scientific and professional evidence in the courtroom only when scientists and lawyers, judges and the lay public understand each other better and can communicate so as to bring their expectations together. Science, by its nature, asks more questions than it can answer, each new answer opening up a range of new and unresolved questions. That is what science does. The courtroom, by contrast, demands certainty – or at least the elimination of reasonable doubt. The two approaches are not incompatible but a serious growth in mutual understanding is required if conflicting expectations are to be reconciled.

A great step forward will be taken as judges and lawyers grow in their understanding not just of basic scientific concepts but also of the potential and the boundaries of different categories of forensic specialist. In that process the development of an effective regulatory system – which at the least must give the outside world insight into what different types of practitioner can do, what constitutes current competence and what are the limitations of particular specialties – could, if it is allowed to do so, play a major part.

Of one thing I am in no doubt: if we had now a system in which the use only of accredited forensic practitioners was the norm, and recourse to the unaccredited highly exceptional, no one would be arguing for the abandonment of that system in favour of an arrangement in which potential users might or might not hit upon a competent practitioner, and might or might not get a good result. Professional standards matter. In the courtroom society demands no less.

## Notes

1 *Buckley v. Rice Thomas* (1554) 1 Plowden 118, 124, 75 ER 182.
2 *Folkes v. Chadd* (1782) 3 Doug 157, 159, 160.
3 *Thorne v. Worthing Skating Rink* (1877) 6 Ch D 415, 416–18, cited as a footnote to *Plimpton v. Spiller* (1877) Ch D 412.
4 *Abbey National Mortgages plc v. Key Surveyors Nationwide Ltd.* [1996] 3 All ER 184, 191.
5 *Daubert v. Merrell Dow Pharmaceuticals* 509 US 579 (1993).
6 *Kumho Tire Co v. Carmichael* 526 US 137 (1999).
7 Notably *The Ikarian Reefer* [1993] 2 Lloyd's Rep.

## References

Academy of Experts (2008) Homepage available at http://www. academy-experts.org [accessed 15 December 2008].

Association of Chief Police Officers (2008) Homepage available at http://www.acpo. police.uk [accessed 15 December 2008].

Bar Council (2008) Homepage available at http://www. barcouncil.org.uk [accessed 15 December 2008].

Bradshaw, S. (2008) 'How to fake a living', *Times Online*, 3 February. Available at http://www.timesonline.co.uk/tol/news/uk/crime/article3277057.ece [accessed 15 December 2008].

British Association of Forensic Odontologists (2008) Homepage available at http:// www.bafo.org.uk [accessed 15 December 2008].

Caddy, B. (1996) *Assessment and Implications of Centrifuge Contamination in the Trace Explosives Section of the Forensic Explosives Laboratory at Fort Halstead*, Cm 3491. London: HMSO.

City and Guilds Institute (2008) Homepage available at http://www.city-and-guilds. co.uk [accessed 15 December 2008].

Civil Procedure Rules (1998) *Civil Procedure Rules* (SI 1998/3132). London: HMSO.

Eddleston, J.J. (2000) *Blind Justice: Miscarriages of Justice in Twentieth-Century Britain?* Oxford: ABC-Clio.

Expert Witness Institute (2008) EWI homepage available at http://www.ewi.org.uk [accessed 15 December 2008).

Fingerprint Society (2008) Homepage available at http://www.fpsociety.org.uk [accessed 15 December 2008].

Forensic Science Service (2008) Homepage available at http://www.forensic.gov.uk [accessed 15 December 2008].

Forensic Science Society (2008) Homepage available at http://www.forensic-science-society.org.uk [accessed 15 December 2008].

General Dental Council (2008) Homepage available at http://www.gdc-uk.org [accessed 15 December 2008].

General Medical Council (2008) Homepage available at http://www.gmc-uk.org [accessed 15 December 2008].

Golan, T. (2004) *Laws of Men and Laws of Nature: the History of Scientific Expert Testimony in England and America*. Cambridge, Mass: Harvard University Press.

House of Commons Home Affairs Committee (1989) House of Commons Session 1988–89. London: HMSO.

House of Commons Select Committee on Science and Technology (2005) *Forensic Science on Trial: Seventh Report of Session 2004–05*. London: HMSO.

House of Lords (1993) *House of Lords Session 1992–93 5th Report*, HL Paper 24, printed 3 February.

Institute of Biology (2008) Homepage available at http://www.iob.org [accessed 15 December 2008].

Institute of Physics (2008) Homepage available at http://www.iop.org [accessed 15 December 2008].

Institute of Traffic Accident Investigators (2008) Homepage available at http://www.itai.org [accessed 15 December 2008].

Kennedy, I. (2001) *Learning from Bristol: The report of the public inquiry into children's heart surgery at the Bristol Royal Infirmary 1984–1995*. London: Department of Health.

Kings College London (2008) Homepage available at http://www.kcl.ac.uk [accessed 15 December 2008].

Law Society (2008) Homepage available at http://www.lawsociety.org.uk [accessed 15 December 2008].

Letheby, H. (1859) Letter to *The Times*, 27 August.

Lewis of Newnham, Lord (1997) *Report of the Forensic Science Working Group*. London: Royal Society of Chemistry.

Lister, S. (2005) ' "Professor" jailed for £1.5m swindle', *Times Online*, 27 January. Available at http://www.timesonline.co.uk/tol/news/uk/article507063.ece [accessed 15 December 2008].

Nursing and Midwifery Council (2008) Homepage available at http://www.nmc-uk.org [accessed 15 December 2008].

Royal College of Veterinary Surgeons (2008) Homepage available at http://www.rcvs.org.uk [accessed 15 December 2008].

Royal Commission on Criminal Justice (1993) *Report of the Royal Commission on Criminal Justice*, Cm 2263. London: HMSO.

Royal Society of Chemistry (2008) Homepage available at http://www.rsc.org [accessed 15 December 2008].

Smith, R.A. (1860) Address to the Royal Society of Arts, *Journal of the Society of Arts*, 135: 136–157.

Society of Expert Witnesses (2008) Homepage available at http://www.sew.org.uk [accessed 15 December 2008].

Strathclyde University (2008) Homepage available at http://www.strath.ac.uk [accessed 15 December 2008].

UK Register of Expert Witnesses (2008) Available at http://www.jspubs.com [accessed 15 December 2008].

United Kingdom Accreditation Service (2008) Homepage available at http:// www.ukas.com [accessed 15 December 2008].

Woolf, Right Honourable the Lord (1996) *Access to Justice Report*. London: HMSO, available at http://www. dca.gov.uk/civil/final/index.htm [accessed 15 December 2008).

# Chapter 21

# The development and enhancement of forensic expertise: higher education and in-service training

*Claude Roux and James Robertson*

### Introduction: forensic science – a real discipline?

Forensic science is a complex area. This complexity arises from two distinct sources. Firstly, the random and disorganised nature of crime makes the application of scientific techniques to the analysis of evidence complex. And secondly, there is the requirement for the scientific results to be expressed within the legal domain that has complex rules and protocols that are different to the process of scientific reasoning.

There has been much debate as to whether or not forensic science is indeed a separate discipline. Louis Pasteur said, 'No category of sciences exists to which one could give the name of applied sciences. There are sciences and the application of science, linked together as fruit is to the tree that has borne it.' (Pasteur 1871). Pasteur's Quadrant (Figure 21.1) shows how the consideration of use and the quest for fundamental understanding are related. This is highly relevant, and fundamental to the development of forensic expertise. If there is no separate discipline of forensic science then it could be properly argued that there is no need for separate forensic science education and training. This argument is dismissed by Margot who, in support for specialised education, training and research, said that forensic science

> has all the requirements for a true single scientific discipline: events are studied as a function of hypotheses; the observations made are used to test the hypotheses; decisions are taken as to what evidence can be found and what tests are to be undertaken to falsify or strengthen one hypothesis. Then the data is considered in light of other circumstantial evidence pertaining to the case. Finally, the data is interpreted and evaluated to ultimately answer the fundamental, essential question (which I assert that forensic science is intended to answer): What is the weight of the evidence?' (Margot 1994).

We would argue that the debate is largely semantic and easily dealt with. Science is science. There can be no argument that anyone who wishes to work at a professional level in any branch of science must have underpinning fundamental science knowledge. However, there are many arguments about what students need to know and how best to deliver this. There is also considerable debate about why science enrolments, and student interest in science, have fallen over recent years. There is a growing consensus that the way forward to improve this situation has to include an examination of how school students are exposed to science. This needs to place a greater emphasis on principles and less emphasis on learning of facts and figures. A recent paper in *Science* (Denofrio *et al.* 2007) looked at how to increase student interest through linking it to science curricula. It proposed working within existing traditional curricula but helping students identify courses and groups to match their particular interests. Interestingly they used forensic science as an example of an area of student interest. Hence, in our view there is no competition between accepting the role of traditional science curricula – although this should not stop its evolution – and recognising that forensic science has its own context that qualifies it as a discipline in its own right. The development and enhancement of forensic expertise cannot be isolated from the underpinning sciences and, arguably, other disciplines such as communications, ethics, logic, etc.

What are then some of the unique characteristics of this forensic discipline? A capable forensic scientist must be able to reason within the inherent uncertainties that exist in criminal investigations and recognise and examine

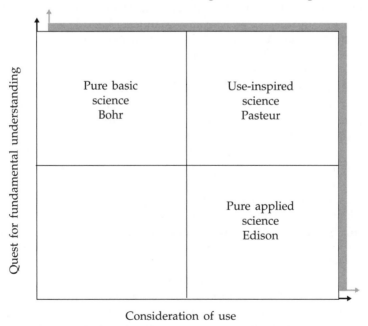

Consideration of use

**Figure 21.1** Relation between the consideration of use and the quest for fundamental understanding in science. The major part of forensic science falls in the use-inspired quadrant.
*Source*: Adapted from Stokes (1997)

evidence upon which to base his or her propositions. In this context, the ability to, first, develop hypotheses about a case and, then, detect relevant evidence to confirm or falsify these hypotheses is crucial. Further, upon completing the scientific analysis, the forensic scientist presents his or her findings in a legal context, through an expert witness report and/or in a courtroom situation. This often requires the use of data gathered through past empirical research, or even undertaking new research in some cases. As Inman and Rudin point out: 'The germane questions are legal questions. The role of forensic science is to translate the relevant legal questions into a scientific question. If this cannot be done then forensic science has no role to play' (Inman and Rudin 2001).

The unique challenges encountered in forensic investigations, combined with the social relevance of the scientific outcomes themselves, make forensic science an exciting and meaningful discipline to pursue, either academically or professionally. Career opportunities in forensic science that were once upon a time viewed as limited have been discussed in *Nature* (Myers 2003).

Of course, the public profile of forensic science has also reached an all-time high. Finding a forensic-free night on television these days is a real challenge. Popular culture has embraced forensic science with an almost obsessive fervour. Judging by the TV guide, the public just cannot get enough. Crime shows have become synonymous with forensic science – it provides the magic bullet solution to catching a culprit. While the limelight may bring some positive benefits to the discipline, it also brings new challenges of increased scrutiny and false or unrealistic expectations. In this context, education has an important role to play in providing more realistic and balanced information to the public, to the legal profession and, of course, to those wishing to study forensic science in all of its many manifestations. It is arguable that a noticeable effect of the TV shows has been to increase the level of interest in forensic science among school students.

Beside the enrolment considerations, forensic science is also a sought-after discipline by universities as it fits very well with current academic trends which often favour industry readiness, multi-skilling, social relevance, etc. For example, the mission statement of the University of Technology, Sydney, Australia, states: 'Our educational model emphasises a holistic concept of learning that educates forward-thinking, industry-ready professionals, promotes international student mobility, and conducts high quality collaborative research in niche areas.' There is little doubt that forensic science is a prime candidate here. However, one should ask the question: Is a high level of industry readiness easily achievable? And is it even desirable?

Many universities around the world have recently attempted to focus on the need for high-quality education (and research) expressed by relevant industries and the interest and demand from the general public and potential students in particular. However, the rapid growth in forensic science programmes has also attracted some criticism from potential employers of a lack of consistency and clarity in the vast range of forensic courses on offer, thus leading to difficulties in determining what skills a graduate might have obtained. This is due to the 'broad brush' approach offered by many of these courses where most of the difficult and relatively unattractive fundamental sciences have been removed from the curricula. How can we address this issue?

An interesting point is that, for science-based curricula, the vast majority of academic forensic programmes appear to be chemistry-based as opposed to biology-based, despite the fact that following the advent of forensic DNA analysis most forensic science jobs are in forensic biology. Why has this happened? Many students of forensic science do not want to work in laboratories at all and are attracted to the field disciplines of crime scene, fingerprints and firearms examination. Although previously the domain of sworn police,[1] in many parts of the world these roles are now being filled by non-sworn[2] or civilian personnel. The need for education and in-service training is vital regardless of sworn status. The important point is that most recent recruitment is of graduates for non-sworn roles. This has obvious implications for employer obligations for education and in-service training.

This chapter will review the current status of forensic science education and training, with references to some historical aspects. It will also try to answer the questions asked above, along with the following:

- What is forensic science education as opposed to training?
- What is the appropriate role of higher education in forensic science education and training?
- How does forensic science education relate to in-house training?

This discussion will consider forensic science including field services such as scenes of crime investigation and traditionally police-managed areas (e.g. firearms, fingerprints, etc.). However, it will not include forensic pathology, which is generally considered as a medical subdiscipline.


## History

This section does not intend to be a comprehensive historical review of forensic science education and training. Its purpose is to provide an overview of how forensic education has developed in an historical, global sense; this may give some insights into the 'why' question!

### General development

Most pioneers in forensic science were medical examiners with an interest in solving crime: André Vesale (1514–1564) in Belgium and Ambroise Paré (1510–1590) in France. It was only at the end of the eighteenth century that chemistry entered the field of scientific examination of crime, the natural link with medicine being toxicology with Mathieu Orfila (1787–1853). During the nineteenth century, to a large extent forensic science was still closely identified with forensic medicine. By the end of the nineteenth century, an increasing number of scientists with expertise outside the area of medicine emerged. The first important developments that had a significant impact on routine police work were those methods that are able to identify a person: photography by Niepce and Daguerre (1816 to 1839), criminal anthropometry by Bertillon (1879 to 1888), and dactyloscopy by Faulds, Vucetich, Galton and

Henry (1880 to 1900). The forensic science specialty was further advanced and emerged as a holistic discipline through the famous pioneering work of Gross in Austria, Locard in France and Reiss in Switzerland (1893 to 1920). In the United Kingdom forensic science remained largely the domain of forensic pathology through the first half of the twentieth century with famous names such as the Glaisters, Sydney Smith and Bernard Spilsbury. The Metropolitan Police Forensic Science Laboratory dates from before the Second World War but the emergence of forensic science in the UK largely had to wait until the late 1950s and 1960s. In Scotland the first police forensic science laboratory was only established in 1968. This brief summary illustrates how, from a medical specialty, forensic science was shaped by what today is often called identification sciences and then by physical evidence and criminalistics. This explains the historical significance of medicine, photography and natural sciences in the development of forensic science.

In 1895 during a congress of the international union of criminal law in Linz (Austria), Hanns Gross suggested teaching 'criminalistics' based on the model of optional courses he had introduced in 1894 in Vienna. However, the first academic School of Forensic Science was created at the University of Lausanne, Switzerland, in 1909 by Professor Reiss under the name of the Institute of Forensic Photography, which later became the 'Institut de Police Scientifique' (School of Forensic Science). In his letter to the University's Vice-Chancellor, Reiss demonstrated his extraordinary vision, and his words are still relevant today:

> Forensic methods attract a growing interest from professional circles. Many young people focus on this career from the start of their study [...]. It becomes absolutely necessary for them to obtain a specialised grade at the end of their specialised study. (translated from Mathyer 2001)

In 1913, Gross created a similar school in Graz (Austria), followed by Heindl in Munich (Germany) and Locard in Lyon (France). Unfortunately, what appeared to be a very promising start did not fully develop because of the Second World War. Only the School of Forensic Science in Lausanne survived this troubled period. After the war, a number of programmes were developed around the world but few gained and sustained an international dimension; the notable exceptions were Paul Kirk's programme at the University of California, Berkeley, USA, the programme at the University of Strathclyde, Scotland, and the School of Forensic Science in Lausanne. The situation did not significantly evolve until the extraordinary explosion in the number of forensic science programmes that has occurred since the mid 1990s. In the UK alone, there are now over 50 BSc degree programmes and over 350 possible course combinations with a forensic aspect to them. There now also appear to be over 100 Masters programmes where until a few years ago there was only a handful. Similar trends can be observed in the USA, in Australia and in other countries.

### From police technicians to scientists

Many forensic science roles, especially those applied to crime scene and fingerprints, were originally considered as technical sub-specialties developed by police officers. In this context photography was initially the most important technical expertise. The situation evolved in parallel to various scientific and technological developments. It has since become common for forensic scientists to possess a pass or a postgraduate degree with some kind of forensic specialisation, the latter being more or less formalised. Today, it is common for forensic scientists to hold a forensic science degree, or at least to have attended specialised forensic training during their studies (although it is recognised that this situation is variable depending on the country).

The main drivers for this evolution over the years have been:

- *Scientific and technological developments*: the emergence of advanced analytical techniques in the mid 1960s moved the focus of scientific education to these new technological areas. The demand for specialised courses increased at the same time as the various techniques broadened their application areas.

- *The advent of forensic DNA profiling*: this caused a major expansion in how forensic science was used, particularly the development and implementation of national DNA databases. This expansion has generated thousands of new forensic positions around the world in a short period of time, and still requires regular training updates.

- *Development and generalisation of quality assurance systems*: shifting the professional focus towards the development of more standardised protocols generated a more structured framework which assisted education institutions to better identify the industry requirements when developing forensic science programmes. The trend of personnel certification created a further incentive for specialised education and training.

- *Significant changes in policing models*: civilianisation and professionalisation of policing created a fertile environment for higher education and training programmes, as shown by recent reviews in various parts of the world (Science, Engineering, Manufacturing Technologies Alliance 2004; National Institute of Justice 2004; National Institute of Forensic Science 2005a).

- *Increased need for independent forensic examination*: in line with the previous point, in some countries there has been an increased requirement for police forces to have exhibits analysed by independent forensic organisations due to the public dissatisfaction in police investigations after a number of miscarriages of justice.

- *Significant changes in education funding*: in most countries, higher education institutions have been forced to develop business acumen because of insufficient government funding. From a business viewpoint forensic science is an excellent discipline to offer as an undergraduate programme because of its popularity with recent school leavers.

### Opportunistic development or concerted approach?

It is therefore interesting to note that, at least in recent years, the global development of higher education and training in forensic science has been more the result of concomitant external drivers than the outcome of a coherent and concerted approach from education institutions. This *ad hoc* situation contains a certain level of risk because it gives the impression that forensic science programmes are driven by technology and by the underpinning sciences with little consideration of the fundamental principles of the forensic science discipline itself. This current situation may be in response to a demand and make good use of university resources but it cannot, in the long term, drive the forensic science discipline to significant increases in knowledge. The wide variety of programmes on offer is not necessarily negative. However, a critical number of these programmes must teach core fundamental forensic principles, for example concepts of trace evidence, identification, exchange, association, if academia is to have a significant role in developing and enhancing the forensic expertise.

## Forensic science in higher education

### The importance of the education system

It is recognised that education systems and organisational structures vary from country to country, and it is therefore impossible to describe every single system here. However, in most countries, formal education is provided by three main sectors:

- Secondary schools sector;
- Vocational education and training sector;
- Higher education sector.

Forensic science has recently attracted some interest from the secondary schools sector as a way to make science curricula more interesting. Although this may generate some seminal interest amongst some students who go on to study forensic science later, the introduction of forensic subjects in secondary schools has little or no effect on the forensic science profession. This subject will therefore not be discussed further in this chapter.

The vocational education and training sector mainly relies on a competency-based approach, whereby students' competencies and skills are assessed irrespective of the time they spend studying. Programmes in the Vocational Education and Training (VET) sector also tend to be more practically based and often involve industry stakeholders at a higher level of interaction than is offered by the higher education sector. These attributes fit well with the nature of forensic science. For this reason, in some countries some well-respected programmes have been developed by this sector in collaboration with the forensic science industry over the years. For example, the Canberra Institute of Technology (CIT), a VET provider, has long been involved in forensic education and training and was instrumental in the development and delivery of a National Diploma of Applied Science (Forensic Investigation) in Australia.

In Australia crime scene examiners are sworn police officers in some States and Territories and non-sworn scientists in other States and Territories. In New South Wales there are two levels of crime scene personnel, sworn crime scene examiners and non-sworn scene of crime officers (SOCOs). For each of these groups a National Diploma is incorporated in their training although most will have obtained a degree qualification prior to employment. In the Australian Federal Police a degree qualification is a requirement to work in most areas of forensic science. An exception can be made in emerging areas such as computer forensics. In the UK crime scene work has been largely civilianised and most new entrants would possess at least a Bachelor's degree. The situation in North America and many other parts of the world is more varied but the work of crime scene examination is still largely carried out by police officers.

Most programmes offered in the higher education sector are not competency-based but generally follow traditional academic assessment and progression patterns (practical reports, mid semester and end of semester exams, etc.). They also tend to be more theoretical and less flexible in their delivery mode (for example work-based programmes are rare in universities) than programmes offered by the VET sector. From an employer's perspective, higher education (HE) programmes compensate for these apparent weaknesses by focusing on the development of research and critical thinking skills amongst their graduates, as well as offering higher degrees that are increasingly seen as a currency in today's world.

Despite the distinction made above between the VET and the HE sectors, it should be recognised that traditional boundaries are increasingly poorly defined. For example, we may find vocational institutions offering forensic science degrees; or universities delivering extracurricular training courses on some specific aspects of forensic science. The latter can even be formalised in a way whereby a whole suite of courses can be offered from the Diploma (typically a vocational qualification) to the Master's level (typically a university qualification), through the spectrum of tertiary qualifications depending on the exit level. In addition, with the increase of forensic personnel holding university degrees, vocational forensic science programmes solely offered by non-university (i.e. VET) organisations may lose their relevance in the future. Staff with degrees (i.e. those who are a product of HE) may not see such vocational programmes as very attractive because VET programmes would give them qualifications that are below theirs in the pecking order. These staff would rather target postgraduate programmes, in particular those that would retain some traditional aspects of vocational courses such as work-based training, for example, but in the HE environment. As an illustration, the Australian Qualifications Framework (AQF) describes how these different levels of tertiary and higher education may be linked together.

**What's new about the Australian Qualifications Framework (AQF)**

Work-based qualifications and academic qualifications are now part of a single system, allowing maximum flexibility in career planning and continuous learning.

The following changes in vocational education and training have most affected the system of qualifications:

- Vocational qualifications are now *industry-based*, with specified combinations of *units of competency* required by each industry for each qualification;

- These qualifications are designed in a *sequence*, allowing you to move steadily from one qualification to the next. Sometimes an individual will want to 'mix and match' units of competency. Whatever units are chosen, these will accumulate in the individual record of achievement with the potential to improve performance, career prospects and further learning;

- To be deemed competent for one of the vocational qualifications, an individual must demonstrate effective use of skills and knowledge under workplace conditions; consequently, much of the training takes place in the workplace. Assessment of skills and knowledge already gained informally in previous work can also take place. This assessment process is known as recognition of prior learning (RPL);

- Registered Training Organisations (RTOs) are accredited to provide training and issue qualifications according to the requirements of the AQF.

The key objectives of the AQF are to:

- Provide nationally consistent recognition of outcomes achieved in post-compulsory education;

- Help with developing flexible pathways which assist people to move more easily between education and training sectors and between those sectors and the labour market by providing the basis for recognition of prior learning, including credit transfer and work and life experience;

- Integrate and streamline the requirements of participating providers, employers and employees, individuals and interested organisations;

- Offer flexibility to suit the diversity of purpose of education and training;

- Encourage individuals to progress through the levels of education and training by improving access to qualifications, clearly defining avenues for achievement, and generally contributing to lifelong learning;

- Encourage the provision of more and higher quality vocational education and training through qualifications that normally meet workplace requirements and vocational needs, thus contributing to national economic performance; and

- Promote national and international recognition of qualifications offered in Australia.

Figure 21.2 provides a schematic view of the qualifications available and the most likely pathways available for students. A recent change to the Australian system is also to recognise a vocational graduate certificate and vocational graduate diploma. Hence, postgraduate options are available from the vocational and university systems in Australia. This has obvious implications with respect to in-service training as the former are competency based and include higher levels of practical skills learning. Table 21.1 shows a comparison of the distinguishing features of Australian vocational qualifications.

### Education or training?

Perhaps more relevant to forensic science is the distinction between education and training. Although these two terms are often used interchangeably, in an educational setting, their meaning is different. Brightman (NIFS 2005a) defines 'training' as the instruction of observable skills or behaviours through structured incremental practice to achieve mastery, while 'education' refers more broadly to cognitive development that enables an individual to think and adapt to different situations and solve problems. In other words, training is more specific, more vocationally oriented, and distils the necessary information to individuals so that they can undertake a particular task or range of tasks in a job. Education, informal and formal, is a lifelong process, and in a broad sense, is preparing an individual for the future. So, from a learning perspective, what is more suited to forensic science – training or education? Forensic science is an excellent example of a discipline that requires learners to strike a balance between education and training. The interesting aspect here is that training can often be an integral component of an educational programme. In fact, most forensic programmes at university could be seen as a forensic science training component embedded in a science degree. Is this training sufficient to produce a student ready for the workplace? The answer is 'no'; however, depending on the level and relevance of the practical component, the student can be 'primed' to make the transition to practitioner a smoother pathway.

### Tertiary education programmes and their role

Simplistically, tertiary education programmes in forensic science can broadly be defined as:

- *Generic programmes* (Bachelor): in these programmes, forensic science is typically used as a vehicle to enrich the content of the curriculum and engage the students. Relevant classes may include a few law and forensic units. However, in reality, these programmes are limited and cannot provide sound understanding of forensic science principles or the necessary skills and personal attributes to become a professional forensic scientist.

- *Specialised forensic programmes* (Bachelor, Honours, and Masters): these programmes vary in their structure as well as in their qualification level. They can provide a comprehensive coverage of forensic science, or offer a science degree with a strong emphasis on forensic science. These programmes share broad similarities in the sense that they all aim at a

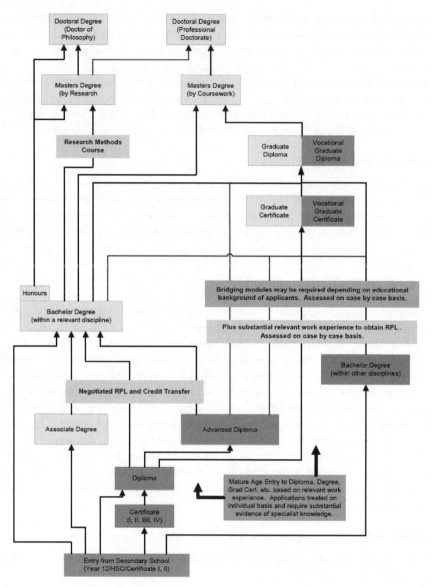

**Figure 21.2** Schematic diagram of educational pathways
*Source*: NIFS (2005a)

higher level of professional readiness than generic programmes. Specialised forensic programmes typically provide a more in-depth coverage of core forensic units or modules and favour the development of research skills and critical thinking.

It should be emphasised at this point that not all forensic science graduates end up working in forensic science. This is where it may be useful to differentiate between science education and science professionalisation. A programme may accept a large intake of students in first year and lead them to a pass

**Table 21.1** Comparison of Advanced Diploma, Vocational Graduate Certificate and Vocational Graduate Diploma

| Advanced Diploma | Vocational Graduate Certificate | Vocational Graduate Diploma |
|---|---|---|
| Competencies or Learning Outcomes enable an individual with this qualification to: | Competencies or Learning Outcomes enable an individual with this qualification to: | Competencies or Learning Outcomes enable an individual with this qualification to: |
| • demonstrate understanding of specialised knowledge with depth in some areas; | • demonstrate the self-directed development and achievement of broad and/or specialised areas of knowledge and skills building on prior knowledge and skills; | • demonstrate the self-directed development and achievement of broad and/or highly specialised areas of knowledge and skills building on prior knowledge and skills; |
| • analyse, diagnose, design and execute judgements across a broad range of technical or management functions; | • initiate, analyse, design, plan and evaluate major, broad or specialised technical and/or management functions in highly varied and/or highly specialised contexts; | • initiate, analyse, design, plan, execute and evaluate major functions either broad and/or highly specialised within highly varied and/or highly specialised contexts; |
| • generate ideas through the analysis of information and concepts at an abstract level; | • generate and evaluate ideas through the analysis of information and concepts at an abstract level; | • generate and evaluate complex ideas through the analysis of information and concepts at an abstract level; |
| • demonstrate a command of wide-ranging highly specialised technical, creative or conceptual skills; | • demonstrate a command of wide-ranging highly specialised technical, creative or conceptual skills in complex contexts; | • demonstrate an expert command of wide-ranging, highly specialised, technical, creative or conceptual skills in complex and/or highly specialised or varied contexts; |
| • demonstrate accountability for personal outputs within broad parameters; and | • demonstrate responsibility and broad ranging accountability for personal outputs; and | • demonstrate full responsibility and accountability for personal outputs; and |
| • demonstrate accountability for personal and group outcomes within broad parameters. | • demonstrate responsibility and broad ranging accountability for the structure, management and output of the work of others and/or functions. | • demonstrate responsibility and accountability for all aspects of work of others and functions including planning, budgeting and strategy. |

*Source:* NIFS (2005a)

degree (science education), but it does not start to deliver the professionally relevant units until Honours level. This is an acceptable pattern so long as universities are honest about it and inform students about the limitations of the programme. However, there is some anecdotal evidence that the latter is not always the case.

Sometimes questions arise whether it is better to attend a Master's programme as opposed to an undergraduate degree. The reality is that it probably does not matter so much. The differences between these two types of qualifications depend on the education system and no facile answer can be provided. In terms of skills and attributes gained during their studies, it is not evident that a Master's graduate will necessarily have an advantage over an Honours graduate. It is however interesting to note that a review of forensic science entitled *Forensic Science on Trial* by a parliamentary committee in the UK (House of Commons 2005) expressed the view, based on industry opinion, that Master's was the appropriate level. Within about two years the number of Master's programmes in the UK had risen about tenfold (Nic Daéid 2007).

It should also be emphasised that the main danger of any postgraduate degree by coursework is to use it to revisit missing fundamental concepts and material from undergraduate teaching. Master's degrees should not be seen as corrective degrees and the foundations should not be built at the Master's level but much earlier. A Master's should rather be used to enhance relevant professional aspects of the discipline and/or to enable the graduate to specialise in a more specific subdiscipline (such as forensic toxicology, forensic DNA, etc.). For example, in the UK, in science, Masters degrees are gradually replacing Honours degrees as the main currency. Many of these are integrated programmes for example MChem, MEng (not a one-year addition). Another option that lies between undergraduate and Master's level are graduate certificates and diplomas. Typically the latter courses consist of one year's full-time study. Certificate courses may be shorter. As previously discussed these are also available in Australia as vocational qualifications. Even with the now large number of forensic science degree courses many entrants to the forensic science industry will not have studied forensic science at undergraduate level. Indeed some employers would prefer to employ graduates who they would argue have a stronger primary discipline founded degree. Postgraduate certificates and diplomas are a useful part of the educational continuum. Either in whole, or by selecting modules or units, they may help fill gaps or enhance fundamental academic knowledge, they may build knowledge of specific forensic relevance and they may provide an academic entry point for mature staff who may lack a primary academic qualification. When offered 'on line' these courses can be an attractive option for a working scientist and to an employer who may be reluctant to release staff for lengthy periods to attend an academic programme.

Another temptation for universities, especially those offering generic programmes, is to use forensic units or modules to replace relatively traditional and unattractive science components. Although this may have a positive effect on science enrolments, it creates real academic and credibility issues. This 'soft' approach also tends to generate graduates who are almost unemployable. For these reasons, forensic science should not be used to lower the level of science to make a soft science degree. There is clear evidence that this has happened in the UK (SEMTA 2004).

In general, this is echoed by forensic science laboratory managers who favour new appointees with a strong foundation in core science disciplines (Higgins and Selavka 1988; Siegel 1988; Furton *et al.* 1999; Almirall and Furton 2003). They often see the forensic content of a programme as a value added feature, which may assist them to rank job applicants further. However, they generally warn against degrees that compromise the level of underpinning sciences. In general, employers are prepared to address gaps in the forensic training undertaken during university studies especially where, historically, they have been used to providing full training in house. However, they do not have the capacity to teach fundamental scientific concepts to their trainees; this should remain the primary role of tertiary education.

Obviously a balance must be struck and, from an employability viewpoint, the most successful programmes are those which combine a solid core of science with a strong forensic science component. Such programmes can be seen as double degrees combining 'the best of both worlds', in most cases a chemistry or a biology foundation with a forensic focus. To this end, a strong partnership with the forensic science industry is highly desirable, if not essential, to ensure the relevance of the forensic component. It is however recognised that designing such programmes is challenging, especially for a three-year degree – a limitation that is imposed by the education system.

It is worth noting at this stage that the majority of such programmes have been chemistry-based degrees as opposed to biology-based ones. For example, out of 61 education programmes listed on the National Institute of Forensic Science website (http://www.nifs.com.au), only 13 have an apparent biology or medical focus (including anthropology and odontology). Similar trends are observed in North America and in the UK. As previously described, this appears to be an anomaly with respect to the fact that jobs in forensic DNA laboratories generally outnumber forensic chemistry employment opportunities. One explanation could be that universities rightly identified that modern forensic DNA profiling mainly applies chemistry processes and that chemistry-based degrees would offer the best overall compromise. However, another simpler and perhaps more cynical reason is that the tertiary sector has seen a significant falling demand for chemistry degrees around the world over the past 10 years (Royal Australian Chemical Institute 2005), while there has been a sustained relatively high demand for biology degrees due to growths in biotechnology, biomedical sciences, and high-profile research such as the human genome project. In other words, the universities' increasing interest in forensic science and the resulting change of focus for chemistry degrees have been primarily dictated by financial pressures and market considerations. The main outcome is, however, not necessarily negative. In modern forensic science, there is a shift of analytical procedures from the laboratory to the crime scene to provide a quick, if not real-time response, as well as assisting with evidence recovery, triage, etc. In this context, a sound education in analytical sciences, especially with a chemistry focus, is undoubtedly an asset. However, the full effect on employment still remains to be seen.

In summary, there are currently an unprecedented number of options offered to anyone who wishes to undertake forensic science studies. In general this is positive progress and assists in the development and enhancement of forensic expertise. In some countries, graduates from the most relevant and well-regarded forensic programmes have been extensively employed within the forensic sector. This can also be seen as a sign of maturity for forensic science. However, the situation brings new challenges for potential students and for employers who must now be very wary in their choices. Some solutions to address this challenge are presented below (see the section on quality of education and training provision).

## In-service training

A university degree is increasingly becoming a necessary entry requirement for the forensic science profession, including crime scene investigation in some parts of the world. However, qualifying with a degree, even in forensic science, does not mean that a graduate has reached the minimum level of expertise and proficiency that is required of a professional forensic scientist. Just as a fresh graduate in medicine will need to undergo further training, internship and specialisations to gradually become a fully trained doctor, (forensic) science graduates will generally undertake some kind of training programme at their workplace and/or at a collaborating educational institution.[3] This initial training programme can be defined as 'the formal, structured process through which a forensic scientist reaches a level of scientific knowledge and expertise required to conduct specific forensic analyses' (NIJ 2004).

The form and length of such training can vary greatly depending on the educational background of the trainee, on the institutional resources and environment and, sometimes, on the legal requirements of the jurisdiction. Typically, a trainee who graduated with a degree which contains a major and relevant forensic science component should require less training than one who had little or no previous exposure to forensic science.

Brightman (NIFS 2005a) identified that, to be effective, training must be:

- connected to the structural and strategic objectives of an organisation and provide a return to the organisation;
- relevant to the needs of the staff undertaking it and provide skills that can be utilised in the workplace, broader than a token response to a sudden need, or focusing on developing specific skills;
- planned, supported and be part of an integrated learning environment that contributes towards the philosophy of continuous improvement in the workplace.

In-service training can contain an educational element to take account of the background differences in new staff. However, it will typically focus on specialisation and specific hands-on skills that are relevant to the forensic scientist's daily activities. It is also important for such training to include material and concepts that are relevant to the forensic science profession, such as ethics, scientific methods, philosophy of science, organisational values, science communication, witness testimony, etc. Mentoring by experienced staff is also a desirable feature throughout this training. At the end of the initial training period, which may take up to two years, and upon fulfilling all assessment requirements (e.g. practical tests, exams, etc.), the forensic scientist may undertake his/her own casework independently.

In the UK there is a national approach to the training of scene of crime and fingerprints staff with training programmes being run at the National Training Centre (NTC) of the National Police Improvement Agency (NPIA) in Harperley Hall. A foundation degree in fingerprint identification is offered in partnership with the University of Teesside. Two Diploma programmes are also available in partnership with Durham University to crime scene investigators and fingerprint experts who have completed the relevant foundation training with the NPIA.

In theory, such a national approach should deliver obvious benefits in achieving consistency. Core academic content of in-service training may have to evolve over time as more entrants to the forensic profession have a higher level of forensic specific knowledge. In the absence of a national approach the employer will necessarily have to conduct some form of training needs analysis and practical assessment of new staff. A balance needs to be reached between a 'one size fits all' approach and a more resource intensive approach based on the individual. In specialist areas various advisory groups are developing guidance on training programme content. These include the Technical and Scientific Working Groups (SWGs) in North America (some with international members) and the scientific working groups of ENFSI (European Network of Forensic Science Institutes). In Australia and New Zealand the Scientific Advisory Groups (SAGs) of the Senior Managers Australian and New Zealand Forensic Science Laboratories (SMANZFL) also play a role in training. SMANZFL works closely with the National Institute of Forensic Science (NIFS) in training and education. NIFS historically developed the National Diploma in Applied Science, Forensic Investigation that is the foundation for most crime scene training in Australia. All fingerprint examiners are also required to have at least the equivalent qualification for their discipline. NIFS also support numerous practical workshops, which help produce a more uniform approach in Australia and New Zealand.

It is entirely the responsibility of the employer to authorise scientists to conduct specific types of examination and analysis. For some roles in many jurisdictions, this must include appropriate proficiency testing. It is highly desirable that all aspects of training and case authorisation are part of an overall accredited quality system.

### The role of continuing education

Education is a lifelong experience. It is likely that during his or her professional career, a forensic scientist will experience significant changes in both criminal activity and technology as well as organisational changes. It is therefore necessary, even for a fully trained and experienced forensic scientist, to stay abreast of the most recent developments. This is the reason why continuing professional development, the mechanisms through which forensic scientists remain current or advance their expertise (NIJ 2004), is highly desirable. According to the Technical Working Group for Education and Training in Forensic Science (TWGED), forensic scientists should even consider continuing professional development as an ongoing obligation.

Continuing professional development may take an informal form such as reading the forensic and broader scientific literature. It is also complemented by a more formal form such as attending conferences and seminars, or by a training element such as taking part in short courses and workshops. Overall the process should be structured, measurable and documented. It is however recognised that these requirements are certainly not applied everywhere around the world or across all the forensic disciplines.

Various topic- or discipline-specific short courses are regularly offered by a number of associations and professional bodies around the world. These courses are often designed and delivered in collaboration with an educational provider, for example a tertiary institution. They may also be offered in conjunction with a scientific symposium. Typical examples include short courses or workshops on fingerprint detection techniques, DNA statistics, fire debris analysis, interpretation and presentation of forensic evidence, etc.

An interesting development is that training is increasingly aligned with competency frameworks (i.e. a system allowing an employee to demonstrate that he or she is competent to undertake a given task or job), certification of forensic personnel as well as promotion prospects. For example, in the generic document entitled 'Performance Based Standards for Forensic Science Practitioners' (ENFSI 2004), the European Network of Forensic Science Institutes (ENFSI) suggests that these standards 'should be used to inform the design and application of all forensic science education and training (whether delivered in forensic science institutions or in an academic environment). Qualification design and certification programmes should also use these activities and standards as the basis for their development.' A number of organisations and groups have also defined competency levels or desirable training requirements for their discipline. For example, the Scientific Working Group for Materials Analysis (SWGMAT), Fiber Subgroup, sponsored by the Federal Bureau of Investigation (FBI), published a document to assist in training people to carry out forensic fibre examinations. Other examples include the training guidelines or equivalent documents published by Scientific Working Groups (SWGs) in the following disciplines: fire and explosives (SWGFEX), illicit drugs (SWGDRUG), latent fingerprints (SWGFAST), firearms and tool marks (SWGGUN) and digital and multimedia evidence (SWGDE/SWGIT). In some cases, the requirements may be very specific, for example, the certification of a bloodstain pattern examiner by the International Association of Identification (IAI) includes the requirement to attend 240 hours of discipline-specific education followed by 40 hours of theory, study and practice of flight characteristics and stain patterns, examination and identification of bloodstain evidence, and documentation of bloodstains and patterns.

The main challenge for in-service training is to offer a programme that is well structured and tailored to the forensic specialty to be effective while at the same time it remains flexible enough to account for the diverse educational backgrounds of the trainees and to address competing demands on time and resources within the forensic organisation. Time pressures constitute probably the most important limitation for any such organisation, although most managers would accept that 'training is not a cost but a sound business investment' (Burns 1995). It is, however, unfortunate that some operational organisations still do not consider initial training as their primary obligation.

An additional challenge, especially for training providers, is to realise that trainees mainly constitute an adult market, as opposed to recent school leavers in degree programmes. Most trainees start their training programme with a higher level of relevant prior learning, personal and professional experience than is the case for recent school leavers. The former also tend to have less time available for their study than the latter. This means that providers should adapt their teaching style and delivery format and avoid the temptation to 'recycle' their existing undergraduate units or modules. This is becoming even more important with the increase of graduate intake into operational forensic science organisations. What is the value for them to sit in classes which are very similar or identical to the units or modules they already undertook at university? Good examples include the use of short and sharp practical sessions, complemented by well-focused lectures and tutorials. There are also opportunities to develop training materials as part of online education packages. Some interesting initiatives have been recently developed around the world. A typical example would be the online Master's and Certificate offered by the University of Florida in five focused areas: Environmental Forensics, Forensic Toxicology, Forensic Drug Chemistry, Forensic DNA and Serology and Forensic Death Investigation. It is however recognised that some discipline areas or specific subjects lend themselves to online delivery better than others. Similarly, trainees in general still indicate a preference for face-to-face delivery (NIFS 2005a).

In summary, in-service training is an essential part of any induction or professional programme and should also be seen as a crucial element of continuing professional development. To be effective, training must be well structured, assessable, with clear learning outcomes, and preferably be developed and delivered in partnership with educational institutions. Training should also be supported by corporate values and management, as well as complying with competency frameworks and support career progression. If these conditions are met, there is little doubt that training contributes to the development and enhancement of forensic expertise.

## Quality of education and training provision

Besides the advantages previously described, the growth in forensic programmes around the world since the mid-1990s has also raised a number of issues. For example, in most countries there is currently a disparity in supply and demand of forensic graduates. Although it is recognised that the role of universities is much broader than producing only graduates ending up working as professionals, this disparity should be a serious ethical concern for any university offering a forensic programme. Is it ethically responsible for universities to attract a large number of students to study in an area where the job opportunities appear to be scarce? For this reason, many universities have designed their programmes in such a way that their graduates obtain generic and scientific skills and personal attributes, which suit them to a wide range of potential careers. In addition to forensic science careers, such graduates may go on to careers in the pharmaceutical industry, occupational health and safety, environmental sciences, science education, etc. The success of such a strategy obviously depends on the content of the programme, and, more broadly, on the quality of the offering.

Ensuring the quality of a forensic science programme is another problem that has been exacerbated by the growth in forensic programmes. It should be pointed out at this stage that, in many countries, the quality of higher education delivery is overseen by a national authority that is often linked to the Ministry or Department of Education. The mandate of such authorities is often broad and focuses more on the institutional level than on the actual programme quality. While universities enjoy such academic freedom, the delivery of programmes from vocational institutions is generally more tightly controlled.

Potential employers have recently criticised the lack of consistency and clarity in the vast range of forensic courses on offer, thus leading to difficulties in determining what skills a graduate might have (SEMTA 2004). These concerns have led to significant reviews of forensic science education and training in the UK, USA and Australia, respectively:

- *Forensic Science: Implications for Higher Education* by the Science, Engineering, Manufacturing Technologies Alliance (SEMTA 2004);

- *Education and Training in Forensic Science: A Guide for Forensic Science Laboratories, Educational Institutions, and Students* by the US National Institute of Justice (Developed and Approved by the Technical Working Group for Education and Training in Forensic Science – (NIJ 2004); and

- *Australian Forensic Science – Education and Training for the Future* by the National Institute of Forensic Science (NIFS 2005a).

Beyond national peculiarities, a number of key findings of these reviews are in broad agreement, and include recommendations about:

- quality assurance and consistency of forensic science degree content;

- close liaison and consultation between forensic science employers and education and training providers to discuss the content and the outcomes of forensic science programmes;

- the need for strong natural science foundations complemented by forensic science discipline-specific training and education;

- the importance of training programmes in professional development; for example, the need for training that is 'structured, measurable and documented'; establishment of training programmes designed to deliver the full range of technical/laboratory skills required in employment.

The main purpose of TWGED was to provide best practice guidance for educating and training forensic scientists. As such, their document also defines the minimum requirements for the core curriculum of a model forensic sciences degree. For example, Table 21.2 below shows the requirements for an undergraduate degree in forensic science.

In parallel to TWGED, in 2002 the American Academy of Forensic Sciences (AAFS) established a committee, the Forensic Education Program Accreditation Committee (FEPAC), which subsequently became the Forensic Science Education Accreditation Commission whose mission is to 'maintain and to enhance the quality of forensic science education through a formal evaluation and accreditation system for college-level academic programs that lead to a baccalaureate or graduate degree.' (FEPAC 2003). To achieve these aims, FEPAC largely use the TWGED curriculum guidelines. Overall FEPAC is a success and nearly self-sustaining for costs. There are currently 17 programmes at 16 American institutions accredited at the graduate and undergraduate levels. FEPAC is also seeking recognition as an accrediting agency by the Council of Higher Education Accreditors (CHEA). In the UK, the Forensic Science Society is offering an accreditation system for academic institutions that deliver forensic science undergraduate and postgraduate courses. The system is based on a set of criteria identified in three different components: crime scene investigation; interpretation, evaluation and presentation of evidence; and laboratory analysis. There are currently 36 programmes accredited at 13 British universities (Forensic Science Society 2008).

While there is no doubt that students need to be more accurately informed, it is, however, recognised that a formal accreditation process may not be feasible nor viable for some jurisdictions as it requires significant resources and input from all stakeholders. An alternative option to accreditation has been identified and is now used in Australia. Forensic science employers and educators have identified (through the auspices of the Australian and New Zealand Association of Forensic Educators and Researchers and the National Institute of Forensic Science) a list of questions and suitable answers to assist prospective students and parents to assess the content and structure of tertiary forensic science programmes. This can be done against standards that are directly related to what employers are looking for in graduates. In this model the onus is on the students to do their homework. It is also more flexible as the questions and answers can be easily modified whenever required. It should however be emphasised that these questions should not be seen as 'accreditation', but they constitute a pragmatic solution which seems effective in a country like Australia. The current questions are shown in Table 21.3 below.

Overall, there is little doubt that both educational institutions and the forensic science industry consider the broad concept of quality assurance for forensic science programmes as an increasingly important issue. A parallel with the generalised advent of QA systems in operational forensics science can be identified. This is a long process, and the challenge is to avoid an overly bureaucratic system which would eventually have little meaning with respect to the actual quality of a given forensic science programme. There is no fast solution and the 'devil is in the details'!

**Table 21.2** Sample curriculum for undergraduate forensic sciences degree proposed by TWGED

| | Biology | Chemistry/Trace Evidence/Controlled Substances | Toxicology | Firearms/Impression Evidence/Questioned Documents/Prints |
|---|---|---|---|---|
| University General Education (36–40 hrs) | Courses required by the university, which may include language, humanities, social sciences, technical writing, mathematics, computer science, and public speaking. Credit hours required will vary from university to university. Some forensic degree coursework may count toward fulfilling these requirements. | | | |
| Natural Science Core (34–38 hrs) | Biology, I, II[b]<br>Calculus<br>General Chemistry I, II[b]<br>Organic Chemistry I, II[b]<br>Physics I, II[b]<br>Statistics | Biology I<br>Calculus<br>General Chemistry I, II<br>Organic Chemistry I, II<br>Physics I, II<br>Statistics | Biology I<br>Calculus<br>General Chemistry I, II<br>Organic Chemistry I, II<br>Physics I, II<br>Statistics | Biology I<br>Calculus<br>General Chemistry I, II<br>Organic Chemistry I, II<br>Physics, I, II<br>Statistics |
| Specialized Core (12 hrs) | Biochemistry<br>Genetics<br>Instrumental Analysis<br>Molecular Biology | Analytic Chemistry Quantitative[b]<br>Inorganic Chemistry<br>Instrumental Analysis<br>Physical Chemistry | Analytic Chemistry Quantitative<br>Biochemistry<br>Instrumental Analysis<br>Physical Chemistry | Inorganic Chemistry<br>Instrumental Analysis<br>Optics/Lasers<br>Physical Chemistry |
| Forensic Sciences Core (6 hrs) | Forensic Science Survey<br>Forensic Professional Practice[c] | Forensic Science Survey<br>Forensic Professional Practice | Forensic Science Survey<br>Forensic Professional Practice | Forensic Science Survey<br>Forensic Professional Practice |
| Forensic Laboratory Science (9 hrs) | Forensic Biology<br>Internship<br>Microscopy<br>Physical Methods | Forensic Chemistry<br>Internship<br>Microscopy<br>Physical Methods | Forensic Chemistry<br>Internship<br>Microscopy<br>Physical Methods | Internship<br>Microscopy<br>Physical Methods |

| Additional Courses[d] (19 hrs) | Cell Biology | Advanced Instrumental Analysis Drugs | Advanced Instrumental Analysis Drugs | Crime Scene Image Analysis |
|---|---|---|---|---|
| | Introduction to Criminal Jusice | Introduction to Criminal Justice | Introduction to Criminal Justice | Introduction to Criminal Justice |
| | Legal Evidence | Legal Evidence | Legal Evidence | Legal Evidence |
| | Microbiology | Analytical Toxicology | Analytical Toxicology | Materials Science |
| | Population Genetics | Materials Science | Pharmacology | |
| | Immunology | Pharmacology | Public Speaking | |
| | Public Speaking | Public Speaking | | |

[a] These examples are based on a minimum of 120 semester hours to obtain a degree. Credit hours as described above are meant to indicate semester credit hours.
[b] Laboratory courses.
[c] This course includes ethics, testimony, evidence, chain of custody, etc.
[d] Electives listed here are not exhaustive, and students may wish to tailor courses according to their areas of concentration.
*Source:* NIJ (2004)

**Table 21.3** Questions and answers from the industry sector assist prospective students and parents assess the content and structure of tertiary forensic science programmes in Australia

| Question | Desirable answer from the industry's viewpoint |
| --- | --- |
| 1 What is the name of your course(s)? | |
| 2 What is the level (BSc, MSc, etc.) and duration of your course(s)? | |
| 3 Is there a specific focus for your course? If so, what is it? | *Ensure the specific focus of the course is relevant for your intended career path* |
| 4 Is it offered in part-time mode? | |
| 5 Is it offered in distance education mode? | |
| 6 What are the entry requirements? | |
| 7 Do you recognise relevant prior learning (i.e. can you give exemptions for subjects already passed at other institutions)? If yes, can you name the institutions for which this applies? | *The general expectation is that equivalent subjects at an equivalent level will be recognised* |
| 8 Do you have any formal arrangement for transfer or exchanges with other institutions? If yes, can you name the institutions for which this applies? | |
| 9 How many units of general science subjects (e.g. chemistry, biology, physics) are in the course and at what level? | *This answer will be course dependent (e.g. undergraduate v. postgraduate). For a 3-year Bachelor's degree, at least half of the units should be general science subjects* |
| 10 How many units of specialised forensic science subjects (e.g. physical evidence, crime scene, toxicology, forensic biology, expert evidence presentation, etc.) are in the course? | *This answer will be course dependent (e.g. undergraduate v. postgraduate). For a 1-year Graduate Diploma all units may be specialised forensic subjects)* |

|  |  |
|---|---|
| 11 What electives or additional subjects (e.g. psychology, law, statistics, criminology) are offered in the course? | *Electives or additional subjects should be relevant for your intended career path* |
| 12 What is the percentage of practical v. theory | *Laboratory/field science subjects or courses should have a strong practical component* |
| 13 Does the course include a research component? | *For employment in the forensic industry, a course that includes a research component is highly desirable* |
| 14 Does the course include an industry-based component? For example placements, internships, laboratory visits, etc. | *Some form of industry-based component is highly desirable* |
| 15 Do you involve industry-based personnel in teaching and/or project supervision? If so, to what extent? | *The involvement of industry-based personnel is highly desirable. The extent of this involvement should be appropriate for the level and aims of the course* |
| 16 Do you have academic staff with experience in forensic casework? If so, please provide details | *It is highly desirable that academic staff delivering specialised forensic subjects have forensic casework experience* |
| 17 Do you have a Course Advisory Committee or equivalent and who are members of this group? Do they include operational forensic service managers? | *There should be a Course Advisory Committee or equivalent and membership should include operational forensic service managers* |
| 18 What career opportunities will this course give me? | *The career opportunities should be consistent with your intended career path* |
| 19 What is the level of graduate employment on completion of this course? Can you give me some specific examples of graduate employment outcomes? | *The level of graduate employment should be high and specific examples should be provided that are consistent with your intended career path* |
| 20 Can graduates pursue research degrees after this course? If so, what are the options? | *This answer will be course dependent. For an undergraduate degree, there should be a clear progression path to a research programme* |

Ultimately, a 'good' forensic science programme can be identified when:

- it generates graduates who are employed in the forensic industry;
- it generates graduates who have enough scientific skills and knowledge to be employed in other scientific industries;
- it genuinely contributes to the advancement of relevant knowledge;
- it has acquired over the years national and international reputations.

## Research and development

Nowadays, most employers see research skills as essential for graduates seeking employment in forensic science. The ability to identify hypotheses and to design experiments to test them in a given context is unquestionably crucial in routine forensic practice. As a result, forensic education should, whenever possible, include a research training component. The scope and length of this research training obviously depends on the duration and on the structure of the educational programme. For example, traditionally, the vocational sector does not have a strong research culture, and research projects in this environment will be less sophisticated and smaller in scope than those offered by the higher education sector. They will often be considered as development (i.e. the creation of new knowledge is very limited) rather than research (the creation of new knowledge is tangible). A typical example would be a project testing and comparing different fingerprint powders on a variety of surfaces. Similarly, three-year pass degrees will offer fewer opportunities to include a genuine research project than postgraduate degrees. Honours and Master's Degrees are the first levels at which research training really occurs. However, from an academic standpoint, a research programme is not sustainable and does not attract the respect from academic peers and major research funding bodies until it offers doctoral degrees. Such degrees rarely include the word 'forensic' on the testamur and are generally simply obtained in 'science'. However, the topic or the thesis title as well as the research group, academic unit or centre where the project was actually undertaken would identify the forensic science nature of the research. Ultimately, the capacity to carry out high-level research in forensic science requires the ability to attract major funding which in turn allows employers to employ experienced professional researchers such as post-doctoral fellows, research assistants and the like. It is however fair to say that, in most countries, it is still difficult to attract major funding for forensic science research through traditional research funding bodies.

Despite this funding issue, nowadays there are ample opportunities to carry out research at different levels, and undertake smaller scale projects catering for the diverse needs and demand from the forensic science industry. This is a positive development because it is essential for any profession to develop research skills at all levels.

It is interesting to note that one of the most positive outcomes of the explosion of forensic science programmes at university over the past 15 years is the associated critical mass of research that has been generated around the world. This has assisted forensic science to grow into a more respected academic discipline. A noticeable result has been the significant increase of attendees and research papers presented at national and international forensic science symposia over the past 15 years. For example, the Australian and New Zealand Forensic Science Society symposia typically attracted 350 attendees before the development of academic forensic science research in the mid-1990s. They now almost reach the 1,000 mark. Similar trends can be observed in Europe and America. A similar comment could be made with respect to the number of papers published in forensic and broad science journals. For example, there was an increase of 35 per cent in the number of publications in *Forensic Science International* between 2004 and 2007 (ISI Web of Knowledge), while during the same period a number of forensic science papers were published in non-forensic journals such as *Chemical Communications*.

In addition to the mere numbers, this increased research capacity is crucial for the development and enhancement of the forensic science discipline. Occasionally, academic institutions with a very strong forensic focus can drive the forensic profession by developing and proposing new models or processes which do not only improve forensic services, but also have a genuine positive effect on the delivery of policing and the criminal justice system as a whole. An example would be recent research in forensic intelligence highlighting the value of integrating the laboratory sciences with other dimensions of the investigative process (Walsh *et al.* 2002; Ribaux *et al.* 2003). This research-driven professional development may even come from outside 'pure forensic science' research. The extraordinary and rapid universal acceptance of forensic DNA profiling evidence after the original work in genetics by Sir Alec Jeffreys and colleagues at the University of Leicester (UK) would be the most extreme example of this kind (Jeffreys *et al.* 1985a, 1985b). In other cases, forensic science research can be more industry or casework driven. This type of research includes projects aiming at improving existing methods and standard operating procedures (e.g. developing a new capillary electrophoresis method for drug analysis) and case- or evidence-specific issues (e.g. investigating the significance of finding fibres on a murder victim's shoe soles). In any case, the most successful and relevant research outcomes are obtained when a close partnership exists between academic and operational institutions. In some countries, in recent years, major collaborations between a number of partners from academia, operational forensic science and support bodies have leveraged this capacity. A typical example would be the project 'Improved Monitoring and Detection Capabilities to Minimise the Potential Criminal Use of Explosives in Australia' (NIFS 2004 and NIFS 2005b) led by the National Institute of Forensic Science. Not only did this project deliver significant operational outcomes, but it also allowed each of the different participating universities to attract further major grants to pursue research in this discipline area.

In summary, active research activities are crucial for the development and enhancement of forensic expertise; and the best outcomes are achieved when there is a strong and healthy partnership between research providers and the broad forensic science community.

## Conclusions and future directions

The role played by forensic science in the criminal justice system is of increasing significance. So too is its public and political profile. This is a new phase for our discipline and one that brings exciting prospects for expansion and development. However, also associated with this increased role comes an added responsibility; a responsibility that is shared equally by all who are involved with forensic science. The contribution of forensic science educators and researchers to the development of this discipline is no less relevant than that of operational forensic scientists.

Educational institutions offering forensic science programmes must clearly consider their role in the teaching and learning process and realise their responsibilities when generating graduates who are 'industry-ready'. In doing so, the education sector must address the content of their programmes and balance underpinning sciences and core forensic science. In our opinion the challenge to provide sound education can be greatly assisted by understanding and applying the fundamental principles of the forensic discipline itself. However, this must not be achieved by compromising the quality of education in fundamental science disciplines.

The education sector must consider multiple and novel delivery methods for their programmes to meet the reality that students often have to work during their study. Continuing professional development is also an important aspect in the modern practice of forensic science. Although there is still some degree of scepticism, the development of online courses may bring some interesting solutions in this area.

Forensic science programmes must also support practical experience and at the same time generate graduates who can think critically in a variety of situations. The latter criterion is seen as pivotal in forensic science education and training. It is argued that field forensic science (i.e. scenes of crime) is the area of our discipline that is going to grow the most in the near future. In particular, future demands in the field will include the need for an improved and quicker selection, triage and assessment of exhibits, and the whole process relies heavily on a high level of critical thinking based on a situational approach. In addition, not only is critical thinking necessary to become a good professional forensic scientist, but it is also important if educational institutions wish to make their product available to other parts of the world which are not necessarily rich or as technologically advanced as the Western world.

In recent years, the rapid growth in forensic science degrees has attracted some criticism from the industry sector. Improved information to students, better communication with the industry sector and the development of quality assurance systems may all assist in solving many of these issues. Ultimately market forces (i.e. students making their choices) will determine the fate of the plethora of forensic science programmes.

The critical requirements for sustained high-quality education in forensic science are:

- a strong foundation in fundamental sciences (i.e. chemistry, biology, mathematics); and
- a strong collaboration with the forensic science industry to ensure the relevance of the forensic component.

Failure to address these issues will result in only a short-term success. Conversely, successful forensic science education and training as well as research and development programmes will play a crucial part in answering those observers and critics who do not recognise forensic science as a specialist area of expertise.

It is our belief that academic programmes in forensic science should include strong practical content. We recognise that the principle focus of an academic programme should be on education and that 'preparing students for industry' practical content is not synonymous with training. Even at the vocational level, which is more competency based, it should not be expected that the student will emerge with industry level competency. If nothing else 'practice makes perfect' and the employer has a minimum requirement to test employees' competency in their environment. Our view is that best practice demands a partnership between the academic and industry, a partnership based on a mutually shared understanding of the role of an educational provider and the practical needs of an employer. Ultimately it is the responsibility of the employer to ensure appropriate in-service training. In an effective partnership with academia, the employer will be able to target in-service training more effectively and potentially reduce the length of initial training.

This partnership approach goes beyond that of academia and the employer and must also include the employee. This is especially so with ongoing and continuing professional development. There needs to be a social contract between employer and employee that recognises their dual and shared responsibilities. The employer must accept primary responsibility for induction and early career training. The employee should accept that they have a higher level of personal responsibility as their career progresses, especially if they wish to undertake further academic study. Ideally employer and employee will develop a long-term agreed development strategy appropriate to the individual. This will include in-service training and it may well include some form of ongoing academic component. Both are necessary elements to truly develop forensic expertise.

## Notes

1 The term 'sworn' is used here to characterise a police employee who has police power; i.e. an officer who can, amongst other things, arrest criminals. This term is commonly used because police officers are generally sworn to an oath. In most jurisdictions, sworn officers have typically attended a Police Academy or specific Police School to acquire general and specific policing skills.
2 In contrast to 'sworn', the term 'non-sworn' or 'civilian' is applied here to a police employee who does not have police power, but is crucially contributing to police functions through his or her skills specific to a specialised area, e.g. crime scene investigation.

3 It is however recognised that few scientific professions, including in forensic science, are structured and integrated to professional bodies to the same level as in medicine.

## References

Almirall, J.R. and Furton, K.G. (2003) 'Trends in Forensic Science Education: Expansion and Increased Accountability', *Analytical and Bioanalytical Chemistry*, 376: 1156–1159.

Burns, R. (1995) *The Adult Learner at Work: A Comprehensive Guide to the Context, Psychology and Methods of Learning for the Workplace*. Chatswood, NSW, Australia: Business and Professional Publishing, pp. 296–297.

Denofrio, L.A., Russell, B., Lopatto, D. and Lu, Y. (2007) 'Linking Student Interests to Science Curricula', *Science*, 318: 1872–1873.

ENFSI Standing Committee for Quality and Competence (2004) *Performance Based Standards for Forensic Science Practitioners*, European Network of Forensic Science Institutes.

Forensic Science Education Accreditation Commission (FEPAC) (2003) *Policies and Procedures*, American Academy of Forensic Sciences.

Forensic Science Society (2008) 'University Course Accreditation Scheme. List of Accredited Universities', available at http://www.forensic-science-society.org.uk/Resources/Forensic%20Science/Accredited%20Courses%20291008.pdf, [accessed 10 November 2008].

Furton, K.G., Hsu, Y.L. and Cole, M.D. (1999) 'What Educational Background Do Crime Laboratory Directors Require from Applicants?', *Journal of Forensic Sciences*, 44: 128–132.

Higgins, K.M. and Selavka, C.M. (1988) 'Do Forensic Science Graduate Programs Fulfil the Needs of the Forensic Science Community?' *Journal of Forensic Sciences*, 33: 1015–21.

House of Commons (2005) *Science and Technology Committee, Forensic Science on Trial. Seventh Report of Session 2004–05*. London: HMSO.

Inman, K. and Rudin, N. (2001) *Principles and Practice of Criminalistics: The Profession of Forensic Science*. Boca Raton, Florida: CRC Press.

International Association of Identification (IAI) (2008) 'Bloodstain Pattern Examiner Certification Requirements', available at http://www.theiai.org/certifications/bloodstain/requirements.php [accessed 10 November 2008].

ISI Web of Knowledge (2008) Homepage available at.http://www.isiwebofknowledge.com/, [accessed 10 November 2008].

Jeffreys, A.J., Wilson, V. and Thein, S.L. (1985a) 'Individual-Specific "Fingerprints" of Human DNA', *Nature*, 316 (6023): 76–79.

Jeffreys, A.J., Brookfield, J.F. and Semeonoff, R. (1985b) 'Positive Identification of an Immigration Test-Case Using Human DNA Fingerprints', *Nature*, 317 (6040): 818–819.

Margot, P. (1994) 'Forensic Science Education … or How Do We Foster Quality', Proceedings of the 3rd meeting of the European Network of Forensic Science Institutes, Linköping, pp. 31–37.

Mathyer, J. (2001) *Rodolphe A. Reiss – Pionnier de la criminalistique*. IPSC, University of Lausanne: Lausanne.

Myers, S. (2003) 'Special Report – Forensic Science', *Nature*, 421: 872–873.

National Institute of Forensic Science (NIFS) (2004) *Improved Monitoring and Detection Capabilities to Minimise the Potential Criminal Use of Explosives in Australia. Phase 1.*

National Institute of Forensic Science (2005a) *Australian Forensic Science – Education and Training for the Future.* NIFS.

National Institute of Forensic Science (NIFS) (2005b) *Improved Monitoring and Detection Capabilities to Minimise the Potential Criminal Use of Explosives in Australia:Phase 2.*

National Institute of Justice (NIJ) (2004) *Education and Training in Forensic Science: A Guide for Forensic Science Laboratories, Educational Institutions, and Students: Developed and Approved by the Technical Working Group for Education and Training in Forensic Science.* Washington, DC: National Institute of Justice.

Nic Daéid, N. (2007) 'Higher education and forensic science, the UK experience', Forensic Science Society Spring Meeting, Bahrain.

Pasteur L. (1871) Pourquoi la France n'a pas trouvé d'hommes supérieurs au moment du péril. Salut public, Section IV, http://www.pasteur-international.org/Publications/declaration.pdf. [accessed 2 April 2008].

Ribaux, O., Girod, A., Walsh, S.J., Margot, P., Mizrahi, S. and Clivaz, V. (2003) 'Forensic Intelligence and Crime Analysis', *Law, Probability and Risk*, 2: 47–60.

Royal Australian Chemical Institute (2005) *Future of Chemistry Study – Supply and Demand of Chemists*, Final Report.

Science, Engineering, Manufacturing Technologies Alliance (SEMTA) (2004) *Forensic Science: Implications for Higher Education.*

Scientific Working Group for Firearms and Toolmarks (SWGGUN) (2001) *Recommended Guidelines for Developing a Training Manual for Forensic Laboratories.*

Scientific Working Group for Materials Analysis (SWGMAT) (2004) *A Forensic Fiber Examiner Training Program.*

Scientific Working Group for the Analysis of Seized Drugs (SWGDRUG) (2006) *Training and Education.*

Scientific Working Group on Digital Evidence and Imaging Technology (SWGDE/SWGIT) (2004) *Guidelines and Recommendations for Training in Digital and Multimedia Evidence.*

Scientific Working Group on Friction Ridge Analysis, Study and Technology (SWGFAST) (2002) *Training to Competency for Latent Print Examiners.*

Siegel, J.A. (1988) 'The Appropriate Educational Background for Entry Level Forensic Scientists: A Survey of Practitioners', *Journal of Forensic Sciences*, 33: 1065–68.

Smith, R. (2007) 'Crime Scene Investigators', *Nature*, 445: 794.

Stokes, D.E. (1997) *Pasteur's Quadrant: Basic Science and Technological Innovation.* Washington, D.C.: Brookings Institution Press.

Technical and Scientific Working Group for Fire and Explosives (SWGFEX) (2006) *Training Guidelines for the Fire Debris Analyst.*

Walsh, S.J., Moss, D.S., Kleim, C. and Vintiner, G.M. (2002) 'The Collation of Forensic DNA Case Data into a Multi-Dimensional Intelligence Database', *Science and Justice*, 42: 205–14.

# Chapter 22

# The future(s) of forensic investigations

*Jim Fraser and Robin Williams*

## Introduction

In this final chapter we briefly describe and reflect on some of the recent and ongoing trends in the development of forensic science and its application to criminal investigations. A full analysis of the impact of these developments in individual countries or jurisdictions is beyond the scope of this chapter. Therefore we concentrate on a single jurisdiction (England and Wales) while also noting significant developments elsewhere which affect the more local trajectory. In doing so we draw on the previous chapters in this Handbook as well as a number of other recent official and academic publications. Many of the current trends in forensic investigations are the instantiation of long-standing scientific and investigative preoccupations and ambitions; others are of more recent origin and reflect the contemporary challenges faced by scientists, policymakers, and criminal investigators. All have to be understood against the background of constant and sometimes unexpected changes in the material, intellectual, political, social, and organisational contexts within which new forms and uses of forensic science are developed and applied.

The unpredictability of knowledge growth, combined with the instability of these conditioning features, means that the futures of the various applied disciplines included in the category 'forensic science' necessarily remain uncertain. Forensic science practitioners, or the wider scientific community in which they are located, may make startling new discoveries and/or throw doubt on the validity and reliability of currently accepted knowledge and techniques. Equally the ways in which the wide variety of disciplines discussed in this Handbook are brought to bear on investigations and prosecutions remain subject to circumstances external to the sciences themselves. Judicial authorities may begin to question previous verities or challenge the reliability of new claims to knowledge; governments may decide to invest more or less in the use of forensic science as a servant to criminal justice; regulatory, auditing and credentialing bodies may exert new demands on innovators and users; new forms of governance which affect the collection or use of forensic science data may be demanded by civil society actors; changing threats to social order and individual security may be identified and novel kinds of forensic science resource recruited to combat them; and legislators may gain or lose confidence in public support for risk management practices that depend on particular features of forensic science and technology for their effective operation.

Foresight is always a hazardous enterprise, and especially so in the realm of science and technology where discoveries and inventions are notoriously difficult to anticipate, where the time taken to translate validated theoretical insights into routine practice is often longer than promised, and where unanticipated consequences of the translation and application process regularly confound prior promises of utility. However, despite such chronic uncertainties, many of those who write about (and even try to future-cast) the history of socio-scientific enterprises persist in the use of terms like 'watershed', 'critical conjuncture', 'paradigm shift', 'crossroad', and (most fashionable at the moment) 'tipping point'. Those who have speculated about the future prospects for forensic science have often employed these and other similar terms and they have done so regardless of the many uncertainties that we have described above.

None of those expressions shall be found in this chapter despite our interest in the possible futures of the application of forensic science to criminal investigations. Instead, we want to illuminate the possible near future of forensic science and its uses by reference to our understanding of the factors that have influenced the recent development of the investigative and prosecutorial deployment of forensic science in England and Wales over the past two decades or so.

Following an outline account of the most significant recent developments in the context, substance, and uses of forensic science, we go on to note a series of recurrent contradictions and problems that have accompanied expansions in the scope and application of this body of knowledge and practice. Only the irrationally optimistic can imagine a future in which all of these contradictions are dissolved or problems solved. In our view, such challenges are firmly entrenched both into what it is that constitutes the 'forensic' in forensic science and also into the many efforts to integrate scientific expertise and technological innovation into the practical exigencies of criminal investigation. However, there may be ways in which criminal justice policymakers and practitioners can minimise some of the troubles that lie at the heart of the forensic science enterprise, and in this way improve current efforts by its practitioners and users to inform and direct the investigation of crime.

## Recent developments

Table 22.1 below identifies the major factors relevant to the recent development of forensic science in England and Wales albeit in a simplified manner. The factors we describe in this table are largely external to changes in the theoretical substrate of forensic science knowledge and practice. Many of these latter changes have already been described in the chapters that make up the first

**Table 22.1**   Factors influencing the recent development of forensic science in England and Wales

| Period | Technological | Professional | Organisational | Policing |
|---|---|---|---|---|
| 1980s | Introduction of new analytical methods largely based on technical criteria | Individual and artisan roles but growing recognition of a need for standardisation of analytical methods<br><br>Gradual introduction of formal quality management systems<br><br>Ramsey and Touche Ross Reports<br><br>Review of fingerprint standards by Evett & Williams | Managers traditionally derived from technical specialists without specific training and with general ambivalence to management roles | Introduction of devolved budgets for major operations such as homicide<br><br>HOLMES introduced following Byford Report<br><br>Increased reliance on independent evidence from experts |
| 1990s | | General diminution of influence of specialists | Rise of 'management culture'<br><br>Introduction of cost-benefit considerations | Publication of critical reviews of police use of forensic science (e.g. UFSE) |
| | Switch to PCR from SLP makes DNA database feasible<br><br>Introduction of robotic technology in DNA analysis<br><br>Technical improvements of DNA profiling takes place leading to SGM*plus* ® and LCN | New models of working introduced e.g. evidence recovery units<br><br>Council for the Registration of Forensic Practitioners belatedly introduced<br><br>Major expansion of police use of forensic science (in addition to DNA) in volume crime | Introduction of account managers by FSS<br><br>Rise of 'customer service' models and forensic science 'marketing'<br><br>Widespread adoption of professional management terminology. E.g. directors of laboratories now become Heads of Operations | Scientific Support Manager Forensic submission units established<br><br>Performance measurement in scientific support<br><br>Cold case review process established<br><br>Inceptive use of forensic science (especially DNA and fingerprints) gradually develops<br><br>Murder Investigation Manual<br><br>Macpherson Report |
| 2000 to present | NAFIS implemented<br><br>IDENT1 implemented<br><br>Development of expert systems for DNA interpretation<br><br>Development of internet crime and digital technologies | Expert reviews of forensic science shortcomings in significant prosecutions<br><br>Forensic Science Regulator appointed in response to proposed privatisation of FSS and creation of the 'forensic marketplace'<br><br>CRFP formally announces closure of register | Consolidation of market models for service provision<br><br>Embedding of commercial vocabularies in professional discourse<br><br>Forensic commodities versus forensic services models | Fingerprint non-numeric standard introduced<br><br>Murder of Damilola Taylor<br><br>NCPE founded – development of 'investigative doctrines'<br><br>Inception of NPIA. Seeming acceptance of the need to address significant defects in police forensic knowledge |

| Period | Social | Political | Legal | Economic |
|--------|--------|-----------|-------|----------|
| 1980s | Rising crime rates and expenditure on law and order<br><br>Rise of 'authoritarian populism'<br><br>Globalisation as an economic and cultural process | Application of market models to public sector<br><br>Large-scale privatisation of many public sector bodies by Conservative government | Independent Prosecution Service (CPS) introduced | Major State provision of forensic science independent of police force budgets.<br><br>Very small commercial forensic sector |
| 1990s | Prominent miscarriages and efforts to restore public confidence through 1993 Royal Commission on Criminal Justice<br><br>Growing concerns over forensic DNA data storage despite widespread acceptance of 'benefits'<br><br>Rising popularity of University 'forensic' degree programmes<br><br>The 'CSI effect' | Intensification of neo-liberal efforts at auditing and managing public service provision<br><br>Introduction of widespread performance measurement in criminal justice by new Labour government | Enabling legislation for the creation of a National DNA database<br><br>CPIA codifies role of investigator and requirements of disclosure<br><br>Best Value legislation requires constant review of public sector organisations | Agency status for major forensic science providers<br><br><br><br><br><br>Reductions in cost of DNA analysis |
| 2000 to present | The rise of Post 9/11 security agendas<br><br>ECtHR challenges to DNA retention policy<br><br>Introduction of the 'Hague Principle' governing the exchange of police data between EU States<br><br>Critiques of the 'surveillance society' | Shift in presentation of DNA database from 'criminal database' to information database<br><br>Numerous reports suggest 'benefits' of DNA database but no conclusive study carried out<br><br>First Home Office Science & Technology strategy published<br><br>Introduction of Home Office Police Standards Unit<br><br>Home Office 'Forensic Integration Program' superseded by NPIA 'Forensics21' | Continued developments in legislation allow increasing scope of DNA use<br><br><br><br>Judicial critique of Low Copy Number DNA profiling and other aspects of forensic science work at Omagh<br><br>The UK Government lose in the case of 'S and Marper' | Major funding for DNA Expansion Programme<br><br>Development of competitive market in forensic science provision<br><br>Quinquennial review of FSS recommends 'privatisation'<br><br>Large-scale procurement of forensic services by the police become formalised and contractual<br><br>Police forces 'in-source' aspects of forensic services |

three sections of this Handbook. Instead we have drawn particular attention to those events and processes that have conditioned forensic science provision: the willingness of key actors and agencies to invest in its development, the organisational forms within which the science is put to use, and the changing levels of political, judicial and public confidence in its validity, reliability and proportional uses within the criminal justice system.

The current and emerging configurations of forensic science provision, their organisational structures and governance, the scope and use of services, the relationships between providers and users, are the consequence of multiple influences that vary from country to country. The extent to which these influences have individually or collectively shaped, supported or constrained the role and contribution of forensic science to criminal justice also varies considerably between countries. The very range, complexity and interrelatedness of factors belies any single or simple narrative account of the development of forensic science during this time. By taking this historical perspective we can reflect on the extent to which external and internal influences have acted individually or in concert in a developmental trajectory which has led to what we think of as the industrialisation of forensic science in England and Wales. By industrialisation we mean the large-scale provision of a standardised service or commodity in which the relationship between actors involved in its production is articulated in modern business or economic terms.

Some of these factors are simply the instantiation of wider social processes that affect a range of governmental and commercial endeavours (for example, the imperatives of new discourses and apparatuses of both national and international security following the attack on the World Trade Centre in 2001 and a series of other terrorist actions in Madrid, London and elsewhere since then); some are reflections of changing organisational imperatives within government in general or in policing in particular (for example, efforts to respond to growing levels of violent crimes involving the use of knives and guns); others are internal to the production and functioning of forensic science itself (for example concerns about the adequacy of the research base of some forensic science disciplines as well as the effects of the marketisation of forensic science in England and Wales).

The forensic science sector in England and Wales was, until the late 1970s, an essentially artisan enterprise. A number of factors constrained the perceived relevance of forensic science, especially the heterogeneity of disciplinary bases (and the esoteric nature of many of them), the low level of usage for largely corroborative purposes by police with limited understanding of the potential of such technologies, and the lack of professional infrastructure to secure practitioner authority. Early reviews in the latter part of the twentieth century (e.g. Ramsay 1987; Touche Ross 1987) were a consequence of a general political desire to increase the efficiency and effectiveness of public sector organisations as opposed to an effort to address the potential contributions of forensic science to criminal justice. Constantly rising demands from the police, and the inability of laboratories to control or influence this demand, featured highly in these reports, whereas the potential benefits of well-managed forensic science to the ends of criminal justice attracted less attention. At the same time, the disconnection of forensic science from the more general scientific world (which was by now seeking to standardise procedures and practices) was one source of significant variation among forensic science practitioners. Early quality assurance trials in forensic science identified extensive variation in the manner in which scientists carried out analyses, and interpretation was largely based on individual experience with very few databases of evidence and an absence of rigorous and reproducible processes. In this environment the individual scientist was sovereign: it was *their* case, *their* statement, *their* opinion.

A growing trend in the general scientific environment during the 1970s was the introduction of quality management systems, a process accelerated in forensic science following criticism resulting from a number of notorious miscarriages of justice, many of which were significant in the decision to establish the Royal Commission on Criminal Justice which reported in 1993. An attentiveness to issues of quality management resulted in a much more standardised approach to the examination and reporting of findings, a development which in part met the need to regain public and political confidence in forensic science. While there was some resistance to the introduction of standardised procedures, such procedures were soon embedded in core forensic disciplines. This development not only fundamentally changed the professional culture by naturally restricting the extent of individual action; it also altered the relationship between forensic scientists and the police and criminal justice actors by restricting the use of non-validated methodologies.

The introduction of transactional charging (payment by police organisations to laboratories for services provided) from 1991 onwards took place as the major provider of forensic science in England and Wales moved from being a public sector department to an independent agency. Charging was seen as a key mechanism to control demand on the part of the police and to compel the traditionally internally focused laboratories to respond to the needs of their 'customers'. The use of the term 'customer' was not initially widely accepted and still remains controversial in many countries outside the UK. There is little doubt that the introduction of transactional charging was effective in general terms. However, it also had specific drawbacks, for example an unhealthy focus on the price of products as opposed to their potential benefits, and an insidious erosion of trust between providers and users. One of the more marked dysfunctional outcomes was the fragmentation of cases by the police into packages of work that could be obtained from cheaper, often non- accredited and relatively inexperienced, providers.

These changes gradually altered the traditional structures, hierarchies and culture of the institutions (laboratories and police), creating new management structures, roles, vocabularies and relationships. Professional vocabulary was supplanted with management terminology, and customer service and marketing departments came into being, directors of laboratories (traditionally a scientific function) became heads of operations, examination requirements became 'products' selected by the customer from an approved list and influential SIOs sought financial discounts for their cases. These changes can be seen in the light of organisational models described by management writers such as Mintzberg.[1] In this case the Forensic Science Service moved from being an organisation whose operating core was 'professional' and sought standardisation of skills, to one whose operating core could be described as a 'technostructure' which sought standardisation and control of work processes.

A major change in the political environment took place in 1997 in the UK with the election of the Labour government. New Labour introduced extensive reforms in the public sector including a very strong focus on performance measurement. The same government also identified the potential of the embryonic national DNA database to provide a significant new resource for crime control. In addition to new legislation, significant funding for expansion of the DNA database was provided on the basis of business cases which linked the funding to performance outcomes. Use of this dedicated funding was not limited to DNA analysis but also provided human resources, equipment (computers, vehicles) and training. This 'DNA Expansion Programme' funding spawned a variety of new support roles: in the recovery of DNA (and later finger marks); in accounting for funds; and in the collation and distribution of DNA intelligence. The rapid expansion of DNA activities in turn widened the use of forensic science in the investigation of both volume and serious crime. More scene examiners resulted in more fingerprints, shoe marks and DNA being recovered and crimes being detected. Yet many of these business cases were speculative and superficial and there has never been any formal evaluation of the impact of the £300 million or so spent expanding the DNA database.

In 2003 an independent review of the FSS (Home Office 2003) recommended that they become a private commercial organisation. By this time there were already two other major forensic science providers in the private sector, Forensic Alliance and The Laboratory of the Government Chemist (LGC). LGC, previously a public sector organisation, became an independent agency which crept into the private sector, in forensic terms, almost unnoticed. In 2005, LGC acquired Forensic Alliance in the first real sign that the free market was at work.

In summary, the ultimate outcome of the complex web of factors included in Table 22.1, only a few of which have been discussed here, was that the main provision of forensic science in England and Wales shifted from being based in public sector organisations to private (or privatising) companies, over a period of 10–15 years. Although the general criteria which influenced this decision regarding the criminal justice system can be identified, including quality and reliability, service levels (in particular customer turnaround time requirements), value for money and increased innovation, no 'business case' with tangible outcomes was articulated. Therefore the value of such a transformation remains untested. However, at this stage, we can note at least one positive outcome from this process. The legacy of most public sector forensic science laboratories around the world is one of case backlogs and slow turnaround times, often counted in weeks or months. In England and Wales turnaround times can be counted in days (if not hours) and backlogs have been banished. If justice delayed is justice denied then this must be considered a sign of success (Fraser 2005). Privatisation remains a matter of debate and some controversy outside England and Wales although there are indications that at least one major continental European forensic science laboratory sees this as their future approach. Outside England and Wales, objections to privatisation are usually on the principled grounds that profiting commercially from participation in the criminal justice system is unethical. Yet many other participants in the criminal justice system are also commercial actors, and this fact alone does not invalidate their participation. The other major objection is that commercial motives will ultimately undermine and degrade standards. The obvious counter-example to this latter objection is the airline industry, which is extensively commercialised on a global scale and yet has maintained extremely high technical standards. Of course the role of regulation in maintaining standards in forensic science has to be recognised as a crucial one in this respect.

In summary, England and Wales has witnessed a combination of new technology, additional funding, growth in use, some sense of a positive contribution to crime detection, and a mixture of deliberate and fortuitous political imperatives. Together these have eventuated in commercial corporate industrial-scale forensic science provision. How these factors will continue to influence the course of forensic science in this jurisdiction is difficult to anticipate, as is the way in which they will interact with yet unknown scientific discoveries and technological innovations. What we can be surer about, however, is that the several long-standing concerns that currently trouble efforts to shape the way in which forensic science is produced and interacts with police investigatory practice will remain the subject of academic, policy, and practical interest for the foreseeable future. In the following paragraphs we describe these recurrent long-standing tribulations. We pay particular attention to their recent and current dimensions, and also consider their continuing significance for the near future of forensic investigations. We also believe these issues are relevant for developments beyond England and Wales.

## Recurrent tribulations

Forensic science is conducted, or at least the results of its application are necessarily applied and evaluated, within two of the most dramatic (and much dramatised) socially organised encounters in contemporary society: those between the police, victims and suspects in the course of criminal investigations; and those between accused persons and judicial actors in courtroom deliberations. For this reason, if for no other, we should not be surprised at the intensity of the recurrent tribulations to which forensic science is subject. The potential (and often actual) significance of its work is too great to expect anything else. These tribulations, and the anxieties that arise from them, will not vanish over time even if their detailed expression changes in intensity and focus. We can identify a number of them.

### *Producing forensic goods and services*

First, there are those concerning the modes of production and delivery of forensic science and technology commodities and services – especially new ones – to the criminal justice system in general and to police investigators in particular. We have already suggested that forensic science in England and Wales is an increasingly marketised activity in which earlier efforts to introduce quasi-market disciplines to control police demands on government forensic suppliers have been replaced by more direct market mechanisms. There has been a change in the position of the Forensic Science Service, and the number of other private forensic science companies has risen rapidly in the past few years. Product innovation is central to the success of all manufacturers and suppliers operating within market systems and producers of forensic technologies are not exempted from this requirement. Indeed the underlying drive for new knowledge in science and new technological applications of such knowledge to the criminal justice system means that entrepreneurial efforts to expand business dovetail nicely with regular demands by investigators for ingenious solutions to the many problems faced in the course of criminal investigations. Investigative and prosecutorial demands for material and intellectual technologies capable of resolving significant uncertainties are limitless, and any forensic science provider capable of meeting at least some of these demands will gain a significant edge over their competitors.

However, this emerging marketplace in England and Wales is populated not only by new commercial companies but by a range of other institutional actors who seek to influence its priorities and, indirectly, its working. Some of these actors are new, and the most significant of these is the Forensic Science Regulator, a 'public appointee whose function is to ensure that the provision of forensic science services across the criminal justice system is subject to an appropriate regime of scientific quality standards' (Home Office 2009a). The Forensic Science Regulator, supported by a budget of £1.3 million has already commissioned and published one review of a forensic science product (a review of 'Low Template DNA Analysis' by Caddy, Taylor and Linacre 2008), and has issued a draft of a Manual of Regulation (see Home Office 2009b), and a business plan which looks forward to 2011 (Home Office 2008). The Regulator aims to 'establish and monitor compliance with' quality standards applied to forensic service provision and to national forensic intelligence databases. In addition, this office has also been given significant responsibility for the provision of advice on forensic science to other key bodies and actors, including government ministers.

Assessing the current (and anticipating the future) significance of the office of the Forensic Science Regulator is made more difficult by the fact that this new role operates in a public policy space already crowded by a number of other actors with an established interest in the provision and use of forensic science. Many of these actors already participate in the formation and delivery of the Police Science and Technology Strategy which provides an overarching framework for shaping government investment and encouraging the development and deployment of forensic science (see Home Office 2004) and brings together a range of operational, academic and private-sector stakeholders (including ACPO, government departments, the research councils, professional associations and commercial companies). Recently these agencies have been joined by the National Policing Improvement Agency whose strategic document 'Forensics21' is driven by the ambition to 'deliver a police-led forensic service fit for the twenty-first century' (National Policing Improvement Agency 2008).

While all of these actors jostle for position in efforts to shape the form and implementation of forensic science innovation, they will continue collectively to face the problem that innovation in forensic science – just like innovation in other socio-scientific realms – is accomplished by a variety of means and by a variety of participants, many of which cannot be planned and many of whom cannot be managed. However, this domain presents particular problems that arise from the fact that forensic technologies are – by definition – subject to the constraints and requirements of the legal communities by which they are to be used, and whose interests they are to serve. The early trajectory of DNA profiling was disrupted by claims and counter-claims regarding utility and validity which remained largely unresolved until a subsequent technological change – from RFLPs to STRs – took place (see Lynch *et al.* 2008). Although the infrastructure for validation of new techniques within laboratories combined with current quality management systems is likely to prevent a recurrence of some of the issues that arose during this period, the absence of systematic criteria for legal admissibility allows new technology to creep into the criminal justice system in an *ad hoc* manner with the police acting as agents of 'technology-pull' and the courts as agents of restraint. In the absence of such criteria, which would necessarily weigh risk against benefits, these difficulties appear certain to be repeated with each fresh cycle of new technology and innovation.

A further matter that merits comment is that the regulatory system is confined to the quality of forensic science provision and has no remit in the economic regulation of forensic science. Nor apparently will it seek to set standards for the *use* of forensic science by the police. Both of these areas therefore represent uncontrolled risks. There are a number of practices which exist in other arenas such as the pharmaceutical industry which presage the likely hazards. We can expect commercial organisations to present information on new products and services in the form of marketing material, rather than against any set of objective criteria. There is no compulsion for them to do the latter. In seeking to recoup their investment, 'sunk cost' bias (consciously or unconsciously) is likely to result in the exaggeration of benefits, and minimisation of the negative aspects, of any product. Furthermore, as anyone who has recently purchased a mobile phone will know, companies frequently present their products in a manner which renders them incomparable with others (or too complex or too time-consuming to compare). This means that purchasing decisions may be made on readily accessible criteria such as price as value is simply too difficult to assess. Lessons from the pharmaceutical industry also show that customers who are not well informed about the technical nature of a product are easier to hoodwink than those who are. It is well known that in relation to pharmaceutical products, the general public are easier to fool than health professionals and since knowledge of forensic science in the police service in general is poor the risks are potentially high here. Besides education of police officers, the obvious solution to this problem is to have a standardised costing and benefits model (such as that used by the National Institute for Clinical Excellence to appraise medicines) in order to at least describe and cost, if not evaluate, new products and services.

In short, in our view, the ongoing maintenance of quality is not a simple issue of scientific standards of service provision but is intimately linked with broader aspects of the commercialisation and use of forensic science. The regulation of quality standards must be responsive to these issues as well as new developments in supply and use in order to maintain standards of forensic service and commodity provision fit for the criminal justice system.

### Forensic science teaching and research

The second set of recurrent troubles concerning forensic science in England and Wales (and elsewhere) swarms around criticism and questions about the current provision of education and training in forensic science, as well as the research base that underpins and informs the dissemination of this body of scientific and technical knowledge to students and practitioners. In the past decade or so the number of higher education institutions (HEIs) providing forensic science programmes in the UK has risen from a handful to many hundreds.[2] Strong criticism of the relevance, content and standards of these programmes has come from a range of sources including the House of Commons Science and Technology Committee's review of forensic science (House of Commons 2005). An unexpected and ironic consequence of this publication, which expressed the view (from the Forensic Science Service) that 'any forensic science qualification should be at Masters level', may have been further rapid expansion (from three in three institutions in 1993 to 109 in 24 institutions in 2007) of the number of programmes at Master's level (Nic Daéid 2007). Although the Forensic Science Society introduced an accreditation programme for forensic science programmes, the take-up of this has been poor.[3] The value of these programmes in educational terms both to the individuals who study them and the forensic science profession remains unclear and unevaluated.

Earlier in this chapter we have drawn attention to the new role of the Forensic Science Regulator in England and Wales, amongst whose responsibilities is the maintenance of 'scientific standards' in the provision of forensic science. However, it would not be possible or appropriate for the office of the Regulator itself to act as a peer reviewer in the way that journals or major grant-awarding bodies operate when they seek to evaluate the standard of scientific research proposals or publications. Insofar as the Regulator seeks the advice of appropriately qualified academics, then the office becomes dependent on prior decisions in the wider academic community about what and whose expert work is deserving of support or recognition. Whereas such reliance may be unproblematic in those academic disciplines that have dedicated research councils, relevant research excellence framework panels and well-established university departments, forensic science, at least in England and Wales, does not have the advantage of such stable institutional embeddedness. Despite the growth of postgraduate university courses in forensic science described above, there are no dedicated PhD programmes in this domain, and university-based research activity remains limited compared to other science enterprises.

A cursory survey of recent forensic science research outputs by UK institutions (Fraser 2008) indicates that virtually no institution could claim to be 'research intensive' in this domain. In the light of this, the teaching provided by them cannot be 'research led'. If we also accept that forensic science practice largely remains dissociated from the general scientific world, with a limited evidence base and underdeveloped tradition of research and publishing, this raises another critical question: what is the source and validity of knowledge on which these institutions base their pedagogy? If the knowledge does not arise from research and the quality of knowledge that arises from practice is of untested validity, then such programmes may be doing no more than recycling conventional forensic science wisdom. The global explosion in the number of academic institutions offering teaching in forensic science has done little to improve this situation. Whilst there has been recent recognition of these uncomfortable facts by the European Network of Forensic Science Institutes and by the US National Academies of Science, the same is not true of the UK at present. It is difficult to know what pressures may occasion a realisation of current failings and the establishment of a strategy for their repair. However, the shortcomings are comparatively straightforward to identify. They include the following:

- Funding – very few research councils in the UK will fund forensic science research and there are limited other sources of funds.

- Complexity – by definition forensic science is an interdisciplinary enterprise therefore relevant research which takes this into account is likely to involve complex collaborations that cross traditional research council remits.

- Sensitivity – there are issues of confidentiality and sensitivity which require the development of close collaboration and trust between stakeholders and which may have direct implications for the criminal justice process.

- Imbalance – historically, most forensic research has been focused on technical or scientific issues which improve analytical standards or sensitivity. The relevance, value or potential benefits of such research for the investigation and prosecution of crime is much less often studied.

Accordingly we can safely assert that systematic knowledge and understanding of how forensic science is *actually* deployed (as opposed to the many espoused and anecdotal accounts) in the investigation of crime and the preparation and presentation of courtroom evidence, remains fundamentally lacking.

The commercialisation of forensic science in England and Wales raises particular issues about research and related matters. The forensic science industry is expected to exploit commercially any new products or services; this is how markets work. Publication of new research is generally regarded as information that can be used objectively to evaluate techniques and methodologies and therefore exerts a powerful influence on potential users. Again, with reference to the pharmaceutical industry, it is possible to see some of the undesired effects of marketised behaviour on research activity. For example, publication bias,[4] in which information is selectively published or published in multiple journals, may give the impression that work is of more significance than it truly is. This and other similar practices currently are outside the recurrent remit of the Forensic Science Rregulator but can impinge on quality standards in an indirect manner. A mechanism for managing this and other risks described above would be to compel forensic science providers to make publicly available all research (the broad aims and methodologies, if not the full details) in which they are engaged. Failure to publish outcomes would be a good indication of failure of research aims and therefore limitations in value to potential users. Better still would be a forensic science equivalent to the Medical Research Council Clinical Trials Unit which could encourage and support high-quality research with the aim of maintaining and improving standards and contributing to criminal justice.

### Securing standards in the application of forensic science

A third area of anxiety for policymakers and users of contemporary forensic science concerns the existence of varying standards of practice applied in different jurisdictions and in different substantive areas of forensic science. This issue has been highlighted as an unintended consequence of the successful development of DNA profiling which since the discovery and implementation of PCR has followed a model trajectory for the delivery of new science: research, laboratory testing and validation, field testing and peer-reviewed publication of each of these stages. The challenges to DNA as a tool for the investigation of crime which took place in the 'DNA wars' were seen as a normal and valuable aspect of its testing, integration and acceptance by the wider scientific community and criminal justice system. The development of DNA contrasts markedly with the introduction and use of many (if not most) other forensic techniques, some of which have not been tested, let alone peer reviewed in any systematic manner.

Such an artisan approach to many areas of forensic science has already been described above as a historical aspect of the development of forensic science in England and Wales, yet it remains significant. Many practitioners continue to use techniques based on historic preferences and which lack an evidence base consistent with currently preferred scientific methodologies. The most conspicuous instance of this is the case of fingerprint examination. From its earliest days (around the turn of the nineteenth century) up to the 1980s (with the introduction of the first AFIS systems) fingerprint examination has largely remained (procedurally, legally and conceptually) unchanged. Even with the advances provided by computerisation, the development of fingerprints as an investigative tool was restricted to geographically local provision until the very end of the twentieth century: the implementation of a national fingerprint database in the UK *followed* the implementation of the DNA database. At least one of the reasons for this slow pace of change is the conservatism of fingerprint practitioners visible in their professional resistance to many of the advances made elsewhere in forensic science. The provision of fingerprint examination is considered a 'strategic asset' by the police service but it is still unclear how this contradictory position can persist without undermining benefits to the investigation of crime. It may well be that the historical difference between standards applied to fingerprint examination and those applied elsewhere to laboratory-based disciplines will continue to be eroded as forensic science providers are increasingly involved in aspects of fingerprint examination and are likely to be increasingly innovative in technological and service delivery terms. If private providers are capable of providing a reliable fingerprint service more quickly and cheaply than do current police organisations, it is possible that they will play a larger part in the provision of this kind of forensic science service in the future, and that different scientific standards will accompany this change.

In addition to the detailed standards that apply to particular technologies and practices within forensic science, there remains an issue that troubles all of them: that of how any and all such evidence types are to be evaluated. There are three important aspects to this: feasibility (whether probabilistic methodologies can be developed for evidence types which traditionally use categoric methods); validity (whether categorical judgements are justifiable for any evidence type); and necessity (whether there is a compelling need always to use probabilistic methodologies when they do become available).

The debate here divides into two camps: one which has recourse to the reason and logic of science; the other which relies on the kind of pragmatic common sense valued by the law. The debate is further confused by the entrenched positions occupied by some groups of practitioners. Whilst we cannot predict the future we think it increasingly obvious that many areas that traditionally use categoric evaluation will soon be amenable to probabilistic modelling and decision making. Current research in relation to fingerprints is well advanced and, in our view, in the long run is likely to prevail. However, even if the issue of feasibility is resolved, those of validity and necessity remain.

The prospects for resolving these issues in turn depend on the success or failure of three current schools of thought: universalism, tradionalism and pragmatism. Universalists take the view that all evidence should be evaluated by probabilistic means and that this is the only rational way to approach the issue. They are perhaps best exemplified by the group which originated in the Forensic Science Service and developed the Case Assessment and Interpretation (CAI) approach and which included Evett, Jackson, Jones, Cook and a number of others. Traditionalists consider categoric evaluation valid, are resistant to probabilistic approaches and typically uninformed about the methodologies which may be used for probabilistic evaluation. Most fingerprint experts and many marks examiners fall into this category although there is variation from country to country. Pragmatists take the view that few professions can claim to have universal standards and that there is such inherent variation in criminal justice systems that although probabilistic evaluation is desirable, it is not necessary in every case given the differing epistemic systems of science and law.

Standardisation is not exclusively an issue for forensic practitioners as it has been demonstrated that police practices can have a positive or negative influence on how forensic evidence is used. It remains the case that with rare exceptions (Senior Investigating Officers and Senior Crime Scene Investigators) the level of knowledge of the police is a significant constraining factor on the contribution forensic science makes to criminal justice. This must be seen as part of a broader context of policing which is based largely on a combination of historical practices, common sense and political imperatives, and rarely on evidence-based practice.

### Researching the investigative uses of forensic science

The final group of tribulations relates to the quantity and quality of research evidence concerning the effective uses of forensic science in the course of criminal investigations. A number of evaluative studies of the effectiveness of recent administrative and technical innovations in forensic science support have been carried out in the past 10 years, and it may safely be assumed that such studies will continue to be carried out by individual forces, by academic researchers and other stakeholders. However, much of the recent work has focused attention on the collection and analysis of a restricted range of contact trace material regularly recovered at crime scenes. The studies have also shared an underlying commitment to the development of improved measures of performance outputs and outcomes as part of their attempt to construct a model of the contribution of more varied forensic information to the detection, prosecution and reduction of volume crime. This 'attrition model'[5] of the forensic process encourages the collection and analysis of data showing the proportion of recorded crime scenes attended, the proportion of scenes attended from which forensic artefacts are recovered, the proportion of these artefacts that facilitated the identification of suspects or linked scenes, and the proportion of such identifications that led to detections. Especially detailed results of its application in the collection and analysis of DNA evidence are available in Burrows *et al.* (2005).[6] Barrow (2005) and Green (2007) also provide attrition data relating to DNA profiles, finger mark and footwear mark collection, comparison and use, and Rix (2004) has focused particularly on the latter technology. Finally, a systematic effort to apply the model to the whole forensic process has informed work undertaken for the Home Office by a private company – Lanner Group Ltd. The work has eventuated in the introduction of management software (Scientific Work Improvement Package) available to all forces in England and Wales, but at the time of writing, the Home Office report which evaluated this resource remains restricted in its circulation.

The previous interest taken by HMIC and other Home Office actors in the use of this approach to researching forensic science has been strongly influenced by developments in the public services in general in which increasingly rigorous (and imaginative) efforts have been made to develop indicators of the efficiency and effectiveness (including cost-effectiveness) of a variety of forms of service provision. At the beginning of this century, the government's crime reduction strategy (Home Office 2000) explicitly commended the beneficial results of the introduction of performance league tables and regular monitoring of performance in the health service and in education and looks forward to the results expected to derive from the enhanced application of such approaches in the field of policing. The later introduction of 'Best Value' into policing provided a powerful statutory framework for consideration of target setting within police authorities, and scientific support staff are subject to this overall framework. The orientation of senior management to such a framework in turn ensures that measures of labour effort and labour output of scientific support staff are considered alongside the effort and output of other staff groups in contemporary discussions of police performance and its overall outcome.

Attention to these issues is unquestionably legitimate, and where properly understood and managed, will be positive both for the attainment of overall organisational aims and for the everyday work of employees. However, enthusiasm for the constant monitoring of individual staff performance by reference to currently available performance indicators needs to be tempered by the acknowledgement of a number of shortcomings in the current repertoire of indicators and of the unintended consequences that can arise when individual staff members treat such performance criteria as a guide to their actions. These include: the diminution of professional autonomy in task performance; a neglect of the contribution to individual performance made by differing forms of collective effort; the resource dependency of individual levels of measured performance. A stronger research base, less influenced by the methodologies embedded in the attrition approach and the performance data that these methodologies require, is an essential element for the informed future of forensic investigations. There are some fugitive signs that some key police bodies (e.g. NPIA) recognise this requirement but it is too early to say how productive will be their influence on research policy in this domain. The other bodies that can be expected to encourage and shape research policy in this aspect of policing are two recently formed academic bodies – the Scottish Institute for Policing Research and the Universities' Police Science Institute – both of which have strong interests in the police uses of forensic science and who are developing research agendas in this domain.

## Conclusion

Central to the form and expression of all of the tribulations described above is a recurrent tension between the forensic science 'imaginary' (a range of representations of the potential of forensic science to deliver truth to justice through the rigorous application of increasingly accurate and reliable technical resources) and the actuality of forensic science provision and its uses by police actors in concrete circumstances of use. The social and policy significance of imaginaries, along with similar notions of 'expectations', 'anticipations' etc., has been discussed elsewhere, and in one case, with specific reference to individual forensic domains (e.g. Borup et al. 2006; Castoriadis 1998; Gerlach 2004; Taylor 2004). There are many policy actors with strong aspirations to contribute to security, safety, crime control and the management of 'risky' individuals by the demonstrably effective use of current and emerging technologies able to capture and interrogate a range of material and informational attributes of individuals and their actions.

Such a forensic imaginary, carried in 'images, stories and legends' (Taylor 2004: 23), fuelled as it is by hopes, worries, desires and a range of other emotional energies, contributes hugely to the willingness of governments to resource forensic science developments and ambitions. But at the same time, the inevitable failure to deliver the full range of expected benefits can make for difficulty in retaining confidence in the capacity of forensic science institutions to contribute to criminal justice in the way previously imagined. Accordingly, the current and future shapes of forensic science and the investigations that rely on it are heavily determined by attentiveness of key actors to promises and hopes as well as to the demands of the realities to which such expectations can be compared.

A seemingly ineradicable feature of this forensic imaginary – despite previous and anticipated failures – is the continued promise of new solutions to old problems, and of the extension of scientific knowledge into areas previously considered to present intractable resistance. We can safely assert that the essential restlessness of scientific work along with diverse efforts to apply it to aspects of criminal justice will continue apace. In this sense it seems likely that the next years will witness an increase in the range (and perhaps the significance) of forensic science knowledge. Waiting in the wings to join the forensic canon are numerous technologies which, according to their developers and advocates, have the potential to provide dramatic solutions to many current policing problems. The most visible of these are: microfluidics[7] (so called 'lab on a chip') and isotope ratio mass spectrometry (IRMS).[8] The first of these developments promises, above all else, major increases in the speed at which samples can be analysed and interrogated, thus responding to common investigative demands for the fast processing and delivery of forensic provision in this domain. The potential claimed for the latter technology – IRMS – is much more dramatic insofar as it promises to offer reliable and definitive accounts of the commonality or difference of sources or origins, as in the case of materials like drugs, plastics, fibres, paint, glass, explosives, etc. The successful development and application of IRMS technology would certainly – in principle – resolve many shortcomings in the currently available technologies for determining and visualising these relational properties.

But we have already emphasised the fact that the landscape covered by this Handbook is both complex and subject to constant change. These factors contribute to the uncertainty of the futures of forensic science and the uses of its associated technologies by criminal justice actors. Despite the attention we have given in this chapter to the recurrent tribulations of forensic science, we remain confident that there will continue to be an expansion of forensic science knowledge, and that its uses will grow in the foreseeable future. Forensic science – in its different forms and with varying degrees of reliability – will play an increasingly valuable role in resolving the inherent problems and complexities that affect criminal investigations and prosecutions. There is widespread expert and lay confidence in its general potential, despite doubts about the epistemic claims of particular sub-disciplines or local problems in the application of particular forensic techniques to individual cases. Even the recent and heavily critical scientific evaluation of the current condition of forensic science in the United States (National Research Council 2009) asserts what they regard as the scientific and technological weaknesses of some (but not all) areas to be repairable. While their preferred solution is the establishment of a national scientific body able to evaluate the claims and credentials of the heterogeneous forms of knowledge and practice that constitute contemporary forensic science, the emerging regulatory regime in England and Wales seeks to deal with these issues rather differently. A less central place is given to the notion of expert self-governance on which the US proposal rests, and more attention is given to the expectations of police and judicial users. Nevertheless, the regime in England and Wales co-opts relevant scientific experts to provide advice and guidance on matters within their areas of competence.

Alongside our own and others' optimism about the potential for forensic science to secure further gains on behalf of the criminal justice system, there remain a number of significant local challenges to its effective provision in England and Wales. Most of these arise from the four tribulations that we have described above, but some also derive from the recent social and ethical interrogations of forensic science that began with the establishment and expansion of the NDNAD, were subsequently extended to consider the collection, storage and use of other forms of bioinformation for criminal justice purposes, and are also being influenced by other global developments. The most important of the local challenges are listed below.

- The current disconnection between the research base of forensic science alongside increasing expectations of the contribution of practitioners risks a loss of confidence in the application of particular technologies by investigators and/or the courts.

- The desire to accredit institutions and individuals may be undermined by the courts due to their reluctance to accept restrictions on the potential types of evidence or witnesses they may hear.

- The urgent demand by policymakers for 'better' data on police uses of forensic science may be frustrated by a lack of funding for relevant independent studies as well as changes in policing priorities.

- In the absence of systematic sources of knowledge and data, evidence-based practice could remain fugitive, especially if controlled by commercial suppliers who seek to differentiate rather than standardise forensic services and commodities.

- The 'immaturity' of the emerging forensic marketplace and the scientific and commercial inexperience of police 'customers' might lead to uncertainty, market fragmentation and unacceptable levels of quality variation which cannot be ameliorated by maintenance of scientific standards alone and may require some form of economic regulatory activity.

- Operational police users of forensic science may be insufficiently well supported in the decisions to deploy particular technologies by independent evaluations of the potentials and risks of new forensic commodities and services.

- Instabilities in the institutional framework for the accreditation of forensic expertise could compromise necessary efforts to evaluate the expertise of individual practitioners.[9]

• The validity and relevance of forensic science degree programmes to the development of forensic knowledge and practice and their educational value to individual students may remain unclear and unevaluated.

Responses to these challenges will provide the structure for the immediate future of the production and application of forensic science in this jurisdiction. Most can be met by the actions of key stakeholders within the criminal justice arena; others require partnerships with agencies outside of this domain. Stronger connections between police users, forensic providers, policymakers and academic researchers would increase the robustness of these responses, but developing existing connections and establishing new ones requires effort and resources to be provided by all relevant parties.

Yet, however much work is done to secure the validity of the science, the reliability of the technology and the competence of forensic science practitioners, the actual contribution of forensic science to criminal investigations remains dependent on the attitudes and attributes of non-scientific users – the police and the courts. Because of this it is likely that its uses will remain persistently suboptimal, attenuated as they are by the fragmented subroutines of dissonant cultural and professional norms and the chronic lack of congruence between the methodologies of science and law for the determination of truth and justice. The primary limiting factor at work here remains the underdevelopment of those kinds of reciprocal knowledge and understanding that would enable interdependent and coordinated action on the part of the major actors – laboratory scientists, the police, prosecuting authorities, advocates and judges – involved in the application of forensic science in the criminal justice system. It is difficult to see how this underdevelopment can be addressed by any realistic or economically feasible mechanism at present; in its absence, policymakers and practitioners may continue, unencumbered by knowledge, to support and apply practices based on tenacious orthodoxies rather than on well-founded theoretical understanding and empirical evidence.

For this reason, if for no other, it is vital that both experts and laypeople have the best possible grasp of exactly what the practitioners of forensic science can (and cannot) achieve in each instance of their application. In addition it is important that we understand the sources and implications of whatever legitimate authority may be granted to such experts and the kind of tribulations faced by those who seek to produce and use forensic science. We hope that this Handbook contributes to informed debate about all these matters.

## Notes

1 For a review of his and other related concepts, see Pugh and Hickson (1996).
2 Undergraduate courses rose from three at three institutions in 1993 to 474 at 71 institutions in 2007. Almost 90 per cent of post-1992 universities teach forensic science compared to 30 per cent of the older universities. The names of some of these programmes have gained folklore status including 'Dance and Movement Studies with Forensic Studies' and 'Forensic Studies with healing Arts'.

3 Currently accredited are 14 institutions that provide 38 courses (around 20 per cent of providing institutions and 8 per cent of all programs). Most of the accredited institutions are post 1992 universities. (See http://www.forensic-science-society.org.uk/Resources/Forensic%20Science/Accredited%20Courses%20161108.pdf – accessed 7 March 2009.)

4 For a brief introduction to this issue see Goldacre (2008).

5 See Burrows, Hopkins, Hubbard, Robinson, Speed and Tilley (2005).

6 Despite this work, there has yet to be a systematic assessment of the contribution of DNA in general, and of the DNA Expansion Programme in particular, to the criminal justice system of England and Wales. Several studies provide statistics which give strong indications of the usefulness of DNA in criminal investigations, and there are many individual cases in which DNA profiling has played a crucial part. However, it is noticeable that the European Court of Human Rights Judgement in the case of 'S' and Marper reiterated the view of the Nuffield Council on Bioethics Report on the Use of Forensic Bioinformation that the quality of currently available data on this question was disappointing, and that there were many problems surrounding its interpretation.

7 For a review of this topic in relation to DNA analysis see Horsman, K.M. et al. (2007).

8 See Benson, S. et al. (2005).

9 The rise and demise of the Council for Registration of Forensic Practitioners is an indication of the potent influence of government (and other stakeholders) and the lack of influence of professionals in this domain. Such a registration body was first recommended by the 1993 Royal Commission and was implemented some five or so years later. There was early resistance from the police service (largely on financial grounds) and from staff associations regarding matters of discipline etc. Support by professionals was initially ambivalent although it was later embraced by all key institutions. By 2008 its future was already in doubt following rumours of financial difficulties and resignations of senior posts. Soon afterwards the Home Office, NPIA and ACPO effectively withdrew their support and CRFP announced formal closure of the register in March 2009. What was lauded as a distinctive solution to setting standards in a complex area lasted less than a decade. It is currently proposed that individual registration will be incorporated into organisational governance structures under UKAS accreditation.

## References

Barrow, K. (2005) *Study into Intelligence Packages*. London: Home Office.

Benson, S. et al. (2005) 'Forensic applications of isotope ratio mass spectrometry – a review', *Forensic Science International*, 157(1): 1–22.

Borup, M., Brown, N., Konrad, K. and Van Lente, H. (2006) 'The sociology of expectations in science and technology', *Technology Analysis and Strategic Management*, 18: 285–298.

Burrows, J., Hopkins, M., Hubbard, R., Robinson, A., Speed, M. and Tilley, N. (2005) *Understanding the attrition process in volume crime investigations*. London: Home Office.

Caddy, B., Taylor, G.R. and Linacre, A.M.T. (2008) *A Review of the Science of Low Template DNA Analysis*. London: Home Office.

Castoriadis, C. (1998) *The Imaginary Institution of Society*. Cambridge: Cambridge University Press

Fraser, J. (2005) 'Who guards the guards?', *Science and Justice*, 45(3): 119.

Fraser, J (2008) Why we need more research. Forensic Science Society AGM, Wyboston.

Gerlach, N. (2004) *The Genetic Imaginary: DNA in the Canadian Criminal Justice System.* Toronto: University of Toronto Press.

Goldacre, B. (2008) *Bad Science.* London: Fourth Estate.

Green, R. (2007) 'Forensic Investigation in the UK', pp. 338–356, in T. Newburn, T. Williamson and A. Wright (eds), *Handbook of Criminal Investigation.* Cullompton: Willan.

Home Office (2000) *The Government's Crime Reduction Strategy.* http://www.homeoffice.gov.uk/crimprev Last consulted 6 January 2006.

Home Office (2003) Review of the Forensic Science Service Executive Summary. http://police.homeoffice.gov.uk/publications/operational-policing/reviewfssjuly2003.pdf Last consulted 7 March 2009.

Home Office (2004) Police Science and Technology Strategy 2004–2009. http://www.homeoffice.gov.uk/documents/PoliceST_S2_part11.pdf?view=Binary Last consulted 4 March 2009.

Home Office (2008) Forensic Science Regulator's Business Plan 2008/9 to 2010/2011. http://police.homeoffice.gov.uk/publications/operational-policing/Forensic_Science_Regulator_3.pdf?view=Binary Last consulted 4 March 2009.

Home Office (2009a) http://police.homeoffice.gov.uk/operational-policing/forensic-science-regulator/ Last consulted 4 March 2009.

Home Office (2009b) The Forensic Science Regulator's Draft Manual of Regulation. http://police.homeoffice.gov.uk/publications/operational-policing/Manual_of_Regulation_22.9.08.pdf?view=Binary Last consulted 4 March 2009.

Horsman, K.M. *et al.* (2007) 'Forensic DNA analysis on microfluidic devices: a review', *J Forensic Sci*, 52: 784–789.

House of Commons (2005) *Forensic Science on Trial*, p. 46. London: The Stationery Office.

Lynch, M., Cole, S., McNally, R. and Jordan, K. (2008) *Truth Machine: The Contentious History of DNA Fingerprinting.* Chicago: Chicago University Press.

National Policing Improvement Agency (2008) http://www.npia.police.uk/en/10432.htm Last consulted 4 March 2009.

National Research Council (2009) *Strengthening Forensic Science in the United States: A Path Forward.* Washington: The National Academies Press.

Nic Daéid, N. (2007) Higher Education and Forensic Science – the UK Experience, Joint conference of the Forensic Science Society and the Ministry of the Interior, Kingdom of Bahrain: 'Forensic Science Against Crime'. Bahrain, March 2007.

Pugh, D.S. and Hickson, D.J. (1996) *Writers on Organisations.* London: Penguin Books.

Ramsay, M. (1987) The Effectiveness of the Forensic Science Service, Home Office Research Study No. 92. London: HMSO.

Rix, B. (2004) *The Contribution of Shoemark Data to Police Intelligence, Crime Detection and Prosecution.* London: Home Office.

Touche Ross (1987) Review of Scientific Support for the Police. London: Home Office.

Taylor, C. 2004. *Modern Social Imaginaries.* Durham, NC: Duke University Press.

# Glossary

**Abduction (or abductive inference)**  A term associated with the philosopher Charles Sanders Peirce to describe a type of logic associated with inference. Most frequently explained as 'inference to best explanation'.

**Acid phosphatase (AP)**  An enzyme which removes phosphate groups from molecules that forms the basis of a presumptive test for **semen**.

**Association of Chief Police Officers (ACPO)**  The body representing senior officers of assistant chief constable rank and above in England and Wales. ACPO works on behalf of the police service as a whole, and is funded by a combination of a Home Office grant, contributions from all of the 44 police authorities, membership subscriptions and the proceeds of its annual exhibition. The equivalent organisation in Scotland is ACPOS.

**Acrosome**  A cap-like structure which covers the head of the spermatocyte (sperm), and contains digestive enzymes which enable sperm cells to penetrate the outer wall of the ovum and transfer nuclear material for fertilisation.

**Activity level**  A term used in the **Case Assessment and Interpretation (CAI)** model. In this context the activity level constitutes the second tier of the **hierarchy of propositions**. This level concerns the formulation of propositions that attempt to account for an activity allegedly performed in an incident under investigation, and will be informed by **likelihood ratio** estimates obtained at **source**, and possibly **sub-source levels.**

**Adventitious match**  The occurrence of a random coincidental DNA profile match.

**Aerosolisation**  The process by which a liquid (such as blood) is formed into an aerosol.

**Alcohol back calculation**  A calculation of the concentration of alcohol in the bloodstream at the time a particular incident occurred.

**Allele**  One member of a pair of genes that occupies the same relative position on homologous chromosomes and is responsible for alternative genetic characteristics.

**Amelogenin**  A protein found in tooth enamel. The gene for amelogenin, present on the x and y chromosomes, can be used to determine the sex of the donor of a DNA profile.

**Amplicon**  DNA formed during the process of amplification of genetic material, either naturally or via synthetic means, such as the **Polymerase Chain Reaction** (PCR).

**Amylase**  An enzyme which breaks down starch into sugars, and which is present in saliva. Detection of amylase forms the basis of **presumptive tests** for the identification of saliva.

**Anagen**  The initial active phase of hair growth, in which the **follicle** produces new cells and pushes them up the hair shaft to become incorporated into the hair.

**Ante-mortem trauma**  Pertaining to injuries or insults to the body in the period prior to death.

**Anthropometric system**  An identification system developed by Alphonse Bertillon in the nineteenth century based on measurement of a number of different parts of the body.

**Antigen**  A molecule which stimulates an immune response.

**Arc**  A term used to describe the arrows in Bayesian networks which show the relationship of conditionality, or dependency, between **nodes** indicating to probabilistic measures of evidence.

**Arrest**  An action of the police, or person acting under the law, to take a person into custody, usually for the purpose of further inquiries. In the United Kingdom a person must be 'cautioned' when being arrested unless impractical to do so, e.g. due to violence or drunkenness.

**Artefact**  A structure or feature, visible only as a result of external action or experimental error. Alternatively, a man-made item.

**Arterial staining**  Bloodstain patterns of characteristic appearance that are the result of traumatic damage to arteries.

**Aspermia**  A rare medical condition resulting in inability to produce semen. **Azoospermia**, the absence of sperm in semen, is more commonly encountered in forensic examinations.

**Associative evidence**  Evidence which links objects or individuals.

**Audit Commission**  A non-departmental public body established in the 1980s to promote economy and efficiency in the public services. Its 1993 paper *Helping with Enquiries: Tackling Crime Effectively* was influential particularly in relation to the investigation of high-volume crime.

**Base pair**  A pair of the complementary bases (A,T or G,C) in DNA. A unit by which the length of a **DNA** double helix can be measured.

**Bayes' Theorem**  A probabilistic theorem used to assess subjective beliefs as measures of probability. (See **Bayesian**).

**Bayesian networks**  A method involving Directed Acyclic Graphs which uses a Bayesian system to calculate conditional probability estimates relating to a specific incident.

**Becke line**  With regard to refractive index measurement of glass, a line visible under the microscope which can be used to determine the edge of the fragment.

**Behavioural Investigative Adviser (BIA)**  A practitioner who specialises in offender profiling. BIAs may use psychological methods as well as advising investigative teams on interview tactics, DNA intelligence led screening, media strategy, risk assessments, geographical analysis and the veracity of victim statements.

**Beta distribution**  A type of continuous **probability distribution** parametrised by two non-negative shape parameters, typically designated $\alpha$ and $\beta$.

**Bifurcate**  The splitting of a fingerprint ridge into two separate ridges. Used as one of the comparison characteristics or **minutiae**.

**Binder**  A substance used in paints to facilitate even distribution of pigment across a surface.

**Bioinformation**  Information about an individual which may be derived from biological samples (see **biometrics**).

**Biometrics**  The application of technology which uses numerical measurement to identify individuals, e.g. fingerprints, iris scans (see anthropometric system).

**Binomial distribution**  The discrete probability distribution of the number of particular outcomes in a sequence of $N$ independent experiments in which there may be only two outcomes. For example the tossing of a coin multiple times to establish how often it lands on 'heads' displays a binomial distribution.

**Bloodstain pattern analysis (BPA)**  The examination and interpretation of bloodstains with the aim of establishing the potential mechanisms that caused the staining.

**Brachial artery**  The artery found in the inner aspects of each arm.

**Brentamine Test (AP test)**  A chemical test used to detect **acid phosphatase** in seminal fluid.

**Carotid artery**  The major artery found in the neck which supplies blood to the head.

**Case Assessment and Interpretation (CAI) model**  An approach to forensic science decision-making developed by Forensic Science Service scientists and based on the use of Bayesian principles. (see **Heirachy of propositions**).

**Cast-off staining** (Also referred to as 'in-line staining'). A pattern of bloodstaining caused by wet blood being thrown from an object, typically a weapon when it is swung.

**Catagen** The second phase of hair growth. During the catagen phase, the follicle shuts down production of cells and the root condenses into a bulb-shaped structure.

**Cementum** The calcified substance covering the root of the tooth.

**Charge** A formal accusation preceding a criminal prosecution.

**Chemiluminescence** The emission of light resulting from a chemical reaction.

**Chemometrics** The application of mathematical or statistical methods to chemical data.

**Child node** The term used to describe a node of a **Bayesian network** that depicts a probabilistic event conditioned by an antecedent event, itself represented as a **parent node**.

**Chromatography** The generic name given to a group of techniques used to separate mixtures of chemicals such as drugs or flammable liquids.

**Chromosome** The structure in which the **DNA** and **genes** of a cell are packaged.

**Criminal Investigation Department (CID)** The branch in UK police forces responsible for the investigation of crime.

**Clearcoat** Unpigmented coatings used to improve the gloss and durability of a vehicle's coating.

**'Cold case'** A criminal case which has been unsolved for a significant period of time.

**Comitology** The process by which the European Commission, the executive arm of the European Union (EU), is advised on legislative development and implementation by a series of committees.

**Complement** The term used in probability theory to describe the mutually exclusive opposing proposition for a probabilistic event.

**Conditional probability** The probability of one event, given the occurrence of another event.

**Converging connections** A type of relationship found in **Bayesian Networks**, where two **parent nodes** demonstrate **conditional dependence** on a **child node.**

**Core(s)** The morphological feature which constitutes the centre of a loop fingerprint pattern.

**Cortex** Spindle-shaped cells which make up the bulk of human hair.

**Costochondral junction** The junction between the anterior end of the rib and the cartilage connecting it to the sternum.

**Council for the Registration of Forensic Practitioners (CRFP)** A UK body set up in response to the 1993 Royal Commission for the regulation of forensic practitioners and closed in 2009.

**Crime analysis** The systematic analysis of police information and other data to identify crime patterns and trends to support enforcement and investigative activities.

**Crime management** The notion that investigations can be managed proactively, with resource deployment according to an agreed set of priorities.

**Crime mapping** The technologies and practices employed to gain understanding of the geographical and temporal distribution of crime, in order to aid the targeting, deployment and allocation of law enforcement resources.

**Crime (scene) sample** Sample obtained from examination of a crime scene usually collected by a **Scenes of Crime Officer**. Also refers to samples retrieved by medical examination of an individual which do not originate from that individual, and from scientific examination of items such as clothing or weapons. A crime sample would normally be compared or examined in conjunction with a control or reference, or subject sample.

**Crime Scene Investigator/Examiner** (see **Scenes of Crime Officer**).

**Crime Scene Manager** The individual responsible for controlling the scene of an incident, coordinating forensic investigative activities and subsequent submission of items for examination to a forensic science laboratory. In the UK this role is typically delegated by the investigating police officer to a specially trained civilian (i.e. non-sworn) officer.

**Criminalistics** An American term often used as a synonym for forensic science, but which more specifically refers to scientific investigations relating to trace evidence.

**Cuticle** The series of overlapping scales that form a protective covering of a hair.

**Decision theory** The application of statistical and mathematical models to decision-making, particularly in conditions of uncertainty.

**Deductive inference** The process of reasoning from premises which, if true, entail that the conclusion must be true.

**Defence fallacy** An informal fallacy. The erroneous assertion of a probability of innocence, by failing to account for all the evidence relevant to a criminal case (see **Prosecutor's fallacy**).

**Delta(s)** Part of a fingerprint where **friction ridges** diverge.

**Dentine**   The layer of the tooth located underneath the surface enamel.

**Deoxyribonucleic acid (DNA)**   The substance that carries an individual's genetic information. Most cells of the body contain a complete copy of that information (the genome). A DNA molecule consists of a long chain of units called nucleotides or bases (chemically a base is part of a nucleotide, but for purposes of characterising a piece of DNA, the terms are often used interchangeably). There are four sorts of units, usually designated A, T, G and C (see **base pair**).

**Dermatoglyphics**   The study or practice of fingerprint examination.

**Diaphyseal**   Pertaining to the shaft of a long bone.

**Diode array detector (DAD)**   A device that may be incorporated into a chromatographic instrument to measure electromagnetic radiation which has passed through the sample and to generate spectral data across a range of wavelengths in order to identify compounds.

**Discriminating power**   A measure of the ability of an evidential type to discriminate between items of that type that come from different sources. Its value may be assessed empirically through a series of pairwise comparisons of items whose source is known.

**Distal phalanges**   Bones found in most vertebrate animals. In humans, these are located furthest from the shoulder joint and comprise the fingertip.

**Diverging connections**   Used in discussions of **Bayesian networks** to describe the way in which two **child nodes** that describe two unrelated events, exhibit **conditional dependence** on a common **parent node**.

**DNA profile**   The result of a series of individual analyses of genetic loci usually carried out simultaneously (by multiplex). This can be used to identify individuals, carry out kinship analyses (paternity, maternity etc.) and associate or eliminate individuals with sources of biological material e.g. blood or semen. A full (**SGMplus®**) profile from an individual stored on the **National DNA Database (NDNAD)** consists of a series of 20 numbers, recording the size of particular marker sections of **DNA**, plus a sex indicator.

**Drip pattern**   A bloodstain pattern caused by blood falling from an object under the influence of gravity.

**Eccrine glands**   Glands in the skin involved in temperature regulation. In humans, eccrine glands are abundant on the palms of the hand, soles of the feet and the forehead and play a role in the deposition of finger marks.

**Edges**   In **Bayesian network** analysis, a synonym for **arcs**.

**Electrostatic detection apparatus (ESDA)**   An apparatus used to reveal otherwise invisible impressions made by a variety of means such as handwriting on documents and shoe marks on floors.

**Eosin**   A red dye used in the microscopic analysis of cells to stain cytoplasm, collagen and muscle fibres. In a forensic context most widely used in the identification of **sperm** and **epithelial cells** from the mouth or vagina.

**Epidermis**   The outermost layer of the skin.

**Epigenetic**   Changes in gene expression caused by external environmental influences.

**Epiphyseal**   Pertaining to a cartilaginous plate located in the metaphyses (the part of the bone that grows during childhood) of children and adolescents.

**Epithelial cells**   The cells which comprise the epithelium, the tissues which line the inner surfaces and cavities of the body such as the mouth and vagina.

**Ethnicity**   A population or group of individuals with a common heritage typically deriving from religion, language, or culture.

**Europol**   The European Union law enforcement organisation that deals with criminal investigation, and assists law enforcement authorities in the investigation and prevention of organised crime.

**Evaluative mode**   The stage in a criminal investigation as specified in the **Case Assessment and Interpretation** (CAI) model, where a suspect has been identified and **likelihood ratios (Lrs)** are assessed in relation to the various stages of a **hierarchy of propositions**.

**Exculpatory**   Pertaining to evidence which may exonerate a suspect.

**External auditory meatus**   The ear canal which runs from the outer to the middle ear.

**Familial searching** The tracing of biological relatives through the identification of 'close matches' between a **crime scene sample** and subject samples on the **National DNA Database (NDNAD)**.

**Fast Fourier Transform (FFT)**   A mathematical function used by various analytical instruments to aid the identification of substances (see **Fourier-transform infrared spectroscopy**).

**Femoral artery**   The artery located in the inside part of each leg, running between the groin and the knee.

**Flat prior**   The assumption of a uniform prior probability in Bayesian analysis.

**Fluid dynamics**   The scientific study of the mechanics of fluid flow.

**Fluorescence in situ hybridisation**   A technique which uses fluorescent chemical probes to identify the presence or absence of specific DNA sequences on chromosomes.

**Fly speck**   Stains caused by material produced by flies following the regurgitation or defecation of human blood.

**Follicle**   The structure, located within the skin, where hairs develop and grow.

**Force Linked Intelligence System (FLINTS)**  A computer system used by some UK police forces to access a number of linked databases encompassing a wide-ranging array of information.

**Forensic anthropology**  The application of physical anthropology (the anthropological study of mechanisms of human evolution) and osteology to crime investigation, particularly in cases where human remains may be skeletonised.

**Forensic archaeology**  The application of archaeological techniques to the investigation of crime, particularly with regard to their use to recover and interpret evidence at crime scenes.

**Forensic entomology**  The application of knowledge of insect biology to criminal investigations, particularly in relation to their colonisation and development in corpses to establish time of body deposition or death. In practice this is not restricted to examination of insects but includes other invertebrates such as arachnids.

**Forensic odontology**  The application of knowledge of dentistry in the course of criminal investigation. Most frequently used to identify individuals from their dentition and the examination of bitemarks.

**Forensic osteology**  The application of knowledge of bones and related areas to criminal investigations. This is most frequently used for the purposes of establishing the species of a bone or the identity of a skeleton.

**Forensic palynology**  The scientific study of pollen, for example to determine whether a certain object (most notably a body) was in a certain place at a certain time.

**Forensic reconstruction**  The practice of using forensic methods to gain an understanding of the sequence of events leading to or during the course of a criminal incident.

**Forensic Science Service (FSS)**  Until recently the main external provider of forensic science services to police forces in England and Wales. Since the 1990s the FSS has become, through a number of stages, an independent government agency charging police forces for their services and subsequently a **GovCo**.

**Forensic strategy**  The process of linking investigative objectives with specific forensic examinations or procedures in a systematic manner in order to achieve aims such as the identification of individuals or the elimination of lines of inquiry.

**Fourier-transform infrared spectroscopy (FTIR)**  A non-destructive instrumental method used for analysing the chemical structure of polymers and other substances.

**Friction ridge**  The raised ridge patterns located on the epidermis of the fingers, palms and soles of the feet.

**Fossa**  A hollow or depressed area in bone.

**Frequentist** A school of thought in statistics, characterised by the view that considers the probability P of an uncertain event A is defined by the frequency of that event based on previous observations. This contrasts with the Bayesian view which considers that probability is related to degree of belief, i.e. it is a measure of the plausibility of an event given incomplete knowledge.

**Galton points** A commonly used term to describe the **minutiae** of fingerprints.

**Gas chromatography** A form of **chromatography** in which the mobile phase is a gas and the sample to be analysed is converted to a gas through the action of heat before being introduced in to the instrument.

**Gene** A unit of heredity composed of **DNA**.

**Genetic** Pertaining to **genes**.

**GovCo** Short for 'government company', a commercial, profit-making organisation which is wholly owned by the government. The **Forensic Science Service** became a GovCo in 2005.

**Haematoxylin** A dye commonly used in histological analyses to stain cell nuclei. Used in combination with **eosin** to identify **sperm** and **epithelial cells** (see **Histology**).

**Haplotype** The set of **alleles** on one of a pair of homologous **chromosomes**.

**Her Majesty's Inspectorate of Constabulary (HMIC)** The main body responsible for auditing and improving efficiency of police forces in England and Wales. There is an equivalent body in Scotland.

**Hierarchy of propositions** A term used in the context of **Bayesian** evaluation of evidence, and particularly associated with the **Case Assessment and Interpretation** (CAI) model. The **hierarchy of propositions** is the sequence of stages which represents all aspects of the process of evidence interpretation, starting with the **source** (which may itself be preceded by the sub-source level), proceeding to the **activity** level and ultimately to the **offence** level.

**Histology** The microscopic study of the cells and tissues of plants and animals.

**Home Office** The UK government department with responsibility (among other things) for policing, forensic science and forensic pathology in England and Wales. In Scotland these functions are the responsibility of the Scottish government. The recently formed Ministry of Justice in England and Wales was formerly part of the Home Office.

**Home Office Large Major Enquiry System (HOLMES)** The computer system used by all UK police forces for the investigation of major incidents. Introduced in the 1980s following the Byford Report into the 'Yorkshire Ripper' investigation.

**Hydroponics**   A method for growing plants in the absence of soil in nutrient-rich water.

**Hypergeometric distribution**   A discrete probability distribution that describes the number of successful outcomes from a sequence of $N$ draws without replacement.

**IBIS**   (See **Integrated Ballistics Identification System**).

**IDENT1**   The software 'platform' that hosts a number of police **biometric** databases, including the national fingerprint database, the PALMS database (of palm prints) and FIND, a facial images database. These police databases are overseen by the **National Policing Improvement Agency** (NPIA).

**Ilium**   In osteology, the main component of the pelvis.

**Immunochromatography**   A form of chromatography that utilises immunochemistry.

**Impact spatter**   The characteristic bloodstain pattern caused when a source of blood is subjected to an impact.

**Inculpatory**   Pertaining to evidence which implicates an individual in a crime.

**Individualisation**   The practice of ascribing unique identity to an individual, object or substance. A term peculiar to forensic science and coined by Paul Kirk. Kirk distinguishes individualisation from 'identification' which he considered to be more accurately described as 'classification'. Kirk claimed criminalistics to be the 'science of individualisation' in 1963.

**Inductive inference**   The method of reasoning which moves from a number of empirical observations to a generalisation.

**Infrared (IR) spectroscopy**   A form of spectroscopy that employs the infrared part of the electromagnetic spectrum. This detects and can be used to analyse characteristic molecular vibrations which are used to classify and identify substances. (See **Fast Fourier Transform**).

**Integrated Ballistics Identification System (IBIS)**   A type of automated firearms identification system. IBIS digitally captures images of fired bullets and cartridge cases from crime scenes and fired from recovered weapons. These images are then stored on a database to enable the comparison of firearms evidence (see also **National Firearms Forensic Intelligence Database**).

**Intelligence**   In a policing context, the collection, analysis and evaluation of information about crime or criminals to inform operational activities.

**Intelligence-led policing**   A policing model which uses proactively acquired intelligence to inform tactics, resource allocations and direct operational activities.

**International Criminal Police Organisation (ICPO-Interpol)**   INTERPOL is the world's largest international police organisation, with 187 member countries. Created in 1923, it facilitates cross-border police cooperation, and supports and assists all organisations, authorities and services whose mission is to prevent international crime.

**International Society for Forensic Genetics**   An international association which promotes scientific knowledge on the forensic applications of genetics.

**Investigative mode**   Used in the context of the **CAI** to describe the stage of an investigation prior to the identification of a suspect.

**Iquanta**   An internet-based analysis tool developed and maintained by the Home Office Police and Crime Standards Directorate to analyse data on police performance.

**Isotope ratio mass spectrometry (IRMS)**   An analytical technique that can be used to determine the isotopic ratios of various common elements within a sample to aid in the determination of geographical origin of natural substances and the chemical and geographic profile of synthetic substances.

**Kastle-Meyer Test**   A presumptive test for the identification of blood.

**Keratin**   A fibrous protein found in hair, feathers, nails and animal horns.

**Kyphosis**   A common condition involving curvature of the upper spine.

**Lamellae**   Thin layers of bone or tissue.

**Laser micro dissection (LMD)**   A process used to dissect tissues at microscopic level. LMD has been used by forensic scientists to separate sperm cells for analysis from female epithelial cells in mixed stains from sexual assaults.

**Latent mark**   A crime scene mark that is not readily visible. This applies to a range of marks from a range of sources including fingers and footwear. Marks can be visualised using chemical, physical and optical methods.

**Laurell technique**   A chemical test used to identify particular proteins, using antibodies, as a marker for seminal fluid.

**Leucomalachite green (LMG)**   A presumptive test for blood.

**Likelihood**   In Bayesian reasoning, the probability of obtaining the scientific evidence (E) given that a proposition (H) is true, and given some background information (I).

**Likelihood ratio**   In Bayesian reasoning, the ratio of the probability of the scientific evidence (E) given that a prosecution proposition ($H_p$) is true and the probability of the evidence given its alternative (defence) proposition ($H_D$), were true, and given some background information (I).

**LIVESCAN**   The technology used to electronically capture and transmit fingerprints and palm prints. In the UK, livescan facilities allow fingerprints to be compared by **IDENT1** 'in real time'.

**Locard's Principle**   The concept attributed to Locard that suggests that in any contact between two (or more) items material from each is transferred to the other. This is generally formulated as 'every contact leaves a trace' but there is little evidence that Locard used this exact expression.

**Locus/loci** (pl)   The specific site of a **gene** on a **chromosome**. **Alleles** occupy the same site on homologous chromosomes.

**Low Copy Number (LCN)**   A more sensitive extension of the **SGMplus®** profiling technique that enables scientists to produce **DNA profiles** from samples containing very few cells. Now more commonly referred to as low template DNA profiling.

**Luminol**   A chemical agent which can be used to detect bloodstains and is typically used to examine faint or latent staining. The technique produces weak fluorescence which fades and therefore must be speedily photographed.

**Magnetometry**   The scientific technique of measuring the strength and direction of magnetic fields.

**Major Incident Room (MIR)**   The term used to describe the co-location of various roles required to carry out a major investigation using HOLMES. The MIR forms the centre of any investigation into a serious criminal offence.

**Major Incident Room Standard Operating Procedures**   One of the recommendations of the Byford Report. Superseded by MIRSAP – below.

**Major Incident Room Standardised Administrative Procedures (MIRSAP)**   The procedures used in the investigation of serious crimes.

**Marker (genetic)** Informally, the specific sites (**loci**) on a chromosome that are analysed to generate a **DNA profile** consisting of repeated short sequences of **DNA** that vary in length between different people. See **short tandem repeats**.

**Mass spectrometry**   The generic name given to analytical techniques which identify substances by fragmentation into molecular ions and measuring their mass/charge ratio.

**Match probability**   In relation to DNA profiles, a calculation which is undertaken using a database and knowledge of population genetics to estimate the probability of a chance match.

**Melanin**   The pigment from which skin and hair acquire their colour.

**Melanocytes**   Specialised cells which produce **melanin**.

**Methyl umbelliferyl phosphate reagent (MUP)**   A chemical reagent that may be used to detect **acid phosphatase** by producing fluorescence.

**Microspectrophotometry**   A technique used to analyse and compare spectral colour characteristics of trace evidence such as fibres and paint fragments.

**Minutiae**   A collective term for the characteristic features of fingerprint ridges – bifurcations, ridge endings, lakes etc., used to identify fingerprints or marks. (See **Galton points**).

**Mitochondrial DNA (mtDNA)**   DNA present in mitochondria (a cell organelle) and which is inherited through the maternal line. Siblings will have the same mitochondrial DNA type as their mother, as will any relative linked through the female line. Can be used for identification of bodies and tissues from bone, teeth and hair shafts if there is insufficient chromosomal DNA.

**Mixed DNA sample** A biological sample containing the **DNA** of more than one individual.

**Morphogenesis** The study of the processes which control the spatial distribution of cells and the development of tissues and organs in the body.

**Multiplex** The simultaneous examination of multiple genetic loci in a 'single' reaction tube. This is a standard process in STR testing.

**Murder Investigation Manual (MIM)** The first compilation of national guidance on the investigation of homicide published by ACPO in 1999.

**Mutagenic** The property of causing genetic mutations.

**National Automated Fingerprint Identification System (NAFIS)** The integrated criminal record and fingerprint identification system that supports all law enforcement organisations in the UK. This has been superseded by **IDENT1**.

**National Centre for Policing Excellence (NCPE)** A body with a role to develop standards in policing introduced by the Government in the 2001 White Paper *Policing a New Century: A Blueprint for Reform.* Now part of **NPIA.**

**National Crime and Operations Faculty (NCOF)** Formerly part of **NCPE** which provided specialist operational support to the police service including forensic aspects of major investigations. Now part of **NPIA** Operational Policing Services.

**National DNA Database** An intelligence database of **DNA profiles** consisting of **subject samples** and **crime samples** used for the investigation, prevention and detection of crime.

**National Firearms Forensic Intelligence Database (NFFID)** The NFFID consists of two parts. The first part is a database which collates data on firearms, such as the type of weapon, make, model and calibre, plus details of any modifications or conversions and details of the incident in which it was involved. The second part of the NFFID is the **Integrated Ballistics Identification System (IBIS).**

**National Injuries Database** A national information resource used to support crime investigations by the identification of weapons and interpretation of wounds. It currently combines police, medical and forensic reports along with photographs, X-rays and video footage.

**National Intelligence Model (NIM)** An intelligence-led business model for law enforcement widely used in the UK.

**National Policing Improvement Agency (NPIA)** A UK non-departmental body which exists to provide support to the police in areas such as information technology, professional development, operational standards, recruitment and training.

**Nodes** The device used in **Bayesian networks** to represent probabilistic events.

**Nominal** An individual whose details are recorded on a police database, e.g. IDENT1.

**Nuchal** Pertaining to the powerful ligament which joins the occipital bone to the dorsal thoracic spines.

**Occipital bone** The curved, trapezoidal compound bone which forms the lower posterior part of the skull.

**Offence level** The highest level in the **hierarchy of propositions**, which addresses the question of whether an individual (or individuals) committed an offence.

**Oligozoospermia** A condition in which a male individual exhibits a low sperm cell count.

**Osteobiography** The interpretation of skeletons to determine the life history and conditions experienced by an individual or population.

**Osteons** The functional unit of compact bone consisting of concentric layers of **lamellae** (thin plate-like structures) that surround a central (Haversian) canal.

**Osteophytosis** The abnormal outgrowth of bone.

**PALMS** The police database hosted by **IDENT1**, which contains palm prints obtained from arrestees, convicted individuals and crime scenes.

**Patent** A crime scene mark (finger marks, footwear) which is visible to the naked eye.

**Pathfinder Project** A Forensic Science Service project which explored ways of reducing crime, and the issue of attrition (the shortfall between the number of crimes reported and those prosecuted). Pathfinder focused on **LCN DNA profiling**, footwear evidence, tool mark evidence, and the linking of crime scene information by technologies such as **FLINTS**.

**Perineum** The surface region between the pubic symphysis and the coccyx.

**Phosphorylchlorine** A compound found in abundant quantities in **semen**, which is converted, on ejaculation, into choline and orthophosphate by **acid phosphatase** (AP).

**Physiologically altered bloodstains (PABS)** Recognisable bloodstain patterns formed from blood which has clotted or coagulated, or has become mixed with another bodily fluid.

**Piperonylmethylketone (PMK or 3,4-methylenedioxyphenyl-2-propanone)** The major chemical precursor for the production of the drug ecstasy.

**Police and Criminal Evidence (PACE) Act (1984)** This Act established a legislative framework in England and Wales for the exercise of police powers, as well as providing codes of practice for the use of those powers (PACE

Act Code of Practice 1984). PACE made particular provisions for dealing with suspected offenders regarding their arrest, detention, questioning and obtaining samples for forensic examination. The Act applies to the police and other investigative agencies.

**Police Information Technology Organisation (PITO)** An organisation, now subsumed into **NPIA,** which was responsible for the development, implementation and ongoing management of major technological systems (e.g. NAFIS) for the police service.

**Police and Partnership Standards Unit (PPSU)** A board set up following the merger of the Police Standards Unit (PSU) and Partnership Performance Support Unit, to support police forces and related groups to meet performance targets.

**Polymerase chain reaction (PCR)** The technique that produces millions of copies of a particular target area or sequence of **DNA**. This enables **DNA profiles** to be obtained from extremely small and degraded **crime scene samples**.

**Population substructure** The deviation from random distribution of alleles within a population. Sub-populations are caused by groups of individuals who have inherited alleles from common ancestors.

**Poroscopy** The examination and comparison of features in fingerprints and marks related to pores in friction ridge skin.

**Posterior probability** In Bayesian reasoning, the probability of a proposition (hypothesis, view, assertion, scenario) (H), given some background information (I) and given the scientific evidence (E).

**Preauricular sulcus** A groove in the pelvic surface of the ilium which is more pronounced in females.

**Presumptive testing** In a forensic context (e.g. street drugs, body fluids); tests which give an indication of the nature of a substance or material but do not provide absolute identification without further confirmatory tests.

**Primer (DNA)** A short section of single-stranded DNA which binds to a complementary strand and acts as a site for initiation of DNA synthesis. Two primers are used to amplify a locus using PCR.

**Primer (paint)** A component of paints which can be analysed and used to discriminate or match paint fragments.

**Prior probability** In Bayesian reasoning, the probability of a proposition, (hypothesis, view, assertion, scenario etc.) before any background information or scientific evidence is taken into account.

**Probability** The likelihood of a particular event occurring, e.g. obtaining a six from the roll of a die.

**Probability Density Function** A function that displays a **probability distribution** in terms of integrals.

637

**Probability distribution** A function which displays the probabilities of possible values a random variable may take, with this range being either discrete or continuous.

**Probative** Pertaining to proof, or the measure of proof.

**Proposition** The term used in the context of the **CAI** to describe the statements formed which constitute prosecution and defence hypotheses to account for an event.

**Prosecutor's fallacy** The transposition of the conditional. In the forensic context this is often taken to mean the confusion between 'the probability of some evidence if an individual is innocent' with the 'probability of innocence if some piece of evidence is available' i.e. $P(E \mid H) = P(H \mid E)$.

**Prostate Specific Antigen (PSA)** A protein produced by cells of the prostate gland, which can act as an indicator of the amount of semen present on an intimate swab and can also be used to estimate the time elapsed since intercourse. A more specific test for semen compared to **acid phosphatase**.

**Proteinase K** An enzyme which can be used to denature epithelial cell membranes in cell-rich preparations, allowing easier identification of sperm cells.

**Prüm Convention** An agreement originally signed by Germany, Spain, France, Luxembourg, the Netherlands, Austria and Belgium which facilitates cooperation in certain matters of security and anti-terrorism. It potentially enables the countries involved to exchange fingerprint and DNA data on possible suspects, and allows for the deployment of armed sky marshals on flights between these nations. It also allows for joint police patrols, and for the entry of armed police officers across the borders of other states, and cooperation in the event of mass disasters. It was adopted into EU regulation in June 2007.

**Pubic symphysis** The joint formed by a union of the bodies of the pubis in the median plane by a thick mass of fibrocartilage. The pubic symphysis connects the left and right pubic bones.

**Public–Private Partnerships (PPPs)** A mechanism for using the private sector to deliver outcomes for the public sector, usually on the basis of a long-term funding agreement.

**P-value** In statistical hypothesis testing, the probability of obtaining a result in an experiment due to chance alone, given that the null hypothesis is true.

**Pyrolysis-gas chromatography** A technique used for identifying the chemical structure of polymers and other substances following thermal degradation of the solid substance and separation of the components produced.

**Quadruplex** The first multi-locus system to be developed by the **Forensic Science Service** for forensic **DNA profiling** was termed a 'Quadruplex', due to the fact that it examined four loci.

**Radial artery** The artery located in the inner part of each wrist.

**Random Man Not Excluded (RMNE)** A frequentist method for the interpretation of mixed DNA profiles. This method uses exclusion probabilities, defined as 'the probability that a random person would be excluded as a contributor to the observed DNA mixture' and does not require the interpretation of the mixed DNA profile.

**Recordable offence** In England and Wales, all offences that carry the possibility of a custodial sentence are recordable (or 'notifiable'), plus 52 other, non-imprisonable offences specified in the Schedule to the National Police Records (Recordable Offences) (Amendment) Regulations 2005.

**Relative frequency** The number of times a particular event $p$ occurs in a run of $n$ trials in an experiment.

**Ridgeology** An evaluative method of friction ridge identification (Ashbaugh 1999).

**Sacroiliac joint** The joint located between the **sacrum** and the **ilium**.

**Sacrum** The large triangular bone located at the base of the spine and the upper back part of the pelvic cavity, inserted between the two hip bones.

**Satellite stain** A small separate bloodstain which has been projected from a larger stain, e.g. due to impact with a surface.

**Scanning Electron Microscopy/Energy Dispersive X-ray Spectrometry (SEM/EDS)** A microscope which uses an electron beam (instead of light) to produce an image of a sample. The same instrument can also be used to to carry out elemental analysis and is used in forensic work e.g. identification of firearms discharge residues.

**Scenes of Crime Officer (SOCO)** The role, typically civilian (or non-sworn), responsible for the examination of incident scenes and recovery of forensic evidence in police investigations. SOCOs may be known by other titles, such as **Crime Scene Examiners** (CSEs), Forensic Investigators, or **Crime Scene Investigators** (CSIs).

**Schmorl's nodes** The protrusion of intervertebral disc material through breaks in the **subchondral bone** plate, with displacement of this material into the vertebral body, leading to an abnormal contour of the spine on radiographs.

**Scientific Support Units/Departments (SSUs/SSDs)** The functional unit within a police organisation in the UK usually responsible for the examination and management of crime scenes, photography and imaging, and fingerprint examination. The detailed roles and activities in departments vary considerably as do their titles.

**Scientific Work Improvement Movement (SWIM)** A process improvement methodology developed for **scientific support departments** by the **Home Office**.

**Scoliosis** A condition in which a person's spine is curved from side to side, and may even be partially rotated.

**Sebaceous glands** Small glands in the skin which produce oily secretions that contribute to finger mark deposition.

**Second Generation Multiplex (SGM)** A **DNA profiling** system that examined seven **loci; six STRs** and amelogenin.

**Secondary spatter** A pattern of **satellite bloodstains.**

**Semen** A fluid produced by the male consisting of sperm and seminal fluid.

**Seminal acid phosphatase** See **acid phosphatase.**

**Senior Investigating Officer (SIO)** The police officer with responsibility for the effective investigation of a serious or major crime, typically a Detective Chief Inspector or more senior rank.

**Sexual Assault Referral Centres (SARCs)** A 'one-stop' location where victims of sexual assault can receive medical care, counselling and forensic examination.

**SGM Plus® (SGM+)** The current technique for DNA profiling of samples for the National DNA Database (NDNAD) which replaced the **SGM** system in June 1999. It examines 11 **loci** (10 loci plus a sex indicator locus) to give a **DNA profile.** The **discriminating power** of a full **SGMPlus®** profile exceeds one in a billion.

**Short tandem repeat (STR)** A region of **DNA** consisting of multiple repetitions of short core sequences of DNA (2–6 bases). Differences in the number of repetitions arise from different alleles and form the basis of DNA (**SGM** and **SGM Plus®**) profiling.

**Significance testing** The use of statistical methods to test whether an alternative hypothesis achieves a predetermined level in order to be accepted in preference to the null hypothesis.

**Single nucleotide polymorphisms (SNPs)** The occurrence of two or more alleles at a single base position in the genome. A particular base might be 'A' in some people and 'G' in others. There are about ten million SNPs in human **DNA**. They are catalogued in dbSNP, a publicly accessible database. SNPs are not currently used for routine DNA profiling.

**Source level** One of three levels of evidential evaluation which concerns itself with the source of evidence found on a suspect or at a crime scene. (See **hierarchy of propositions** and **case assessment and interpretation.**)

**Sperm** (Spermatozoa, spermatozoon) The mature mobile reproductive cell in male animals.

**Sphenooccipital synchondrosis** The fusion of cartilage between the sphenoid and occipital bones in the skull. In 95 per cent of humans this normally occurs between 20 and 25 years of age, and hence can be used as an indicator of age.

**Spinneret**  The device used to extrude polymers from a solution to form fibres.

**Squalene**  A fatty hydrocarbon found in some finger mark residues.

**Squamous**  With reference to epithelial cells, 'flat' cells which line the membranes of the body including the mouth (buccal) and vaginal cavities.

**Striation marks**  A pattern of fine linear marks caused by protrusions and imperfections on one surface after contact with another. Typical examples include marks from tools and on bullet casings. These marks are used in forensic comparisons.

**Stringing technique**  With reference to **BPA**, a technique which uses string to establish the area in two- or three-dimensional space from which a blood pattern originated.

**Subchondral bone**  The bone located below the cartilage.

**Subject sample**  A biological sample from an individual for analysis and storage. This includes samples from arrested persons, volunteers or victims.

**Superciliary**  Pertaining to the eyebrow.

**Surfactant**  A substance that increases the spreading or wetting properties of a liquid.

**Suture**  The immovable junctions between bones in the skull.

**Taphonomy**  The study of the biological, chemical and physical processes that change organisms after death.

**t-distribution (or Student's t-distribution)**  A probability distribution that arises from the problem of estimating the mean of a normally distributed population when the sample size is small.

**Telogen**  The third and final phase of hair growth, where cell production stops.

**Temporal artery**  The major artery of the head.

**Teratogenic**  The property of causing congenital abnormalities to the embryo or foetus by environmental agent, e.g. chemicals or radiation.

**Tetrahydrocannabinol ($\Delta$9-THC)**  The major active ingredient in cannabis.

**Topcoat**  The final coating of paint applied to a vehicle. It is this last layer which people normally associate with the vehicle's colour.

**Trabecular**  The bone material located in the inner cavity of long bones, where most of the arteries and veins of the bone are located. The external trabecular bone also contains red bone marrow.

**Trail pattern**  A distribution of bloodstaining that arises when blood falls from a moving object (including an individual) typically forming a linear pattern (see also **Drip pattern**).

**Transfer Principle**  (see Locard's Principle).

**Transnational crime**  Organised criminal activity which crosses or exploits national boundaries.

**Transnational policing**  Policing activities which focus on the investigation, detection and gathering of intelligence of relevance to transnational crime.

**Trichomes**  Hair-like projections that can be used to identify, cannabis plants, resin and related products.

**Urethra**  The duct in mammals that conveys urine from the bladder to be discharged outside the body.

**Vehicle**  The solvents, resins and other substances added to paint which form a continuous film, and bind the pigment to surfaces.

**Victimology**  The study of victimisation, the relationship between victims and offenders.

**Volar surfaces**  The surfaces of the fingertips, thumbs, palms, soles of the feet and toes.

**'Volume' crime**  Crimes that make up the majority of offences recorded in official crime statistics, most commonly domestic burglaries, vehicle thefts and thefts from vehicles, etc.

**Y chromosome**  The **chromosome** present only in males and which remains largely unchanged as it passes through the male line. Different **DNA** variants on the **Y chromosome** can help with research into the evolution and movement of human populations. **Y chromosome** profiling is a sensitive means to examine the male-specific component in male/female mixtures, often encountered in rape cases.

**Zygomatic arch** A junction in the skull found between the zygomatic bone (cheekbone) and temporal bone (situated at the sides of the skull).

# Index